Introduction to Intellectual Property

Introduction to Intellectual Property

Theory and Practice

Third Edition

World Intellectual Property Organization

Wolters Kluwer

Published by:
Kluwer Law International B.V.
PO Box 316
2400 AH Alphen aan den Rijn
The Netherlands
E-mail: lrs-sales@wolterskluwer.com
Website: www.wolterskluwer.com/en/solutions/kluwerlawinternational

Sold and distributed by:
Wolters Kluwer Legal & Regulatory U.S.
920 Links Avenue
Landisville, PA 17538
United States of America
E-mail: customer.service@wolterskluwer.com

ISBN 978-94-035-3636-1

e-Book: ISBN 978-94-035-4226-3
web-PDF: ISBN 978-94-035-4236-2

Table of Contents

Foreword

In the time it takes to read this foreword, approximately forty-five intellectual property (IP) applications will be made somewhere in the world. This striking figure reflects the fact that for some years now global IP activity has been at its peak, with at least twenty-three million applications filed annually since 2020.

Just as remarkable is the quiet but major shift in the engines of IP growth. As recently as twenty years ago, around 50% of all IP filings came from North America and Europe. Last year, almost 80% originated from Asia, Africa and Latin America.

What this means is that, today, more people are innovating and creating in more parts of the world than ever before, generating bold new ideas that are changing not just how we work, live and play, but also how we address common, global challenges and support the Sustainable Development Goals.

Yet, as this new edition captures, IP theory and practice—for all their growing influence and dynamism—remain highly technical areas of work, requiring specialized knowledge of law and regulation, as well as a deep appreciation of how IP intersects with factors like economic, innovation and trade policy.

As the UN agency for intellectual property, WIPO is at the heart of these trends. Our vision is of a balanced and effective IP ecosystem that works for everyone, everywhere, and that serves as a powerful catalyst for job creation, business growth, economic dynamism and sustainable development. We also help build the requisite skills and knowledge to achieve these ends, supporting and empowering stakeholders at every level of innovation ecosystems to leverage IP effectively.

This book reflects these commitments and IP's role in an evolving world. Produced in partnership with Kluwer Law International, it offers a comprehensive overview of IP rights, their theory and practice, and how they are used by enterprises and entrepreneurs across the globe. It also traces the history of the global IP ecosystem, from the Paris Convention of 1883 to the two new multilateral treaties agreed by WIPO in 2024.

Our aim is to provide access to critical facts and information in a way that deepens understanding, inspires engagement and demystifies the complexities inherent in IP law and practice. Whether you are an IP practitioner, a student or simply curious about understanding more, we hope you find this resource a valuable and detailed guide to the conceptual, economic and social dimensions of intellectual property.

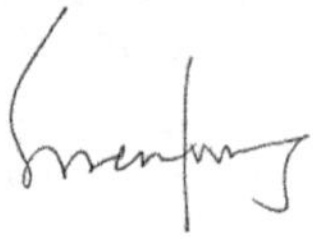

Daren Tang
WIPO Director General

Part I Intellectual Property, Its Functions and Components

CHAPTER 1
The Concept and Functions of Intellectual Property

This chapter offers a bird's eye view of the concept of intellectual property (IP) and its various branches and sub-branches as an introduction to the whole book. Those branches and sub-branches will be the subject of special chapters that will look at the details of each subject matter.

§1.01 THE CONCEPT OF INTELLECTUAL PROPERTY

Generally, the concept of IP is defined by means of two approaches. The most common approach is to associate IP with legal rights that result from intellectual activity in the industrial, scientific, literary, and artistic fields. The second approach is linking it to the promotion, as a deliberate act of Government policy, of creativity and the dissemination and application of its results and encouraging fair trading in a way that contributes to economic and social development.

As generalized as those two approaches may be, they beg for rethinking. The first approach is too broad and fails to explain why so many products of intellectual activity, such as telephone directories, lists of clients, and statistical data, are not IP subject matter. The second approach is too narrow because it does not take into account those relevant fields of IP protection that have nothing to do with creativity, such as trademarks, geographical indications (GIs) and purely commercial trade secrets.

IP is characterized by a combination of four elements. First, its subject matter is formed by intangible elements. Second, its subject matter is proprietary, to the extent it gives rise to a right to exclude others from using (in a broad sense) the protected matter. Third, it is subject to be used in trade. And, fourth, it covers all those intangible elements that are introduced by merchants, producers, creators in the products and services so as to attract customers and/or persuade customers not to acquire competitors' products and services.

The subject matter of IP is intangible or material in the sense it cannot be apprehended or controlled by hand. IP covers ideas, their expressions and their uses, not the objects in which it is embodied or that display it. The immaterial nature of the subject matter of intellectual property gives rise to a fundamental characteristic of the rights that are granted to its owners: those are not the rights of economically exploiting the protected subject matter but the rights of prohibiting others from economically exploiting that subject matter. In this sense, IPRs can be said to have a *negative* nature. Actually, they differ sharply from property rights in tangible goods. Law is about the regulation of social conduct. Every time one wishes to do something that interferes with (and consequently reduces) other persons' freedom, one needs permission from the law. It follows that the law must give him/her the power to use his/her tangible property because such a use is naturally exclusive and rivalrous in nature and thus interferes with other persons' freedom: possession over a tangible good is rivalrous and therefore de facto excludes others per se from possessing it. For example, if a person erects a house on a piece of land, no one else can erect another house in the same place. There is simply no space for that. That is why property rights in tangible goods are primarily defined as rights *to use and exploit*. There is no need for the law to establish the right to prevent others from using a piece of land as a primary prerogative because that exclusion is a natural (if not physical) consequence of possession. By contrast, IPRs are property rights in *intangible* goods. Being intangible, the possession of their subject matter does not de facto impede per se others from possessing them simultaneously. In economics jargon, IPRs cover non-rival subject matter. Therefore, the right in that subject matter must be, primarily, protected by a legal right *to exclude* others from using (or copying) them, for possession alone is not enough to secure exclusivity. This explains why IPRs are usually stated in a negative manner (i.e., the right to exclude others from doing something rather than the positive right to do something), as opposed to rights in tangible goods. In other words, this explains why the essence of IPRs is the right to say "no"—this negative dimension corresponds to the very intangible nature of the subject matter protected.

IP is *proprietary* in the sense above mentioned: it gives the right to exclude others from economically exploiting the protected subject matter. Therefore, IP is generally put on the same ground as property in tangible objects. Accordingly, the civil laws of some countries qualify IPRs as property rights in chattels. This is quite an appropriate conceptual parallel, but one should not forget that the intangible nature of IPRs remits them to a unique category, with unique attributes. One of those attributes was mentioned above: the laws define IPRs as the right to exclude others rather than the rights to use, enjoy and dispose, which correspond to property rights in tangible goods. Another attribute is that, unlike rights in tangible goods, IPRs are sometimes conceived as rights of primarily obtaining revenue. In this sense, third parties may use the protected subject matter provided they pay the owners the adjusted remuneration. Only if third parties fail to do so, IPR owners have their rights to exclude fully established.

The third characteristic element of IPRs is their susceptibility of being used in trade or, in broader and more correct terms, of being put to economic exploitation in the production and circulation of goods and services. The rules of IP, for example, do not apply to disputes involving the use of signs of political parties, or the use of civil names, or the assignment of inventions through succession. Those rules may be used as analogical references, but they are not employed as such. IPRs are about economic exploitation with a purpose of producing and circulating goods and services.

Finally, IP is about differentiation. This is, perhaps, the least acknowledged characteristic of IP, and yet it is essential to its correct understanding. If products were absolutely identical regarding their technical and esthetical features, as well as prices, consumers would select them indifferently. Any attempt by a competitor to do something different—by introducing a new technical function or simply reducing the price—would be immediately followed by other producers. It is this scenario that economists call *perfect competition*. However, perfect competition does not exist in the real world because rival manufacturers and merchants inevitably seek to increase sales and/or profits. And they can do so only by introducing differences that lure new customers (and persuade clients not to look for competing products or services). Those differences can be of many sorts, from new technical features, new designs, new processes, new materials or ingredients (the so-called *internal differences*) to prices, location, reputation, origin, technical assistance, special courtesy treatment to clients (the so-called *external differences*). When intangible, those differences are directly or indirectly protected by IP. These include prices and location, which are indirectly subject matter of IPRs. Certain trademarks designate low prices. Other trademarks identify high prices. Location is designated by shop names. Shop signs may be physically embedded in the buildings that host the commercial establishments, but they are intangible to the extent that it is the information they provide to customers that matters. And they can be displaced when the shop is relocated. Today's shop signs are found on the Internet, known as *domain names* and *hashtags*. Like traditional shop signs, domain names and hashtags identify (virtual) places of business and serve to inform customers where those places can be found.

In other words, and because it serves a differentiating purpose, IP is the cornerstone of an economy based on private entrepreneurship. Without IP there is no enterprise—enterprise being understood as an organized combination of assets with the purpose of carrying business. An enterprise must be identified and so must the assets that differentiate it from its rivals. Enterprise was invented in Sumer, when for the first time, merchants and artisans started to engage in trade with the purpose of collecting private revenue (by contrast with merchants in other parts of the Pre-Classical world, who would trade on behalf of the sovereigns—the pharaoh, in Egypt; the emperor, in China). Museums across the world are rich in specimens of seals that Sumerian merchants would use in the course of their businesses. And the Code of Hammurabi had one provision ensuring (indirectly) artisans the private appropriation of the secrets of their business in a way that does not sound very different, if the anachronism is tolerated, from footnote 10 to the Agreement on Trade-Related Aspects of Intellectual Property Rights (TRIPS Agreement), which prohibits the interference with contracts.

Therefore, the primary function that IPRs serve is *differentiation* of products and services. All other functions designated to IP are secondary to differentiation and ultimately contribute to or result from it. Patents and utility models, for example, protect those internal differences in products that correspond to different (i.e., new) technical features. In this sense, patents promote differentiation by invention. Copyright protects internal differences that result from creative styles and organization of information. In this sense, copyright promotes creativity. The public policies that speak to generating broader access to inventions and literary works, for example, are only possible in the view of differentiation. Trademarks help consumers choose the products and services they want to acquire. They differentiate by relying on external differences like origin, reputation, quality, and any other characteristic that consumers have learned to associate with the branded goods or services. The repression of unfair competition, likewise, aims at preventing the elimination of differences by dishonest competitors. This vastest and oldest component of industrial property was traditionally employed to protect those elements of industrial property that did not count with formal recognition, such as unregistered trademarks and trade names, but as it will be shown in Chapter 13, this notion has been replaced by the modern tendency of making the repression of unfair competition a complementary mechanism of IP enforcement.

This fundamental notion of IP as a tool of differentiation is corroborated by a simple fact: all the components of IP must comply with a single substantive condition in order to be eligible for protection. That single condition is *to be different*. Therefore, where the law says inventions must be *new* to be patentable, what the law actually says is that inventions must be *different* from what exists in the prior art. When the same law says that inventions must be *sufficiently inventive*, it actually says that inventions must be *genuinely different* from the prior art. When the law requires works to be *creative* and *original* in order to be copyrighted, it actually requires works to be *different* from what other authors have created. *Originality* means a link between the work and its specific origin or its specific author—and not to a different origin or author. The specificity of this linkage is, therefore, equivalent to creativity, and that is why creativity and originality are used to mean the substantive condition that works must meet in order to be copyrightable. And the same can be said of trademarks, geographical signs, plant varieties, and all other components of IP: it is the difference that they represent that makes them eligible for protection. This includes trade secrets. After all, a secret is something that one knows that is different from what others know.

It is this essential factor of IP that explains why those two general approaches aforementioned are incorrect. On the one hand, many products of intellectual activity, such as telephone directories, lists of clients, and statistical data, are not protected because they are not differentiating. Therefore, linking IP to the protection of the results of human mental activity is too broad. Only those results that are differentiating are eligible for intellectual protection. On the other hand, associating IP with the promotion of invention and creation is reductionist. The reason is that IP protects differentiation, and inventions and creations are just two of many intangible differentiating factors introduced in products and services.

One final introductory notion about IP results from this. Contrary to a general misperception of the anticompetitive nature of IP, eventually associated with its exclusive (or, rather, excluding) nature, IP is inherently and essentially pro-competitive. IP promotes competition by differentiation. In doing so, it prohibits competition by imitation and parasitism.

IP is traditionally divided into two branches, "industrial property" and "copyright."

"Industrial property" embraces protection of inventions by means of patents, protection of certain commercial interests by means of trademark law and law on trade names, and the law on protection of industrial designs. In addition, industrial property embraces the repression of unfair competition. Industrial property corresponds to ideas, and it translates into the rights of excluding others from *using* those ideas.

"Copyright" grants authors and other creators of works of the mind (literature, music, art) certain rights to authorize or prohibit, for a certain limited time, certain uses made of their works. Copyright, broadly speaking, embraces the provisions on the protection of copyright in the strict sense of the word and also the protection of what is usually referred to as "related or neighboring rights." Unlike industrial property, copyright—with a few exceptions—does not cover ideas but their expression. Therefore, the exclusive rights granted by copyright are not against the use but against the reproduction (in various modalities) of the protected works. This dichotomy is expressed in Article 9.2 of the TRIPS Agreement. Recent advances, however, have brought copyright closer to protecting ideas, such as copyright in computer programs and the creative organization of databases.

The Convention Establishing the World Intellectual Property Organization (WIPO), concluded in Stockholm on July 14, 1967 (Article 2(viii)), provides that "'intellectual property' shall include rights relating to:

(1) literary, artistic and scientific works;
(2) performances of performing artists, phonograms, and broadcasts;
(3) inventions in all fields of human endeavor;
(4) scientific discoveries;
(5) industrial designs;
(6) trademarks, service marks, and commercial names and designations;
(7) protection against unfair competition;

and all other rights resulting from intellectual activity in the industrial, scientific, literary or artistic fields."

The areas mentioned under (1) belong to the copyright branch of IP. The areas mentioned in (2) are usually called "related or neighboring rights," that is, rights related to or neighboring on copyright. The areas mentioned under (3), (5) and (6) constitute the industrial property branch of IP. The area mentioned under (7) may also be considered as belonging to that branch, the more so as Article 1(2) of the Paris Convention for the Protection of Industrial Property (Stockholm Act of 1967) (the "Paris Convention") includes "the repression of unfair competition" among the areas of "the protection of industrial property"; the said Convention states that "any act of competition contrary to honest practices in industrial and commercial matters constitutes an act of unfair competition" (Article 10*bis*(2)).

The expression "industrial property" is sometimes misunderstood as relating to movable or immovable property used for industrial production, such as factories and equipment for production. However, industrial property is a kind of IP and thus relates to intangible elements. Those elements include inventions and industrial designs. Simply stated, inventions are new solutions to technical problems, and industrial designs are aesthetic creations determining the appearance of industrial products. In addition, industrial property includes trademarks, service marks, commercial names and designations, including indications of source and appellations of origin (AOs), and the protection against unfair competition. Here, the protection concerns signs transmitting information to consumers, in particular, as regards products and services offered on the market, and it is directed against unauthorized use of such signs which is likely to mislead consumers, as well as against practices that consist of misleading practices in general. The Paris Convention (Article 1(2)) provides that "the protection of industrial property has as its object patents, utility models, industrial designs, trademarks, service marks, trade names, indications of source or AOs, and the repression of unfair competition."

The area mentioned in the WIPO Convention under (4)—scientific discoveries—belongs to neither of the two branches of IP. The reason is another fundamental consequence of the differentiating and pro-competitive nature of IP. Given their inherently differentiating nature, all IP subject matter is—or should be—susceptible of being alternated by competitors. In the face of a commercially successful patented invention, competitors should be able to invent competing, alternative, non-infringing alternative technical solutions. In the face of a commercially successful copyrighted work, competing authors should be able to create their own works. This condition of alternativeness is not possible for scientific discoveries. Discoveries are findings of the inventions made by Nature. They are not susceptible of being reinvented by men or women. Therefore, they are not differentiating per se. Of course, the introduction of a natural feature in a given product by its artificial introduction may become an invention, if sufficiently inventive, or different. That is why the Geneva Treaty on the International Recording of Scientific Discoveries (1978), which defines a scientific discovery as "the recognition of phenomena, properties or laws of the material universe not hitherto recognized and capable of verification" (Article 1(1)(i)), has not attempted to attribute ownership as regards the findings themselves, but merely introduced a mechanism of recognition of discoverers' merits.

§1.02 COPYRIGHT AND RELATED RIGHTS

Copyright relates to literary and artistic creations, such as poems, novels, music, paintings, films, and computer software. In most European languages other than English, copyright is called "author's rights." The expression "copyright" refers to the main act which, in respect of literary and artistic creations, may be made only by the author or with the author's authorization. That act is the making of *copies* of the literary or artistic work, such as a book, a painting, a sculpture, a photograph, or a film. The second expression, "author's rights" refers to the person who is the creator of the literary or artistic work, its author, thus underlining the fact, recognized in most laws, that the author has certain specific rights in the creation, for example, the right to prevent a distorted reproduction, which can be exercised only by the author, whereas other rights, such as the right to make copies, can be exercised by other persons, for example, a publisher who has obtained a license to this effect from the author. The term "copyright" is generally used in this book, but the subtle nuances and distinctions in the language used to refer to these rights have their roots in the historical development of the rights of authors and creators and can still be seen in the operation of various national legal systems.

"Related rights," also called "neighboring rights," protect the legal interests of certain persons and legal entities that contribute to making works available to the public or that produce subject matter which contains sufficient creativity or technical and organizational skill to justify recognition of a copyright-like property right. The related rights recognize that the productions that result from the activities of such persons and entities merit legal protection as they are *related* to the works protected by copyright. The full expression would be "rights related to copyright" or "rights neighboring on copyright." It is generally understood that three kinds of rights are covered by the concept of related rights: the rights of performing artists in their performances; the rights of producers of phonograms in their phonograms; and the rights of broadcasting organizations in their radio and television broadcasts.

The protection of authors' interests does not consist merely in preventing the unauthorized use of their works. Their works are intended to be made available to the public at large and the rights contribute to this process. The various categories of works are made accessible to the public in different ways. For example, a publisher reproduces the manuscript of a literary work in its final form without adding to the expression of the work as created by the author. The interests of book publishers are protected on the basis of the rights assigned or licensed to them by authors.

The situation is slightly different in the case of dramatic and musical works. Where such works are to be communicated to the public, they have to be performed or recited with the aid of performers. In such cases, the interests of the performers themselves should also be taken into account in relation to the use of their individual interpretations of the works concerned.

The development of sound recording techniques and the possibility of relatively easy reproduction of such recordings have also raised the need for protection of producers of sound recordings, which also are referred to as "phonograms." The easy availability in the market of increasingly efficient recording devices and platforms created the growing problem of piracy of sound recordings, which by now has become a worldwide problem especially with the advent of the Internet and ever-changing new technologies that facilitate the immediate sharing of perfect digital copies. Furthermore, sound recordings are frequently used by broadcasting organizations and other service aggregators such as mobile phone companies and Internet service providers, among others; while such uses may provide publicity for the sound recordings and for their producers, they also have become an essential ingredient of the daily programs of broadcasting organizations and other service aggregators. Consequently, just as the performers were seeking their own protection, producers of sound recordings began to pursue the case of their protection against unauthorized duplication of their sound recordings and also for a right to remuneration for the use of sound recordings for purposes of broadcasting and other communication to the public. These concerns were addressed to an extent by the WIPO Copyright Treaty (WCT) and the WIPO Performances and Phonograms Treaty (WPPT), which are discussed in more detail herein.

Related rights also encompass the interests of broadcasting organizations with respect to their broadcasts. The broadcasting organizations are also seeking protection against the unauthorized retransmission and reproduction of their broadcasts. Piracy with regard to these broadcasts has also increased substantially, to the point where perfect digital copies of broadcasts of major sports events are often streamed on the Internet.

A fundamental point is that ideas, as such, are not protected by copyright. This distinction is sometimes referred to as the "idea *versus* expression dichotomy." Generally speaking, it is the expression of the author's ideas that is protected by copyright rather than his/her ideas. For example, if an author writes an article setting forth ideas on how to build a radio receiver or music aggregator, the copyright the author has in the article published in a review will not prevent a third party from using the author's ideas to use the ideas to build a receiver or music aggregator, but the copyright will protect the author against the reproduction of copies of the article without consent. As for the invention itself, it does not enjoy copyright protection but may be protected on other grounds in the industrial property context. Absent patent protection, a person who has made ideas public, for example, in a public lecture, has no means of stopping others from using them. But once an idea has been expressed in tangible form, copyright protection exists for the words, musical notes, drawings, etc., in which it is clothed. For a work to enjoy copyright protection, however, it must be an original creation.

The final fixation of a work in a material form (writing, printing, photography, sound or visual recording, digital file, sculpture, construction, painting, graphic reproduction, etc.) is not necessarily a prerequisite for protection. However, certain countries, notably those that historically followed the model of the Anglo-American legal system, require, mainly for reasons of proof, some fixation of the work before protection is assured.

Copyright protection is independent of the quality or the value attaching to the work—it will be protected whether it be considered, according to taste, a good or a bad literary or musical work—and even of the purpose for which it is intended because the use to which a work may be put has nothing to do with its protection.

Rights are made to be respected and if they are not, the imposition of sanctions ensues. Any unauthorized use of works protected by copyright, when authorization of such use is required by law, constitutes what is called a copyright infringement (for instance, reproduction, public performance, broadcasting or any other communication to the public effected without permission, adaptation in any other form without the consent of the author, plagiarism, etc.). Legislation specifies sanctions to remedy the prejudice caused by such infringements, and the sanctions may be civil or criminal depending on the legal system and the importance of the infringement or violation.

Finally, it is generally accepted that the whole set of prerogatives that constitute copyright has to be recognized and protected at least throughout the life of the author. After the author's death, the work continues in principle to be protected for a certain time. The term of protection is regarded as being a fair balance between the preservation of the economic rights conferred on the author and society's need to have access to the expression of a culture whose essential aspects will have a more lasting effect than transitory successes. On expiry of the term of protection, the work falls into the public domain; that is, it can be used by anyone without any authorization. The period of protection is generally the life of the author plus fifty years, which is the period provided for many works in the Berne Convention, although in recent years many countries have adopted a term of the life of the author plus seventy years. Related rights also enjoy various terms of protection, which in general tend to be shorter than the terms for copyright rights. The application of terms of protection to moral rights varies by jurisdiction; in some national systems, these rights are perpetual.

The international copyright treaties and national legal systems generally provide for a variety of flexibilities in the form of "limitations and exceptions" to the exclusive rights provided by copyright law. These limitations and exceptions, which are most frequently applied to economic rights, have developed based on the recognition that under certain circumstances copyright restrictions should not apply. In general, such circumstances are expected to be special cases that do not conflict with the normal exploitation of the copyrighted work and do not unreasonably prejudice the legitimate interests of the author. For example, many countries allow for copyrighted works to be adapted without the permission of the author or rights holder in order to create versions that are accessible to blind, visually impaired, and print disabled people. This type of limitation or exception is the subject of a new international treaty adopted by WIPO Member States (*see* Chapter 30).

§1.03 PATENTS AND RELATED CONCEPTS

[A] Patents for Invention

An invention is an idea that permits the practical solution of a specific problem in a field of technology. Inventions are characteristically protected by patents, also called "patents for invention." Every country which gives legal protection to inventions gives such protection through patents, although there are a few countries in which protection may also be given by means other than patents, as will be seen below.

The basic function and role of the patent system are simple and reasonable. It is desirable in the public interest that industrial techniques should be improved. As seen, entrepreneurs feel the natural pressure to improve the products they sell so as to differentiate them and lure clients, and increase profits. In order to encourage improvement, and to encourage also the disclosure of improvements in preference to their use in secret, any person devising an improvement in a manufactured article, or a method of making it, or a new substance and/or the process of making that substance, may, upon disclosure of the details to the public through the Patent Office of a country and compliance with the requirements stipulated in the applicable law, be given a set of exclusive rights for a certain period of time. After that period expires, the invention passes into the public domain. The exclusive rights are justified on the grounds that if it had not been for the inventor who devised and disclosed the improvement, nobody would have been able to use it at that or any other time since it and the manner of producing it may have remained unknown. In addition, the giving of the exclusive right encourages the putting into practice of the invention since the only way the applicant can make a profit is by putting the invention into practice, either by using it himself/herself and deriving an advantage over his/her competitors by its use, or by allowing others to use it in return for royalties.

Not all inventions are patentable. Generally, laws require that, in order to be patentable, the invention must be new, it must involve an inventive step (or it must be non-obvious), and it must be industrially applicable. These three requirements are sometimes called the *substantive conditions of patentability* because compliance with those requirements is a necessary condition of patentability. They are listed in Article 27.1 of the TRIPS Agreement as mandatory requirements or conditions of patentability. Furthermore, the laws of some countries exclude certain specific kinds of inventions from the possibility of patenting: for example, inventions which comprise substances obtained by nuclear transformation. In this way, the nature of the subject matter may also constitute a substantive condition of patentability. These conditions are *substantive* because they concern the claimed inventions. In addition to *substantive* conditions, patent laws also impose *formal* conditions and requirements. They are *formal* because they refer to the manner in which the application is formulated. They are many, like the components of the application (description, designs, claims, and abstract) and their contents, power of attorney, address and designation of agent for notice, fees, forms, unity of invention. Article 29.1 of the TRIPS Agreement makes the enabling disclosure (or description) of the invention a mandatory formal requirement or condition of patentability. The Patent Cooperation Treaty (PCT), in Articles 4-7, also designates some formal requirements as mandatory conditions concerning international patent applications.

It is customary to distinguish between inventions that consist of products and inventions that consist of processes. An invention that consists of a new alloy is an example of a product invention. An invention that consists of a new method or process of making a known or new alloy is a process invention. The corresponding patents are usually referred to as a *product patent* and a *process patent*, respectively.

Under the protection conferred by a patent for invention, anyone who wishes to commercially exploit the invention must obtain the authorization of the person who received the patent—called *the patentee* or *the owner of the patent*. If anyone exploits the patented invention without such authorization, he/she commits an illegal act. Such protection is limited in time. In most countries, following the minimum term established by Article 33 of the TRIPS Agreement, it is of twenty years from the date of filing the application for patent protection. The rights conferred by a patent are described in the patent law of the country in which the patent for invention was granted. The rights, usually called *exclusive rights of exploitation*, generally consist:

(1) in the case of product patents, of the right to make, use, sell, offer for sale, import and export the product that includes the invention; and
(2) in the case of process patents, of the right to use the process that comprises the invention as well as the right to make, use, sell, offer for sale, import, and export products which were made by the process that comprises the invention.

In 1994, Article 28.1 of the TRIPS Agreement introduced harmonized language as regards the exclusive rights conferred by patents which correspond in general to the description given in the previous paragraph. Actually, Article 28 does not refer to stockpiling, but a WTO Panel construed its language as comprising the prohibition of stockpiling (*Canada—Patent Protection of Pharmaceutical Products*, Report of the Panel adopted on April 7, 2000, WT/DS114/R, of March 17, 2000). As a corollary of the right to say "no," patent owners are also entitled to say "yes," by licensing and assigning inventions. Article 28.1, in the context of process patents, refers to the making of products using, at least, the claimed process *directly*. Members of the WTO may, however, extend the provision to the indirect use of the claimed process. The second exception is the submission of the exclusive right to import to the exhaustion of rights. Those WTO Members that adopt international exhaustion—the termination of exclusive rights as a consequence of the legitimate transfer of title in patented products in other territories by the patent owner or by someone with the owner's permission or under the owner's control—reduce thereby the exclusive right to import.

Another important notion is that the term "exclusive rights of exploitation" is a technical one and does not mean exactly what it says. Patents do not confer a right to exploit the inventions. As said above, patents confer a negative right to exclude others from exploitation. The right to exploit an invention results from economic freedom. For example, an inventor creates a new product or device that applies in an industry that is covered by a state monopoly. That inventor will not be allowed to economically exploit his/her invention. But he/she will be allowed to deny the exploitation of the patented invention. In the case the country's law denies the patentee the right to refuse to license, he/she will be entitled to an adequate remuneration for the compulsory license that will necessarily ensue.

It has been mentioned earlier that if anyone exploits the patented invention without the authorization of the owner of the patent for invention, he/she commits an illegal act. However, as already stated, there are exceptions to this principle because patent laws may provide for cases in which a patented invention may be exploited without the patentee's authorization, for example, exploitation in the public interest by or on behalf of the government, or exploitation on the basis of a compulsory license. A compulsory license is an authorization to exploit the invention, given by a governmental authority, generally only in very special cases, defined in the law, and only where the entity wishing to exploit the patented invention is unable to obtain the authorization of the owner of the patent for invention under reasonable commercial terms. The conditions of the granting of compulsory licenses are also regulated in detail in laws that provide for them. In particular, the decision granting a compulsory license usually has to fix adequate remuneration for the patentee, and that decision usually may be the subject of an appeal. These topics are covered in some detail by Article 31 of the TRIPS Agreement.

[B] Utility Models

A second form of protection for inventions consists in the registration, or the granting, of a patent for a *utility model*. The expression "utility model" is merely a name given to certain inventions, namely—according to the laws of most countries which contain provisions on utility models—inventions in the mechanical field. Utility models generally cover external features introduced in previously known objects and that increase their utility. This is why the objects of utility models are sometimes described as devices or useful objects. Another type of protection which is sometimes considered similar to utility model patents (or certificates) is referred to as a *petty patent*. Petty patents, however, are not necessarily the same as utility models. In a number of countries, petty patents were introduced to simplify the complex procedure necessary for procuring a normal patent, in particular, its technical examination as to the substantive conditions of patentability. Petty patents are generally granted upon a mere statement by the applicant that he/she believes to have invented the claimed (and described) invention—i.e., without an *ex ante* examination. Petty patents have a shorter term and are not directly enforceable. When the owner of a petty patent wishes to claim the exclusivity of his/her rights against an alleged infringer, he/she must previously seek a technically positive analysis by the patent office. Petty patents, therefore, do not provide for legal security and cannot be used to seek capital investment in new technological ventures. So, petty patents have not proved useful, and their legal protection has been dropped in some countries, such as Australia.

Utility models usually differ from inventions for which ordinary patents for invention are available mainly in three respects: *first*, in the case of an invention called "utility model," the inventive step required is smaller than in the case of an invention for which a patent for invention is available; *second*, the maximum term of protection provided in the law for a utility model is generally much shorter than the maximum term of protection provided in the law for an invention for which a patent for invention is available; and *third*, the fees required for obtaining and maintaining the rights are generally lower than those applicable to ordinary patents. Moreover, in certain countries, there is also a substantial difference in the procedure for obtaining protection for a utility model: this procedure is generally shorter and simpler than the procedure for obtaining patents for invention.

Utility models can encourage inventors and investors to invest in and protect technical developments which do not fulfill the strict requirements of patentability and to obtain protection both at a lower cost and more quickly. Consequently, utility models are of particular interest to small- and medium-sized industries and can promote technical development in developing countries. Utility models can fill a gap in the protection of inventions which occurs when the requirements relating to inventive step for patents mean that certain inventions which do not comply with those requirements cannot be protected. Moreover, this form of protection prevents the patent system from being devalued by being applied to minor technical inventions.

§1.04 INDUSTRIAL DESIGNS

Generally speaking, an industrial design is the ornamental or aesthetic aspect of a useful article. The ornamental aspect may consist of the shape and/or pattern and/or color of the article. The ornamental or aesthetic aspect must appeal to the sense of sight. The article must be reproducible by industrial means, which is why the design is called "industrial"—in other words, it is the mold for the serial production of goods. If this latter element is missing, the creation may rather come under the category of a work of art that is protected by copyright law rather than by a law on industrial property. In order to be protectable, an industrial design must, according to some laws, be new and, according to other laws, original. This corresponds to the language of Article 25.1 of the TRIPS Agreement. A few WTO Members, in transposing Article 25.1 to their national systems, adopted the two conditions: industrial designs must be new *and* original. The double condition may mean a stricter examination for registrability.

In accordance with Article 26.1 of the TRIPS Agreement, industrial designs must be protected against unauthorized copying or imitation undertaken for commercial purposes. The protection must last at least ten years (Article 26.3 of the TRIPS Agreement). Countries tend to make protection available in multiples of five-year periods.

The document that certifies the protection of an industrial design may be called a registration certificate or a patent. If it is called a patent, one must, in order to distinguish it from a patent for invention, always specify that it is a patent for an industrial design.

With the remarkable evolution in design art in recent years, consumers have become more and more interested in a combination of utility and pleasing aesthetic appearance in the articles they buy. This tendency results in an increasing investment by manufacturers in design development and in a corresponding necessity to protect the result of their creative work through the registration of the relevant designs.

§1.05 BUSINESS IDENTIFIERS: TRADEMARKS, TRADE NAMES, TRADE DRESS, AND GIs

[A] Trademarks

The concept of a mark is not a new one. For centuries, merchants and manufacturers in various parts of the world have labeled their products with signs of one kind or another to distinguish them from those of their competitors. However, the use made of marks long remained a limited phenomenon relating only to certain types of goods that were sold far from their place of production. Most goods were consumed at the place they were produced, and no marks were used. The modern concept of a mark, that is to say, the mark as we know it today, first appeared in the eighteenth century as a result of the increased possibilities for communication and the adoption of laws guaranteeing freedom of commerce and industry. It is the result of the evolution of trademark systems introduced in the Middle Ages (specifically, as a result of the social change caused by the Commercial Revolution) to identify, differentiate and certify the works of artisans and merchants inserted in guilds or corporations. The two basic principles of trademark law—distinctiveness and veracity—were imported from the law of heraldry. Indeed, the very first treatise on trademark law, authored by Bartolo da Sassoferrato, in the fourteenth century, dealt with the law of heraldry (*De Insignis et De Armis*). As from that time, trade became more developed, both within States and between States, and the increased circulation of goods of all kinds made it necessary to place marks on those products so that they could be identified, in both the interests of producers and traders and also those of the consumers.

Since the end of the Second World War, the unprecedented development of international trade has led to an even greater use of marks in all countries and in all fields of activity. Although we are not always aware of the fact, marks today assume a preponderant role in our day-to-day life, and we enter into contact with a host of marks, not only in supermarkets and public places where we are faced with posters but also in the press, on radio and on television, that enter into the home.

[1] Functions of Marks

A trademark serves several purposes. From the viewpoint of the person who is interested in buying goods, the trademark serves the purpose of guiding him/her in taking the decision to buy. Such a decision is based on the expected characteristics or other properties of the goods (size, weight, color, fragrance, taste, durability, degree of efficiency in the operations in which the goods are used, etc.). In other words, one may say that what the prospective buyer is looking for is a certain quality or other characteristic of the goods. So, one of the functions of a trademark is to convey a feeling of that quality or characteristic or a remembrance of a previous experience as to that quality or characteristic. One of the functions of a trademark is to distinguish the goods with that quality or characteristic from other comparable goods. While it is often said that a trademark must enable anyone to distinguish the goods of one enterprise from goods of the same kind produced by another enterprise, the consumer does not necessarily know the name of the firm that manufactures or markets the product, apart from which the mark may yet serve to distinguish goods from other goods that come from the same firm. This means that trademarks do not necessarily indicate the origin of the goods or services they designate.

A second function of the trademark is to allow the manufacturer to identify goods manufactured by him/her once they are no longer in his/her possession but already in the possession of others, for example, the shops that sell it.

A third function of the trademark is to allow the authorities responsible for controlling the quality or other characteristics of the goods sold under a trademark to do their job.

But enterprises do not only deal with goods, they also render services. Services may be of almost any kind: travel, advertising, transport, insurance, treatment of materials, etc. A *service mark* is thus a sign used by enterprises offering services (hotels, restaurants, airlines, travel agencies, car-rental agencies, laundries and dry-cleaners) in order to identify their services on the market.

As it was said above for patents, trademark rights are rights to exclude others from their unauthorized use for the purposes of selling or advertising goods and services. A trademark certificate does not grant its owner the right to use the registered sign. Such right also arises from economic freedom, i.e., from the laws that regulate the economy. Governmental authorities may impose restrictions upon—and even abolish—the use of trademarks when such use is contrary to public policies, namely in health and food sectors. Article 20 of the TRIPS Agreement has language that, in this regard, provides trademark owners with the guaranty that restrictions on the use should not be arbitrary. They may be imposed, but only if they are justified (namely on public health reasons). This is the case in particular of tobacco and food trademarks, where restrictions may be imposed by international rules adopted by the World Health Organization (WHO). In any event, where they impose (justifiable) restrictions on the use of certain signs, governments are still obliged to make them registrable (Article 15.4 of the TRIPS Agreement) and keep the registrations alive (Article 19.1 of the TRIPS Agreement).

[2] Economic Importance of Marks

Marks are nowadays widely used in practically all countries—whether developing or industrialized countries, market-economy or planned-economy countries—and they play an important economic part in marketing and trade. However, as a matter of course, the intensity of the use of trademarks is directly related to the level of economic freedom in a given economy. In centrally planned economies, dictated by equalitarian ideologies, the main social goal is to achieve uniformity among citizens. This leads to a severe undermining of differentiation of products and services, which destroys the value of IP. As said, IP protection is fundamentally a tool of private entrepreneurship, whether it covers literary, art or scientific works, inventions, signs, reputation, origin because the exclusive rights it provides can only be fully enforced in an environment of rivalry, of free competition. Marks serve equally the purposes of those who offer goods or services on the market—such as manufacturers, producers, distributors, wholesalers and retailers—and the interests of consumers, public authorities and the economy in general. A mark enables the enterprise that uses it to draw the attention of possible consumers to the existence of the goods bearing that mark, to hold their attention once they have become acquainted with the products and, finally, to distinguish them from products of the same type that are offered on the market. An enterprise may, in this way, acquire a reputation for the products it offers under a given mark. The value represented by the mark derives from this association between a mark and a product and thereby enables demand for the goods bearing that mark to be maintained and expanded and to compete with other enterprises that offer goods of the same type. Once a mark has already acquired a firm reputation, it also makes it easier to penetrate new markets and thus stimulate export activities.

Marks also meet the interests of consumers in various ways and to a not inconsiderable extent. The use and promotion of marks helps to make consumers aware of the goods and services available on the market, to more readily identify their origin and to effect a choice between similar goods and services. These are all factors that stimulate competition. In the long term, this may lead to an increase in the number and types of consumer goods and bring about an eventual drop in prices. The use of marks may also stimulate competition between users in respect of quality, which, in the long term, can help to improve the overall quality of goods and services.

An effective trademark system likewise contributes to the protection of consumers against various forms of unfair trading practices (e.g., the use of misleading marks or confusingly similar marks). Many countries do not have specific legislation on consumer protection, or where such legislation does exist, the consumers are frequently not in a position to assert their rights. In such cases, trademark legislation can constitute one of the rare sources of law available to protect the consumer.

Marks are equally useful to the national authorities, particularly to those responsible for verifying the quality and other characteristics of goods and services. The use of marks may assist them, for example, in identifying, as a result of complaints that have been received or of tests that have been carried out, those goods and services that do not comply with the statutory requirements, from among the goods and services that are identical or that belong to the same category. Finally, the registration of marks constitutes a useful source of statistical and economic information for the national authorities.

Every country has therefore an interest in setting up an effective system to ensure that marks are protected and used in a way that satisfies the legitimate interests of producers and consumers and which enables the best use to be made of the contribution trademarks can make to economic development.

[B] Trade Names

Trade names are generally names, terms or designations which serve to identify and distinguish an enterprise and its business activities from those of other enterprises. Whereas marks distinguish the goods or services of an enterprise, a trade name identifies the entire enterprise without necessarily any reference to the goods or services it puts on the market and symbolizes the reputation and goodwill of the business as a whole. Thus, a trade name is a valuable asset for the enterprise it identifies. It is also a useful source of information for consumers. Therefore, it is in the interest of both business enterprises and consumers that trade names be protected and that legal measures be adopted to prevent the use of trade names in ways that are likely to confuse or mislead consumers.

Trade names are protected under most national laws. However, the legal regimes governing trade names vary considerably from country to country. They are typically determined by a combination of provisions of civil, commercial, company, trademark and/or unfair competition laws and/or special laws on trade names. Many countries provide for a registration system of trade names, although the systems vary significantly as to both their territorial scope (local and/or national) and the legal consequences of registration.

In some countries, trade name protection is extended to the protection of shop signs, i.e., the names of specific places of business. But in other countries, in the absence of a specific regime of registration and protection of shop signs, the law of repression of unfair competition applies. The geographical scope of protection of shop signs does not go beyond the limits of the area of influence of the business in question—being understood that beyond those limits, customers would not be misguided by the existence of a similar or identical shop sign for the same sort of business. Those limits may not go beyond one given street, or a neighborhood, and, in rare cases, an entire city.

In the modern economy, the regime of shop signs overlaps with that of trademarks, and this explains that a sui generis protection for shop signs, which existed in various countries in the middle of the twentieth century, was gradually abandoned. But shop signs, as such, have not disappeared. One of its modern expressions is domain names—the name of places where e-business is conducted.

Trade name protection very frequently overlaps with trademark protection because of the coincidence of their respective expressions. However, they are conceptually different, as are their geographical scope as well as the means of evidence of infringement. This is what Article 8 of the Paris Convention says when it says that trade names are to be protected "whether or not [they form] part of a trademark."

[C] Trade Dress

Trade dress—a creation of jurisprudence—is the name given to the combination of elements that, as a whole, permit the identification of a product or a commercial establishment. Generally, those elements are visually perceptible, but not necessarily. For example, the unique scent of the fragrances used by companies like Abercrombie & Fitch (a United States (US) lifestyle retailer) and Uno de 50 (a Spanish fashion jewelry maker and retailer) are an integral part of the trade dress of the firms' stores. Under the law of some countries, trade dress may be registered as trademarks, but in general, it is covered by the large umbrella of repression of unfair competition.

[D] Geographical Indications

Among the types of commercial designations are indications of source and AOs. Before the entry of the TRIPS Agreement into force, indications of source and AOs together formed what were referred to as *GIs*. However, Articles 22-24 of the TRIPS Agreement introduced a legal regime for GIs that lies somewhere between indications of source, which protection stems almost exclusively from rules of repression of unfair competition, and AOs, whose rules were set in the Lisbon Agreement for the Protection of Appellations of Origin and their International Registration, of 1958. A revision to the Lisbon Agreement has approached GIs and AOs (*see* the Act of Geneva, 2015).

An indication of source is constituted by any denomination, expression or sign indicating that a product or service originates in a country, a region or a specific place (for instance, "made in ..."). As a general rule, the use of a false or deceptive indication of source is unlawful.

An AO is constituted by the denomination of a country, a region or a specific place that serves to designate a product originating therein, the characteristic qualities of which are due exclusively or essentially to the geographical environment, in other words, to natural and/or human factors. The use of an AO is lawful only for a certain circle of persons or enterprises located in the geographical area concerned and only in connection with the specific products originating in that area (for instance, "Bordeaux," "Champagne").

GIs, as per the TRIPS Agreement, do not necessarily consist of denominations of a country, region or place. Any word that has acquired the meaning of origin may serve as a GI. The word "Basmati," for example, which means aromatic rice, is not an AO in a strict sense but serves as a GI to the extent it is associated with a particular variety of rice that grows in the region of Punjab, comprising parts of the territories of India and Pakistan.

Indications of source, GIs, and AOs serve to identify the source or origin of the products or services for which they are used. AOs, however, have an additional function. Whereas an indication of source shows only from where a product comes, an AO indicates, in addition, the characteristic qualities of a product which are determined by the geographical area from which it comes and to which the appellation refers. Furthermore, while any expression or sign evoking the geographical source of a product may constitute an indication of source (e.g., a national emblem), an AO is always a geographical name (generally the name of the country, region or place from which the product originates, although, in some cases, it can refer to a specific geographical area without actually indicating its name).

The legal recognition and protection of indications of source, GIs and AO are in the general interest. They convey very important information to consumers on the geographical origin of goods and services and, indirectly, on their inherent quality and characteristics. Therefore, if properly used, GIs can help the public in its purchasing decisions and frequently exercise a strong influence thereon. However, the wrongful use of GIs can mislead consumers as to the geographical source of goods or services, sometimes thereby causing serious damage to consumers. Furthermore, an enterprise which wrongfully uses a GI might not only mislead the public but might also gain an unfair advantage over its competitors, including those from the geographical area covered by the indication, who, over a period of time, may lose the whole or part of their custom and the goodwill and reputation symbolized by such indication.

§1.06 IP "HYBRIDS": CHARACTER MERCHANDISING AND LAYOUT-DESIGN (TOPOGRAPHIES) OF INTEGRATED CIRCUITS

[A] Section I: IP "Hybrids"

Certain intangible assets used by companies and individuals to differentiate their businesses and products touch upon several specialties of IP. Along this book, we will have the opportunity to discuss a few of them, such as traditional knowledge (TK), traditional cultural expressions (TCEs) and layout-designs (topographies) on integrated circuits. Because of their hybrid nature, those assets may be protected under several forms of IP. Another example of hybrid IP is character merchandising.

[B] Section II: Character Merchandising

[1] The Notion of Character

[a] Definition

Broadly speaking, the term "character" covers both fictional humans (e.g., Tarzan or James Bond) or non-humans (e.g., Donald Duck or Bugs Bunny) and real persons (e.g., famous personalities in the film or music business, sportsmen).

In the context of the merchandising of characters, it is mainly the essential personality features easily recognized by the public at large which will be relevant. Those personality features are, for example, the name, image, appearance or voice of a character or symbols permitting the recognition of such characters.

[b] Sources and Primary Use of Characters

The main sources of fictional characters are:

(1) literary works (such as Pinocchio by Collodi or Tarzan by E.R. Burroughs);
(2) strip cartoons (such as Tintin by Hergé or Astérix by Uderzo and Goscinny);
(3) artistic works (such as paintings (Mona Lisa by Leonardo da Vinci)) or drawings (the panda of the World Wide Fund for Nature (WWF) or the young boy Fido Dido by Joanna Ferrone and Susan Rose);
(4) cinematographic works (such as Crocodile Dundee, King Kong, Indiana Jones or E.T. with respect to movies, House MD or Seinfeld with respect to television series or Finding Nemo with respect to motion picture cartoons).

It should be noted that, in the case of cinematographic works, the character may, and in fact often does, originate in a literary work (such as the character Oliver Twist by Charles Dickens) or in a strip cartoon (such as the character Batman).

As regards the primary use of a fictional character, it can in most cases be referred to as an "entertainment function." Such a character may appear in a novel, a tale or a strip cartoon (e.g., the character Tarzan in the novel entitled *Tarzan, the Lord of the Jungle*, the character Mr. Brown in the tale entitled *Squirrel Nutkin* or the characters named James Bond or Tintin), and the success gained by the work depicting the character generally leads to new stories. Such primary use will be made by the creator of the character, although where a character has reached a high degree of reputation and the creator has died, the heirs, if any, or the holders of the publishing rights, may organize by means of contracts the "survival" of the character in new stories (e.g., the books featuring James Bond after the death of Ian Fleming). Other creators, on the contrary, may wish that the characters they have created should not be the subject of new stories after their death (e.g., Hergé, the creator of Tintin). The situation is somewhat different in the case of cinematographic works, where it is seldom the creator of a character (the maker of the original drawings or scripts) who makes the primary use (but exceptions do exist, such as the "little man" character created by Charlie Chaplin).

In other cases, the primary uses of a fictional character can sometimes be referred to as "promotional, advertising and recognition functions." This will concern, for example, characters which are closely linked to a certain company (such as the "Michelin Man," the Exxon (Esso) tiger or the Peugeot lion), to a certain product (such as the character Johnnie Walker to a Scotch whisky) or to a given event (such as the mascots used to personalize Olympic Games or World Cup football). Those characters are created with a view to popularizing legal entities, products or services, and activities. Generally, the primary use will not originate from the creator of the character, i.e., the person entrusted with the task of creating the character.

The main sources, where the character is a real person, are the movie and show businesses and sporting activities. In the case of real persons, one should speak of "primary activity" in preference to "primary use." The difficulty with real persons is that actors, for example, may enjoy a reputation both as persons and as the character they may have portrayed in a movie or television series. In some cases, the real person is only referred to under the name of the character portrayed (*see* developments below on the types of character merchandising).

[2] The Concept of Character Merchandising

[a] Definition

Character merchandising can be defined as the adaptation or secondary exploitation, by the creator of a fictional character or by a real person or by one or several authorized third parties, of the essential personality features (such as the name, image or appearance) of a character in relation to various goods and/or services with a view to creating in prospective customers a desire to acquire those goods and/or to use those services because of the customers' affinity with that character.

It should already be emphasized that the person or legal entity which will organize the merchandising activity (the merchandiser) will very seldom be the creator of the fictional character or the real person concerned. The various property or personality rights vesting in the character will be the subject of contracts (such as transfer or license agreements or product or service endorsement agreements), enabling one or several interested third parties to be regarded as authorized users of the character.

The following examples of character merchandising can be given:

(1) a toy is the three-dimensional reproduction of the fictional character Mickey Mouse;
(2) a T-shirt bears the name or image of the fictional characters Ninja Turtles;
(3) the label attached to a perfume bottle bears the name "Beyoncé";
(4) tennis shoes bear the name "André Agassi";
(5) a box of chocolates bears the name and the photo of Cristiano Ronaldo;
(6) an advertising movie campaign for the drink Coca Cola Light shows the pop star Elton John drinking Coca Cola Light.

[b] A Brief History of Character Merchandising

As an organized system, character merchandising originated and was initiated in the United States of America (USA) in the 1930s at the Walt Disney Studios in Burbank (California). When this company created its cartoon characters (Mickey, Minnie, Donald), one of its employees, Kay Kamen, established a department specialized in the secondary commercial exploitation of those characters and, to the surprise of most, succeeded in granting an important number of licenses for the manufacture and distribution of low-priced mass market merchandise (posters, T-shirts, toys, buttons, badges, drinks).

Of course, the idea of secondary exploitation of the reputation of a character existed before the twentieth century, but the reasons were not directly commercial. In South East Asia, for example, the religious characters of "Ramayana," such as Prince Rama, Vishnu and Sita, have for centuries been represented in the form of sculptures, puppets or toys. Furthermore, in more recent times (the late nineteenth century), some industrialists, with a view to popularizing the goods they manufactured, decided to create fictional characters which would be represented on the goods, the packaging or any documents and would be used to generate secondary exploitation for functional or ornamental goods such as decorative plates, articles of clothing, clocks, and puppets (e.g., in France, the character Pierrot Gourmand (a famous mark for lollipops) or the Michelin Man of the tire manufacturer). Furthermore, the exploitation of literary characters probably started with the works of Beatrix Potter (the books *Peter Rabbit* and *Squirrel Nutkin* with the animal characters which became and still are represented in the form of soft toys or other articles for children) or with the work of Lewis Carroll (*Alice in Wonderland*), the characters of which also became soft toys and were later adapted into a motion picture cartoon.

This phenomenon developed rapidly during the twentieth century. In the 1950s, political, movie and show-business personalities authorized, for example, the reproduction of their names or images on articles of clothing (so-called tie-in advertising).

Today, famous sports persons commercialize entire lines of products, like apparel and accessories, under their name, like CR7, which results from the addition of Cristiano Ronaldo's acronym with the number he displays on the back of his football uniforms. In the 1970s and the 1980s, "merchandising" programs were set up on the basis of famous characters from films (e.g., Star Wars, E.T. or Rambo). The financial consequences are very significant, and frequently movie companies obtain more revenues from merchandising goods bearing the names or images of the famous characters created in their studios than from movie ticket sales.

Furthermore, the range of goods or services covered by "merchandising" expanded considerably since, for example, in the USA, it concerns at least twenty-nine of the forty-two classes of the International Classification of Goods and Services established by the Nice Agreement.

Today, "merchandising" programs (whether or not they include the use of the essential personality features of a character) may concern a great variety of goods and services:

(1) universities (in the USA, merchandising of Washington University in St. Louis, Missouri) with its name and logo on t-shirts and mugs;
(2) organizations (advertising campaign for Amnesty International in France with the participation of famous film actors, or merchandising of the representation of a panda by the WWF);
(3) sports events (merchandising of the mascots of the 2016 Olympic Games in Rio de Janeiro (Brazil));
(4) social events (wedding of Prince Charles and Lady Diana in the United Kingdom (UK));
(5) art exhibitions (merchandising of the images of Van Gogh or Toulouse-Lautrec);
(6) natural events (merchandising in connection with Halley's Comet), scientific events (the comic strip character Snoopy was the mascot of the first American astronauts);
(7) personalities in many fields of activity (actors, pop stars, sportsmen, etc., whose names and images are reproduced on various goods, packaging, documents or other material).

This historical introduction can be concluded with four examples showing the impact and importance of character merchandising. First, in the USA, after the wide advertising campaign made by the IBM Company for its computers, using a look-alike of Charlie Chaplin, the character who appeared was sometimes referred to no longer as Charlie Chaplin but as "the IBM Guy." Second, in the case of the Euro Disney Park which was inaugurated in April 1992 near Paris, a company obtained, for the whole of Europe, the exclusive right to reproduce the Walt Disney characters. Third, the profits made in France from a Toulouse-Lautrec retrospective exhibition (mainly by the sales of merchandised products relating to the image of the painter) enabled the Louvre Museum to purchase an important painting for its collection. Finally, the Sony

Corporation, like other entertainment companies, has formed a character merchandising unit that will sell products based on its music, film and video businesses.

[c] Types of Character Merchandising

From a commercial or marketing point of view, character merchandising can probably be dealt with in a single category. However, from the legal point of view it is important to differentiate between the various subjects of merchandising since the scope and duration of legal protection may vary according to the subject involved.

Two main categories exist depending on whether the merchandising involves the use of fictional characters or real personalities (generally referred to as "personality merchandising"). Between those two categories, a third hybrid category exists which is generally referred to as "image merchandising."

[i] Merchandising of Fictional Characters

This is the oldest and the best-known form of merchandising. It involves the use of the essential personality features (name, image, etc.) of fictional characters in the marketing and/or advertising of goods or services.

Originally, the practice of character merchandising, as an organized system of promotion, developed as a means of exploiting the popularity of cartoon characters, drawings of attractive figures and the like. Such cartoon characters originated:

(1) in a literary work being adapted to the cartoon form (for the purpose of a movie or a comic strip) such as the characters Pinocchio or Alice in Wonderland;
(2) in a work created as a cartoon character, originally for films (Mickey Mouse, Donald Duck, Pluto) or for comic strips (Tintin, Snoopy, Astérix, Batman);
(3) in a film character, later reproduced or adapted as a cartoon for advertising and merchandising purposes (the character Zorro or even a real creature such as the shark in the film "Jaws");
(4) in a videogame, such as Angry Birds and Minecraft, where characters were not initially individualized, but the success of the games on various platforms triggered their commercial exploitation in a multitude of forms, such as toys, board games, and books;
(5) in a cartoon character created mainly for the purpose of merchandising and not, originally, intended for a movie or comic strip (e.g., the character Fido Dido, exploited by Fido Dido, Inc. for a number of goods including the drink "Seven-Up" which was the subject of a worldwide advertising campaign, or the numerous mascots created and used in respect of various events, such as sports competitions);
(6) in a puppet or doll character designed for a film or a television show (e.g., the character E.T., the Gremlins or the Muppets).

Character merchandising with cartoon characters involves mainly the use of the name, image and appearance of the character. The appearance may involve two-dimensional reproduction (drawings, stickers, etc.) or three-dimensional reproduction (dolls, key rings, etc.).

[ii] Personality Merchandising

This form of merchandising involves the use of the essential attributes (name, image, voice and other personality features) of real persons (in other words, the true identity of an individual) in the marketing and/or advertising of goods and services. In general, the real person whose attributes are "commercialized" is well known to the public at large; this is the reason why this form of merchandising has sometimes been referred to as "reputation merchandising." In fact, from a commercial point of view, merchandisers believe that the main reason for a person to buy low-priced mass goods (mugs, scarves, badges, T-shirts, etc.) is not because of the product itself but because the name or image of a celebrity appealing to that person is reproduced on the product.

This category can be subdivided into two forms. The first form consists in the use of the name, image (in two or three dimensions) or symbol of a real person. This form relates mainly to famous persons in the film or music industries. However, persons connected with other fields of activity may be concerned (e.g., members of a royal family). As indicated above, it is not so much the product which is of principal importance to the consumer, but rather the name or image that it bears is the main marketing and advertising vehicle. The second form occurs where specialists in certain fields, such as famous sports or music personalities, appear in advertising campaigns in relation to goods or services. The appeal for the potential consumer is that the personality represented endorses the product or service concerned and is regarded as an expert. Of course, the more the product or service advertised is linked with the activity of the personality, the more the potential consumer will consider that the said product or service is endorsed and approved by that personality (advertising for tennis shoes or rackets by a tennis champion, advertising for an energy drink by a cross-country runner or advertising for high-fidelity equipment or musical instruments by a pop star).

[iii] Image Merchandising

This is another form of merchandising. It involves the use of fictional film or television characters, played by real actors, in the marketing and advertising of goods or services. In those cases, the public sometimes finds it difficult to differentiate the actor/actress (real person) from the role he/she plays (character portrayed). Sometimes, however, there is a complete association, and the real person is referred to and known by the name of the character. The following examples can be given to illustrate this notion: from the film industries, Laurel and Hardy, the Marx Brothers, Crocodile Dundee, James Bond 007 played by Sean Connery and Roger Moore, Frankenstein's monster by Boris Karloff and Tarzan by Johnny Weissmuller; from television series, Columbo played by Peter Falk, the character J.R. in "Dallas," played by Larry Hagman, or the character McGy ver played by Richard Dean Anderson. In the case of the latter, a T-shirt bearing the image of R.D. Anderson would be referred to as a "McGyver T-shirt," while packs of dairy products reproducing the image of R.D. Anderson would mention the name McGyver, the purchasing of such product giving the possibility of winning secondary "McGyver" products such as T-shirts or travel bags.

In the case of image merchandising, goods or services will be marketed with the merchandising of distinctive elements of a film or series (appearance and dress of the actor/actress when playing the character coupled with memorable aspects of a scene (e.g., introductory scenes of the James Bond movies, the appearance and weapons of Rambo or the "knife scene" in Crocodile Dundee)).

[3] Forms of Legal Protection

[a] Copyright

In the context of copyright, the most relevant aspects of the merchandising of fictional characters and image merchandising are books, pamphlets and other writings, audiovisual works, works of drawing and photographic works. As regards personality merchandising, the relevance of copyright is primarily in the sphere of photographic and audiovisual works.

Furthermore, the notion of adaptation is very important. Article 2(3) of the Berne Convention reads as follows:

> Translations, adaptations, arrangements of music and other alterations of a literary or artistic work shall be protected as original works without prejudice to the copyright in the original work.

The multiplicity of communication media offers, at the present time, a great number of possibilities for the creation of adaptations (derivative works). Many film adaptations are probably more well known than the novel or short story on which they were based (e.g., the Pinocchio and Cinderella cartoons by the Walt Disney Studios are probably better known to many children than the original stories, written by Collodi and Charles Perrault, respectively). Some famous artistic figures have been widely merchandised once they have fallen into the public domain. For some goods or services, a fictional character may be the subject of a monopoly (through trademark protection), but generally it may be exploited by anybody. For example, the famous Mona Lisa (La Gioconda) by Leonardo da Vinci has been, and still is, used on various goods or their packaging (postcards, card games, dolls, alcoholic beverages, chocolate or fruit boxes, mineral water, diaries); it has also been the subject of multiple transformations (cartoons, caricatures, fancy photographs, etc.).

Drawings or cartoons (two-dimensional works) may be protected independently if they meet the substantive requirements of copyright protection. In that respect, it should be emphasized that a work which is original is not necessarily new since a graphic adaptation of an already existing literary character (whether or not that character has fallen in the public domain) may qualify for copyright protection (e.g., the literary characters Pinocchio or Cinderella adapted to the cartoon form by the Walt Disney Company). The same will apply to the drawing of a common creature (e.g., the cartoon character Donald Duck). Furthermore, it should be noted that, mainly in the case of cartoon strips and animated cartoons, copyright protects each different original pose adopted by the character.

Three-dimensional works (mainly sculptures, dolls, puppets or robots), which may be original works or original adaptations of two-dimensional or audiovisual fictional characters, will generally enjoy copyright protection independently of the work in which they appear if they meet the required criteria.

Audiovisual works including fictional characters (films, video games, photographs, film frames or stills) will, as a whole (image and soundtrack), generally enjoy copyright protection if they meet the required criteria. This will be all the more probable since audiovisual fictional characters will often have "started life" as drawings (storyboards or strip cartoons) or been described in a literary work. Copyright protection may extend to the individual visual attributes or to the physical or pictorial appearances (costumes, disguises or masks) of a fictional character.

The relevance of copyright protection in the case of personality merchandising is limited because copyright does not vest in the real person concerned but in the person who created the work in which the essential personality features of a real person appear (e.g., in the case of a biography, copyright belongs to the author; in the case of a sculpture, drawing or painting representing a real person, the copyright belongs to the artist; in the case of a film or television series, the copyright of the work generally belongs to the person who made it possible for the work to be made and who supervised and directed the work of the actors (author or film producer)). However, in the latter example, as a performer, an actor/actress has some rights if the law of the country of which he/she is a national provides for performers' rights or if that country is party to the Rome Convention of October 26, 1961, for the Protection of Performers, Producers of Phonograms and Broadcasting Organizations. Once the Beijing Treaty for Audiovisual Performances comes into force, it will provide additional protection for audiovisual performers, including those who perform in films and television programs.

The question is probably more debatable in respect of photographic works. The reply will depend on who owns the copyright. In most cases, the author of the photographs will own the copyright. If a photograph is commissioned for private and domestic purposes, the commissioning party usually has a right to prevent the making of copies of the photograph or its being shown in public. A final problem relates to the case where the party commissioning the work is not the person who is the subject of the photograph. In any case, forms of protection other than copyright are available for the control of the commercial use of photographic works.

[b] *Trademarks and Service Marks (Marks)*

The essential personality features of a fictional character may, under certain conditions (mainly of a substantive nature), be registered as marks. As regards the essential personality features of a real person, the question seems more debatable, mainly with respect to the image (portrait). In the context of merchandising, the trend has been to adopt stage names and personalized logos which may be more easily registrable (e.g., in the pop music area, such stage names as the Beatles and the Rolling Stones with their respective "Apple" and "Tongue and Lip" logos). Another way for a real person to protect his/her name is to obtain registration of the nickname by which he/she is known (e.g., in the USA, the famous football player Elroy Hirsch, known as "Crazy Legs," or, as mentioned above, CR7 for Cristiano Ronaldo).

In countries where rights only result from registration, the main impediment however is the time needed to obtain registration because, in the context of merchandising, delays should be as short as possible since the public's recognition of many characters (such as E.T., Dick Tracy or Batman) and their popularity are of limited duration. However, there are some exceptions, such as the cartoon characters of Walt Disney or the literary characters of Beatrix Potter.

Some of the conditions of form to be met by a mark which is the subject of an application will have an important impact in the context of merchandising. One of those conditions which exists in a few countries concerns the relation which should exist between the goods or services to which the mark applies and the business of the owner of the mark. Generally, neither a merchandising agency nor the creator of a character will themselves be engaged in the manufacture or marketing of secondary products, and it will therefore be difficult for them to acquire trademark rights in a fictional character because they will not themselves be dealing with the goods or services. Furthermore, the activity carried out by a licensee will not be considered as business generated by the licensor, unless the latter becomes a joint owner of the licensee's business.

The modern trend is more favorable, however, since it is more and more widely recognized that a mark can be applied to an unlimited number of goods or services, independently of the true activity of the applicant but notwithstanding the provisions which may exist with respect to the non-use of a registered mark. However, a difficulty may arise in those countries, like the US, which require that the licensor exercises quality control in the use of the mark by the licensee. Absence of such control, or of any activity that ensures compliance with minimum quality standards by the licensee, may give rise to a situation of *naked license*, and the licensor may lose the mark.

In view of the "aesthetic functionality" doctrine (mainly in the toy or doll area) or the "primarily functional" external appearance of goods, three-dimensional configurations of goods (applied for in the form of two-dimensional graphic representations) are in principle not accepted for registration as trademarks in many countries, except where the trademark has acquired secondary meaning in connection with the goods.

Further conditions are of a substantive nature. One of the main conditions is that a mark should be distinctive, in other words, neither generic nor descriptive in respect of the goods or services covered. Furthermore, a mark should not be misleading (capable of deceiving the public) or contrary to public order or morality.

In some countries, however, distinctiveness alone is not sufficient and the personality features of a fictional character will be registrable as marks only if they have acquired a secondary meaning. In other countries, the acquisition of a secondary meaning can remedy the inherent lack of distinctiveness of the essential features of a fictional character.

A number of countries have a more favorable approach, and most names and appearances of fictional characters are considered fanciful and therefore sufficiently distinctive.

As regards the essential features of a real person, the latter, or the person or entity entitled to act in his/her name, may obtain the registration of his/her name or appearance as a mark in some countries. However, where a surname (which can also be a trade name) is registered as a mark, the exclusive right of the holder may be limited since other persons bearing the same name may, under certain conditions, continue to use their names, unless the registered mark concerns a well-known personality and/or trade name and the other persons intend to take advantage of the reputation of the registered mark by parasitic means.

In countries where proof of use is required in order to obtain protection, the use made by authorized users such as licensees or merchandisers is considered as use of the mark made by its holder (*see* Article 19.1 of the TRIPS Agreement), provided that the use if kept by the holder under certain sort of control (but without the need for a formal license agreement). This provision is most relevant to holders engaged in merchandising programs.

[c] Industrial Designs

Industrial design protection is mainly relevant for cartoon characters represented in the form of aesthetic designs for three-dimensional articles which mainly belong to the toy or costume jewelry areas (dolls, robots, puppets, action figures, brooches, "pins") which generally originate in cartoons, but which may sometimes represent real persons. The relevance of design protection will be of importance notably when copyright protection is excluded or reduced, mainly when a character has been created with the intention of being industrially exploited. Furthermore, since design protection is often subject to registration, a design application will be helpful to establish prima facie evidence of ownership as from the date of the application, although effective protection will only commence on the date of registration of the design.

[d] Other Forms of Protection

Many countries have enacted provisions, either under general law (Constitution, Civil Code, etc.) or under specific statutes, which enable a real person as such to be protected against the unauthorized commercial or advertising use of the essential features of his or her personality (name, pseudonym or nickname, image, symbols, etc.) or a real, recognizable person portraying a character against the unauthorized commercial or advertising use of the essential features of the character portrayed. Those rights will, in general, supplement the protection which may be available within the scope of IP in its broadest sense (including marks, industrial designs, copyright, unfair competition). Such protection may be achieved through the notions of defamation or libel, privacy rights and personality or publicity rights.

[C] Section III: Layout-Designs (Topographies) of Integrated Circuits

[1] Introduction

Although prefabricated components of electrical circuitry have been used for a long time in the manufacture of electrical equipment (e.g., radios), large-scale integration of a multitude of electrical functions in a very small component became possible as a result of advances in semiconductor technology. Integrated circuits are manufactured in accordance with very detailed plans or "layout-designs."

The layout-designs of integrated circuits are creations of the human mind. They are usually the result of an enormous investment, both in terms of the time of highly qualified experts and financially. There is a continuing need for the creation of new layout-designs which reduce the dimensions of existing integrated circuits and simultaneously increase their functions. The smaller an integrated circuit, the less the material needed for its manufacture, and the smaller the space needed to accommodate it. Integrated circuits are utilized in a large range of products, including articles of everyday use, such as watches, television sets, washing machines, automobiles, as well as sophisticated data processing equipment.

Whereas the creation of a new layout-design for an integrated circuit involves an important investment, the copying of such a layout-design may cost only a fraction of that investment. Copying may be done by photographing each layer of an integrated circuit and preparing masks for the production of the integrated circuit on the basis of the photographs obtained. The possibility of such copying is the main reason for the introduction of legislation for the protection of layout-designs.

Layout-designs of integrated circuits are not considered to be industrial designs in the sense of the laws providing for the registration of industrial designs. This is because they do not determine the external appearance of integrated circuits but rather the physical location, within the integrated circuit, of each element with an electronic function. Moreover, layout-designs of integrated circuits are not normally patentable inventions because their creation usually does not involve an inventive step, although it requires a great deal of work by an expert. Further, copyright protection may not apply if national law determines that layout-designs cannot be copyrighted.

[2] The Treaty on Intellectual Property in Respect of Integrated Circuits

[a] Introduction

At the international level, the Treaty on Intellectual Property in Respect of Integrated Circuits ("IPIC Treaty") was adopted under WIPO's auspices on May 26, 1989, in Washington, D.C. This was the result of an extensive preparatory phase that included four meetings of an ad hoc Committee of Experts, consultations with developing countries and the preparation of special studies by the WIPO Secretariat. The Treaty has not entered into force but its substantive provisions have, to a large extent, been incorporated by reference in the TRIPS, which was concluded in 1994.

The preparatory meetings highlighted the critical attitude of developing countries, which questioned the need for a Treaty on this issue.

Developing countries considered that protection of investment in layout-designs for chips did not in itself justify the creation of a special IP title. It was argued that not every creation justified departure from the principle of free competition. Because of the implications of absolute rights in an intellectual creation, only certain specified intellectual creations should enjoy such treatment.

The weakness of the creative foundation on which exclusive rights would be based was also the subject of criticism since in the sui generis regime layout-designs for protectable integrated circuits did not require novelty nor inventive level. It was also pointed out that the creation and application of layout-designs for semiconductors presented a number of technological specificities that affected the legal context. For example, the growing use of computer design systems (especially silicon compilers) diminishes the individual contribution to chip design. The trend toward incorporating software (increasingly protected under copyright) in chips has also brought closer together protection of the former and possible protection of the latter.

As far as the draft Treaty itself was concerned, the main issues related to the definition of protectable objects, the ambiguity of the required provisions ("intellectual effort"), the scope of the requirement regarding "fixing" of the layout-design in a chip, failure to disclose completely, the duration proposed (ten years) and, especially, the content of the rights granted to the owner of the layout-design.

One subject of special concern was the extension of the protection provided for in Article 4 of the draft Treaty to objects that incorporated an unauthorized copy of the microchip. It was considered that this would put developing countries in an extremely disadvantageous situation. Developing countries are net importers of electronic goods and local production capacity only exists in a few of them. To require such countries to assume responsibility for chips incorporated within equipment that they import would be to confront them with the almost impossible task of taking apart and verifying the origin of all the equipment's components. It would be far more reasonable to act against those who in the first-place produce and distribute such equipment.

Taking into account the results of the preparatory work, the expectations of many observers with regard to the Washington Conference included, on the one hand, the hypothesis of relatively easy concordance among industrialized countries and, on the other hand, a defensive position (if not a blockade) on the part of developing countries. The reality was quite different. On the basis of an energetic stand by the Group of seventy-seven, Group B (developed countries) suffered an important division, mainly in connection with the provision on nonvoluntary licenses. The US and Japan voted against (the only two countries to do so), while the Treaty met with firm support from developing countries and the European Community (EC).

Although, as mentioned above, the Group of seventy-seven was far from seeking the adoption of a Treaty on the issue, it considered that the text negotiated represented a reasonable compromise, particularly with regard to the provisions finally adopted on nonvoluntary licenses, "innocent offenders," the duration of protection and conditions of disclosure.

The Treaty lays down international norms approved by the majority of countries, even though they are rejected by the two countries that are currently the world's largest producers of semiconductors. The work carried out and the results achieved obviate the need to deal with the matter in other forums, for example, within the Uruguay Round. Moreover, reopening the discussion would be highly inadvisable and might incite a number of developing countries to reject any form of protection for layout-designs of integrated circuits.

[b] Scope of Protection

[i] Object Protected

In accordance with legislation enacted in developed countries and with the Treaty adopted, layout-design of integrated circuits is protectable. US law, influenced by the technology that predominated at the time of its adoption, refers to protection of the masks and not the layout-designs. The most recent laws in European countries, however, refer to the topography of integrated circuits, which gives an idea of their three-dimensional nature. In any event, the subject of protection is not the technology used to manufacture chips but the layout-design. The objective is to prevent slavish copies of integrated circuits, which can be done at a low cost in comparison with the need to create a new design.

In conformity with a number of laws (although not those of the US nor Japan) and the Treaty, protection does not depend on whether or not the layout-design is fixed in a semiconductor. The protection of layout-designs that are not fixed, therefore intangible, was considered by many delegations at the Washington Conference to be appropriate for the layout-design industry (as opposed to semiconductor manufacturing) emerging in some countries.

Legal control concerns layout-designs for both finished chips and intermediate chips such as gate arrays.

[ii] Protection Requirements

In conformity with legislation adopted and the Treaty, the only requirement for protecting a layout-design is that it should be original or considered to be the equivalent and should be the result of intellectual effort. In contrast to the patent system, therefore, neither novelty nor inventive level is required.

[iii] Type of Protection

It has already been stated that legislation adopted establishes a sui generis title. A number of developing countries questioned the need for establishing such special protection. For example, India considered that integrated circuits could be protected under copyright (a solution that was also proposed by Great Britain). Argentina argued that the provisions on unfair competition contained in the Paris Convention applied. In the case of Switzerland, it was stated that the Federal law of 1983 on unfair competition allowed the distortions resulting from unlawful copying of layout-designs of integrated circuits to be rectified.

The WIPO Treaty leaves each country free to decide on the legal framework (patents, copyright, etc.) under which protection is to be granted, subject to minimum rules laid down in the Treaty and, where appropriate, to international agreements governing the respective field (patents, copyright, unfair competition, etc.). At that time, it was thought that, in view of these restrictions, it was not likely that a country would choose any of these alternative forms of control because it would then have to respect not only the provisions of the Washington Treaty but also those of the other agreements concerned. However, the practice of protection of layout-designs after the entry of the TRIPS Agreement into force proves that idea was wrong: even though many WTO Members have adopted a sui generis regime for the protection of layout-designs, their use is very scarce. In many WTO Members, not one single registration has ever been applied for.

[iv] Rights Granted

In conformity with the legislation mentioned, the owner of a layout-design has the exclusive right to reproduce the design in question, to incorporate it in a chip and to market the semiconductors incorporating it. According to some laws (e.g., the Semiconductor Chips Protection Act (SCPA)), the owner has the right to reproduce and market not only the chips but also the industrial goods incorporating the semiconductor concerned. This is one of the issues that met with the greatest resistance on the part of developing countries during negotiations on the Washington Treaty.

In accordance with the rules proposed for the Treaty, a person acquiring in good faith industrial goods incorporating an infringing semiconductor may be liable vis-à-vis the original owner of the semiconductor (and may have to pay fees). Although it is obvious that any importer of such goods does not in most cases have any real possibility of investigating whether or not the semiconductor incorporated is original, unless he/she takes the equipment apart, he/she is made liable for payment of compensation to the owner of the original circuit when the existence of infringement has been notified.

The final text of the Treaty makes it clear that protection is independent of "whether or not the integrated circuit is incorporated in an article" (Article 3.1(b)), although by not explicitly laying down procedures or penalties, it gives a certain leeway to national laws and judges to determine the legal effects of such a situation.

[v] Obligations of the Owner and Nonvoluntary Licenses

Unlike the patent system, which lays down the obligation to exploit the patent granted, the special protection mentioned does not include any form of obligation regarding exploitation or anything else.

However, some national statutes provide for the possibility of granting nonvoluntary licenses, as is the case in copyright laws under certain circumstances and in patent laws.

The WIPO Treaty also provides for this possibility in one of the articles that prompted the rejection of the Treaty by the US. Article 6.3 provides the following:

> (a) Notwithstanding paragraph (1), any Contracting Party may, in its legislation, provide for the possibility of its executive or judicial authority granting a non-exclusive license, in circumstances that are not ordinary, for the performance of any of the acts referred to in paragraph (1) by a third party without the authorization of the holder of the right ("non-voluntary license"), after unsuccessful efforts, made by the said party in line with normal commercial practices, to obtain such authorization, where the granting of the non-voluntary license is found, by the granting authority, to be necessary to safeguard a national purpose deemed to be vital by that authority; the non-voluntary license shall be available for exploitation only in the territory of that country and shall be subject to the payment of an equitable remuneration by the third party to the holder of the right.
>
> (b) The provisions of this Treaty shall not affect the freedom of any Contracting Party to apply measures, including the granting, after a formal proceeding by its executive or judicial authority, of a non-voluntary license, in application of its laws in order to secure free competition and to prevent abuses by the holder of the right.
>
> (c) The granting of any non-voluntary license referred to in subparagraph (a) or subparagraph (b) shall be subject to judicial review. Any non-voluntary license referred to in subparagraph (a) shall be revoked when the conditions referred to in that subparagraph cease to exist.

[vi] Reverse Engineering

One important limitation on the rights granted under the laws and the Treaty is the admissibility of reverse engineering when it leads to the creation of a new integrated circuit. Reverse engineering has been accepted in practice as a legitimate method of competition in the semiconductor industry. However, it requires technological capabilities and resources that are beyond the majority of developing countries.

[vii] Disclosure

In this field as well the sui generis system is totally innovatory. In some laws, registration of the relevant documentation is not a requirement for protection because protection follows upon the marketing of the product; in other cases, it is possible to withhold from registration any information that the owner considers confidential, thereby virtually making protection a system for the protection of trade secrets. This also weakens one of the fundamental principles of industrial property, namely, the disclosure of knowledge, a principle that has been one of the cornerstones of the search for a balance between public and private interests involved in the granting of monopolies for inventions. In the case of integrated circuits, under some legislation, it is up to the holder of the right to decide what information can be made available to the public and what he/she wishes to keep to himself/herself.

Article 7.2 of the Treaty manages to achieve a certain balance:

> Any Contracting Party shall be free not to protect a layout-design (topography) until the layout-design (topography) has been the subject of an application for registration, filed in due form with the competent public authority, or of a registration with that authority; it may be required that the application be accompanied by the filing of a copy or drawing of the layout-design (topography) and, where the integrated circuit has been commercially exploited, of a sample of that integrated circuit, along with information defining the electronic function which the integrated circuit is intended to perform; however, the applicant may exclude such parts of the copy or drawing that relate to the manner of manufacture of the integrated circuit, provided that the parts submitted are sufficient to allow the identification of the layout-design (topography).

[viii] Duration

The systems in force usually provide for a period of ten years from the date on which the layout-design was first commercialized (or an application for protection was made). If one takes into account the curve of obsolescence of many semiconductors, however, this period could be too long. The Treaty provides for a minimum duration of eight years, without specifying the moment at which the period begins (it could be from the time of the layout-design's creation). As we shall see, this is one of the Treaty provisions that the TRIPS Agreement has modified.

[c] Implications of the Legal Regime

The sui generis regimes adopted in developed countries and in the relevant WIPO Treaty basically establish a right to prevent slavish copying of the protected layout-design. As we have seen, unlike patents, they do not grant exclusivity of exploitation, nor do they prevent independent development of layout-designs (even if they turn out to be identical to other designs already protected), nor "reverse engineering" based on a prior layout-design.

Paradoxically, cases of slavish copying of layout-designs of integrated circuits appear to be infrequent. Generally, litigation involving layout-designs is directly related to the breach of trade secrets.

The lack of effective application of the sui generis regime to semiconductors and the realization that copying is virtually non-existent led two US experts to ask whether the SCPA was not in fact "a solution in search of a problem."

It is not possible to affirm with certainty that the situation described above will alter significantly in the future as a result of technological change.

Only a handful of developing countries are at present manufacturing integrated circuits, and it is unlikely that many more will in the future embark upon a venture that requires considerable investment and is subject to a basically unstable market. Although the layout-design (but not the manufacture) of circuits is taking place in an increasing number of developing countries, it concerns designs for custom and semi-custom circuits, generally protected under contracts between the designer and the company interested in a special application (in the case of individuals). In other words, proprietary technology concerning integrated circuits is in the hands of a small group of companies, based in an even smaller group of countries.

Finally, it should be borne in mind, as we have already said, that "reverse engineering" requires a high level of technological capability and investment. It is outside the capabilities (and the interests) of the majority of developing countries.

The "TRIPS" Agreement concluded as part of the 1994 Uruguay Round of General Agreement on Tariffs and Trade (GATT) incorporates many of the substantive provisions of the Washington Treaty. However, the TRIPS Agreement does not include the provisions of the Treaty that deal with compulsory licenses—which were, as said, one of the major points of contention among Contracting Parties and which led Japan and the US to refuse support to its entry into force.

§1.07 PROTECTION AGAINST UNFAIR COMPETITION

Protection against unfair competition has been recognized as forming part of industrial property protection for more than a century. It was in 1900, at the Brussels Diplomatic Conference for the Revision of the Paris Convention for the Protection of Industrial Property (hereinafter referred to as "the Paris Convention"), that this recognition was first manifested by the insertion of Article 10*bis* in the Convention. In its original version, as adopted at the Brussels Diplomatic Conference, that Article read as follows: "Nationals of the Convention (Articles 2 and 3) shall enjoy, in all the States of the Union, the protection granted to nationals against unfair competition." As a result of the subsequent revision conferences, the article now reads as follows (in the Stockholm Act (1967) of the Paris Convention):

> (1) The countries of the Union are bound to assure to nationals of such countries effective protection against unfair competition.
> (2) Any act of competition contrary to honest practices in industrial or commercial matters constitutes an act of unfair competition.
> (3) The following in particular shall be prohibited:
> 1. all acts of such a nature as to create confusion by any means whatever with the establishment, the goods, or the industrial or commercial activities, of a competitor;
> 2. false allegations in the course of trade of such a nature as to discredit the establishment, the goods, or the industrial or commercial activities, of a competitor;
> 3. indications or allegations the use of which in the course of trade is liable to mislead the public as to the nature, the manufacturing process, the characteristics, the suitability for their purpose, or the quantity, of the goods.

An additional twelve practices are identified as unfair competition in the commentary to the Model Law for Developing Countries on Marks, Trade Names, and Acts of Unfair Competition. They are:

(1) bribing the buyers of a competitor, to secure or retain their patronage;
(2) obtaining the business secrets or trade secrets of a competitor by espionage, or by bribing his/her employees;
(3) using or disclosing, without authorization, the secret technical "know-how" of a competitor;
(4) inducing employees of a competitor to violate their employment contracts or to leave their employer;
(5) threatening competitors with suits for patent or trademark infringement, if done in bad faith and for the purpose of reducing trade by them and hindering competition;
(6) boycotting trade to prevent or hinder competition;
(7) dumping, that is, selling below cost, with the intent and effect of harming or suppressing a competitor;
(8) creating the impression that the customer is being offered an opportunity to make purchases under unusually favorable conditions, when such is not the case;
(9) slavishly copying goods, services, publicity, or other features of the trade of a competitor;
(10) encouraging or utilizing breach of contract by competitors;
(11) effecting publicity which makes comparisons with goods or services of competitors;
(12) violating legal provisions not directly concerning competition to obtain, through such violation, an unfair advantage over other competitors.

Whereas certain industrial property entitlements, such as patents, are granted on application by industrial property offices and confer exclusive rights with respect to the subject matter concerned, protection against unfair competition is based not on such grants of titles but on the consideration—either stated in legislative provisions or recognized as a general principle of law—that acts contrary to honest business practices are to be prohibited. Fair play in the marketplace cannot be ensured only by the protection of registered industrial property rights. A wide range of unfair acts, such as misleading advertising and the violation of trade secrets, also undermine differentiation and therefore must be repressed for the sake of fair and free competition, either under specific laws on industrial property or under general principles on fairness and honesty in trade.

The link between the two kinds of protection is clear when certain cases of unfair competition are considered. For example, in many countries, unauthorized use of a trademark that has not been registered is considered illegal on the basis of general principles which belong to the field of protection against unfair competition (in a number of countries such unauthorized use is called "passing-off"). There is another example of this kind in the field of inventions: if an invention is not disclosed to the public and is considered to constitute a trade secret, the unauthorized performance by third parties of certain acts in relation to that trade secret may be illegal. However, by contrast with patent protection, it is not the performance of those acts per se that is deemed illegal but the dishonest manner of acquiring the secret information, generally through breach of confidence. On this important topic, it is strongly recommended to confer *Gurry on Breach of Confidence*, Tanya Aplin et al., Oxford Univ. Press, 2012.

What is unfair or dishonest largely depends on the economic and social realities at a given time and place. This makes unfair competition law particularly adaptable to changing circumstances and realities. Unfair competition law can furnish a solid legal framework and yet provide a sufficiently flexible standard for formulating and applying measures which can be at the same time sensitive to the particular and ever-changing social and economic conditions in a particular country and effective to combat the specific types of dishonest trade practices which give rise to concern.

The law on the repression of unfair competition is evolving significantly and rapidly, namely in the direction of increasingly becoming a tool for the promotion of *free* competition, rather than of *fair* competition. On the one hand, this brings unfair competition law very close to competition law or antitrust law. On the other hand, unfair competition law is also very closely associated with consumer law.

CHAPTER 2

The History and Evolution of IP

Although the following paragraphs will look at the evolution of three different branches of IP (patents, trademarks, and copyright), the truth is that in spite of them performing the same function—which is differentiating products and services—those different branches may evolve under different circumstances and in different periods. What determines the evolution of IP is social change and, in particular, change in the way society does business. Thus, even though merchants and manufacturers have used business identifiers of various sorts (trade names, trademarks, trade dress, slogans) since Antiquity, we can detect the birth of trademark law in tandem with the emergence of the Commercial Revolution, between the eleventh and the thirteenth centuries. The gradual increase in wealth and in population of Europe, the opening of new fronts of trade (with the Arab countries, in the South of Europe, and in fairs), and the admission of foreign merchants in major cities, led to the adoption of new legal tools of trade, such as insurance contracts, letters of credit—and trademark law. Soon, the guilds that formed the economic structure for trade and manufacture in Medieval Europe started including rules on the use of trademarks by guild masters. As the first treatise ever written on trademark law, *De Insigniis et Armis* (authored by Bartolo da Sassoferrato and published in 1358, one year after his death), explains, the function of trademarks is the same as that of coats of arms. It is not a surprise, therefore, that trademark law has inherited its fundamental legal principle of distinctiveness from heraldry. As Bartolo explained, a confusion between two similar coats of arms could bring their bearers to death by mistake.

As the economy of Europe grew, cities (and countries) started competing with each other. Not only sovereigns had to intervene and settle disputes between cities as far as the use of certain brands were concerned, but they also started to grant incentives to foreign artisans so that they could bring their knowledge (and, in many cases, their families, their tools, and their apprentices) from their cities of origin and teach local artisans. These were industrial privileges, which were granted in the form of *privileges*, in the sense they constituted special favors to certain artisans who were authorized to carry on their businesses in the granting city without belonging to the local corporation.

As privileges, they targeted specific individuals. The first law that promised that sort of privileges to a technical field in general—textiles—was the Cloth Act, passed by Edward III, of England, in 1337. Soon, the practice of granting industrial privileges, which seems to have appeared for the first time in Bordeaux, in 1236, spread throughout Europe. In practice, those privileges operated as tools for technology transfer (TT).

The next major social change with an impact on IP can be detected in that period in which Europe moved from the Middle Ages to the Modern Ages, that is to say, the period that corresponds to the so-called Renaissance. From an economic standing, the factors that triggered such change were again the increase in demography, the expansion of trade routes, and the sudden introduction of new commodities resulting from the Discoveries. In that period, trademarks became business assets, and for the first time their licensing and assignment outside the corporations were authorized. Also, the first rules on the registration of masters' trademarks with a central office were adopted, either in the guild's office or in an office at the municipal authority. The granting of industrial privileges became a matter of administrative routine, and the first statutes concerning them appeared (in Venice, in 1474 and in England, in 1623). Also, very importantly, the reinvention of the movable printing characters, by Gutenberg, and the strong demand for books (first, of translation of classical authors, and, subsequently, of original works) caused the application of a sort of industrial privileges to books. The first printing privileges appeared in Venice (in 1469). In 1544, the Great Council of Venice passed what we could call a predecessor of copyright: a statute that made the printing of new books dependent on the previous permission, in writing, by the authors or their successors. But most printing privileges were granted for specific works, such as the *Lusiads* (1571), the epic poem by Luís Vaz de Camões, and *El Ingenioso Hidalgo de La Mancha* (1606), by Miguel de Cervantes.

The second major social change occurred in the sequence of the period called Enlightenment, when the Scientific Revolution took shape, and the subsequent Industrial Revolution emerged and developed. It is in this era that we can detect the birth of modern patent law, which was dictated by a combination of the globalization of trade with the need of disposing of the surpluses that resulted from industrial production.

Between each of these major changes, IP has gone (and is still going) through incremental changes, in response to new technologies that are sufficiently relevant to justify special IP protection but not enough to cause a major change in the way society does business, such as new types of IP titles that come and go (such as awards and medals, which were the direct product of nineteenth-century international fairs, and were absorbed by the rules of repression of unfair competition in the course of the twentieth century), or new forms of protection that society experiments with (such as the sui generis regime of topographies of integrated circuits).

Anyway, we should never forget that any trends in IP protection are dictated through a bottom-up approach. It is entrepreneurs (small and big, poor and rich) who, in their daily businesses, feel the need for IP protection. It is them who put social pressure on law makers to adopt new laws, or change old laws, or forget them.

This means that it is the society that decides where and how IP is to be established, protected, and used. And as society changes, so does IP. It is the manner in which society uses IP that dictates its evolution.

§2.01 THE HISTORY AND EVOLUTION OF PATENTS

Three periods stand out as important in the history and evolution of patents:

(1) Industrial privileges (thirteenth to eighteenth centuries): sovereign and local authorities granted privileges with the specific purpose of luring foreign artisans, thus circumventing the strict norms that regulated production by guilds or corporations; those privileges conveyed primarily the right to use (as an exception to the quasi-monopolistic regimes of guilds); the right to exclude was a secondary mechanism.

(2) National Patents (eighteenth century to 1883): every inventor was entitled to apply for a patent, the grant of which depended solely on objective conditions; protection of domestic inventions abroad was not entertained; with very exceptions, such as England (Statute of Monopolies, 1624) and Brazil (Decree of 1809), countries would provide for discriminatory treatment against foreign inventors. Patents conveyed primarily the right to exclude, as the regime of corporations gradually disappeared in England and was abolished in France (1789). Economic freedom slowly and gradually emerged. English courts, in the eighteenth century, established basic conditions of patentability, such as enabling disclosure, and US courts, in the nineteenth century, imposed novelty.

(3) Internationalization (1883 to the present): protection of inventions outside their country of origin was developed along with international trade; worldwide or regional conventions assist this development.

[A] Industrial Privileges

Titles of private appropriation of knowledge appeared relatively recently in history, especially if compared to trademarks. The reason is that even if invention has always supported the progress of human societies, the idea of identifying the inventor and bestowing upon him a proprietary right is relatively recent. Obviously, the names of pre-historic inventors did not reach us, even though they existed in profusion, as the enormous quantity of shapes of stone and bone tools, like hammers and saws, shows. But even after the human being developed writing, it was not until the Middle Ages that social leaders started granting proprietary titles in new techniques to their introducers (and, eventually, their inventors) as tools of public policy. There are early notices of such initiatives, like the "law" that was enacted in Sybaris, a Greek colony in southern Italy, in the sixth century B.C. In *The Deipsonophists*, Athenaeus of Naucratis wrote about a statute promising those who created new and especially delicious recipes to be served in official banquets the exclusive right of making those recipes for one year. In spite of its similarities with a modern patent statute, the real reason for Sybaris' statute is the way that society at that time looked at cooks: unlike other artisans, cooks were seen and treated as artists. In parallel with playwrights and poets, who submitted their works to the audiences' approval and patrons' rewards through competitions held on stages, Sybaris' cooks presented their new recipes to public banquets.

Classical writers, such as Pliny the Elder, refer to other examples of cooks being rewarded because of their inventive (and delicious) recipes.

To identify in Sybaris' statute an early patent law, therefore, is an anachronism. Nevertheless, such initiative is worth mentioning in a historical reference to patents because of its background idea of exclusivity—i.e., of appropriation—attributed to the creator of something new. Later, in Alexandria, the Ptolemy dynasty would gather many inventors in the Museum, some of whom would be the greatest inventors of all times, like Ctesibius and Hero. The Museum operated like a modern research institution, and those inventors left written testimonies of extraordinary technical achievements, but they were remunerated by salaries and special privileges—not the right to exclude others. Many of those inventions were to be used in temples and had the objective of awing the faithful. Imhotep, inventor of the pyramid, who worked as a leading administrative official and architect for Egyptian pharaoh Djoser, received great privileges of a financial and social nature—perhaps having his name inscribed in a stela after the name of the pharaoh being the most precious of all prizes that could be granted in Egypt—but he was ultimately an employed inventor. The names of several architects and their technical solutions to construction problems were mentioned by the Roman architect Vitruvius in his treatise *De Architectura* (first century B.C.), but no references to special rewards were made.

The vast commercial network built around the shores of the Mediterranean Sea during the Roman Empire served a genuine society of consumption, as the profusion of objects for daily use by the Romans that are conserved in museums illustrate. But inventions would belong to those who had ordered the construction or making of objects. It was only in the Middle Ages, when the Commercial Revolution (eleventh to thirteenth centuries) gave rise to the opening of new trade routes and gave birth to the first forms of capitalism, that sovereigns, with the objective of broadening the tax basis and, hence, increasing their revenue, started granting special titles to the introducers of new techniques. Those titles would generally be issued by means of *littera patens* or open letters—a letter whose contents would be made public so that all the subjects could know them. Those titles would grant rights of very differing kinds to the beneficiaries, in particular exemption from guild rules, exemption from taxation, allocation of land, interest-free loans, naturalization and even titles of nobility. Some patentees would also receive the right to live within the walls of the granting city. This was, indeed, an important grant because many foreign artisans would migrate at the peril of their lives, for cities would try to keep secret some of the most coveted techniques, like those of working the glass in the Murano style, or the silk, in the manner of Northern Italian cities. Those patents made no distinction between an inventor in the modern sense of the word and the person who introduced a technique already known abroad. However, foreign artisans were the main addressees of letters patent. Manufacture, in general, was the exclusivity of the members of local guilds and therefore was subject to the corresponding rules. Guilds were not necessarily adversary to invention, but the rigidity of their by-laws, which described in detail the standards of production and imposed heavy sanctions on their infringement, would naturally discourage the introduction of significant changes in products and processes.

In exchange for the favors or privileges received, foreign artisans would be under the obligation of hiring local apprentices and teaching them their knowledge. In other words, as said, medieval privileges were essentially a mechanism of TT and dissemination. Indeed, because of the natural restrictions imposed on productive activities by non-guild members, industrial privileges were primarily permissions to use the techniques—and it is here essentially that industrial privileges differ from modern patents: whereas the former granted primarily the right to us, the latter accord primarily the right to exclude. Today, the right to use stems essentially from the laws on the freedom of work.

It was by resorting to industrial privileges that England was successful in establishing its wool industry as from the fourteenth century by luring Flemish artisans with their tools, apprentices and families. The first general statute that promised all sorts of privileges to Flemish artisans who wished to migrate to England and produce wool was enacted by Edward III, in 1327.

Industrial privileges became a fairly usual tool of public policies across Europe. England was perhaps the pioneer, with the earliest known patent having been granted to a certain Bonafusus de Sancta Columba by the city of Bordeaux, in 1234, and confirmed by Henry III, in 1236. The privilege concerned the exclusive making and buying of wool cloth in the manner of the Flemish, the French or the English and had a term of fifteen years.

France, Pisa, Florence, Portugal, Spain, etc., would also grant privileges with the same objectives and under similar conditions. With hindsight, some of those titles were conceptually very interesting and contained aspects that are very modern. For example, a patent granted by John II, king of Portugal, in 1490, for a term of forty years, concerning devices for extracting water from rivers and wells, provided for a compulsory license in favor of those who used the devices for using the water in homes. Users were nonetheless obliged to pay to the patentees the remuneration of two gold florins.

The city of Florence, in 1421, granted a privilege to Brunelleschi, the famous architect of the *duomo*. The privilege had a term of three years and concerned a boat for hauling marble along river Arno. Interestingly, the document contains its own justification: the privilege was granted by the city council because otherwise Brunelleschi would have kept his invention secret. The invention, however, was never put into practice: at his first attempt of building a boat, Brunelleschi saw it sinking in the river.

In 1474, the Republic of Venice adopted a statute establishing the granting of privileges to inventors for ten years. That statute is generally considered the first modern patent statute, but that is an anachronism. Even though the statute established the conditions for the granting of privileges, the Senate would grant them on a case-by-case basis, with different privileges and terms for each patent. The adoption of that Statute and its declared objective of luring foreign skilled artisans was an attempt by Venice to stop its economic decline, caused by the Portuguese success in reaching India by sea and thus destroying Venice's monopoly in the trade of spices. Numerous privileges were indeed granted under the statute, but they would concern the common needs of the city, namely the construction and dredging of canals and the building and operation of mills. Those were important inventions, but they could not serve as the basis for the economic growth of a Republic. It is important to note that the main industries of Venice, in which its artisans excelled, were not benefited by patents: glass (in Murano) and ship building (at the Arsenal). The reason is the same that was mentioned in respect of the Museum of Alexandria: the inventors of new techniques eventually introduced in Murano and in the Arsenal were paid salaries, because they were hired inventors. Nevertheless, the statute of 1474 presented already some aspects of modern patent laws. Besides setting a uniform term (which was not obeyed, as said), it provided for the right to exclude, established penalties for infringement, and foresaw the possibility of compulsory licenses in favor of the Republic (the statute, however, ensured that in the event a compulsory license was granted, the invention would still be operated by the inventor).

In England, in addition to privileges granted with the aim of supporting the expansion of industrial production by the introduction of new techniques, sovereigns would accord monopolies for the exclusive carrying out of commercial activities of many sorts. Those monopolies would frequently cover articles and services that were already provided to citizens, thereby harming the interests of established merchants and manufacturers. A strong reaction against those abusive monopolies, which were granted by the king without consulting with the Parliament, arose in courts, for they were deemed in violation of the common law.

One important trial resulting from that controversy occurred in the case of *The Case of the Tailors of Habits & of Ipswich*, in 1614, in which the King's Bench rejected the guild's plea against Taylor because he had not followed the period of apprenticeship required by the by-laws. Based on a statute enacted under Queen Elizabeth, the court held that reserving work for those who had complied with guilds' by-laws was illegal. This was the end of the corporative regime and the beginning of entrepreneurship. In France this would happen more than one century and a half later, in 1789.

Another significant trial was *Darcy v. Allen*, of 1603. In this case, the King's Bench held the monopoly of making, importing and selling playing cards granted to Darcy to be unlawful on four grounds: (i) the monopoly was against English citizens' freedom to work, as courts had already held in various opportunities; (ii) monopolies were generally harmful to society because they only ensured the private gains of a few individuals; (iii) monopolies could not be granted in so a manner that prejudiced the rights of previously established professionals (thus implying, for the first time, the idea of novelty); and (iv) there could be no justification in giving exclusivity in the trade of cards for twenty-one years to someone who did not possess any special technical skills and knowledge in making cards.

The Parliament reacted against those abusive monopolies by enacting, in 1624, the Statute of Monopolies. Except for a few monopolies that the Statute explicitly preserved from invalidation, it declared all monopolies, dispensations and grants to be void other than:

> any letters patent and grants of privilege for the term of fourteen years or under, hereafter to be made, of the sole working or making of any manner of new manufactures within this realm, to the true and first inventor of such manufactures which others at the time of making such letters patent and grants shall not use.

This statute had remarkable longevity (from 1624 to 1852). In spite of its vagueness (or perhaps exactly because of its broad language), it permitted that courts construed the modern system of patents. The old economic regime presided by the corporative spirit was defeated by the spirit of entrepreneurship that gave rise to the Industrial Revolution, and courts corresponded by building rules in favor of titles that were supportive of innovation and its dissemination. Some fundamental opinions construing the 1624 Statute continue having an impact today, such as the opinion that made the submission of specifications mandatory (*Liardet v. Johnson*, 1778) and the opinion that admitted that processes could also be patented (*Boulton and Watt v. Bull*, 1795).

From 1760, the number of patents granted in England grew rapidly in direct relation to the Industrial Revolution. In the other countries, however, where industrialization began at a later date, the number of patents remained low; in France, the discredit expressed in general in respect of all hindrances to the freedom of production and trade, together with the poor results generally obtained by the owners of "letters patent," led the monarch to decide that these beneficiaries would lose their rights if they had not put their invention into application within a period of one year (declaration of 1762) and to reject a large number of requests for privileges. In an attempt to improve the quality of patents granted, the opinion of the French Academy of Sciences was required—it is here, actually, that we can detect the origins of the modern Patent Office. The Academy's by-laws of 1699 contained an explicit clause referring to the *ex ante* examination of patent applications.

[B] National Patents

Almost simultaneously, the US (1790) and France (1791) adopted patent laws based on the grant of a patent to all inventors, provided that certain objective conditions were met. Article 1 of the French Law of January 7, 1791, was particularly significant: "any discovery or new invention, in all kinds of industry, shall be the property of its author; consequently, the law shall guarantee to him the full and complete enjoyment thereof, in accordance with the conditions and for the time to be determined hereafter."

However, lawmakers had nationalist concerns: a 1793 amendment to the law in the US afforded patents to citizens only; in France, the person introducing foreign techniques was treated on an equal footing with the true inventor, but an inventor who obtained a patent for the invention abroad after having obtained a French patent would lose the enjoyment of the latter. The French regime was undeniably aimed at free riding on English inventions: patent owners could be authorized to keep their inventions secret so that English rivals could not learn about them; moreover, French patent owners were requested to exploit their inventions in France, and the import of patented goods would lead to the invalidation of the patent. Interestingly, an English inventor asked an English court to be granted an extended period for submitting the specifications, thereby keeping his invention secret for a longer period, so as to prevent his French rivals from copying his invention, thus destroying his head-start and the consequent advantage. The court refused. In the court's view, French practices should not be allowed to determine the public policies of the English patent system (*In re Lacy's Patent*, Court of Chancery, 1816).

The new system was extended throughout the early decades of the nineteenth century, particularly as a result of French law being applied in the countries conquered by Napoleon. In the monarchies, either those that had been maintained or had been restored after 1815, the principle of privileges continued, but, in practice, the right to a patent was acknowledged everywhere. As the Industrial Revolution extended to further countries, a quantitative explosion in the number of patents took place: in the years 1815-1820, the US, France and Britain were the only countries that granted more than hundred patents a year. Between 1850 and 1854, these three countries each exceeded thousand, and several other countries granted some hundreds. At the same time as this quantitative development took place, qualitative improvements were introduced. Simple importers of techniques ceased to be treated in the same way as inventors; the concept of novelty was developed; and certain formalities were redefined and, in some cases, simplified. Almost everywhere, except in the US, where substantive examination had been introduced in 1836, a system of registration predominated. France, in 1791, abolished the regime of patent *ex ante* examination as a reaction against the guild regime. The reason was that the *ex ante* examination of patent applications was considered to have similarity with the master work examination under the guild regime. Although foreigners were generally able to obtain domestic patents, it remained fairly rare for one and the same invention to be patented in more than one country. The reason was in part because the complexities of the procedure made multiple protection a complicated matter and one of uncertain effectiveness.

However, the existence of patents was felt to constitute a hindrance to international trade. In the Member States of the Zollverein, the Customs Union of the German States prior to the constitution of a unified Empire in the nineteenth century, the patentee lost the right to oppose imports of goods covered by the patent where they were produced in another Member State of the Zollverein. With the success of free trade, for which England had given the example, it seemed that the patent system would be abandoned at the same time as the customs barriers. However, the inventors and their associates, the industrialists of the technically most developed countries, reacted and launched the idea of international protection for inventions. At the 1873 Universal Exposition in Vienna, a patent congress debated on various ideas in that respect. At the same time, an international economic crisis led to a retreat in the idea of free trade and caused any idea of abolishing patents to be rejected. At Paris, during another universal exposition, an international congress began drawing up a solution for the international protection of industrial property. Developments continued in 1880, and a diplomatic conference finally led, on March 20, 1883, to the signing of the convention that created the Union for the Protection of Industrial Property. The major achievement of that Convention was the adoption of the national treatment principle, which, in the field of patents, had the clear objective of defeating the design of some patent regimes under an undisguised free-riding perspective.

[C] Internationalization

With the signing of the Paris Convention, a period began of internationalization of industrial property and, in particular, of the patent system. The Paris Union provided the framework within which progress was achieved, by means of the periodical revisions of the Convention, rendering the protection of inventions originating in one member country of the Union more readily obtainable and more effective in the other member countries.

At the Stockholm Diplomatic Conference in 1967, an agreement was concluded to create the WIPO (which has become a specialized agency of the United Nations (UN)), providing the industrial property and copyright Unions (the latter having been established under the Berne Convention, of 1996) with a permanent structure. The special needs and aims of the developing countries have been one of the major features of WIPO's activities.

Ever since its creation, the Paris Convention provided the possibility for Member States of the Paris Union to conclude "special agreements" between themselves as regards industrial property. This possibility has been extensively used, particularly for the conclusion of the PCT (1970; administered by WIPO) and the European Patent Convention (EPC) (1973; administered by the European Patent Office (EPO)). These special agreements enable progress to be achieved within a restricted framework where not all Member States of the Paris Union feel the need to increase their international commitment; except where such agreements have a geographical basis, they are accessible to all member countries of the Paris Union.

Regardless of its success in enabling the filing of patent applications in other countries, the Paris Convention still contained a major shortcoming, unacceptable in a globalized commercial environment. The shortcoming was in the way that the national treatment principle operated. Paris Contracting Parties were obliged to grant to foreign or non-resident inventors the same treatment they granted to their own nationals. This meant that where a government wished to abolish patent protection, it could do so, provided it did not grant patents to its own subjects. This aspect was exploited by several countries, which thereby for many years continued free riding on foreign inventions, in particular in the chemical and pharmaceutical sectors. While this was confined to a few countries, the situation was tolerable to the major exporting powers. But the economic growth of a few emerging developing countries, with their own technological capacities, and the newly acquired ability to reverse engineer foreign inventions, and the increase in the number of independent nations gave rise to tensions and concerns as regards the inadequacy of the Paris Convention in a globalized world.

This inadequacy of the patent system was corrected by the adoption of the 1994 TRIPS Agreement, which is Annex 1C to the Agreement that Established the WTO. Besides incorporating the national treatment principle of the Paris Convention, the TRIPS Agreement established its own national treatment principle, in accordance with which WTO Members are obliged to grant to the nationals and those assimilated to residents of the other Members at least the minimum standards of protection that the Agreement contains, and never less than those granted to nationals.

As the international patent system evolved and became more sophisticated, voices were heard in the sense of adding legal security and cohesion to the titles that protected inventions of global value, in particular those that integrate the global chains of value—i.e., those that are integrated in end-products whose assembly lines are not found in one country only but are the result of manufacture disseminated in various national territories.

That was when the idea of a global patent—parallel to the global trademark, under the Madrid system; the global design, under the Hague system; and the global appellation of origin, under the Lisbon system—was born. The PCT represented already a step in that direction, but it was too hesitant because ultimately the decision to grant patents lied in national (or regional) patent offices, and, in spite of the harmonization brought by the TRIPS Agreement, the rights resulting from those titles may vary greatly in strength and duration. However, a significant number of countries rejected either the idea of moving toward a global patent or the proposal of giving binding effects to the searches and preliminary examinations carried out by patent offices that integrate the PCT system. It was when the IP5 group—the group of the five patent offices from the US, Europe, Japan, Korea, and the People's Republic of China—proposed to set a (voluntary) mechanism of sharing information between the participating offices. Under that mechanism—designated as Patent Prosecution Highway (PPH)—once a patent application receives a positive appraisal (in part or in totality) by one of the participating offices, the patent applicant can submit to another office a request for his/her application to be inserted into a *fast-tracking* procedure.

The PPH is still very far from the global patent, but it permits to accelerate the examination of patent applications—a very significant favor in an era when many patent offices are facing backlog issues given the increase in the numbers of patent applications—and increase the quality and the consistency of titles issued.

§2.02 THE HISTORY AND EVOLUTION OF TRADEMARKS

Trademarks are not a creation of our times, even though their current omnipresence is of rather recent origin.

Trademarks, as marks of origin, were affixed by the makers of bricks, leather, weapons, cooking-ware and other things even in the ancient cultures. These marks were either letters, usually initials, or other symbolic signs stamped on the goods to signify the maker of the product. In Sumer, marks (in the shape of seals) were stamped on clay tablets containing contracts, thereby representing the merchants in deals made at a long distance. Privately owned seals were profusely used in Sumer, the first civilization where private trade was carried by merchants who did not operate for the temples or the palace but for their own gain. By contrast, in old Egypt and China, the economy was mainly directed by the sovereign, which explains that relatively few trade-related signs have been found in the territories where those grated civilizations exercised influence, other than public symbols, such as the stamps of the sovereigns and public officials. Certainly, these marks did not exercise their present-day function of facilitating the distribution of goods in a complex economy by distinguishing the goods of one manufacturer or merchant from those of other manufacturers and merchants. Nevertheless, they signify an important element in trademark law, still valid today, namely, that marks create a relationship between goods and their maker. More importantly, those signs were instruments of private entrepreneurship. Such markings were also used as signs of ownership. The English word "brand," often used synonymously with "trademark," even today, reflects this usage: "brand" was the marking placed on cattle by their owners with hot irons.

Trademarks—although not yet called by that "term of art," a word created only in the nineteenth century—continued to play a similar role throughout the greater part of history, including medieval times and the centuries beyond. The modern principles of trademark protection—primarily, the condition of distinctiveness, and, secondarily, the requirement of veracity—were inherited from the law of heraldry in the Middle Ages. Significantly, as already said, the first treatise ever written on trademark law, *De Insigniis et Armis*, by Bartolo da Sassoferrato (published posthumously in 1358), dealt with heraldry.

Marks were of particular significance in the growing production of goods for export. Thus, metal goods were made in England long before the industrial age and the production of steel, and weapons and cutlery carried the traditional signs of their English makers. This is true also of goods made of precious metals. Even today, the marks affixed by the makers of silver teapots or trays in Augsburg, Braunschweig, London, Paris, Amsterdam or Saint Petersburg, in the sixteenth and seventeenth centuries, still serve as the guidelines for ascertaining the quality and origin of such goods.

The guilds constituted the principal form of craft production from the time at which town life began to be reorganized, based on trades, headed by master craftsmen, who achieved that status usually (but not always) following apprenticeship and the completion of a masterpiece. The conditions of manufacture were verified by the guilds' inspectors or jurors. Various marks were used: the guild mark, the master craftsman's mark chosen once and for all when the master's status was conferred upon him/her; occasionally, a journeyman's mark or a local mark (indicating the geographical origin). These marks could take the shape of seals attached to pieces of material or hallmarks on articles of precious metal.

The aim was to check that the organization of the profession was respected both as regards the rules of manufacture and compliance with the distribution of tasks between the various trades. These marks, aimed at making the craftsmen feel responsible, were mostly compulsory and do not seem to have played any significant part in winning customers, except in the case of local marks, representing the city's arms. Indeed, the guild regime discouraged competition within the city, but the goods manufactured by the local guild would compete with the goods made in other cities at the fairs and at the halls.

It was forbidden to use a mark belonging to someone else, and the severity of penalties laid down in the sixteenth century for counterfeits shows that the transgression of the rules spread with the decline of the guilds. Examples are the 1544 Edict of Charles V, which dictated exclusion from the trade and severance of the right hand, and the 1564 Royal Edict of France which imposed the death sentence for counterfeit marks on gold cloth.

In France, the guilds were abolished by the Law of March 17, 1791, and the privileges of the English guilds disappeared entirely in 1835. However, as said above, well before those dates, the guild system was already declining, losing ground to non-regulated professions, to international trade and, starting with the Industrial Revolution, to large-scale undertakings. The disappearance of the guild rules led to that of the guild marks, which were replaced by more modern types of trademarks in the eighteenth century.

Trademarks began to assume their present-day role in the course of the last century. The advent of mass production, the establishment of a more complicated system of distribution of goods from the producer to the buyer, and the growing trade in goods all brought with them the need for a universally applicable identification of the goods.

With the increasing use of trademarks, there also came an increase in copying. Cheap knives and forks could be passed off as cutlery from, for example, Sheffield by copying the marks of the makers of Sheffield. The cases were numerous. Usually, the rightful users of the marks had no means of stopping the counterfeiters. The marking of their goods provided them with no legally recognized right, and the general law was hardly developed anywhere to such an extent that such counterfeiting could be pursued as an act of deceit or, in our present language, as an act contrary to honest business practices. Commercial morality usually also did not consider such acts as wrong. However, in the course of time, remedies were developed by the courts, or the legislatures acted to stop the infringement of trademark rights.

In England, a remedy against such infringement was developed by the courts beginning in the middle of the nineteenth century. It is sufficient to point out that a time came when the user of a trademark was seen as entitled to exclude others from willfully taking away the reputation he/she had developed under the mark. This was the birth of the famous action of passing-off: no person is entitled to pass off his/her goods as those of another.

British law at that time was in force in many countries, including the region of North America which became the US.

After the independence of the US in 1776, it was only a slow process which resulted in separate legal development in that country. Presently, of course, the legal system of the US, while still having many things in common with the legal system of the UK, is totally separate and independent. In the field of trademarks, similar court decisions developed as in the UK. Eventually, the coalition of trademark owners became strong enough to convince the federal legislature, the Congress, to pass a trademark act. This was done in 1870, but that act lasted only for seven years, when it was declared unconstitutional. In any event, it took until 1905 before a new comprehensive trademark act was enacted. This was, interestingly enough, the same year that the UK adopted a new trademark act.

On the European continent, as a result of the absence of a system like the British common law, trademark protection could be adopted only by the legislatures. One of the first countries to enact a comprehensive law was France, whose 1857 law remained in force for more than hundred years. Many European countries, such as Germany and Italy, still had to find their national unity. Thus, in Germany, the first legislative protection provided for registered trademarks was a Prussian ordinance of 1874. The first "Reichsgesetz" of 1874, only three years after the formation of the German Reich, was quite limited in scope and allowed only pictorial marks to be registered. The first comprehensive enactment in Germany was that of 1896. The development in the neighboring countries was quite similar.

The development in trademark law in this century can be summarized under a few headings: use or registration as the basis for the creation of rights; recognition of modern ways of exploiting trademarks (assignment, licensing); recognition of new theories of trademark protection.

These developments were not only those by legislatures; very often, the significant lines were established by court decisions.

As far as the recognition of new theories of trademark protection in the twentieth century is concerned, reference could be made to the British Act of 1938 and the Benelux Trademark Act of 1970.

The British Act for the first time created new rights for the trademark owner, namely the right to exclude any trademark use, whatever, regardless of whether there was a likelihood of confusion or not. Thus, in the British law, it seems that where a competitor refers to a trademarked product in order to present the advantages of his/her own product, he/she could be enjoined for trademark infringement. The Benelux Act has also created a new right, namely, the right to enjoin any use which is causing damage to the trademark owner, regardless of the similarity of goods. These examples show that the traditional notion of trademarks as signs indicating origin, and nothing else, is no longer quite true, even as far as present trademark legislation is concerned.

National developments in trademark law have been influenced to a substantial degree by developments in the international field. Particular reference should be made to the Paris Convention. The Paris Convention is the basic international convention in the field of industrial property, including trademarks. It is supplemented by the Madrid Agreement on the International Registration of Marks, signed in 1891, a special union for members of the Paris Convention. The international recognition of foreign trademarks started hesitantly in the seventeenth century by means of bilateral agreements. The idea behind those agreements was to ensure that trade benefits granted to one specific contracting country should not be diverted to benefit goods originating in other countries. Therefore, contracting parties would provide reciprocal and automatic recognition to the trademarks registered in their countries of origin. This concept lies behind the idea of protection of trademark "as is" (*telle quelle*) that the Paris Convention still keeps, as a sort of a legal fossil. In 1994, the TRIPS Agreement added a few important elements to the Paris Convention provisions on trademarks, such as the protection of well-known trademarks against dilution, the exception to rights as regards the use of third parties' trademarks for purely informative purposes, and the prohibition of compulsory licenses of trademarks.

The important point under the aspect of the history of trademark law is that the ratification of these international treaties and their transformation into national legislation has contributed substantially to making the field of industrial property law as international as it is today. The international conventions embody the common views of the international community in industrial property law, and the standards of these treaties were carried into national legislation again and again, especially when the conventions were revised.

§2.03 THE HISTORY AND EVOLUTION OF COPYRIGHT

The idea of copyright protection only began to emerge with the invention of printing, which made it possible for literary works to be duplicated by mechanical processes instead of being copied by hand. This led to the appearance of a new trade—that of printers and booksellers, in England called "stationers." These entrepreneurs invested considerable sums in the purchase of paper, in buying or building presses, and in the employment of labor, involving an outlay which could be recouped with a reasonable return over a period of time. In this situation, without any form of protection against competition from the sales of unauthorized copies, the investment in the printing and selling of books was a precarious and speculative venture, and many stationers were ruined. The pressures grew for some form of protection, and this came in the shape of privileges granted by the various authorities: in England and in France by the kings; and in Germany by the princes of the various States. These privileges gave the beneficiaries exclusive rights of reproduction and distribution, for limited terms, with remedies available for enforcement by means of fines, seizure, confiscation of infringing copies, and possibly damages. The resulting situation exhibited many of the basic features of the copyright system as we know it today.

By the end of the seventeenth century, the system of privileges—i.e., the grant of monopoly rights by the Crown—was being criticized more and more, and the voices of authors asserting their rights began increasingly to be heard. This led in England in 1709 to what is acknowledged to be the first copyright statute—the Statute of Anne.[1]

1. Strictly speaking, one can find the real birth of modern copyright law in the statutes of the United States, in 1790, and of France, in 1793. The reason is that the Statute of Anne continued identifying the right with the books, as opposed to those two Statutes that acknowledged that the copyright and the books were different entities. Indeed, the core language of the Statute of Anne read:

> the author of any book or books already printed, who hath not transferred to any other *the copy or copies of such book or books* [...].

The object of this law was expressed in the long title of the Bill as being for the encouragement of learning and for securing the property of copies of books to the rightful owners thereof. Its principal effect was to provide that the author of a book enjoyed the sole right to print and publish it for fourteen years from the date of its first publication; the author could, and usually did, sell that right to a bookseller. The Act also provided that at the end of that first period of fourteen years, a second protection period commenced which again belonged initially to the author, if living, so that the overall effect was to create a period of copyright protection running for twenty-eight years from the date of the first publication. In the case of books already printed when the Act was passed, there was a single protection period of twenty-one years. The emphasis of the Act was therefore on the protection against unauthorized copying of published works, and in practice the principal beneficiaries were the publisher/booksellers. It should be noted that the Act imposed both a registration and a deposit condition; published books had to be registered at Stationers Hall, and copies had to be deposited for the use of universities and libraries (rising ultimately to a total of nine deposit copies).

In the eighteenth century, there was continuous dispute and litigation over the relationship between copyright subsisting at common law and copyright under the Statute of Anne. This was finally settled by the House of Lords in the case of *Donaldson v. Beckett* in 1774 with the ruling that at common law the author had the sole right of printing and publishing books, but that once a book was published, the rights in it were exclusively regulated by the Statute. This common law right in unpublished works lasted until the Copyright Act 1911, which abolished it, and today in England, copyright subsists solely by statute.

In France, the evolution from the system of privileges to a system of copyright was part of the general changes in French life brought about by the Revolution which abolished privileges of all kinds, including the privileges of publishers. In 1791 and 1793, the Constituent Assembly passed two decrees which laid the foundations for the French copyright system. The Decree of 1791 secured for the author a right of public performance throughout the author's lifetime and for five years after death for the benefit of the author's heirs or assigns, and the Decree of 1793 gave the author an

---

By contrast, although using language clearly inspired in the Statute of Anne, the US copyright Act of 1790 read:

> the author and authors [...] who halt or have not transferred to any other person *the copyright of such map, chart, book or books*, [...].

The French statute of 1793 made the separation between the right and the physical object that fixed the creation even clearer:

> The authors of writings of all kinds, composers of music, painters and designers, who have paintings or drawings engraved, shall enjoy during their entire life the exclusive right to sell, have sold, distribute their works in the territory of the Republic and to transfer ownership of them in whole or in part.

In other words, under the Statute of Anne, the right was transferred with the book, whereas in the United States and in France, the right and the book were independent.

exclusive right to reproduce works throughout the author's lifetime and for ten years after death for the benefit of the author's heirs or assigns. We can see immediately a difference in approach from that of the Statute of Anne. In France, these rights are described as "author's rights," and they are enjoyed throughout the author's lifetime and do not depend upon either publication or upon compliance with formalities such as registration.

However, both in England and in France, the rights were seen essentially as property rights, securing for the author or the author's heir or assignee the economic value of the work protected.

The next development to note was the appearance in Germany of philosophic concepts by philosophers such as Kant and Hegel, who saw copyright or author's rights as not merely a form of property securing an economic benefit for the author or right owner. They regarded an author's literary and other creative work as an extension of, or reflection of, the author's personality, in respect of which the author was entitled by natural justice to be protected as a part of his/her personality. This concept greatly influenced the development of copyright in continental Europe and, in particular, led to the development of the *droit moral* or moral rights (the non-economic rights of authors).

To complete this brief historical survey, one should turn to the US and observe that until 1976, when the current US Copyright Act was enacted, the law of copyright in the US was closely based upon the original provisions in the English Statute of Anne. Thus, the first federal law in the US, enacted in 1790, provided for the protection of books, maps and charts for a period of fourteen years from the date of first publication, which could be renewed for a further term if the author was still alive on the expiry of the first term, and subject to strict requirements of registration and deposit. Those features remained in the US law until 1976 when the present law was enacted which changed the duration of protection to the life of the author plus fifty years, thus bringing it into line with virtually all other countries with copyright laws; the duration of protection was extended again in 1998 to the life of the author plus seventy years. The 1976 Act amended to implement the Berne Convention removed the previous formalities for copyright protection, making registration voluntary and setting up a separate system for mandatory deposit.

The essence of the conceptual differences between the historic common law and civil law systems is as follows: the common law countries treated copyright, in effect as a form of property, capable of being created by an individual or a corporate author, and once created, susceptible to commercial exploitation in the same way as any other form of property, the component rights being exclusively directed to securing enjoyment of the economic potential of the property. In civil law countries, the author's right was also regarded as having "property" characteristics. Copyright law seeks to protect the economic content of that property to the same extent as does the common law system, but there is a difference, which lies in an added dimension of authors' rights—i.e., the intellectual or philosophical concept that the work of an author is an expression of the author's personality which by natural justice requires protection just as much as the economic potential of the work. These rights were embodied in the *droit moral* or the author's moral rights. These different philosophical strains are apparent in many national copyright laws today.

The international period of copyright protection began with the signing in 1886 of the Berne Convention for the Protection of Literary and Artistic Works (Berne Convention), while international related rights protection dates back to the signing in 1961 of the International Convention for the Protection of Performers, Producers of Phonograms and Broadcasting Organizations, generally referred to as the "Rome Convention." Subsequent revisions of the Berne Convention have continued to improve the international system of protection of copyright and related rights in light of continued technological developments through its last revision in 1971. Although the historic distinction between common law and civil law systems can still be seen in many national laws, these international agreements have had a harmonizing effect. All parties to the Berne Convention must protect both the economic and moral rights of authors.

Subsequent international instruments dealing with copyright and related rights subjects have been adopted over the years since the adoption of the Berne Convention and the Rome Convention. These include the TRIPS Agreement, administered by the WTO, which made it compulsory for all WTO Member States to provide for the minimum standards of protection set out in the Berne Convention (Paris revision of 1971). The WCT and the WPPT, also sometimes referred to as the "WIPO Internet Treaties," were adopted in 1996 to address some of the challenges to the international copyright and related rights system in the digital era. In 2012, the WIPO Beijing Treaty on Audiovisual Performances (BTAP or Beijing Treaty) was adopted with a similar objective. While the aforementioned instruments generally focus on providing minimum levels of copyright and related rights protection, in 2013, an instrument with a different objective was concluded, namely the WIPO Marrakesh Treaty to Facilitate Access to Published Works for Persons Who Are Blind, Visually Impaired, or Otherwise Print Disabled (MVT or Marrakesh Treaty). This treaty focuses on limitations and exceptions to copyright.

CHAPTER 3

The Effect of IP Protection on Economic and Technological Development

§3.01 INTELLECTUAL PROPERTY AND DEVELOPMENT

Innovation is a central driver of economic growth and development. It also has the potential to mitigate some of the emerging problems related to health, energy and the environment faced by both richer and poorer countries.[2]

Although the term "innovation" can have varying definitions depending on the context, most innovation economists tend to adhere to the definition provided in the Organisation for Economic Co-operation and Development's (OECD's) Oslo Manual (2018). This manual defines innovation as "a new or improved product or process (or a combination thereof) that differs significantly from the unit's previous products or processes and that has been made available to potential users (product) or brought into use by the unit (process)." Innovation and its diffusion are essential contributors to long-run economic growth and development, manifesting in various areas. For example, it may enhance economic productivity, lead to quality improvements, or result in entirely new process and product categories. While innovation may not always be reflected in productivity statistics, it often results in a higher level of utility for consumers.

Innovation influences productivity, which is defined as the efficiency of converting inputs into outputs, through various channels. A substantial body of empirical literature has explored the relationship between innovative activity and productivity growth at the firm, industry, and country levels.[3] Economists and policymakers consider innovation and its diffusion as critical elements for economic growth and

2. This chapter was initially drafted upon the World Intellectual Property Report (2011) but has been updated to reflect newer versions of the Report.
3. *See* Schumpeter (2013). The endogenous growth models and quality ladder models theorize that innovation drives long-run aggregate productivity and economic growth. *See* Grossman and

development. Investments in research and development (R&D) yield positive spillover outcomes both locally and globally, facilitating the broader accumulation of knowledge. The advantages of such innovative endeavors, referred to as "spillovers," extend beyond the investing firms or countries.[4]

Most empirical studies examining the link between innovation and productivity have focused on the manufacturing sector of the developed countries, revealing a strong correlation between innovation, productivity, and economic development. These findings were similarly found in several developing economies.[5]

As early as the mid-1990s, research suggests that 80% of productivity growth in these countries can be accounted for by innovation. This productivity growth, in turn, accounted for some 80% of the countries' gross domestic product (GDP) growth.[6] In addition, increases in R&D spending have been shown to have a significant and positive effect on the countries' level of output and productivity.[7]

At the firm level, there is evidence that demonstrates the positive links between R&D, innovation, and productivity.[8] Innovative firms are able to improve their competitive edge by increasing their efficiency and hence overtaking their less efficient rivals. Moreover, firms that invest in innovation are also more likely to introduce new technological advances or processes, which tend to yield increased labor productivity.[9]

Innovation-driven growth is also taking place in less developed countries. Research has demonstrated that catch-up growth, and the broader dissemination of technology across countries can occur more faster than ever before, as seen in the cases of the Republic of Korea and China.[10]

Differences in innovative activity and related technological gaps between countries are significant factors in explaining cross-country variation in income and productivity levels. Studies have shown that roughly half of cross-country differences in per capita income and growth can be explained by differences in total factor productivity growth, a measure of an economy's long-term technological change or dynamism.[11] In addition, the variation in the growth rate of GDP per capita is shown to increase with the distance from the technology frontier. Countries with fewer technological and inventive capabilities generally see lower and more economic growth than do richer countries.

Helpman (1994); Romer (1986); Romer (2010); Grossman and Helpman (1991); and Aghion and Howitt (1990). *See* a complete reference to the sources used in this chapter in Additional Readings, *infra*.

4. *See* Edquist (2013); Freeman (1987); Lundvall (1992); and Fagerberg et al. (2006).
5. These studies include Benavente (2006); Chudnovsky et al. (2006); Crespi et al. (2016); Crespi and Zuniga (2012); Grazzi and Jung (2016); Raffo et al. (2008) on Latin America, Cirera et al. (2016) on Africa; and Jefferson et al. (2006); Han et al. (2002); Zhou et al. (2017) on Asia.
6. *See* Freeman (1994).
7. For an overview, *see* Khan and Luintel (2006) and at the firm level, studies such as Criscuolo et al. (2010) and Bronzini and Piselli (2016).
8. *See* Crépon et al. (1998); Griffith et al. (2006); Mairesse and Mohnen (2010); and OECD (2010).
9. *See* Benavente and Lauterbach (2008).
10. *See* Romer (1986); Long (1988); and Jones and Romer (2010).
11. *See* Jones and Romer (2010); Guinet et al. (2009); and Bresnahan and Trajtenberg (1995).

Empirical evidence demonstrates that while there has been a convergence in technology adoption delays between rich and poor countries, there has also been a divergence in penetration rates. Furthermore, the pattern of technology diffusion accounts for 80% of the significant income disparity between rich and poor countries over the past two centuries.[12] Total factor productivity depends to a large degree on the ability of countries, industries or firms to adopt technologies and production techniques of countries and firms with higher levels of technological development.

These spillovers are frequently driven by knowledge acquired through channels such as foreign direct investment (FDI), trade, licensing, joint ventures, the presence of multinationals, migration and/or collaboration with firms from higher-income countries.

Strategies for acquiring, adapting, imitating and improving technologies and existing techniques in relation to local conditions are key for innovation. Developing innovative capacity requires complementary in-house innovation activity.

Certain framework conditions, adequate human capital and absorptive capacity are necessary at the country- and firm-levels in order to benefit from innovation spillovers. Absorptive capacity is the "ability of a firm, and by extension country, to recognize the value of new, external information, assimilate it, and apply it to commercial ends is critical to its innovative capabilities."[13]

In addition, the literature refers to the necessary presence of functioning "national innovation systems" with linkages between innovation actors and a government policy that underpins innovation activity.[14]

In general, knowledge spillover effects—situations where knowledge flows from one firm or individual to another without direct compensation to the originator—can lead to a wide dissemination of new ideas, which in turn can result in greater and faster innovative activities and economic growth. However, spillovers are often a two-way street, involving give and take. Policymakers must balance incentives for creating knowledge against the rapid diffusion of knowledge. Generating spillovers is one of the main elements of open innovation strategies: firms can be better innovators by engaging with others—even if that involves some sharing of proprietary knowledge. Patent system allows firms to flexibly control which knowledge to guard and which to share so as to maximize knowledge.

What is needed is a means of harnessing available resources and overcoming barriers to innovation to encourage these activities.

§3.02 GOVERNMENT SUPPORT FOR INVENTIVE ACTIVITIES

Inventive process—viewed as the production of problem-solving information—faces two fundamental difficulties. First, it is a *risky process*: when embarking on a problem-solving exercise, it is uncertain whether a solution can really be found.

12. *See* Comin and Mestieri (2018).
13. *See* Cohen and Levinthal (1990).
14. *See* Jones and Romer (2010).

Second, information related to problem-solving possesses characteristics of what economists call a public good: many people can simultaneously use it, and the problem solver often cannot prevent reproduction of the information. The latter characteristic is also known as the *appropriability dilemma* of inventive activity.

Given this, it has been argued that markets—when left alone—would underinvest in inventive activity relative to what would be socially desirable. Firms operating in competitive markets may forgo inventive opportunities when their returns to investment are small. This would especially be the case in situations where resources available to the firm are limited, success of a problem-solving effort is uncertain and where competitors can immediately free ride by imitating the successful solution.

There are mechanisms for reducing these risks and appropriating inventive efforts in private markets. For example, the pooling of inventive activity within larger firms diminishes the uncertainty of inventive outcomes, as successes make up for failures. In addition, being the first to introduce a new good or service on the market may be sufficient to generate enough profits to make an inventive investment worthwhile.

But, the problems of appropriability and risk in innovative activity persist even where private markets offer certain innovation incentives. To begin with, although individuals may invent purely out of curiosity, they also need to earn a living. Pushing the limits of the world's knowledge frontier requires talent, but often it also demands years of experience, collaboration within larger research teams and expensive equipment. In addition, successful innovation in modern economies requires not only smart inventions but also substantial investment in the subsequent development and commercialization of new products. In many cases, market mechanisms are bound to be insufficient for inducing innovation that is in society's best interest, thus providing a rationale for government intervention.

In general, one can broadly distinguish three mechanisms for promoting innovation. First, there is publicly funded innovation carried out by academic institutions and public research organizations. Second, governments can fund research undertaken by private firms—notably through public procurement, research subsidies, soft loans, R&D tax credits and innovation prizes. And third, the IP system is the one mechanism that promotes privately executed R&D which is financed through the marketplace rather than government revenues.

The choice of policy instrument should depend on the circumstances in which the innovative activity is conducted.

In fact, the different means to promote innovation can be complementary. For instance, basic research that does not immediately lead to commercial application is largely undertaken by academia and public research organizations, which in turn are oftentimes subsidized by governments. But some academic research may result in patents and subsequent licensing for commercial development.

Important differences exist in how R&D of the innovative activity is financed. Certain policy instruments—notably, prizes, R&D tax credits and IP rights—require firms to initially fund R&D activity on their own or through financial markets. These instruments may therefore be less effective for large and highly risky R&D projects and in economies with underdeveloped financial markets. The other instruments provide upfront public financing of R&D, reducing *ex ante* risk and avoiding the problems of imperfect credit markets.

In general, no single policy instrument works best in all circumstances. In considering which instrument to employ, policymakers need to take into account financing conditions, risk levels, possible information failures, performance incentives and other variables. Each instrument has its rewards and drawbacks. The key challenge for policymakers is to mix policies so that they effectively complement one another.

§3.03 INTELLECTUAL PROPERTY PROTECTION AS AN INNOVATION POLICY

IP protection is a policy initiative that provides incentive for undertaking creative and innovative activity. IP laws enable individuals and organizations to obtain exclusive rights to their inventive and creative output. Ownership of intellectual assets limits the extent to which competitors can free ride on problem-solving and related information, enabling owners to profit from their efforts and addressing the appropriability dilemma at its heart.

IP rights are an elegant means for governments to mobilize market forces to guide innovative and creative activity. It allows decisions on which innovative opportunities to pursue to be taken in a decentralized way. To the extent that individuals and firms operating at the knowledge frontier are best informed about the likely success of innovative projects, the IP system promotes an efficient allocation of resources for inventive and creative activity.

This has traditionally been the key economic rationale for protecting IP rights. However, there are a number of additional considerations, some of which strengthen the case for exclusive rights, while others weaken it.

First, while IP rights do not directly solve the problem of risk associated with inventive activity, they can improve the functioning of financial markets in mobilizing resources for risky innovation. In particular, the grant of a patent at an early stage in the innovation process can serve to reassure investors that a start-up firm is in a position to generate profits if the invention is successfully commercialized. In addition, it provides an independent certification that an invention pushes the limits of the knowledge frontier—something that investors may not be able to assess on their own.

Second, inventing sometimes means finding solutions to stand-alone problems. More often, however, it is a cumulative process, whereby researchers build on existing knowledge to develop new technologies or products. The IP system plays an important role in the process of cumulative innovation.

For example, the disclosure requirement for patent protection on an invention can be used to learn about the latest technological knowledge in the field. This technical document may then promote follow-on innovation in that inventors may build on the existing body of knowledge available through patent documentations.

But patent protection granted on an invention may create a barrier for follow-on innovation. Notably, certain technology fields are characterized by complex patent landscapes, generating uncertainty about whether potential new inventive output could clash with existing proprietary rights. A related problem arises where the commercialization of an invention requires use of third-party proprietary technology. Other right holders may refuse to license their technologies or may demand royalties that render the innovation unprofitable—leading to the so-called *holdup problem*. Even where they are willing to license, coordinating the participation of a large number of right holders may be too costly.

Third, the IP system facilitates firm specialization in different stages of the innovation process. The traditional view of research, development and commercialization undertaken by a single firm does not reflect innovation processes in modern economies. For example, while a given firm may find it is particularly good at figuring out how to extend the life of batteries, other companies might be better at turning the underlying inventions into components for different consumer electronics. Specialization allows firms to maximize an inherent advantage, ultimately enhancing the economy-wide productivity of the innovation process.

However, specialization implies that firms will have to license in or license out their know-how from external sources. This implies high transaction costs on the firms attempting to do so—in the form of information, search, bargaining, enforcement, and related costs.

To some extent, IP rights can reduce these costs. In the absence of patent rights, for instance, firms would be reluctant to disclose secret but easy-to-copy technologies to other firms when negotiating licensing contracts. As a result, licensing agreements from which all parties stand to benefit might never materialize.

In addition, while inventive and creative assets can, in principle, be transferred through private contracts independent of any IP right, IP titles offer a delineation of these assets combined with an assurance of market exclusivity. IP rights thus convey important information that can facilitate the drawing up of contracts and reduce the uncertainty of contracting parties as to the commercial value of the licensed assets.

Fourth, the grant of exclusive IP rights affords firms market power, viewed by economists as the ability to set prices above marginal production costs. In many cases, market power emanating from an IP right is limited, as companies face competition from similar products or technologies.

However, IP rights impose certain costs on the society. In particular, the exclusive rights create a so-called deadweight loss in the market by allowing for marked-up prices for goods and services—above their costs of production. This creates a distortion in the allocation of resources in the market.

There is thus a trade-off for providing IP protection—reward individuals for their geniuses at the expense of society's ability to freely profit from them. The role of economic analysis is to understand under which circumstances IP protection is most beneficial to society. Indeed, studies have shown that the impact of IP protection on innovation and development differs in important ways across industries and countries.

It is important to note that the IP system is a vital element in the stimulation of invention and innovation; many other factors in practice combine to contribute to successful innovation. External factors such as economic, technical, or regulatory matters, which are beyond the control of the innovator, may affect the success or failure of the innovation.

For example, economic research has shown that there is a difference between how IP protection affects firms in developed and developing countries. This has to do, in part, with the firms' absorptive and innovative capacities in those groups of countries. Firms that have sufficient levels of absorptive and innovative capacities are more likely to benefit from the IP system than those which do not.

In particular, firms in the high-income country group—as defined by the World Bank—tend to have strong innovative capabilities and use the IP system more frequently than the rest. The firms located in this group of countries usually operate and produce new-to-the-world types of innovation.

Others, firms in the lower- and middle-income group brackets, have varying degrees of innovative capabilities and use the Patent system to a lesser extent than their high-income counterparts. This group of countries may not create or produce patentable innovation to the same extent as high-income countries, but they use the utility model, trademark, industrial design, and other forms of IP to protect their innovations and access new and existing innovation from abroad. They may learn from existing innovations, eventually developing their own and thus profit from using the IP protection system. Moreover, there are significant differences in the use of the IP system among middle-income economies, particularly between China, India, and others.

Then, there are firms in the low-income countries that have little absorptive and innovative capacities. This group of countries is less likely to use the IP system as vigorously or frequently as the other two. Here, the influence of IP protection on their economic development may be limited. And the benefit of implementing and enforcing IP protection may not be as relevant as for the others.

However, this does not imply that countries with little innovative capabilities do not innovate or create. In fact, anecdotal evidence argues that firms in low-income countries have been known to show ingenuity in overcoming obstacles in difficult economic environments. However, the types of local innovation and creative activities produced may not require the use of the IP system. Moreover, many innovative and creative activities usually take place in the informal economy. Thus, recourse to the IP system may not be an option for these firms.

Countries with limited resources may benefit from the implementation of IP protection to encourage FDI. FDI could help countries' economic development through so-called spillover effects. Local talents that are hired and trained would have skills that they may impart to other segments of the economy. Even businesses that provide services to foreign firms are likely to improve their efficiencies and benefit from foreign investment.

In addition, IP protection can encourage foreign TT. Foreign firms that are located in the countries can help the economies build their local innovative capabilities. Economic studies show that IP protection is a relatively important factor in firms' R&D

location decisions. And it is these R&D labs that help locals build their innovative capabilities. However, the diffusion of foreign technologies to local firms, which could stimulate home-grown innovation, would depend on the foreign firms' management of their intellectual assets. Several East Asian countries, for example, have successfully insisted on and benefited from FDI when they conditioned the entry of foreign firms on the transfer of technology. However, it remains open whether these policies can be replicated elsewhere.

[A] IP Instruments and What They Protect

Table 3.1 describes the five forms of IP most relevant to innovation—patents and utility models, industrial designs, copyrights, plant variety rights and trade secrets. These IP forms have emerged historically to accommodate different forms of innovative and creative output.

Table 3.1 Main Forms of IP Rights Available to Innovators

IP Right	*Subject Matter*	*Acquisition of Right*	*Nature of Right: Prevent Others From ...*
Patents and utility models	Inventions that are new, non-obvious and industrially applicable	Granted by government authority, typically following substantive examination	... making, using, selling, offering for sale or importing
Industrial designs	Industrial designs that are new and/or original	Granted by government authority upon registration, with or without substantive examination	... making, selling or importing
Copyrights	Creative expressions	Automatically, upon creation	... reproducing and related acts
Plant variety rights	Plant varieties that are new, distinct, uniform and stable	Granted by government authority following substantive examination	... using and multiplying propagating materials
Trade secrets	Any valuable confidential business information	Automatically, upon creation	... unlawfully disclosing

Note: This table offers an intuitive overview of the main forms of IP and, only incompletely, describes the legal character of these rights as established through national laws and international treaties.

Source: WIPO IP Report (2011).

Another IP instrument that is also relevant—albeit indirectly—to innovation is trademark. The economic rationale for trademark protection is to resolve problems of asymmetric information between market participants.

The principle of asymmetry of information is that information is sticky and may not flow freely among market participants. For instance, the information that a seller has about his/her product is different from what the buyer knows and can perceive visually. And, in order to decide whether to purchase the good, the buyer would have to spend time and money to research different product offerings; this is known as the buyer's search costs.

Trademark protection addresses this issue of information asymmetry by reducing the buyer's search costs. First, it grants exclusive rights to names, signs and other identifiers in commerce subject to certain procedural rules and limitations on certain goods and services. Second, it pushes producers and sellers toward creating concise identifiers for specific goods or services. For example, instead of asking for the location of a "coffee store belonging to a firm headquartered in the US city of Seattle," consumers can simply search for "Starbucks" and will be perfectly understood.

Trademarks thus improve communication about goods and services. And, they help consumers to distinguish between different product offerings and, in this way, they promote orderly competition between sellers.

A similar rationale to trademark exists for the protection of GIs. Like trademarks, GIs seek to reduce consumers' search costs and provide incentives for product differentiation. One key difference is that the right to use a GI belongs to a group of producers located within a certain geographical boundary rather than a single entity.

[B] How Patent Protection Affects Innovation

Most economic research on IP protection has focused on patents to better understand what is behind the increasing patenting activity and, more generally, how innovation works. In addition, the construction of new databases—often combining unit record data on patents with firm-level information on innovative behavior and economic performance—has enabled richer investigations into the effects of patent protection.

First, patent protection affects firm performance, and this impact varies across industries. Surveys of manufacturing firms in developed economies show that the two most important appropriation mechanisms are lead time and sales and service activities. In industries with short product life cycles—for example, electronics—patents appear to be of lesser importance; indeed, technologies may be obsolete by the time patents are granted. By contrast, patent protection is critically important in the chemical and pharmaceutical industries.

In sectors where patents play a crucial role in innovation such as the pharmaceutical industry, there is a positive correlation between prospects of securing patent rights and higher investments in R&D.

These findings are true for developed countries where pre-existing innovative capacity and level of education are higher. Lower-income countries, however, do not see any change in the incentives for R&D.

Second, patent strategies change where innovation is cumulative. On the one hand, patent documents reveal technical information that may be useful in developing follow-on innovation.

On the other hand, econometric evidence suggests that dense webs of overlapping patent rights—so-called patent thickets—can indeed slow or even forestall cumulative innovation processes. High transaction costs have made it difficult for some—especially small—firms to obtain the licenses necessary for prior and complementary technologies; the latter include patented research tools that, for example, are of special relevance to biotechnology research.

Third, patent rights shape the interplay between competition and innovation. For instance, they foster a healthy competitive balance. IP rights prevent competition of the free-riding type that undermines the appropriation of R&D investment. But they permit competition between substitute products each of which may be protected by different patent rights.

In addition, certain features of the patent system directly promote competitive market forces: the disclosure requirement enables firms to learn from the inventions of rivals; and the limited protection term ensures that the economic rent associated with a patent is time bound, inducing firms to stay ahead by constantly innovating.

But, patent ownership can, in certain situations, significantly curtail competition. While rare, patent rights to key technologies for which few substitutes exist can lead to concentrated market structures.

Moreover, the emergence of patent thickets, as outlined above, can negatively affect competition by marginalizing those firms that do not have a sufficiently large patent portfolio as a bargaining tool. Where patent rights overly restrict competition, society loses twice: through higher prices and less choice in product markets; and through insufficient competitive pressure on firms to innovate.

Fourth, patents play a role in technology markets and open innovation strategies. The exclusive right on a patented invention minimizes the risk that a patented intellectual asset will be easily appropriated, which in turn provides some assurance for the buyer to invest in the asset and later recover its investment on this innovation.

Generating spillovers is a second important element of open innovation strategies: firms can be better innovators by engaging with others—even if that involves some sharing of proprietary knowledge. Indeed, patent rights are at the heart of the trade-off between guarding and sharing knowledge. They allow firms to flexibly control which technologies to share, with whom and on what terms.

It is important to mention that economic research provides only limited guidance on how different patent-based knowledge sharing activities—especially those associated with more recent open innovation strategies—affect spillovers and innovation. This is partly the result of insufficient data; in particular, patent licenses are often confidential and escape statistical measurement.

[C] Importance of IP Institutions

Patent laws set the basic rules on what can be patented, for how long and under what conditions. However, the incentives created by the patent system are critically dependent on how these rules are implemented. This is largely the responsibility of patent offices and courts.

Patent institutions best serve innovation when they promote two broad principles: rigorous examination leading to the grant of quality patents and balanced dispute resolution.

Promoting the first principle has two important elements. First, patent offices should grant patents only for those inventions that strictly meet the standards of patentability—namely, novelty, inventive step (non-obviousness) and industrial applicability. This sounds straightforward, but for patent offices, it is not: the complexity of technology is constantly on the rise, and many entities in different parts of the world create new knowledge that may be relevant prior art. Second, patent documents should clearly delineate the patent's inventive claims and describe the invention in a transparent way. Patents granted which meet both criteria can be considered quality patents.

The second principle recognizes that disputes over patent rights invariably occur. But when they do, they should be resolved in a way that balances the interests of all parties involved. In particular, the parties should have easy access to dispute resolution mechanisms, but those mechanisms should minimize bad faith initiation of disputes, and remedies should be proportionate to any damage suffered.

Why do these two principles matter? Poor-quality patents—including patents for trivial inventions or those with overly broad or ambiguously drafted claims—can harm innovation. At worst, they may lead firms to refrain from certain research activities or from commercializing a new technology for fear of violating patent rights; at best, they burden innovating companies by leading to extra royalty payments and legal costs. Poor-quality patents may also increase the risk of anticompetitive uses of patent rights. Vague descriptions of inventions in patent documents, in turn, may curtail the spillover benefits of patent disclosure.

Imbalanced dispute resolution can have more varied effects on innovative behavior. For example, if dispute resolution is overly costly, it may bias the system against smaller firms—whether they are claimants or defendants. Smaller firms may thus innovate less, either because they have difficulty enforcing their patent rights or they are more exposed to infringement accusations from competitors. Enforcement costs may be an especially binding constraint for firms in more resource-constrained low- and middle-income countries, which explains why many of them do not apply for patent rights in the first place.

Promoting patent quality is bound to reinforce more balanced dispute resolution and vice versa. Quality patents that have undergone rigorous examination are less likely to be challenged in court. Conversely, effective dispute settlement preempts the filing of poor-quality patents, as the prospect of enforcing them is low.

CHAPTER 4

The Contribution of Industrial Property to the Transfer and Dissemination of Technology

§4.01 INTRODUCTION

Article 7 of the TRIPS Agreement provides that "The protection and enforcement of intellectual property rights should contribute to the promotion of technological innovation and to the transfer and dissemination of technology [...]." This language must be read with care because it contains two elements that are generally overlooked. The first element is that the provision expresses a reductionist view of IP, which was mentioned in Chapter 1. IP is not only about innovation. There are several fields of IP that are not necessarily related to innovation or transfer and dissemination of technology, such as GIs, business-related trade secrets, and trademarks. Therefore, where Article 7 refers to "intellectual property," it actually refers to those areas of IP with a technical content. The second element is the presence of the term "should contribute." This means that the negotiators of the TRIPS Agreement were aware that some aspects of IP protection may indeed contribute to the promotion of technological innovation and the transfer and dissemination of technology, but they do not do so necessarily. It is up to States to: (a) set the social, technical, and economic structures that permit the transfer and the absorption of technology; and (b) adopt the adequate legal institutions that make IP protection an instrument of development. With a view to a shift toward the knowledge-based economy in this century, the assimilation of knowledge and the creation of new technology have become essential elements for companies to survive and grow in the market environment where competition has been increasing domestically as well as internationally. Consequently, many countries have been investing in knowledge creation as a priority under national economic, technological and development policy and strategy. Simply stated, to acquire a new technology, there are two ways to do so: either to create such technology by oneself or to acquire it from others.

Creating the technology by oneself may have the advantage of having the possibility to better control, in terms of the duration, geographical coverage and scope, the developed technology through IP protection, including trade secrets. It also avoids being dependent on technologies which have been created and owned by others. However, investment in research and development can be expensive. There is no guarantee that such investment would bring any fruitful results. In addition, if a company has no expertise in the field of technology under research, it may take a long time to develop such expertise. Sometimes, that is not a viable option because competitors' technical capability and the market may develop much faster than the speed of their own research.

Another path, that is, to acquire technology from others, is indeed an option if the required technology is available and accessible in a less risky, more efficient, and more economic manner. While the importance of self-developed technology for maintaining a competitive edge cannot be denied, the importance of the transfer of technology in the innovation system has been widely recognized partly because of changes in technological and economic environments. First, the technology becomes more complex and develops in a cross-cutting area which goes beyond the traditional fields of technology. The complexity of technology used in a product requires a company to cooperate with others which have expertise in other technical fields. Second, the ongoing integration of domestic and international markets through continuing liberalization and de-regulation of markets enhanced competition at the national and international levels. In certain fields of technology, competition within the sector is so strong that new products with new functions and designs appear in the market regularly in a short cycle. To keep up with the speed of technological development and global competition, acquiring new technology from others may allow companies to go beyond their own R&D to find the best technologies, and integrate them into the company's own settings. Consequently, while many companies have been integrating both mechanisms into their innovation processes, namely, in-house innovation and technology acquisition from others, the latter is used more and more strategically with a view to the company's overall business model. Open and collaborative innovation mechanisms have been explored by many private companies. The strategic cooperation between the transferor and the transferee of the technology may bring mutual benefits to both parties by utilizing the expertise of the other.

The term "transfer of technology" may be understood in a narrow or broad sense when used in the context of IP, in particular, patents. Broadly stated, the transfer of technology is a series of processes for sharing ideas, knowledge, technology, and skills with another individual or institution (e.g., a company, a university or a governmental body) and of acquisition by the other of such ideas, knowledge, technologies and skills. In the context of transferring technologies from the public sector and universities to the private sector, the term "transfer of technology" is sometimes used in a narrower sense: as a synonym to "technology commercialization" whereby basic scientific research outcomes from universities and public research institutions are applied to practical, commercial products for the market by private companies.

The transfer of technology may occur within national borders or internationally. Since, in general, a bigger pool of technology is available internationally than nationally, international procurement of technology is a natural solution to obtain new technology and to foster innovation based on the acquired technology, particularly with a view to increasing competition at the global level. Due to a disparity in technological capacity among countries, at the macro level, technological knowledge generally flows from a higher technological capacity country to a lower technology capacity country, i.e., in a simplistic manner, from a party in a developed country to a party in a developing country. Such a description, however, may be too simplistic and static. Hoekman et al. (Bernard Hoekman, Keith Maskus, Kamal Saggi "Transfer of technology to developing countries: unilateral and multilateral policy options," World Bank Policy Research Working Paper 3332, June 2004) gathered data on the flow of technology trade among high-income OECD countries and between high-income OECD countries and (i) upper-middle income countries; (ii) lower-middle income countries; (iii) low-income countries; and (iv) sub-Saharan states, respectively, and compared the data between 1971 and 2001. They found that upper-middle income countries constituted the fastest-growing market for technology-intensive exports from OECD countries and, at the same time, they had become suppliers of technology-intensive products together with lower-middle income countries. While middle-income countries collected royalty income of USD 12.7 billion from OECD countries in 2001, the amount collected by low-income countries was USD 2 billion. Another researcher reported some specific cases where a technology holder in a developing country transferred his/her technology to a party in a developed country.

The successful transfer of technology to a given country is largely dependent on the availability of indigenous technological capacities, and the process of transferring selected imported technology should thus be complementary to national research and development efforts and the development of an indigenous technological capability. The transfer and development process involves a sequence of interlinked activities, such as the identification of technological needs in light of development objectives; the obtaining of information on alternative sources of technology, including local sources; the evaluation and selection of the most appropriate technology; the unpackaging of technology packages in order to assess the suitability, costs, and conditions of their components; the negotiation of the best possible terms and conditions; the adaptation and absorption of imported technology and stimulation of the development of indigenous technology; and the dissemination of newly available technology to potential users. The successful evaluation, selection, development, adaptation, and application of technology requires indigenous national capacities for research and development (R & D) and the formulation of appropriate national policies in science as well as in technology.

The process of TT is fundamentally the flow of human knowledge from one human being to another, whether a transferor or a transferee is an individual, an enterprise, small or large, a university, a research institution, or any other party. Such a flow of knowledge may occur through various channels as described below.

[A] Transfer Through Tangible and Intangible Property

Transfer and acquisition of technology can take place with the transfer of ownership of properties, such as a purchase of production lines, an acquisition of a factory or a merger and acquisition (M&A) of a whole company. In many instances, those tangible assets inherently involve both implicit and explicit technological knowledge. In the case of M&A, transfer of intangible property, such as patents, would normally occur together with the transfer of tangible property. This would allow the new patent owner to obtain exclusive rights to prevent others from using, making etc. the patented invention without the new owner's consent. The mere acquisition of a patent per se, however, may not play much of a role in transferring new technological knowledge to the new patent owner, since the technological information relating to that patent has already been published by the patent office concerned. However, actual "use" of the patented technology by the new owner may lead to him or her understanding the relevant technology better and gaining technical know-how related to such technology.

[B] Transfer Through Technology Licensing

Technology licenses mainly involve patents, trade secrets and know-how.[15] Simply stated, in the IP context, a license constitutes permission by the IP owner (e.g., of a patent) to another party to conduct one or more activities covered by the exclusive rights under the agreed terms and conditions, such as the amount of royalty payment, the duration of the license, geographical coverage, the scope of use, etc. A patent license per se only constitutes permission to use the patented technology in a specific way. However, as previously stated, the actual use of the patented technology by the licensee may facilitate better understanding of the relevant technology and increase the capacity of the licensee to absorb new technology. Technology licenses play a crucial role in joint venture agreements and collaborative research agreements, which are also important ways to transfer technology in a win-win environment. In an increasingly complex world, innovation and rapid market responsiveness are regarded as keys to global competitiveness. These factors have contributed to the development of various initiatives to address research in a more collective way at different levels, with the objective of establishing excellence in research projects and networks that would attract researchers and investments. Joint ventures and collaborative research support the exchange of knowledge, know-how and expertise of researchers participating in the collaboration, and stimulate the creation of new ideas through such exchange of knowledge.

[C] Transfer Through the Public Domain

Anyone can use and build upon ideas and innovations over which no person has any property rights. In relation to a patent granted in one country, after the expiration or

15. However, software licensing frequently also involves copyright.

abandonment of the patent in a given country, or in any other country in which a patent has not been granted or has no legal effect, third parties are not required to obtain the consent of the patent holder for the exploitation of the patented invention. However, it should be noted that if the exploitation of the patented invention infringes another valid patent that claims a broader scope of technology covering the said invention, the consent by the owner of such broader patent is required to exploit the off-patent invention. Public domain technologies may be transferred through technical publications and literatures or through products that exhibit their embedded technologies. For example, technology may be transferred by studying and examining technologies used in the acquired product (so-called reverse engineering). Such a form of transfer, however, requires an absorptive capacity on the part of the transferee to explore, understand and imitate the embedded technologies. There is usually a learning curve that increases the absorptive capacity by means of repeated "trials and errors."

The abovementioned channels are typical channels through which technologies are transferred from one party to another, although they are neither exhaustive nor mutually exclusive since various channels may be exploited simultaneously. In those channels, it is crucial for parties seeking TT to better understand the market in which they wish to seek TT. IP information can provide useful intelligence to prepare such business strategy for successful transfer of technology. IP information contained in patent, trademark or industrial design databases, made available by Intellectual Property Offices (IPOs) and WIPO make it possible to grasp a general idea of the current state of relevant technologies, to locate major players who are contributing to technological developments in the interested fields of technology, or who are offering opportunities of licensing out, or who are potential business partners, and to obtain detailed information of technologies, including those that have entered the public domain. Such information can be obtained from publicly available IP databases which allow the public to search, retrieve, analyze, and learn from vast amount of information generated from patent, trademark, and industrial design documents all over the world.

Access to new technologies is considered crucial in effectively responding to global challenges, such as development, climate change, health, and food security. Indeed, new technologies can be a solution to a number of, if not all, challenges prescribed in the UN Millennium Development Goals (MDGs). In particular, Goal 8 of the MDGs states that UN Member States are committed to developing a global partnership, and Target 8f indicates: "in cooperation with the private sector, make available the benefits of new technologies, especially information and communications." As a specialized agency of the UN, the effective use of IP for economic, social, and cultural development has been a key concern of WIPO. In particular, the WIPO Development Agenda aims to ensure that development considerations form an integral part of WIPO's work. Forty-five recommendations adopted by the WIPO General Assembly in October 2007 contain a number of recommendations that relate to the transfer of technology. Specifically, Cluster C "Technology Transfer, Information and Communication Technologies and Access to Knowledge" highlights the concerns of WIPO Member States and recommends actions in this area. A considerable number of

Development Agenda projects relate to recommendations under Cluster C, but two projects in particular are directly relevant to the transfer of technology. They are the "Project on Innovation and Technology Transfer Support Structure for National Institutions" and the "Project on Intellectual Property and Technology Transfer: Common Challenges—Building Solutions." These projects have led to the launch of initiatives contributing to innovation and TT capacity including the Access to Research for Development and Innovation (ARDI) and Access to Specialized Patent Information (ASPI) programs for free or low-cost access to scientific and technical content and patent databases, respectively, as well as the establishment of Technology and Innovation Support Centers (TISCs), offering technology information and related services in numerous countries worldwide.

ARDI is coordinated by WIPO together with its partners in the publishing industry with the aim to increase the availability of scientific and technical information in developing countries. By improving access to scholarly literature from diverse fields of science and technology, ARDI seeks to: reinforce the capacity of developing countries to participate in the global knowledge economy; and support researchers in developing countries in creating and developing new solutions to technical challenges faced on a local and global level. As of August 2023, 103 publishers were providing access to as many as sixty thousand journals, books, and reference works for developing countries and territories through ARDI and its partners in the Research4Life partnership.

ASPI is a public-private partnership administered by WIPO and made possible through cooperation with leading patent information providers. Through ASPI, eligible patent offices and academic and research institutions in developing countries can receive free or low-cost access to sophisticated tools and services for retrieving and analyzing patent data.

The WIPO TISC program supports developing countries to establish locally based, high-quality technology information and related services, helping their innovators to exploit their innovative potential and to create, protect, and manage their IP rights. Services offered by TISCs may include: Access to online patent and non-patent (scientific and technical) resources and IP-related publications; Assistance in searching and retrieving technology information; On-demand searches (novelty, state of the art and infringement); Monitoring technology and competitors; On-demand patent analytics; Basic information on industrial property laws, management and strategy, and technology commercialization and marketing; and other technology and innovation support services.

In order to facilitate the sharing of knowledge and the adaptation, transfer and diffusion of technologies, WIPO has been developing platforms that build on partnerships and collaborations between technology holders and technology users. There are at present two such collaborative platforms developed or being developed by WIPO: *WIPO Re:Search* in the field of health and *WIPO Green* relating to environmental technology. *WIPO Re:Search*—Sharing Innovation in the Fight Against Neglected Tropical Diseases 154 was formed in 2011, and creates a partnership among WIPO, pharmaceutical companies, research and academic institutions and a nongovernmental organization, BIO Ventures for Global Health. It provides access to IP for pharmaceutical compounds, technologies, know-how and data available for research and development for neglected tropical diseases, tuberculosis and malaria. *WIPO Green* is a technology marketplace that provides access to a broad range of environmental technology solutions. Its key objectives are the accelerated adaptation, adoption and deployment of environmental technologies particularly in developing countries and emerging economies. Technology holders will offer their technology on WIPO Green as a package, which may include associated know-how and services, and the terms of access to the technology for research, manufacture and/or sale will be governed by individually negotiated agreements.

§4.02 THE USE OF INDUSTRIAL PROPERTY INFORMATION

Many different governmental authorities are potential users of IP information, particularly those authorities involved in encouraging innovative activities. The competent governmental authority involved in encouraging innovative activities can use patent information as a means of creating an interest in innovation in technical training courses at universities and technical colleges. Moreover, access to national patent database and global patent database can be provided in specialist public libraries. The government can assist national industries to increase exports to other developing or to industrialized countries by assisting them in obtaining patent rights in those countries and by upgrading the role of its Patent Office. The government can support the efforts of big national industries to build up their own collections of patent documents and it may facilitate for them the acquisition of these documents. A number of countries have developed TISCs with support from WIPO, while others have independently developed IP and technology information services to provide assistance to local innovators.

In business circles, IP information is widely used in formulating a firm's IP strategy, as an input into research and development processes, to facilitate licensing and technology transactions, for TT and for analysis of markets and competitors in order to support important business decisions. Further, the availability of information concerning ownership and rights and obligations associated with a patent (e.g., licensing agreements or security interest), which may be found in national patent registries, may support the transparency of the market and the legal certainty of transactions of so-called intangible assets.

Although all information that is needed to analyze the technical contents of patents as well as the status of such patents (and patent applications) or trademark registrations is held by IPOs, if such information is published on paper, in practical terms, it can be difficult to access, particularly from abroad. Digitization of national IP documents facilitates access to IP information as well as the statistical/analytical use of such information. IP information is increasingly available via easily accessible services that are delivered over the Internet. WIPO has created global IP databases to increase the availability of IP information and its accessibility to the public since the beginning of this century. PATENTSCOPE, WIPO's global patent database, as well as WIPO's

Global Brands Database and Global Design Database provide access not only to international patent applications and international trademark and industrial design registrations but also to similar data from national and regional IP offices.

Patent documents are an important source of information on new inventions made in a wide range of fields of technology. Indeed, in certain fields of technology, the majority of such breakthroughs are disclosed through patent documents rather than scholarly publications. University researchers in particular are often not aware of this fact and do not systematically integrate patent information into their research activities. Increasing the awareness of university researchers about the value of patent information could increase the efficiency and impact of their research and also benefit their industry partners, who often rely on universities to give expert opinions or perform research tasks on their behalf.

Universities also play an important role in the introduction of the use of IP information at all levels within the country, because they generate the engineers and researchers who will be the future potential beneficiaries of such use. Therefore, educational material at the engineering faculties could include patent information as one of its major components.

§4.03 PATENT DATABASES

Patent information comprises all information that has been published in patent and related documents or can be derived from analyzing patent filing statistics. It can be used for a variety of purposes, including:

Legal: e.g., to improve the quality of patent applications, to avoid infringing the patent rights of others, and identify inventions in the public domain.
Technical: e.g., to improve the efficiency of research by avoiding "re-inventing the wheel."
Business: e.g., to identify potential partners and competitors, to determine value of patents or patent portfolios, and uncover commercial opportunities.
Public policy: e.g., to assess developments and trends in specific areas of technology for industrial policy planning and other purposes.

Patent documents contain a wide range of information, systematically organized into different sections of the document, including:

Applicant. Name of the individual or company applying to have a particular invention protected.
Inventor. Name of the person or persons who developed the invention.
Description. Clear and concise explanation of known existing technologies related to the new invention and explanation of how this invention could be applied to solve problems not addressed by the existing technologies; specific embodiments of the new technology are also usually given.
Claims. Legal definition of the subject matter for which protection is sought or granted; each claim is a single sentence in a legalistic form that defines an

invention and its unique technical features; claims must be clear and concise and fully supported by the description.
Priority date. Date of the first filing from which the one-year priority period for further applications starts.
Filing date. A reference to the patent document or patent documents on the basis of which the applicant is claiming the "right of priority," by virtue of which the applicant can make subsequent patent applications while maintaining the effective filing date of the original application or applications.
Publication date: The date on which the patent document was published.
Grant date: The date on which the patent was granted, as applicable.
Patent classification: A symbol or set of symbols, consisting of a series of letters and/or numbers, representing the technical subject matter disclosed in the patent document and facilitating the retrieval of patent documents according to their subject matter.
Designated states. The patent offices at which the patent applicant can seek to obtain protection for their invention on the basis of the patent application. Applies to regional or international patent applications.
Legal status. Indication of whether the patent has been granted or not; if granted, the countries or regions in which the patent has been granted; and whether it is still valid or has expired or been invalidated in a particular country or region.
Citations and references. Certain patent documents also include references to related technology information uncovered by the applicant or by a patent examiner during the patent granting procedure; these references and citations include both patent and non-patent documents.
Document codes. Used to distinguish published patent documents according to type and status (codes according to WIPO Standard ST.16); for example, with respect to published international applications under the PCT, the code A1 denotes an international application published with the International Search Report (ISR), while the code A2 indicates an international application published without the ISR, and the code A3 designates an ISR published with a revised front page.
INID codes ("Internationally agreed Numbers for the Identification of [bibliographic] Data"). Identify different elements of bibliographic data (*see* WIPO Standard ST.9); for example, the code 11 is associated with the patent number and the code 54 is associated with the title of the invention.
Country codes. Specify different countries by a unique two-letter country code for example, the code "WO" indicates the International Bureau of WIPO; a list of country codes is given in WIPO Standard ST.3 available on the WIPO website.

The dual nature of patent information (i.e., its technical and legal components) plays a fundamental role in the checks-and-balance mechanism of the patent system. First, it informs the public of the owner, extent and technical scope of existing rights.

Such information is essential for third parties to avoid infringing the patent rights of others, and to contact the owner to negotiate a license or a transfer of the rights.

Second, somewhat as a mirror of the first, patent information indicates the extent to which third parties may exploit the technical knowledge contained in the patent document without infringing the patent. After the expiration or abandonment of the patent in a given country, or in any other country in which the patent has no legal effect, third parties are not required to obtain the consent of the patent holder for the exploitation of the patented invention (this is often referred to as the public domain). Further, if the applicable national patent law provides exceptions and limitations to the rights, third parties who are using or making a patented invention that falls under an exception or limitation would not be regarded as infringing the patent right concerned.

Third, patent information is essential for ensuring the quality of granted patents. By searching existing technology in patent information databases prior to drafting and filing a patent application, applicants can obtain a better indication of the prior art and increase the likelihood of obtaining valid patents for their inventions, and at the same time, assist the patent office's examination procedure. Moreover, applicants may save the costs of filing patent applications with no prospect of obtaining patent protection. During the examination stage, patent examiners use patent information to search prior art and to examine the patentability of inventions. Further, based on the information obtained from published patents, third parties may initiate opposition or revocation procedures if they believe that a granted patent does not meet the patentability requirements under the applicable law. Similarly, in some countries, third parties can make contributions to the examination procedure by submitting relevant prior art information. Of course, such contributions are possible only where the public has access to the information contained in patent applications.

Patent information is made available to the public through a variety of databases. Each database covers a particular set of patent documents. At present no database has complete coverage of all patent documents ever published worldwide. Thus, it may be necessary to consult multiple databases in order to find and then access patent documents relevant to your interests. Many national and regional IPOs provide free online access to their own patent collections as well as to selected patent documents from other offices.[16]

WIPO offers free online access to all international patent applications within the framework of the PCT and their related documents and patent collections from National and Regional Offices through its PATENTSCOPE search service.[17]

A number of commercial and nonprofit providers also offer free patent information databases online. Certain commercial providers have established value-added services for access on a fee-paying basis including translations of patent information and additional systematic classification, for instance, by chemical structures and reactions or biological sequences. Moreover, professional search services exist that can

16. An extensive list of national patent databases can be found at www.wipo.int/patentscope/en/national_databases.html.
17. *See* patentscope.wipo.int/search/en/search.jsf.

perform prior art searches on behalf of potential patent applicants and may be useful if an initial search does not produce desired results.[18]

§4.04 BRAND DATABASES

In view of the penetration of the Internet to merchandizing and advertisement, and globalized market places in many fields of goods and services, the value of brands protected by trademarks increased in many countries. At the same time, companies in low- and middle-income economies increasingly seek to develop their own brands—or to acquire them from abroad. The globalization of economic activity has prompted trademark holders to take their brands to more and more places. This includes trademark holders from low- and middle-income countries, who account for an increasing proportion of non-resident filings throughout the world. The emergence of the Internet has spurred trademark filings in a number of ways. It has spearheaded the creation of new firms, business models and services. The digital marketplace has increased the importance of brand reputation, as consumers engage in transactions at a distance. At the same time, brand owners face online sales of counterfeit goods and other forms of misuse of their trademarks, increasing their need for legal protection.

Given that the use of trademarks for the sale of goods and services on the Internet became common, branding strategy requires global protection of trademarks, prevention and avoidance of confusingly similar Internet domain names. These issues arising from the cyber space in this century also make it necessary to expand the scope of trademark information search from national domain to global market place and cyber space.

As the Internet domain names continue to suffer from cybersquatting, trademark holders also get involved in disputes which have never been more complex before. WIPO has facilitated global trademark search by creating Global Brands Database including national trademark data. The goal is to allow any person wishing to perform global search of similar marks or signs and to make sure their domain name candidates to avoid any infringement with registered trademarks.

As a first step to protecting trademarks, it is advisable to conduct a trademark search to make sure that the mark in question is not already in use by another enterprise in the target market(s). Trademark offices in many countries register marks without comparing them with existing trademark registrations and applications received earlier, but leave it to potential competitors to give notice of opposition once the mark or the application has been published or registered. Therefore, obtaining trademark registration in such countries is no guarantee that the trademark will not be infringing on the rights of others. It is therefore important, wherever possible, to search national trademark databases prior to using a trademark for your export operations.

18. WIPO's study and survey of patent databases may be found at www.wipo.int/edocs/mdocs/mdocs/en/cdip_3/cdip_3_inf_2study_iii_inf_1.pdf.

Trademark searches may be conducted through national or regional (such as TMView of OHIM) databases or WIPO's global brand database all of which are public and free of charge, or specialized commercial trademark databases.

§4.05 STATISTICS FOR IP INFORMATION

According to recent statistics, in 2013, patent applications filed worldwide amounted to around 2.57 million, up 9% from 2012, after passing the 2 million mark in 2011. Driving that strong growth were filings in China and the US. China and the US received the most applications. The State Intellectual Property Office of the People's Republic of China (SIPO) received the most applications in 2013, followed by the United States Patent and Trademark Office (USPTO), the Japan Patent Office (JPO), the Korean Intellectual Property Organization (KIPO) and the EPO. The EPO received around a fifth of SIPO's total. The gap between SIPO and the other offices has widened considerably since 2011, when SIPO became number one. The top twenty list includes patent offices from thirteen high-income countries and seven low- and middle-income countries, such as Brazil and India. One notable change of the top twenty list is the entry of Indonesia, which replaces South Africa. SIPO increased its share in the world total, while the JPO and the EPO saw theirs decline. The top five offices accounted for 81% of the world total in 2013. Around 40% of applications filed worldwide in 2013 were at offices in low- and middle-income countries. Among those offices, Malaysia and South Africa each received around 7,200. Bangladesh, Kenya and Nepal received only a few hundred. As the number of patent applications grows, the amount of patent information contained in published applications also grows, which in turn contributes to the expansion of knowledge of technology which is accessible to the public.

It is also important to note that a large number of granted patents enter the public domain every year. Patent rights generally last up to twenty years from the date of filing. The estimated number of patents in force worldwide rose from 8.72 million in 2012 to 9.45 million in 2013, when the USPTO recorded the most, with 2.39 million patents (26% of the total) followed by the JPO with 1.84 million (19%). Holders must pay maintenance fees to maintain the validity of their patents but may opt to let a patent lapse before the end of the full term. For seventy-seven offices that reported data, more than half the grants they issued remained in force for at least seven years after the application date, and about a sixth lasted the full twenty years. This means that 80% of granted patents expire before twenty years from the filing.

The PCT offers applicants an advantageous route for seeking patent protection internationally as an alternative to the Paris Convention for pursuing patent rights in different countries. PCT's world share now exceeds 55%, meaning more than half of foreign filing are made through PCT. China and the US drove record PCT filings in 2013, when total PCT applications surpassed 200,000 for the first time, at 205,256, up 5.1% from 2012. With more than 57,000 PCT international applications, the US exceeded in 2013 its previous filing peak of just over 54,000 in 2007. Japan is the second-largest user, and China surpassed Germany to become the third largest. After China, India is the largest user of the PCT system among the BRICS countries (Brazil, the Russian Federation, India, China and South Africa).

An estimated 4.87 million trademark applications were filed worldwide in 2013, 7.6% more than in 2012. Since 1995, applications have more than doubled. A trademark application may refer to different goods or services classes. Many offices use the Nice Classification, an international classification of goods and services for registering trademarks and service marks. Applications received by these offices are classified in one or more of the forty-five Nice classes. Some offices allow for only a single-class filing, which requires applicants to file a separate application for each class. Others permit multiclass filings, which enable applicants to file a single application in which a number of classes can be specified. To make better international comparisons between numbers of applications received, it helps to compare class counts across offices. Class counts are also used to make trademark registration activity internationally comparable. The total number of classes specified in applications surpassed 7 million, a nearly 60% increase on the 4.47 million recorded in 2004—the first year complete class counts became available. The increase in trademark filing activity (measured in application class counts) has been largely influenced by China, which has accounted for more than half the annual increases in global trademark filing activity since 2010. In 2013, China's office registered trademarks in which just over 1 million classes were specified, followed distantly by OHIM (280,623), the USPTO (274,430) and the office of Turkey (172,588).

To obtain trademark protection in multiple countries or jurisdictions, applicants can file their applications either directly at each individual office—the Paris route—or file an application for international registration through the Madrid system—the Madrid route. The nearly 47,000 international trademark applications filed through the Madrid system in 2013 were up 6.4% on 2012, reflecting growing membership and a general upward trend in applications worldwide. About one-third of the growth is from the two countries with the most applicants using the Madrid route in 2013—Germany accounted for 10% and the US for 22% of total growth. In all, 44,414 international registrations were recorded in 2013, an increase of 5.9% and the fourth consecutive year of growth.

§4.06 LICENSING AND THE TRANSFER OF TECHNOLOGY

[A] Introduction

One means for accomplishing economic development through the transfer of technology is the commercial transfer and acquisition of technology. Of course, technology can also be transferred and acquired by other than commercial methods. Personnel can be educated or trained at research and development institutions, technical institutes, or centers of high learning. Such personnel can in turn study books, periodicals, or other publications on special scientific and technical subjects, or read patent documents, and in that way acquire knowledge of specific technology. But these methods will inevitably fall short of enabling those personnel or others to apply that knowledge, especially the inventions described in patent documents, to manufacture products, produce goods or render services.

This is true for two reasons. First, the exclusive rights to work an invention belong to the owner of that invention. Without the authorization of the owner, his/her invention cannot be put into practice by others. Second, as has been mentioned, not all the knowledge—the know-how—which facilitates or is otherwise useful for the working of the invention is set forth in the description of the invention that is found in the patent document. Hence, it becomes necessary to buy those rights, or to buy the permission to use the invention, or to buy the know-how that enables the invention to be put into practice in the most efficient way.

[B] The Commercial Transfer and Acquisition of Technology[19]

[1] In General

The commercial transfer and acquisition of technology, that is, the selling and buying of the exclusive rights to a patented invention or of the permission to use the invention or of the know-how, takes place through certain legal methods.

Those legal methods give rise to legal relationships between the owner of the exclusive rights or the supplier or the know-how who transfers the exclusive rights or gives the permission or supplies that know-how—called the transferor—and the person or legal entity which acquires those rights or that permission or receives that know-how—called the "transferee." Those legal relationships are essentially contractual in nature.

By "contractual" in nature it is meant that the transferor of the technology consents to transfer and the transferee consents to acquire the rights, the permission or the know-how in question.

There are three principal legal methods that can be used to bring about a commercial transfer and acquisition of technology.

[2] The Sale: Assignment

The first legal method is the sale by the owner of all his/her exclusive rights to a patented invention and the purchase of those rights by another person or legal entity.

When all the exclusive rights conferred by the grant of a patent for invention are transferred, without any restriction in time or other condition, by the owner of the patented invention to another person or legal entity, it is said that an "assignment" has taken place. The word "assignment" is a typically English expression that covers the legal concept that has just been described. That concept is recognized in the laws of many countries. It applies also to the exclusive rights in utility models, industrial designs and trademarks, as well as other objects of industrial property. For the sake of

19. Material Transfer Agreements (MTAs), Collaboration Agreements (CAs), and some contracts covering technical assistance and maintenance may also imply the transfer of technology.

simplicity, however, the further explanation of this legal concept will be confined to the principles and characteristics of the assignment of the patented invention. Similar principles and characteristics apply to the assignment of other objects of industrial property.

The legal act whereby the owner of the patented invention transfers those rights to another is evidenced by a writing in the form of a legal document generally referred to as an "instrument of assignment of patent rights" or "assignment of patent rights" or, more simply yet, as an "assignment." The transferor, that is the owner of the patented invention, is called the "assignor" and the other person or entity, the transferee who or which acquires all the exclusive rights, is called the "assignee." When an assignment takes place, the transferor—the so-called assignor—no longer has any rights in respect of the patented invention. The transferee—the so-called assignee—becomes the new owner of the patented invention and is entitled to exercise all the exclusive rights conferred by the grant of the patent for invention.

[3] The License Contract

The second legal method is through a license, that is, the giving by the owner of a patented invention to another person or legal entity of the permission to perform, in the country and for a limited period of time, one or more of the acts which are covered by the exclusive rights of the owner of the invention patented in that country. When that permission is given, a "license" has been granted. It may be recalled that those acts are the making or using of a product that includes the invention, the making of products by a process that includes the invention, or the use of the process that includes the invention. Here, again, the word "license" is a typically English expression that covers the legal concept that has just been described. That concept is also recognized in the laws of many countries. It applies also to the exclusive rights in other objects of industrial property. Again, for the sake of simplicity, the remaining explanations of the principles and characteristics of the license will be limited to the patented invention. Similar principles and characteristics do apply, however, to the license of other objects of industrial property.

Where a license is granted, the legal document evidencing the permission given by the owner of the patented invention is usually referred to as a "license contract" or, more simply yet, as a "license." The owner of the patented invention who gives that permission is referred to as "the licensor." The person or legal entity who or which receives that permission is referred to as "the licensee."

It is formally called a "license contract" because two types of legal acts or transactions are usually involved. First, there is the *giving* by the owner of the patented invention to another person or entity *of the permission* to perform one or more of the acts covered by the exclusive rights of the patented invention. That permission or authorization is referred to as "a license." Second, the license is usually granted subject to certain conditions which will be set out in the written document by which the license is granted to the licensee.

One of the conditions will obviously be related to the payment by the licensee of money in return for the license that is granted. Thus, the licensee may promise to pay a fixed sum of money at a stated time or at stated times in the future or the licensee may promise to pay a sum of money, the amount of which will depend on the degree of working of the patented invention.

Another condition might be that the invention will be used by the licensee only for the manufacture of products destined for a specific use, as for example, the manufacture of a pharmaceutical product for use in humans but not for use in animals. Another condition might be that the licensee must work the invention in certain factories only or sell the product embodying the invention in certain defined areas only.

The conditions that have just been mentioned call for promises to be made or action to be taken by the licensee. It is also possible that the conditions may relate to promises to be made or action to be taken by the licensor. For example, the licensor may promise to defend in court a lawsuit brought by a third person against the licensee in which that third person claims that the working of the invention by the licensee violates the exclusive rights already conferred by the grant of another—a separate or distinct—patent for invention which is owned by that third person.

[4] The Know-How Contract

The third of the three principal legal methods for the transfer and acquisition of technology concerns know-how.

It is possible to include provisions concerning know-how in a writing or document that is separate from a license contract. It is also possible to include such provisions in a license contract. In the case where the know-how relates to a patented invention or a registered trademark or industrial design, the provisions are usually found in the license contract that deals with that patented invention or other object of industrial property. This is particularly so—and it is very often the case—when the owner of the patented invention or other object of industrial property is also the developer and holder of that know-how. For a variety of reasons, however, even in such a case, the provisions concerning the know-how might be placed in a separate or distinct writing or document. Whenever provisions concerning know-how appear in a separate or distinct writing or document, that writing or document is normally called a "know-how contract."

Through such provisions, one party—the supplier of the know-how—undertakes, that is, promises, to communicate the know-how to another party—the recipient of the know-how—for the use by that other party.

The know-how may be communicated in a tangible form. Documents, photographs, blueprints, computer cards, and microfilm, among others, are illustrations of tangible forms. Examples of know-how that could be transmitted in such forms are architectural plans of the factory buildings, the diagrams of the layout of the equipment in the factory, drawings or blueprints of machines, lists of spare parts, manuals or instructions for the operation of machines or the assembly of components, lists and specifications of new materials, labor and machine time calculations, process flow charts, packaging and storing instructions, reports on stability and environmental aspects, and job descriptions for technical and professional personnel. Such know-how in tangible form is sometimes referred to as "technical information or data."

The know-how might also be communicated in an intangible form. Examples of the transmittal of know-how in such a form would be an engineer of the supplier of the know-how explaining a process to an engineer of the recipient or the manufacturing engineer of the recipient witnessing a production line in the enterprise of the supplier. Another example would be training in the factory of the recipient, or at the enterprise of the supplier, of personnel of the recipient.

Know-how in intangible form relating to the demonstration of, or advice on, manufacturing and other operations is sometimes referred to as "technical services." Know-how in intangible form relating to training is sometimes referred to as "technical assistance." Where the know-how in intangible form is to consist of the actual direction of manufacturing operations or other operations, such as planning, or financial and personal administration, or marketing, it is sometimes referred to as "management services."

The provisions on these various forms of know-how can be rather lengthy and may refer to annexes, schedules or tables that are attached to the contract document and which set forth in detail the technical information or data, or the service or assistance that is agreed to be provided.

The provisions concerning the transmittal of know-how in tangible form, on the one hand, and in intangible form, on the other, might be subject of separate writings or documents. Indeed, under the laws of certain countries, such provisions must be the subject of distinct contracts or agreements, each covering separately, the different forms, commonly called, respectively, "the technical information contract" (or more loosely, "the know-how contract"), "the technical services contract (or agreement)," "the technical assistance contract (or agreement)" and "the management contract (or agreement)."

The provisions concerning the know-how to be communicated are not limited, however, to a description of the know-how and how it will be transmitted. They will extend as well to the price to be paid by the recipient for that know-how and to certain other matters relating to its disclosure to third persons.

The possibility that the know-how to be communicated by the supplier to the recipient might be disclosed, accidentally or otherwise, to third persons, is a very real concern to the supplier of the know-how.

The know-how of the supplier has usually been acquired or developed by the supplier during research and development activities and through experience in the application of industrial and business techniques in the operations of the supplier's enterprise. The know-how may very well be the reason for the current competitive position, if not leadership, of the supplier in the technology field concerned. As such, it is a valuable asset of the supplier to be preserved. At the same time, it is a resource which the supplier is willing to part with in exchange for an agreed price from the recipient and others who may wish to use it. Its supply to the recipient is consequently the result of a bargain. The price is not just the payment by the recipient of a monetary remuneration fixed by agreement between the supplier and the recipient. It is also the commitment by the recipient not to disclose the know-how to third persons except under certain conditions or with the consent of the supplier.

The provisions concerning know-how will thus cover various measures to safeguard against the disclosure of the know-how to unauthorized persons. Certain safeguard measures may even have to be taken prior to, as well as during the negotiations. Those measures will thus have to be agreed to even before the execution of the know-how contract itself.

In a number of countries, the legal form of the document evidencing an assignment or a license contract and other formalities and requirements concerning an assignment or license are prescribed by the patent law or by the commercial law.

Thus, a requirement may be imposed that an instrument of assignment of patent rights be executed in a particular manner, as for instance, it may be required that the instrument be signed not just by the assignor but also by the assignee.

Further, a requirement might be imposed that a public official certify, in the case where the assignor is a physical person, that the signature affixed as the signature of the assignor is the signature of the person who purports to be the assignor. In the case where the assignor is a legal entity, the law might require that the representative of that legal entity give evidence to a public official that the representative has the authority to sign on behalf of the legal entity.

Similar requirements might be imposed by the law in respect of the license contract and the licensor and the licensee.

In addition, in a number of countries, the patent law may require that an instrument of assignment of patent rights or a license contract be presented to the patent office for registration. By the act of registration, the assignee or the licensee is recognized by the Government as the transferee or holder of the rights transferred by the assignment or of the rights conferred by the license contract.

In addition, in a number of countries, the law may require that the terms and conditions set forth in the instrument of assignment or in the license contract be reviewed or examined and approved by one or more designated government authorities. For instance, where technology is to be acquired from abroad or where payments in foreign exchange must be made, the law might require the foreign investment commission or the central bank or both review and approve the provisions of the assignment or the license contract.

As in the case of the assignment and the license contract, the law may require that the know-how contract—or the separate contracts or agreements covering the different forms of know-how—be signed in a specified way. So also, law may require that the know-how contract—or those separate contracts or agreements—be registered or reviewed or examined and approved by one or more designated government authorities.

[C] TT in Other Contexts

[1] Sale and Import of Capital Goods

The commercial transfer and acquisition of technology can take place with the sale, purchase and import of equipment and other capital goods. Examples of capital equipment are machinery and tools needed for the manufacture of products or the application of a process.

Raw materials, for example, crude oil or phosphoric acid, can also be considered as capital goods in that although they are products in themselves, they may be necessary for the manufacture of another product, such as gasoline or fertilizer, respectively. So also, intermediate goods, such as cotton or polyester fiber, or woven cloth and leather, which is to be cut and sewn into clothing, and parts or other components, such as tires, batteries, radiators, and engines, which are to be assembled into an automobile, may be considered in the nature of capital goods in that they are needed in the manufacture of other products.

Such sales and purchases of capital goods and their import into the country can be considered, in a sense, TT transactions. They are often accompanied by documentation containing technical information, as for instance, manuals on the installation, operation and maintenance of machinery or other equipment, specifications giving size, quality, color, density and other characteristics of the raw material or intermediate goods in question, or instructions on the assembly of parts or other components of a product. Such documentation contains knowledge essential to the use of capital goods.

Contracts covering the sale and purchase and the import of capital goods are sometimes associated with a license contract or with know-how provisions or a know-how contract. In certain instances, provisions concerning the sale and purchase and the import of capital goods may be found in the license contract or the know-how contract itself.

[2] Franchising and Distributorship

The commercial transfer of technology may also take place in connection with the system of the franchising or distributorship of goods and services.

A franchise or distributorship is a business arrangement whereby the reputation, technical information and expertise of one party are combined with the investment of another party for the purpose of selling goods or rendering services directly to the consumer.

The goods in question may be durable, as in the case of automobiles or home appliances. The goods in question may be consumable in use, as, for example, prepared food or beverages. The services may extend to the rental of capital equipment, for example, automobiles, trucks or other power equipment, or to hotel operations, or dry-cleaning facilities, or secretarial help.

The outlet for the marketing of such goods and services is usually based upon a trademark or service mark or a trade name and a special decor or design of the premises. The license of such a mark or name by its owner is normally combined with the supply by that owner of know-how in some form, either technical information, technical services, technical assistance or management services concerning production, marketing, maintenance and administration. The owner of such a mark or trade name and know-how is called a "franchisor" or "licensor." The party to whom the license is granted and the know-how is supplied is called the "franchisee," "distributor" or "dealer." The franchisee, distributor or dealer may own the premises or contribute money and time as an investment in the business firm. Other aspects of their business relationship, including sharing of the profits of the franchise or distributorship will be agreed to between the franchisor or licensor and the franchisee, distributor or dealer and set forth in a writing or document called a "franchise agreement" or "distributorship agreement."

As in the case of the assignment, the license contract and the know-how contract, the law may require that such franchise or distributorship agreements be registered and reviewed or examined and approved by one or more designated government authorities.

The complexity of many business arrangements and TT transactions, however, often presents problems for the enterprises or other entities and the officials of their government which wish to acquire technology. Their experience in acquiring technology may not be as extensive as those of the enterprises that own technology and are willing to transfer it. Therefore, it may be necessary or advisable for the technology acquirer to seek the assistance of others in planning for and acquiring a given technology. It may even be necessary or advisable to cooperate in a more extensive manner with the technology transferor than the degree of cooperation which normally results from, for instance, the license contract or the know-how contract.

This leads to the explanation of three other kinds of business arrangements that the technology acquirer may resort to. These are "the consultancy arrangement," the "turn-key project" and "the joint venture arrangements."

[3] The Consultancy Arrangement

The help of an individual consultant or a firm of consultants that will give advice and render other services concerning the planning for, and the actual acquisition of, a given technology can be useful, if not indispensable, for such enterprises, entities and governments that wish to acquire technology from enterprises in other countries.

In such a business arrangement not only is help received in acquiring the technology but the experience gained and the lessons learned in engaging and working with the individual consultant or firm of consultants will be valuable knowledge that can serve to better carry out future projects.

As concerns planning, the advice or services may relate to the choice of the product to be manufactured or improved upon and the technology to be used, to the investment required, to the type of business organization or other relationships to be established, and to the suitability of each for the objective or objectives to be attained.

The planning advice or services may extend to recommendations on the type of product to be manufactured, the choice of the technology to be used in that manufacture and its possible sources.

The services might include general surveys of the geographical area or areas under consideration to determine the suitability of the area for the installation of a factory or for the marketing of the product.

The services could include studies of the availability of labor, raw materials, intermediate goods, parts, or components. They might include assessments of the impact of the technology on the environment, including field testing and laboratory analysis. Investment estimates, the identification of sources of financing and other pre-investment type services might also be provided. The consultancy services could also include an evaluation of the types of business relationships that are possible, and which should be entered into. In this connection, recommendations could be made on which of the different legal methods for the acquisition of the technology selected should be used.

The consultancy services might extend also to the implementation of a project. "Design and engineering" services are a typical example. Such services concern the preparation of the plan for the site of the plant, the design of the factory building, the design of machinery and other equipment, the preparation of tender documents for the construction of the building or the equipment and for civil engineering works, the evaluation of bids and advice on the award of contracts, the supervision of the construction of the factory, including the installation of the equipment, the supervision of the start-up and testing of the equipment and making findings on the state of performance of the process utilized, as well as giving advice in the initial period on the operation of particular equipment or the entire factory.

The consultancy services could extend further to actual research and development with a view to improving the product being manufactured or the process being applied or to determining possible uses of by-products or to creating new or related products or processes.

One or more individual consultants or firms of consultants might be engaged to render the services in question. Usually, however, such an individual or firm specializes in a particular type of service, such as investment planning, design and engineering, environmental impact, marketing or business organization and management. In a sense, the consultancy services are forms of know-how. They can thus be considered within the framework of the know-how contract, more particularly, the technical services contract or agreement.

[4] The Turn-Key Project

In certain instances, two or more of the business arrangements, and hence the legal methods that they reflect, can be combined in such a way as to entrust the planning, construction, and operation of a factory to a single technology supplier, or to a very limited number of technology suppliers.

Thus, the "turn-key project" may involve a comprehensive arrangement of certain of the legal methods, whereby one party undertakes to hand over to his/her client—the technology recipient—an entire industrial plant that can operate in accordance with agreed performance standards. More usually, the turn-key project involves the undertaking by one party to supply to the client the design for the industrial plant and the technical information on its operation. In the latter event, supplementary arrangements might also be made for the acquisition of rights to the technology, for civil engineering work and for provision of technical services and assistance concerning the construction of the plant, the purchase and installation of equipment, raw materials or parts and components, training, and supervision of the operation of the plant, at least in its initial stages.

It is called a "turn-key" project because the end result is to "turn" over to the client the "key" to the door of the industrial plant. That is a symbolic way of expressing the completion of the tasks agreed to between the parties.

Of course, it is also possible, depending upon the experience and resources of the technology recipient, that the technology recipient undertakes one or more specific tasks, such as part of the civil engineering work, the construction of the factory building and the purchase and installation of equipment, and even the design of that factory and equipment.

Both the consultancy arrangement and the turn-key project arrangement have their shortcomings. The first does not usually entail the responsibility of the consultant for the results. In the second, the technology supplier or suppliers are so responsible. Neither the first or the second provide means for a continuing involvement of the technology supplier so that access to later advances in its technology can be more readily facilitated. This is because neither contains a commitment to the technology acquirer to provide further advice or services or to provide improved or additional technology. Neither contains measures to provide money or other resources that may be needed for further growth.

Because of these shortcomings and for other reasons, joint venture arrangements can be more attractive means of industrial or commercial cooperation.

[5] Joint Venture Arrangements

The following will explain what is meant by a "joint venture," describe the two forms of arrangements, give examples of the use of the two forms, and how the different legal methods can be used in those arrangements.

First of all, some explanations must be made in connection with what is meant by "joint venture arrangements." In essence, a joint venture arrangement, or as it is more simply termed "a joint venture" is, in a broad sense, as the words imply, the doing together by two or more persons or enterprises of an activity which may or may not succeed. In the sphere of business, it is one kind of business relationship or form of business organization. It consists of an agreement between two or more persons or between two or more enterprises or even between one or more persons and one or more enterprises to combine, in a specified way, a certain kind and amount of their resources in order to manufacture, to produce or to sell a product or to render a service and to share in a specified way the profits that result and the risks that occur.

There are two fundamental forms of joint venture: the equity joint venture and the contractual venture.

The equity joint venture is an arrangement whereby a separate legal entity is created in accordance with the agreement of two or more parties. The parties undertake to provide money or other resources as their contribution to the assets or other capital of that legal entity. That entity is usually established as a limited liability company and is distinct from either of the parties which participated in its creation. That company becomes the owner of the resources that are contributed by each party. Each of the parties in turn become the owners of the company, that is, each is said to have "an equity" in the company.

Where one or more of the parties is a foreign enterprise or entity, such a party is, or such parties are called a "foreign participant" or "the foreign participants." The parties or participants, as they are called, will agree on the purposes and functions of the limited liability company, the proportion of the capital each will contribute to, and the share of each in the profits of, the limited liability company, and on such other matters as its management, operation, duration and termination. One or more of these matters may be governed as well by a joint venture law or by company law and related laws, including laws on taxation and labor relations.

However, the contractual joint venture might be used where the establishment of a separate legal entity is not needed or where it is not possible to create such an entity. This may be the case where the project involves a narrow task or a limited activity or is for a limited time or where the laws of the country in which the business operation is to be conducted do not recognize the ownership of property by foreigners. The relationship between the parties will be set forth in the contract or agreement concluded between them.

The different legal methods for the commercial transfer and acquisition of technology can be used in either form of joint venture arrangement.

An assignment of the exclusive rights to a patented invention, a utility model, industrial design or trademark by one of the participants could constitute a portion of that participant's contribution to the capital of the joint venture company. It is also possible, of course, for one of the participants to grant a license of a patented invention or other object of industrial property or to supply know-how as part of that participant's contribution to the joint venture company. More commonly, however, such a license or the supply of know-how in one or more of its forms will be the subject of one or more contracts made after the joint venture company is established. Those contracts will be concluded between one of the participants as the transferor of the technology in question and the joint venture company. Through such contracts the technology in question can be transferred to the joint venture company which will thus acquire the means to enable it to carry out its operations.

Whether one or more of the legal methods will be used in the establishment of the joint venture company or whether one or more of those legal methods will be used and when so as to enable the joint venture to carry out its operations will be matters for negotiation between the prospective participants. The result of their negotiations will be reflected in the joint venture agreement. The license contract, the know-how contract, the technical services or the technical assistance contract, the franchise contract, and contracts covering other commercial matters, might even form annexes to the joint venture agreement. They would be signed once the joint venture company was established.

Needless to say the joint venture agreement, whether it be for the establishment of a limited liability company or not, and the different contracts of the various legal methods that may be used, must be concluded in accordance with laws and regulations applicable to such companies and to the tax laws concerning those companies or to the laws relating to agency or partnership, as well as to other economic laws, including laws relating to labor, the sales of goods, insurance and to foreign economic and trade contracts.[20]

[D] Negotiation of Licensing Agreements

[1] Introduction

Any technical licensing contract may be analyzed in respect of the following basic elements:

(1) the subject of the contract;
(2) the licensor's obligations;[21]
(3) the obligations common to both parties.[22]

In reality, these elements are frequently spread out through the contract or are even intermingled. Nevertheless, examining a contract from these points of view has the advantage of providing a clear and logical analysis of the essential aspects that have to be considered when negotiating a contract.

The following topics are typically the subject of the negotiations leading to the conclusion of the license contract or which require special attention in drafting its provisions. These provisions are discussed from the point of view of the licensing of patents but they apply also to the other forms of IP.

20. The types of contracts that may imply technology transfer are in vast number. Only a few are mentioned here. One could also add various sorts of research agreements, such as collaborative research, contract research (in consultancy), and sponsored research.
21. Licensees also have obligations, such as, primarily, those of paying the due remuneration, besides those of keeping secrecy, granting-back improvements introduced, and collaborating, as necessary, with the licensor in the defense of its rights (namely, in the case a third party alleges lack of exploitation).
22. This list of licensor obligations is not complete. Those obligations may also include to maintain the licensed IP rights, defend the licensed IP rights against opposition or invalidation, enforce the licensed IP rights against infringement.

[2] *Identification of the Parties*

One of the first points of concern to the negotiators of the license contract will be the identification of the entities or persons which or who will become the parties or, in other words, will sign the license contract and become legally bound to carry out its provisions.

The objective in describing the parties to a license contract is to identify each of them with sufficient certainty, such that the identity of each entity or person from which or whom a given performance can be expected or to which or whom it will be rendered, will not later become a subject of controversy.

This objective assumes particular significance in complex business transactions in which there is more than one entity or person on either side. This is quite likely to be the situation in a licensing and know-how arrangement between entities or persons in different countries.

For example, one side in the negotiations leading to the conclusion of the license contract may be a grouping of legal entities, all organized and located in one foreign country or each organized and located in separate countries, but in either case, with a common ownership, control or other interest. In such cases, it may be contemplated that the patent license will be given by one of the legal entities in the group (or perhaps even by a legal entity outside the group) and that other performances will be undertaken or received by one or more of the other legal entities in the group.

Similar questions will arise where the other side to the negotiations is likely to involve a number of government authorities—ministries, commissions, bureaus or administrations or other government units—or public entities, state enterprises or private entities, including those established as a result of a joint venture with a foreign legal entity.

Further, consideration will have to be given to whether one document setting forth all the terms and conditions and commitments should be prepared and executed between all the parties on both sides or whether several documents, each containing distinct terms and conditions and commitments, should be drawn up and signed by the different parties on each side.

[3] *Objectives of the Parties; Scope of the License*[23]

When the parties are negotiating a license contract, they usually proceed on the basis that certain technology is necessary for the manufacture of a particular product or the application of a particular process from which a product or other result is to be

23. A technology license agreement will generally determine the exclusivity agreed with the licensee (i.e., sole, exclusive, or non-exclusive). The scope of such exclusivity has an impact on licensee's rights and obligations. When the license is exclusive, for example, the licensee acquires standing in court to sue infringers and defend the patent in general. Another important issue is the possibility accorded (or not) to the licensee of sub-licensing the invention From a public policy perspective, the more potential users of the invention are given access to its exploitation the better, but an easy access may have an opposite effect—that of discouraging further investments in new improvements.

obtained. In other words, the ultimate objective of the parties in concluding a license contract is the transfer by the licensor, and the acquisition by the licensee, of a given technology and of the right to exploit that technology in the making, or in the use or sale of a given product or in the application of a given process through which a product or other result will be obtained.

This objective of the parties will be expressed both generally and specifically in the license contract.

Their objective will be reflected in a general way either in a preambular part of the license contract, consisting of a series of provisions often referred to as "recitals" or "whereas clauses," or directly in an operative element of the license contract, consisting of a particular article entitled "background information."

The objective of the parties to the license contract will be expressed more specifically in subsequent provisions that delineate the "scope" of the license contract. One set of those provisions identifies the technical subject matter of the license contract (i.e., the product or the process, the invention or inventions and the know-how and technological advances, if any).

Another group of those provisions will determine which of the parties may perform one or more acts of exploitation, set forth the place or places where that act or those acts may take place, and establish the duration of the exploitation, and specify the purpose or purposes for which the technology may be exploited.

Other provisions will prescribe the level of working of the invention or inventions, specify the means, if any, to assist in the exploitation, fix the remuneration for the exploitation and state the consequences of a failure or of an interference with the exploitation of the technology or with other commitments agreed upon.

[4] Subject Matter

The provisions of the license contract that define its technical subject matter in effect identify the technology which will be the subject of exploitation, and ultimately, if the license contract is fulfilled, that will be transferred from the licensor and acquired by the licensee.

These provisions describe the product to be made, used or sold, or the process to be applied and from which a product will be obtained and in turn used or sold; identify the invention or inventions included in that product or process; describe the know-how, if any, that is to be supplied; and identify the technological advances of one party or the other, and the conditions under which those advances will be made available by that party to the other.

[5] Identification of Product or Processes

Since the ultimate objective of the licensee concerns a product or process, one of the provisions in the license contract will identify in concise terms that product or process. In the typical case, that provision is set forth in the part of the license contract dealing with definitions.

The product might be identified somewhat broadly, as for example, "instruments for the purpose of writing," which would include, for instance, fountain pens, ballpoint pens and felt-tipped pens. The product might be defined more specifically, as for example, only one or more but not all of those kinds of pens.

The process might be identified as a chemical formula according to which certain chemical substances interact when a specified catalyst is introduced resulting in a specified product.

The title and the abstract set forth in the application for the grant of a patent for the invention that is included in the product or the process may be a useful starting point in providing the requisite information to describe the product or the process.

[6] Identification of the Invention(s)

The provision that identifies the invention or inventions included in the product or process usually refers to the number of the patent for invention or the application for the grant of a patent for invention, the country where the patent was granted or registered or where the application was filed, the date of the patent grant or the filing date of the application, and in some cases, the title of the invention and the status of the application. Where the product or the process in question includes a number of inventions, the relevant information in respect of each invention is usually grouped together and set forth in a schedule attached to the license contract.

[7] Description of the Know-How

Under the standard requirements of most patent laws, the description of the invention claimed in an application for the grant of a patent for invention must disclose the invention in a manner sufficiently clear, detailed, and complete to permit a person having ordinary skill in the art to carry out the invention.

Some patent laws go further, and require also that the best mode contemplated by the inventor for carrying out the invention be set forth. But those patent laws do not extend to requiring a description of additional means that may facilitate the carrying out of the invention. Such additional means may consist of the use of technical information and expertise acquired through long experimentation with the invention.

More frequently, the technical information or expertise is not disclosed because it is not known at the time of putting the description together as part of the documentation to be submitted to obtain the grant of a patent for invention. The description of the invention claimed in the application for the grant of a patent for invention is often based on research work carried out under laboratory or small-scale conditions.

Commercial production or even production on a pilot scale may not come until a later stage. It may then be too late for it to be incorporated in the description of the invention in the form of an amendment to the application as filed because the patent for invention has long since been granted. Further, as to whether the invention will be cost-competitive or not, this may not be known at the time of the filing of the application. Commercial costing may not be determinable until commercial production commences and optimum production runs can be reached.

For the foregoing reasons, it will be useful, if not indispensable, that the potential licensee acquires from the licensor or, with its/her assistance, from others, the technical information, data or knowledge resulting from experience or skills, in other words, the "know-how," which is or may in the future be applicable in effectively exploiting the invention or inventions included in the product or process in question.

As regards the description of such know-how, technical information can be identified in terms of the relevant documentation, as for example, diagrams of the layout of the plant, drawings, or blueprints of machines, lists of spare parts, manuals or instructions for the operation of machines or the assembly of components, specifications of raw materials, labor and machine time calculations, packaging and storing instructions and information on stability and environmental aspects.

Job descriptions can be drawn up for each expert whose technical or professional expertise is needed. This information can be set forth in one or more annexes, appendixes or schedules attached to the license contract.

[8] Confidentiality

Know-how is acquired or developed by the licensor during research and development activities or through the application of industrial and business techniques in the operations of the licensor's enterprise. The know-how may often be the reason for the current competitive position, if not superiority, of the licensor in the technology field concerned. As such, it is a valuable asset of the licensor to be preserved. At the same time, it is a resource which the licensor is willing to part with in exchange for an agreed price from the licensee or others who wish to use it. Its supply to the licensee is consequently the result of a bargain in which the price is not just the payment of a monetary remuneration fixed by the license contract but also the commitment by the licensee not to disclose that know-how to third persons except under certain conditions or with the consent of the licensor.

Turning to the terms and conditions of the license contract itself, the parties will need to define which portions of the know-how, whether developed by one or the other, and at what times, should or should not be disclosed, to whom, and for what duration.

The parties will also need to state the effects if an unauthorized disclosure should occur, accidentally or otherwise, including the consequences if the license contract expires or, because of a default of one or the other of the parties, it comes to an end before its stated expiration, including the period agreed upon for non-disclosure.

[9] Access to Technological Advances

The technological advance of immediate concern to the parties to the license contract will normally be one which significantly or substantially affects, for example, in the case of a given product, the volume of its production, the cost of its manufacture or the efficiency of its use, or, in the case of a given process, the material conditions under which that process is applied, or the cost of its application, or the efficiency of its application.

Various approaches can be taken by the parties to the license contract to provide information about and to define their respective rights in technological advances which either may have made or acquired.

The parties might decide that the mutual exchange of information on technological advances is in their best interests, and that each shall be free to exploit, free of charge, the technological advance of the other. This is called cross-licensing. When the obligation to transfer the advances or improvements on the licensed technology falls upon the licensee, it is called "grantback." Under Article 41.2 of the TRIPS Agreement, WTO Members may deem grantback conditions, when exclusive, to be unlawful. However, when the Parties establish exclusivity in a reciprocal manner, such clause should not be prohibited without further analysis. The essence of the contract should be the economic balance of rights and obligations. Therefore, when one clause that is apparently inconvenient to one of the parties is set off by a compensatory measure, it could become pro-competitive.

The parties might also decide that if either party makes available the technological advance of the other to a third person for remuneration, then the other shall be entitled to share in that remuneration in some agreed manner and amount. It is usually provided further that the party making the technological advance should apply for patent protection. If it does not elect to do so, the other party may apply, in the name of either and at the expense of the party applying.

Anyway, access to improvements to the licensed invention by either contracting party may give rise to complex issues and, importantly, may have antitrust implications. So, parties are invited to deal with matter with great care.

[10] Territorial Rights

Which of the parties to the license contract will be able, by virtue of its provisions, to perform what act or acts of exploitation, in what territory or territories, and with what effects on arrangements with third persons in relationship with the licensor or the licensee who are also interested in exploiting the technology are distinct but related questions. They are related because each concerns the exclusive right of the licensor under the patent for invention granted to the licensor and which will be the subject matter of the license contract. A decision on each of these questions must be clearly reflected in the license contract.

[11] Field(s) of Use

A provision on the field or fields of use or activity specifies the purpose or purposes for which the invention or the know-how may be applied. It serves to define the scope of that application by the licensee. At the same time, depending on that defined scope, the licensor may be able to grant a license or supply know-how to each of a number of other licensees, each specializing in different applications of the invention or the know-how in question. That permits the most practical way of exploiting the invention or know-how, given the capabilities of each particular licensee.

It should be noted that the amount to be paid by the licensee for the technology may vary according to the purpose or purposes for which the technology is sought to be exploited. The licensor may be willing to authorize the exploitation of the invention or supply the know-how for application in terms of a given field of use or activity. However, the licensor may be willing to authorize that exploitation in respect of all the purposes for which the invention or the know-how may be applied. In the latter event, it is likely that the price asked for will be higher than where a more limited field of use or activity is agreed upon. In the long run, though, it may be desirable for the licensee to have the opportunity to apply the technology for all purposes. The price asked for in that case, however, must be compared to the lower price which may be asked for if a limited purpose is agreed to. The comparison becomes all the more relevant if the licensee is not currently, nor in the future likely to be, in a position to exploit the technology beyond the limited purpose.

[12] Exploitation

The licensor expects that the licensee will not only exploit the invention and apply the know-how but will do so to the fullest extent permitted by the terms and conditions of the license contract.

The parties might wish to specify that the licensee will make, use, or sell the product that includes the patented invention or will apply the know-how in a certain manner with a view to obtaining a certain result and to exploiting the technology at a certain level. The parties might wish also to set forth the commitments of the licensor the performance of which will assist the licensee in achieving the expected manner and extent of working or other exploitation.

The questions that usually arise in respect of the manner and extent of exploitation are concerned with the following matters: the quality of the product; the volume of production; the making of part of the product by third persons to be authorized by the licensee; the import of the product to meet local demand in the absence of sufficient working in the country itself; and the use of the distribution channels of the licensor.

The quality of the product is a factor in promoting the sale of the product, in establishing the goodwill of the licensee and in maintaining the licensee's competitive position in the market.

Further, the quality of the product may be linked to the reputation of the licensor where the product is to be marketed bearing the trademark of the licensor. From the point of view of the public, a product bearing a trademark carries with it a certain symbol of quality and consistency, for which someone, whether identified or not, holds him/herself responsible.

Consequently, the standard of quality of the product, the know-how to be imparted to meet that standard and the requisite quality will be matters which are usually reflected in appropriate provisions in the license contract.

The license contract might stipulate an agreed quality standard for the product. In that case, the license contract usually also includes a provision that the licensor will inform the licensee of the way in which the product is to be made so that the required quality standard can be attained.

Other ways, although indirect, exist to assure that a given standard of quality for the product is achieved. It might be stipulated that certain production personnel designated by the licensor will be employed by the licensee to supervise certain phases of production.

The licensee might wish to have certain assurances from the licensor concerning the actual working of the patented invention and the application of the know-how. The licensee might wish to have an assurance from the licensor that, by working the patented invention of the licensor and applying the know-how supplied by the licensor, the licensee will be able to fulfill his/her expectations under the license contract to make a given product that includes the patented invention or know-how.

The licensee might wish to have the assurance that by such working and application the licensee will be able to obtain a given product or other result through the process that includes the patented invention or the know-how.

Also of concern to the licensee in respect of the effective exploitation of the patented invention is whether the know-how supplied by the licensor will be adequate or suitable in attaining the objective of the licensee to make the patented product or to obtain a given product or other result through the patented process.

The approach to this question consists essentially of the licensor giving to the licensee an assurance as to the know-how to be supplied. Such an assurance is referred to as a guarantee of know-how.

In this context, a guarantee is an assertion that a given fact or event concerning the know-how exists or that a given performance will take place if the know-how is applied; that assertion is accompanied by a promise that if the fact or event does not exist or the performance does not take place, a correction will be made or some other act will be done in its place.

The guarantee provision of the license contract might be phrased in terms of the conformity of the know-how supplied to the agreed description of what was promised to be supplied. It might be phrased in terms of the results to be attained by the application of the know-how. It might be phrased in terms of the suitability of the know-how to meet the technological requirements of the licensee.

[13] Settlement of Disputes

When non-performance is likely, or does occur, and there is no provision in the license contract which fixes the agreed consequences in respect of that failure of performance, one party might propose a solution that is satisfactory to the other. That solution might be the allowance of additional time to render the performance or the substantial correction of the flaw or flaws in question. It might mean that some other performance in lieu of the defective performance would be acceptable. In these ways, an amicable way of settling the dispute between the parties could be arrived at without recourse to legal remedies in the courts or other tribunals.

Yet circumstances could arise when the party injured by the default in the performance of the other is not offered a satisfactory solution. It could be also that the party alleged to have defaulted, denies that there has been a failure to perform as agreed. In either event, some machinery for the settlement of the dispute should be provided for before recourse is had to the courts or other tribunals. Thus, recourse might have been to the advice of independent experts, or the findings and recommendations of a group consisting of representatives of each side, or to conciliation or to arbitration proceedings or, ultimately, to the courts or other tribunals competent in the matter. In particular, a clause designating the WIPO Arbitration Center as the forum for settling disputes may be added to a license contract.

[E] Remuneration

[1] Introduction

One of the most critical and complex issues to be negotiated between the prospective transferor and the potential transferee is the "price" or the "cost" of the industrial property to be acquired whether outright or by license, and of the technology to be transferred. The "price" or the "cost" is dependent upon a number of factors, including the nature of the industrial property rights and the technology and the relative bargaining power of the two parties. The prospective transferor usually makes a careful assessment in terms of value or the need for the particular technology, the alternative technologies available, the prospect of technological advances and the likely production and profitability of the potential transferee. The prospective transferor also makes detailed projections of production and consequent income flow from other potential licensees or technology recipients.

The potential transferee assesses the total payments that it is likely to make for a particular technology and for advances in that technology against the profitability of the enterprise over a period of time and also evaluates such payments in relation to costs of alternative technology or payments made with respect to similar transactions.

[2] Direct Monetary Compensation

Direct monetary compensation for industrial property rights or for technology may take different forms: (a) "lump-sum payment"—a pre-calculated amount to be paid once or in installments; (b) "royalties"—post-calculated, recurring payments, the amount of which is determined as a function of economic use or result (production units, service units, sales of the product, profits); (c) "fees"—compensation for services and assistance rendered by technical or professional experts, fixed at a specified amount or calculated per person and per period of service.

These forms of remuneration may be combined in a given industrial property license or TT agreement. In some instances, the lump-sum payment form may replace the system of royalties altogether, while in other instances the two might be combined one way or another, as where the licensee or technology recipient may elect to make a lump-sum payment in lieu of one form of royalty or another. In other instances, the licensee or technology recipient may be given the opportunity to elect to pay royalties on production units rather than on sales. The fees for technical services and assistance may be determined separately, either stipulated in advance or negotiated as rendered.

It is to be noted, however, as elaborated below, that under the laws in certain countries governing the transfer of technology the various rights or elements of technology may have to be separately priced or valued and even made the subject of distinct licenses or agreements.

[3] Lump-Sum Payment

The lump-sum amount may be paid, in the case of a transfer or assignment of industrial property rights, at the time of the transfer or assignment of industrial property rights or, in the case of an industrial property license or a TT agreement, upon the conclusion of the license or agreement or shortly or sometime thereafter, either in a single payment or in a series of installment payments. The latter may be staggered in relation to certain events such as the execution of the license or the agreement, or on the delivery of certain technical information.

The lump-sum payment is often made for the outright acquisition of industrial property rights, whether by sale or assignment, as well as in the case of the license of industrial property rights or the transfer of know-how, where the technology can be transferred all at once and the licensee or technology recipient can readily and fully absorb it. Such payment is made for the transfer of rights and know-how concerning technology which is less sophisticated and may be quite appropriate from the viewpoint of the licensee or technology transferee if a continuing supply of technical information concerning technological advances or the marketing of the product or technical services and assistance in support of the licensee or technology recipient is not required of the licensor or technology supplier. For example, a lump-sum payment may be made to obtain the rights in a patented product, or to a patented process or to sets of drawings, specifications or other technical information that are sufficient in themselves to enable the licensee or technology recipient to manufacture and sell certain products.

Under the laws in certain countries governing the transfer of technology, recourse to the form of lump-sum payment for the acquisition of industrial property rights or technology is subject to certain conditions. Under one of these laws, it is provided that, subject to the authorization of a specified governmental unit, a lump-sum amount may be paid if it is determined in advance on the basis of the estimated volume of sales during the period of the license or agreement and provided, further, that the amount is within the maximum limits which may be established for the sector, activity or product. Under another of these laws, a lump-sum payment is permitted in the case of the acquisition of patent rights by transfer or purchase and for certain types of technical services and assistance; otherwise, the remuneration must take the form of royalties in the case of a patent or trademark license or an agreement for the supply of know-how to be applied in the production of consumer goods or materials in general or in the manufacture of machinery, equipment or other capital goods. In the latter cases, however, although a lump-sum amount may be fixed for the technical information initially supplied, it must represent an advance on the royalty remuneration.

[4] Royalties

As indicated previously, royalties are post-calculated, recurring payments, the amount of which is determined as a function of economic use or result.

In order to establish this functional relationship between the recurring amounts and the economic use or result, the provision in the license or agreement may refer to the volume of production, to the sales price of the product that is manufactured incorporating the technology (or, in the case of the trademark license, that is sold bearing the trademark) or to the profits of the licensee or technology recipient.

As noted previously, under the laws in certain countries governing the transfer of technology, royalties are the only form of remuneration which may be provided for in specified types of industrial property licenses or TT agreements. In particular, these laws require that the royalties be ascertained either on a percentage basis or as a fixed value per product unit, but in either case imposed or related to the sales price, or, when applicable, also linked to the profits earned from the sales of the product.

[5] Lump-Sum Payment Compared with Royalties

The lump-sum payment is characterized by the fact that the obligation is fulfilled immediately or fairly shortly. Further, the parties do not have to make continuous accounts or control the calculation or the remittance, as in the case of royalties.

The lump-sum payment, when compared with royalties, may or may not have certain tax advantages. The continuous payment of royalties is considered to be income to the licensor or technology supplier from the viewpoint of taxation and, as such, royalties are subject to income taxes. The single lump-sum payment, and even the lump sum payable in installments, may be considered the counterpart to, or the financial result of, a sale or purchase operation, with the assignment or transfer of the industrial property rights and the supply of the know-how considered analogous to the sale of commercial goods. The licensor or technology supplier will also have to pay taxes on the lump-sum payment. The single lump-sum payment, however, may be subject to a different (often higher) tax rate than income in the form of royalties. Under some tax laws, it may be possible to alleviate the higher or progressive rates on the lump-sum payment if it is split into installments and paid over several tax years and thus subject to lower tax rates.

Where a more or less single performance is the counter value, the lump-sum payment may lead to results economically more justified between the parties. If, for example, unexpected high sales are reached, especially under the influence of monetary fluctuations or other economic circumstances, the system of royalties leads to unexpected and unjustified returns to the licensor or technology supplier. Upon the payment of a lump sum, the licensor or technology supplier would receive only the counter value of its single performance of the licensor or technology supplier. Upon the payment of a lump sum, the licensor or technology supplier would receive only the counter value of its single performance which it thought was justified at the time the agreement was concluded.

However, the lump-sum payment may also entail risks for the licensee or technology recipient if production or sales of the product lag behind expectation and if the lump-sum payment is disproportional to the economic value of the performance of the licensor or technology supplier.

[6] Lump-Sum Payment and Royalties Combined

In many cases, the remuneration for industrial property rights or know-how is a combination of a lump-sum payment and royalties.

The lump-sum payment is often treated as an initial payment for disclosing information that enables the potential licensee or technology recipient to evaluate the technology. The licensor or technology supplier frequently views this payment as the initial remuneration for basic research and development in respect of technology. The actual initial payment varies a great deal from transaction to transaction and may range from a small sum for the delivery of initial technical information to a very large amount for sophisticated technology that has required much research and development. In some instances, the initial lump-sum payment may be viewed as a minimum payment or regarded as a down payment or advance against royalties. Further, the licensee or technology recipient may be given the opportunity to make an additional lump-sum payment, stipulated in advance or negotiated at the time of the election to make that payment, in lieu of royalties, with a credit against the payment of the royalties already made.

In negotiating remuneration in the form of a combined lump-sum payment and royalties, the licensee or technology recipient will need to evaluate carefully the total outflow and incidence of the payments that may be likely for various combinations. The burden of interest charges, for example, is important in determining the size of the lump-sum figure, while projections of production estimates and of cash-flow from sales during the period of the license or agreement are essential in assessing the percentage rate of royalties.

[7] Fees for Technical Services and Assistance

Specific technical services and assistance, to be provided by the licensor or technology supplier, may be necessary in connection with the transfer of the technology or the marketing of the product under a trademark, and may have to be paid for separately.

The fees for specific technical services and assistance related to a patent or trademark license or a technical know-how agreement include: (a) the cost of training programs for the personnel of the licensee or technology recipients; (b) fees for technical services and assistance to be rendered by technical experts of the licensor or technology supplier to the licensee or technology recipient at the latter's industrial plant during the period of the license or agreement; (c) fees for technical services and assistance which concern machinery, equipment or other capital goods needed in the utilization of the technology at the industrial plant of the licensee or technology recipient.

Frequently, in the case the title is invalidated and the licensor has to reimburse the licensee for (undue) payments made, such reimbursement is not full, part of it corresponding to technical services and assistance provided by the licensor that, is spite of the invalidation, are advantageous to the licensee. In this case, the legal principle is the prohibition of unjust enrichment.

[8] Indirect and Non-monetary Compensation

[a] Income from Related Operations

The licensor or technology supplier may receive income from various operations, such as commissions on the sales of the product made on behalf of the licensee or technology recipient through the distribution channels of the licensor or technology supplier, profits from the sale of the product supplied to the latter under exclusive purchase arrangements, profits from the sale to the licensee or technology recipient of related products which complete its marketing program, profits from the sale to the licensee or technology recipient of raw materials, intermediate goods, parts or other components and rentals from machinery, equipment or other capital goods released by the licensor or technology supplier to the licensee or technology recipient.

[b] Dividends

If the licensor or technology supplier assumes a financial participation in the enterprise of the licensee or technology recipient or if they enter into a joint venture, the licensor or technology supplier will obtain, in the event of successful commercial operations, dividends from the financial participation. If an essential part of the commercial operations depends upon the industrial property rights or technology of the licensor or technology supplier, there may be a direct dependency between the amount of the royalties and the amount of the dividends: the higher the royalties the lower the dividends, and vice versa. The degree of participation and financial and tax factors may dictate the relevant amount to be assigned to each and the formation of reserves or the holding back of profits, which may lead to an increase in the value of the financial participation.

In this context, attention is directed to the laws in certain countries governing the transfer of technology which treat as profits payments in respect of the price of industrial property rights or technology made between a subsidiary and its parent, or between subsidiaries; or where there exists economic unity or community of interests between the parties, or where effective technical, administrative, financial and commercial management of the technology transferee is exercised by the technology transferor; or where the technology transferor supplies raw materials or intermediate products used in the process in an amount equal to more than a specified percentage of the total cost of the product. Some of these laws also provide that in such cases the lump-sum payment or royalties may neither be treated as a contribution to capital nor constitute shares in the profits or in the capital of the enterprise of the licensee or technology recipient nor be deducted for the purpose of calculating the tax on its income.

Under the laws in certain other countries governing the transfer of technology, although royalties may be paid by the licensee or technology recipient to the licensor or technology supplier even where the latter has a financial participation in the former, the amount of the royalty payments must be reduced substantially in the event that the licensor or technology supplier has a majority participation in the licensee or technology recipient; in addition royalty payments by a wholly owned subsidiary to its foreign parent company are ordinarily not permitted.

[c] Cost Shifting or Sharing Measures

Certain cost shifting or sharing measures, for example, the expenses in maintaining or defending rights under the patent or the trademark, that are adopted may have the effect of reducing the expenses of the licensor or technology supplier and increasing the cost to the licensee or technology recipient of the TT transaction.

[d] Feed-Back of Technical Information

The technical know-how of the licensee or technology recipient which is to be turned over to the licensor or technology supplier can also constitute a form of income to the latter.

[e] Acquisition of Market Data

The licensor or technology supplier may benefit from data provided by the licensee or technology recipient concerning the marketing of the product in the local area, including new sales promotion techniques, which may prove useful to the marketing of the product in other areas.

[9] Cost Reductions and Savings to the Licensee or Technology Recipient

Some elements of a given TT transaction may have the effect of reducing the operating expenses of the licensee or technology recipient or otherwise lead to savings on the part of the technology transferee.

Mention may be made of such measures as the utilization by the licensee or technology recipient of the channels of sales distribution of the licensor or technology supplier, the use without payment of the trademark of the licensor or technology supplier, the access of the licensee or technology recipient to information concerning improvements to existing inventions, or developments in know-how, or new inventions of the licensor or technology supplier or rights in respect of such technological advances, and the opportunity to benefit from the marketing information and other technical services and assistance of the licensor or technology supplier.

[10] Description of the Currency of the Obligation and of Payment

It is necessary to distinguish two aspects of the question of currency designation. The first concerns the determination of the currency which will serve as the measure of the obligation to pay, and the second relates to the choice of the currency in which payments will be made to discharge that obligation. The currency of obligation and the currency of payment may be one and the same but they need not necessarily be, and in fact may be different, as is often the case in an international commercial transaction.

[11] Currency of Obligation

The currency of the obligation in the case of the lump-sum payment may be the currency of either the country of the licensor or technology supplier, or the country of the licensee or technology recipient or a third country.

In the case of royalties, if the royalty amount is linked to the volume of production, and does not depend on the value of the unit produced, the currency chosen may be either that of the country where production takes place or that of another country. If the royalty amount is linked to sales, the currency chosen may be that of the country where sales take place. If export sales are likely, more than one currency may be chosen—the currency of the country of the licensee or technology recipient where production and domestic sales occur, and the currency or currencies of the country or countries where the export sales are made. If royalties are linked to the profits of the enterprise of the licensee or technology recipient, then the currency of the country where that enterprise is legally organized may be chosen.

As concerns fees for technical services and assistance, the determination will most likely be between the currency of the country of the expert and the currency of the country where the services are performed; however, in the case of services performed by experts sent to the country of the licensee or technology recipient, the amount of the fees will normally be determined in the currency of the country of the expert, with payment in whole or in part in the currency of that country and the remainder, if any, plus the portion attributable to living expenses and other facilities in the country of the licensee or technology recipient.

Under the laws in certain countries governing the transfer of technology, it is provided that the currency of the obligation must be currency of the country of the licensee or technology recipient, though remittance abroad may be made in the equivalent foreign currency; whereas, under the laws in some other of these countries, though the currency of the obligation may be expressed in a foreign currency at least the expenses connected with the maintenance of experts in the country of the licensee or technology recipient must be paid in the currency of that country.

Many factors may play a role in the choice of the currency of payment, such as whether the currency of obligation can be utilized in the country of that currency by the licensor or technology supplier; the inflation rate in the country of the currency of obligation; the stability in the international money markets of that currency in relation to other currencies; the existence of currency exchange controls in the country of the currency of obligation or where the income of the licensee or technology recipient is generated; and the applicability of tax laws which may provide special benefits to one party or the other.

[12] Rate of Exchange

In the event that the currency of payment chosen differs from the currency of obligation, the rate of conversion will normally figure as a provision in the license or agreement. Any one of a number of different exchange rates may be selected; for example, the official rate established by national or international monetary authorities, or an average of the said rates or a commercial rate, such as the telegraphic transfer selling rate or other selling rate or other rate of a specified domestic or foreign commercial bank.

[F] Types of IP Licenses

[1] Introduction

The typical provisions of an IP license are discussed above in general terms. Some provisions are particular to the type of IP being licensed. Some of the more important of these provisions are listed below.

[2] Patent Licenses

Under a patent license, the purpose of the contract is to authorize the use of an invention protected by a patent. The patent involved is identified by stating the name of the country in which it has been granted, together with its number. Generally, the technical subject matter of the invention is briefly stated in the preamble or in the article defining terms used in the contract. Reference is also frequently made to a separate annex when the license concerns a number of patents issued in differing countries. It is advisable to state exactly those countries in which patent applications are still pending and to stipulate which of the parties is responsible for complying with the administrative and legal formalities required for the upkeep of the patent.

A patent affords a set of exclusive rights: to use the invention, to manufacture it, to sell it or place it on the market. Generally, a license provides an authorization for the licensee to carry out all those acts.

A license may be an exclusive license, a sole license or a simple license. An exclusive license guarantees that the licensee will have no competition, not even that of the licensor or of the latter's subsidiaries. This must be stipulated in the agreement. A sole license guarantees the licensee that the licensor will afford no licenses to other manufacturers within the contractual territory. A simple license provides no guarantees in that respect, but simply constitutes an authorization to use the invention.

In such cases, it is recommended to include in the contract what is known as the "most favored licensee clause." Such a clause ensures that the licensee will enjoy the most favorable conditions that may subsequently be granted to a second licensee (for the same territory). This clause thus avoids any distortion of competition that would result from differing contractual conditions for the supply of technology.

[3] Trademark Licenses

Trademark licensing is of fairly recent origin in trademark history. Since the original function of a trademark was to indicate trade origin, goods emanating from a source other than the trademark owner could not, without deception, carry a licensor's mark. Indeed, the grant of a trademark license rendered a licensor vulnerable to the claim of non-user and expungement of its mark. The exercise by a licensor of quality control over the products sold by a licensee to which the mark was affixed opened the door to the fiction that such control was a form of user avoiding expungement of the mark. This fiction formed the basis of the registered user provisions inserted into most trademark statutes in the last forty years.

Most registered user provisions require the license parties to submit their agreements to the Registrar who scrutinizes them to ascertain the nature and extent of the quality controls to be exercised by the licensors. The Registrar is obliged to ensure that registration of such agreements accord with the national interest, and the Registrar is required to refuse registration to agreements which appear to him to facilitate trafficking. It should be noted, however, that registration has been considered not to be essential for validity of a trademark license. The registration provisions have been described as permissive and not mandatory. Provided a licensor maintains control over the quality of the licensed products and the licensor is perceived as retaining a connection with the licensed products expungement can be avoided.

Trademark licenses may be granted as adjuncts to or separately from patent and know-how licenses. Among the provisions particular to most trademark licenses are the following:

> *Permission to Use.* The grant of permission to use the relevant mark or marks is the first-stated provision of most license agreements. The particulars of the mark or marks are usually listed in a schedule to the license agreement, together with the products in respect of which the mark is to be used.

Number of Licensees. It will be important for the licensee to know how many other licensees will be appointed to service the license territory. It will also be important to ascertain whether the licensor intends to distribute within the territory. Finally, it will be important to a licensee where others are to be appointed to ensure that its rivals are appointed on comparable terms.

Quality Control. As mentioned above, at the heart of any registered user agreement is a provision that the licensee will not use the marks on products which do not attain the standard of quality prescribed by the licensor. Quality control provisions will provide that the user receives, on a confidential basis, all specifications, technical data and know-how of the licensor to allow the prescribed quality standards to be met. Policing of this clause will usually require the user to send sample products to the licensor and to permit inspections of the user's factory and warehouses and of methods of production, materials used, storage and packing of finished products. The agreement should permit the user to dispose of products which do not meet the quality standard provided they do not carry the trademark. This is an important topic because under the statutes of some countries the trademark owner that fails to verify the licensee's quality standards is sanctioned with the *abandonment* of the mark.

Marketing. The license will designate the territory in which the trademark may be used. This will usually contain prohibitions against trading outside the designated territory as well as provisions keeping the licensor out of the license territory. Advertising material employed by the licensee may have to receive the licensor's approval.

Financial Arrangements. In addition to a fee or royalties for being permitted to use its trade marks, a licensor may also require payment in respect of the provision of skilled persons to instruct employees of the licensee in the materials required to achieve the prescribed quality standards required in the agreement. Arrangements also have to be made to allocate the cost of the sampling procedure. Finally, the licensee is usually required to keep detailed books and records of sales of the trademarked products.

Infringements. The licensee is normally required to report to the licensor all particulars of infringements which occur and the licensor usually has conduct of all infringement proceedings.

[4] Copyright Licenses (Publishing)

In the case of a publishing contract, the owner of copyright does not need and usually does not intend to part with his or her copyright or even the right to control the publication of his or her work. Under certain copyright laws, which consider the author's economic rights inseparable from his or her moral rights, assignment of the author's right to publish the work may not even be possible. When entering into a publishing contract, the owner of the copyright usually only undertakes to restrict the exercise of his or her right in the work to be published to the minimum extent necessary for the publisher to be able to use the work. At the same time, the ownership of copyright does not change but remains with the author or other owner of the copyright.

Thus, a characteristic publishing contract is a mere license granted to the publisher by the owner of copyright. To be of value to the publisher, a license must also enable the publisher to protect the publishing activity against third persons.

A license is generally understood in the field of copyright as the authorization given by the author or other owner of copyright (licensor) to the user of the work (publisher or other licensee) to use it in a manner and according to conditions agreed upon between them.

The publisher should be granted a license comprising all the rights necessary for optimum realization of the planned publication. Generally, the publisher acquires an exclusive license (providing an exclusive right) to reproduce and publish the work concerned—or, if appropriate, to provide, reproduce and publish its translation—in a standard trade edition, comprising a reasonable number of copies.

The license can be granted for one edition only, or also for subsequent ones. The size of a single—or the first—edition is usually determined in the contract either by fixing the number of copies it should comprise, or by stipulating a minimum and/or maximum number of copies ("the print run"). The agreement on the size of a single—or the first—edition usually takes into account the need to comply with the presumable demand of the public, at costs permitting sales at the usual retail price per copy prevailing in the given book market as regards similar publications.

In the case of a license to publish the work in translation, the language (or languages) of the authorized edition (or editions) must be specified.

In order to promote the dissemination of the work published, and with regard to possible further exploitation of the publication under the contract, the licensee may also acquire certain so-called subsidiary rights. Such rights serve the purpose of reproducing or communicating to the public, or licensing others to reproduce or communicate to the public, the work (or its translation) in specified forms other than the standard trade edition.

Such subsidiary rights may, for instance, comprise: the right of previous and subsequent publication in the press of one or more extracts from the work; serial rights, that is, the right to publish the entire work or parts of it in one or more successive issues of a newspaper or periodical, before or after publication of the work in the standard trade edition; the right to read extracts from the work in sound or television broadcasting; the right to include the published work or a part of it in an anthology; the right to arrange for pocket book or book club editions subsequent to the standard trade edition.

Publishers often request the licensor to confer on them, in the framework of subsidiary rights, the right also to license the reproduction of the published work by means of making microfilms or other reprographic reproductions thereof, for purposes beyond the limits of fair use allowed by the law. The publisher may also request the right to license storage of the work in a computer, accessible to the public. Again, publishers may request the licensor to entitle them to license the reproduction of the work in the form of sound recordings as well. Sometimes, also the right of licensing the reproduction of filmstrips is requested. All these kinds of reproduction by means of modern technology are often referred to in contemporary publishing contracts as "mechanical reproduction" of the work, and the rights involved as "mechanical reproduction rights." This term should not be confused with the notion of the "musical mechanical right," which means the right to reproduce a musical work in the form of sound recordings.

Publishing contracts for many newer works also generally address specifically the licensing of rights to create electronic versions, often known as "e-books" or "talking books," which are versions of the work (either abridged or unabridged) read aloud (sometimes by the author) designed for use with various listening devices. These works were previously distributed on physical media such as cassettes or compact discs, and now are also distributed through streaming on or downloads to computers or various devices that may be dedicated to the purpose or may be used for many purposes (e.g., smartphones). For these and other types of uses that were not anticipated in older publishing contracts, entered into before the advent of various technologies, there have been disputes between authors and publishers as to whether (or which) previous contractual provisions and levels of remuneration apply.

It is a reasonable and usually accepted position not to confer upon the publisher rights to exploit the work in any manner involving its adaptation, such as dramatization rights for stage or film production, or for sound or television broadcasting, or translation rights in general. Strictly speaking, the exploitation of such rights goes beyond the scope of the promotion or direct exploitation of the publisher's own publication of the work.

The grant of "digest rights" (the right to publish an abridgement or shortened form of the work), or of the so-called strip cartoon rights, is often made subject to special authorization in each case, in view of the moral interests of the author relating to the integrity of his/her work.

With regard to the integrity of the work to be published, special stipulations can be incorporated in the contract. This may prove useful especially in countries where no appropriate "moral rights" provisions are established by legislation. For example, it may be agreed that "the publisher shall reproduce the work without any amendment or abbreviation thereof, or addition thereto."

As regards translation of the work, it is usual to agree that "the publisher shall have a precise and faithful translation made at his or her own expense. The title of the translation is subject to the written approval of the Copyright Licensor. Upon request, the final text of the translation shall also be submitted to him or her for approval."

It can also be stipulated that "the Publisher shall ensure that the title of the work and the name of its author shall appear with due prominence on every copy produced." Depending on the circumstances, it also can be added that "the Publisher undertakes to print the name of the original publisher (that is, ...) as well as the year(s) of the previous edition(s) of the work on the verso of the title page."

With regard to certain formalities previously required in a few States as a condition of the full enjoyment of copyright in published works, and in order to provide notice, it is generally stipulated in publishing contracts that an appropriate notice of copyright shall be printed on the title page. The notice consists of the symbol C, the year of the first publication of the work and the name of the owner of the copyright in the work.

As regards distribution of the copies published, it is often stipulated that "the Publisher shall provide for efficient promotion of the work at his or her own expense." In cases where a license has not been confined to one edition only, it is often added that "he or she shall see to it that the book is continuously available, and that new editions are printed in due time, so as to comply with actual demand."

[G] Assessing Abusive Clauses: *Ex Ante Versus Ex Post* Analysis; Per Se *Rules Versus the Rule of Reason*

The first edition of this book added, at this point, a section on the government control of TT agreements. It recommended such intervention, particularly for developing countries, as a way of protecting importing companies, generally with less bargain power vis-à-vis the IP owners, as well as of promoting national public policies. The first edition relied very significantly on proposals made in the WIPO Model Law for Developing Countries on Inventions, a publication of the 1980s. That approach has been deeply revised and even though some precaution is recommended in dealing with TT in a wide context of national public policies, it is generally understood that the contracting parties should be left to decide as to their best interests. Three surveys organized by WIPO and published on its website (Survey on Technology Transfer Agreements and Antitrust (December 2013); WIPO Survey on the Antitrust Dimension of IP Licensing Agreements in Support of Technology Transfer (March 2015); and Survey on IP, Joint R&D and Competition (June 2015)) indicate a trend in eliminating *ex ante* controls of TT-related agreements. The trend, accordingly, is to submit contracts to *ex post* controls, which are naturally triggered only when and if conflicts arise between the parties and abuses are eventually alleged. Moreover, a significant number of countries have inserted in their national laws a (short) list of clauses that are deemed to be per se abusive, hence unlawful, but most clauses are subject to analysis taking into account the circumstances of each case, and in particular the eventual benefits that result to the parties and to the economy in general. In other words, most clauses with an apparent anticompetitive tone are scrutinized under a *rule of reason* approach.

Article 40.2 of the TRIPS Agreement enumerates three clauses that are generally seen as anticompetitive: exclusive grantback conditions; clauses preventing challenges to the validity of the licensed IP right; and coercive package licensing. It is up to countries to decide whether these clauses are per se abusive. In principle that are not necessarily so: for example, grantback conditions can be pro-competitive if they are reciprocal, or if the beneficiary party pays for the transfer. Article 40 of the TRIPS Agreement does not represent an authorization for WTO Members to impose controls on licensing abusive clauses. In fact, Article 40.1 reads: "[A] [WTO] Member may adopt, consistently with the other provisions of this Agreement, appropriate measures to prevent or control [abusive licensing] practices [...]." However, at first sight, measures that are consistent with the TRIPS Agreement should not need an authorization. But this contradiction is only apparent. Article 40.1 speaks to non-violation issues. In other words, it says that Members may adopt measures to prevent or control [abusive licensing] practices that are consistent with the other provisions of the Agreement, even if they impair the benefits that other WTO Members expected from the implementation of the Agreement. Therefore, Article 40.1 accords those measures immunity against non-violation complaints (which are currently under a moratorium).

This is an important aspect because it gives leeway for WTO Members in handling this important issue.

§4.07 IP FOR SMALL AND MEDIUM ENTERPRISES

Regardless of the kind of business a Small and Medium Enterprise (SME) is in, it is likely that in the course of its business it would produce creative content, develop innovative solutions and know-how and acquire business information all of which could be captured by different types of IPRs. It is also likely that it would be using the IP acquired by others. Almost every SME has a trade name or a sign that it uses to distinguish itself from other businesses, it probably has information that enables it to be more competitive such as customers' lists to sales tactics it may have developed creative original designs, or created publications such as advertising material, brochures, posters and some may have developed or improved a new product. The IP system provides for the possibility of appropriating rights over these outputs enabling the SME to use and manage these to further its competitive strategy. Likewise it may be using the software, machines, music and publications of others. In doing so it may be using the IP rights of others for which if it does not have the authorization to use could pose financial, reputational or other risks to its business. Therefore the IP system is clearly of relevance to an SME.

The following types of inventive, innovative and creative output may attract different types of IP rights:

- Innovative products and processes (through patents and utility models).
- Cultural, artistic and literary works including, in most countries, also for computer software and compilation of data (through copyright and related rights protection).
- Creative designs, including textile designs (through copyright and industrial design rights).
- Distinctive signs (mostly through protection of trademarks including collective and certification marks, but in some cases through GIs).
- Microchips (through protection of layout-designs or topographies of integrated circuits).
- Denominations for goods of a given quality or reputation attributable to the geographical origin (through protection of GIs).
- Trade secrets (through protection of undisclosed information of commercial value).

An enterprise that has developed innovative products or processes or created cultural, artistic and literary works, designs or distinctive signs or relies on confidential information would have the possibility of acquiring proprietary rights over them through the different options available under the IP system. These options when used in a strategic sense can go a long way in furthering the competitive position of an SME in the marketplace.

[A] Using IP as a Competitive Tool

Through the effective use of patents, the SME would be able to prevent competitors from using the patented invention for the duration of the patent, a maximum of twenty years. This would allow it to consolidate its market position effectively marginalizing the competition and establishing itself in the market as the preeminent player. Higher price margins and higher returns on investments would follow. In many cases, where an enterprise has merely improved an existing product and the improvement is not sufficiently inventive to be deemed patentable, utility models (or "utility innovations") may be a good alternative for strengthening its market position. Trade secrets are another option and one frequently relied upon by SMEs for protecting innovative products and processes as well as a vast array of confidential business information that a business relies on for its competitive advantage.

Similarly, copyright is available to protect the creative content developed by an SME. These could be product information material, guides for using products, brochures, websites, TV or newspaper advertisements, marketing videos, etc., which are all copyrightable subject matter. As a general rule, copyright protection is automatic and does not depend on registration. Being able to control their use is an important tool for an SME in protecting its competitive space in the market.

Trademarks, however, are business identifiers. They are in many ways the face of the business. They allow its customers to distinguish its products or services from those of its competitors, giving the SME the possibility to better market its goods or services. But trademarks are not just used as identifiers. They are also seen as a guarantee of consistent quality. A customer who is pleased with the quality of the product or service will continue to purchase it relying on the promise of a given quality of the trademark. Great care therefore should be taken in choosing and designing an appropriate trademark, protecting it, using it with care in advertising, and policing its misleading or improper use by others.

Collective marks, in addition, can be used by a group of SMEs (a cooperative or an association of enterprises) making the same or similar products to join together under a joint marketing campaign of a collective mark. This allows the individual member SMEs, usually small enterprises which would otherwise not be able to effectively market themselves, to benefit from a reputation acquired on the basis of the common origin or other common characteristics of the goods produced or services rendered by different enterprises.

Inherent in certain products from a particular region are characteristics that are due to the soil, climate or particular expertise of the people of that area which consumers of those products expect and have confidence in. Here too the SMEs of that region producing goods that have those characteristics can market their products under a GI and benefit from the collective reputation of that GI. It is important to note that in the case of such products, the SME must qualify to use that mark and must maintain the standards and quality expected of goods produced in that region.

An SME could also market under a certification mark which certifies that the product meets certain required standards thus giving consumers an indication that their product has been checked by an organization considered competent to certify the product and has met the necessary requirements. This too may help a company to market its products and improve its image among consumers.

An attractive design captured by an industrial design right is another important means by which an SME could distinguish itself from the competition and ensure market share. A visually attractive design alone may enable the SME to captivate a demanding and extremely diversified clientele and could constitute its single most important distinguishing factor.

It is important to keep in mind that a single product may be protected by various forms of IP rights covering different aspects of that product. For example, a mobile phone would have hundreds of patents protecting its inherent technology, trade secrets protecting the know-how and other confidential business information, designs protecting its appearance, copyright protecting the ring tones, manuals and brochures. All of these forms of IP would together build and nurture the brand of the enterprise symbolized and identified by the trademark and is an important tool for maintaining and strengthening the competitive edge and expanding the market base.

[B] Exploiting IP Assets

These IP rights provide the means by which the inventive and creative output of SMEs embedded in a product are themselves transformed into proprietary products preventing third parties from exploiting them and enabling the SME to carve out a temporary monopoly for that product. In addition, through business identifiers and distinctively identifiable features which are also proprietary under the IP system, it is able to establish its unique identity and strengthen its appeal in the market place. The increased recognition coupled with the trust that is placed by consumers on the brand demands product consistency so as to ensure customer loyalty. This is the principal means by which an SME can benefit from the IP system, which is for strengthening its market position through limiting competition (by raising barriers to entry by competitors, reducing the threat of substitutes) while at the same time increasing its visibility and appeal.

However, this is not the only way IP adds value. The IP rights having transformed different types of intangibles into a type of tangible property can now be dealt with as one would deal with tangible property. One could sell, give others the right to use in exchange for a fee through licensing and franchising agreements, strengthen one's bargaining position in obtaining access to the IP rights of others (cross-licensing) or in entering into joint ventures and also use them as collateral in financial transactions or in simply relying on IP assets to establish sufficient credibility for accessing finance.

A licensing agreement is a partnership between an IPRs owner (licensor) and another who is authorized to use such rights (licensee) in exchange for an agreed payment (fee or royalty). A variety of such licensing agreements are available, which may be broadly categorized as technology license agreements, trademark licensing and franchising agreements and copyright license agreements. The right to use the IP owned by another which is the essence of these agreements opens up possibilities that one would normally have been prohibited from engaging in given that the rights are owned by another. Therefore, the SME can manufacture, sell, import, export, distribute and market various goods or services which it may be prevented from doing otherwise. What is particularly interesting about the possibility of IP licensing is that while the IP system transformed creative and innovative output into property their inherently intangible nature allows for multiple and potentially endless number of users to exploit the IP as the use of one does not prevent the use by another unlike with tangible property where the use by one essentially excludes use by another. Thus, an IP owner can provide the right to use a single IP to as many licensees as he/she wishes potentially adding revenue streams endlessly.

In a technology license agreement, a technology protected more than likely by patents and trade secrets would be licensed. Similarly in a trademark licensing agreement a trademark would be licensed giving the right to the licensee to apply it to certain goods or use it in connection with certain services and a copyright licensing agreement gives another the right to use certain works protected by copyright. In a franchising agreement, however, a franchisor who has developed a certain way of doing business gives another the right to use that business model with the right to use a bundle of IP rights linked to that business along with training and support. In essence, a successful business is replicated and run by a franchisee with the rights to use the IP rights attached to that business under the supervision, control and assistance of the franchisor.

A joint venture may consist of any variety of business relationships that involve two or more enterprises pooling their resources with the objective of implementing a common business purpose. Often, in such agreements, one party will contribute technology or know-how of which he/she is the proprietor and the other party may contribute financial and expertise of his/her own to the project. The joint venture will, therefore, often include a license agreement concluded by the parties concerned to regulate the use of the proprietary information and compensation for its use.

In recent years, there is growing acceptance that IP assets can be used as collateral for securing loans from a financial institution. There has also been a growing trend toward securitization of IP assets. Securitization normally refers to the pooling of different financial assets and the issuance of new securities backed by those assets. In principle, these assets can be any claims that have reasonably predictable cash flows, or even future receivables that are exclusive.[24] Thus, securitization is possible for future royalty payments from licensing a patent, trademark or trade secret, or from musical compositions or recording rights of a musician. In fact, one of the most famous securitizations involved the royalty payments of David Bowie.

IP is also important in securing high risk investment by angel investors and venture capitalists generally in the context of technology-based start-up companies that have potential for high growth. A single IP could be the only asset of value and the foundation of the business proposition. It is necessary, therefore, to include in the business plan being presented to investors that the IP rights have been secured or is in the process of being secured. This gives a strong signal to investors of the seriousness of the SME, that they have taken steps to protect their assets and that they believe in their innovative or creative product and that it is not relying, without authorization, on other companies' trade secrets, copyrighted materials, patents or other IP rights. In some high-tech sectors the risk of infringing on third-party IP rights is high and investors may be reluctant to take the risk unless they are confident that (e.g., through a patent or trademark search) no such risks exist. As such, any indication that confirms due diligence on the part of the SME in the management of IP assets is likely to play an important role in convincing investors of the SME's potential.

In addition, in most countries, the Government provides encouragement and support to high-tech start-ups and other innovative SMEs through grants, guarantees, subsidies and/or soft loan schemes, which are provided via various public funding institutions and banks that directly or indirectly recognize the importance of IP assets.

[C] Valuation of IP Assets

In order to be able sell, license or enter into any commercial arrangements with IP at its base it is necessary to be able to put a value on the IP asset. While there are certain accepted norms that enable with a certain degree of accuracy to value tangible assets such as houses and cars valuing intangible assets poses some challenges. Various methods have evolved for doing so and the principal methods are the cost method, market method and the income method. The cost method establishes the value of an IP asset by calculating the cost of developing a similar (or exact) IP asset either internally or externally. The market method is based on comparison with the actual price paid for a similar IP asset under comparable circumstances. The income method values the IP asset on the basis of the amount of economic income that the IP asset is expected to generate, adjusted to its present-day value. This method is the most commonly used method for IP valuation.

24. It should be noted that real securitization requires packaging of debt instruments into funds and structuring these for investors who have varying appetite for risk. Normally with IP this does not take place, although there have been attempts in that direction. This should not be seen as the same as royalty monetization. Also in this context, patents, trademarks and copyright is discussed, but these separate rights are dealt with very differently in terms of monetization.

[D] Risk Management

Failure to protect its innovative and creative output would be at the SME's cost. If, for example, the SME does not proceed to protect its innovations a competitor may do so and be able to legitimately exclude the SME from the market or ask it to pay a licensing fee for using its own innovative output.

Further, just as much as being an owner of IP rights vests in the company a variety of options for using those rights in a manner that furthers the competitive strategy of the company it also means that respecting the IP rights of others needs to be part of the risk management strategy of an SME. IP therefore also has to be considered in the context of business risk and steps have to be taken to minimize the risk of the unauthorized use of the proprietary assets of others. One assumes that deliberate infringement of the rights of third parties are not tolerated by the SME not only because it is against the law but also because it could be very costly for the SME in terms of legal fees, time lost and damages to be paid if found guilty. However, the SME could face the same costly consequences if it inadvertently infringes the IP rights of others. Therefore, clear steps have to be taken to avoid such eventualities by being vigilant and informed of the IP rights of others. In the case of patents, the company must also be mindful that even if it owns a patent, it does not give it the right to use it as there may be patents owned by others that prevent the use of the patent in question. When deciding on a trademark, a search of the trademark databases is a necessary first step to determine if there are others with that same or similar name that could be considered confusing and give rise to an infringement issue. For some enterprises, the use or exploitation of copyrighted works, sound recordings, broadcasts or performances may be a central part of their daily business activities. For others, it may simply be an occasional tool used for enhancing corporate publications, websites and other marketing devices. For others still, use of copyright material may be confined to the use of their computer software. A common misperception is that works published on the Internet are in the public domain and may therefore be widely used by anybody without the authorization of the right owner. Any works protected by copyright or related rights, ranging from musical compositions, to multimedia products, newspaper articles and audiovisual productions for which the time of protection has not expired, are protected regardless of whether they are published on paper or by other means for example, on the Internet. In each case the authorization of the right owner is required before using these works. As a general rule, every commercial use or exploitation of these rights requires a license or an assignment of the rights from the right owner. Usually these rights are collectively managed by a single organization which simplifies the process of obtaining licenses for various works. Rather than dealing directly with each individual author or right holder, collective management societies offer users a centralized source where rates and terms of use can be negotiated, and where authorizations can be easily and quickly obtained.

Doing business via the internet is practically indispensable for most companies today. This means that an Internet address is required, technically known as a domain name. In spite of their different functions, domain names often conflict with trademarks, the latter being used to identify and distinguish products or services from those of the competitors. The SME should, therefore, avoid using a domain name that is already protected by another enterprise as a mark.

[E] Entering International Markets

An important aspect about IP rights is that they are "territorial," i.e., only available in the country or region in which they had been applied for and granted. Therefore, if the SME is interested in entering foreign markets it is important to keep in mind that the IP rights that it has obtained in its local context will not be valid in the foreign market in question. In order to have IP rights in the foreign market, it would have to seek and obtain protection in that market (except when it is available automatically without the need to comply with formalities, e.g., through an international treaty mechanism such as the Berne Convention for the Protection of Literary and Artistic Works). Thus, once protection has been obtained in the market of interest then the competitive advantages referred to above in the local market will extend to the foreign market. Therefore, any competitor in that market would not be able to engage in business that would infringe the IP right in question unless it secures a license to do so. Conversely, if no IP protection has been obtained in that market, competitors are free to use the IP rights in question. For example, a product protected by a patent and a trademark successfully marketed in country A can be reproduced in country B and marketed under the same trademark if that trademark and patent are not protected in country B. There are exceptions however in the context of what are called famous marks.

This is an important point and bears repeating that there is no such thing as a global patent or trademark or design (the situation is a bit different with copyright) and third parties have the right to use and exploit those rights if they are not protected in the country or region in question. Thus, in the context of licensing, a formal licensing agreement is relevant only if the IPR that is sought to be licensed is protected in that country. If not, it is free to use.

[F] Impact of Electronic Commerce

While the Internet can open a lot of opportunities for SMEs, it may also pose a number of challenges for the effective protection and enforcement of IPRs, in general, and for copyright and related rights, trademarks and patents, in particular. The protection of copyright and related rights in the digital environment, the protectability of e-commerce business methods by patents, the use of trademarks as "metatags" and keywords, the infringement of trademark rights through the use of a sign on the Internet, the scope of protection of well-known marks and unfair competition in electronic commerce are some of the issues and challenges which an SME may have to face.

[G] Dispute Settlement

Despite the best of efforts unfortunately disputes do arise. It may take the form of infringements of the company's IP rights by third parties and the necessity to decide the best way to deal with that or it may take the form of third parties alleging infringement by the company of their IP rights and demanding that it stop and that they be compensated for damage. These are situations that could have been prevented or perhaps not. IP litigations are costly affairs and no small company would willingly go into it as a defendant and even as a complainant. An option that should be considered for such an eventuality is the option of alternative dispute settlement mechanisms such as arbitration and mediation, the possibility for which should ideally be incorporated into contracts when entering into relationships with third parties. Arbitration generally has the advantage of being a less formal procedure than court proceedings, and an arbitral award is more easily enforceable internationally. An advantage of mediation is that the parties retain control of the dispute resolution process. As such, it can help to preserve good business relations with another enterprise with which the SME may like to collaborate in the future.

[H] Developing an IP Strategy

SMEs should generally consider all of these issues not on an ad hoc basis as and when a situation presents itself but in a strategic sense in the context of its long-term business interests and determine whether and to what extent is IP relevant to its business and what it should do about it. In other words. it should put in place an IP strategy.

An important first step in this regard is to identify what potential IP exists in the company. This is done by way of an IP audit. This entails identifying potential IP assets, determining whether they should be protected by IP rights and if so which IP rights, monitoring them, maintaining them, valuing them and in general determining the best strategic approach to be taken given the business interests of the company.

Once potential IP assets have been identified, the SME must, having made a cost benefit analysis, determine whether formal protection will be sought for some or all of them and if so what IP rights will be considered the best way to go and proceed to do so as early as possible. If the SME intends to enter international markets taking steps in a timely manner to secure IP rights in those markets is crucial. It is also important to determine how the IP of the SME is managed vis-à-vis its partners, suppliers, contractors, service providers, clients as well as determine how the SME will manage the IP of these third parties in its interactions with them. These are all important in preventing leakage, determining ownership issues, managing risk of infringement etc.

This should be complemented by a strategy of constantly keeping itself informed of the activities of competitors and other players in the space occupied by the SME by consulting patent and trademark databases regularly. These resources provide rich and timely information on the most recent technical developments opening up licensing opportunities and preventing unnecessary expenses in researching what is already known, finding ready solutions to technical problems, identifying new licensing partners or suppliers, new market opportunities, monitoring activities of competitors, identifying possible infringers, and avoiding infringing competitors' rights etc.

A non-exhaustive check list of issues that should be included in an IP strategy are indicated below:

- Check trademark databases to avoid using an existing trademark and protect trademarks before launching a new product or service with a new brand name. It is important to consider export markets when doing so and avoid using brand names that may have an undesirable meaning in a foreign language.
- Identify patentable subject matter and make sure it is patented early enough to avoid losing the invention to competitors.
- Make sure that patentable inventions are not shared with others or published before filing a patent application. In order to meet the patentability criteria inventions must be considered "new." Early disclosure of an invention (e.g., through publication) will compromise the chances of the invention being considered new, and therefore patentable.
- Make sure that trade secrets are kept within the enterprise and prepare, where appropriate, confidentiality agreements when negotiating and sharing information with business partners in order to protect trade secrets.
- For export-oriented firms, make sure IP is protected in all potential export markets. In the case of patents, it is important to bear in mind that an enterprise generally has twelve months from the date of filing of a national application to file the same patent application in other countries.
- Use your IP portfolio as leverage when seeking sources to finance your business (e.g., include IP assets, particularly patents, utility models and industrial designs, in your business plan as it may help to convince investors of the market opportunities open to your enterprise).
- Use patent information available in patent databases to develop your business strategies.
- When conducting joint research with other enterprises or research institutes, make sure that there is sufficient clarity on who will own potential IP generated from the research project.
- Monitor the market and make sure that your IP assets are not being infringed. If violation of your IP rights is detected it may be advisable to contact a lawyer.
- If you are unsure about how to best protect your company's intangible assets, conducting an IP audit may be a good first step in order to identify all your company's valuable information and to develop an IP strategy. On occasions, companies are unaware of the wealth of assets they possess in the form of information, creative ideas and know-how and may, therefore, not take adequate steps to protect them.

[1] Conclusion

While it cannot be said that IP is equally relevant to all SMEs, it would be more relevant to SMEs that are potentially high growth, innovation based and export oriented, no SME can afford to ignore the IP system. Even if it does not integrate IP into its competitiveness strategy, which would certainly be to its detriment, it should at the very least consider the implications of ignoring the system from a risk management perspective. As such, every SME should take the time to understand the broad contours of the IP system and determine ideally how it could add value to its business proposition and if not what it would cost if it failed to do so.

CHAPTER 5
About WIPO, Its Work and Strategic Goals

§5.01 WIPO

[A] History

The "Convention Establishing the World Intellectual Property Organization" was signed at Stockholm in 1967 and entered into force in 1970. However, the origins of WIPO go back to 1883 when the Paris Convention was adopted, and to 1886 when the Berne Convention was adopted. Both of these conventions provided for the establishment of international secretariats, and both were placed under the supervision of the Swiss Federal Government. The few officials who were needed to carry out the administration of the two conventions were located in Berne, Switzerland.

Initially there were two secretariats (one for industrial property, one for copyright) for the administration of the two conventions. In 1893, the two secretariats united. The name of the organization now known as WIPO has undergone several changes in the course of its history. The most recent of its names, before it became WIPO, was *Bureaux Internationaux Réunis pour la Protection de la Propriété Intellectuelle* (BIRPI), the acronym of the French language version of the name: United International Bureaux for the Protection of Intellectual Property (in English). In 1960, BIRPI was moved from Berne to Geneva.

At the 1967 diplomatic conference in Stockholm, when WIPO was established, the administrative and final clauses of all the then existing multilateral treaties administered by BIRPI were revised. The said clauses had to be revised because Member States wished to make the Organization (WIPO)—which is, of course, an organization of Governments—independent of the Swiss Government, to give it the same status as all the other comparable IGOs, and to pave the way for WIPO to become a specialized agency of the UN system of IGOs.

Among the specialized agencies, some of the best known are the International Labour Organization (ILO), the United Nations Educational, Scientific and Cultural

Organization (UNESCO), the WHO and the Food and Agriculture Organization (FAO). They are called "specialized agencies" because each of them has specialized knowledge and expertise, and has accumulated vast international experience in a particular subject or field of activity of importance to the international community. Thus, ILO is specialized in labor, UNESCO in education, science and culture, WHO in health, FAO in food and agriculture and WIPO in IP.

Most of the IGOs now called specialized agencies did not exist before the Second World War. They were created for the specific purpose of dealing with a particular subject or field of activity at the international level. However, some IGOs, such as the ILO, the Universal Postal Union (UPU) and the International Telecommunication Union (ITU) were in existence, and had become the responsible IGOs in their respective fields of activity, long before the establishment of the UN. After the UN was established, these organizations became specialized agencies of the UN system of organizations.

Similarly, long before the UN was established, BIRPI was the responsible IGO in the field of IP. WIPO, the successor to BIRPI, became a specialized agency of the UN when an agreement was signed to that effect between the UN and WIPO and came into effect on December 17, 1974. An IGO can only become a specialized agency of the UN pursuant to such an agreement.

A specialized agency, although it belongs to the family of UN organizations, retains its independence. Each specialized agency has its own membership. All Member States of the UN are entitled to become members of all the specialized agencies, but in fact not all Member States of the UN are members of all the specialized agencies. Each State decides for itself whether it wants, or does not want, to become a member of any particular specialized agency. For example, even before joining the UN as a member (in September 2002), Switzerland was already a member of WIPO. Each specialized agency has its own constitution, its own governing bodies, its own elected executive head, its own income, its own budget, its own staff, its own programs and activities. Machinery exists for coordinating the activities of all the specialized agencies, among themselves and with the UN, but, basically, each agency remains the master of its own destiny, responsible, under its own constitution, to its own governing bodies which consist, of course, of States members of the organization.

The agreement between the UN and WIPO recognizes that WIPO is, subject to the competence of the UN and its organs, responsible for taking appropriate action in accordance with its basic instrument, treaties and agreements administered by it, *inter alia*, for promoting creative intellectual activity and for facilitating the transfer of technology related to industrial property to the developing countries in order to accelerate economic, social and cultural development.

[B] Structure

The constitution, the "basic instrument," of WIPO is the Convention signed at Stockholm in 1967. In describing WIPO, the following questions will be answered in very general terms: why is an IGO needed? What are the Unions administered by

WIPO? Which States are members of WIPO? What does WIPO do? How is it governed and managed?

Why is an intergovernmental IP organization needed? IPRs are limited territorially; they exist and can be exercised only within the jurisdiction of the country or countries under whose laws they are granted. But works of the mind, including inventive ideas, cross frontiers with ease, and, in a world of interdependent nations, should be encouraged to do so. Moreover, with growing similarity in the approach and procedures governing IP matters in various countries, it makes eminent sense to simplify practice through international standardization and mutual recognition of rights and duties among nations. Therefore, governments have negotiated and adopted multilateral treaties in the various fields of IP, each of which establishes a "Union" of countries which agree to grant to nationals of other countries of the Union the same protection as they grant to their own, as well as to follow certain common rules, standards and practices.

The Unions administered by WIPO are founded on the treaties. A Union consists of all the States that are party to a particular treaty. The name of the Union is, in most cases, taken from the place where the text of the treaty was first adopted (thus the Paris Union, the Berne Union, etc.). The treaties fall into three groups.

The first group of treaties establishes international protection, that is to say, they are treaties which are the source of legal protection agreed between countries at the international level. For instance, three treaties on industrial property fall into this group. They are the Paris Convention, the Madrid Agreement for the Repression of False and Deceptive Indications of Source on Goods and the Lisbon Agreement for the Protection of Appellations of Origin and their International Registration.

The second group consists of treaties which facilitate international protection. For instance, six treaties on industrial property fall into this group. They are the PCT which provides for the filing of international applications for patents, the Madrid Agreement Concerning the International Registration of Marks, the Lisbon Agreement which has already been mentioned because it belongs to both the first and second groups, the Budapest Treaty on the International Recognition of the Deposit of Microorganisms for the Purposes of Patent Procedure and the Hague Agreement Concerning the International Deposit of Industrial Designs.

The third group consists of treaties which establish classification systems and procedures for improving them and keeping them up to date. Four treaties, all dealing with industrial property, fall into this group. They are the International Patent Classification (IPC) Agreement, the Nice Agreement Concerning the International Classification of Goods and Services for the Purposes of the Registration of Marks, the Vienna Agreement Establishing an International Classification of the Figurative Elements of Marks and the Locarno Agreement Establishing an International Classification for Industrial Designs.

Revising these treaties and establishing new ones are tasks which require a constant effort of international cooperation and negotiation, supported by a specialized secretariat. WIPO provides the framework and the services for this work.

[C] Functions

The activities of WIPO are basically of four kinds: global services to protect IP across borders and to resolve disputes; awareness raising, cooperation, and capacity-building programs to enable all countries to use IP for economic, social and cultural development; a policy forum to shape balanced international IP rules for a changing world, and a world reference source for IP information. All these activities serve the overall objectives of WIPO, to maintain and increase respect for IP throughout the world, in order to favor economic and social development by stimulating creative activity and facilitating the transfer of technology and the dissemination of literary and artistic works.

The registration activities of WIPO involve direct services to applicants for, or owners of, industrial property rights. These activities concern the receiving and processing of international applications under the PCT or for the international registration of marks or deposit of industrial designs. Such activities are financed normally from the fees paid by the applicants, which account for about three-fourths of the budget of WIPO.

The main activities in intergovernmental cooperation in the administration of IP are concerned with the management of collections of patent documents used for search and reference, and devising means for making access to the information which they contain easier; the maintenance and updating of international classification systems; the compilation of more and more sophisticated statistics; regional surveys of industrial property and copyright law administration.

WIPO maintains comprehensive collections of industrial property and copyright laws and treaties, as well as of IP judgments, which are available to the public, and are published on WIPO's website (WIPO Lex).[25]

The substantive or program activities of WIPO, which constitute the major part of its activities, include promoting the wider acceptance of existing treaties, updating—where necessary—such treaties through their revision, concluding new treaties, and organizing and participating in development cooperation activities.

As a final remark of this brief introduction to WIPO and its role, an important element should be highlighted. It is frequently said that WIPO's main role is to promote the international protection of IP. By saying this, those persons less informed about WIPO express the belief that WIPO promotes IP for the sake of its protection. That is a misunderstanding. Article 3(1) of the Convention that established the Organization provides that its first objective is "to promote the protection of intellectual property

25. WIPO Lex saw broad gains in database user experience and offerings in 2022/23. Careful attention was given to curating and streamlining the presentation of IP legal data in individual country profiles, and IT developments made the website content more intuitive and searchable on the web. A centralized "WIPO Treaties: Preparatory Documents webpage" was launched in May 2023, providing easy access to important and frequently requested materials generated during the drafting and negotiation of WIPO-administered treaties. The Judgments Collection was further expanded during the biennium; as at end 2023, the collection covered some thirty-five jurisdictions and provided free access to over 1,200 IP court decisions. More information is available in the WIPO Performance Report 2023.

throughout the world through cooperation among States." And Article 4(1) clarifies that, in order to attain that objective, WIPO "shall promote the development of measures designed to facilitate the efficient protection of IP throughout the world." This language imposes without ambiguity two qualifications on the work to be done by WIPO. The first qualification is that the promotion of the protection of IP must be achieved through cooperation among States. In other words, the role of the International Bureau is to facilitate such cooperation. It is up to Member States to define their specific objectives and policies, to be translated into IP norms. The second qualification is provided by the term "efficient protection." WIPO does not seek to facilitate any sort or level of protection, but only protection that is "efficient." The efficiency of the protection of IP is measured by the objectives and goals that system is designed to achieve. And, once again, it is up to WIPO Member States to design those objectives in view of their public policies.

This element is of crucial importance to adequately understand the role of WIPO. Accordingly, the discussions currently held in the various WIPO Standing Committees, which are mentioned throughout this book, such as those dealing with the Agenda for Development and with exceptions and limitations to IP rights, are not dysfunctional interruptions to the work of the Organization.

In a related vein, it is crucial to highlight that WIPO and its Member States are increasingly recognizing the paramount importance of fostering a culture of innovation and actively contributing to the innovation ecosystem through intellectual property. Beyond a narrow legalistic viewpoint, there is a growing acknowledgment of the need to perceive IP through the lens of the broader innovation ecosystem, encompassing diverse stakeholders such as start-ups, SMEs, academia, policymakers, and researchers. This envisions a world where intellectual property serves not only as a legal framework but also as a catalyst for innovation and creativity across various sectors. WIPO stands at the forefront, steering the development of a balanced and effective global intellectual property ecosystem. This commitment is aimed at propelling innovation and creativity for the betterment of humanity and fostering a more sustainable future.

[D] Administration

The Convention establishing WIPO provides for four different organs: the General Assembly; the Conference; the Coordination Committee; and the International Bureau of WIPO (or Secretariat).

The General Assembly is the supreme organ of WIPO. Among its other powers and functions, the General Assembly appoints the Director General upon nomination by the Coordination Committee; it reviews and approves the reports and activities of the Coordination Committee as well as the reports of the Director General concerning WIPO; it adopts the financial regulations of WIPO and the biennial budget of expenses common to the Unions; it approves the measures proposed by the Director General concerning the administration of the international agreements designed to promote the protection of IP; it determines the working languages of the Secretariat taking into consideration the practice of the UN; and it also determines which States are not members of WIPO and which intergovernmental and international nongovernmental organizations (NGOs) shall be admitted to its meetings as observers.

The General Assembly consists of all the States which are members of WIPO and are also members of any of the Unions.

Unlike the General Assembly, the Conference consists of all the States which are members of WIPO whether or not they are members of any of the Unions. The main functions of the Conference could be divided into five groups. First, the Conference constitutes a forum for exchanges of views, between all States members of WIPO, on matters relating to IP, and, in this context, the Conference can, in particular, make any recommendations on such matters, having regard to the competence and autonomy of the Unions. Second, the Conference is the body that establishes the biennial development cooperation program for developing countries and, third, adopts a budget for that purpose. Fourth, the Conference is also competent to adopt amendments to the Convention establishing WIPO. Proposals for the amendment of the Convention may be initiated by any State member of WIPO, by the Coordination Committee or by the Director General. Fifth, the Conference, like the General Assembly, can determine which States and organizations will be admitted to its meetings as observers.

The Coordination Committee is both an advisory organ on questions of general interest and the executive organ of the General Assembly and the Conference. The Coordination Committee gives advice to the various organs of the Unions and WIPO on matters of common interest to two or more of the Unions or to one or more of the Unions and WIPO itself, in particular regarding the budget of expenses common to the Unions. The Coordination Committee also prepares the draft agenda of the General Assembly and of the Conference, as well as the draft program and budget of the Conference.

The fourth organ of WIPO is the International Bureau of WIPO or Secretariat. It is headed by the Director General, with the assistance of eight Sectors Leads, which take care of each of the eight Sectors that form the operational structure of the Organization.[26]

[E] Membership

The Convention establishing WIPO declares that membership shall be open to any State which is a member of any of the Unions, and to any State which is not a member of any of the Unions, provided that it is a member of the UN, any of the specialized agencies of the UN, or the International Atomic Energy Agency, or is a party to the Statute of the International Court of Justice or is invited by the General Assembly of

26. As of June 30, 2024, the workforce of WIPO comprised 1,727 people, recruited according to the principle of equitable geographical (121 nationalities) and gender distribution established in the UN system. On that same date, in Professional and higher categories, and General Service on regular budget funding, 619 women and 503 men worked for the Secretariat. For detailed information on WIPO workforce, *see* wipo-workforce-2024-jun-en-wipo-workforce-2024.pdf.

WIPO to become a member. Thus, only States can be members of WIPO or, indeed, of any other specialized agency of the UN.

To become a member, a State must deposit an instrument of ratification or accession with the Director General of WIPO at Geneva. States party to the Paris or Berne Conventions may become members of WIPO only if they are already bound by, or concurrently ratify or accede to, at least the administrative provisions of the Stockholm (1967) Act of the Paris Convention or of the Paris (1971) Act of the Berne Convention.

As of November 30, 2023, 193 States were party to the Convention Establishing the WIPO.

§5.02 THE STRATEGY OF WIPO, AN ORGANIZATION FOR THE TWENTY-FIRST CENTURY

[A] Introduction

WIPO and its Member States recognize that IP has become an increasingly intricate subject in a world grappling with numerous global challenges. In anticipation of a more dynamic future, the organization, under the leadership of Director General, Daren Tang, has undertaken some strategic shifts. This aims to equip WIPO with greater dynamism and agility, fostering a more holistic perspective in addressing the complexities of intellectual property, ensuring its readiness for the challenges of the future.

In the medium term, the core elements of WIPO's strategy are represented by a Strategy House, which consists of the Organization's Vision, Mission, Strategic Pillars and Foundation. WIPO's Vision is to help create a world where innovation and creativity from anywhere is supported by IP for the good of everyone. To this end, WIPO will continue to lead the development of a balanced and inclusive global IP ecosystem. WIPO works with Member States and other stakeholders to ensure that IP is seen as a tool for every Member State to create jobs, attract investments, drive enterprise growth, and ultimately develop economies and societies for a better and more sustainable future.

The following overview of the global landscape sets out the broader context in which WIPO and its stakeholders operate. It serves as a reminder of the importance of WIPO's strategy in steering the Organization on a course that ensures it remains relevant to, and has an impact on, the fast-moving world in which we live.

[B] Landscape

We are living in a time of crisis and opportunity. The pandemic has wreaked havoc on everyone's lives and livelihoods. Economies, societies, businesses and communities have all been profoundly affected. At the same time, the pandemic has demonstrated the power of human ingenuity, with the development and deployment of vaccines and other therapies in record time.

Indeed, innovation and creativity are the hallmark of humanity. Our relentless quest to innovate and create for a better future has led to many previously unimaginable advances. Over the last century, global living standards have improved more than six-fold and life expectancy has more than doubled. More recently, a shift to digital, accelerated by the pandemic, has transformed the way we work, live and play. As a result, innovation, creativity and IP are now more central than ever to the lives of everyone in the world.

While much has been achieved, many complex global challenges lie ahead of us, as reflected in the UN 2030 Agenda for Sustainable Development. Two stand out in particular: the need to foster broad-based post-pandemic economic recovery, and the need to put the world on an environmentally sustainable footing. In both of these areas, technology, innovation and creativity—and IP—will play an important role.

To meet the promise and challenges of the future, it is no longer tenable for us to look at IP only from a technical, legal perspective, and as a matter of concern for IP professionals and experts alone. Going forward, IP must be seen more broadly as a powerful tool for meeting the global challenges that we collectively face, for growth and development, and as a matter of everyday interest to everyone, everywhere.

As economies become more innovative and creative, IP becomes a more central issue and deserves greater attention from policymakers, business leaders and other stakeholders. IP makes it possible to create value from different intangibles—technological edge, brand reputation and image, design appeal and creative flair. These are the bases on which an increasing number of companies compete and individuals make a living. In the S&P 500, a leading benchmark of market performance, intangible assets make up 90% of business value.[27] The trend is global. In 2020, the total value of intangible assets reached an all-time high of USD 65.7 trillion surpassing the value of tangible assets and accounting for 54% of all global listings.[28]

The increasing importance of IP is well illustrated by the growth in IP filings. In 2022, IP offices around the world received 15,543,300 trademark applications, 3,457,400 patent applications, 3,010,510 utility model application, and 1,482,600 industrial design applications.[29] These figures reflect growing investments in innovative and creative industries and the increasing importance of protecting these investments through IP registration.

Globalization over the past few decades has fueled demand for IP protection both locally and internationally, as enterprises and economies look to the cross-border flow of technology, brands, designs and content. This is reflected in the rise in applications filed under WIPO's Global IP Protection Services, most notably, the PCT, the Madrid (Trademarks) System and the Hague (Designs) System.[30]

27. *See* www.oceantomo.com/intangible-asset-market-value-study.
28. *See* www.ipos.gov.sg/docs/default-source/default-document-library/singapore-ip-strategy-report-2030.pdf.
29. Detailed information updated until the end of 2023 is available at www.wipo.int/edocs/pubdocs/en/wipo-pub-941-2023-en-world-intellectual-property-indicators-2023.pdf.
30. The strength of WIPO's Global IP Protection Services is expressed by the following figures: in 2023, 686,700 PCT applications reached the national phase; in the same year 103,144 industrial

Over the same period, we have also seen broader participation in the IP system globally. Asia continues its rise as a dynamic region for innovation and creativity, now accounting for around two-thirds of global IP filings. But beyond Asia, we are also seeing the emergence of innovative and creative communities in all other regions of the world.

Against this backdrop, multilateral cooperation in IP remains important and WIPO's Global IP Protection Services are highly successful examples of such cooperation. As the global challenges facing us, such as the pandemic, climate change, and other issues, are highly complex and cannot be solved by countries individually but require collective action, such cooperation remains a critical part of our work.

WIPO will therefore seek to continue fostering multilateral cooperation by continuing to act as a neutral, inclusive and transparent facilitator. WIPO also seeks to work more closely with other partners in the international system, including its fellow UN agencies, international organizations (IGOs), and NGOs, in order to contribute to finding holistic solutions to these global challenges.

Shifting the focus away from the multilateral to regional and national contexts, WIPO's work concentrates on helping Member States use IP for growth and development. To do this effectively, WIPO looks at IP as an enabler of a country's innovation ecosystem. As such, WIPO has broadened its support focus beyond laws and regulations, and also addresses other elements like the country's sources of innovation and creativity, its levels of awareness, skills and capabilities around IP, the capacity of its enterprises to create and then commercialize IP for business growth, the use of IP as an asset class, the avenues for IP disputes to be resolved, and so on.

WIPO, moreover, pays close attention to a broader group of stakeholders within the innovation and creative ecosystems. SMEs, for example, constitute 90% of all companies in the world, 70% of employment and close to 50% of global GDP. However, many of them remain unaware of IP or how to use it for business growth. We intend to engage and support this vital but underserved community more extensively, helping them to use IP to take their ideas to the market.

Youth is also a focus of WIPO's attention. They are our future innovators, creators and entrepreneurs, and represent a large percentage of the population in many developing countries. Society as a whole need to ensure that they understand how IP is connected and relevant to their lives and support their aspirations, whether it is to earn a livelihood through innovation and creativity, or to address global challenges.

In sum, as the UN agency for IP, WIPO is committed to driving the development of a balanced and inclusive global IP ecosystem, where IP is recognized and used as a tool for Member States to create jobs, attract investment, support business competitiveness and ultimately contribute to growth and development.

---

designs applications were filed; and in 2020, 1,117,939 trademark applications were filed through the Madrid System. For detailed and regularly updated figures, *see* www.wipo.int/web/ip-statistics.

[C] Strategy House

The Strategy House provides a framework for the Organization to respond to the needs of all stakeholders within the context of the fast-changing external environment outlined above.

WIPO has built itself up over decades to be a widely respected neutral international forum for IP issues. It has a strong mandate at the intersection of innovation, creativity and IP, which are areas of increasing importance to people across the globe. WIPO delivers services that businesses around the world rely on every day. The Organization is financially sound and has the resources to invest in its next stage of growth.

For these reasons, the Strategy House is rooted in continuity but builds on our strengths, charting a future course with new accents and a fresh focus where these are called for.

The Strategy House outlines the Organization's Vision, Mission, Strategic Pillars and Foundation (Figure 5.1).

Figure 5.1 WIPO's Vision, Mission, Strategic Pillars and Foundation

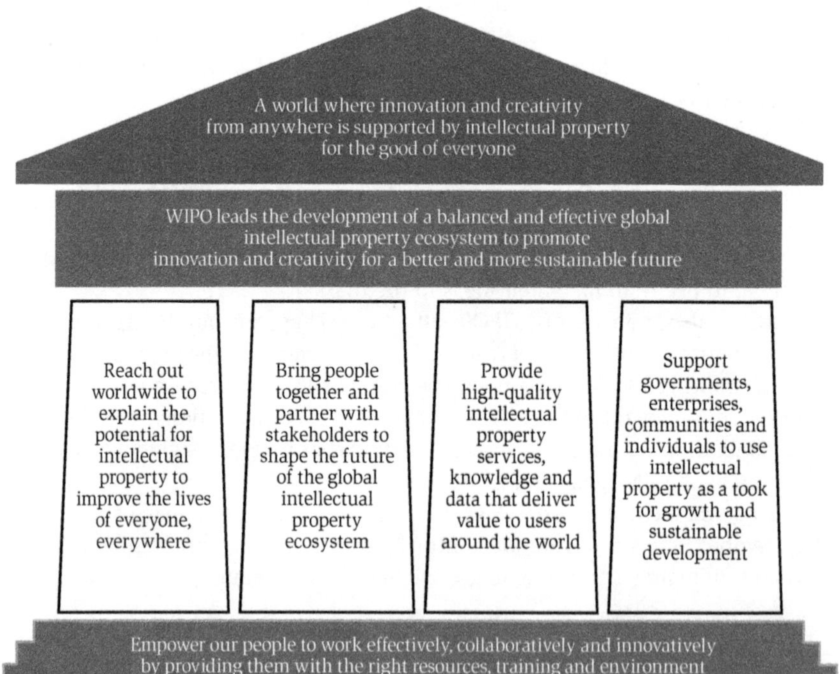

[D] The Vision

A world where innovation and creativity from anywhere is supported by intellectual property, for the good of everyone.

This Vision centers on the world. It is the broadest articulation of the value of our work and our aspirations for the future. It draws on the fact that innovation and creativity are a core part of humanity and our desire for IP to support the use of these fundamental human qualities for the good of everyone.

[E] The Mission

WIPO leads the development of a balanced and effective global intellectual property ecosystem to promote innovation and creativity for a better and more sustainable future.

The Mission describes what WIPO will do to achieve its vision of the future. It recognizes that IP is the core competency of the Organization and a tool to promote innovation and creativity. It does not just refer to an IP system, but an ecosystem, which better describes and encompasses the dynamic interplay between law, policy, practice and other elements required for innovation and creativity to support our future. Our description of the road ahead is also drawn from and inspired by the UN SDGs in line with our role as a UN agency.

[F] The Four Strategic Pillars and Their Foundation

WIPO's Vision and Mission are underpinned by four Strategic Pillars. They represent the Organization's broad areas of strategic focus, which, in turn, are cascaded into Expected Results, and then specific programs and activities. The Foundation is the bedrock of WIPO's Strategy House. It encapsulates all of the work the Secretariat does internally to provide the right type of resources, environment and culture for the Organization's Staff to work well. The Strategic Pillars should not be seen in isolation; they are dynamically interconnected and supported by the Foundation. These are the Pillars:

> Pillar 1: Reach out worldwide to explain the potential for IP to improve the lives of everyone, everywhere.
> Pillar 2: Bring people together and partner with stakeholders to shape the future of the global IP system.
> Pillar 3: Provide high-quality intellectual property services, knowledge and data that deliver value to users around the world.
> Pillar 4: Support governments, enterprises, communities and individuals to use intellectual property as a tool for growth and sustainable development.

[G] Foundation: To Empower WIPO Staff to Work Effectively, Collaboratively, and Innovatively by Providing Them the Right Resources, Training and Environment

[1] Background

The success of WIPO's strategy depends on a strong Foundation, which constitutes the management and administrative functions of WIPO and its organizational culture. This Foundation, in turn, has to evolve to provide the best working environment for WIPO Staff to deliver the Expected Results and impact for Member States.

As with all other organizations, the COVID-19 pandemic has resulted in major changes to the way the Secretariat works. WIPO has invested significantly in automating end-to-end administrative and management business processes, and its Staff have adapted remarkably quickly to the additional demands placed by the pandemic. The adoption of new models for the delivery and implementation of technical assistance and the uninterrupted provision of quality Global IP Protection Services are evidence of this. Increased digitalization and greater agility and responsiveness characterize the services and products the Organization offers. Currently, many parts of the Organization function electronically, but it has not yet transitioned to digital solutions across all business lines to the degree needed.

WIPO's administrative and management frameworks and processes have evolved significantly to better serve internal business owners and external stakeholders. However, a tension remains between strict adherence to UN system approaches and meeting the needs of WIPO's hybrid mandate as a specialized UN agency that delivers competitively priced, high-quality services to a growing number of fee-paying customers. To a large extent, with the guidance of its Member States, WIPO has balanced these needs carefully and effectively.

Strong financial management strategies and frameworks have been put into place; positive financial results over several years have enabled WIPO to build a healthy level of reserves in line with established policies and objectives for financial resilience and risk management. WIPO also has strong business processes with robust controls. However, the regulatory framework is rules-based, overly prescriptive and lags behind organizational needs.

WIPO's organizational structure is results-oriented and vertical. Its culture has tended to be formal, hierarchical, and risk averse, with a legacy of highly centralized decision-making. As such, there is a major opportunity to empower staff to cultivate greater ownership of the organization across all levels.

[2] Future Directions

WIPO intends to focus on three Expected Results.

First, the Organization is building a Secretariat that is empowered through a dynamic corporate culture and provided with the right resources and training to work effectively, collaboratively and innovatively.

Second, WIPO will be digitally enabled and will have a secure and sustainable operating environment and services.

Third, WIPO will continue to exercise sound and prudent financial management and put into place effective corporate governance and oversight systems.

CHAPTER 6
Copyright and Related Rights

§6.01 INTRODUCTION

Copyright and related rights law, which in civil law countries is referred to as author's rights and neighboring rights law, respectively, is a branch of that part of the law that deals with the rights of authors of intellectual creations, performers and others engaging in the diffusion of works. Such rights are respected by the laws of most countries. The reasons for this respect for the rights of authors and related rights holders are the need to stimulate and foster the individual creativity of men and women and the need to make the results of that creativity available by disseminating it on the widest possible scale. Copyright and related rights law deals with particular forms of creativity, including those concerned with mass communication. It affects virtually all forms and methods of public dissemination, including not only distribution of printed publications but also sound and television broadcasting, public exhibition of films in cinemas, use of software and even of databases for the storage and retrieval of information.

Copyright and related rights law deals with the rights of authors of intellectual creations, performers and others engaging in the diffusion of works. Most artistic works, for example books, paintings or drawings, exist only once they are embodied in a physical object, including a digital file. But some works exist without embodiment in a physical object. For example in many jurisdictions music or poems are artistic works even if they are not, or even before they are, written down in a musical notation or words.

Copyright and related rights law, however, protects only the form of expression of ideas, not the ideas themselves. The creativity protected by copyright law is creativity in the expression as well as the choice and arrangement of words, musical notes, colors, shapes and so on. Copyright law protects the owner of economic and moral rights in artistic works against those who "copy"—those who take and use the form in which the original work was expressed by the author, and those who otherwise make use of these works.

§6.02 SUBJECT MATTER OF COPYRIGHT PROTECTION

The subject matter of copyright protection includes every production in the literary, scientific and artistic domain, whatever the mode or form of expression. For a work to enjoy copyright protection, however, it must be an original creation. The ideas in the work do not need to be new but the form, be it literary or artistic, in which they are expressed must be an original creation of the author. And, finally, protection is independent of the quality or the value attaching to the work—it will be protected whether it be considered, according to taste, a good or a bad literary or artistic work—and even of the purpose for which it is intended (e.g., a building for the use as a school building), because the use to which a work may be put has nothing to do with its protection.

Works eligible for copyright protection are, as a rule, all original intellectual creations. A non-exhaustive, illustrative enumeration of these is contained in national copyright laws. To be protected by copyright law, an author's works must be original. This means in most countries of the copyright/common law system that the works must originate from the author; they must have their origin in the labor of the author. But it is not necessary, to qualify for copyright protection, that works should pass a test of imaginativeness or inventiveness. In countries of the civil law system, the mere origin and labor do not suffice, but a given minimum level of creativity must be reached to earn copyright protection. The work is protected irrespective of its quality and also when it has little in common with literature, art or science. Protectable works include purely technical guides or engineering drawings, or even maps. This demonstrates that it is not mere ideas, as such, that are protected by copyright, but the form of expression. Exceptions to the general rule are made in national copyright laws by specific enumeration; thus laws and official decisions or mere news of the day are generally excluded from copyright protection.

Practically all national copyright laws provide for the protection of the following types of works:

(1) *literary works:* novels, short stories, poems, dramatic works and any other writings, irrespective of their content (fiction or non-fiction), length, purpose (amusement, education, information, advertisement, propaganda, etc.), form (handwritten, typed, printed, in braille; book, pamphlet, single sheets, newspaper, magazine); whether published or unpublished; in most countries "oral works," that is, works not "fixed" in a medium such as a writing, are also protected by the copyright law;

(2) *musical works:* whether serious or light; songs, symphonies or other instrumental music, choruses, operas, musicals, operettas; whether for one instrument (solos), a few instruments (trios, quartets, other chamber music, etc.), or many (bands, orchestras);

(3) *artistic works:* whether two-dimensional (drawings, paintings, etchings, lithographs, etc.) or three-dimensional (sculptures, architectural works), irrespective of content (representational or abstract) and destination ("pure" art, for advertisement, etc.);
(4) *maps and technical drawings*;
(5) *photographic works:* irrespective of the subject matter (portraits, landscapes, current events, etc.) and the purpose for which made;
(6) *cinematographic works:* whether silent or with a sound track, and irrespective of their purpose (theatrical exhibition, television broadcasting, etc.), their genre (motion picture or film dramas, documentaries, newsreels, etc.), length, method employed (filming "live," animation, etc.), or technical process used (pictures on transparent film, on electronic video tapes, in digital files, etc.);
(7) *computer programs* (either as a literary work or independently);
(8) *adaptations, translations, and collections of works*: such as musical arrangements, dramatic adaptations of a novel, song books or anthologies.

Many copyright laws also protect "works of applied art" (artistic jewelry, lamps, wallpaper, furniture, etc.) with sufficient originality and creativity, and choreographic and pantomime works. Designs and fashion designs are protected by copyright in some national laws. Some copyright systems also regard sound recording ("phonograms") and broadcasts as works subject to copyright protection, although in most copyright systems they are given related rights protection.

§6.03 RIGHTS COMPRISED IN COPYRIGHT

The owner of copyright in a protected work may use the work as he or she wishes and may exclude others from using it without his or her authorization. However, in certain situations the copyright owner must give due regard to the legally recognized rights and interests of others.

The rights bestowed by law on the owner of copyright in a protected work are frequently described as "exclusive rights" to authorize others to use the protected work. Some laws may, instead of "exclusive rights," recognize a "right to prohibit" under which the owner of the copyright may impede others from using the protected work without the owner's authorization.

In addition to their exclusive rights of an economic character, frequently referred to as "economic" (or "patrimonial") rights, the original authors of works protected by copyright also have "moral rights." What is meant by "using" a work protected by copyright? Most copyright laws define economic rights as covering the acts or "uses" that must not be performed or made by persons other than the copyright owner without the authorization of the copyright owner. Most civil law countries provide for large acts of exploitation both in tangible and non-tangible form and further specify certain concrete acts. Common law countries generally provide for a list of concrete acts.

Such acts, requiring the authorization of the copyright owner, usually include at least the following:

- reproduction of the work in various forms;
- distribution of copies of the work;
- public performance of the work;
- broadcasting or other communication of the work to the public;
- translation of the work into other languages; and
- adaptation of the work.

[A] Reproduction Rights

The right of copyright owners to prevent others from making copies of their works without permission is the most basic right protected by copyright legislation. The right to control the act of reproduction—be it the reproduction of books by a publisher, or the manufacture by a record producer of compact discs containing recorded performances of musical works—is the legal basis for many forms of exploitation of protected works. Reproduction may also occur if a work is copied in a smaller or bigger size, or a different format (for ex., in braille or another accessible format).

The right of reproduction also exists in the digital environment, as set forth in the WCT, the WPPT, and the WIPO BTAP. Accordingly, scanning, copying works on a USB or smartphone, storing them on a hard drive of a computer, uploading, downloading works on a server/in the cloud, etc. are acts of reproduction.

[B] Distribution Rights

Other rights are recognized in national laws in order to ensure that this basic right of reproduction is respected. Many laws include a right to authorize the distribution of copies of works. The right of reproduction would be of little economic value if copyright owners could not control distribution of copies of their works made with their consent.

The right of distribution usually terminates upon first sale or transfer of ownership of a particular physical copy. This means, for example, that when the copyright owner of a book sells or otherwise transfers ownership of a copy of the book, the owner of that copy may give the book away or even resell it without the copyright owner's further permission. The question of applying this concept to digital files is under consideration in various national legal systems. Where digital files are distributed in the form of fixed copies that are put into circulation as tangible objects, such as USB drives or CDs, the distribution right applies; however, where digital files are communicated to the public via electronic communication networks, most countries would follow the rule on the distribution right under the WCT, which excludes application of the distribution right in these cases of intangible use.

Another right that was recognized in many countries in the 1990s, and is included in the WCT, is the right to authorize rental of copies of certain categories of works, such as musical works in sound recordings, audiovisual works and computer programs. This became necessary in order to prevent abuse of the copyright owner's right of reproduction when technological advances made it easy for rental shop customers to copy such works.

The public lending right (PLR) is another form of distribution of hard copies (and much less frequently digital copies) of works that is applied in a number of countries and is gaining increasing attention, though mostly not as an exclusive right to authorize but rather as a statutory remuneration right. A number of countries provide that public libraries or their operators are obliged to pay a given amount of money to collective management organizations (CMOs) of authors for the lending to the public mainly of books, but also of CDs or similar material. This recognizes the economic interests of authors and other copyright owners to participate in the value of often massive uses of works through public lending. A few jurisdictions also extend PLR to publishers.

Finally, some copyright laws include a right to control importation of copies as a means to prevent erosion of the principle of territoriality of copyright. The right is based on the premise that the legitimate economic interests of copyright owners would be endangered were they not able to exercise their rights of reproduction and distribution on a territorial basis.

[C] Right of Public Performance

A public performance is considered under many national laws to include any performance of a work at a place where the public is or can be present, or at a place not open to the public but where a substantial number of persons outside the normal circle of a family and its close acquaintances are present. The right of public performance entitles the author or other copyright owner to authorize live performances of a work, such as a play in a theatre or an orchestra performance of a symphony in a concert hall. Public performance also includes performance by means of a recording. Thus, a musical work is considered publicly performed when a sound recording of that work, or phonogram, is played over amplification equipment, for example in a discotheque, airplane or shopping mall.

[D] Communication to the Public, Broadcasting and Making Available Rights

Another major category of acts covered by copyright protection includes communicating works to the public by means of wires or cable or by wireless means, including broadcasting works, and of making works available to the public. At a national level, terminology differs; for example, some laws do not limit "broadcasting" to wireless communication, but also include cable transmissions.

Against the background of international law, the right of broadcasting covers the transmission for public reception of sounds, or of images and sounds, by wireless means, whether by radio, television or satellite. When a work is communicated to the public, a signal is distributed by wire or wireless means for reception only by persons who possess the equipment necessary to decode the signal. Cable transmission is an example of communication to the public.

Under the Berne Convention, authors have the exclusive right to authorize the public performance, broadcasting and communication of their works to the public. Under some national laws, the exclusive right of the author or other right owner to authorize broadcasting is replaced, in certain circumstances, by a right to equitable remuneration, as permitted by the Berne Convention, although this type of limitation on the broadcasting right has become less common.

As permitted under the Berne Convention, national laws regularly also cover acts of rebroadcasting, retransmission and communication by loudspeaker of broadcast works to a place where the initial communication cannot be received otherwise.

Since the adoption of the WPPT, the rights of broadcasting and communication to the public have been the subject of much debate. New questions have arisen as a result of technological developments, in particular digital technologies, which have introduced interactive communications that enable users to select works to be delivered to their computers or other devices. Opinions diverged as to which right should be applied to this activity. Article 8 of the WCT clarifies that it should be covered by an exclusive right without any exhaustion; the Treaty describes it as the authors' right to authorize the making available of their works to the public "in such a way that members of the public can access these works from a place and at a time individually chosen by them." Most national laws implement this right as a part of the right of communication to the public, although some do so as part of the right of distribution.

[E] Translation and Adaptation Rights

The acts of translating or adapting a work protected by copyright also require the permission of the right owner. Translation means the expression of a work in a language other than that of the original version; the right to authorize translation extends to any method of translation, whether made by a translator or a by means of a translation program. Adaptation is generally understood as the modification of a work to create another work, for example adapting a novel to make a film, or the modification of a work for different conditions of exploitation, e.g., by adapting a textbook originally written for university students to make it suitable for a lower level. Discussions are ongoing about whether an output of an application of artificial intelligence (AI) which resembles an existing work would be an adaptation covered by the author's adaptation right.

Translations and adaptations are themselves works protected by copyright. In order to publish a translation or adaptation, permission must be obtained from both the owner of the copyright in the original work and the owner of copyright in the translation or adaptation.

The scope of the right of adaptation has been the subject of significant discussion in recent years because of the greatly increased possibilities for adapting and transforming works in digital formats. With digital technologies, users can easily manipulate text, sound and images to create user-generated content (UGC). Discussion has focused on achieving an appropriate balance between the rights of the author to control the integrity of a work by authorizing modifications, and the interests of users to make changes that seem to be part of the normal use of a work in digital format. Some of the questions revolve around whether right owner authorization is needed to create new works that use parts of previously existing works, for example through sampling or mash-ups.

[F] Moral Rights

The Berne Convention, in Article 6*bis*, requires its members to grant authors the following rights:

(i) the right to claim authorship of a work (sometimes called the right of paternity or the right of attribution); and
(ii) the right to object to any distortion or modification of a work, or other derogatory action in relation to a work, which would be prejudicial to the author's honor or reputation (sometimes called the right of integrity).

The Berne Convention requires these rights to be independent of authors' economic rights. Moral rights are only accorded to individual authors and in many national laws they remain with the authors even after the authors have transferred their economic rights. This means that even where, for example, a film producer or publisher owns the economic rights in a work, in many jurisdictions the individual author continues to have moral rights.

In addition. some national laws recognize other moral rights besides those prescribed in the Berne Convention, such as the right of disclosure or divulgation of the work, the right to repent or withdraw (retract) works previously made available to the public, and the right of access to the single or a rare copy of the work held by a third party.

In some countries, moral rights have the same duration as economic rights, while in others, they may even last in perpetuity. In some countries, moral rights may be waived, while in others, they are considered so closely bound to the personality of the author that they cannot be waived, and can be transferred only by inheritance.

§6.04 RELATED RIGHTS

Related rights protect the legal interests of certain persons and legal entities that contribute to making works available to the public or that produce subject matter which, while not qualifying as works under the copyright systems of all countries, contains sufficient artistic, creative, or technical and organizational skill or investment to justify recognition of a copyright-like property right. The law of related rights deems that the productions that result from the activities of such persons and entities merit legal protection as they are *related* to the protection of works of authorship under copyright and enable or promote their diffusion.

Some laws make clear, however, that the exercise of related rights should leave intact, and in no way affect, the protection of copyright, as stated in the Rome Convention and other treaties.

Traditionally, related rights have been granted to three categories of beneficiaries:

- performers;
- producers of sound recordings (also referred to as phonograms); and
- broadcasting organizations.

The rights of performers are recognized because their artistic or creative intervention is necessary to give life to, for example, motion pictures or musical, dramatic and choreographic works, and because they have a justifiable interest in the legal protection of their individual interpretations. The rights of producers of sound recordings are recognized because their creative, financial and organizational resources are necessary to make sound recordings, often based on musical works, available to the public in commercial form, and because of their legitimate interest in having the legal resources to take action against unauthorized uses—be this the making and distribution of unauthorized copies (piracy) or the unauthorized broadcasting or communication to the public of their sound recordings. Likewise, the rights of broadcasting organizations are recognized because of their role in making works available to the public, and in light of their justified interest in controlling the transmission and retransmission of their broadcasts.

The first organized international response to the need for legal protection of these three categories of related rights was the conclusion, in 1961, of the Rome Convention. While most international conventions follow in the wake of national legislation and are intended to synthesize existing laws, the Rome Convention was an attempt to establish international regulations in a field in which few national laws existed at the time. This meant that most states had to draft and enact laws before they could accede to the Convention.

In the 1990s, there was a widespread view that the Rome Convention was out of date and in need of revision or replacement by a new set of norms in the field of related rights, even though the Convention was the basis for the inclusion of provisions on the rights of performers, producers of sound recordings (phonograms) and broadcasting organizations in the TRIPS Agreement. The levels of protection granted in the two instruments are similar, but not the same. For two of the categories of beneficiaries, updated protection was then provided by the WPPT, adopted in 1996 along with the WCT (the two are sometimes referred to collectively as the *Internet Treaties*), and the BTAP (Beijing Treaty, adopted in 2012). Discussions continue in the WIPO Standing Committee on Copyright and Related Rights (SCCR) on a new treaty on the rights of broadcasters (*see* Chapter 36, below).

The rights granted in most national laws to the three types of beneficiaries of related rights based on these treaties are generally as follows (although not all rights may be granted under the same law):

- *Performers* have the right to authorize fixation (recording), broadcasting and communication to the public of their live performances without their consent, and the right to authorize reproduction of fixations of their performances, distribution and rental of such fixations. The rights in respect of broadcasting and communication to the public of performances incorporated in recordings often are in the form of equitable remuneration rather than a right to authorize. Many countries also provide for the right of making available fixed performances in such a way that members of the public may access them from a place and at a time individually chosen. Due to the personal nature of their artistic achievements, many national laws also grant performers moral rights (as also required by the WPPT), which may be exercised to claim being named as performer (or stay anonymous or use a pseudonym), or to object to modifications of their performances that present them in an unfavorable light. Most national laws apply performers' protection to performers both in relation to their audio and audiovisual performances.
- *Producers of sound recordings (phonograms)* have the right to authorize or prohibit reproduction, importation, distribution and rental of their sound recordings and copies thereof, and the right to equitable remuneration for broadcasting and communication to the public of their sound recordings. Like performers, they enjoy in most countries the right of making available fixed performances in such a way that members of the public may access them from a place and at a time individually chosen.
- *Broadcasting organizations* have the right to authorize or prohibit rebroadcasting, fixation and reproduction of their broadcasts.

Under some laws, additional rights are granted. As in the case of copyright, the related rights treaties and national laws contain limitations and exceptions to related rights. These limitations allow use of protected performances, phonograms and broadcasts, for example, for teaching, scientific research or private use, and use of short excerpts for reporting current events. Some countries allow the same kinds of limitations on related rights as their laws provide in connection with copyright, including the possibility of nonvoluntary licenses. Under the WPPT, such limitations and exceptions must be restricted to certain special cases that neither conflict with the normal use of the performances or sound recordings nor unreasonably prejudice the legitimate interests of performers or producers.

The duration provided is often fifty years for performers and phonogram producers, following the minimum duration under the WPPT, although a number of national laws provide longer terms in certain cases. For broadcasting organizations, durations of twenty to fifty years are provided under national laws.

Several countries provide for additional related rights, such as for film producers in their film productions, photographs that are not copyright works, scientific editions, sui generis databases, or others.

§6.05 OWNERSHIP AND EXERCISE OF COPYRIGHT

The owner of copyright in a work is generally, at least in the first instance, the creator of a work, i.e., the author. However, this is not always the case. The Berne Convention, in Article 14*bis*, contains rules for determining initial ownership of rights in cinematographic works. Certain national laws also provide that, where a work is created by an author employed for the purpose of creating that work, the employer, not the author, is the owner of the copyright in that work. As noted above, however, in general moral rights belong to the individual author of a work, regardless of who owns the economic rights. An author can only be the natural person who by his or her mind is able to create a work, an intellectual creation. Therefore, most national laws consider that an output of AI without creation of the human author does not lead to authorship of a work and thus is in the public domain. A few jurisdictions consider the author of a computer-generated work to be the person who made the arrangements needed to create the work.

The laws of many countries provide that the initial right owner may transfer all economic rights in a work to a third party, although often moral rights cannot be transferred. Authors may transfer the economic rights in their works to individuals or companies best able to market them, in return for payment. Such payments are often made dependent on actual use of the works and are referred to as royalties. Transfer of copyright may take one of two forms: assignment and licensing.

An assignment is a transfer of a property right. Under an assignment, the right owner transfers the right to authorize or prohibit certain acts covered by one, several or all rights under copyright. The person to whom the rights are assigned becomes the new copyright owner or rightholder. Copyright rights are divisible, so it is possible to have multiple right owners for the same or different rights in the same work.

In some countries, an assignment of copyright is not legally possible, and only licensing is allowed. Licensing means that the copyright owner retains ownership but authorizes a third party to carry out certain acts covered by the economic rights, generally for a specific period of time and for a specific purpose. For example, the author of a novel may grant a publisher a license to make and distribute copies of the novel. At the same time, the author may grant a license to a film producer to make a film based on the novel. Licenses may be exclusive, with the right owner agreeing not to exercise the licensed acts or to authorize any other party to do so; or non-exclusive, which means the right owner may carry out the licensed acts and authorize others to do so. A non-exclusive license, unlike an assignment and an exclusive license, does not generally convey the right to authorize others to carry out acts covered by economic rights.

Licensing may also take the form of collective administration of rights. Under collective administration, authors and other right owners grant exclusive licenses to a single entity that acts on their behalf to grant permission for third-party use, collect and distribute remuneration, prevent and detect infringement of rights, and seek remedies for infringement. Collective administration offers advantages to authors, in particular by providing a single, central source to ensure that mass use of a work takes place only with the necessary, easily obtainable, permission. This is increasingly important as digital technologies allow multiple possibilities for the unauthorized use of copyright-protected works, but at the same time can facilitate collective management through the inclusion of licensing information in metadata. Collective licensing is also being discussed as a solution to massive uses of works on digital platforms to which users upload works, which are being made available to the public often without authorization of right owners. Likewise, collective licensing is being discussed in some countries as a solution to massive copying of works into training databases for the ultimate purpose of enabling generation of AI texts, music or images. In respect of certain mass uses, extended collective licenses (also covering non-members of CMOs under certain circumstances) are also generating growing interest as a solution to facilitate legal uses.

While there are few specific copyright law provisions regarding the possibility of copyright relinquishment, copyright owners may also effectively abandon the exercise of rights, in whole or in part. Such effective abandonment is also characterized as gratuitous licensing to everyone with no or limited conditions for use. The owner may, for example, post copyright-protected material on the Internet and leave it free for anyone to use, or restrict the abandonment to non-commercial use with or without certain additional requirements. Various cooperation projects have been set up according to a licensing model whereby contributors authorize to anyone certain uses described in the licensing terms adopted for the project, such as the Creative Commons licenses and the General Public License (GPL) for free software. Right owners thereby leave their contributions free for others to use and adapt, but with conditions such as requiring that subsequent users must also adhere to the terms of the license. Such projects, including the open-source movement, which specializes in creating computer programs, also build their business models on the existence of copyright protection, because otherwise they could not set specific terms or create an obligation for subsequent users.

§6.06 DURATION AND TERRITORIALITY OF COPYRIGHT

Copyright protection does not continue indefinitely. Copyright laws provide for a period of time during which the rights of the copyright owner exist and may be exploited. The period or duration of copyright begins from the moment the work is created or, under some national laws, when it is expressed or “fixed” in tangible form. Copyright protection continues, in general, until a certain time after the death of the author. The purpose of this provision in the law is to enable the author’s successors to benefit economically from exploitation of the work even after the author’s death. In some countries moral rights continue in perpetuity after the conclusion of the term of economic rights.

In countries party to the Berne Convention, and some other countries, the duration of copyright provided in national law is, as a general rule, the life of the author plus not less than fifty years after the author’s death. There is a trend in a number of countries to lengthen the duration of copyright to the life of the author plus seventy years after the author's death. The Berne Convention and many national laws also establish periods of protection for works such as anonymous, posthumous, cinematographic or co-authorship works where it is not possible to base duration on the life of an individual author.

Works that are no longer subject to copyright protection enter the "public domain," which also includes works that were never subject to copyright protection.

Copyright and related rights also have geographical limitations. In principle, each national law only applies to domestic works or other objects of protection. Due to obligations under the international treaties, protection must extend also to foreign works and objects of protection as defined in the treaties. Accordingly, the relevant "points of attachment" to each jurisdiction must be analyzed when considering copyright protection. If they (and further conditions) are fulfilled, the protection afforded by the Berne Convention and later copyright and related rights multilateral agreements is for an author or rights owner of a work to be afforded the same "national treatment" as would be applied to a national of that jurisdiction, in each country for which protection is sought and which is party to the convention. The owner of the copyright in a work is protected by the law of a country against copyright-relevant acts that are done in that country. For protection against such acts done in another country, the copyright owner must refer to the law of that other country. If both countries are members of one of the international conventions on copyright, the practical problems arising from this geographical limitation are very much eased because a common minimum standard of protection established by the conventions then exists in both countries.

§6.07 LIMITATIONS AND EXCEPTIONS TO COPYRIGHT AND RELATED RIGHTS PROTECTION

There are several types of limitations and exceptions to copyright protection. First, certain categories of works are excluded from copyright protection. In some countries, works are excluded from protection if they are not fixed in a tangible form. For example, a work of choreography would only be protected once the movements were written down in dance notation or recorded on videotape. In some countries, the texts of laws as well as court and administrative decisions are excluded from copyright protection.

Second, certain particular acts of exploitation that usually require the right owner's permission may, under circumstances specified in the law, be carried out without the owner's permission. The two basic types of limitations and exceptions in this category recognized by the Berne Convention are: (a) free use, which carries no obligation to compensate the right owner for the use of the work without permission; and (b) nonvoluntary (or compulsory) licenses, which require that compensation be paid to the right owner for non-authorized exploitation.

Examples of free use include:

- quoting from a protected work, provided that the source of the quotation and the name of the author are mentioned, and that the extent of the quotation is compatible with fair practice;
- use of works by way of illustration for teaching purposes; and
- use of works for the purpose of news reporting.

In respect of free use for reproduction, the Berne Convention contains a general rule rather than an explicit limitation or exception. Article 9(2) states that Member States may provide for free reproduction in certain special cases where that act does not conflict with the normal exploitation of a work and does not unreasonably prejudice the legitimate interests of the author. As noted above, many national laws allow individuals to reproduce a work exclusively for their personal, private and non-commercial use. However, the easy, high-quality individual copying made possible by digital technologies has led some countries to make efforts to address the concern of possible prejudice to the legitimate interests of the authors, including through systems (sometimes referred to as private copy levies) that allow private copying but incorporate a right to remuneration through a mechanism for payment to right owners for the resulting prejudice to their economic interests.

In addition to the specific categories of free use set out in national laws, the laws of mainly common law countries recognize the concepts of fair use (a concept applied in the USA, among others) or fair dealing (a concept applied in some Commonwealth countries, among others, more specific than fair use). These broad, general limitations or exceptions allow the use of works without the right owner's permission, taking into account factors such as (in the case of fair use) the nature and purpose of the use, including whether it is for commercial purposes; the nature of the work used; the amount of the work used in relation to the work as a whole; and the likely effect of the use on the potential commercial value of the work. Fair use has been rendered more concrete through an important body of case law.

Nonvoluntary licenses allow the use of works in certain circumstances without the right owner's permission, but require that compensation be paid for that use. Such licenses are called nonvoluntary because they are allowed within the law and do not result from the exercise of the exclusive right of the copyright owner to authorize particular acts, and thus they are not voluntary on the part of the copyright owner. In the case of compulsory licenses, the law requires the right owner to conclude a licensing agreement for an equitable remuneration. Two nonvoluntary or compulsory licenses are permitted in the Berne Convention, namely, for the mechanical reproduction of musical works and for broadcasting. For broadcasting, these licenses were introduced because the new technology for disseminating works to the public by broadcasting, which is time sensitive, was thought to be possibly hindered by the strong bargaining position of the CMOs. As regards mechanical reproduction, concern was expressed about the practice of exclusive recording licensing agreements, which would prevent recordings of the same music with other artists by competing phonogram producers. Once adopted, these licenses sometimes remained in the law even after the reason for their introduction no longer applied. In some countries, effective alternatives now exist for making works available to the public based on right owners' permission, including in the form of collective administration of rights.

Limitations and exceptions have traditionally focused on national situations. However, the topic has been introduced in the WIPO SCCR with some Member States seeking the harmonization of certain limitations and exceptions across national borders, as well as the ability to transfer copies of protected works made pursuant to such limitations and exceptions across borders under certain conditions. The sub-topics under discussion have included limitations and exceptions for persons with disabilities, libraries and archives, and educational, research and teaching institutions. The topic that was first developed fully was that of limitations and exceptions for persons who are blind, visually impaired, or otherwise print disabled, which was first introduced in the Committee as a treaty proposal in 2008 and resulted in the Marrakesh Treaty, which was adopted by WIPO Member States in June 2013. The Marrakesh Treaty requires its members to adopt limitations and exceptions for the making and cross-border transfer of copies of certain published works in formats accessible to persons who are blind, visually impaired, or otherwise print disabled. The SCCR continues to discuss limitations and exceptions for the benefit of libraries and archives, as well as museums, and for educational and research institutions and persons with other disabilities.

§6.08 COPYRIGHT PROTECTION AND DEVELOPING COUNTRIES

Finally, mention should be made here of the relationship between the protection of copyright and related rights and the interests of developing countries. Many developing countries have vibrant, thriving cultural and creative industries in everything from music, to visual arts, to video games and films. WIPO studies have shown that the culture and creative industries make significant contributions to developing country economies. Absent protection from copyright and related rights, the economic benefits from these works would not always remain in or return to the country in which they originated. Therefore, protection of copyright and related rights serves the twin objectives of preserving and developing national culture and providing a means for commercial exploitation in national and international markets.

The interest of developing countries in the protection of copyright and related rights goes beyond development of domestic cultural industries into the realm of international trade and development. The extent to which a country protects IP rights is inextricably linked to that country's potential to benefit from the rapidly expanding international trade in goods and services protected by such rights. The convergence of telecommunications and computer infrastructure leads to international investment in many sectors of developing country economies, including IP. Businesses and investors often seek evidence of a strong culture of respect for IP when considering whether to invest in businesses that are either based on or dependent on IPRs. They also seek evidence of effective and efficient application of the law, which is also imperative. This can be achieved through setting up of appropriate CMOs for the collection and distribution of remuneration for the works of authors and performers. Protection of copyright and related rights has thus become part of a much larger picture: it is a necessary precondition for participation in the global marketplace and the complex system of international trade and investment.

Another important area in which copyright and related rights may have unique relevance for developing countries is with respect to the largely unwritten and unrecorded cultural expressions of many countries, generally known as TCEs or folklore (the more recent term TCEs will be used except when describing a document or law that used the older term). There are some ways in which TCEs may be protected by copyright and related rights, as well as through other legal mechanisms. These expressions could be indirectly protected by copyright to the extent they are reflected in new creative expressions, even if they are based on a traditional legend or tale. By providing for related rights protection, developing countries may also offer a means of protection for the vast, ancient and invaluable cultural expressions that are the essence of what distinguishes each culture. TCEs may be indirectly protected under related rights as performances, since it is often through performers that they are communicated to the public. Likewise, protecting producers of sound recordings and broadcasting organizations helps to establish the foundation for national industries capable of disseminating TCEs within a country and in foreign markets. Protection for TCEs has been under discussion in the WIPO Intergovernmental Committee on Intellectual Property and Genetic Resources, Traditional Knowledge and Folklore (IGC) for many years (*see* §6.10[C] below).

§6.09 INFRINGEMENT

The rights of an owner of copyright or related rights are infringed when one of the acts requiring authorization of the owner is done by someone else without the owner's consent and when such acts are not permitted by law. Infringements that involve the unauthorized copying of copyrighted materials for commercial purposes and the unauthorized commercial dealing in copied materials are often referred to as "piracy."

[A] Incidence of Piracy

A large proportion of piracy is carried on for commercial gain (although the legal concept of piracy covers a wider spectrum of activities). This element of commercial gain implies that piracy will often be carried out on an organized basis, since not only is the unauthorized reproduction of a work involved, but also the subsequent sale, distribution or other exploitation of the illegally reproduced work, which will often require some form of organized distribution network or contact with potential purchasers. To the consumer, often only the end of the chain of such a distribution network will be visible in the form of a sales outlet selling a pirated product. It is important to bear in mind, however, particularly when addressing the question of the means of dealing effectively with piracy, that often behind one such outlet there is a systematically organized illicit enterprise, which illegally reproduces a copyright-protected work and distributes it to the public via a number of sales outlets.

While piracy is not a recent phenomenon, two developments have occurred which have caused piracy to assume alarming proportions, to the extent that some copyright and related rights owners believe it threatens the basis of the copyright system.

The first of these developments has been the advances in the means by which intellectual works may be communicated. Today, it is possible for most people easily to digitize works by scanners, smart phones, etc., and to upload and make them available on the Internet or other computer networks to the entire world, be it from one's own website, in a cloud with sharing links, or on platforms. The advent of digital technology has had a tremendous impact on the dissemination and other use of works. The medium of the printed word and copies of works in tangible form, such as CDs, has been supplemented progressively by Internet communication of audio and visual recordings or texts in digital forms, including digital files or streams. The results of these advances in the means of communicating intellectual works are undeniably socially beneficial, and have enriched the nature of the relationship that an author may create with the public. One by-product of these advances, however, is the increase in scope for pirates to interfere in the control that authors exercise over the dissemination and use of their works by the public.

Simultaneously with the advances that have occurred in the means of communicating intellectual works, there have been significant advances in the means of reproducing works. While initially, photocopying machines, high-quality and cheap cassette recorders for recording music from live performances, radio or gramophone records, and video recorders allowed members of the public to make copies of works by themselves, the advent and proliferation of devices to make digital copies and to post them on the Internet brought a new dimension to the challenge for right holders. Such copies are in many countries permitted by law if done for private purposes or study, or similar uses, under further conditions, often combined with statutory rights to remuneration (such as the "private copy levy") to reduce the harm of such mass uses for authors and other right holders. However, it is equally easy for internet pirates to make digital copies for the purpose of diffusion on the Internet without authorization and thereby to interfere with the right holders' possibilities of gaining revenues from exploitation of their works and to recover investment costs.

One consequence of these easily available, digital means of reproduction is the difference in cost between, on the one hand, the making of the original recording by an author and his or her business partners and, on the other hand, the reproduction of such a recording by others. In the case of a film, a producer must, through the investment of the producer and any partners, finance the script writer and any other literary author involved, the musical composer, the actors, the support cast, the cost of location and site facilities, and the use of sophisticated visual and sound recording equipment. Once the film is complete and available in a digital file, however, further perfect copies of the work can be reproduced with considerable ease and at little cost. The ability to compress the works and transmit them over the Internet at a nominal cost has contributed to the spread of unauthorized commercial use of copyright-protected works. Thus, advances in recording technology have produced the means whereby pirates can easily produce illegal versions of the original work. Since the pirate has not made, and therefore does not need to recover the cost of, any investment in the production of the original work, the pirated copies may be sold or uploaded on a platform for public access at reduced prices, thereby undermining the original author's and investor's possibility of obtaining a just moral and economic reward for their work and investment. This has a negative impact on the ability of authors and performers to make a living with their original creative achievements, and thus harms the contribution of cultural and creative industries to national economies.

The copyright system has responded to these developments through the 1996 WIPO Internet Treaties, which have been implemented in a large number of countries of the world. The Internet Treaties provide the exclusive right of making works, performances and phonograms available to the public in such a way that members of the public may access them from a place and at a time individually chosen by them. The offering on the Internet and similar networks as well as the subsequent transmission is covered by a right to authorize. Since these uses may not always easily be controlled, and technical means exist to protect the works in order to exercise control over their exploitation, these Treaties also introduced legal protection in case such technical protection measures are circumvented or manipulated, and to prevent interference with related rights management information (RMI). Still, right holders worldwide complain that enforcement of rights on the Internet remains a challenge, given the large scale of Internet piracy and the frequent location of websites or platforms in countries where enforcement is difficult to achieve.

[B] Effects of Copyright Infringement

Large-scale copyright infringement affects all the stakeholders involved in the creation, production and distribution or other exploitation of intellectual works and thus the entire copyright system. These various stakeholders, and the damage inflicted on them by copyright and related rights infringement, are as follows.

[1] Authors and Performers

In illegally reproducing and distributing printed works and audio and visual recordings, and in illegally recording live performances and distributing them for profit, as well as in illegally making any music, films, texts, etc. available to the public on platforms accessible over the internet or other digital networks, infringers pay no remuneration to authors and performers and may affect or destroy legal markets. Authors and performers, of course, are dependent on remuneration in order to derive their living from their creative works. Performers, in particular, lose control over the public exposure of their performances when piracy of the performances takes place, with the result that their employment prospects may be substantially diminished. By depriving authors and performers of the proper economic reward for their work, piracy constitutes a substantial detriment to cultural development and, in particular, to the development of local culture in developing countries.

[2] Publishers and Producers

The investment of publishers in the design, printing and publication of books and other printed works, and the investment of producers in the arrangement and recording of sound and visual works, is often necessary to enable authors and performers to achieve a wide audience for their works and performances. This investment requires not only financial resources, but also skill and judgment in the selection and presentation of works to the public. The possibility of market failure is a risk which must be assumed by publishers and producers and set off against the rewards of the market successes which they have promoted. No similar degree of investment, skill, judgment and risk is assumed by pirates, who are often able to select the works that they will illegally reproduce after the works have been on the market, and success has been established. In addition, digital tools make the financial resources needed to illegally reproduce and make works available minimal, and pirates do not reward the rightholders of the work reproduced as producers and publishers do. In consequence, publishers and producers are often deprived of many of the benefits of their successes, with resultant financial consequences for the risks that they are able to assume in bringing new works onto the market.

[3] Distributors

A further necessary element in the copyright system is distribution outlets for copyright-protected works including books, music, video games, and films. Because pirates are able to distribute and make available these works more cheaply owing to a lack of financial investment in the production of the works, legitimate distributors often cannot compete against the prices charged by the distributors of pirated works. They are even less able to compete with free illegal copies, which are widely available through the Internet. Again, the result is that the system of legitimate diffusion of works to the public, including online transmission channels, is prejudiced, with consequential detriment to authors, publishers and producers alike in obtaining legitimate market coverage for their works. Widespread availability of illegal copies and streams may also hinder new businesses that make works available lawfully online, especially in those countries that are considered smaller markets, as is the case for many least-developed and developing countries. Therefore piracy may prevent the population in some countries from having the same access to lawfully diffused works available in other countries.

[4] Consumers

While consumers may sometimes see short-term benefits in the availability of cheaper works as a result of piracy, not only may the quality of reproductions made by pirates be inferior, but online piracy may also expose consumers to theft of their personal data without their knowledge and vulnerability to files that are harmful to their computers. With widespread piracy, in many cases for free, consumers are also disadvantaged in the long term through a reduction in the availability of lawful works, measured by both quantity and variety. This diversion of economic rewards from authors and their business partners to pirates removes the incentive to invest time, effort, skill and resources in the creation of new works. These effects may harm even famous artists and settled businesses, and they almost certainly have a chilling effect on incipient businesses, including online and local artists and authors.

[5] Governmental Authorities

Since piracy is a clandestine activity, the profits derived by pirates are not subject to tax collection. Among the adverse consequences of this diminution in governmental revenue may be a reduction in the amount of government sponsorship available for the arts, as in some cases the level of such sponsorship may in part be determined by reference to the contribution that is made to the government budget by taxation derived from the distribution or other exploitation of works subject to copyright or related rights protection. In addition, the lawful exploitation of copyright works generates significant employment benefitting the national economy.

Piracy can be seen to have detrimental effects, therefore, on each of the stakeholders that participate in the copyright and related rights system. In consequence, piracy threatens to stultify the evolution and development of the national cultural identity that the copyright system is designed to promote.

§6.10 HISTORICAL EFFORTS TO PROVIDE FOR PROTECTION OF TCEs

[A] Introduction

TCEs are an important cultural heritage of every nation and are still developing—frequently in contemporary forms—even in modern communities all over the world. It is of particular importance to developing countries where TCEs are often a basis of their cultural identity and an important means of self-expression both within their own communities and in their relationship with other parts of the world. TCEs are increasingly important from the point of view of their social identity as well, where TCEs are a living, functional tradition, rather than a mere souvenir of the past.

The accelerating development of technology, especially in the fields of sound and audiovisual recording, broadcasting, cable television and cinematography may lead to improper exploitation of this cultural heritage. TCEs are being commercialized by such means on a worldwide scale without due respect for the cultural or economic interests of the communities in which they originate. In connection with their commercialization, TCEs are often distorted in order to correspond to what is believed to be better for marketing them. And generally no share whatsoever is conceded of the returns from the exploitation of TCEs to the peoples who developed and maintained them.

Under copyright laws, TCEs are generally considered to belong to the public domain. This approach explains why, at least so far, most countries generally have not established working, tailor-made copyright protection of the manifold national or community interests related to the utilization of TCEs. Some countries have attempted to treat TCEs under copyright law, while others have established separate legal regimes for protection of TCEs, either passed on intellectual property or through other areas of law.

In recent decades there have been increasing calls from many countries to respect TCEs as a source of cultural identity, and to find proper legal solutions both nationally and at the international level for the protection of TCEs. Such protection is proposed against any improper utilization of TCEs, including the frequent practice of making profit by commercially exploiting such expressions outside their originating communities without any prior informed consent (PIC) and recompense to such communities. Cultural heritage is a source of inspiration and creativity for parties within and outside the traditional or customary context and covers such areas as entertainment, fashion, publishing, design and other cultural industries. Taking into account the importance of TCEs in social and cultural identity, it has been suggested by some commentators that existing IP law does not adequately protect it and there is need to come up with a sui generis system of protection.

[B] Attempts to Protect TCEs under Copyright Law

The first attempts to explicitly regulate the use of TCEs were made in the framework of certain copyright laws (Tunisia, 1967; Bolivia, 1968 (in respect of musical folklore only); Chile, 1970; Morocco, 1970; Algeria, 1973; Senegal, 1973; Kenya, 1975; Mali, 1977; Burundi, 1978; Ivory Coast, 1978; Guinea, 1980; Tunis Model Law on Copyright for Developing Countries, 1976) and in an international Treaty (the Bangui text of 1977 of the Convention concerning the African Intellectual Property Organization, hereinafter referred to as "the OAPI Convention"). All these texts consider works of folklore as part of the cultural heritage of the nation ("traditional heritage," "cultural patrimony"; in Chile, "cultural public domain," the use of which is subject to payment).

An attempt to protect TCEs by means of copyright law was also undertaken at the international level in the Diplomatic Conference of Stockholm in 1967 for the revision of the Berne Convention. As a result, Article 15(4) of the Stockholm (1967) and Paris (1971) Acts of the Berne Convention contains the following provision: "(a) In the case of unpublished works where the identity of the author is unknown, but where there is every ground to presume that he/she is a national of a country of the Union, it shall be a matter for legislation in that country to designate the competent authority which shall represent the author and shall be entitled to protect and enforce his/her rights in the countries of the Union. (b) Countries of the Union which make such designation under the terms of this provision shall notify the Director General [of WIPO] by means of a written declaration giving full information concerning the authority thus designated. The Director General shall at once communicate this declaration to all other countries of the Union." This article of the Berne Convention implies the possibility of requesting, in certain cases, protection of TCEs.

To cater for the special needs of developing countries and facilitate access of those countries to foreign works protected by copyright, the Tunis Model Law on Copyright for Developing Countries was adopted by the WIPO Committee of Governmental Experts and made specific provisions for the protection of national TCEs.

Finally, related rights cannot fully satisfy the need for legal protection against improper use of TCEs because they cannot prevent the copying of TCEs that are not performed, broadcast or contained in phonograms. Furthermore, the limited duration of the protection of related rights does not fit TCEs for the same reasons as the limited duration of copyright does not fit.

For these and other reasons showing that many aspects of copyright and related rights do not fit the characteristics of TCEs and the needs of local communities, it was thought advisable by many national governments to establish, as regards IP aspects of TCEs, a special sui generis type of law for adequate protection against unauthorized exploitation.

[C] Special Model Provisions for National Laws on the Protection of TCEs Against Illicit Exploitation and Other Prejudicial Actions

[1] Evolution

At the meeting of WIPO's Governing Bodies in 1978 it was felt that despite concern among developing countries as to the need to protect TCEs, few concrete steps had so far been taken to formulate legal norms. Following that meeting, the International Bureau of WIPO prepared a first draft of sui generis model provisions for an intellectual-property-type national protection of folklore against certain unauthorized uses and against distortion.

The first draft of WIPO's model provisions on intellectual-property-type protection of folklore was submitted in Dakar in March 1979 to WIPO's Permanent Committee on Copyright and Neighboring Rights, which recommended that a joint WIPO/UNESCO working group should be convened as soon as possible, and should preferably deal not only with domestic aspects, but also with the international aspects of the legal protection of folklore creations.

In accordance with the decisions of their respective Governing Bodies, WIPO and UNESCO convened a Working Group in 1980 at Geneva, to study the draft of model provisions intended for national legislation prepared by WIPO, as well as international measures for the protection of works of folklore. The said Working Group recommended, in respect of the model provisions for national laws on the protection of creations of folklore, that the Secretariats of WIPO and UNESCO should prepare a revised draft and commentary thereon, taking into consideration all the interventions made in the Working Group.

Accordingly, the Secretariats prepared a revised draft, and a Commentary, which were submitted to the Working Group convened by WIPO and UNESCO for a second meeting at Paris in 1981. The outcome of the meeting was submitted a year later, in June-July 1982, to a Committee of Governmental Experts, convened by WIPO and UNESCO at WIPO headquarters in Geneva, which adopted what is called "Model Provisions for National Laws on the Protection of Expressions of Folklore Against Illicit Exploitation and Other Prejudicial Actions" (hereinafter referred to as "the Model Provisions").

[2] Basic Principles

The basic requirement in providing for legal protection of TCEs is the necessity of maintaining a proper balance between protection against abuses of expressions of folklore, on the one hand, and the freedom and encouragement of their further development, dissemination as well as adaptation for creating original authors' works inspired by folklore, on the other. A major part of TCEs forms a living body of human culture which should not be restricted in its unfolding and/or influence on creativity by too tight a net of protection.

In this context the proposed protection has to be practicable and effective, rather than remaining a system of imaginative requirements removed from reality.

The Model Provisions were designed with the intention of leaving room for national legislation to adopt the system of protection best suiting the conditions existing in a given country.

[3] The Subject of Protection

No generally accepted definition of folklore has yet been found, in spite of countless proposals which have been made to this effect. Consequently, the Model Provisions do not offer any definition of folklore. However, for the purpose of the Model Provisions, section 2 defines the term "expression of folklore" in line with the findings of the Committee of Governmental Experts on the Safeguarding of Folklore, which met in Paris in February 1982, and provides that "expressions of folklore" are understood as productions consisting of characteristic elements of the traditional artistic heritage developed and maintained by a community in the country or by individuals reflecting the traditional artistic expectations of such a community.

This definition of the expressions of folklore embraces the concepts of both collective and individual development of the traditional artistic heritage, since the generally applied criterion of "impersonal" creativity does not always correspond to realities of the evolution of folklore. The personality of the artist is often an important factor in folkloric expression, and individual contributions to the development and maintenance of such expressions may represent a creative source of enrichment of inherited folklore, if they are recognized and adopted by the community as expressions corresponding to its traditional artistic expectations.

The use of the words "expressions" and "productions" rather than "works" is intended to underline the fact that the provisions are sui generis, rather than of copyright, since "works" are the subject matter of copyright. Naturally, the expressions of folklore may, and—in fact—most of the time do, have the same artistic form as "works."

The fact that only "artistic" heritage is being considered, means that, among other things, traditional beliefs, scientific views (e.g., traditional cosmogony), substance of legends or merely practical traditions as such, separated from possible traditional artistic forms of their expression, do not fall within the scope of the proposed definition of "expressions of folklore." However, "artistic" heritage is understood in the widest sense of the term and covers any traditional heritage appealing to the aesthetic sense of man. Verbal expressions, which would qualify as literature if created individually by an author, musical expressions, expressions by action and tangible expressions may all consist of characteristic elements of the traditional artistic heritage and qualify as protected expressions of folklore.

In addition to the definition, for the purposes of the Model Provisions, an illustrative enumeration of the most typical kinds of expression of folklore is offered therein. Such expressions are subdivided into four groups depending on the form of the "expression," namely, expression by words ("verbal"), expressions by musical sounds ("musical"), expressions "by action" (of the human body) and expressions incorporated in a material object ("tangible expressions"). Each must consist of characteristic elements taken from the totality of the traditional artistic heritage. The first three kinds of expression need not be "reduced to material form," that is to say, the words need not be written down, the music need not exist in the form of musical notation and the bodily action—for example, dance—need not exist in a written choreographic notation. However, tangible expressions must be incorporated in a permanent material, such as stone, wood, textile, gold, etc. The provision also gives examples of each of the various forms of expression. They are, first, "folk tales, folk poetry and riddles"; second, "folk songs and instrumental music"; third, "folk dances, plays and artistic forms of rituals"; and fourth, "drawings, paintings, carvings, sculptures, pottery, terracotta, mosaic, woodwork, metalware, jewellery, basket weaving, needlework, textiles, carpets, costumes, musical instruments, architectural forms." The last-named appears in the Model Provisions in square brackets to show the hesitation which accompanied its inclusion, and to leave it to each country to decide whether or not to include it in the realm of protected expressions of folklore.

Identification of expressions of folklore originating in and developed by a community could be achieved by keeping an inventory of them. However, such an inventory being related mainly to conservation of folklore, its regulation does not fall within the scope of the Model Provisions.

[4] Prejudicial Acts

As reflected in the Model Provisions, there are two main categories of acts against which expressions of folklore need to be protected. They are "illicit exploitation" and "other prejudicial actions" (section 1).

"Illicit Exploitation" of an expression of folklore is understood in the Model Provisions (section 3) as any utilization thereof if made both with gainful intent and outside its traditional or customary context, without authorization by a competent authority or the community concerned itself. This means, among other things, that a utilization—even with gainful intent—within the traditional or customary context should not be subject to authorization. However, a utilization, even by members of the community where the expression has been developed and maintained, requires authorization if it is made outside that context and with gainful intent.

"Traditional Context" is understood as the way of using an expression of folklore in its proper artistic framework based on continuous usage by the community. For instance, to use a ritual dance in its traditional context means to perform it in the actual framework of the respective rite. However, the term "customary context" refers rather to the utilization of expressions of folklore in accordance with the practices of everyday life of the community, such as usual ways of selling copies of tangible expressions of folklore by local craftsmen. A customary context may develop and change more rapidly than the traditional ones.

The section under consideration then specifies the acts of utilization which require authorization where such circumstances exist. In doing so, it distinguishes between the case in which copies of the expressions are involved and the case in which copies of such expressions are not necessarily involved. In the first case, the acts requiring authorization are publication (in the broadest sense of the word, so as to cover any form of making available to the public the original, a copy or copies of an expression of folklore embodied in any material form, including recordings), reproduction and distribution; in the second case, the acts requiring authorization are public recitation, public performance, transmission by wireless means or by wire and "any other form of communication to the public."

Permitted Use. The Model Provisions would not prevent indigenous communities from using their traditional cultural heritage in traditional and customary ways and in developing it by continuous imitation. Keeping alive traditional popular art is closely linked with the reproduction, recitation or performance, in a stylistically varying presentation, of traditional expressions in the originating community. An unrestricted requirement for authorization to adapt, arrange, reproduce, recite or perform such creations could place a barrier in the way of the natural evolution of folklore and could not be enforced in societies in which folklore is a part of everyday life. Thus, the Model Provisions allow any member of a community of the country to freely reproduce or perform expressions of the folklore of his or her own community in their traditional or customary context, irrespective of whether he/she does it with or without gainful intent and even if done by means of modern technology, if such technology has been accepted by the community as one of the means of the evolution of its living folklore.

Section 4 sets out four special cases, in which there is no need to obtain authorization, even if the utilization of the expression of folklore was made against payment and outside its traditional or customary context. The four special cases are:

(1) use or utilization for purposes of education;
(2) utilization made "by way of illustration" in any original work of an author, provided that such utilization is compatible with fair practice as it is understood in the country concerned;
(3) where expressions of folklore are "borrowed" for creating an original work of an author. This important exception serves the purpose of allowing the free development of individual creativity inspired by folklore;
(4) "incidental utilization" which typically includes utilization in connection with reporting on current events and utilization of images where the expression of folklore is an object permanently located in a public place.

Other Prejudicial Actions, detrimental to interests related to the use of expressions of folklore are, according to the Model Provisions, four distinct offenses, subject to penal sanctions (section 6).

Section 5 requires, as a rule, that in all printed publications, and in connection with any communication to the public, of any *identifiable* expression of folklore, its source shall be indicated in an appropriate manner, by mentioning the community and/or geographic place from where the expression utilized has been derived. In section 6 noncompliance with the requirement of acknowledgment of the source is made subject to punishment.

Unauthorized utilization of an expression of folklore, where authorization is required, constitutes an offense. It is understood that the offense of using an expression without authorization is also constituted by uses going beyond the limits or that which are contrary to the conditions of an authorization obtained. Deception of the public, by creating the impression that what is involved is an expression of folklore derived from a given community when, in fact, such is not the case, is likewise punishable.

Public utilization distorting the expression of folklore, in any direct or indirect manner "prejudicial to the cultural interests of the community concerned," is an offense. The term "distorting" covers any act of distortion or mutilation or other derogatory action in relation to the expression of folklore published, reproduced, distributed, performed or otherwise communicated to the public by the culprit.

All four kinds of offenses are conditional on willful action. However, as regards noncompliance with the requirement of acknowledgment of source and the need to obtain authorization to use the expression of folklore, the Model Provisions also allow for punishment of acts committed negligently. This takes account of the nature of the offenses concerned and the difficulties involved in proving willfulness in cases of omission.

[5] Implementing the Protection of Expressions of Folklore

Authorizing Utilization of Expressions of Folklore. Concerning the entity entitled to authorize the utilization of expressions of folklore, the Model Provisions alternatively refer to "competent authority" and "community concerned," avoiding the term "owner" of the expression involved. They do not deal with questions of ownership of expressions of folklore since this aspect of the problem may be regulated in different ways from one country to another. In some countries, expressions of folklore may be regarded as the property of the nation, while in other countries the sense of ownership of the traditional artistic heritage may have been more strongly developed in the communities concerned themselves. Who should be entitled to authorize the utilization of expressions of folklore depends very much on the situation as regards ownership of them and necessarily varies according to different legislation on the subject. In countries where aboriginal or other traditional communities are recognized as owners fully entitled to dispose of their folklore and where such communities are sufficiently organized to administer the utilization of the expressions of their folklore, such uses may be subject to authorization by the community itself, which would grant permission to prospective users in a manner similar to authorization given by authors, as a rule, at full discretion. In other countries, where the traditional artistic heritage of a community is basically considered as a part of the cultural heritage of the nation, or where the communities concerned are not prepared to adequately administer the use of their expressions of folklore themselves, "competent authorities" may be designated, to give the necessary authorizations in the form of decisions under public law.

Supervisory Authorities. Section 9 of the Model Provisions provides for the designation of the competent authority if that alternative is preferred by the legislator. The same section also provides for designation of a "supervisory authority," if this should become necessary owing to the adoption of certain subsequent provisions suggested alternatively as regards activities to be carried out by such an authority.

According to the Model Provisions, the tasks of the *competent* authority (provided such an authority has been designated) are to grant authorizations for certain kinds of utilization of expressions of folklore, to receive applications for authorization of such utilizations, decide on them and, where authorization is granted, to fix and collect a fee—where required by law.

As far as the *supervisory* authority is concerned, the Model Provisions offer the possibility of providing in the law that the supervisory authority shall establish a tariff of the fees payable for authorizations of utilizations, or shall approve such tariff (without indication in the Model Provisions as to who will, in such case, propose the tariff, although it was understood by the experts adopting the Model Provisions that, in such a case, the competent authority would propose the tariff) (section 10), and that the supervisory authority's decision may be appealed to a court (section 11, paragraph 1).

Which authority or authorities will be designated in a given country will largely depend on the legal system existing in that country. A possible solution would be to set up a special authority for the purpose of dealing with the tasks laid down in the Model Provisions and to designate a ministry, for example, the Ministry of Culture, as the supervisory authority. As far as the competent authority is concerned it could be the Ministry of Culture, any public institution for matters related to folklore, authors' society or similar institution. A representative body of the community concerned could likewise be designated, even where, for whatever reason, the legislator had preferred not to recognize the community itself, in its capacity of owner of its expressions of folklore, as being entitled to directly authorize utilizations of such expressions.

It would seem eminently useful and logical if representatives of the various folklore communities of the country were to be associated and given an important role in the work of any competent authority or authorities. Furthermore, representatives of cultural and ethnological institutions, including museums, having experience in certain aspects of the protection of folklore, could likewise be associated in the work of the competent authority or authorities.

If the legislator decided that the community as such was entitled to permit or prevent utilizations of its expressions of folklore subject to authorization, the community would act in its capacity of owner of the expressions concerned and would be free to decide how to proceed. There would be no supervisory authority to control how the community exercises its relevant rights. However, the experts were of the opinion that if it was not the community as such, but a designated representative body thereof, which was entitled by legislation to give the necessary authorization, such a body would qualify as a competent authority, subject to the relevant procedural rules laid down in the Model Provisions.

Process of Authorization. As regards the process of authorization it follows from section 10(1) of the Model Provisions that an authorization must be preceded by an "application" submitted to the competent authority. The authorization to be applied for may be "individual" or "blanket," the first meaning an ad hoc authorization, the second intended for customary utilizers such as cultural institutions, theaters, ballet groups and broadcasting and television organizations. In this latter context, national legislators may also consider the applicability of systems of nonvoluntary licensing possibly existing in the country concerning utilization of works protected by copyright, with special regard to certain kinds of uses by broadcasting organizations and cable systems.

Remuneration. The Model Provisions (section 10, paragraph 2) allow, but do not make mandatory, the collecting of fees for authorizations. Presumably, where a fee is fixed, the authorization will be effective only on condition of payment. Authorizations may be granted free of the obligation of paying a fee. Even in such cases, the system of authorization is justified since it may prevent such utilizations as would distort the expressions of folklore or otherwise be unworthy of their dignity. Where fees are charged, they must be fixed according to a tariff established or approved—as already mentioned—by the supervisory authority.

The Model Provisions deal, in the same paragraph, also with the purpose for which the collected fees must be used. They offer a choice between the promoting or safeguarding of national culture or of national folklore. Naturally, national folklore is part of national culture, but national culture concerns a greater number of potential beneficiaries than national folklore. It is advisable, in any case, to secure by decree that a certain percentage of any fee collected by the competent authority is to go to that community from which the expression of folklore for the utilization of which the fee was paid originates. The relevant decree may allow the competent authority to retain part of the collected fees to cover the costs of administering the authorization system. Where there is no competent authority designated and both authorization and collection of relevant fees is carried out directly by the community as such, it seems obvious that the employment of the collected fees should also be decided by the community. The State should secure its share of such revenues, if at all, by imposing on them taxes or by providing for other appropriate measures.

[6] Sanctions

The two main types of possible punishments appear to be fine and imprisonment. Which of these sanctions should apply, what kinds of other punishments could be provided for and whether the sanctions should be applicable separately or also in conjunction, depends on the nature of the offense, the importance of the interests to be protected and the solutions already adopted in a given country for similar offenses. The minimum and maximum amounts of fines or terms of imprisonment would likewise depend on the actual practice of each country. Consequently, the Model Provisions do not suggest any specific punishment; they are confined to the requirement of penal remedy, leaving it to national legislation to specify its form and measure.

As regards seizure and other actions, however, the Model Provisions are somewhat more explicit. The relevant section 7 applies in the case of any violation of the law to both objects and receipts.

[D] Regional and International Protection of TCEs

The Model Provisions should pave the way for sub-regional, regional and international protection. It is of paramount importance to protect TCEs against illicit commercialization and distortion beyond the frontiers of the country in which they originate. Regional and international protection of TCEs serves to protect TCEs against illicit use that takes place abroad. However, national legislation on the protection of TCEs also provides the necessary basis for protecting the expressions of folklore of communities. By appropriate extension of their applicability under the principle of national treatment, national provisions may provide the substance of regional or international protection.

In order to further such a process, the Model Provisions provide for their application as regards expressions of folklore of foreign origin either subject to reciprocity or on the basis of international treaties (section 14). Actual reciprocity in the relations of two or more countries already protecting their national folklore may sometimes be established and declared more easily than mutual protection by means of concluding and ratifying international treaties. However, a number of experts stressed that international measures are an indispensable means of extending the protection of expressions of folklore of a given country beyond the borders of the country concerned. Consequently, it is advisable to endeavor to conclude multilateral treaties based on national laws protecting expressions of folklore, in order to secure such protection in a greater number of countries. In this context, the possibility of developing existing intergovernmental cultural or other appropriate agreements, so as to cover also reciprocal protection of expressions of folklore, should likewise be considered.

Additional information on the current work of WIPO on the protection of expressions of folklore (or TCEs), which, after many years of intensive discussions in the IGC, has advanced significantly when compared to the Model Provisions, can be found in Chapters 12 and 35.

CHAPTER 7
Patents

§7.01 INTRODUCTION

A patent is a document issued, upon application, by a government office (or a regional office acting for several countries), which describes an invention and creates a legal situation in which the patented invention can normally only be exploited (manufactured, used, sold, imported) with the authorization of the owner of the patent. "Invention" means a solution to a specific problem in the field of technology. An invention may relate to a product or a process. An invention is "patentable" if it is new, involves an inventive step (i.e., it is not obvious) and is industrially applicable. The protection conferred by the patent is limited in time (generally twenty years from the filing date).

In a number of countries, inventions are also protectable through registration as "utility models." The requirements are less strict than for "patentable" inventions, the fees are usually lower than for patents, and the duration of protection is shorter than in the case of patents, but otherwise the rights under the utility model are similar to those under a patent.

Patents are frequently referred to as "monopolies," but nowhere, in most laws, is the inventor or the owner of a patented invention given the right to make, use or sell anything. Under the principle of territoriality, the effects of the grant of a patent are that the patented invention may not be exploited in the country (or in the WTO territory) by persons other than the owner of the patent unless the owner agrees to such exploitation. Thus, while the owner is not given a statutory right to practice his/her invention, he/she is given a statutory right to prevent others from exploiting his/her invention, which is frequently referred to as a right to exclude others from making, using or selling the invention. The right to take action against any person exploiting the patented invention in the country without his/her agreement constitutes the patent owner's most important right, since it permits him/her to derive material benefits as a reward for his/her intellectual effort and work, and compensation for the expenses which his/her research and experimentation leading to the invention have entailed.

The following illustration may be helpful in trying to understand this concept. When Alexander Graham Bell received his patent for the telephone, he/she had the power to prevent anyone else from making, using or selling a telephone. Assume that someone else later invented a dial telephone for which that person also received a patent as an improvement on Bell's telephone. This second person would then be able to prevent anyone else, including Bell, from making, using or selling a dial telephone in accordance with that patent. This sets up the necessity and importance of licensing. In these circumstances, Bell would need a license from the owner of the dial telephone patent in order to make a dial telephone, and the owner of the dial telephone patent would need a license from Bell under Bell's basic telephone patent in order to make, use or sell the dial telephone.

It should be emphasized, however, that while the State may grant patent rights, it does not automatically enforce them, and it is up to the owner of a patent to bring an action, usually under civil law, for any infringement of his/her patent rights. The patentee must therefore be his/her own "policeman." This notion is confirmed by the specific language of paragraph four of the Preamble of the TRIPS Agreement, which recognizes IPRs as "private rights."

Simply put, a patent is the title issued by the State on an invention, according to an inventor, or their successor in title, the right to exclude for a limited period, in return for the disclosure of the invention, so that the invention, upon the patent's expiry or lapse, is available for the public to use.

In a number of countries protection may be obtained for "utility models." In essence "utility model" is merely a name given to certain inventions, namely—according to the laws of most countries which contain provisions on utility models—inventions in the mechanical field. This is why the objects of utility models are sometimes described as devices or useful objects. Utility models differ from inventions for which patents for invention are available mainly in two respects: first, in the case of an invention called "utility model," the technological progress required tends to be smaller than the technological progress ("inventive step") required in the case of an invention for which a patent for invention is available; second, the maximum term of protection provided in the law for a utility model is generally much shorter than the maximum term of protection provided in the law for an invention for which a patent for invention is available.

The titles issued for protecting utility models may be designated as "utility model patents" or as "utility model certificates."

§7.02 CONDITIONS OF PATENTABILITY

An invention must meet several criteria if it is to be eligible for patent protection. These include, most significantly, that the invention must consist of patentable subject matter, the invention must be industrially applicable (useful), it must be new (novel), it must exhibit a sufficient "inventive step" (be non-obvious), and the disclosure of the invention in the patent application must meet certain standards.

[A] Patentable Subject Matter

In order to be eligible for patent protection, an invention must fall within the scope of patentable subject matter. Patentable subject matter is established by statute, and is usually defined in terms of the exceptions to patentability, the general rule being that patent protection shall be available for inventions in all fields of technology.

Examples of technical developments that may be excluded from the scope of patentable subject matter include the following:

(1) discoveries of materials or substances already existing in nature;
(2) scientific theories or mathematical methods;
(3) plant or animal varieties, or essentially biological processes for the production of such plant or animal varieties, other than microbiological processes;
(4) schemes, rules or methods, such as those for doing business, performing purely mental acts or playing games;
(5) methods of treatment for humans or animals, or diagnostic methods practiced on humans or animals (but not products for use in such methods).

Some of these technical developments are not inventions per se, such as scientific discoveries and materials that exist in nature. Others are inventions in a broad sense, but they are excluded because they do not relate to the *making of things* or they do not provide a *technical solution to a technical problem*. In view of their abstract nature (in spite of their leading to concrete economic results) they are excluded from patentability. This concerns methods of doing businesses, as well as business schemes, such as banking and insurance contracts. However, in some jurisdictions those kinds of abstract inventions are patentable, provided they are implemented through (corporeal) devices, such as computers.

[B] Industrial Applicability (Utility)

An invention, in order to be patentable, must be of a kind which can be applied for practical purposes. In other words, the invention cannot be purely theoretical. It must be an invention that can be carried out in practice. If the invention is intended to be a product or part of a product, that product must be capable of being made. And if the invention is intended to be a process or part of a process, that process must be capable of being carried out—"used," as it is generally said—in practice.

The industrial applicability or utility of an invention does not mean that the invention in question has to perform better than the prior art. For an invention to have utility, therefore, it suffices that it works. However, things may become more complex in certain fields of technology, namely in the pharmaceutical sector. In those areas, a description of an invention may be submitted to a patent office that includes its results, namely that it has a certain prophylactic effect.

It is the possibility of making or manufacturing in practice, and this possibility of carrying out or using in practice, that are reflected in the word "applicability" in the expression "industrial applicability."

The word "industrial" in the same expression, refers to not only the feasibility, but also the reproducibility of the invention, and has a broad multi-sectoral scope that usually expressly encompasses agriculture. To some extent, the term "industrial" also implies a prohibition to grant patents for abstract inventions, i.e., inventions the use of which does not comprise the handling of material, tangible substances.

[C] Novelty

Novelty is a fundamental requirement in any examination as to substance and is an undisputed condition of patentability. It must be emphasized, however, that novelty is not something which can be proved or established; only its absence can be proved. Generally speaking, new means anything not found in the prior art, that is, the sum of information in any form. The prior art is also relevant of another condition of patentability: the inventive step (non-obviousness).

An invention is new if it is not anticipated by the prior art. "Prior art" simply stated is all the knowledge that had been disclosed prior to the relevant filing or priority date of a patent application in a way that makes it accessible to the public, whether it existed by way of written or oral disclosure or simply public use of the invention. The question of what should constitute "prior art" at a given time is one which has been the subject of some debate, depending on the IP title in question.

One viewpoint is that the determination of prior art should be made against a background of what is known only in the protecting country. This would exclude knowledge from other countries, if it was not imported into the country before the making of the invention, even if that knowledge was available abroad before the date of the making of the invention.

Another viewpoint is based on the differentiation between printed publications and other disclosures such as oral disclosures and prior use, and where such publications or disclosures occurred.

The disclosure of an invention such that it becomes part of the prior art may take place in three ways, namely:

(1) by a description of the invention in a published writing or publication in other tangible form;
(2) by a description of the invention in spoken words uttered in public, such a disclosure being called an oral disclosure;
(3) by the use of the invention in public, or by putting the public in a position that any member of the public may use it, such a disclosure being a "disclosure by use."

Publication in tangible form requires that there be some physical carrier for the information, a document in the broad sense of the term, and that document must have been published, that is to say, made available to the public in any manner such as by offering for sale or deposit in a public collection. Publications include issued patents or published patent applications, writings (whether they be manuscript, typescript, or printed matter), pictures including photographs, drawings or films, and recording, whether they be discs or tapes or any other devices in either spoken or coded language.

Oral disclosure, as the expression suggests, implies that the words or form of the disclosure are not necessarily recorded as such and includes lectures and radio broadcasts.

Disclosure by use is essentially a public, visual disclosure such as by display, sale, demonstration, unrecorded television broadcasts and actual public use, in a manner that discloses the invention's working.

A document will only destroy the novelty of any invention claimed if the subject matter is explicitly and entirely contained in the document. The subject matter set forth in a claim of an application under examination is thus compared element by element with the contents of each individual publication. Lack of novelty can only be found if the publication by itself contains all the characteristics of that claim, that is, if it anticipates the subject matter of the claim.

Lack of novelty may however be implicit in the publication in the sense that, in carrying out the "teaching" of the publication, a person having ordinary skill in the art would inevitably arrive at a result falling within the terms of the claim. Generally speaking, lack of novelty of this kind will only be raised by the Patent Office where there is no reasonable doubt as to the practical effect of the prior "teaching."

It should be noted that in considering novelty, it is not permissible to combine separate items of prior art together.

[D] Inventive Step (Non-obviousness)

In relation to the requirement of inventive step (also referred to as "non-obviousness"), the question as to whether or not the invention "would have been obvious to a person having ordinary skill in the art" is perhaps the most difficult of the standards to determine in the examination as to substance.

The inclusion of a requirement like this in patent legislation is based on the premise that protection should not be given either to what is already known as part of the prior art, or to anything that the person with ordinary skill could deduce as an obvious consequence or derivation thereof.

The person having ordinary skill in the art is a person with appropriate technical training and practical experience, and having access to all the information available in the scientific field at the date of the patent application's priority date. The expression "ordinary skill" is intended to exclude the "best" expert that can be found. In the absence of an international treaty defining novelty as a universal criterion, the term "ordinary skill" is intended that the person be limited to one having the average level of skill reached in the field in the country concerned.

It should be noted that novelty and inventive step are different criteria. Novelty exists if there is any difference between the invention and the prior art. The question, "is there inventive step?" only arises if there is novelty. The expression "inventive step" conveys the idea that it is not enough that the claimed invention is new, that is, different from what exists in the state of the art, but that this difference must have two characteristics. First, it must be "inventive," that is, the result of a creative idea, and it must be a step; that is, it must be noticeable. There must be a clearly noticeable difference between the state of the art and the claimed invention. This is why, in some jurisdictions, there is the concept of an "advance" or "progress" over the prior art.

Second, it is required that this advance or progress be significant and essential to the invention.

In order to assess the nature of the differences which are relied upon as constituting an inventive step, account has to be taken of the prior art as a whole. Thus, as distinct from the assessment of novelty, the subject matter of the claim under examination is compared not with each publication or other disclosure separately, but with the combinations thereof, insofar as each such combination is obvious to the person having ordinary skill in the art. The combination may be global, whereas the claim may define a set of subject matter known separately, for instance, a new form of washing machine including a particular type of motor coupled to a particular type of pump. For inventive step to be destroyed, it is necessary that not only the combination but also the choice of the combined elements is obvious. It is the sum of the differences that have been discovered which must be compared with the prior art and judged as to obviousness, and not each of the new elements taken individually, except where there is no technical link between them.

The evaluation of the differences should not neglect any of the three aspects that typify all inventions, namely:

(1) a problem to be solved;
(2) a solution to that problem; and
(3) a result guaranteed by the application of that solution.

If the problem is known or obvious, the examination will bear on the originality of the solution claimed. If no inventive step is found in the solution, the question becomes whether or not the result is obvious or whether it is surprising either by its nature or by its extent. If a person having ordinary skill in the art would have been able to pose the problem, solve it in the manner claimed, and foresee the result, the inventive step is lacking.

[E] Disclosure of the Invention

An additional requirement of patentability is whether or not the invention is sufficiently disclosed in the application.

A disclosure in an application, to be complete, must contain such description and details as to enable any person skilled in the art to which the invention relates to make and use the invention as of the filing date of the application.

While the prior art setting may be mentioned in general terms in the description, the essential novelty, the essence of the invention, must be described in such detail, including proportions and techniques where appropriate, as to enable those persons skilled in the art to make and use the invention.

Specific operative embodiments or examples of the invention must be set out in the description. Examples and other descriptive passages should be of sufficient scope as to justify the scope of the claims.

So that oppositions may be filed, the public must be informed of the content of the application, and this is done by the Patent Office by publication of a notice in an official journal or gazette to the effect that:

(1) the application is open to public inspection; and/or
(2) the Patent Office will, unless opposition is filed within a prescribed period, grant a patent; or
(3) a patent has been granted on the application.

The grounds upon which an opposition may be filed are limited by the relevant legislation. Generally speaking, it should be possible for an opposition to be based on noncompliance with any substantive requirement. However, the law in some countries only allows an opposition to be based on noncompliance with only certain substantive requirements. Typically these grounds are lack of novelty, inventive step or industrial applicability, insufficient disclosure of the invention, or the fact that an amendment made to a patent application has gone beyond the original disclosure in the application as filed. Some jurisdictions make it possible to file an opposition on the ground that the applicant has no right to a patent.

§7.03 DRAFTING AND FILING A PATENT APPLICATION

[A] Identification of the Invention

The first task in drafting a patent application is the identification of the invention. This involves:

(1) summarizing all the necessary features which in combination solve a particular technical problem; and
(2) an examination of this combination to determine whether it would, according to one's own judgment, fulfill the requirements for patentability, especially inventive step.

It is during this process that a full comprehension of the essence of the invention is obtained, and this is important in helping to draft the description and claims.

Generally speaking, an inventor may be so much involved in his/her own considerations that he/she may be prejudiced by the direct result of his/her work. The result of this is a limited understanding by the inventor of his/her own invention, particularly the specific problem which he/she attempted to solve and all the specific features which lead to the most effective solution.

Often the invention contains many new features. It is essential to identify the critical feature or features and to have an explanation of why they contribute to an effective solution to the problem. There are two important reasons for this. First, the claims should be as broad as possible; the broadest claim is the one restricted by the least number of features. Second, having identified the critical features and their effect, it is then necessary to ask how else may this effect be achieved, that is, can the specific features be substituted or altered while still achieving the same end result. This is important not only in drafting the claims, which must be wide enough to cover these substitutes or alternatives, but also in the description of the invention which must include details of the substitutes or alternatives so that the broad claim can be supported by the description.

[B] Practical Aspects of Drafting Patent Applications

Drafting practices and requirements differ from country to country. However, there are typically three basic requirements to be complied with in the drafting of a patent application.

First, there is a requirement that the application should relate to one invention only, or to a group of inventions so linked as to form a single general inventive concept. This requirement, referred to as "unity of invention," is particularly important when claims are being drafted.

Second, the description should disclose the invention in a manner sufficiently clear and complete for the invention to be evaluated, and to be carried out by a person having ordinary skill in the art. This is of fundamental importance, since one of the main functions of the description is to provide new technical information to third parties. An important phrase to note in this requirement is "a person having ordinary skill in the art." This allows for a simplified description since it can be assumed that the reader will be an informed reader having the background knowledge which makes it unnecessary to describe every basic detail of the invention. This description, which is generally referred to as "enabling disclosure," has become a mandatory formal requirement of patentability under international law, in accordance with Article 29.1 of the TRIPS Agreement.

Third, the application must contain claims which determine the scope of the protection, in view and presented as a difference to the state of the art.

[1] Description

The first section of the description typically contains two elements, namely, the title of the invention and a brief statement of the technical field in which the invention lies.

Usually this statement is in the form of a short introductory paragraph which commences with the phrase "This invention relates to ..."

In the second section, the background of the invention is described. In drafting this section, the patent agent usually sets out any existing problems or difficulties which the invention overcomes. Previous solutions to those problems or difficulties should be described, preferably in a way which clearly sets out the difference between the present invention and those previous solutions. This section may also describe the object of the invention, that is to say, what the invention sets out to achieve. The second section of the description is important to provide a good understanding of the invention and to put it into perspective against the prior art.

The third section of the description provides a summary of the invention in such terms that it may be readily understood. The patent agent will normally describe the invention first in general terms which correspond to those he/she intends to use in the main claim. By using this technique, the agent can avoid any disputes that might arise based on differences between the invention described and the invention as defined in the claims. This description of the invention in general terms is usually followed by a series of paragraphs which set out different preferred features of the invention. These paragraphs usually form the basis for dependent claims which follow the broad main claim.

In the fourth section of the description, two elements are generally found, namely a brief description of the drawings, if drawings are appropriate, and a detailed description of one or more embodiments of the invention.

It is usual for the description of the embodiment to include a passage which briefly describes the actual operation of the invention. If the device, for example, is a machine or an electrical circuit, the manner in which the machine or electrical circuit operates is extremely helpful in understanding the invention.

[2] Drawings

Extensive use of drawings can assist in describing details of the invention. If the invention relates to some form of mechanical object, for example, drawings illustrating plan, elevation and sectional views of that object could be used. Elements of the drawings which are described are numbered in the drawings and these numbers utilized in the description of the embodiment.

Where the invention is an electrical circuit, drawings can be used effectively to show the connections between the various elements or components of the circuit. Again these elements or components should be numbered for ease of reference. Normally the drawings should contain no textual matter. Exceptions, however, may be made when single descriptive words can be used where they do not interfere with the lines of the drawings. Thus in any drawing illustrating an electrical circuit, for example, standard components may be indicated in the drawings by boxes which may be labeled. Similarly, where the invention relates to a process, drawings may show a block, schematic or flow-sheet diagram, and blocks or boxes contained therein may be labeled as appropriate.

Where the invention is in the chemical field, the drawing may be a graph, and, more specifically, where the invention is of a metallurgical nature, the drawing may be a diagram such as a phase diagram.

[3] Claims

The claims must be clear and concise and fully supported by the description. This third basic requirement is important since the claims are the basis of interpretation of patent protection. It is from the claims that third parties are able to know what they may do and what they may not do. The claims may not be significantly broader or different from that which has been described.

The claims are the center or the heart of any granted patent because they define the protection which is the purpose of the patent, that is to say, they define clearly the scope of the exclusive right provided by the patent. Therefore, it is the most important task within the work of the patent agent when preparing the application, to produce a wording of the claims which defines the invention in terms of the technical features disclosed in the description and which do not contain any reference to commercial advantages.

The series of claims drafted by the patent agent generally commences with a broad main claim followed by a number of claims of narrower scope. The broad claim is drafted so as to just avoid the prior art known at the time of preparing the application. The patent agent drafts the succeeding claims more narrowly, and hopefully this results in stronger claims which could withstand any anticipation by more relevant prior art which might be produced by a Patent Office during examination, or by third parties during any opposition or invalidation proceeding. It should be emphasized that there must be some element of additional invention in each succeeding claim in order for it to be stronger.

The narrower claims following the broad main claim usually refer back to one or more of the preceding claims. Because of this they are usually called dependent claims. The features introduced in each of the dependent claims must find some basis in the description. There it is usually explained that these are preferred features which produce a better technical form of the invention.

The manner in which claims are drafted is of the essence in the determination of the rights. For example, a third party can infringe a patent only in part, to the extent that the product manufactured and/or sold by that party reproduces only several of the claims of a patented invention, but not all. Moreover, only independent claims can be infringed. If a third party reproduces the contents of one dependent claim only without embodying the limitations of the independent claim referred to, there is no infringement. But it is not possible to infringe one independent claim only in part. For example, if one claim describes four components of an invention, e.g., A-B-C-D, a third party shall not be deemed of infringement if he/she reproduces A-B-C, or A-B-D, or just A-D, or any other combination of those components, provided they are not entirely reproduced. This rule results from the so-called principle of indivisibility of claims. But, by contrast, it is possible to infringe claims partly by means of the combination of two or more infringers, and provided the combination results in the reproduction of all the characteristics listed in one given claim. For example, one third party reproduces elements A and B, and another third party, in an arrangement with the first, reproduces C and D, with the intent of, together, obtaining the result achieved by the claimed invention. This would be a case of infringement by combination, although, individually, none of the third parties had actually infringed the whole claim.

The last element of a patent is the abstract. The abstract presents a short summary of the description and the claims. It serves the purpose of enabling third parties to obtain quick information about the essential contents of the invention. It must be emphasized that it is not used to interpret the scope of protection. The guiding principle is that the abstract should be so drafted that it can efficiently serve as a scanning tool for purposes of searching in the particular art. Thus the abstract has to be as concise as the disclosure permits. Generally speaking, it should contain between 50 and 150 words.

§7.04 EXAMINATION OF A PATENT APPLICATION

[A] Examination as to Form; The Filing Date and Priority Date

It is now useful to follow the progress of an application through the Patent Office. There are three main areas of activity worthy of some comment, namely:

(1) examination as to form;
(2) search; and
(3) examination as to substance.

In each of these areas of activity, the normal procedure is for a dialogue to be carried out, mainly in writing, between an examiner in the Patent Office, and the applicant. The patent agent acts as a go-between in the sense that he/she receives communications from the Patent Office, advises the applicant as to the appropriate course of action, takes the applicant's instructions, and responds accordingly to the Patent Office's communications.

Prior to examination as to form, the application is checked to ensure that all the requirements necessary to accord the application a filing date, have been satisfied. This is a fundamental check since if a filing date is not established, the application will be treated as if it had not been filed, and it proceeds no further. The filing date is important in the general scheme of things since it constitutes the date from which certain actions are calculated, such as the term of the patent, and, where appropriate, determines the priority date of any subsequent application in another country under the terms of the Paris Convention for the Protection of Industrial Property (Paris Convention). The filing date (or priority date) is also relevant to the evaluation of novelty and inventive step.

The priority date is also important in the general scheme of things. The right of priority may be based on a national, regional or international application filed less than twelve months earlier. Its effect is to substitute the date of the earlier filing for the date of the subsequent filing, shielding the application from events of disclosure and competing applications made between the priority date and the actual filing date. This is particularly important with respect to the relevant prior art for evaluating novelty and inventive step, whereby the priority date will be serving as the reference point.

It must be emphasized that the right of priority is only available in those countries which are party to the Paris Convention (or members of the WTO). It should be noted however, that under some national laws, priority rights are granted on a bilateral basis of reciprocity for countries not parties to the Paris Convention or Members of the WTO.

The right of priority, as defined by Article 4(B) of the Paris Convention ("any subsequent filing in any of the other countries of the Union [or Members of the WTO] ... shall not be invalidated by reason of any acts accomplished in the interval") offers great practical advantages to an applicant who seeks protection in several countries. The applicant is not required to present all applications in his/her own country and in foreign countries at the same time, since he/she has up to twelve months to decide in which foreign countries he/she desires protection. The applicant can use that period to organize, with due care, the steps to be taken to secure protection in the various countries of interest to him/her.

Examination as to form is normally carried out as soon as an application has been accorded a filing date. Basically, this covers the following points: the language requirements, the representation, the content of the request, the statement concerning the inventor, the physical requirements governing the description, the claims and the drawings, and the inclusion of an abstract. The applicant is given an opportunity to correct any defects identified during examination as to form, and if such defects are not corrected within a specified time, the Patent Office rejects the application.

[B] Search

Depending on the examination procedure provided in the relevant law, the search will be conducted either separate from and prior to, or at the same time as, the examination as to substance. In either case, the objective of the search is to determine the prior art in the specific field to which the invention relates. In conducting the search, the Patent Office checks its documentation holdings to ascertain whether any documents exist which describe a solution which is the same as or similar to that described in the application.

If the search is conducted separately to the examination as to substance, a search report will be forwarded to the applicant setting out:

(1) a list of the documents located during the search, which disclose subject matter the same as or closely resembling the invention; and
(2) the claims in the application that should be compared with each of those documents.

The report may also give an indication of the scope of the search, that is the type of documents which may have been searched, the time span covered, and the specific areas of technology searched.

The codes indicating the relevance of the prior art to the invention (A, X, Y, etc.) are also a significant feature of the search report.

The search itself is a documentary search in a collection of patent documents that is primarily arranged for search purposes according to the specific areas of technology. These patent documents may be supplemented by articles from technical journals and other so-called non-patent documents. This total collection of documents that are linked to the invention is usually referred to as "the search file."

The Patent Office conducts the search only in respect of documents in the search file. The search does not extend to disclosures other than publications and, in particular, does not seek to determine whether disclosure has taken place by public use. This type of disclosure, if any, will only be taken into account during the examination as to substance phase, and then only if that use has been brought to the attention of the Patent Office by some third party's action.

The search itself will first cover all directly relevant technical fields, and may then have to be extended to analogous fields, but the need for such extension must be judged by the examiner in each individual case, taking into account the outcome of the search in the directly relevant areas of technology. It must be realized that whilst completeness is the ideal of the search, this ideal may not necessarily be obtained because of such factors as the inevitable imperfections of any classification and information retrieval system, and may not be economically justified if the cost is to be kept within reasonable bounds.

[C] Examination as to Substance

The aim of the examination as to substance procedure is to ensure that the application satisfies certain conditions of patentability. In essence, this is to prevent the grant of a patent where:

(1) the invention is excluded from patent protection by specific provisions in the legislation;
(2) the invention is not new, does not involve an inventive step and/or is not industrially applicable;
(3) the invention is not sufficiently disclosed in a clear and complete manner in the documents filed.

As with examination as to form, the applicant is given the opportunity to remove any objections raised during the examination as to substance phase, and if he/she fails to do so within a specified time, the Patent Office will refuse the grant of a patent.

It is in the interest of both the applicant and the public that there exists the possibility to amend the application. Not only can deficiencies be eliminated and thus a better patent grant secured, but also amendments to clarify the disclosure will result in a better description of the invention and a more precise definition of the scope of protection.

Not all amendments are permissible. As a general rule, an amendment is not allowable if it goes beyond the original disclosure in the application.

It should be noted that since the purpose of any patent law is to protect inventions, the Patent Office will refuse to grant a patent if the results of the examination clearly preclude the grant. Any doubt is resolved in the applicant's favor, since final adjudication on the validity or otherwise of a patent is usually possible via the courts (unless, of course, the general interests of the public are somehow involved).

[D] Grant and Publication

If and when the examination process has reached a conclusion favorable to the applicant, that is to say all the necessary requirements as to form and substance have been fulfilled, and assuming no opposition has been filed or that any opposition has been unsuccessful (where the law allows for pre-grant opposition), the Patent Office will grant a patent on the application. This involves certain actions on the part of the Patent Office.

First, when the patent is granted, the details of the patent are entered into the Patent Register (which contains already the data relating to applications that are publicly accessible after their publication).

The Register usually contains bibliographic data such as the patent number, the name and address of the applicant/patentee, the name of the inventor, the original application number, the filing date, certain priority application details and the title of the invention. The Register does not contain any technical information unless it is fully electronic, when it may contain the links to all the technical details of the application or the patent.

Additionally in countries where annual fee payments are required in order to maintain the patent in force, the Register will contain details of when such fees have been paid. In those countries where licenses and assignments or other rights in rem must be recorded, details in that regard are included.

The Register can thus be very useful to third parties especially competitors of the patentee, because it reveals the actual status of the patent. In some countries the courts accept a certified copy of an extract from the Register as being proof of the correctness of the position recorded in respect of the patent.

Second, the Patent Office publishes in an Official Gazette, a reference to the grant of the patent with the prescribed bibliographic data. The entry in the Official Gazette may also contain the abstract or the main claim, and if there are drawings, the most illustrative drawing.

Third, a Certificate of Grant is issued to the applicant, which is the legal document establishing his/her ownership of the patent. A copy of the granted patent is also issued at the same time.

Lastly, the Patent Office publishes the patent document itself in printed form. Copies of the patent document are made available by the Patent Office for use by Patent

Libraries, etc., as a source of technical information, and to third parties subject to the payment of a fee. In an increasing number of jurisdictions, however, electronic solutions enable Patent Offices to provide the same information in a more streamlined way, with less costs and higher accessibility.

As stated above, in order to keep the patent in force, each year, for the term of the patent, a prescribed renewal or maintenance fee, usually has to be paid to the Patent Office. In some countries, the maintenance fee is payable even before the patent is granted. In some countries the maintenance fee is not required annually but may be paid, for example, say every three to five years. A small number of countries do not require the payment of maintenance fees.

§7.05 OPPOSITIONS, THIRD-PARTY OBSERVATIONS AND APPEALS

Many countries provide opposition mechanisms in their patent systems. Opposition systems *stricto sensu* offer third parties an opportunity to oppose the grant of a patent at the granting authority within a certain *period of time* provided by the applicable law. An opponent must allege at least one of the grounds for opposition among those that are prescribed in the applicable law. Opposition procedures are closely related to the patent granting procedure. An opposition may be requested shortly before the grant of a patent (pre-grant opposition) or after the grant of a patent (post-grant opposition). In some countries, an opposition may be filed pre-grant, within a certain time period immediately after the publication of the application for a patent and before the examination phase, in which case the procedure resembles, to a certain extent, the so-called third-party observation system. It is possible to combine pre-grant and post-grant opposition systems. India, for example, provides both a pre-grant and a post-grant opposition system. One of the main objectives of the opposition system is to provide a simple, quick and inexpensive administrative mechanism that ensures the quality and validity of granted patents by allowing for the avoidance of granting or an early rectification of invalid patents. In general, opposition proceedings are *inter partes* procedures conducted before the patent office, not a court.

Pre-grant opposition often starts once the examination of a patent application has been completed by a positive result. The Office publishes its intention to grant the patent on the claimed invention contained in the application, and provides a certain time period during which an opposition can be filed. The opponent shall state the grounds for opposition and submit any evidence. If no opposition is filed during that period, the patent will be granted. If an opposition is filed, the applicant will be notified of that fact, together with the grounds for opposition and the evidence (e.g., prior art documents that demonstrate lack of inventive step). The applicant will be given the opportunity to comply with the requirements under the applicable law, and to make observations, within the prescribed time limit. In accordance with the applicable law, the opponent has the possibility to respond to the observations made by the applicant. Based on the submissions by the opponent and the applicant, an examiner or any other person entrusted to decide on opposition cases under the applicable law will make a decision as to whether the patent shall be granted or not.

In some countries, the pre-grant opposition system is designed in such a way that it starts after the publication of the patent application and before substantive examination. Once the patent application is published, an opposition may be filed within a certain time period prescribed under the applicable law. The opponent shall state the grounds for opposition and submit any evidence. If no opposition is filed during that period, the substantive examination will be carried out. If an opposition is filed, the applicant will be notified, and given an opportunity to make observations and/or amend the application within the prescribed time period.

Post-grant opposition starts once the patent is granted. Once the fact that a patent has been granted is published, an opposition may be filed with evidence within a certain time period prescribed in the applicable law. Similar to the pre-grant opposition, the patentee will be notified about that fact, and be given the opportunity to comply with the requirements under the applicable law, and to make observations, within the prescribed time limit. In accordance with the applicable law, the opponent has the possibility to respond to the observations made by the patentee. Based on the submissions by the opponent and the applicant, whoever is entrusted to decide on opposition cases under the applicable law will make a decision as to whether the patent shall be maintained, amended or revoked.

Since one of the objectives of the opposition system is to provide a simple mechanism to ensure the quality and validity of granted patents, procedural and substantive requirements provided by the applicable laws regarding opposition systems have certain common aspects. However, there are differences in the details. Some of these differences are the following:

(i) the time frame during which an opposition may be filed: the opposition period may start immediately after the publication of the patent application, after the completion of the substantive examination with a positive result and/or after the grant of the patent;
(ii) entitlement to file an opposition: in many national laws, any party, including the applicant or the patentee, may file an opposition. However, some laws provide that any third party (excluding the applicant or the patentee) may file an opposition, provided such party demonstrate a legitimate interest;
(iii) the threshold for opposition: In many countries the opponent has to provide full evidence of the grounds. With respect to admissibility, in some countries the request has to be sufficiently substantiated, and in some cases accompanied by written documents or/and other evidence while in other countries, the criteria of admissibility are not defined in their patent laws;
(iv) the disclosure of the identity of the requester. In some countries, it is possible for the opponent, the true party in interest, not to disclose his/her identity, which may be in favor of continuing good business relationship between the opponent and the patent applicant or patentee;
(v) the length of the opposition period: the length of the opposition period varies from country to country. Among the countries listed in Chapter V,

the duration varies from two to six months for pre-grant opposition and from six to twelve months for post-grant opposition;

(vi) the grounds for an opposition: in many countries, the requirements regarding novelty, inventive step, industrial applicability, sufficiency of disclosure and addition of new matter going beyond the original disclosure are grounds for an opposition. Noncompliance with the requirements concerning the exclusions from patentable subject matter also forms part of the grounds for an opposition in many countries. Some countries accept an opposition on the grounds that an applicant/patentee is not entitled to the right to a patent, or on other grounds covering all requirements that should be fulfilled to obtain a patent. They include, for example, the fact that information regarding corresponding foreign applications was not submitted, the source or geographical origin of biological material used in the invention was not disclosed, or the essential formalities were not complied with;

(vii) reviewing officers: the opposition may be conducted by an examination division or the proceedings may be held before a special opposition board; the board may include technical and legal examiners or judges;

(viii) *inter partes* procedural requirements: formal and procedural requirements relating to, for example, a request, notification to parties, arguments, evidence, oral hearing and final decision depends on the applicable law;

(ix) opposition fee: in many countries, the payment of an opposition fee is required to file an opposition; but The rules relating to the bearing of costs after the resolution of the opposition can also be different, whether it is the "losing party" that needs to bear the fees (and other costs, e.g., representation) or all parties bear their own costs;

(x) the effect of the opposition on civil actions: in some countries the opposition has an estoppel effect or an effect for civil proceedings to stay. In other countries both administrative and civil proceedings could be pursued independently and in parallel; and

(xi) the time frame for an opposition: in one country the final determination has to be issued within one year, extendable up to six months; in many countries, no time limits for a final administrative decision is specified.

An appeal against the final decision of the opposition body is generally possible, often to a court. It should be noted that, according to Article 62.5 of the TRIPS Agreement, final administrative decisions in procedures concerning the acquisition and maintenance of IPRs as well as the administrative revocation and *inter partes* procedures shall be subject to review by a judicial or quasi-judicial authority.

The number of patent applications/patents in respect of which oppositions are filed is not very high. For example, the number of patents opposed at the EPO in 2017 corresponded to 3.7% of patents granted (*see* <report-archive.epo.org/about-us/annual-reports-statistics/annual-report/2017/statistics/searches.html>).

In a larger sense, the opposition system may be complemented by related mechanisms which allow third parties to intervene in the patent examination process before the grant of a patent or to challenge the grant of a patent after its grant. Those mechanisms are similar to the opposition system, but may differ in some criteria from the opposition system *stricto sensu*, which is an *inter partes*, time-bound review system. Three types of related mechanisms could be distinguished:

(i) Third-party observations: many patent systems provide the opportunity for third parties to submit prior art documents or other related information, including comments and observations during the patent examination process. Those pre-issuance submissions by third parties are considered to contribute to the higher quality of patents as they assist the patent examination by submitting information on prior art, for example, published patent applications and other printed publications of potential relevance. The third-party observations do not trigger a specific review process, but are in most countries made available to the public and included in the file. In some countries, additional mechanisms are provided beyond the third-party observations. For example, in the USA, it is further possible to submit a protest and to contribute to the patent examination in a peer-to-patent pilot project and to file a protest against a published patent application. In summary, third-party observations are distinct from an opposition system as they are not triggering a review process, are generally related to prior art documents, and the submitting third party is not becoming party of the process (ex parte).

(ii) Re-examination: in some countries, re-examination procedures provide the post-grant opportunity for third parties to request a re-examination of the patent in view of new pieces of prior art. In general, the main difference between the re-examination and a post-grant opposition system consists in the fact that the post-grant opposition can be raised within a certain time period, while a re-examination may be requested during the lifetime of a patent. Re-examination could be conducted ex parte, largely without the participation of the requester in the conduct of the re-examination or *inter partes*, with greater participation of the respective parties. The ex parte re-examination often has the nature of re-conducting the substantive examination at the administration level on the basis of the prior art submitted by the requester of the re-examination. The *inter partes* re-examination in certain countries may resemble administrative revocation or invalidation mechanisms in some other countries in the sense that both provide for a wide range of substantive grounds and *inter partes* proceedings which allow third parties to challenge a patent before an administrative body. However, the proceedings of the *inter partes* re-examination are generally more conducted as a second examination by the patent office itself than as a full *inter partes* administrative review by a specialized board. Further, in one country, an *inter partes* re-examination is also limited to the grounds of novelty and the inventive step. In some countries, *inter partes* re-examination mechanisms complement the opposition system after the opposition period has lapsed.

(iii) Administrative revocation and invalidation: some countries provide for administrative revocation and invalidation mechanisms available after the grant of a patent without a time limit, in some countries even after expiry of a patent. Those mechanisms provide for similar *inter partes* opportunities for third parties to challenge a patent in an administrative, non-judicial procedure. For example, Japan provides for the possibility for an administrative appeal for revocation called "trial for invalidity." Administrative review mechanisms might complement a system of third-party observations or a pre-grant opposition system, such as in some countries in Asia such as China, Japan, the Philippines and the Republic of Korea, or in Costa Rica. In general, the administrative review is conducted by a specialized board which reviews certain grounds of invalidity. Therefore, those mechanisms are sometimes called "administrative appeal for revocation." In addition, in most countries, an appeal to the administrative review decision is possible, which is handled by a court, which may be a specialized patents court in some countries.

Invalidation of a patent may also be pursued in courts, either through direct invalidation lawsuits or through counterclaims in infringement lawsuits. The connection between the two types of actions is a matter of national laws. In some jurisdictions, in the face of a counterclaim, the court takes hold of the invalidity allegation and decides it as a preliminary matter. In other countries, where the judicial competence for examining the validity of patents belongs to a special jurisdiction (that is the case, for example, of Brazil), a counterclaim of invalidity in an infringement suit leads to the suspension of this process until a federal court decides on the validity issue.

No international treaty regulates opposition systems as such. Countries are free to provide, or not to provide, an opposition mechanism in their national laws. While substantive requirements with respect to opposition proceedings are not dealt with in existing treaties, some general procedural requirements prescribed in the TRIPS Agreement and the Patent Law Treaty (PLT) may also be applicable to opposition procedures.

Article 62.4 of the TRIPS Agreement provides that, where a Member's law provides administrative revocation and *inter partes* procedures such as opposition, revocation and cancellation, they shall be governed by the general principles set out in Article 41.2 and 3. Article 41.2 and 3 reads:

> 2. Procedures concerning the enforcement of intellectual property rights shall be fair and equitable. They shall not be unnecessarily complicated or costly, or entail unreasonable time-limits or unwarranted delays.
> 3. Decisions on the merits of a case shall preferably be in writing and reasoned. They shall be made available at least to the parties to the proceeding without undue delay. Decisions on the merits of a case shall be based only on evidence in respect of which parties were offered the opportunity to be heard.

Further, Article 62.5 states that final administrative decisions in the above procedures referred to under Article 62.4, including administrative revocation and *inter partes* opposition procedures, shall be subject to review by a judicial or quasi-judicial authority. However, there shall be no obligation to provide an opportunity for such review of decisions in cases of unsuccessful opposition or administrative revocation, provided that the grounds for such procedures can be the subject of invalidation procedures.

In addition, as a general rule, according to Article 62.2, Members shall ensure that the procedures for grant, subject to compliance with the substantive conditions for acquisition of the right, permit the granting of the right within a reasonable period of time so as to avoid unwarranted curtailment of the period of protection.

According to PLT Article 10(1), noncompliance with certain formal requirements with respect to an application may not be a ground for revocation or invalidation of a patent, either totally or in part, except where the noncompliance with the formal requirement occurred as a result of a fraudulent intention. Those formal requirements are: (i) form or contents of application (PLT Article 6(1)); (ii) formal requirements relating to request form, fees and priority document (PLT Article 6(2), (4) and (5)); (iii) form and means of transmittal of communications (PLT Article 8(1) and (3)); and (iv) language and signature of communications (PLT Article 8(2) and (4)). In other words, once a patent is granted, it shall not be revoked or invalidated on the grounds of noncompliance with the above formal requirements.

In addition, PLT Article 10(2) provides that a patent may not be revoked or invalidated, either totally or in part, without the owner being given the opportunity to make observations on the intended revocation or invalidation, and to make amendments and corrections where permitted under the applicable law, within a reasonable time limit.

Further, PLT Article 11 provides the extension of a time limit for an applicant's action before the patent office under certain conditions, and PLT Article 12 requires Contracting Parties to provide reinstatement of rights where an applicant lost his/her rights because of the failure to observe a time limit, if the failure occurred in spite of due care required by the circumstances or was unintentional. However, in accordance with PLT Rules 12(5)(vi) and 13(iv), no Contracting parties shall be required to grant a relief under PLT Article 11 or reinstatement of rights under Article 12 in respect of a time limit for an action in *inter partes* proceedings. In other words, a Contracting party is free to provide, or not to provide, the extension of a time limit and/or the reinstatement of rights regarding a time limit for an action in *inter partes* opposition proceedings.

However, when adopting these Rules, the Diplomatic Conference adopted Agreed Statement No. 5, stating that while it was appropriate to exclude actions in relation to *inter partes* proceedings from the relief provided by Articles 11 and 12, it was desirable that the applicable laws of the Contracting Parties provide appropriate relief in those circumstances which takes into account the competing interests of third parties, as well as the interests of others who are not parties to the proceedings.

§7.06 EXPLOITATION OF THE PATENTED INVENTION

Although the topic of this section is not about the law of patents or the use of the rights that result from them, but rather about the practical use of their subject matters, it is worthy that we spend a couple of paragraphs looking into it. Indeed, the exploitation of patented inventions has been in the center of debates about the policy of the patent systems. Society has to gain from the very existence of the system, that is true, because of the disclosure requirement and the consequent dissemination of technology. Therefore, the fact that most patents are not exploited does not invalidate the system. But society has to gain even more when the inventions are put on the market, through licensing, assignment of through their industrial and commercial exploitation. After all, it is the practice of patented inventions that brings to consumers new and better or cheaper products and services, and wealth and job creation in general. Today's national strategies on IP that many countries are adopting and implementing dedicate entire chapters to the practical use of inventions. And some countries have established entities (or departments within their patent offices) that help individual inventors and small companies to look for economic opportunities for the exploitation of their patents.

[A] Exploring the Market for an Invention

New ideas or innovations have to be marketed just like any other product or property. The larger and potentially more rewarding the market for the inventor's "industrial property" is, the more vigorous and professional must be his/her selling efforts. Major corporations and small businesses alike are well aware that the new product market is a key to their continued growth and even survival. Many companies make more than half their current sales with products developed within the past ten years, and new products and product variations are essential for continued sales growth.

The big corporation explores the potential market for a new product in a thorough and objective way and may spend millions of dollars in product planning, testing, market research and advertising. The small company can adapt the same techniques and processes to suit its own scale of operation. Above all, the independent entrepreneur should approach the problem with the same thoroughness, patience and emotional detachment that large corporations employ. Individual inventors and innovators should do likewise.

While major companies generally try to discover what it is the public wants and then develop a product to meet the need, the independent more often dreams up a product and then sets about trying to sell it. He has probably worked lovingly on his/her idea for years, perhaps gone through the painstaking and lengthy procedure of obtaining a patent and has an unshakable belief in its usefulness and commercial value. This emotional relationship between the inventor and his/her product can easily interfere with the rationality and effectiveness of his/her marketing approach. One of the key qualities he/she must retain is objectivity. Without it, he/she may be tempted to rush into situations without proper evaluation and prior research.

[B] The Feasibility/Marketability of an Invention

In assessing the feasibility/marketability of his/her product, the inventor should consider the following points:

(1) Does the product fill a need? Or, can a need be stimulated by means of clever promotion and advertising? The frisbee (a hand-tossed flying disc) was not needed but it caught the public imagination nonetheless.
(2) Is the product timely? Many products fail because they hit the market too soon or too late.
(3) What competition will the product have? If it will compete with similar products already on the market, is it substantially better, cheaper or otherwise more attractive?
(4) What are the economics of production? What are the problems inherent in the product's design? Can the product be made at a cost that is adequately covered by its retail selling price? How interested will financing sources be in backing it?

One of the concomitants of the size and dynamism of any large market is that successful products can be the creators of fortunes, and failures can prove unbelievably costly. One only has to consider some of the classic case histories from the US motor industry, for example, to appreciate this. Unfortunately, one of the failings of many individual inventors, is their belief that their invention will have a large market.

Given that the risk of new product failure is quite high, it is understandable that businessmen may be reluctant to outlay a large sum for an invention if the probable selling price of the product when it ultimately reaches the marketplace is unlikely to exceed by a reasonable margin the expected cost of its production.

If the invented product caters to a very limited market, if well-entrenched alternative products are competitively priced, or if high marketing and distribution costs are likely to be involved, it is unlikely that the invention will be greeted with much enthusiasm by businessmen. Similarly, it may not meet with a particularly good reception if it represents only a minor advance on the state of the art in a field of rapid technological development.

At all times it is necessary for the inventor to realize that what counts in any market is not the ingenuity which has found expression in the invention, its technical merit, or the aesthetics of the product, but the projected "bottom line" economic results.

It should be emphasized that every product has a life cycle. Its market reaches a peak of profitability, and sooner or later goes into a decline. Customer "brand or product loyalty" can keep some products around for years. Others, such as novelty or fad items, peak fast and are completely forgotten a few years later. Toys are a good example and most, these days, have a rapid turnover. It is said that up to 40% of the items in a toy store at any given time have probably been introduced within the past year.

Life cycles, particularly of consumer products, are becoming shorter, and products are continually pre-empted by newer ones or beaten into a low profit generating stage by competitors with similar products.

It should be apparent from the foregoing, that one of the essential elements for consideration before marketing a product is a proper assessment of the product.

[C] Selling an Invention

It is not enough, however, to assess the product itself; the inventor should also discover whether there is an adequate market for the product covered by his/her invention. For example, he/she should consider the following questions.

Who will buy the product? The prime users of the product will have a significant effect on how it is packaged, presented and promoted, as well as its price. The potential market is a question that should be studied carefully since many product developers have jumped to conclusions, albeit the wrong ones, concerning who will buy their products, and even how they will be used.

How many people make up the potential market? This is a difficult figure to assess but is one of the keys to product survival. Statistics on local populations and potential market segments published by the relevant government agencies, as well as surveys by private firms, can provide the basis for a study of the proposed market areas by age group, marital status and so on.

In his/her enthusiasm for his/her "brain-child," the inventor often rushes to find a market for it before it has been translated from an idea on paper into at least a prototype if not a production item. Obviously the earlier the point in time from the germination of the idea, the more limited the demand will be for the particular invention. A businessperson who by nature of his/her interests is exposed to many new product ideas is likely to be less willing to pay good money for a paper idea than he/she would be to compensate an inventor for an invention which has been brought to the stage of successful manufacture and marketing with many, if not all, of the design and production problems solved.

However, for some of the more sophisticated technology, research establishments, multinational corporations and the like are showing increasing interest in taking up embryo or partially developed technology with the object of completing development and thus gaining from the research effort and securing a significant lead over competitors.

"Test marketing" is a stage that many larger companies go through before commencing full scale production. They introduce the product in limited quantities to those viewed as a typical segment of their potential market. The small businessman also should consider using this technique before he/she commits too much time and money launching a product that ultimately may not sell.

Depending on the type of product involved, a prototype or sample might be constructed to enable the individual inventor to demonstrate the capacity and special features of the product incorporating the invention to possible buyers and users. In other instances, explicit engineering drawings are an adequate substitute.

In the case of a consumer product, a sample presented to a cross-section of retailers for their reactions can give a good indication of possible customer acceptance and sales. If the response to a widespread survey of this type is enthusiastic the inventor is ready to take the next step and consider full scale production either by him/herself or by someone else.

Basically, there are two methods the inventor can use to get his/her idea into production. He/she can sell or license, his/her product idea to a company equipped to manufacture it. Alternatively, he/she can become a manufacturer him/herself, either establishing a factory or contracting out production to a job or machine shop if appropriate.

Despite the fact that almost all manufacturing companies are constantly on the lookout for new products to complement their existing line, and are dependent upon them for future profits, the independent inventor is not always welcomed with open arms. Getting to see the person with the necessary knowledge and authority to appraise and accept the proposed product often takes tact and time.

The reason why some companies receive new product ideas with coolness is many sided. Often, companies are besieged with unsolicited ideas from the public, very few of which are even worth serious consideration. Larger corporations frequently have research and development departments in which substantial sums of money have been invested. Management, naturally, favors in-house developments. Other companies are wary of inventors who may claim that their ideas have been stolen, when in fact the company may have been already working on the same idea.

Larger corporations often publish their policies and procedures regarding new product ideas from outside sources. Some have "submitted ideas departments." Most companies would prefer that the inventor merely send them a copy of his/her patent on a new idea. Alternatively, the inventor can submit a copy of his/her patent application as soon as it has been filed.

When submitting an idea which is not patentable, the inventor should be aware of the company's policy regarding unsolicited ideas before he/she sends it. Some companies reserve the right to make arbitrary payment for ideas as they see fit.

If a patented idea is accepted, the inventor may be able to choose whether he/she wishes to sell his/her patent outright for a lump sum, or enter into a licensing agreement with the company.

§7.07 COMPULSORY LICENSES

Licenses that are granted by the owner of the patent are considered "voluntary," as distinguished from "compulsory" or "nonvoluntary" licenses. The beneficiary of a voluntary license has the right to perform acts covered by the exclusive right under an authorization from the owner of the patent for invention. The authorization in a contract is generally called a license contract concluded between the owner of the patent for invention and the beneficiary of the license (or the licensee granted a right to sub-license). In contrast, the beneficiary of a nonvoluntary license has the right to perform acts covered by the exclusive right under an authorization given by a government authority against or independently from the will of the owner of the patent for invention.

In countries where the grant of nonvoluntary licenses is provided for, the grounds for granting such licenses generally fall into three categories:

Abuse of Patent rights: Some countries provide for the grant of compulsory licenses to prevent the abuses which might result from the exercise of the exclusive rights conferred by the patent. Under Article 5A(2) of the Paris Convention, failure to work is given as an example of such an abuse;

Public Interest: Some countries provide for the grant of a nonvoluntary license in the case where a nonvoluntary license is deemed necessary for reasons of public welfare, including health, defense, and development of the economy.

Dependency of Patents: the TRIPS Agreement determines the possibility of granting a compulsory license to permit the exploitation of a patent which cannot be exploited without infringing a previously granted patent.

It should be noted that there is a conceptual distinction between compulsory licenses *stricto sensu* and government use—the latter not requiring a formal "license" or authorization to be granted, given that they result from the use of a governmental prerogative set in the law (and that is exactly the reason that explains why the TRIPS Agreement does not use the expression "compulsory licenses"). However, Article 31 of the TRIPS Agreement has approached those two concepts and treated them exactly the same way In general, conditions for the granting of compulsory licenses of patents are found in Article 31 of the TRIPS Agreement. Specific conditions for compulsory licenses granted for absence of or insufficient exploitation are found in Article 5(A) of the Paris Convention. The last sentence of Article 27.1 of the TRIPS Agreement is also considered by a number of authors to have an impact on those compulsory licenses, namely in that it would prohibit the granting of compulsory licenses on the ground of absence of industrial exploitation (i.e., manufacturing the claimed product or using the claimed process to make a product) in the country in question. This is, however, a matter of controversy among WTO Members, as the disputes initiated by the US against Brazil (in 2000) and by Brazil against the US (in 2001) in the WTO Settlement Mechanism reveal. Other compulsory licenses that are the subject of special rules are those granted for the exporting of pharmaceutical products in order to address problems of public health in other countries. *See Implementation of Paragraph 6 of the Doha Declaration on the TRIPS Agreement and Public Health*, Decision of the WTO General Council of August 30, 2003 (WT/L/540). This Decision has been replaced by Article 31*bis* of the TRIPS Agreement for the WTO Members that have accepted it. Article 31*bis* establishes a waiver from patent owners' rights under Article 31(f) (on the prohibition of granting compulsory licenses with the predominant objective of exporting). Such waiver benefits those WTO Members that face problems of public health and have not or have insufficient capacity of production of pharmaceutical products. Where two parallel compulsory licenses have to be granted, only one remuneration is to be paid, which will take into account the economic value of the authorization in the importing WTO Member.

[A] The Grant of Nonvoluntary Licenses to Remedy Abuses Resulting from the Exercise of the Patent Right

Article 5A of the Paris Convention gives countries of the Paris Union the right to legislate against the abuses which might result from the exercise of the exclusive rights conferred by the patent, for example failure to work, as provided as follows in paragraph (2):

> (2) Each country of the Union shall have the right to take legislative measures providing for the grant of compulsory licenses to prevent the abuses which might result from the exercise of the exclusive rights conferred by the patent, for example, failure to work.

The question as to what constitutes such an "abuse" is one left to national law. Apparently Article 5A(2) indicates that failure to work is considered one type of such "abuse," but this interpretation is not without challenges. Actually, it can be argued that only failure to work that is abusive may be sanctioned. Failure to work, therefore, would require some qualification—namely, that the enforcement or the refusal to license a non-worked invention would create serious problems to the establishment of a new industry or would create an impediment to the availability on the market of an important product.

[1] Non-working of a Patent

While the definition of "working" is generally a matter of national law, it usually means at least, in the case of a patent directed to a product, the making of the product and, in the case of a patent having been granted in respect of a process, the use of the process. While the laws of some countries specifically provide that the importation of a product that includes the invention does not constitute working, the current trend is away from this requirement. As a rule, the working requirement may be fulfilled through the working of the patented invention either by the owner of the patent for invention or by another entity or person under a license contract.

At the outset it should be recalled that a patent must disclose the invention in a manner such that one skilled in the art can carry it out. Thus patents, even apart from their being worked, are considered beneficial to industry, as their publication may inspire other inventions. Moreover, the inventions described in patents fall into the public domain after the expiration of their term. That is, after their expiration, the technology disclosed in a patent can be freely used by anyone without obtaining the patent owner's permission.

Despite these benefits, it is believed in some countries that, in order to be fully justified the patented invention should be worked in the country where the patent is granted, and not serve only as an exclusive right to prevent others from doing so or to control importation. The principal goal of requiring local working of a patented invention is the transfer of technology, the actual working of patented inventions in a given country being seen as the most efficient way of accomplishing such a transfer to that country.

The arguments against compulsory working of an invention in a particular country or territory are threefold: first, that such compulsory working of inventions may work against the goal of transferring technology; second, that it may not be economically feasible to do so; and, third, it runs against the rationale behind the promotion of free trade of goods, patented or not.

The first argument against nonvoluntary licenses is that they are less effective than voluntary licensing in encouraging the transfer of technology, and may, indeed, even be counterproductive to that goal. Stated another way, voluntary licensing clearly offers one means whereby the transfer of technology can be facilitated, whereas nonvoluntary licensing should not be viewed as playing such a role but should be limited to correcting abuses which may arise in the exercise of patent rights.

The transfer of technology is best done in an atmosphere of cooperation between the transferor and the transferee. In the present context, that means between the patent owner and the potential licensee. That cooperation generally leads to the disclosure of non-patented "know-how" which is necessary to make a commercially viable product, but which was not necessary to satisfy the disclosure requirement to obtain the patent. In the case of a nonvoluntary license the atmosphere of cooperation, and hence the disclosure of non-patented know-how, is absent. Thus, the grant of a nonvoluntary license under a patent results in a bare right to work the patented invention, which is likely to be an insufficient vehicle for the full transfer of technology.

An example is the know-how required to switch from the use of CFCs (which are seen as being harmful to the earth's ozone layer) as a refrigerant to other substances, which often have a lower molecular size. While the basic refrigeration cycle remains the same, devices, such as air conditioners, using the new refrigerants would have to be redesigned to, among other things, provide tighter fits between parts which come into contact with the refrigerant so as to prevent leaks. While the patent may fully describe the new substances useful as refrigerants, and the way in which they can be made, it need not disclose the know-how needed to make air conditioners which can operate using them.

Moreover, it may not be economically feasible to require a patent owner to manufacture products in accordance with his/her patent in every country in which patent protection has been obtained. Such a requirement does not allow cognizance to be taken of regional or international integration of markets or of comparative advantages of countries or regions. That is, a patent owner may find that products incorporating a patented invention, or made by a patented process, may be made cheaper if production is consolidated in one facility in one country, with the demand in other countries being satisfied by importation. Indeed, the patent owner may find that individual components of his/her product, which are themselves protected by patents, may be best manufactured in several countries or regions, with final assembly being conducted in one facility or on a regional or national basis.

An example is the manufacture of photovoltaic cells for the conversion of light into electrical power. A significant element in the cost of production is the capital equipment used to make such cells and the training of personnel to operate the equipment. A requirement of local working with respect to patents covering photovoltaic cells, or processes for their manufacture, would, in many countries, increase the cost of such devices to a point where they would be beyond the means of local people to afford.

The third argument is specific to the WTO: if all patents were locally exploited, there would be no international trade of patented goods. This explains the specific language of the last sentence of Article 27.1 of the TRIPS Agreement, which prohibits the discriminatory treatment of patent rights depending on whether the products are locally made or imported. This language is the translation into the TRIPS Agreement of the principle of national treatment of goods, as set by Article III.4 of the GATT 1994. In 2000 and 2001 the US and Brazil initiated reciprocally WTO dispute settlement procedures against each other involving provisions in their respective national patent statutes allegedly imposing the local exploitation of patents. Because those two countries settled the matter (the US dropped its request for a panel dispute against Brazil, and Brazil promised not to pursue its consultations with the US), there is no explicit interpretation of the last sentence of Article 27.1 by a WTO panel.

In response to these criticisms of nonvoluntary license provisions, two points are often made. First, since in countries with such provisions they are seldom applied for and even less likely to be granted, they are of little practical importance. Second, such provisions do serve as a legal possibility which may encourage a patent owner to more readily enter into a voluntary license agreement, even if those provisions are seldom applied. Nonetheless, the environment of cooperation usually found in the case of voluntary licensing is more effective than the environment of coercion present in the case of nonvoluntary licensing to promote the full and continuing transfer of technology.

Article 5A(2) of the Paris Convention specifically provides that countries of the Paris Union may provide for the grant of nonvoluntary licenses to prevent abuses resulting from the exercise of patent rights, including failure to work. Article 5A(4) provides that compulsory licenses for failure to work or insufficient working of the invention may not be requested before a certain period of time of non-working or insufficient working has elapsed. This time limit expires either four years from the date of filing of the patent application or three years from the date of the grant of the patent for invention. The applicable time is the one which, in the individual case, expires last.

The time limit of three or four years is a minimum time limit which recognizes that it may take some time for the owner of a patent to begin working the patented invention in each country where he/she has obtained patent protection. The patent owner must be given a longer time limit, if he/she can give legitimate reasons for his/her inaction, for example, that legal, economic or technical obstacles prevent working, or working more intensively, the invention in the country. If that is proven, the request for a compulsory license must be rejected, at least for the time being. The time limit of three or four years is a minimum time limit also in that sense that national law can provide for a longer time limit.

Article 5 A(4) further provides that the compulsory license for non-working or insufficient working must be a non-exclusive license and can only be transferred together with the part of the enterprise benefiting from the compulsory license. The patent owner must retain the right to grant other non-exclusive licenses and to work the invention him/herself. Moreover, because the compulsory license has been granted to a particular enterprise on the basis of its known capacities, it is bound to that enterprise and cannot be transferred separately from that enterprise. These limitations are intended to prevent a compulsory licensee from obtaining a stronger position on the market than is warranted by the purpose of the compulsory license, namely to ensure sufficient working of the invention in the country.

[2] Procedural Safeguards and Compensation

The grant of a nonvoluntary license results in the use of a very valuable property right of the patent owner. Since the grant of such a license is without the consent of the patent owner, reasonable procedural safeguards, including an effective independent (preferably judicial) review procedure, should be established to ensure that nonvoluntary licenses are properly granted and executed.

In particular, the granting authority, such as a patent office, should ensure that the conditions for the grant of a nonvoluntary license are met, allowing the patent owner to state his/her position in this regard. Moreover, the granting authority should ensure that adequate payment by the beneficiary of the nonvoluntary license is made to the patent owner and provide means whereby the nonvoluntary license may be canceled if the grounds for the grant of the nonvoluntary license no longer exist or if the obligations under the nonvoluntary license are not met by the beneficiary thereof.

The grant of a nonvoluntary license does not mean that the beneficiary (the licensee) need not pay royalties. On the contrary, national laws dealing with this question generally require that the licensee make payments to the patent owner on the basis of the working of the invention. Article 31(h) of the TRIPS Agreement provides that, when a compulsory license is granted "the right holder shall be paid adequate remuneration in the circumstances of each case, taking into account the economic value of the authorization." Article 31(k) adds that "The need to correct anti-competitive practices may be taken into account in determining the amount of remuneration in such cases."

[3] Forfeiture or Revocation of Patent in the Event of Abuses

While it is anticipated that the grant of a compulsory license would, in most instances, be sufficient to correct abuses, Article 5A(3) of the Paris Convention allows the forfeiture or revocation of the patent in cases where the grant of such compulsory licenses is not sufficient. That paragraph further provides that "[n]o proceedings for the forfeiture or revocation of a patent may be instituted before the expiration of two years from the grant of the first compulsory license."

[4] Compulsory Licenses in the Event of Anticompetitive Abuses

When a compulsory license is granted to correct an abusive use of patent rights that is considered anticompetitive—meaning that the abuse was practiced by a patentee with dominant power in the relevant market or with the intention of acquiring such power—Article 31(k) of the TRIPS Agreement requires that the decision to grant be preceded by a process of a judicial or administrative nature. In this event, two of the conditions that apply to compulsory licenses in general—such as the need to seek a voluntary license on reasonable conditions and terms and the predominantly purpose of supplying the domestic market—do not apply. Moreover, the remuneration may be set on lower levels than those determined by Article 31(h).

[5] Compulsory Licenses in the Event of Dependent Patents

Compulsory licenses for dependent patents are submitted by Article 31(l) of the TRIPS Agreement to a number of restrictions, namely that:

(i) the invention claimed in the second patent shall involve an important technical advance of considerable economic significance in relation to the invention claimed in the first patent;
(ii) the owner of the first patent shall be entitled to a cross-license on reasonable terms to use the invention claimed in the second patent; and
(iii) the use authorized in respect of the first patent shall be non-assignable except with the assignment of the second patent.

[B] The Grant of Nonvoluntary Licenses in the Public Interest

Some countries provide for a compulsory license when there has been no "abuse" of the patent right but where the grant of a nonvoluntary license is deemed necessary to protect the public interest. In general, nonvoluntary licenses granted in the public interest can be granted in favor of private parties or in favor of the government itself (or in favor of a person acting on behalf of the government).

[1] Nonvoluntary Licenses Granted in the Public Interest in Favor of Private Parties

By contrast with the grounds mentioned above, which are set specifically in international treaties, compulsory licenses may also be granted where the public interest in general recommends so. One of those grounds is the need to attend the interest of society in certain sectors of a vital interest, such as health, food and climate protection. Another ground is the setting of certain patented inventions as mandatory technical standards, when the exclusivity that stems from the patent may prevent standard implementors to apply it, thus depriving consumers from its benefits.

[2] Nonvoluntary Licenses Granted in the Public Interest in Favor of the Government, or on Its Behalf

A number of countries allow the government to exploit inventions without the consent of the owner of the patent, or to have third parties exploit the invention on its behalf, in the public interest. Under certain laws, this is called *crown use* or *government use*. There are typically three fields in which this may occur: national defense, national economy and public health.

In most cases of public interest, it should be sufficient for the State to authorize, against the will of the owner of the patent for invention, any entity or person designated by the Government, to perform any of the acts which are covered by the patent for invention. In each specific case, the Government will decide which of those acts may be performed.

This kind of measure in the public interest suits situations that arise in cases of national emergency particularly well. To take the example of medical equipment, it might be necessary to import that equipment very quickly in case of a sudden epidemic. If the owner of the patent is not willing to import or to conclude a license contract for importation on reasonable terms, the Government might decide to ask another entity to import the apparatus or might decide to import it itself. Once the epidemic has been brought under control, however, there is no reason to maintain the measure, and the owner of the patent for invention will recover the full control of the rights attached to the patent.

By contrast with compulsory licenses granted in favor of private parties, the use by governments (or by government contractors) does not need to be preceded by a formal act of grant. In this sense, Article 44.2 of the TRIPS Agreement provides that "Members may limit the remedies available against such use [by governments, or by third parties authorized by a government] to payment of remuneration in accordance with subparagraph (h) of Article 31."

[3] Procedural Safeguards and Compensation

Because the grant of nonvoluntary licenses confers the right to use a valuable property right of the patent owner, without his/her consent, procedural safeguards should be established to ensure that the grant of such licenses is done only when, and for as long as, the conditions warrant it. Moreover, provisions should be made for the compensation of the patent owner for the use of his/her property rights. Language in this sense is found in Article 31(h) of the TRIPS Agreement.

CHAPTER 8
Trademarks

§8.01 INTRODUCTION

As noted above, trademarks already existed in the ancient world. Even at times when people either prepared what they needed themselves or, more usually, acquired it from local craftsmen, there were already creative entrepreneurs who marketed their goods beyond their localities and sometimes over considerable distances. As long as three thousand years ago, Indian craftsmen used to engrave their signatures on their artistic creations before sending them to Iran. Manufacturers from China sold goods bearing their marks in the Mediterranean area over three thousand years ago and at one time about a thousand different Roman pottery marks were in use, including the FORTIS brand, which became so famous that it was copied and counterfeited. With the flourishing trade of the Middle Ages, the use of signs to distinguish the goods of merchants and manufacturers likewise expanded several hundred years ago. Their economic importance was still limited, however.

Trademarks started to play an important role with industrialization, and they have since become a key factor in the modern world of international trade and market-oriented economies. Industrialization and the growth of the system of the market-oriented economy allow competing manufacturers and traders to offer consumers a variety of goods in the same category. Often without any apparent differences for the consumer they do generally differ in quality, price and other characteristics. Clearly consumers need to be given the guidance that will allow them to consider the alternatives and make their choice between the competing goods. Consequently, the goods must be named. The medium for naming goods on the market is precisely the trademark.

Businesses also need trademarks to individualize their products, however, in order to reach out to consumers and communicate with them. So, trademarks serve their owners in the advertising and selling of goods, and they serve the economy in a general sense by helping to rationalize the commercialization of goods.

By enabling consumers to make their choice between the various goods available on the market, trademarks encourage their owners to maintain and improve the quality of the products sold under the trademark, in order to meet consumer expectations. In a market that offers a choice, a consumer who is disappointed will not buy the same product again. One who is satisfied will tend to rely on the trademark for his/her future purchase decisions. Thus, trademarks reward the manufacturer who constantly produces high-quality goods, and as a result they stimulate economic progress.

§8.02 DEFINITIONS

[A] Trademarks

The first edition of this book has put emphasis on a dual function of trademarks: to designate the source of the goods or services it designates and to distinguish them from competing goods or services. It was said, however, that this does not mean that the trademark must inform the consumer of the actual person who has manufactured the product or even the one who is trading in it: the consumer in fact often does not know the name of the manufacturer, still less the geographical location of the factory in which the product was made. It is not necessary for the trademark to fulfill a purpose of indicating (geographical or physical) origin. The point was that it is sufficient that the consumer can trust a given enterprise, not necessarily known to him, being responsible for the product sold under the trademark. The origin function as described above presupposes that the trademark distinguishes the goods of the given enterprise from those of other enterprises; only if it allows the consumer to distinguish a product sold under it from the goods of other enterprises offered on the market can the trademark fulfill its origin function. This shows that the distinguishing function and the origin function cannot really be separated. For practical purposes one can even simply rely on the distinguishing function of the trademark, and define it as "A sign which serves to distinguish the goods of one enterprise from those of other enterprises."

This is confirmed by the language of Article 15.1 of the TRIPS Agreement. However, the function of trademarks has to be characterized not as a duality of elements, but rather as a unitary function. Distinctiveness is of the essence. Not infrequently, trademarks distinguish products and services sold by the same undertaking. It happens that, in the context of antitrust proceedings, competition authorities determine that a given company keeps a product on the market, in competition with another product of a company with which it has merged or that it has acquired. This is *intrabrand* competition, and trademarks also have a role to play in this particular context.

[B] Service Marks

In modern trade, consumers are confronted not only with a vast choice of goods of all kinds, but also with an increasing variety of services which tend more and more to be offered on a national and even international scale. There is therefore also a need for signs that enable the consumers to distinguish between the different services such as insurance companies, car-rental firms, airlines, etc. These signs are called service marks, and fulfill essentially the same origin-indicating and distinguishing function for services as trademarks do for goods. It is widely recognized that there is a need for protection of service marks as there is for trademarks, and modern trademark laws give protection to the marks for services in the same way as to the marks that identify goods.

Since service marks are signs that are very similar in nature to trademarks, basically the same criteria can be applied, so service mark protection has sometimes been introduced by a very short amendment to the existing trademark law, simply providing for the application to service marks, *mutatis mutandis*, of the provisions on the protection of trademarks.

It follows from the above principle that service marks can be registered, renewed and cancelled in the same way as trademarks; they can moreover be assigned and licensed under the same conditions. Rules devised for trademarks therefore apply equally, in principle, to service marks.

[C] Collective Marks and Certification Marks

Trademarks typically identify individual enterprises as the origin of marked goods or services. Some countries provide for the registration of collective and certification marks, which are used to indicate the affiliation of enterprises using the mark or which refer to identifiable standards met by the products with which a mark is used.

Collective marks and certification marks are not defined in the same way by national legislations. However, the following are the most common features in the relevant provisions of national law on this topic.

[1] Collective Marks

Collective marks can be said to be signs which serve to distinguish the goods or services of members of an association, which is the proprietor of the mark, from those of other undertakings. The main feature of a collective mark is that it is used as an indication to the relevant public that goods or services originate from a member of a particular association. Additional features may include common quality or accuracy, geographical origin or other characteristics set by the association. An enterprise entitled to use the collective mark may in addition also use its own trademark.

The regulations concerning the use of the collective mark normally have to be included in an application for the registration of the collective mark and any modifications to the regulations have to be notified to the Trademark Office. In several countries, the registration of a collective mark may be cancelled if that mark is used contrary to the provisions of the regulations or in a manner which misleads the public. Collective marks, therefore, play an important role in the protection of consumers against misleading practices.

The Paris Convention contains provisions on collective marks in its Article 7*bis*. Those provisions, in particular, ensure that collective marks are to be admitted for registration and protection in countries other than the country where the association owning the collective mark has been established. This means that the fact that the said association has not been established in accordance with the law of the country where protection is sought is no reason for refusing such protection. However, the Convention expressly states the right of each Member State to apply its own conditions of protection and to refuse protection if the collective mark is contrary to the public interest.

[2] Certification Marks

A certification mark may be said to constitute a sign which is used or intended to be used to distinguish goods or services dealt with or provided in the course of trade and certified by the proprietor of the certification mark in relation to origin, material, mode of manufacture of goods or performance of services, quality, accuracy or other characteristics, from other goods or services dealt with or provided in the course of trade but no so certified. The certification mark may only be used in accordance with the defined standards.

The definition of "certification mark" is not the same in all countries. In most systems, however, an important requirement for the registration of a certification mark is that the entity which applies for registration is "competent to certify" the products concerned. In most systems, the certifying entity is the holder of the certification mark, but may not use itself the certification mark. This is an important safeguard for the protection of the public against misleading practices.

§8.03 SIGNS THAT MAY SERVE AS TRADEMARKS

It follows from the purpose of the trademark that virtually any sign that can serve to distinguish goods or services from other goods or services is capable of constituting a trademark. Trademark laws should not therefore attempt to draw up an exhaustive list of signs admitted for registration. If examples are given, they should be a practical illustration of what can be registered, without being exhaustive. If there are to be limitations, they should be based on practical considerations only, such as the need for a workable register and the need for publication of the registered trademark.

If we adhere strictly to the principle that the sign must serve to distinguish the goods or services of a given enterprise from those of others, the following types and categories of signs can be imagined:

(1) *Words*: This category includes company names, surnames, forenames, geographical names and any other words or sets of words, whether invented or not, titles and slogans.
(2) *Letters and Numerals*: Examples are one or more letters, one or more numerals or any combination thereof.
(3) *Devices*: This category includes fancy devices, drawings and symbols and also two-dimensional representations of goods or containers.

(4) *Combinations* of any of those listed under (1), (2) and (3), Including logotypes and labels.
(5) *Colored Marks*: This category includes words, devices and any combinations thereof in color, as well as color combinations and color as such.
(6) *Three-Dimensional Signs*: A typical category of three-dimensional signs is the shape of the goods or their packaging. However, other three-dimensional signs such as the three-pointed Mercedes star can serve as a trademark.
(7) *Audible Signs (Sounds Marks)*: Two typical categories of sound marks can be distinguished, namely those that can be transcribed in musical notes or other symbols and others (e.g., the cry of an animal).
(8) *Olfactory Marks (Smell Marks)*: Imagine that a company sells its goods (e.g., writing paper) with a certain fragrance and the consumer becomes accustomed to recognizing the goods by their smell.
(9) *Other (Invisible) Signs*: Examples of these are signs recognized by touch.

As mentioned before, countries may set limits on registrability for practical purposes. The majority of countries allow the registration only of signs that can be represented graphically, since only they can be physically registered and published in a trademark journal to inform the public of the registration of the trademark.

A number of countries allow the registration of three-dimensional trademarks, obliging the applicant either to submit a two-dimensional representation of the three-dimensional sign (drawing, picture or any other representation capable of being printed) or a description (or both). In practice, however, it is not always clear what is protected by the registration of a three-dimensional sign.

A similar problem exists for audible signs. A sequence of notes can of course be registered as a device mark, but that registration does not normally give protection to the actual musical phrases so expressed. What is protected is the sequence of notes, as registered, against the use of similar devices. Sound marks clearly can serve as trademarks, however, and the USA, for example, allows their registration. In practical terms, this means that the sound must be recorded and submitted in a sound device to the USPTO for registration.

The TRIPS Agreement (Article 15.1) provides for a limited list of signs that WTO Members are obliged to register: words (including personal names), numerals, figurative elements, combinations of colors as well as any combination of those signs. WTO Members are, therefore, not obliged to register colors or combination of colors as such, as well as signs that are not visually perceptible.

§8.04 CRITERIA OF PROTECTABILITY

The requirements that a sign must fulfill in order to be capable of serving as a trademark are reasonably standard throughout the world.

Generally speaking, two different kinds of requirement are to be distinguished.

The first kind of requirement relates to the basic function of a trademark, namely, its function to distinguish the products or services of one enterprise from the products or services of other enterprises. From that function it follows that a trademark must be distinctive or capable of distinguishing different products or services.

The second kind of requirement relates to the possible harmful effects of a trademark if it has a misleading character or if it violates public order or morality.

These two kinds of requirement exist in practically all national trademark laws. They also appear in Article *6quinquies* B of the Paris Convention, where it is stated that trademarks enjoying protection under Article *6quinquies* A may be denied registration only if "they are devoid of any distinctive character" or if "they are contrary to morality or public order and, in particular, of such a nature as to deceive the public."

[A] Requirement of Distinctiveness

We have seen that the trademark serves to distinguish the goods or services of one enterprise from those of others, so, in order to function as a trademark, it must be distinctive. A sign that is not distinctive cannot help the consumer to identify the goods or services of his/her choice. The word "apple" or the shape of an apple cannot be registered for apples, but it is highly distinctive for computers and cell phones. This shows that the distinctive character must be evaluated in relation to the goods or services to which the trademark is applied.

The test of whether a trademark is distinctive is bound to depend on the understanding of the consumers, or at least the persons to whom the sign is addressed. Very often, however, a sign has not been used before it is filed for registration, and so the question can only be whether it is capable of distinguishing the goods or services to which it is to be applied.

In conclusion, a sign is distinctive for the goods or services to which it is to be applied when it is recognized by those to whom it is addressed as identifying goods or services from a particular trade source, or is capable of being so recognized.

The distinctiveness of a sign is not an absolute and unchangeable factor. It is a purely circumstantial matter. Depending on the steps taken by the user of the sign or third parties, it can be acquired or increased or even lost. Circumstances such as (possibly long and intensive) use of the sign have to be taken into account when the registrar is of the opinion that the sign lacks the necessary distinctiveness, that is, if it is regarded as being not inherently distinctive. Article 15.1 of the TRIPS Agreement allows WTO Members to make registrability depend of distinctiveness acquired through use (the so-called secondary meaning).

There are, of course, different degrees of distinctiveness, and the question is how distinctive a sign must be in order to be registrable, regardless of its possible use. In that connection a distinction is generally made between certain typical categories of marks, such as arbitrary or fanciful (whose meaning does not exist, like IBM, for computers and related services, or does not correspond to the nature of product and service they designate, like APPLE, for electronic devices), suggestive (which require the consumer to use some imagination to find a characteristic in the product, such as FRESHIE for fruit juice), generic (words usually taken from the dictionary that describe the product in question), and descriptive (words that describe the product or service and its characteristics) trademarks.

Fanciful trademarks may not be the favorites of the marketing people, since they require heavy advertising investment to become known to consumers. They inherently enjoy very strong legal protection, however.

Marketing people are generally fond of brand names that somehow generate a positive association with the product in the mind of the consumer. They tend therefore to choose more or less descriptive terms. If the sign is exclusively descriptive, it lacks distinctiveness and cannot be registered as such as a trademark. However, not all signs that are neither meaningless nor arbitrarily used necessarily lack distinctiveness: there is an intermediate category of signs that are suggestive, by association, of the goods for which they are to be used, and of the nature, quality, origin or any other characteristic, of those goods, without being actually descriptive. Those signs are registrable. The crucial question in practice is whether a trademark is suggestive or descriptive of the goods or services applied for. This question has to be judged according to the local law and jurisprudence of the country and all the circumstances of the specific case. If the registrar has a doubt, or is convinced that the term is descriptive rather than suggestive, he/she has to consider whether and to what extent the term is descriptive rather than suggestive, he/she has to consider whether and to what extent the term has already been used by the applicant. As a general rule, it can be said that a descriptive term is distinctive for the goods or services concerned if it has acquired a secondary meaning, that is, if those to whom it is addressed have come to recognize it as indicating that the goods for which it is used are from a particular trade source.

In case of doubt as to whether a term is descriptive or suggestive, the very fact that the mark has been used in the course of trade for a certain period of time may be sufficient for accepting it for registration.

However, the more descriptive the term is, the more difficult it will be to prove secondary meaning, and a higher percentage of consumer awareness will be necessary.

If a sign is not distinctive, it cannot function as a trademark and its registration should be refused. This is a ground for refusal of registration that would be typically raised by the registrar upon examining the application. In order to overcome such a ground of refusal, the applicant would have to demonstrate that the trademark is distinctive, for example because of acquired distinctiveness or secondary meaning.

Next, we will see the criteria governing the refusal of registration for lack of distinctiveness.

[1] Generic Terms

A sign is generic when it defines a category or type to which the goods belong. It is essential to the trade and also to consumers that nobody should be allowed to monopolize such a generic term.

Examples of generic terms are "furniture" (for furniture in general, and also for tables, chairs, etc.) and "chair" (for chairs). Other examples would be "drinks," "coffee" and "instant coffee," which shows that there are larger and narrower categories and groups of goods, all having in common that the broad term consistently used to describe those goods is generic.

These signs are totally lacking in distinctiveness, and some jurisdictions hold that, even if they are used intensively and may have acquired a secondary meaning, they cannot be registered since, in view of the absolute need of the trade to be able to use them, they must not be monopolized.[31]

[2] Descriptive Signs

Descriptive signs are those that serve in trade to designate the kind, quality, intended purpose, value, place of origin, time of production or any other characteristic of the goods or services for which the sign is intended to be used or is being used.

In line with the definition of the distinctive sign given earlier, the test to be applied must establish whether consumers are likely to regard a sign as a reference to the commercial origin of the product or services (distinctive sign) or whether they will rather look on it as a reference to the characteristics of the goods or services or their geographical origin (descriptive sign). The term "consumer" is used here as an abbreviation denoting the relevant circles to be considered in a specific case, namely those to whom the sign is addressed (and in certain cases also those who are otherwise reached by the sign).

The fact that other traders may have a legitimate interest in the fair use of a term can therefore be used as a kind of additional ground when making the decisive test of whether consumers are likely to regard the sign as a reference to the commercial origin or as a reference to characteristics of the goods or services. It should not, however, be used on its own as a basis for a decision to refuse the registration of a term when it is not clear that consumers are also likely to regard the term as descriptive.

[3] Other Signs Lacking Distinctiveness

Signs may lack distinctiveness for other reasons. This is true of a device which, owing to its simplicity or pure illustrative or ornamental character, may not capture the consumer's attention at all as a sign referring to the commercial origin of the product or service, but rather as a mere illustrative part of the packaging of the goods offered to him.

An example (with regard to words) would be a relatively long advertising slogan recommending the goods to the consumer which, even when reproduced on the packaging, would be much too complex to be understood by consumers as a reference to the origin of the product.

---

31. A good hint about the genericism of a term for designating goods and services, other that its appearance as an entry in a dictionary, is the presence of that term in the class index of the classification of goods and services for the purpose of trademark registration. That, of course, is not the only criterion nor is the definitive, but it offers a good lead.

In practice the authorities have to deal with certain other typical categories of cases which in many laws are expressly listed as grounds for refusal, and which are dealt with below.

[4] Reference to Geographical Origin

References to geographical origin (as opposed to the commercial origin of the goods or services in the sense of the origin-indicating function) are basically not distinctive when they are truthful. They convey to the consumer an association with the geographical name, indicated either as the place of manufacture of the goods in question or of ingredients used in their production, or—depending on factual circumstances—with certain characteristics of the goods attributable to their origin.

However, certain countries allow geographical names and landscape-related figures to be registered as trademarks where the products obey to specific requirements as regards the place of production and the origin of the ingredients or parts. Switzerland, for example, as called this sort of requirements as the "Swissness" of trademarks.

However, geographical names are accepted as distinctive trademarks when the products or services they designate keep no relation with the place they designate.

[5] Foreign Script and Transliterations

Imagine the use of a Thai script mark in India or Sri Lanka, the use of Chinese characters in Switzerland, Singhala characters in the USA or Japanese characters (Katakana, Kandi) anywhere but in Japan. For the great majority of ordinary consumers these marks are purely fanciful devices. However, this matter should be understood with a grain of salt. Indeed, the laws of some countries require that the translation of non-fanciful trademarks be indicated in the act of filing. Moreover, trademarks in foreign characters must be accompanied by a transliteration. The principle that presides over these trademarks is, of course, that of avoiding consumer confusion, mas some countries impose some constraints based on the need for protecting the national language. Significantly, neither the Paris Convention (Article *6quinquies*) nor the TRIPS Agreement (Article 15) contain rules associating the mandatory protection of trademarks to questions of language.

Since these marks are distinctive, they are basically registrable. The registrar may, however, ask for a translation (a description of its meaning) or transliteration in local script.

[6] Colors

The use of words and/or devices in colors or combined with colors generally increases their distinctiveness. Consequently, applications for such signs claiming the colors shown or described in the application are easier to register. The first trademark registered in the UK in 1876 (and still on the register) was a triangle (a basic geometrical shape) in red. However, protection is then in principle restricted to the actual colors in which the mark is registered. Signs that might have been regarded as confusingly similar to the registered mark, had it been in black and white may therefore fall outside the scope of protection in view of the use of different colors. Since signs registered in black and white are protected against the registration and use of confusingly similar signs regardless of color, and since the registered owners of such signs can normally use them in any color they may wish to use, the usual practice is not to register signs in color. However, a given color or combination of colors may be an important element of a trademark, constantly used by its owner, and therefore liable to be imitated by competitors. This shows that a trademark owner may have a real interest in registering such a mark in the distinctive colors in which it is used, even where the mark was distinctive enough to be registrable in black and white. In order to eliminate the previously mentioned risk of restricting the scope of protection of such a mark, its owner may register the mark both in black and white and in the colors actually used.

[7] Names, Surnames

Company names and trade names are registrable, except where they are deceptive or not distinctive.

Common surnames are not normally registrable, since they are not distinctive. In some countries, this may even constitute an absolute ground for refusal of the registration. As for less common surnames, it is important to establish whether another meaning in everyday language will be overwhelmingly recognized by consumers. If there is such a dominant meaning, the sign is registrable on the condition that the meaning in question is not descriptive of the goods for which the mark is to be used.

[B] Exclusions from Registration on Other Grounds: Public Interest

[1] Deceptiveness

Trademarks that are likely to deceive the public as to the nature, quality or any other characteristics of the goods or their geographical origin do not, in the interest of the public, qualify for registration.

The test here is for intrinsic deception, inherent in the trademark itself when associated with the goods or services for which it is proposed. This test should be clearly distinguished from the test for the risk of confusing customers by the use of identical or similar trademarks for identical or similar goods or services.

It is true that fanciful trademarks or marks with an arbitrary meaning for the goods or services proposed cannot be deceptive. And yet trademarks that have a descriptive meaning, even if they are only evocative or suggestive and therefore distinctive, may still be deceptive. Such trademarks have therefore to be examined from two angles: first they must be distinctive, and second, they must not be deceptive.

As a rule, it can be said that the more descriptive a trademark is, the more easily it will deceive if it is not used for the goods with the characteristics described.

[2] Reference to Deceptive Geographical Origin

Signs that are descriptive or indicative of geographical origin are false for products or services that do not come from the region described or indicated. In such cases the consumer will be deceived if the reference to the geographical origin has the wrong connotations for him.

This is particularly true if the region or locality has a reputation. Famous examples of such signs are "Champagne" and "Swiss Chocolate."

In practice, such cases of direct reference to geographical origin are relatively rare. More often indirect references are made, and these cases are more problematic. A reference to a famous Swiss mountain for chocolate would still deceive consumers, as would a device mark consisting of a typical alpine landscape. *See*, in this regard, what was said above about the "Swissness" of trademarks, as imposed by an amendment to the Swiss trademark law.

Indeed, even the use of foreign words can, under certain circumstances, be deceptive without any reference to a specific geographical origin. The very fact that a word comes obviously from a particular foreign language may give consumers the impression that the product comes from the country where that language is spoken. Consumers will therefore be deceived if the country concerned has a reputation for the goods concerned.

However, it should be realized that, in addition to being spoken in many different countries all over the world, English is also the modern international marketing language, with the result that many trademarks have an English-language connotation quite independent of the geographical origin of the goods marked with it, and that consumers are generally aware of the fact.

[3] Partial Deceptiveness

We have seen that the question whether or not a trademark is inherently deceptive must be examined in relation to the goods or services in respect of which the application is made. Depending on the list of goods or services, therefore, an application may be distinctive for some, descriptive for others and/or deceptive for still others. In such cases the examiner has to require a limitation of the list of goods. Should the applicant not agree to such limitation, the examiner refuses the whole application in some countries. In others, he/she accepts the application only for the goods or services for which, in his/her opinion, the mark is not deceptive and refuses it for the others.

[4] Signs Contrary to Morality or Public Policy

Trademark laws generally deny registration to signs that are contrary to morality or public policy. Article 6*quinquies* of the Paris Convention, as seen, accepts this ground of refusal. Examples of those signs are obscene pictures, and emblems of public authorities or of forbidden political parties as examples.

It should be emphasized that here the discussion concerns the offense to morality or public policy caused by the sign itself, not by the products or services it designates. In this regard, the solution is offered by Article 15.4 of the TRIPS Agreement—which, contrary to what it appears, is not an absolute solution.

[5] Functional Elements of a Product or of a Package

The shapes and other visual elements of a product or of its packaging are also generally denied protection and registration by trademark laws. Those shapes are functional in nature, i.e., they have a particular shape because of the function they are determined to play. They lack, therefore, arbitrariness, which is a fundamental aspect that underlies distinctiveness.

That was the reason that led to the refusal of the registration of the LEGO brick shape as a trademark. That was also the ground for the debate concerning the application for the registration of the sound of the Harley-Davidson motorbike engine as a sound trademark (which the company has abandoned).

[6] Signs Reserved for Use by the State, Public Institutions or IGOs

A country generally protects its national flag, its official name and the names of official institutions in its own interest. Furthermore, countries are obliged by Article *6ter* of the Paris Convention also to prevent that the signs covered by that provision are registered or used as trademarks, or as element of trademarks, without the authorization of the competent authority.

§8.05 PROTECTION OF TRADEMARK RIGHTS

A trademark can be protected on the basis of either use or registration. Both approaches have developed historically, but today trademark protection systems generally combine both elements. The Paris Convention places contracting countries under the obligation to provide for a trademark register. Over one hundred States have adhered to the Paris Convention. Nearly all countries today provide for a trademark register, and full trademark protection is properly secured only by registration.

Use does still play an important role, however: first of all, in countries that have traditionally based trademark protection on use, the registration of a trademark merely confirms the trademark right that has been acquired by use. Consequently, in principle, in the countries based on a trademark protection on use, the first user has priority in a trademark dispute, not the one who first registered the trademark.

In the event of a conflict between an unregistered distinctive sign but previously used as a trademark and a registered trademark, it is the latter which in principle has priority. However, in some jurisdictions, the person who first used the sign is authorized to continue the use he/she has made of it.

§8.06 USE REQUIREMENTS

[A] Need for an Obligation to Use

Trademark protection is not an end in itself. Even though trademark laws generally do not require use as a condition for the application for trademark registration, or even the actual registration, the ultimate reason for trademark protection is the function of distinguishing the goods on which the trademark is used from others. It makes no economic sense, therefore, to protect trademarks by registration without imposing the obligation to use them. Unused trademarks are an artificial barrier to the registration of new marks. There is therefore an absolute need to provide for a use obligation in trademark law.

At the same time trademark owners need a period after registration before the use obligation comes into effect. This is especially true of the many companies that are active in international trade. They cannot normally introduce a new product in the market in numerous countries at the same time. In order to avoid loopholes in the protection of their new trademarks of which competitors could take advantage, they must from the very beginning apply for the registration of their new trademarks in all countries of potential future use. Without a reasonable period for the use obligation written into the law, internationally active companies would obviously have enormous difficulties. Indeed, even in their own countries companies often need several years before they can properly launch a newly developed product on the market. This is especially true of pharmaceutical companies, which have to make clinical tests and have to apply for approval of their product by the health authorities.

The period granted in trademark laws that provide for a use obligation is sometimes three years (*see* the second sentence of Article 15.3 of the TRIPS Agreement), but more often five years.

The TRIPS Agreement has set the use requirement in two different ways: as a requirement to *obtain* the registration and as a requirement to *maintain* the registration.

As regards use as a requirement to obtain the registration, Article 15.3 has three different rules:

- WTO Members may make registrability depend on use;
- actual use of a trademark shall not be a condition for filing an application for registration (however, in the period before the application and the grant of the registration WTO Members may require evidence of use or of intent of use);
- an application shall not be refused solely on the ground that intended use has not taken place before the expiry of a period of three years from the date of application.

Under Article 19 of the TRIPS Agreement, as a requirement for maintaining the registration, trademarks shall not be cancelled before the expiry of an uninterrupted period of at least three years (i.e., Members may provide for a longer period) of non-use. However, cancellation does not apply when trademark owners have valid reasons for not using them. Reasons are valid when they refer to circumstances arising independently of the will of the owner of the trademark which constitute an obstacle to the use of the trademark, such as import restrictions or other government requirements.

[B] Practical Use Requirements

In principle, the trademark must be used in the country of registration. The use must be made in relation to the goods or services. Normally, the trademark will be affixed to the goods or to their packaging. In the case of certain goods (gasoline, etc.) or services use on accompanying documents or in advertising may be sufficient.

The use must be made publicly, that is, the goods or services must be offered for sale through normal trade channels. This does not mean that they must be available everywhere. It is sufficient if the goods are sold or services provided in certain specialty shops, from a restricted number of outlets or through some special trade channels (for instance, to restaurants in the food service business). It is not sufficient, however, to use a trademark exclusively on goods offered in the shop or restaurant of the company that is the owner of the trademark, and available to its employees alone. This same note also applies to services: these must be provided to clients, regardless of their number, in the course of business.

Use solely in advertising should be sufficient only if it the advertising is for a future sale and the process of launching the goods or services on the market has started. Advertisement, when effective, must also be admitted as evidence of notoriety for the purposes of considering a trademark as well known, under Article 6*bis* of the Paris Convention (Article 16.2 of the TRIPS Agreement).

The use must be genuine; token use is not sufficient. Market tests, if made in order to determine the acceptance of the product or services by consumers (and not with the sole intention of safeguarding the protection of the trademark), should be recognized as genuine use, as well as clinical trials of pharmaceutical products.

In order to safeguard the protection of a registered trademark, it must be used for at least one of the goods or services for which it is registered. Use for one of the goods or services for which the trademark is registered should safeguard protection for all goods or services on the list of registered goods or services that are similar to the one used. In order to avoid unnecessarily weakening the effect of the use obligation, however, it may be going too far to provide that use for one product safeguards the registration for the whole class or for all goods or services for which the trademark is registered, and which may cover several classes. Nevertheless, it should be noted that what determines the scope of protection of a trademark is the product or service itself and the risk of confusion, not the classes in which that good or service belongs.

The trademark must in principle be used as registered. However, the Paris Convention provides in its Article 5C(2) that the "use of a trademark by the proprietor in a form differing in elements which do not alter the distinctive character of the mark in the form in which it was registered (...) shall not entail invalidation of the registration and shall not diminish the protection granted to the mark."

Word marks can be used in any form, type face or colors and in combination with additional elements (trade names, descriptive terms), provided that the registered mark maintains its distinctive character. If a word mark and a device mark are registered separately but always used together, that use is sufficient for the purpose of protection of the registered trademarks.

The majority of national laws allow the use to be made by the trademark owner him/herself or by a third party with his/her consent. Sometimes such use by third parties is formalized. If trademark law requires a formalized agreement, and if the agreement is legally invalid under unfair competition law or other rules such as food and drug regulations, it should be sufficient that the third party is effectively and genuinely entitled to use the mark on behalf of the trademark owner, irrespective of whether or not the agreement is legally valid. This solution is made mandatory for WTO Members by Article 19.2 of the TRIPS Agreement.

[C] Consequences of Non-use

The principal consequence of unjustified non-use is that the registration is open to cancellation at the request of a person with a legitimate interest. There is moreover a tendency to require of the registered owner that he/she prove use, since it is very difficult for the interested third party to prove non-use. In the interest of removing "deadwood" from the register, such reversal of the burden of proof is justified.

The burden of proof should be on the trademark owner not only in cancellation proceedings but also in any other proceedings where the owner is alleged to have taken advantage of his/her unused trademark right (opposition procedure, infringement action).

No evidence of use should be required for the renewal of a trademark registration, however. This is an administrative complication which is unnecessary in view of the fact that an interested person can at any time at all take appropriate action against an unused trademark registration.

Non-use does not always lead to invalidation of the trademark right. Non-use can be justified in the case of force majeure, and any other circumstance that is not due to fault or negligence on the part of the proprietor of the mark, such as import restrictions or special legal requirements within the country.

[D] Proper Use of Trademarks

Non-use can lead to the loss of trademark rights. Improper use can have the same result, however. A mark may become liable for removal from the Register if the registered owner has provoked or tolerated its transformation into a generic name for one or more of the goods or services in respect of which the mark is registered, so that, in trade circles and in the eyes of the public, its significance as a mark has been lost.

Basically, two things can cause genericness: namely, improper use by the owner, provoking transformation of the mark into a generic term, and improper use by third parties that is tolerated by the owner.

In order to avoid improper use, everyone in the company owning the trademark who is involved in advertising or publicizing the brand must follow some rules.

The basic rule is that the trademark should not be used as, or instead of, the product or service designation. By systematically using a product or service designation in addition to the trademark, the proprietor clearly informs the public that his/her mark identifies a specific product or service as one in a certain category. This is especially important if the trademark proprietor has invented a totally new product or service which at the outset is the only one in the category. Trademarks such as FRIGID AIRE, CELLOPHANE and LINOLEUM became generic terms because they were the only product in their category, and no additional name was given to the category by its proprietors. When instant coffee, also called soluble coffee, was invented in 1938, the first product marketed by the company that invented it was called NESCAFE. However, from the start the company systematically used a product designation such as "instant coffee" or "soluble coffee" on its labels.

A second important rule is that trademarks should always be used as true adjectives and never as nouns, in other words the trademark should not be used with an article, and the possessive "s" and the plural form should be avoided. It would be wrong to talk about NESCAFE'S flavor or about three NESCAFES instead of three varieties of NESCAFE.

Furthermore, it is advisable always to highlight the trademark, that is, to make it stand out from its surroundings.

Finally, a trademark should be identified as such by a trademark notice. Only a few laws provide for such notices, and making their use on goods compulsory is prohibited by Article 5D of the Paris Convention. Trademark law in the USA allows the use of a long statement (such as "Registered with the United States Patent and Trademark Office") to be replaced by a short symbol, namely, the circled R. Over the years this symbol has spread throughout the world and become a widely recognized symbol for a registered trademark. Its use is recommended for registered trademarks as a warning to competitors not to engage in any act that would infringe the mark.

However, it is not enough just to follow these rules: the trademark owner must also ensure that third parties and the public do not misuse his/her mark. It is specifically important that the trademark should not be used as or instead of the product or service description in dictionaries, official publications, journals, etc.

Consumers tend to use well-known marks as product designations. Many consumers all over the world refer to instant coffee as NESCAFE. Basically, the trademark owner can be proud of such use as it shows the strength of his mark. However, the more famous a mark is, the more it is in danger of turning into a generic term. This is why it is so important, in such cases, that companies should apply a very strict policy of proper use on their own part, and intervene against third parties (other than consumers) in the event of abuse. According to generally accepted rules of law and practice, the transformation of a trademark into a generic term occurs only if all the trade circles involved and the general public have become used to using the sign as a generic term. The proprietors of the trademark NESCAFE, for instance, have traditionally applied such a strict policy and this trademark, which is one of the best known in the world, has consequently remained a protected trademark which enjoys strong protection, despite the habit of many consumers to refer to instant coffee in general as NESCAFE. Another example of this kind of trademark that continues to enjoy strong protection is Coca Cola, probably the best-known trademark in the world.

§8.07 TRADEMARK REGISTRATION

[A] Introduction

Applications for registration of a trademark are to be filed with the government authority competent to receive and process industrial property applications. Usually, it is called "Industrial Property Office" or "Patent and Trademark Office" or "Trademark Office."

The tasks of the Office are defined by the applicable law, which is supplemented by regulations and administrative instructions. Usually, that law contains detailed provisions on the requirements of an application, on the processing of the application until the decision by the Office whether the trademark can be registered or not, and on any further procedures relating to trademark registrations.

[B] Application for Registration

In general, countries provide for an application form, the use of which is mandatory in certain countries. The application form has to be completed with the name and address of the applicant. Foreigners have either to give an address for service in the country or to use an agent holding a power of attorney to be signed by the applicant. Often further formalities were imposed, such as authentication by a notary public and legalization. However, since such requirements can be burdensome, they are now often eliminated from modern legislations and are even prohibited by the Trademark Law Treaty (TLT) and the Singapore Treaty on the Law of Trademarks for their respective contracting parties.

The sign filed for registration must appear in the application form or in an annex to it. If it is intended that the sign should be registered in color, the colors must be claimed and a specimen in color or the description of the color(s) must be submitted. The graphic representation is not a universal requirement, as an increasing number of laws provide for the requirement of a representation "in a manner which enables the competent authorities and the public to determine the clear and precise subject matter of the protection."

The type of the sign for which registration is sought should be indicated, provided that this category is accepted under the applicable legislation. The specific requirements concerning the representation are usually defined in the implementing regulations.

The applicant has also to list the goods or services for which the sign is to be registered. Trademark laws generally require the applicant to group the goods or services according the classification system used by the national office, which can either be its own system or the system established under the Nice Agreement concerning the Classification of Goods and Services for the Purposes of the Registration of Marks (whether the country is a party of such Agreement or not).

Finally, one or more fees have to be paid for the registration of a trademark. A country may provide for a single, all-embracing fee or several (application fee, class fee, examination fee, registration fee, etc.). Both systems have advantages and disadvantages. On the one hand, it is simpler and more cost-efficient to charge a single fee. On the other hand, this may lead to unjust consequences for applicants who decide to withdraw the application totally or partially during the registration procedure (e.g., because of an objection from the owner of a prior right, or because of insurmountable objections from the registrar). In such cases at least partial reimbursement of the fee paid should be provided for.

An increasing number of trademark offices accepts registration applications through the Internet.

[C] Examination

[1] Examination as to Form

Countries generally accept an application for registration of a trademark at least if the formal requirements are fulfilled.

[2] Examination as to Substance

Most countries examine trademark applications as to substance in the interest of both the public and competitors.

One has to make a clear distinction between two types of grounds for refusal.

As discussed in section §8.04, above, Trademarks may be examined for absolute, objective grounds for refusal, that is, whether they are sufficiently distinctive, not deceptive, not immoral, etc. Such an examination is highly desirable in the interest of consumer protection, but for competitors too, and the trade in general, it is important that nobody should be able to monopolize a descriptive or even a generic term by a simple administrative act.

The laws of many countries provide also for examination on relative grounds, that is, whether the rights applied for are identical or similar to prior rights that have been applied for or granted for identical or similar goods or services. Such examination may either made ex officio and/or on the basis of an opposition procedure.

In general, three typical approaches can be observed internationally:

- a system, providing for examination by the office for absolute and relative grounds, and also for an opposition procedure;
- under a second approach the office examines only for absolute grounds, the law provides for no opposition procedure and it is left to the owner of the prior rights to bring a cancellation or infringement action against the registration or use of a more recent sign;
- the third system provides for examination by the office for absolute grounds and also for an administrative opposition procedure, in which the owner of prior rights can oppose the infringing trademark application by means of a simplified and not too costly procedure. This system is a compromise between the more extreme systems mentioned before, and follows a modern trend which is reflected in the proposed European Community Trade Mark (CTM) system.

Under Article 15.5 of the TRIPS Agreement, WTO Members are obliged to provide for a "reasonable opportunity for petitions to cancel the registration." In addition, it provides that "Members may afford an opportunity for the registration of a trademark to be opposed."

Industry in general prefers the third system, since it is less time-consuming and much more flexible. In view of the many trademarks on the registers of countries all over the world, it is in any case advisable to carry out a search for prior rights before applying for registration of a trademark, and even more so before beginning to use it. Most applicants do such searches regularly, while companies have at least their more important registered trademarks watched, either by their trademark agents or by one of the international watching services, in order to keep themselves informed of applications for registration of potentially conflicting similar marks.

The standards to be applied by the registrar when examining whether a trademark application is to be refused because of a prior right are the same, in principle, as those to be applied in an opposition procedure or by a judge in an infringement action (even though in the latter case the factual circumstances of the infringement will play an additional role).

Since it is very difficult for trademark examiners in practice with the broad definition of confusing similarity, some rules have been developed which help to define in specific cases whether, in view of the similarity of the two marks, confusion is likely to arise.

The fundamental criterion is that the examiner must look at the trademark in question from the standing point of the average consumer.

An important point is that usually the consumer does not compare trademarks side by side; he/she is generally confronted with the infringing mark in the shop without seeing the product bearing the mark that he/she knows and remembers more or less accurately. He mistakes the products offered under the infringing mark for the genuine product that he/she actually wants to buy. In this context it must be taken into account that the average consumer also has an average memory, and that it must be sufficient for him to doubt whether the trademark with which he/she is confronted is the one he/she knows.

Since the average consumer generally does not at first glance recognize differences between the marks that he/she might spot if he/she took his/her time to study the mark and the product offered under it more carefully, the first impression that he/she gains must be decisive. This is especially true for mass-consumption goods offered in self-service stores.

Furthermore, unsophisticated, poorly educated consumers and also children are more liable to be confused. The purchaser of a sophisticated and costly machine, car or aircraft will no doubt be more attentive than the consumer in the self-service store. In those fields, therefore, very similar trademarks do coexist, which would probably be easily confused if applied to mass-consumption goods.

Another interesting example of how the category of goods can influence the testing of confusing similarity is to be found in the field of pharmaceuticals. Prescription drugs are normally sold to the consumer (on prescription by doctors) by educated pharmacists, who are less likely to be misled by relatively similar brand names used for medicines for different indications, so the testing of similarity can be more generous. For drugs sold over the counter, the contrary is true. In view of the potentially serious consequences for the uneducated consumer if he/she buys a wrong product, the testing of similarity must be particularly strict.

The second important point when testing the similarity of trademarks is that they should be compared as a whole, and that more weight should be given to common elements which may lead to confusion, while differences overlooked by the average consumer should not be emphasized. Notwithstanding this basic rule of comparing trademarks as a whole and not dividing them into parts, the structure of the signs is important. Common prefixes are normally more important than common suffixes; if two signs are very similar or identical at the beginning, they are more likely to be confused than if the similarity is in their endings. Long words with common or similar beginnings are more likely to be confused than short words with different initial letters.

The third important point is that highly distinctive marks (coined or arbitrarily used marks) are more likely to be confused than marks with associative meanings in relation to the goods or services for which they are registered.

The same is true if a mark contains a highly distinctive part (part of the word mark or one of several words forming the mark), and that highly distinctive element is exactly or almost exactly duplicated by the infringing mark. If, however, the common element of the two signs is descriptive, the consumer's attention tends to focus on the rest of the mark.

When trademarks with a common element are compared, it also has to be established whether there are other trademarks on the register and used by different owners that have the same common element. If so the consumer will have become accustomed to the use of this element by different proprietors, and will no longer pay special attention to it as a distinctive element of the mark.

The situation is different, however, if all marks having such a common element (normally a prefix or suffix) are registered and used by the same proprietor (or with his/her consent). This is the special case of the series mark, where the consumers may have become accustomed to associate the series with a common source, and will tend to make the same assumption about any new trademark containing the same element. However, the mere fact of somebody using a series of trademarks that have a common element is not, as such, sufficient to exclude the use of the same element by a competitor as a component of a mark which on the whole is very different. The use of such a common element can only constitute infringement if consumers really have come to recognize the common element of the series of marks used by the registered owner as indicating the source of the goods or services offered by him under the different marks containing that element.

The fourth important point is that confusion can arise from similarity in the writing, the pronunciation and in the meaning of the sign, and that similarity in one of those areas is sufficient for infringement if it misleads the public.

With regard to similarity in writing, the graphic presentation of the trademark plays an important part. Similarity in pronunciation is important because trademarks that are written differently may be pronounced in the same way, and pronunciation counts in oral communication: even if similarity in writing is avoided by the use of very different graphic presentations, this does not make any difference when the two trademarks are compared orally.

Similarity in meaning may lead to confusion if the same idea is conveyed by both trademarks (DREAMLAND and SLUMBERLAND for mattresses). Conversely, a totally different meaning can preclude confusion between two marks that would normally be regarded as confusingly similar.

Independently of the above rules, some special aspects have to be taken into account for figurative marks (devices).

For purely fanciful marks the graphical impression conveyed by the two marks is decisive.

For composite marks the similarity of the word part is normally sufficient, as similarity in pronunciation constitutes trademark infringement. Similarity in the figurative part can only lead to confusion if that figurative part is a distinctive element of the mark. Furthermore, in the case of composite marks any similarity in the word parts of the two marks is likely to be emphasized if the figurative parts of the marks are also similar. Even though the words might not be confused in writing or pronunciation, the marks as a whole can be confusingly similar in view of the similarity of their figurative elements.

A special case is the device that can be named by a word. A star device will normally be designated by the word "star," and will therefore be confusingly similar to a word mark STAR. Also lion or tiger devices would be confusingly similar to the word marks LION and TIGER. The situation is different when two device marks are compared which both feature an animal. Case law generally hesitates to grant a monopoly on an animal device as such. Consequently, two such devices, for instance, two tiger or lion or cow devices (there are numerous cow devices registered for milk products) must be sufficiently similar for there to be confusion. So should the use of the corresponding word as a trademark nevertheless be prohibited, and should the owner of a word mark TIGER really be able to object to all possible graphic presentations of a tiger in a device mark? To avoid any possible problem of restricted protection, the owner of a device mark should also secure trademark protection for the name of the animal shown in the device.

[D] Refusal of Registration

Before issuing a total or partial refusal of the application, the office should give the applicant an opportunity to make observations.

The decision refusing an application either partly or totally must be open to appeal. Depending on the legal system of the country, the appeal may be lodged with the registrar, with an administrative appeal board or with the court.

[E] Date of Registration

If the application leads to registration, the office issues a certificate to the owner. The owner's exclusive right exists from the date of registration. However, the priority of the right should date back to the date of filing for registration. While it is true that the application is not normally a sufficient basis for bringing an infringement action against a later right, it must be a valid basis for an opposition procedure. And, even more importantly, the date of the application for registration will be decisive in a later court case. The time that passes before an application leads to registration varies a great deal, and in certain cases can be very long. A later application can for various reasons lead to registration sooner (for instance, where the earlier application was refused by the examiner and finally granted on appeal). Clearly, the owner of the earlier application must have the prior right in relation to the owner of a later application.

Furthermore, the applicant can claim the priority of his/her national registration under Article 4 of the Paris Convention if the application in the foreign country is made within six months of the filing date of the first application. The right of priority means that, on the basis of a regular first application filed *in one* of the Contracting States, the applicant may, within a certain period of time (six months), apply for protection *in any of the other* Contracting States. The subsequent application will be regarded as if it has been filed on the same day as the first application. In other words, it will have priority (hence the expression "right of priority") over applications filed by others during the said period of time for the same mark. Moreover, the subsequent application, being based on the first application, will not be affected by any event that takes place in the interval, such as the sale of articles bearing a mark. One of the great practical advantages of this provision is that applicants seeking trademark protection in several countries are not required to present all of their applications at the same time but have six months to decide in which countries they wish to seek protection, and to organize with due care the steps necessary for securing protection.

[F] Duration and Renewal

The validity of trademarks, subject to renewals, has no time limits. For administrative reasons, a time limit is generally provided for in trademark laws (the TRIPS Agreement, for example, set a term of no less than seven years—Article 18), but it is possible to renew registrations indefinitely when the time limit expires.

One of the reasons for imposing such time limits is that the office can charge a fee for renewal, and this is a welcome source of revenue. Furthermore, the registration of trademarks without a time limit would lead to an undesirable amount of trademark registrations that are no longer of any interest to their owners. Even if unused marks may be removed from the register, such a procedure would be costly and time-consuming for the interested party, and not always successful.

Consequently, the requirement of renewal and the payment of a renewal fee is a welcome opportunity for a trademark owner to consider whether it is still worth having his/her registration renewed, as the trademark may have been superseded, or may even be no longer in use. For this reason, the renewal fee should be not too low, indeed probably even higher than the original registration fee. Excessive fees should also be avoided, however. In any case, renewals should be made simply on payment of the fee, without any new examination of the mark for absolute or relative grounds for refusal. Of course, it should be possible for the owner to make a voluntary restriction of the list of goods or services of the original registration, when the mark is no longer used for some goods or services. Such restriction can save fees.

[G] Publication and Access to the Register

It is important for owners of prior rights and the public that all relevant data contained in the register, concerning applications, registrations, renewals and changes of name, address and ownership, should be published in an official gazette. This enables owners of prior rights to take the necessary steps, including opposition (if provided for) or an action for cancellation. The publication of applications and registrations should contain all the important data, such as the name and address of the applicant, a representation of the mark, the goods or services grouped according to the classification system, the colors claimed (where appropriate), an indication of the type of mark, and where the priority is claimed (Paris Convention, Article 4), a statement to that effect.

The register of marks should, moreover, be accessible to the public. To ensure that owners of prior rights are properly informed it is indispensable that the register contain up-to-date information, namely all recorded data not only on registrations, but also on the contents of pending applications, regardless of the medium on which the data are stored.

[H] Removal of the Trademark from the Register

The cancellation of a trademark registration is a serious matter for its owner, as it leads to a loss of his/her rights under the registration. Nevertheless, there are a number of grounds on which a trademark can be removed from the register.

[1] Removal for Failure to Renew

It has been shown that, for administrative reasons, a trademark is registered for a certain period of time only. When that period expires, the trademark can be renewed and a renewal fee has to be paid. If the owner fails to renew his/her trademark registration and more specifically fails to pay the renewal fee, this leads to the removal of the trademark from the register. Registries generally allow a period of grace for payment of the renewal fee (usually with a surcharge).

If the law permits renewal of the trademark registration for just some of the registered goods or services (to be encouraged as a means of removing "dead wood" from the register), this leads to a partial cancellation of the trademark registration for all the goods or services in respect of which it is not renewed.

[2] Removal at the Request of the Registered Owner

The registered owner can him/herself, at any time, renounce his/her registration for either all or some of the goods or services for which the mark is registered. At the request of the registered owner, therefore, the authorities will in principle remove the mark from the register either wholly or in part.

[3] Removal for Failure to Use

If the owner of a trademark fails to use his/her mark within the prescribed period, provided for in the law, any interested party can, in principle, ask for its cancellation. If the owner cannot justify the non-use, removal of the registration is ordered by the court. If the owner can prove use or justify the non-use, but only for some of the registered goods or services, the court orders partial cancellation. Partial cancellation extends either to all registered goods or services for which use cannot be proved or at least to all those not similar to the goods or services that the registered owner has used.

This does not mean that the registered owner's rights would be strictly limited to the goods or services used, or even to a single product on which his/her trademark has been used. Even if his/her registration is cancelled for all but the one product for which he/she can prove use, he/she can still defend his/her exclusive right to the registered trademark against the registration and use of an identical or confusingly similar trademark by a competitor for all goods or services that are identical or similar to the product for which his/her trademark is registered and used.

[4] *Invalidation*

If a trademark consists of a sign that should not have been registered, it can be invalidated by the court at the request of any interested party. Sometimes trademark laws also provide an ex officio procedure for that purpose. As a consequence of the invalidation, the trademark is removed from the register.

If the grounds for invalidity exist only with respect to some of the registered goods or services, the registration is removed for those goods or services only.

Normally, removal from the register is ordered only if the grounds for invalidity already existed when the trademark was registered. Moreover, even if the trademark should not have been registered owing to lack of distinctiveness, its invalidation is excluded if in the meantime it has become distinctive by use.

Such acquired distinctiveness cannot, however, prevent the removal from the register of trademarks that consist of generic or deceptive terms. And yet there can be exceptional cases in which the deceptive meaning that would have prevented trademark registration at the outset has been lost in the meantime.

[I] Rights Arising from the Trademark Registration

The registered owner has the exclusive right to prevent others from the use of an identical or similar trademark without his/her consent, for identical or similar goods or services, where such use would result in a likelihood of confusion. This is the language that, with some minor deviations, is found in Article 16.1 of the TRIPS Agreement. The meaning of this language is unequivocal, as already noted: trademark owners do not receive from the trademark office a right to use the signs they register, but rather a right to exclude others. The reason is that the right to use trademarks or any other assets (intangible or tangible) results from the statutes that regulate the economy. This is found in Article 20 of the TRIPS Agreement, which only requires from WTO Members that the encumbrances be somehow justified. Justifications based on public health spring immediately to mind, such as those that a number of countries have imposed on trademarks designating tobacco products.

It follows from the mark's basic function of distinguishing the goods or services of its owner from those of others that he/she must be able to object to the use of confusingly similar marks in order to prevent consumers and the public in general from being misled. This is the essence of the exclusive right afforded to the trademark owner by registration. He must be able to object to any use of his/her trademark by a third party for goods or services for which it is protected, to the affixing of the mark on such goods or services, to its use in relation to the goods or services and to the offering of the goods or services for sale under the mark, or the use of the mark in advertising, business papers or any other kind of document. Furthermore, since consumers are to be protected against confusion, protection generally extends to the use of similar trademarks for similar goods or services, if such use is likely to confuse the consumer.

It must be underlined, however, that the trademark owner cannot unconditionally object to the use of his/her trademark or a similar mark for the goods or services for which his/her trademark is registered or for identical or similar goods or services. Depending on the procedural system in the country, the trademark owner may be able to rely on those formal rights for goods or services for which the mark is registered but not used, but he/she could face a counterattack leading to partial cancellation of his/her trademark for non-use.

The exclusive rights of the trademark owner can be exercised by means of an infringement action. The trademark is infringed if, owing to the use of an identical or similar sign for identical or similar goods or services, there is a risk or a likelihood of the public being misled. The test to be applied in an infringement action is narrower than in an administrative procedure (examination ex officio, opposition procedure). The test is not a hypothetical one, but has to deal with the reality of infringement in the marketplace. Consequently, the court has to consider how the infringer is actually using the trademark, and the extent of use of the infringed mark may also be significant.

Many laws not only provide for an infringement action, but also offer an administrative opposition procedure against an application for the registration of a confusingly similar trademark. In that case, the test is much broader, because allowance has to be made for the risk of confusion that could arise from any use that the applicant might possibly make of his/her trademark if it were registered. The test is in fact the same as is applied by the office in its examination for prior third-party rights. However, there is more justification for applying such a broad test in opposition procedures, since it is the owner of the right who opposes the application and therefore demonstrates his/her interest in defending his/her right against the registration of a confusingly similar trademark.

Together with the question whether a trademark is distinctive, the question whether a trademark is confusingly similar to an earlier right is one of the cornerstones of practical trademark protection.

[1] Similarity of Goods or Services

Trademarks are registered for goods or services in certain classes which have been established for purely administrative purposes. The classification of goods and services cannot therefore be decisive for the question of similarity. Sometimes totally different goods or services are listed in the same class (for instance, computers, eyeglasses, fire extinguishers and telephones in class 9), while similar goods or services can clearly be listed in different classes (adhesives may fall into classes 1, 3, 5 and 16).

The test of whether goods or services are similar is based on the assumption that identical marks are used. Even identical marks are unlikely to create confusion as to the origin of the goods or services if the goods or services are very different. As a general rule goods or services are similar if, when offered for sale under an identical mark, the consuming public would be likely to believe that they came from the same source. All the circumstances of the case must be taken into account, including the nature of the goods or services, the purpose for which they are used and the trade channels through which they are marketed, but especially the usual origin of the goods or services, and the usual point of sale.

As far as the latter criterion is concerned, the problem is that in modern supermarkets, drugstores and department stores, goods of all kinds are sold together, so the usual point of sale is less relevant to whether consumers regard goods as coming from the same source as their usual origin. Still, the criterion does remain valid in many cases where goods are exclusively or at least commonly sold in specialty shops. In such cases, consumers may tend to believe the origin of goods to be the same if they are both sold in the same specialty shops, and may tend to deny that sameness of origin if they are not usually sold in the same shops.

If different goods are all manufactured by the same type of enterprise, or if consumers expect them to be typically manufactured by the same enterprise, they will generally be regarded as having a common origin.

A further aspect is the nature and composition of goods. If they are largely made of the same substance, they will generally be held to be similar, even if they are used for different purposes. Raw materials and finished goods manufactured out of the raw materials are not normally similar, however, since they are generally not marketed by the same enterprise.

The paragraphs above apply, *mutatis mutandis*, to services, as frequently they are provided as bundles—for example, the use of computer applications by subscription associated with technical assistance, and services of inspection and maintenance. Consumers tend to believe that the whole bundle come from a single source.

Depending on the circumstances of the specific case, one or more of the aspects mentioned may determine the decision on whether goods or services are similar or not. Generally, however, they will all have to be taken into account.

[2] Similarity of Trademarks

Trademarks can be more or less similar to each other. The test, of course, is whether they are confusingly similar. A trademark is confusingly similar to a prior mark if it is used for similar goods or services and so closely resembles the prior mark that there is a likelihood of consumers being misled as to the origin of the goods or services. If the consumer is confused, the distinguishing role of the trademark is not functioning, and the consumer may fail to buy the product that he/she wants. This is bad for the consumer, but also for the trademark owner who loses the sale.

No intention to confuse on the part of the infringer is necessary, nor is actual confusion. The likelihood of confusion is the test. That is the only way for the system to function.

Of course, phrases such as "likelihood of confusion of the consumer" (or "of the public") have to be interpreted. "The consumer" does not exist, and the public as such cannot be confused. Confusion arises, or is likely to arise, always in a section of the public. It has to be determined in the specific case what the relevant part of the public is that has to be considered, in other words who are actually addressed or reached by the trademark.

[3] *Influence of Use and Non-use*

Confusion in the marketplace can only arise from actual use on similar goods or services. To prevent confusion, however, it is still necessary that the trademark protection system allow the trademark owner or interested third parties to object to an application for registration of a trademark which is based on mere intention to use the mark.

For the same preventive purpose, many trademark laws allow the owner of a registered trademark to object in opposition procedures to the filing, and in infringement actions to the use, of similar marks for goods or services identical or even similar to all goods or services covered by the existing registration, regardless of the use of the latter. The defendant who is aware of the total or partial non-use may counterattack by introducing an invalidation action seeking partial or total cancellation of the existing trademark registration for non-use.

More modern conceptions allow the trademark owner, after the prescribed period has expired, to object by opposition or court action to an application for registration, or to the use, of an identical or similar mark for goods or services identical or similar only to those on which the owner is actually using his/hers. If the owner is not using his/her trademark, the opposition is refused, and if he/she is using it on one or several of the goods or services for which it is registered, only those on which it is used are taken into consideration for the test of confusing similarity. The burden of proof of use in an opposition procedure is on the owner of the right.

Many laws also allow the defendant in trademark infringement actions to claim non-use of the trademark on which the action is based, and the owner can then only succeed in his/her infringement action if he/she can prove use of his/her mark.

If the infringed trademark is being used, the extent of the use can influence the test of confusing similarity. Intensive use increases the distinctiveness of the mark, and confusion with well-known marks is more likely even if the goods or services on which the infringing mark is used are less similar or if the similarity of the marks is less apparent.

[4] *Protection Beyond the Scope of Confusing Similarity*

Well-known or famous marks, which are highly reputed, are in some countries given protection that goes beyond the scope of similarity of the goods or services. Such far-reaching protection should only be given if the use of the same mark or a nearly identical mark for other, dissimilar goods or services would be prejudicial to its distinctiveness or its reputation or otherwise is likely to cause damage and the consumer is led to perceive a connection between those products and the owner of the well-known mark. This extended protection does not necessarily cover all possible goods or services. It could well be that the use of a mark identical to the well-known mark would do unjustified harm in relation to a certain category of goods or services, whereas the same use on totally dissimilar goods or services might not be against the interests of the registered owner of the well-known mark. The decision has to be determined by all the circumstances of the specific case, including the extent of reputation of the mark, the type of goods or services for which it is used by the infringer, the manner in which he/she presents his/her goods or services, and so on. In this regard, the Joint Recommendation Concerning Provisions on the Protection of Well-Known Mark, which establishes different factors to determine whether a mark is considered well known in a particular jurisdiction.

At present, the practice in most countries is to grant protection that goes beyond the scope of similarity of goods or services only in exceptional cases of famous or highly reputed marks. Yet reputation is not sufficient on its own, of course; broader protection is justified only where the use of a sign without due cause would take unfair advantage of, or be detrimental to, the distinctive character or the reputation of the trademark. The language of Article 16.3 in this context should be taken into consideration.

[J] Restriction of the Exclusive Right in the Public Interest

In the same way as the owner's right to use his/her trademark can be restricted by other rights, his/her right to prevent third parties from using his/her mark can be restricted by the legitimate interests of others. Article 17 of the TRIPS Agreement provides that "Members may provide limited exceptions to the rights conferred by a trademark, such as fair use of descriptive terms, provided that such exceptions take account of the legitimate interests of the owner of the trademark and of third parties."

The trademark owner also cannot prevent third parties who are not his/her competitors from referring to his/her trademark by acts such as the listing of the mark in a compendium of trademarks or in dictionaries, or to use it in newspaper articles or in books or other publications.

In this sense, it is relevant to note the language of Article 17 of the TRIPS Agreement, which provides for exceptions to rights conferred to trademark owners. As an example of exceptional use by third parties, the Agreement mentions the fair use of descriptive terms—in the sense not of using descriptive trademarks, because they are not susceptible of registration, but of using distinctive trademarks as a way of describing certain activities, such as those mentioned in the previous paragraph. Exceptions, however, are exceptional—they must take account of the legitimate interests of the owner (such as those mentioned in the next paragraph) and of third parties.

Since the trademark owner has a justified interest in preventing his/her mark from becoming generic, he/she can, in certain cases, demand that it be properly used. Some legislations recognize a right of the trademark owner to have his/her trademark identified as such in dictionaries; if a dictionary lists a trademark without stating that it is one, its owner has the right to ask for a correction in the next edition of the dictionary.

[K] Remedies for Trademark Infringement

A successful infringement action leads to prohibition of the use of the confusingly similar mark. If the infringing mark is registered, cancellation of the registration is ordered.

The trademark owner can also, in principle, ask for compensation for damages. Damages are difficult to prove in trademark infringement cases, however, so this remedy is not very important in practice.

The situation is of course different in cases of counterfeiting, as it will be discussed below, in the context of enforcement of IPRs.

CHAPTER 9

Industrial Designs

§9.01 INTRODUCTION

In a lay or general sense, industrial designs relate to the creative activity of achieving an aesthetic or ornamental appearance for mass-produced items that satisfies both the need to appeal to potential consumers and the need to perform efficiently its intended function. In a legal sense, an industrial design constitutes the ornamental or aesthetic aspect of an article. An industrial design may consist of three-dimensional features, such as the shape of an article, or two-dimensional features, such as patterns, lines or color. Although they may also concern handicraft items, industrial designs generally relate to articles of manufacture that can be produced by industrial means on a large scale, such as packages, containers, furnishing and household goods, lighting equipment, jewelry, electronic devices and textiles. Industrial designs may also be relevant to ornamentation, graphic symbols, graphical user interfaces (GUI), icons and logos.

Appearance is one of the elements that influence the decision of consumers to prefer one product over another, particularly in areas where a range of products performing the same function is available in the market. In these latter situations, if the technical performance of the various products offered by different manufacturers is relatively equal, appearance, along with, of course, cost, will determine the consumer's choice.

Protecting industrial designs amounts to protect one of the elements by which manufacturers achieve market success. In so doing, by rewarding the designer for his/her efforts in creating the industrial design, protection serves as an incentive to the investment of time and resources in fostering the design element of production.

§9.02 EVOLUTION OF DESIGN PROTECTION

The first statutes dealing with the protection of industrial designs appeared in the sixteenth and seventeenth centuries, and were associated with an industry that at that time acquired enormous importance in Flandres and France: the industry of tapestry. The first norms that provided protection of designs against copying was introduced in the by-laws of the guild of tapestry weavers of Brussels, in 1525. One of the provisions of the by-laws prohibited workers and apprentices from copying the designs that masters gave them to weave into the fabrics; moreover, even when the carpets were made on request—as most of them were, because of their very high price—the purchaser was not allowed to keep a blueprint or copy of the figurative ornaments woven into the carpets; these had to remain with the master who designed them. More than one century later, in 1664, France introduced the exclusive right to industrial designs applied to tapestry. The reason was the establishment of a tapestry factory in Beauvais. In 1730 similar rules were included in the regulations pertaining to the tapestry of Aubusson.

However, these were isolated initiatives and were specifically connected with one industry. The emergence of protection for industrial designs in a more general way had to wait for the Industrial Revolution, with the growth of industrialization and methods of mass production. In the UK, the first law giving protection to industrial designs was the Designing and Printing of Linens, Cotton, Calicoes and Muslins Act of 1787, which gave protection for a period of two months to "every person who shall invent, design and print, or cause to be invented, designed and printed, and become the Proprietor of any new and original pattern or patterns for printing Linens, Cottons, Calicoes or Muslins." The contribution and importance of design in the growing textile industries was thereby recognized.

The small area of industry covered by this first law in the UK was extended soon after, in 1798, by the Sculpture Copyright Act, which gave protection to new models, copies or casts of "human and animal figures." The importance of the pottery and porcelain industries, and the integral role of design in these industries, was further recognized by the extension of the protection under this Act in 1840 to new models, copies or casts of "any subject being matter of invention in sculpture."

Growing recognition of the expansion of industrialization and of the possible application of methods of mass production to most areas of manufacture lead to the gradual extension of design protection to other fields of endeavor up until the consolidation achieved in the Designs Act of 1842, which extended protection to "any new and original design whether such design be applicable to the ornamenting of any article of manufacture, or of any substance, artificial or natural, or partly artificial and partly natural, and that whether such design be so applicable for the pattern, or for the shape or configuration, or for the ornament thereof, or for any two or more of such purposes and by whatever means such design may be so applicable, whether by printing, or by painting, or by embroidery, or by weaving, or by sewing, or by modeling, or by casting, or by embossing, or by engraving, or by staining, or by any other means whatsoever, manual, mechanical, or chemical, separate or combined." Design was thereby recognized as a fundamental element of all production and manufacture.

A somewhat similar evolution of design protection took place in France. The Law on Literary and Artistic Property of 1793 was applied in certain cases to the protection of designs. The growth of the textile industries, in particular, soon led to the enactment in 1806 of a special law dealing with industrial designs. The Law of March 18, 1806, established a special council (Conciliation Board or *Conseil de Prud'hommes)* in Lyon responsible for receiving deposits of designs and for regulating disputes between manufacturers concerning designs. While initially destined for industries in Lyon, particularly those manufacturing silk, the system of deposit and regulation by special council was extended to other cities and, through judicial interpretation, to two- and three-dimensional designs in all areas of industrial activity.

§9.03 THE LEGAL PROTECTION OF INDUSTRIAL DESIGNS

The formulation of a legal system for the protection of industrial designs, like the provision of legal protection for all forms of IP, requires the establishment of a balance of interests. On the one hand, there is the need to provide efficient and effective protection, in order that the law may fulfill its function of promoting the design element in production. On the other hand, there is the need to ensure that the law does not unnecessarily extend protection beyond what is necessary to create the required incentive for design activity, so that the least number of impediments are introduced to the free use of available designs. The establishment of this balance requires careful consideration of a number of matters, of which the most important are:

(1) the definition of the subject matter of protection;
(2) the rights which are granted to the owner of the subject matter;
(3) the duration of such rights;
(4) the entitlement to such rights; and
(5) the method of acquisition of such rights.

[A] Definition of Subject Matter of Protection

[1] Design as Appearance of an Article

As an industrial design is the ornamental or aesthetic aspect of an article, the subject matter of protection is not the articles or products, but rather the design which is applied to or embodied in such articles or products.

The emphasis is on the appearance of the article. Protection of an industrial design does not apply to articles or products in such a way as to grant the owner of the design exclusive rights over the commercial exploitation of those articles or products. Rather, the protection only applies to such articles or products as they embody or reproduce the industrial design. Protection does not, therefore, prevent other manufacturers from making, selling or importing similar articles fulfilling the same utilitarian function, provided that such articles do not embody or reproduce the protected industrial design or substantially a copy of it.

[2] Application to or Embodiment in an Article

One of the basic purposes of industrial design protection is the stimulation of the design element of *production*. Although some industrial designs also concern handicraft items, a feature of some industrial design laws is that a design can be protected only if it concerns articles produced by industrial means on a large scale.

Some industrial design laws therefore require that a design must be applied to utilitarian articles or articles of manufacture in order to be protected.

[3] Judgment of the Design by Its Appearance

It is usually a condition of the protection of industrial designs that the design that is applied to or embodied in an article must have an appearance which is capable of visual judgment. The purpose of this requirement is to emphasize that industrial design protection is concerned solely with *appearance* or *aspect* of articles, and not with their function.

[4] Exclusion of Designs Dictated by Technical or Functional Considerations

The concern of industrial design protection with appearance only is also apparent from the requirement, commonly found in industrial design laws, that designs which are dictated solely by the function which the article is to perform shall be excluded from protection. In this respect, the TRIPS Agreement allows members of the WTO to provide that the protection shall not extend to designs dictated essentially by technical or functional considerations (Article 25.1 of the TRIPS Agreement).

A fundamental purpose is served by the exclusion from protection of designs dictated solely by the function which the article is to perform. Many articles to which designs are applied are produced by a large number of different manufacturers. Belts, shoes, screws and piston rings, for example, may be produced by hundreds of different manufacturers, and all articles within each class are intended to perform the same function. If a design for one such article, for example, screws, is dictated purely by the function which the screw is intended to perform, protection for that design would have the effect of excluding all other manufacturers from producing items intended to perform the same function. Technical or functional features of a product are the proper province of patent law, and not industrial design law, which is concerned only with appearance.

The assessment of the exclusion varies from country to country. In some jurisdictions, the theory of the multiplicity of forms applies: if the given function or technical effect can be achieved by another design, the design in question is not essentially dictated by technical or functional considerations and can therefore be protected. Other theories based on the degree of freedom of the creator, the aim of the creator or the lack of aesthetic considerations apply throughout the world.

[B] Novelty or Originality Requirement

In order to be protected, it is required that industrial designs be independently created and new or original (Article 25.1 of the TRIPS Agreement). In some countries or regions, the industrial design must be new to be protectable. In others, it must be original. In certain jurisdictions, the industrial design is required to be both new and original.

According to Article 25.1 of the TRIPS Agreement, members of the WTO may provide that designs are not new or original if they do not significantly differ from known designs or combinations of known design features. The definition and assessment of the novelty or originality requirement vary from country to country.

In general, an industrial design is considered to be new if it has not previously been disclosed to the public and it may be considered original if it significantly differs from known designs or combinations of known design features. The difficulty in evaluating originality lies in the measure of the significance in the difference between new and old designs. Originality is a concept taken from copyright, and usually means that the work may be attributed to a specific author, or origin. But if this requirement, put in these terms, would be adequate to ensure the independence of creation, it would not be enough to ensure differentiation. That is why some national laws require "significance" as a qualifier of the type of difference. The general idea is that "significant difference" does not mean a radical or absolute difference, otherwise only entirely new and revolutionary designs could be protected. "Significant difference," in the context of industrial designs, means that the difference is enough for the average consumer—not for the person with technical skills in the art—to be able to acknowledge a different design as compared to those that were available on the market. It should be noted, for the sake of precision, that in some legislations (as is the case of the European Union (EU) Regulation) the criterion is not the "average consumer" but the informed "user." In this way, industrial design protection is available for those new products that represent an acknowledgeable esthetical or ornamental evolution from previous products, rather than breakthroughs. Examples of products that fall under the category of evolutionary—and no less deserving protection—designs are collections of fashion apparel (which evolve at each new season) and car facelifts (which change the external appearance in several details of previous car models every year or two years, by refreshing their appearance but without breaking with the general visual impression they cause on consumers). In this context one should not forget that the TRIPS Agreement Section that deals with industrial designs was exactly motivated by the concerns of the fashion industry, worried with the administrative and legal difficulties in protecting designs that are mostly of an evolutionary and fleeting nature.

The nature of the novelty may differ among the industrial design laws of various countries. In some jurisdictions, the novelty required is absolute or universal, meaning that the design for which protection is sought must be new as against all other designs disclosed in all other parts of the world at any previous time. In other jurisdictions, a qualified standard of novelty is sometimes provided for. In this latter situation, the qualification may relate to time, meaning that novelty is judged by reference to designs disclosed within a limited preceding period of time. It may relate to territory, meaning that novelty is judged by reference to all designs disclosed within the relevant jurisdiction, as opposed to anywhere in the world.

§9.04 RIGHTS IN INDUSTRIAL DESIGNS

The rights which are accorded to the owner of a protected industrial design again emphasize the essential purpose of design law in promoting and protecting the design element of industrial production (*s*ee Article 26.1 of the TRIPS Agreement: "The owner of a *protected* industrial design shall have the right …"). Thus, whereas copyright accords to an author the right to prevent the copying of a work, industrial design law accords to the owner the exclusive right to prevent the unauthorized exploitation of the design in industrial articles.

[A] Entitlement to Rights

The right to legal protection in respect of an industrial design belongs to the creator (or author) of the industrial design. Two questions concerning the operation of this principle arise and are often the subject of particular legislative provisions.

First, there is the question of the entitlement to legal protection in respect of an industrial design that has been created by an employee, or by a contractor pursuant to a commission. In these situations, the law usually provides that the entitlement to legal protection of the design shall belong the employer, or to the person who has commissioned the design. The basis for this rule is that the creation of the design falls within the duties which the employee is paid to perform, so that the employee should seek the reward for his/her creative activity in an appropriate level of remuneration, responsibility and other conditions of employment. Likewise, in the case of the contractor, the thing for which the contractor is being paid is the creation of the design for the use of the person commissioning the design.

Second, many contemporary designs are produced with the assistance of computers. The question arises whether it can be said that there is an author or creator who is entitled to legal protection in respect of designs generated with the assistance of a computer. One approach to this question is to treat the computer like any other tool which may be used by a designer to assist in the process of generating a design. On this basis, the person who is responsible for manipulating the computer's capacity to produce a design would be considered to be the creator of the design.

[B] Acquisition of Rights

[1] Filing of an Application for Registration of a Design or for the Grant of a Design Patent

The acquisition of industrial design rights generally requires the compliance with formalities and procedures. The protection is granted pursuant to the filing of an application for the registration of the industrial design or for the grant of a design patent. Industrial design registrations or design patents are usually granted by the IPO of the country or region where an application is filed.

Timing is very important. Taking into account the novelty and/or originality requirement for industrial designs in most legislations, it is in general crucial to file an application for registration or for the grant of a design patent of an industrial design before publicly disclosing it, so as to avoid destroying its novelty/originality. If the industrial design has already been disclosed to the public, it may no longer be considered as "new" or "original." Some countries, however, allow for a so-called grace period—which lasts usually six or twelve months—to file after disclosure of the industrial design. Such a period provides a safeguard for applicants who have disclosed their industrial design before filing an application. The TRIPS Agreement, having in mind the fashion industry, as said above, has language that addresses concerns with the issue of timing and opportunity, requiring that WTO Members adopt procedures that are not burdensome and costly. In this token, some laws provide for the possibility of multiple designs sharing common characteristics, to be filed in one single application. The laws of countries vary in this regard, admitting the multiple application of twenty, fifty or hundred designs in one filing.

IPOs may carry out an examination of the application. The scope of the examination varies from country to country. In some countries, the law provides for a formal examination only of the application, so as to ensure that it meets the formalities imposed by the relevant law. In that case, the IPO checks, for instance, whether the application contains indications allowing the identity of the applicant to be established and a representation of the industrial design concerned. In certain countries, IPOs carry out a substantive examination so as to determine whether the requirement of novelty or originality is satisfied by the industrial design for which protection is sought.

A system requiring only formal examination has the effect of shifting the burden of assessing novelty or originality to those interested persons in the market who may wish to use, or who may have used, the industrial design concerned or a substantially similar design. Any person interested in using such a design will have the opportunity either to oppose the registration or the grant of a design patent of the industrial design for which application has been made, if the relevant industrial design law provides for an opposition procedure, or of bringing proceedings for the cancellation of a registration or a design patent which it is alleged is invalid. Moreover, the system offers a solution to the problem of maintaining an adequate search system and skilled manpower to undertake a substantive examination of the novelty or originality of designs. Such a search system can very often be almost impossible to maintain, since, if absolute or universal novelty is required, it would imply including all designs publicly disclosed at any time in any part of the world.

The alternative system of examination provides for a search of past designs and an examination of the design for which registration is sought to ascertain whether it satisfies the required condition of novelty. It necessitates the maintenance of a search file and sufficient skilled manpower to undertake the substantive examination.

[2] Unregistered Industrial Design Rights

In some countries or regions, industrial designs may be protected without any formality. Industrial design laws applicable in these jurisdictions grant—without registration—a time- and scope-limited protection to so-called unregistered industrial designs. These rights are primarily aimed at protecting designs for short life cycle products such as in the fashion industry. The protection is limited in time (usually, a few years) and in scope, as it usually allows the owner only to prevent third parties not having his/her consent from copying his/her industrial design.

[3] Copyright

Depending on the particular national law and the kind of design, industrial designs may, in certain countries, also be protected by copyright. In principle, the enjoyment and the exercise of copyright are not subject to any formality (Article 5.2 of the Berne Convention for the Protection of Literary and Artistic Work). Therefore, no application for the acquisition of exclusive rights in the design is required. The TRIPS Agreement mentions this duality of approach: WTO Members may opt for an industrial property or for a copyright regime.

The relation between protection under copyright law and industrial design law varies from country to country.

In certain countries, full cumulative protection is allowed so that industrial designs may also enjoy copyright protection. Cumulative protection first means that the design is protected simultaneously and concurrently by both laws in the sense that the creator can invoke the protection of either or both laws. It also means that, if the creator has failed to obtain the protection of the industrial design law by failing to apply for its registration or for the grant of a design patent, he/she can claim the protection of copyright law, which is available without compliance with any formality, provided that the industrial design complies with the requirements of the copyright law in the concerned jurisdiction. Finally, it means that, after the expiration of the term of protection under industrial design law, the creator may still claim the protection of the copyright law.

In other countries, cumulative protection is allowed under specific conditions such as the requirement for the industrial design to have a high artistic character or to be conceptually separable from the article. Finally, in some jurisdictions, cumulative protection is not allowed, but the creator may choose that his/her industrial design be protected either by the industrial design law or by the copyright law.

The main differences between protection by copyright law and protection by industrial design law are the following:

(1) under industrial design laws, protection is lost unless the industrial design is applied for registration or for the grant of a design patent by the applicant before its public disclosure (at least) in the country or region where protection

is sought. In principle, copyright protection is not subject to any formality. No application is necessary;

(2) industrial design protection is granted for a limited period of time which amounts in principle to at least ten years. Copyright endures in most countries for the life of the author and fifty years after his/her death;

(3) under industrial design laws, there is infringement whether or not there has been deliberate copying, even though the infringer acted independently and without knowledge of the protected industrial design. Under copyright law, there is infringement only in the reproduction of the work in which copyright subsists.

[C] Content of the Right

The owner of a protected industrial design has the right to prevent third parties not having his/her consent from exploiting the industrial design. In principle, this encompasses the exclusive right to prevent third parties from making, selling or importing articles bearing or embodying a design which is a copy, or substantially a copy, of the protected design, when such acts are undertaken for commercial purposes (Article 26.1 of the TRIPS Agreement).

The owner's rights extend not only to the unauthorized exploitation of the protected industrial design itself, but also to the unauthorized exploitation of any substantial copy of such a design.

In parallel with patent rights, and with almost the same language, the TRIPS Agreement allows WTO Members to provide limited exceptions to rights conferred in industrial designs (Article 26.2).

[D] Duration of Rights

Industrial rights are granted for a limited period. The duration of protection of industrial design rights varies from country to country. However, the duration of protection of industrial designs shall amount to at least ten years (Article 26.3 of the TRIPS Agreement). Many jurisdictions provide longer periods of protection (fifteen or twenty-five years). In some jurisdictions, the total duration is divided into successive periods (e.g., successive five-year periods), allowing the owner of the industrial design rights to renew the registration.

§9.05 THE RIYADH DESIGN LAW TREATY

On November 22, 2024, WIPO Member States today approved the Riyadh Design Law Treaty, which will make it easier, faster and more affordable for designers the world over to protect their designs both at home and abroad, marking a major step forward in empowering designers and fostering international collaboration in design.

The new Treaty, which represents a breakthrough of negotiations that took more than twenty years, will make it significantly easier for designers, especially smaller scale designers and micro, SMEs, to register and protect their creations.

Today, the process for protecting designs varies from one country to another. In some countries, designs are filed as "registered designs." Registration systems may involve the examination of design applications by the IP office, involving procedures that vary from country to country. In other jurisdictions, designs are protected under patent law as "design patents," which are usually only granted after a thorough examination of the design application by the IP office. This lack of international consistency is standards of protection leads to legal insecurity and constitutes an obstacle to the international trade of design-based goods.

In addition, designers generally must follow the filing procedures set by the IP office of the country in which they are seeking protection. Because design rights are territorial and thus limited to the country or region in which protection was obtained, designers must go through the same process in each country or region where they wish to protect their designs—thus making it difficult, if not impossible, for small creation-based SMEs to overpass national boundaries.

The Riyadh Treaty will help make the framework for design protection procedures more predictable and make the procedures themselves less complex and more affordable. It will be easier for designers to file applications in several different jurisdictions.

These are the fundamental features of the Riyadh Treaty:

- It sets a maximum list of indications or elements that designers must submit with an application. Establishing a closed list of elements will help to create a predictable framework for design protection procedures: designers wishing to file an application will know exactly what indications or elements may be required.
- It allows applicants to choose how they represent the design in an application (drawings, photographs or, if admitted by the IP office, video).
- It allows applicants to include several designs in a single application, under certain conditions.
- It sets out requirements for the granting of a filing date. Keeping the list of filing date requirements for design applications to a minimum is crucial because, in the field of design, postponing the filing date can result in a definitive loss of rights.
- It provides for a grace period of twelve months following a first disclosure of the design, during which such disclosure will not affect its validity for registration.
- It allows applicants to keep their designs unpublished for at least six months after having secured a filing date.
- It provides relief measures and offer some flexibility to applicants to prevent them from losing their rights if they miss a deadline. Without such measures, missing a time limit generally results in a loss of rights. In the case of designs, that loss is irreparable.

- It simplifies the procedure for requesting the renewal of a design registration.
- It furthers the introduction of e-filing systems for designs and the electronic exchange of priority documents.

The Treaty foresees the availability of technical assistance to developing and least-developed countries for the implementation of the Treaty.

Moreover, the Riyadh Design Law Treaty expressly interfaces design protection with the protection of TK and TCEs. This is achieved through a provision under which contracting parties may require applicants to file information on TCEs and TK relevant to the eligibility for registration of the design.[32,33]

The Treaty requires the accession by fifteen contracting parties to enter into force.

32. Earlier in 2024, WIPO Member States agreed on a new WIPO Treaty on Intellectual Property, Genetic Resources and Associated Traditional Knowledge. This is the first WIPO Treaty to address the interface between IP, GRs and associated TK and applications for patents, and the first WIPO Treaty to include provisions specifically for Indigenous Peoples as well as local communities. *See infra* §35.05[A].
33. The opportunity of this provision is illustrated by two recent episodes: (i) one concerned the well-known fashion designer Tory Burch, who on her website offered sweaters for sale that were an imitation of those traditionally made by the local community of Póvoa do Varzim, Portugal; (ii) the other was the advertisement by ADIDAS of tennis shoes ornamented with a *molas* figurative pattern, originally developed by the community of the kunas, of Panama. *See Tory Burch removes sweater after being accused of stealing traditional Portuguese design*, available at evoke.ie/2021/03/31/style/ (accessed November 2024). For information on the original sweaters from Póvoa do Varzim, *see* www.cm-pvarzim.pt/. (accessed November 2024) *See also* Janel Martinez, on June 21, 2019, at www.adweek.com/ (accessed October 2024). Both fashion houses dropped their articles from the market, implicitly acknowledging traditional communities' rights in their traditional designs. The molas, actually, are protected under especial legislation in Panama, but, in the absence of an international agreement, it could not produce effects beyond national borders. Eventually, with the entry into force of the new Riyadh Treaty, other countries may feel inclined to follow Panama's pioneer example. Alternatively, the solution found in the Australian case *Milpurrurru v. Indofurn Pty Ltd* (1995) 30 IPR 209, cited above (*see* 11.05[A][2]), where the claims of copyright infringement and unfair trade practices were successful, could be followed. Nevertheless, copyright is time bound, whereas unfair trade practice claims depend on proof of competition and unfairness.

CHAPTER 10
Geographical Indications

§10.01 INTRODUCTION

"Champagne," "Cognac," "Roquefort," "Chianti," "Pilsen," "Porto," "Sheffield," "Havana," "Tequila," "Darjeeling"—some well-known examples for names which are associated throughout the world with products of a certain nature, quality and geographical origin. One common feature of all those names is their geographical connotation, that is to say, their function of designating existing places, towns, regions or countries.

Such GIs can acquire high reputation, and thus may be valuable commercial assets. For this very reason, they are often exposed to counterfeiting and their protection—national as well as international—is highly desirable.

[A] Can GIs Only Be Used for Agricultural Products?

Agricultural products typically have qualities that derive from their place of production and are influenced by specific local, geographical factors such as climate and soil. It is therefore not surprising that a majority of GIs throughout the world are applied to agricultural products, foodstuffs, wine and spirit drinks.

However, the use of GIs is not limited to agricultural products. A GI may also highlight specific qualities of a product that are due to human factors found in the product's place of origin, such as specific manufacturing skills and traditions. That is the case, for instance, for handicrafts, which are generally handmade using local natural resources and usually embedded in the traditions of local communities.

§10.02 DEVELOPING A GI: WHY?

Interest in GIs has thrived in recent years. The obligation, under the TRIPS Agreement, for Members of the WTO to protect GIs has, to a large extent, triggered this attention.

But beyond that, what creates the attraction? The short answer is that they are seen as useful tools in marketing strategies and public policies, for which there has been growing interest in the last two to three decades.

[A] GIs as Differentiation Tools in Marketing Strategies: From Mere Source Indicators to Brands

Consumers pay increasing attention to the geographical origin of products, and care about specific characteristics present in the products they buy. In some cases, the "place of origin" suggests to consumers that the product will have a particular quality or characteristic that they may value. Often, consumers are prepared to pay more for such products. This has favored the development of specific markets for products with certain characteristics linked to their place of origin.

Brand recognition is an essential aspect of marketing. GIs convey information about the origin-bound characteristics of a product. They therefore function as product differentiators on the market by enabling consumers to distinguish between products with geographical origin-based characteristics and others without those characteristics. GIs can thus be a key element in developing brands for quality-bound-to-origin products.

[B] GIs as a Factor of Rural Development

A number of studies indicate that, under appropriate conditions, GIs can contribute to development in rural areas. The entitlement to use a GI generally lies with regional producers, and the added value generated by the GI accrues therefore to all such producers.

Because GI products tend to generate a premium brand price, they contribute to local employment creation, which ultimately may help to prevent rural exodus. In addition, GI products often have important spin-off effects, for example in the areas of tourism and gastronomy.

GIs may bring value to a region not only in terms of jobs and higher income, but also by promoting the region as a whole. In this regard, GIs may contribute to the creation of a "regional brand."

A word of caution is, however, needed. The mere fact of developing a GI for a product does not guarantee automatic success or development for the region. For GIs to contribute to development, several conditions must be present in the region and in the way in which the specific GI scheme is designed.

[C] GIs as a Means to Preserve TK and TCEs

Products identified by a GI are often the result of traditional processes and knowledge carried forward by a community in a particular region from generation to generation.

Similarly, some products identified by a GI may embody characteristic elements of the traditional artistic heritage developed in a given region, known as "TCEs." This is particularly true for tangible products such as handicrafts, made using natural resources and having qualities derived from their geographical origin. In addition, certain TCEs—such as indigenous and traditional names, signs and symbols—may also be protected as GIs despite their having no direct geographical meaning.

GIs are compatible with the nature of TK and TCEs in that they provide protection that is potentially unlimited in time, as long as the qualitative link between the products and the place is maintained and the indication has not fallen into genericity. They work as a collective right, there is no provision for a right to license or assign and the product-quality-place link underlying the protection of a GI prohibits the transfer of the indication to producers outside the demarcated region.

While GIs do not directly protect the subject matter generally associated with TK or TCEs, which remains in the public domain under conventional IP systems and is open to misappropriation by third parties, they can indirectly contribute to their protection in several ways.

First, GI protection recognizes the cultural significance of TK and TCEs and can help preserve them for future generations. For example, in designing a GI scheme for a product, the production standards, also known as the "code of practice" or "regulations of use," may include a description of a traditional process or TK.

In addition, through the added value of a GI scheme, producers are less tempted to replace traditional processes by possibly less costly ones. In India, for example, cheap powerloom-produced sarees are sold as highly reputed "Banarsi" handloom sarees within and outside the Varanasi region (where authentic Banarsi sarees are produced). Powerloom imitations cost only one-tenth of the price of real handloom Banarsi sarees, thereby jeopardizing the business of local craftsmen and potentially causing the production of handloom sarees to become unsustainable, and the skills and knowledge involved in the technique to be lost.

GIs can provide protection for TK and TCEs against misleading and deceptive trading practices. They can also benefit indigenous communities by facilitating the commercial exploitation of TK and TCEs, and encouraging TK-based economic development. GIs provide indigenous communities with a means to differentiate their products and benefit from their commercialization, thereby improving their economic position.

§10.03 THE RATIONALE BEHIND THE PROTECTION OF GIs

GIs are more than just a name or a symbol. They reflect a reputation strongly linked to geographical areas of varying sizes, thus giving them an emotional component. A GI's reputation is a collective, intangible asset. If not protected, it could be used without restriction and its value diminished and eventually lost.

Use of GIs by unauthorized parties is detrimental to legitimate producers and to consumers. Such use deceives consumers and leads them to believe they are buying a genuine product with specific qualities and characteristics, whereas they get an imitation. Producers suffer damage because valuable business is taken away from them, and the established reputation of their products is affected. Producers may even be prevented from using the indication themselves, for instance, if it is registered as an individual trademark by a company.

Protecting a GI enables those who have the right to use the indication to take measures against others who use it without permission and benefit from its reputation free of charge ("free-riders"). Protecting a GI is also a way to forestall registration of the indication as a trademark by a third party and to limit the risk of the indication becoming a generic term.

[A] Deterring Free Riding

A GI's reputation is the result of efforts undertaken by producers in a given region. Producers who do not work according to the specifications for that GI, which are sometimes restrictive, or who are not located in the defined production region may be tempted to use the GI to free ride on its reputation. Often, such use is made in connection with lower-quality products.

It is important for several reasons that those who have the right to use a GI prevent its unauthorized use, not only to avoid losing business, but also, in the longer term, to ensure the GI is used only in relation to products that possess the qualities or characteristics to which it owes its reputation. Use of a GI for lower or different-quality products most likely results in tarnishing its reputation.

[B] Forestalling Registration of the GI as a Trademark by a Third Party

An unprotected GI may be registered as a trademark by an individual producer or company, for goods identical or similar to those identified by the GI. This is likely to occur at the international level for indications protected in one jurisdiction but not in others. For jurisdictions in which the GI is not protected, the indication may be considered a distinctive sign available for registration as a trademark. The first to file for registration would obtain the trademark, which might give them the right to exclude use of the indication by anyone else, including the producers who had historically used it in their country of origin.

[C] Limiting the Risk of the GI Becoming a Generic Term

Where a GI is no longer associated with a product characteristically linked to a geographical origin but used instead as the common name to designate the product, it is said to have become a generic term. In such a case, the indication can be used by anyone to designate a type of product rather than a product with a distinct geographical origin and specific geographical qualities or characteristics. It can no longer serve as a distinctive sign or be used in a product differentiation strategy. Protecting a GI and enforcing the right obtained over it contribute to reducing the risk of that indication becoming a generic term.

[D] What Does a Protected GI Enable You to Do? What Does It Not Enable You to Do?

Protection for a GI is usually obtained by acquiring a right over the sign that constitutes the indication. That right can be a *specific* right designed for GIs (a sui generis right), which may be called, for instance, a protected GI, a denomination of origin or an AO. The right acquired can also be a collective or a certification mark.

A GI right enables those who have the right to use the indication to prevent its use by a third party whose product does not conform to the applicable standards. For example, in the jurisdictions in which the Darjeeling GI is protected, producers of Darjeeling tea can exclude use of the term "Darjeeling" for tea not grown in the tea gardens of Darjeeling or not produced according to the standards set out in the code of practice for the Darjeeling GI. However, a protected GI does not enable the holder to prevent someone from making a product using the same techniques as those set out in the GI standards.

§10.04 PROTECTION OF GIS ON THE NATIONAL LEVEL

GIs are protected in different countries and regional systems through a wide variety of approaches—often by a combination of two or more approaches. Those approaches have been developed in accordance with different legal traditions and within a framework of certain historical and economic conditions.

There are three main modalities of protection for GIs: (a) so-called sui generis systems; (b) collective and certification marks; and (c) modalities focusing on business practices including administrative product approval schemes. These approaches involve differences with respect to important questions, such as the conditions for protection or the scope of protection. However, two of the modes of protection, namely sui generis systems and collective or certification mark systems, share some common features, such as the fact that they set up rights for collective use by those who comply with defined standards.

[A] Sui Generis Systems of Protection

In certain jurisdictions, GIs may be protected through a system that applies specifically and exclusively to them—a sui generis system of protection. Such systems establish a specific right, a sui generis right, over GIs, separate from a trademark right or any other IP right. A sui generis protection system exists in the EU with regard to GIs for wines and spirits, agricultural products and foodstuffs. Many other jurisdictions throughout the world, such as India, Switzerland, the Andean Community countries and the

African Intellectual Property Organization (OAPI, *Organisation Africaine de la Propriété Intellectuelle*), among others, also have sui generis systems of protection.

The terminology used to refer to sui generis rights over GIs is not uniform. Terms such as *appellations of origin, controlled appellations of origin, protected designations of origin, protected GIs* or simply *GIs*, are used in different legislation.

Generally, an application for registration of a sui generis right should contain a delimitation of the geographical area within which the product identified by the GI is produced; a description of the product's characteristics, quality or reputation; and the standards of production with which users of the right should conform. In certain jurisdictions, the link between the product's characteristics and the geographical area must be substantiated. All those elements are contained in a document, which is sometimes called "the product specification."

In addition, sui generis systems of protection usually require that verification and control schemes be put into place to ensure that users of the GI comply with the agreed standards of production.

A sui generis right protects at the very least against any use of the GI that would mislead consumers as to the true geographical origin of the product, or that constitutes an act of unfair competition. GIs identifying wines and spirits are further protected against any use by an ineligible or unauthorized person, even where such use does not result in consumers being misled or in an act of unfair competition. In some jurisdictions with a sui generis system, such "additional protection" is afforded to GIs that identify other types of products as well. Furthermore, some sui generis systems protect GIs against use in a translation, or against imitation or evocation.

[B] Collective Marks and Certification Marks

Some countries protect GIs under trademark law, more specifically through collective marks or certification marks. This is the case, for example, in Australia, Canada, China and the USA.

What is meant by a collective mark or certification mark (or, in some countries, guarantee mark) differs from country to country. However, a common feature of these types of marks is that they may be used by more than one person, as long as the users comply with the regulations of use or standards established by the holder. Those regulations or standards may require that the mark be used only in connection with goods that have a particular geographical origin or specific characteristics.

In some jurisdictions, the main difference between collective marks and certification marks is that the former may only be used by members of an association, while certification marks may be used by anyone who complies with the standards defined by the holder of the mark. The holder, which may be a private or a public entity, acts as a certifier verifying that the mark is used according to established standards. Generally, the holder of a certification mark does not itself have the right to use the mark.

Protection for GIs registered as collective or certification marks is provided for under general trademark law. In other words, protection is afforded against use in the course of trade by third parties without the owner's consent, of identical or similar signs for identical or similar goods, where such use would result in a likelihood of confusion.

[C] Laws Focusing on Business Practices

GIs may be protected through certain laws that focus on business practices, such as laws relating to the repression of unfair competition, consumer protection laws or laws on the labeling of products.

These laws do not create an individual industrial property right over the GI. However, they indirectly protect GIs insofar as they prohibit certain acts that may involve their unauthorized use.

§10.05 THE INTERNATIONAL LEGAL FRAMEWORK

[A] The Paris Convention for the Protection of Industrial Property (1883)

The Paris Convention was the first international multilateral treaty to include provisions relating to indications of geographical origin. Article 1(2) of the Convention recognizes "indications of source" and "appellations of origin" as subject matter for industrial property. The Paris Convention does not directly define either of these terms, although it contains language that allows one to infer the following definition of an indication of source: *"an indication referring to a country, or to a place situated therein as being the country or place of origin of a product."*

An *indication of source* provides information about the geographical origin of a product, but does not imply any special quality or characteristic of the product for which it is used. Examples of indications of source are the mention, on a product, of the name of a country, or indications such as "made in ...," "product of ... ." An indication of source can also be composed of symbols or iconic emblems associated with the area of geographical origin.

The Paris Convention stipulates that, in cases of use of false indications of source on goods, the goods in question are to be seized upon importation or, ultimately, to be subject to the actions and remedies available in the country of importation. It further sets forth the obligation of Member States to ensure appropriate legal remedies for repressing the use of false indications of source.

The Paris Convention also requires its members to ensure effective protection against unfair competition. For example, the use of an indication of source on a good such that it could mislead the public as to the true geographical origin of the good could be considered an act of unfair competition.

[B] The Madrid Agreement for the Repression of False or Deceptive Indications of Source on Goods (1891)

The Madrid Agreement for the Repression of False or Deceptive Indications of Source on Goods extends the protection afforded to false indications of source under the Paris Convention to deceptive indications of source as well. Deceptive indications are those which, although literally true, may be misleading. This would be the case where, for example, there are homonymous place names in two different countries, but only one place is known for the production of a particular good. If the name were used on goods from the similarly named place, the indication of source would be considered deceptive as the public would likely be led to believe that the good came from a different place.

[C] The TRIPS Agreement (1994)

The TRIPS Agreement, one of the WTO Agreements, is applicable to all WTO Members. It includes a section on the protection of GIs (Part II, section 3).

Section 3 of the TRIPS Agreement sets forth a definition of a GI and contains a general obligation for WTO Members to provide protection against misleading use of a GI and against use that constitutes an act of unfair competition. It also requires Members to refuse or invalidate registration of a trademark that contains or consists of a GI with respect to goods not originating in the territory indicated, if use of the indication on the trademark for such goods might mislead the public as to the true place of origin.

In addition to that general obligation, section 3 of the TRIPS Agreement requires WTO Members to provide protection against any use of GIs for wines and spirits and against registration as trademarks of those indications, even if such use or registration does not mislead the public as to the true origin of the goods.

Finally, the TRIPS Agreement contains exceptions to the obligation to provide protection for GIs. A first exception applies to GIs for wines and spirits only, for those WTO Members in which the indications have been used in a continuing and similar manner for a number of years. A second exception applies where a trademark has been acquired in good faith in the territory of a WTO Member before the date of application of the TRIPS Agreement in that WTO Member, or before the GI is protected in the country of origin. A third exception applies where the indication is considered by a WTO Member to be the customary term in common language (the common name) for the identified goods or services.

[D] The Lisbon System

The Lisbon Agreement for the Protection of Appellations of Origin and Their International Registration, adopted in 1958 and revised at Stockholm in 1967, provides for a relatively high level of protection for AOs and makes it possible to protect them in multiple countries, regardless of the nature of the goods to which they apply, through an international registration mechanism covering all its Contracting Parties.

The Geneva Act of the Lisbon Agreement on Appellations of Origin and Geographical Indications, adopted on May 20, 2015, updates and enhances the existing international registration system. It allows for the international registration of GIs alongside AOs, to better take into account national and regional systems for the protection of distinctive designations in respect of origin-based quality products. In addition, the Geneva Act accommodates the needs of countries that use the trademark system to protect GIs. The Geneva Act also allows certain IGOs to join, making the international system of protection more inclusive.

[E] The Madrid System

GIs can be protected in several countries as collective or certification marks through the Madrid Agreement Concerning the International Registration of Marks, concluded in 1891, and the Protocol relating to the Madrid Agreement, adopted in 1989. Both treaties constitute the Madrid system and are administered by WIPO.

For further information on the Madrid system please refer to Chapter 20.

§10.06 PROTECTION OF GIs ON THE INTERNATIONAL LEVEL THROUGH THE PROVISIONS OF BILATERAL AGREEMENTS

A further possibility of international protection of GIs is the conclusion of bilateral agreements between two states, typically those engaged in trade partnerships. Such agreements may be independent treaties or form part of a wider trade agreement. A number of countries have entered into such agreements. In general, such bilateral agreements consist of lists of GIs compiled by the Contracting Parties and an undertaking to protect the GIs of the respective Contracting Party. The agreement usually also specifies the kind of protection that is to be granted. In certain instances, they might encompass the prohibition of use of the other party's GIs or they could go beyond and provide for rules and principles of protection, along with mechanisms for enforcing such protection.

CHAPTER 11

Plant Varieties: The International Convention for the Protection of New Varieties of Plants (1991 Act)

§11.01 INTRODUCTION

[A] Why Do Farmers and Growers Need New Plant Varieties?

New varieties of plants with features such as improved yield, resistance to plant pests and diseases, salt and drought tolerance, or better adaptation to climatic stress are a key element in increasing productivity and product quality in agriculture, horticulture and forestry, whilst minimizing the pressure on the natural environment. Due to the continuous evolution of new pests and diseases as well as changes in climatic conditions and users' needs, there is a continuous demand by farmers/growers of new plant varieties and development by breeders of such new plant varieties.

The tremendous progress in agricultural productivity in various parts of the world is largely based on improved varieties, together with improved farming practices, and future food security depend on them.

Successful breeding requires great skill and knowledge. In addition, large-scale breeding calls for significant investment in land, specialized equipment (e.g., greenhouses, growth chambers and laboratories), and skilled, scientific manpower.

[B] Why Is PVP Necessary?

It takes a long time to develop a successful plant variety (ten to fifteen years in the case of many plant species). Yet not all new plant varieties are successful and, even where the varieties show significant improvements, changes in market requirements may eliminate the possibility of a return on investment. This makes it necessary to balance the benefits with the return of the original high investment. Generally, however, plant breeding results in the availability of varieties with increased output and improved quality for the benefit of the society.

Sustained and long-term breeding efforts are only worthwhile if there is a chance to be rewarded for the investment made. To recover the costs of this research and development, the breeder may seek protection to obtain exclusive rights for the new variety.

At the same time, a new variety, once released, can often be easily reproduced by others. The original breeder is thus deprived of the fair opportunity to benefit from his or her investment. It is, therefore, critical to provide an effective plant variety protection ("PVP") system, which encourages the development of new varieties of plants thereby benefiting the breeder and society at large.

In addition to making PVP available, other measures to encourage plant breeding activities include increased public funding for plant breeding, facilitating access to genetic resources (GRs) and encouraging public-private partnerships (PPP).

§11.02 THE UPOV

[A] Background

The International Union for the Protection of New Varieties of Plants (UPOV) PVP system came into being with the adoption of the International Convention for the Protection of New Varieties of Plants by a Diplomatic Conference in Paris on December 2, 1961 (the "UPOV Convention"). This was the point at which there was recognition of the IPRs of plant breeders in their varieties on an international basis. The UPOV Convention 1961 was revised at Geneva in 1972, 1978 and 1991.

The UPOV Convention provides the basis for members to encourage plant breeding by granting breeders of new plant varieties an IPR: the plant breeder's right (hereinafter "breeders' right").

Any State or IGO wishing to become a member of UPOV needs to obtain a positive advice of the Council of UPOV on the conformity of its laws with the provisions of the UPOV Convention prior to depositing its instrument of accession. There are presently seventy-eight UPOV members, seventy-six countries and two IGOs. The UPOV website provides a summary of the situation.

With the exception of India and Zimbabwe, which might be permitted to deposit their instruments of accession to the 1978 Act of the UPOV Convention "provided that the depositing State had [...] acted expeditiously to complete its legislation and any UPOV formalities and to effect the deposit" (*see* documents C/33/18 "Report," paragraph 21(b) and C(Extr.)/25/10 "Report," paragraph 22), States and IGOs wishing to join UPOV need to deposit their instrument of accession to the 1991 Act of the UPOV Convention.

[B] What Is UPOV?

UPOV is an IGO having legal personality and based in Geneva, Switzerland. Pursuant to an agreement concluded between the WIPO and UPOV, the Director General of WIPO is the Secretary-General of UPOV and WIPO provides administrative services to UPOV.

The mission of UPOV is to provide and promote an effective PVP system of, with the aim of encouraging the development of new varieties of plants, for the benefit of society.

[C] What Does UPOV Do?

UPOV implements the abovementioned mission statement. The main objectives of UPOV are, in accordance with the UPOV Convention, to:

- provide and develop the legal, administrative and technical basis for international cooperation in PVP;
- assist States and organizations in the development of legislation and the implementation of an effective PVP system; and
- enhance public awareness and understanding of the UPOV PVP system.

To implement these objectives UPOV is engaged in activities such as the adoption and publishing, on its website, of explanatory notes, information materials, test guidelines, communication on benefits of UPOV and other relevant information. IT tools have also been developed to facilitate the exchange of data between UPOV members and to facilitate for breeders to make applications for breeders' rights through a UPOV portal.

§11.03 HOW DOES PVP WORK?

The breeder's right means that the authorization of the breeder is required to propagate the variety for commercial purposes. The UPOV Convention specifies the acts that require the breeder's authorization in respect of the propagating material of a protected variety and, under certain conditions, in respect of the harvested material. UPOV members may also decide to extend protection to products made directly from harvested material, under certain conditions.

In order to obtain protection, the breeder needs to file individual applications with the authorities of UPOV members entrusted with the task of granting breeders' rights.

[A] What Are the Requirements for Protecting a New Plant Variety?

Under the UPOV Convention, the breeder's right is only granted where the variety is: (i) new; (ii) distinct; (iii) uniform; (iv) stable and has a suitable denomination.

[B] What Are the Benefits of PVP and UPOV Membership?

The UPOV Report on the Impact of PVP demonstrated that in order to enjoy the full benefits which PVP is able to generate, both implementation of the UPOV Convention and membership of UPOV are important. The introduction of the UPOV system of PVP and UPOV membership were found to be associated with:

(a) increased breeding activities;
(b) greater availability of improved varieties;
(c) increased number of new varieties;
(d) diversification of types of breeders (e.g., private breeders, researchers);
(e) increased number of foreign new varieties;
(f) encouraging the development of a new industry competitiveness on foreign markets; and
(g) improved access to foreign plant varieties and enhanced domestic breeding programs.

In order to become a UPOV member the advice of the UPOV Council in respect of the conformity of the law of a future member with the provisions of the UPOV Convention is required. This procedure leads, in itself, to a high degree of harmony in those laws, thus facilitating cooperation between members in the implementation of the system.

§11.04 THE CRITERIA FOR PROTECTION

[A] Definitions

[1] The Notion of Breeder

Only the breeder as defined in Article 1(iv) of the 1991 Act of the UPOV Convention is entitled to be granted a breeder's right. The 1991 Act of the UPOV Convention provides, under its Article 21(1)(iii), that "[e]ach Contracting Party shall declare a breeder's right granted by it null and void when it is established [...] (iii) that the breeder's right has been granted to a person who is not entitled to it, unless it is transferred to the person who is so entitled."

The *person* who can apply for plant breeders' rights is the one who bred the new variety i.e., the "breeder." The definition of "breeder" is important because it identifies who is entitled to apply for and, if the conditions are fulfilled, obtain, a breeder's right. Article 1(iv) of the 1991 Act of the UPOV Convention defines a breeder as: "the person who bred, or discovered and developed, a variety, the person who is the employer of the aforementioned person or who has commissioned the latter's work, where the laws of the relevant Contracting Party so provide, or the successor in title of the first or second aforementioned person, as the case may be."

It is important to note that the concept of *person* embraces both physical persons and legal persons (i.e., companies). The breeder might be, for example, an amateur gardener, a farmer, a scientist, a plant breeding institute or an enterprise specialized in plant breeding.

The plant breeding techniques used can range from traditional breeding techniques, such as crossing and selection, through to new technologies, such as genetic engineering. The UPOV Convention makes no restrictions in this regard.

Discoveries can be the initial step in the process of breeding a variety. However, the phrase "the person who bred, *or discovered and developed*, ..." means that a mere discovery or find would not entitle the person to protection. Development of the variety by the breeder is necessary for a breeder to be entitled to obtain protection.

As indicated in Article 1(iv) of the 1991 Act of the UPOV Convention, the person entitled to protection may, in certain circumstances, be different from the person who actually bred the variety. Under particular circumstances, the *employer* of the breeder or the *successor in title* of the breeder may be entitled to apply for protection. For example:

(a) where the breeder is an employee, entitlement to the breeder's right shall be determined by the employment relationship in the context of which the variety was bred, or discovered and developed, and in accordance with the law applicable to that relationship;
(b) when the actual person who obtained the variety transfers the right to someone else (the successor in title), e.g., to another person or company.

The definition of breeder gives no consideration to the process used for obtaining the plant variety. The process for the granting of the plant breeders' rights will not take into account whether the plant variety was bred using modern techniques, implying considerable financial resources, or whether it was the outcome of a simple selection process. What is relevant is the outcome itself, i.e., the attainment of a new plant variety, entitling the breeder to apply for a plant breeder's right.

[2] The Notion of Plant Variety

The plant kingdom is vast and has been classified by a ranking system containing many divisions and subdivisions. A "Family" is a division within the plant kingdom, which is subdivided into "Genera," which are further subdivided into "Species." Species is the division which is most familiar to people. A species is a group of plants which are reproductively isolated. Thus, plants of different species, such as apple, potato, rose, wheat, do not inter-breed by natural means.

Although the rank of species is an important botanical classification, it is clear that the plants within a species can be very different. Farmers and growers need plants that are adapted to the growing conditions in their local environment and which are suited to the cultivation practices employed. Therefore, farmers and growers use a more precisely defined group of plants, selected from within a species, called a plant "variety."

The UPOV Convention definition of a plant variety starts by stating that it is "a plant grouping within a single botanical taxon of the lowest known rank, ..." thus confirming that a plant variety falls within the lowest subdivision of the species. Thus, a variety may not consist of plants of more than one species. However, to understand more completely what a plant variety is, the 1991 Act of the UPOV Convention (Article 1(vi)) defines "variety" as: "a plant grouping within a single botanical taxon of the lowest known rank, which grouping, irrespective of whether the conditions for the grant of a breeder's right are fully met, can be defined by the expression of the characteristics resulting from a given genotype or combination of genotypes, distinguished from any other plant grouping by the expression of at least one of the said characteristics, and considered as a unit with regard to its suitability for being propagated unchanged."

Let us explain in more depth the concept of variety:

(1) [Plant grouping] A plant variety is a group of plants within a single botanical taxon of the lowest rank. The definition means that this is *irrespective of whether the conditions for the grant of a breeder's right are fully met*. Thus, the definition of a "variety" is wider than "protectable variety."
(2) [Characteristics] For any variety to be capable of protection, it must first be clearly defined and must fulfill the criteria for distinctness, uniformity and stability (DUS) required for protection. All Acts of the UPOV Convention have established that a variety is defined by its characteristics and that those characteristics are therefore the basis on which a variety can be examined for DUS. The 1991 Act of the UPOV Convention makes this clear by stating in Article 1(vi) that a variety is a plant grouping that can be "defined by the expression of the characteristics resulting from a given genotype or combination of genotypes" and can be "distinguished from any other plant grouping by the expression of at least one of the said characteristics." To consider characteristics for plant varieties in a more concrete way, think about potatoes; a different type of tuber is produced by each different variety.
(3) [Capable of being propagated unchanged] The group of plants should be capable of being propagated unchanged; in other words, the expression of the characteristics by which the variety has been defined should be maintained throughout generations.

If a plant grouping does not meet these criteria, it is not considered to be a variety within the UPOV system. In order to be protected, the variety must meet the conditions of novelty, DUS and be designated with a suitable denomination.

§11.05 THE BASIC OBLIGATION OF CONTRACTING PARTIES

Article 2 of the UPOV Convention requires that "Each Contracting Party shall grant and protect breeders' rights."

[A] Implementation of the Convention

[1] Measures of Implementation

The Convention (Article 30) provides that:

> (1) [Measures of implementation] Each Contracting Party shall adopt all measures necessary for the implementation of this Convention; in particular, it shall:
> (i) provide for appropriate legal remedies for the effective enforcement of breeders' rights;
> (ii) maintain an authority entrusted with the task of granting breeders' rights or entrust the said task to an authority maintained by another Contracting Party;
> (iii) ensure that the public is informed through the regular publication of information concerning
> - applications for and grants of breeders' rights, and
> - proposed and approved denominations.

In addition, UPOV publishes a Plant Variety Database on the UPOV website (PLUTO Plant Variety Database—a non-official database) which contains information from UPOV members on, *among other things*, applications for and grants of breeders' rights and proposed and approved denominations.

[2] Conformity of the Laws

The Convention (Article 30(2)) provides that it "shall be understood that, on depositing its instrument of ratification, acceptance, approval or accession, as the case may be, each State or IGO must be in a position, under its laws, to give effect to the provisions of this Convention."

§11.06 GENERA AND SPECIES TO BE PROTECTED

The 1991 Act of the UPOV Convention requires that, within a certain period, protection should be available to varieties of all plant genera and species. UPOV members bound by Acts other than the 1991 Act of the UPOV Convention have five years from becoming bound by the 1991 Act of the UPOV Convention to meet that requirement. New UPOV members have ten years, in which to offer protection to all genera and species and in the interim are required to offer protection to at least fifteen plant genera and species.

[A] Right of Priority

Article 11 of the UPOV Convention provides for a right of priority of one year, based upon an earlier application for the same variety with another UPOV member; hence a subsequent application is treated as if it were filed on the date of the earlier application. The right of priority provides benefits in relation to the examination of the novelty and distinctness conditions. Thus, the examination of subsequent applications will relate to the filing date of the first application. Other benefits of the right of priority are that, in relation to subsequent applications, the breeder has at least three months to send the relevant documents and can defer the examination for up to two years after the expiration of the priority period. It is important to note that, in order to benefit from the right of priority based upon a first application, the breeder must claim it in the subsequent applications. Should the breeder fail to do so, the subsequent application will be considered as filed on the application date of that subsequent application.

§11.07 CONDITIONS FOR THE GRANT OF THE BREEDER'S RIGHT

[A] Introduction

The conditions for protection are specially tailored according to the nature of plant varieties and plant breeding. If a legal right is to be granted in respect of a variety and if that right is subsequently to be effectively enforced, the identity of the variety must be well established and maintained during the whole period of protection.

The UPOV Convention accordingly establishes DUS as criteria to be satisfied. The two other criteria are novelty, i.e., that the variety must be "new" in the sense that it must not have been sold or disposed of to others during a specified period prior to the filing date of the application, and the variety must be given a suitable denomination. The grant of protection *shall not be subject to any further conditions*, provided that the applicant complies with all the formalities and pays the required fees (Article 5).

The conditions for the grant of the breeder's right are stated in Article 5 of the UPOV Convention: The breeder's right shall be granted where the variety is:

(i) new;
(ii) distinct;
(iii) uniform; and
(iv) stable.

Novelty is defined in Article 6 of the UPOV Convention. Paragraph (1) provides that: "The variety shall be deemed to be new if, at the date of filing of the application for a breeder's right, propagating or harvested material of the variety has not been sold or otherwise disposed of to others, by or with the consent of the breeder, for purposes of exploitation of the variety, (i) in the territory of the Contracting Party in which the application has been filed earlier than one year before that date and (ii) in a territory other than that of the Contracting Party in which the application has been filed earlier than four years or, in the case of trees or of vines, earlier than six years before the said date."

When a Contracting Party applies the UPOV Convention to a plant genus or species to which it did not previously apply the 1991 Act or an earlier Act, it may consider a variety of recent creation existing at the date of such extension of protection to satisfy the condition of novelty defined in paragraph (1) even where the sale or

disposal to others described in that paragraph took place earlier than the time limits defined in that paragraph.

The different grace periods (Article 6(1)(i) and (ii)) for selling or disposing of the variety in the territory of the Contracting Party where the application is filed and in other territories without affecting the novelty have been established in recognition of the lengthy nature of the evaluation by the breeder of the variety in each territory in order to take a decision to seek protection. The longer period for trees and vines takes into consideration the slower growth and longer evaluation needed for these types of plants.

Under Article 7 of the UPOV Convention: "The variety shall be deemed to be distinct if it is clearly distinguishable from any other variety whose existence is a matter of common knowledge at the time of the filing of the application. In particular, the filing of an application for the granting of a breeder's right or for the entering of another variety in an official register of varieties, in any country, shall be deemed to render that other variety a matter of common knowledge from the date of the application, provided that the application leads to the granting of a breeder's right or to the entering of the said other variety in the official register of varieties, as the case may be."

According to the UPOV Convention (Article 7), to satisfy the requirement of distinctness, a variety must be clearly distinguishable from any other variety whose existence is a matter of common knowledge.

A variety whose existence is a matter of common knowledge (variety of common knowledge) must satisfy the definition of a variety set out in Article 1(vi) of the 1991 Act of the UPOV Convention, but does not necessarily have to fulfill the DUS criteria required for the grant of a breeder's right under the UPOV Convention.

Article 8 of the UPOV Convention defines uniformity as follows: "The variety shall be deemed to be uniform if, subject to the variation that may be expected from the particular features of its propagation, it is sufficiently uniform in its relevant characteristics." The notion of uniformity ensures that the variety can be defined as far as is it necessary for the purpose of protection. This is indicated by the notion of sufficiently uniformity, i.e., the criterion for uniformity does not seek absolute uniformity.

The UPOV Convention links the uniformity requirement for a variety to the particular features of its propagation. This means that the level of uniformity required for truly self-pollinated varieties, mainly self-pollinated varieties, inbred lines of hybrid varieties, vegetatively propagated varieties, cross-pollinated varieties, mainly cross-pollinated varieties, synthetic varieties and hybrid varieties will, in general, be different. Furthermore, it relates only to the characteristics which are relevant for the protection of the variety.

Article 9 of the UPOV Convention defines stability as follows: "The variety shall be deemed to be stable if its relevant characteristics remain unchanged after repeated propagation or, in the case of a particular cycle of propagation, at the end of each such cycle." As with the uniformity requirement, the criterion for stability has been developed to establish the identity of the variety as the subject matter of protection. Thus, the criterion for stability relates only to the relevant characteristics of a variety.

The DUS test is essentially based on characteristics examined by means of growing trials. The UPOV Office issues test guidelines used by its members when assessing if the technical criteria for protection are complied with.

[B] Variety Denomination

The UPOV Convention requires that a variety shall be designated by a variety denomination, which will be its generic designation. The use of the variety denomination to commercialize propagating material of the protected variety is mandatory under the UPOV Convention, even after the period of protection has expired. If the breeder fails to provide a suitable variety denomination, the application will be rejected.

Variety denomination requirements are dealt with in Article 20 of the UPOV Convention.

[C] Other Conditions

The UPOV Convention provides that the granting of plant breeders' rights shall not be subject to conditions other than the ones mentioned above, provided that the applicant complies with the formalities provided for by the law of the Contracting Party with whose authority the application has been filed, and that he/she pays the required fees (*see* Article 5).

§11.08 PROVISIONAL PROTECTION

Provisional protection is provided to the breeder during the period between the filing or the publication of the application and the granting of the plant breeder's right. The UPOV Convention provides (*see* Article 13) that in respect of the period between the filing or the publication of the application and the grant of the breeder's right, the breeder is entitled at least to equitable remuneration from any person who, during that period, carries out acts which, once the right has been granted, would require the breeder's authorization as provided in Article 14 of the UPOV Convention. This provisional protection takes effect only if protection is granted, i.e., if the application is rejected, provisional protection is not available.

§11.09 SCOPE OF THE BREEDER'S RIGHT

[A] Introduction

Even a person with only basic knowledge about plant reproduction and multiplication can easily reproduce the variety. This means that, once released, a protected variety can be multiplied, i.e., propagating material of the variety can be produced, without the authorization of the breeder and that may infringe the breeder's right. We can compare the situation with other forms of IP. For example, a book protected by copyright can be photocopied without the authorization of the author and that may infringe the copyright. In the case of plant varieties, an equivalent act could be taking cuttings from a rose bush to produce new plants. However, a variety is a living entity and it can even reproduce itself. In many cases, the only action needed to reproduce the variety is simply to cultivate it and allow it to produce seed, tubers, etc., which can then simply be replanted to produce a new crop. For some species, the product sold by farmers after cultivation is the same part of the plant used to reproduce the variety.

[B] Plant Breeder's Right on the Propagating Material (Article 14(1))

The plant breeder's right is a right to exclude others from performing certain acts. The list of acts which require the authorization of the breeder when being performed with the propagating material are listed below. It should, however, be emphasized that the breeder's right does not give a breeder the right to grow or commercialize the variety. The section on "Protection and Exploitation of Protected Varieties" below addresses this issue.

The UPOV Convention (*see* Article 14) specifies the acts in respect of the propagating material (e.g., seed, bulbs, tubers, cuttings, etc.) of a protected variety which require the prior authorization of the breeder. Those acts are the following: production or reproduction (multiplication), conditioning for the purpose of propagation, offering for sale, selling or other marketing, exporting, importing, and stocking for any of the above purposes. As a result, breeders may decide to exploit the variety themselves or grant licenses to another party (or other parties) to exploit the variety on an agreed basis.

[C] Plant Breeder's Right on Harvested Material (Article 14(2)) and Certain Products (Article 14(3))

The use of propagating material without the authorization of the breeder triggers an extension of the breeder's right to the harvested material obtained from that propagating material (i.e., the unauthorized propagating material) of the protected variety. This is explained further in the following sections.

In the absence of extension of the right to harvested material, the material of a protected variety could be exported from country A, without the authorization of the title holder, to country B, where plant breeders' rights are not available. The material could then be freely reproduced in country B to produce cut flowers (harvested material), which were exported back to country A. If cut flowers did not fall within the scope of the breeder's right, the breeder could not do anything to stop this practice. The result would be that the breeder would go unrewarded and would lose his/her breeding investment.

The UPOV Convention, in its Article 14(2), provides that the breeder's right extends to harvested material: (i) if the material is obtained through the unauthorized use of propagating material, and (ii) if the breeder has not had reasonable opportunity to exercise his/her right in relation to the propagating material. The result in the situation described above is that the breeder would have the right to stop the importation of the flowers produced from propagating material on which he/she did not have the chance to exercise the breeder's right.

In addition, Article 14(3) of the UPOV Convention contains an optional provision which allows members of the Union to extend the scope of the breeder's right to products made directly from harvested material, if they have been obtained through the unauthorized use of harvested material of the protected variety which has itself been obtained from unauthorized use of propagating material, unless the breeder has had reasonable opportunity to exercise his/her right in relation to the harvested material.

The provisions under Article 14(2) and (3) constitute what has been called a "cascade." The notion of "cascade" implies that breeders can only exercise their right in relation to the harvested material if they have not been able to exercise their right in relation to the propagating material, and can only exercise their right in relation to a product made directly from the harvested material if they were unable to exercise their right in relation to the harvested material.

§11.10 VARIETIES COVERED WITHIN THE SCOPE OF THE PLANT BREEDER'S RIGHT

In addition to the protected variety itself, the scope of breeder's right also applies to the following varieties as stated in Article 14(5) of the 1991 Act of the UPOV Convention: varieties which are not clearly distinguishable from the protected variety; varieties whose production requires the repeated use of the protected variety; and essentially derived varieties. Article 14(5)(b) of the 1991 Act of the UPOV Convention provides as follows:

[Essentially derived and certain other varieties]

(a) The provisions of paragraphs (1) to (4) shall also apply in relation to
  (i) varieties which are essentially derived from the protected variety, where the protected variety is not itself an essentially derived variety,
  (ii) varieties which are not clearly distinguishable in accordance with Article 7 from the protected variety and
  (iii) varieties whose production requires the repeated use of the protected variety.

(b) For the purposes of subparagraph (a)(i), a variety shall be deemed to be essentially derived from another variety ("the initial variety") when
  (i) it is predominantly derived from the initial variety, or from a variety that is itself predominantly derived from the initial variety, while retaining the expression of the essential characteristics that result from the genotype or combination of genotypes of the initial variety,
  (ii) it is clearly distinguishable from the initial variety and
  (iii) except for the differences which result from the act of derivation, it conforms to the initial variety in the expression of the essential characteristics that result from the genotype or combination of genotypes of the initial variety.

(c) Essentially derived varieties may be obtained for example by the selection of a natural or induced mutant, or of a somaclonal variant, the selection of a variant individual from plants of the initial variety, backcrossing, or transformation by genetic engineering.

§11.11 EXCEPTIONS TO THE BREEDER'S RIGHT

The UPOV Convention establishes compulsory and optional exceptions to the breeder's right.

[A] Compulsory Exceptions

UPOV members must provide for these exceptions. The compulsory exceptions are established in Article 15(1): acts done privately and for non-commercial purposes; acts done for experimental purposes, and acts done for the purpose of breeding other varieties, and, except where the provisions of Article 14(5) apply, acts referred to in Article 14(1) to (4) in respect of such other varieties.

The wording of Article 15(1)(i) indicates that acts which are *both* of a private nature *and* for non-commercial purposes are covered by the exception. Thus, non-private acts, even where for non-commercial purposes, may be outside the scope of the exception. Furthermore, the wording indicates that private acts which are undertaken for commercial purposes do not fall within the exception. The use of the protected variety for experimental purposes is not covered by the plant breeder's right.

The exception under Article 15(1)(iii) includes acts done for the purpose of breeding other varieties, and, except where the provisions of Article 14(5) apply, acts referred to in Article 14(1) to (4) in respect of such other varieties. This is a fundamental element of the UPOV PVP system and is known as the "breeder's exemption," whereby there are no restrictions on the use of protected varieties for the purpose of breeding new plant varieties.

The second part of Article 15(1)(iii) clarifies that, except for the particular varieties provided for in Article 14(5), i.e., essentially derived varieties, varieties which are not clearly distinguishable of the protected variety and varieties whose production requires the repeated use of the protected variety, the new varieties obtained can be commercially exploited without the authorization of the title holder of the protected variety used to create those new varieties.

[B] Optional Exception

Article 15(2) of the UPOV Convention provides an optional exception, which permits members of the Union to exclude, for example, farm-saving of seed from the scope of the breeder's right, subject to certain conditions. This exception covers three aspects: the farmer's holding—where it can take place; the product of the harvest—the material involved; and the limits and safeguarding.

The optional exception is restricted to the following permission: "farmers to use for propagating purposes, on their own holdings, the product of the harvest which they have obtained by planting, on their own holdings, the protected variety or a variety covered by Article 14(5)*(a)*(i) or (ii)."

The wording of the Convention clarifies that the optional exception relates to the use of the product of the harvest by the farmer on his/her own holding. Thus, the optional exception may be considered by UPOV members not to extend to a transfer of the product of the harvest to another farmer for that other farmer to use for propagating purposes.

Article 15(2) states that "each Contracting Party may, [...] restrict the breeder's right in relation to any variety in order to permit farmers to use for propagating purposes, on their own holdings, the product of the harvest which they have obtained by planting, on their own holdings, the protected variety or a variety covered by Article 14(5)*(a)*(i) or (ii)." This wording indicates that the optional exception may be considered to relate to crops where the product of the harvest is used for propagating purposes, for example small-grained cereals where the harvested grain can equally be used as seed, i.e., propagating material.

Article 15(2) states that "Notwithstanding Article 14, each Contracting Party may, within reasonable limits and subject to the safeguarding of the legitimate interests of the breeder, restrict the breeder's right [...]." Where it is decided that the optional exception would be appropriate, there are various factors that might be considered in relation to reasonable limits and safeguarding of the legitimate interests of the breeder.

§11.12 RESTRICTIONS (EXCEPTIONS AND LIMITATIONS) TO THE PLANT BREEDER'S RIGHT

Restrictions to the plant breeder's right are established in Article 17 of the UPOV Convention. Those may be imposed by Contracting Parties on grounds of public interest. However, where the restriction has the effect of authorizing a third party to perform any act for which the breeder's authorization is required, the breeder is entitled to receive "equitable remuneration." In addition, the breeder's right is subject to exhaustion and limits of duration.

[A] Exhaustion of the Breeder's Right

Under Article 16 of the UPOV Convention, the breeder's right does not extend to acts concerning material the protected variety or other varieties covered by the scope of protection of the protected variety, which have been sold or otherwise marketed by the breeder or with his/her consent in the territory of the member of the Union concerned, or any material derived from the said material, unless such acts: (i) involve further propagation of the variety in question; or (ii) involve an export of material of the variety, which enables the propagation of the variety, into a country which does not protect varieties of the plant genus or species to which the variety belongs, except where the exported material is for final consumption purposes. The rule of exhaustion which is common to IP law is aimed at ensuring that holders of a breeder's right can only exercise their right—and receive remuneration—once in each stage of propagation. The exhaustion rule also ensures that the breeder's right to prohibit further or unauthorized propagation of the variety is never exhausted.

[B] Duration of the Breeder's Right

The minimum period of protection of the breeder's right, under Article 19 of the 1991 Act of the UPOV Convention, is designed to ensure an adequate incentive for the long-term investment that is necessary in plant breeding. The term is of twenty-five years for trees and vines and twenty years for other plants. This period starts from the date of grant.

CHAPTER 12

Traditional Knowledge, Traditional Cultural Expressions, and Genetic Resources

§12.01 THE ISSUE IN A NUTSHELL: IP FOR TRADITIONAL FORMS OF CREATIVITY AND INNOVATION

Many Indigenous Peoples, local communities, and governments have called for greater respect and recognition for the rights and interests of the holders of TK, TCEs and GRs whose needs and expectations are quite unique in relation to IP. Indeed, they face challenges unlike any other that IP law has yet presented: the protection of TK and TCEs intersect every category of IP and often involve other legal issues, as well as ethical and cultural sensitivities, reaching well beyond IP. The relationship between IP and GRs is also complex and raises specific issues for IP.

Claims are increasingly being made for the IP protection of traditional forms of creativity and innovation, which, under the conventional IP system, are not fully protected; in fact TK and TCEs are generally regarded as being in the public domain, and thus free for anyone to use, yet this "public domain" status is highly contested, especially by Indigenous Peoples as well as local communities.

This lack of protection makes TK and TCEs vulnerable to misappropriation and misuse, examples of which could include:

- a traditional remedy could be appropriated by a pharmaceutical company and the resulting invention patented by that company;
- an indigenous folk song could be adapted and the derivative original work protected by copyright, without any acknowledgement of the indigenous community which created the song and without sharing any of the benefits arising from the exploitation of the song with the community;

- inventions derived from GRs could be patented by third parties, raising questions as to the relationship between the patent system and the conservation and sustainable use of biodiversity and the equitable sharing of benefits.

The debate about protection centers on whether, and how, changes should be made to the existing IP system. Recognizing traditional elements as IP would enable their holders to have a say over their use by others. This does not mean that conventional IP systems are being forced upon TK, TCEs and GRs, but rather that values and principles embedded in IP law could be adapted for new subject matter and for new beneficiaries.

In fact, the discussion over their protection is inscribed in a broad policy context. The preservation, management and sustainable use of GRs and associated TK, as well as the sharing of the benefits, are topics that occupy public debate in sectors such as food and agriculture, biological diversity and environment, innovation and regulation in biotechnology, and economic, social and cultural development. With the rise of modern biotechnology, GRs have taken on increasing economic, scientific and commercial value.

Several important international instruments exist in the area of biological diversity. These include the 1992 Convention on Biological Diversity (CBD) and its 2010 Nagoya Protocol on Access to Genetic Resources and the Fair and Equitable Sharing of Benefits Arising from their Utilization to the CBD (the Nagoya Protocol), the International Treaty on Plant Genetic Resources for Food and Agriculture of the FAO, the UPOV Convention, the 1994 UN Convention to Combat Desertification (UNCCD) and the Agreement under the United Nations Convention of the Law of the Sea on the Conservation and Sustainable Use of Marine Biological Diversity of Areas beyond National Jurisdiction, which was adopted in 2023.

TK, TCEs and GRs are also raised in the context of the WTO Agreement on TRIPS. While the TRIPS Agreement has no provisions on the issue of TK, the Doha Declaration, in 2001, instructed the TRIPS Council to examine the protection of TK and TCEs. Furthermore, discussions on the relationship between the TRIPS Agreement and the CBD are taking place within the TRIPS Council since the built-in review of Article 27.3(b) in 1999.

The protection of TCEs raises issues related to the preservation and safeguarding of intangible cultural heritage, notably within the ambit of the UNESCO World Heritage Convention (1972) and Convention for the Safeguarding of Intangible Cultural Heritage (2003). It also forms part of the context of the promotion of cultural diversity and of the UNESCO Convention on the Protection and Promotion of the Diversity of Cultural Expressions (2005). TCEs protection is discussed in such contexts as the respect for cultural rights, the promotion of artistic development and cultural exchange and the promotion of tradition-based creativity and innovation as ingredients of sustainable economic development.

Human rights also form a crucial part of the context for the protection of TK, TCEs and GRs at WIPO. The 2007 UN Declaration on the Rights of Indigenous Peoples recognizes that "Indigenous peoples and individuals are free and equal to all other peoples and individuals and have the right to be free from any kind of discrimination, in the exercise of their rights, in particular that based on their indigenous origin or identity" (Article 2). Article 31 provides that Indigenous Peoples "have the right to maintain, control, protect and develop their intellectual property over such cultural heritage, traditional knowledge and traditional cultural expressions."

In May 2024, WIPO Member States adopted, by consensus, a historic new WIPO Treaty on Intellectual Property, Genetic Resources and Associated Traditional Knowledge (*see* further below and in Chapter 35).

§12.02 WHAT ARE TK, TCEs AND GRs?

No single definition would do justice to the diverse forms of knowledge and expressions that are held by Indigenous Peoples as well as local communities throughout the world.

The terms "TK" and "TCEs" potentially cover an enormous variety of customs, traditions, forms of artistic expression, knowledge, beliefs, products, and processes of production. There is not, as yet, any generally accepted, formal definition of these terms, but WIPO uses working descriptions in its work.

What makes knowledge or cultural expressions "traditional" is not their antiquity: much of them are not ancient or inert, but a vital, dynamic part of the lives of many communities. The concept of "tradition" refers to the particular link that knowledge or expressions may have with a community: the fact that they are developed, sustained and passed on within a community and transmitted through the generations, sometimes through specific customary systems of transmission. In short, it is the relationship with the community and the mode of transmission that make knowledge or cultural expressions "traditional."

[A] TK

The term "TK" is sometimes used as shorthand for the entire field of TK and TCEs. The term, as a broad description of subject matter, generally includes the intellectual cultural heritage, practices and knowledge systems of Indigenous Peoples and also local communities.

WIPO distinguishes between TK and TCEs, because, from an IP standpoint, a different set of policy questions arises and distinct legal tools are likely to apply. Be that as it may, this is not to suggest that these are distinguished in the traditional context, where a holistic view of an integrated, inseparable heritage prevails. For example, a traditional tool, like an axe or hammer, may embody TK (its method of fabrication and its method of use) but also may be seen as a TCE in itself, because of its design and ornamentation.

In the narrow sense, TK is a living body of knowledge that is developed, sustained and passed on from generation to generation within a community, often forming part of its cultural or spiritual identity. In a few words, TK is understood as:

- knowledge, know-how, skills, innovations or practices;
- that are passed between generations, whether consecutively or not;
- in a traditional context; and
- that form part of the traditional lifestyle of Indigenous Peoples and local communities who act as their guardian or custodian.

TK is not limited to any specific technical field, and can be found in a wide variety of contexts, including: agricultural; scientific; technical; ecological; medicinal, including related medicines and remedies; and biodiversity-related knowledge or knowledge associated with GRs. Examples include, among thousands of others:

- knowledge about traditional medicines;
- traditional hunting or fishing techniques;
- knowledge about animal migration patterns, environmental stewardship, climate change and water management.

[B] TCEs

TCEs may be succinctly described as the creative or artistic form (the "expression") in which traditional culture is embodied or expressed. TCEs are seen as integral to the cultural and social identities and heritage of Indigenous Peoples and local communities, reflecting values and beliefs. TCEs are characteristic of the cultural or social identity of a community that still bears, maintains and practices them. TCEs are handed down through the generations, and are maintained, used or developed by their holders. They are constantly evolving, developing and being recreated.

TCEs may be tangible, intangible, or a combination of the two. Indeed, in any material object, there is often a symbolic or religious element from which it cannot be separated.

Although "expressions of folklore" was the term used in international discussions and is found in many national laws, some have expressed reservations about the negative connotations associated with the word "folklore." WIPO nowadays uses the neutral working term "TCEs." "Expressions of folklore" is understood as a synonym.

Examples of TCEs could include, among many other artistic or cultural expressions: stories, poetry, riddles, songs, dances, plays, rituals and ceremonies, drawings, paintings, carvings, textiles, designs, sculptures, crafts, costumes, musical instruments, architectural forms, etc.

[C] GRs

GRs are defined in the CBD. In short, they are parts of biological materials that:

- contain genetic information of value; and
- are capable of reproducing or being reproduced.

Examples include material of plant, animal, or microbial origin, such as medicinal plants, agricultural crops and animal breeds.

Some TK is closely associated with GRs: through the utilization and conservation of the resource, often over generations, and through their common use in modern scientific research.

§12.03 WHO ARE THE HOLDERS OF TK AND TCEs?

One central issue in the debate over the protection of TK and TCEs is the identity of their holders, owners, bearers or custodians.

It is generally agreed that protection should principally benefit TK/TCEs holders, in particular the Indigenous Peoples, as well as local communities, that develop, maintain and identify culturally with them and seek to pass them on between generations, whether consecutively or not.

TK/TCEs are usually regarded as collectively originated and held, so that any rights and interests in this material should vest in communities rather than in individuals. In some instances though, beneficiaries may also include recognized individuals within the communities, such as certain traditional healers or individual farmers working within the community. Typically, this recognition arises through customary law.

It could be that more than one community qualifies for protection of their TK/TCEs, including communities which share the same or similar TK/TCEs in different countries.

§12.04 WHAT DOES "PROTECTION" MEAN?

[A] Protection of TK and TCEs

At WIPO the term "protection" refers to the use of IP tools and principles to prevent unauthorized or inappropriate uses of TK/TCEs by third parties. Put differently, the form of protection being developed is the application of IP law, values and principles to prevent misuse, misappropriation, or other kind of illicit exploitation. The objective, in short, is to make sure that the intellectual innovation and creativity embodied in TK or TCEs are not wrongly used.

IP protection can entail exclusive rights, as well as nonproprietary forms of protection like moral rights, equitable compensation schemes and protection against unfair competition.

In brief, IP laws typically establish:

(1) *exclusive property rights* in creations and innovations in order to:
   - grant control over their exploitation, particularly commercial exploitation;
   - provide incentives for further creativity.

(2) *other forms of protection*, for example:
- moral rights protection;
- equitable compensation; and
- protection against unfair competition.

IP protection could make it possible, for example, to protect traditional remedies and indigenous crafts and music against misappropriation, and enable communities to control and benefit collectively from their commercial exploitation, if they so wish.

Protection is different from "preservation" or "safeguarding," which are the identification, documentation, transmission, revitalization and promotion of cultural heritage in order to ensure its maintenance or viability. The objective, in that case, is to make sure that the TK or TCEs do not disappear, are lost or degrade, and to ensure that they are maintained and promoted.

The IP system can be approached from two different angles to ensure protection of TK and TCEs. These two approaches—generally referred to as "positive" and "defensive" protection—can well be undertaken together in a complementary way.

Under a first approach—"positive protection"—the IP system is designed to enable holders to acquire and assert IP rights in their TK and TCEs. This can allow them to prevent unwanted, unauthorized or inappropriate uses by third parties and/or to exploit TK/TCEs commercially, for example through the granting of licenses. In brief, positive protection is the granting of rights that empower communities to promote their TK/TCEs, control their uses by third parties and benefit from their commercial exploitation, if that is what they wish to do.

A second approach—"defensive protection"—is designed to prevent the illegitimate acquisition or maintaining of IP rights by third parties. Defensive protection aims to stop people outside the community from acquiring IP rights over TK and TCEs. India, for example, has compiled a searchable database of traditional medical knowledge that can be used as evidence of prior art by patent examiners when assessing patent applications. This database is described further below. Defensive strategies might also be used to protect sacred cultural manifestations from being registered as trademarks.

[B] Protection of GRs

The relationship between IP and GRs raises distinct questions as compared with those that arise at the nexus of IP and TK/TCEs. GRs are subject to access and benefit-sharing regulations, in particular within the international frameworks defined by the CBD and its Nagoya Protocol, as well as by the FAO International Treaty on Genetic Resources for Food and Agriculture.

GRs as encountered in nature are not IP. As they are not creations of the human mind, they cannot be directly protected as IP. WIPO is not involved in the regulation of access to GRs or their direct "protection" as such. However, inventions based on or developed using GRs may be patentable or protected by plant breeders' rights.

There are two main IP issues directly associated with GRs. The first is "defensive protection" of GRs: this refers to preventing patents from being granted over inventions based on or developed using GRs (and associated TK) which do not fulfill the existing patent requirements of novelty and inventiveness.

The second concerns the consistency and synergy between the IP system and the CBD: a number of countries have enacted domestic legislation putting into effect the CBD's obligations that access to a country's GRs should depend on securing that country's PIC, and agreeing to fair and equitable benefit-sharing (Agreement on fair and equitable benefit sharing (ABS)) (Article 15). The principle of PIC concerning access to GRs is one of the cornerstones of the CBD. According to this principle, holders should be fully consulted before their GR is accessed or used by third parties and an agreement should be reached on appropriate terms; they should also be fully informed about the consequences of the intended use. ABS regulates exchanges of genetic material between a legitimate holder and a subsequent user of GRs. The CBD and its Nagoya Protocol lay out the broad principles that countries are to respect when requesting and granting each other access to their GRs. The question arises as to whether the IP system should be used to support and implement CBD obligations, and whether patent applications that do not comply with these obligations should be disqualified.

In order to address those two separate issues, three mechanisms are being developed. The first mechanism is the creation, implementation and use of databases/information systems, information exchange, patent examination practices, and the adjustment of search tools and patent classification systems, all with the aim of helping patent examiners find relevant prior art and avoid the granting of erroneous patents. WIPO, for example, has improved its own search tools and patent classification system. In 2003, TK classification tools were integrated within IPC.

The second mechanism is the implementation of a mandatory disclosure requirement, i.e., to make it mandatory for patent applications to show the source or origin of GRs, as well as, perhaps, evidence of PIC and a benefit-sharing agreement. Such a disclosure requirement and variations thereof are found in several national and regional patent laws. The WIPO Treaty on Intellectual Property, Genetic Resources and Associated Traditional Knowledge, adopted in May 2024, addresses both information systems/databases and disclosure requirements related to GRs and associated TK (*see* further below and in Chapter 35).

The third mechanism is the management of patent/IP rights through contract (IP clauses in mutually agreed terms). WIPO has gathered examples of relevant contractual practices and model IP clauses which may be considered for inclusion in contractual agreements when mutually agreed terms are being negotiated. WIPO also has draft guidelines on IP clauses in ABS agreements.

[C] What Is the Objective of Protection?

Protection is not undertaken as an end in itself, but as a means to reach broader policy goals and to respond to the needs of their holders. Stakeholders have expressed a variety of policy objectives underlying the protection of TK and TCEs, including:

- Wealth creation, trading opportunities and sustainable economic development, including promotion of equitable benefit-sharing from use of TK/TCEs.
- Preservation, promotion and development of TK/TCEs.
- Prevention and repression of misappropriation and unauthorized exploitation, illicit use and abuse, as well as other unfair and inequitable uses of TK/TCEs.
- Protection of tradition-based creativity and innovation.
- Recognition of value and promotion of respect for TK/TCEs and the communities that preserve them.
- Prevention of false and misleading claims to authenticity and origin; prevention of third-party failure to acknowledge the source.

§12.05 OPTIONS FOR THE IP PROTECTION OF TK AND TCEs

No form of legal protection system can replace the complex customary systems that sustain TK and TCEs within their traditional context. This is why IP protection complements those systems, and operates beyond the community: it is not aimed to supplant the community's own customs and practices.

There are nonetheless concerns that attempts to protect TK/TCEs within the IP system could turn it into an asset sought by third parties, thereby separating it from their communities, and consequently depriving them of vital benefits. Thus, communities maintain that any protection should remain true to its roots.

Diversity being the very essence of TK and TCEs, it is not surprising that no single template or comprehensive "one-size-fits-all" solution is likely to suit all the needs of holders in all parts of the world. This diversity requires flexibility in fashioning an international IP instrument, which also aims to be enforceable, especially from the viewpoint of beneficiaries, and not to create burdens for them and for administrators.

Non-IP options are also available, such as trade practices, consumer protection and labeling laws, the use of contracts, customary and indigenous laws and protocols, cultural heritage preservation, civil liability and common law remedies, criminal law, and biodiversity-related legislation. These may be used alone or in combination with IP law to afford appropriate protection to TK and TCEs.

The options for IP protection include:

- existing IP laws and systems;
- extended or adapted IP rights specifically focused on TK/TCEs; and
- new, stand-alone sui generis systems specifically designed for TK/TCEs.

[A] Existing Conventional IP Systems

Existing IP laws have been used to protect against some forms of misuse and misappropriation of TK and TCEs, including through the laws of patent, copyright, trademarks, GIs, industrial designs, and trade secrets. Various holders have found existing IP rights useful and their protection strategies make some use of the IP system.

[1] Patent Law

When people innovate within the traditional framework, they may be able to use the patent system to protect their innovations. In other words, innovations based on TK or TCEs may benefit from patent protection. In Australia, the Jarlmadanghah Burru community, together with Griffith University, were granted a patent for new compounds having analgesic benefits. The compounds were obtained from a plant well known to the Jarlmadanghah Burru community for its healing properties, including pain relief. The community had initially explored the commercial benefits of the plant after one its members used the plant to stop pain after his finger was bitten off by a crocodile. In South India the medicinal knowledge of the Kani tribes led to the development of a sports drug named Jeevani, an anti-stress and anti-fatigue agent, based on the herbal medicinal plant arogyapacha. Indian scientists used the tribal know-how to develop the drug, and filed two patent applications on the drug. The technology was then licensed to the Arya Vaidya Pharmacy, Ltd., an Indian pharmaceutical manufacturer and a trust fund was established to share the benefits arising from the commercialization of the TK-based drug.

Equally, systems have been developed to ensure that illegitimate patent rights are not granted over TK subject matter that is not a true invention. For example, India's database on traditional medicinal knowledge, the Traditional Knowledge Digital Library (TKDL), plays such a role within the existing patent system.

[2] Copyright and Related Rights

In some national laws, TCEs are referred to as a type of copyright work, and most of the usual rules of copyright apply to them. Examples are Barbados, Côte d'Ivoire, Indonesia and the Islamic Republic of Iran. Another group of countries have included within their copyright legislation provisions specifically designed for TCEs: Burkina Faso, Ghana, Kenya, Mexico, Mozambique, Namibia, Nigeria, Senegal, Sri Lanka, Togo, the United Republic of Tanzania, and Viet Nam. In most of these cases, the provisions are based upon the Tunis Model Law of 1976 or the 1982 WIPO-UNESCO Model Provisions, but the national modalities of protection may differ.

A contemporary expression derived from or inspired by pre-existing traditional materials and which incorporates new elements can often be sufficiently original to qualify as a protected copyright work. However, the protection afforded to such derivative works vests only in their new material or aspects. While the adaptation of a protected work is the exclusive right of the copyright holder, this does not prevent, in general, creators from being inspired by other works or from borrowing from them.

Copyright, through moral rights, can provide protection against insulting, derogatory, offensive, demeaning or degrading use of a work, an issue that is often of concern for TCEs which embody spiritual qualities and the cultural identity of a community. Preventing such misuse, and promoting respect for cultural values, may be the principal goal of protection for some.

There are examples of communities successfully protecting songs, graphic works and other works through copyright. For instance, the Australian case *Milpurrurru v. Indofurn Pty Ltd* (1995) 30 IPR 209 involved the importation into Australia of carpets manufactured in Viet Nam which reproduced, without permission, works created by indigenous artists. The artists successfully claimed infringement of copyright and unfair trade practices. The judgment recognized the concept of "cultural harm" and awarded collective damages to all the artists to be distributed according to their cultural practices.

Performances of TCEs may come under international related rights protection, as provided under the WPPT, 2002, and the BTAP, 2012.

Article 15.4 of the Berne Convention for the Protection of Literary and Artistic Works (1971) provides a mechanism for the international protection of unpublished and anonymous works. This provision aims at providing international protection for TCEs.

[3] Distinctive Signs, Designs and Unfair Competition

Laws for the protection of marks, GIs, and industrial designs, as well as unfair competition law may offer protection. These aim at the protection of established reputation, distinctiveness and goodwill, such as may be enjoyed by a community in the production of handicrafts, artworks and other traditional products. Distinctive names, signs and symbols associated with TK/TCEs can be protected under trademark law and safeguarded against third parties' claims. For instance, the Seri people of Mexico registered the "*Arte Seri*" mark to protect authentic ironwood products that are produced by traditional methods from the *Olneya tesota* tree.

In many countries, trademarks, particularly certification marks, are used to safeguard the authenticity and quality of indigenous arts and crafts. For instance, the registered certification mark "Toi Iho" was used in New Zealand to promote and market authentic, quality Maori arts and crafts.

Unfair competition law, trade practices and labeling laws allow for action to be taken against false or misleading claims that a product is authentically indigenous, or has been produced or endorsed by, or is otherwise associated with a particular community.

GIs can be used, in particular for products such as handicrafts that have qualities or characteristics derived from their geographical origin.

The design, shape and visual characteristics of textiles, carvings, sculptures, pottery, woodwork, metalwork, jewelry, basket weaving and other handicraft could be protected as industrial designs.

The law of confidentiality and trade secrets has been used to protect non-disclosed TK, including secret and sacred TK. Courts may award remedies for breach of confidence when customary laws of secrecy are violated. For example, publication of sacred or secret materials has been successfully prevented using a breach of confidence action. In *Foster v. Mountford and Rigby Ltd (1976) 29 FLR 233 FC* members of the Pitjantjatjara Council obtained an interlocutory injunction, on the basis of breach of confidence, to restrain the publication of a book entitled *Nomads of the Australian Desert*.

[B] Adaptation of Existing IP

The limitations of existing IP laws in meeting all the needs and expectations of TK/TCEs holders have been underlined and some consider that adaptations of existing rights may be necessary.

A number of countries have adapted existing IP systems to suit the particularities of TK and TCEs. For example, some have included within their copyright legislation provisions specifically designed for TCEs, following largely the 1982 WIPO-UNESCO Model Provisions.

Adaptations to the copyright law may provide protection for collective works or works that have not been fixed and special remedies for infringement that is also culturally offensive.

In trademark law, a Database of Official Insignia of Native American Tribes prevents others from registering these insignia or confusingly similar marks as trademarks in the USA. New Zealand's trademark law was amended to provide for the refusal to register a trademark where its use would be likely to offend a significant section of the community, including the Maori. A similar mechanism exists in New Zealand for patents.

Several States already provide specific legal protection for TK within their national patent legislation. For example, approximately thirty-five countries and regional organizations have included disclosure requirements related to TK and GRs within their patent laws.

At the international level, the principal tool for locating technical information for patent examination purposes, the IPC, has been expanded to take better account of TK, in particular concerning medicinal products based on plant extracts. This increases the likelihood that patent examiners locate published TK that is relevant to claimed inventions in patent applications, without adversely affecting the legal status of TK from the point of view of its holders.

The PCT provides for an international search and examination, which takes into account TK-related information resources, thus increasing the likelihood that relevant TK will be located. Since 2003, TK documentation is included in the non-patent literature part of the PCT Minimum Documentation.

[C] Sui Generis Systems

In most cases, conventional IP systems and their adaptations are not considered sufficient to cater to the unique character of TK/TCEs.

A number of countries and regions have developed their own distinct new sui generis systems. Upon request, WIPO offers legal and technical assistance in this respect.

The international legal instruments for the effective protection of TK and TCEs which are being negotiated in the WIPO IGC follow a sui generis approach and are described in the following paragraphs and, more fully, in Chapter 35.

§12.06 THE WORK OF WIPO IN THE FIELD OF TK, TCEs AND GRs

In 1997, the UNESCO-WIPO World Forum on the Protection of Folklore was held in Phuket, Thailand, following which, in 1998, WIPO established a program addressing, for the first time in a comprehensive and consolidated manner, the subjects of TK, TCEs and GRs. During 1998 and 1999, WIPO conducted fact-finding missions in twenty-eight countries to identify the IP-related needs and expectations of TK holders. Indigenous Peoples, local communities, NGOs, governmental representatives, academics, researchers and private sector representatives were among the more than three thousand persons consulted on these missions. The results of the missions are in the WIPO report "Intellectual Property Needs and Expectations of Traditional Knowledge Holders: WIPO Report on Fact-finding Missions (1998-1999)," a report that still guides WIPO's activities today.

[A] WIPO's TK Division

Nowadays, WIPO's TK Division:

- facilitates a normative process among Member States aimed at developing international legal instrument/s: this takes place within the WIPO IGC. These negotiations led to the adoption in May 2024 of the new WIPO Treaty already referred to (and *see* further Chapter 35);
- provides training, mentoring and matchmaking programs, other capacity-strengthening activities and technical assistance; and
- maintains inter-agency and external relations (with OHCHR, CBD, UNESCO, WHO, WTO, FAO, United Nations Conference on Trade and Development (UNCTAD), UN Permanent Forum on Indigenous Issues, etc.).

[B] The Intergovernmental Committee

Because the existing international IP system does not fully protect TK and TCEs, many communities and governments have called for an international legal instrument or instruments to provide sui generis protection. Many argue that, because of the international scale of misappropriation and misuse, there is a need for well-established, culturally appropriate and predictable rules at the international level.

Similarly, in relation to GRs, many argue that clarity on the relationship between IP and GRs would improve the efficacy, transparency and quality of the patent system and prevent the erroneous grant of patents for inventions that are not novel or inventive with regard to GRs and associated TK.

In order to identify and address the IP issues relating to TK, TCEs and GRs, WIPO Member States established the IGC in September 2000. More information on the IGC process is provided in Chapter 35.

[C] Projects and Activities: The Practical Work of WIPO

WIPO's Traditional Knowledge Division offers several practical programs specifically for Indigenous Peoples as well as local communities. These are distinct from any administrative support WIPO provides for these stakeholders in the context of the IGC's negotiations (for which *see* Chapter 35).

A training, mentoring and matchmaking program for entrepreneurs from Indigenous Peoples, and also local communities, provides practical in-person training on the strategic use of existing IP systems, business and life skills, branding, marketing, ethics and communications in support of their businesses for the ultimate benefit of their communities. Each trainee is then paired with a mentor for a year. WIPO matches the trainees with external partners for their specific needs, such as pro bono lawyers. Direct support is provided to the trainees' projects and businesses that support and sustain communities.

This program has been particularly addressed to women entrepreneurs. It forms part of an extensive skills development and capacity-building program offered for Indigenous Peoples and local communities by the Traditional Knowledge Division.

For Indigenous and local community youth in particular, an annual Photography Prize invites members of these communities who are 35 years or younger to enter their photographs on a given theme. The winners receive prizes, and in some cases are able to license their photographs for additional remuneration. All participants receive training on the features and benefits of the copyright system.

The WIPO Creative Heritage Project provides practical support and IP-related advice for communities wishing to record their TK and/or TCEs.

Other important beneficiaries of WIPO's capacity-building activities are governments, as well as research, scientific and cultural institutions, academia, NGOs and other members of civil society.

As part of this program, upon request, and within its budgetary limits, WIPO organizes workshops and seminars, develops information materials as well as other types of resources, including information databases, and provides policy and legislative assistance, education and training. WIPO's work includes assistance to develop and strengthen national and regional systems for the protection of TK and TCEs (policies, laws, information systems and practical tools). Furthermore, the Traditional Knowledge Division offers two distance learning (DL) programs on TK, TCEs and GRs in cooperation with the WIPO Academy.

WIPO also makes available a suite of information materials. A series of Briefs and a short animation provide an accessible introduction to the issues. *Protect and Promote your Culture* (WIPO Pub. No. 1048) and the *WIPO TK Documentation Toolkit* (WIPO Pub. No. 1049) provide practical advice to Indigenous Peoples as well as local communities on use of the current IP system and on managing the IP implications of their documentation work, respectively. *Intellectual Property and the Safeguarding of Traditional Cultures—Legal Issues and Practical Options for Museums, Libraries and Archives* (WIPO Pub. No. 1023) presents legal information and best practices for such institutions. *Intellectual Property and Folk, Arts and Cultural Festivals—A Practical Guide* (WIPO Pub. No. 1043) offers insights for festival organizers to develop appropriate IP management strategies and tools to deal with the various IP issues that can arise around such events. A *Guide to Intellectual Property in Access and Benefit-sharing Agreements* (WIPO Pub. No. 1052) and a complementary database provide empirical information on how IP issues are dealt with in access and benefit-sharing contracts. *Developing Patent Disclosure Requirements related to Genetic Resources and Traditional Knowledge—Key Questions* is a widely consulted resource in the context of policy development, including in relation to the IGC's negotiations. The pages of the WIPO website devoted to TK, TCEs and GRs carry many other resources, including a searchable database of sui generis laws. The Traditional Knowledge Division is active on social media in order to provide information to stakeholders, especially Indigenous Peoples and local communities.

Disputes between holders and third-party users of TK, GRs and TCEs over ownership and control, access and benefit-sharing can emerge. Such disputes bring about not only legal, but also cultural and ethical questions. For example, inappropriate use of a sacred cultural artifact, symbol or design may not cause financial loss but can cause considerable spiritual offense. Therefore remedy through litigation in a national court is not always desirable. Alternative Dispute Resolution (ADR) offers an option for tackling the disputes that arise in relation to TK, TCEs and GRs. The WIPO Arbitration and Mediation Center and Traditional Knowledge Division can assist parties in the resolution of disputes through a dedicated service for art and cultural heritage disputes.

[D] Indigenous Participation in WIPO

WIPO's work is founded on a deep appreciation for the experiences, perspectives, rights and interests of the representatives of Indigenous Peoples as well as local communities who are permanent observers to WIPO or specifically accredited to the IGC. WIPO's work often refers to and takes into consideration the UN Declaration on the Rights of Indigenous Peoples.

Accredited representatives are assisted by the *WIPO Voluntary Fund for Accredited Indigenous and Local Communities* to attend the WIPO negotiations and related meetings. Sessions of the IGC commence with presentations by a panel of representatives of Indigenous Peoples and also local communities.

Launched in 2009, the WIPO Indigenous Intellectual Property Law Fellowship aims to ensure that Indigenous Peoples are actively and effectively involved in the work of WIPO on issues that matter to them. It recognizes the legal expertise that exists within indigenous communities, and offers an opportunity for a professional experience and a practical role within the WIPO Secretariat, including the WIPO IGC. It responds to the needs for stronger capacity in the domain of indigenous IP law and for strengthened capacity on IP law and policy for indigenous lawyers and policy advisors.

CHAPTER 13
Protection Against Unfair Competition

§13.01 INTRODUCTION

Protection against unfair competition has been recognized as forming part of industrial property protection for almost a century. It was in 1900, at the Brussels Diplomatic Conference for the Revision of the Paris Convention for the Protection of Industrial Property (hereinafter referred to as "the Paris Convention"), that this recognition was first manifested by the insertion of Article 10*bis* in the Convention. In its original version, as adopted at the Brussels Diplomatic Conference, the article read as follows: "Nationals of the Convention (Articles 2 and 3) shall enjoy, in all the States of the Union, the protection granted to nationals against unfair competition." As a result of the subsequent revision conferences, the article now reads as follows (in the Stockholm Act (1967) of the Paris Convention):

> The countries of the Union are bound to assure to nationals of such countries effective protection against unfair competition.
> (1) Any act of competition contrary to honest practices in industrial or commercial matters constitutes an act of unfair competition.
> (2) The following in particular shall be prohibited:
> 1. all acts of such a nature as to create confusion by any means whatever with the establishment, the goods, or the industrial or commercial activities, of a competitor;
> 2. false allegations in the course of trade of such a nature as to discredit the establishment, the goods, or the industrial or commercial activities, of a competitor;
> 3. indications or allegations the use of which in the course of trade is liable to mislead the public as to the nature, the manufacturing process, the characteristics, the suitability for their purpose, or the quantity, of the goods.

At first glance, there seem to be basic differences between the protection of industrial property rights, such as patents, registered industrial designs, registered trademarks, etc., on the one hand, and protection against acts of unfair competition on the other. Whereas industrial property rights, such as patents, are granted on application by industrial property offices and confer exclusive rights with respect to the subject matter concerned, protection against unfair competition is based not on such grants of rights but on the consideration—either stated in legislative provisions or recognized as a general principle of law—that acts contrary to honest business practice are to be prohibited. Nevertheless, the link between the two kinds of protection is clear when certain cases of unfair competition are considered. For example, in many countries unauthorized use of a trademark that has not been registered is considered illegal on the basis of general principles that belong to the field of protection against unfair competition (in a number of countries such unauthorized use is called "passing-off"). There is another example of this kind in the field of inventions: if an invention is not disclosed to the public and is considered to constitute a trade secret, the unauthorized performance by third parties of certain acts in relation to that trade secret may be illegal. Indeed, the performance of certain acts in relation to an invention that has been disclosed to the public and is not patented or in respect of which the patent has expired, may under very special circumstances also be illegal (as an act of "slavish imitation").

The above examples show that protection against unfair competition effectively supplements the protection of industrial property rights, such as patents and registered trademarks, in cases where an invention or a sign is not protected by such a right. There are, of course, other cases of unfair competition, for example the case referred to in Article 10*bis*(3)2 of the Paris Convention, namely that of a false allegation in the course of trade of such a nature as to discredit a competitor, in which protection against unfair competition does not perform such a supplementary function. This is due to the fact that the notion of unfair competition covers a great variety of acts, as will be discussed in the analysis below.

§13.02 THE NEED FOR PROTECTION AGAINST UNFAIR COMPETITION

Free competition between enterprises is considered the best means of satisfying supply and demand in the economy and of serving the interests of consumers and the economy as a whole. However, where there is competition, acts of unfair competition are liable to occur. This phenomenon has been discernible in all countries and at all times, regardless of prevailing political or social systems.

Sometimes economic competition has been compared to competition in sport, because in both the best should win. In economic competition, that should be the enterprise providing the most useful and effective product or service on the most economical and (to the consumer) satisfying terms. This result can only be achieved, however, if all participants play according to a certain set of basic rules; and also as in sport, it may be tempting to disregard the rules. Violations of the basic rules of economic competition can take various forms, ranging from illegal but harmless acts (which can be committed by the most honest and careful entrepreneur) to malicious fouls, intended to harm competitors or mislead consumers. They may consist in a direct attack on an individual competitor or in a surreptitious deception of the "referee," who in economic competition typically is the consumer. Whatever form such violations may take, it is in the interest of the honest entrepreneur, the consumer and the public at large that they should be prevented as early and as effectively as possible.

Experience has shown that there is little hope of fairness in competition being achieved solely by the free play of market forces. In theory consumers, in their role as referees of economic play, could deter dishonest entrepreneurs by disregarding their goods or services and favoring those of honest competitors. Reality, however, is different. As an economic situation becomes more complex, consumers become less able to act as referees. Often they are not even in a position to detect by themselves acts of unfair competition, let alone react accordingly. Indeed, it is the consumer who—along with the honest competitor—has to be protected against unfair competition.

Self-regulation has sometimes been referred to as a remedy but it has not proved to be a sufficient safeguard against unfair competition. Without doubt, self-regulation by associations of enterprises can play an important role in ensuring honest business conduct: if self-regulation is well developed and generally observed, it can even be faster, less expensive and more efficient than any court system. Yet it stands or falls on continuing observance by all participants.

In order to prevent unfair competition effectively, self-regulation must, at least in certain areas, be supplemented by a system of legal enforcement. Only such a system can assure honest entrepreneurs that their chances of success will be determined by their own efforts, and assure consumers that they can make optimum buying choices, thus avoiding the waste of scarce resources, and ensuring improved market transparency and maximum economic welfare.

The rules on the prevention of unfair competition and those on the prevention of restrictive business practices (antitrust law) are interrelated: both aim at ensuring the efficient operation of a market economy. They do so in different ways, however: antitrust law is concerned with the preservation of the freedom of competition by combating restraints on trade and abuses of economic power, while unfair competition law is concerned with ensuring fairness in competition by forcing all participants to play according to the same rules. Yet both laws are equally important, although in different respects, and supplement each other. Countries setting up a system of market economy need an antitrust law, but one cannot rely on antitrust law alone to ensure fairness of competition as a side effect: that can be achieved only by distinct rules providing for protection against unfair competition.

Industrial property laws protecting inventions, industrial designs, marks, trade names, GIs, etc., are insufficiently comprehensive on their own to ensure honest practice in the marketplace. It is true that the protection of industrial property rights is in the interest not only of their owners, but also of consumers and of the public at large, and thus also serves the objective of ensuring fairness in competition. In particular, the unauthorized use of a trademark for a competing product not only constitutes undue exploitation of the trademark owner's goodwill, but also deceives the public as to the commercial origin of the product (and hence its characteristics). It can therefore be argued that trademark law is a specific part of the larger field of unfair competition law and that the enforcement of trademark protection serves to prevent acts of unfair competition, in particular, passing-off and dilution of distinctive quality or advertising value. The same is true, to a lesser extent, of other industrial property rights, such as patents, which protect inventors against undue exploitation of their efforts.

However, in spite of these common objectives, fair play in the marketplace cannot be ensured only by the protection of industrial property rights. A wide range of unfair acts, such as misleading advertising and the violation of trade secrets, are usually not dealt with by the specific laws on industrial property. Unfair competition law is therefore necessary either to supplement the laws on industrial property or to grant a type of protection that no such law can provide. In order to fulfill this function, unfair competition law must be flexible, and protection thereunder must be independent of any formality such as registration. In particular, unfair competition law must be able to adapt to all new forms of market behavior. Such flexibility does not necessarily entail a lack of predictability. Of course, unfair competition law can never be as specific as patent law or trademark law; yet experience in many countries has shown that it is possible to develop an efficient and flexible system of unfair competition law and at the same time to ensure sufficient predictability.

§13.03 THE LEGAL BASIS FOR PROTECTION

[A] Development of Unfair Competition Law

All countries that have established market-economy systems have devised some kind of safeguard against unfair business practices. In doing so, however, they have chosen quite different approaches. While in other areas of industrial property law, such as those dealing with patents, designs or marks, it is generally agreed that protection is best afforded by a specific, comprehensive statute, the legal basis for the repression of unfair competition can range from a succinct general tort provision to detailed regulation in a special statute. The reason for this diversity of approaches is often purely historical.

The concept of unfair competition law emerged first in France around 1850. Although at that time there was no specific prohibition of dishonest business practices, the French courts were able to develop a comprehensive and effective system of unfair competition law on the basis of the general provision contained in Article 1382 of the French Civil Code, according to which unlawful acts entail an obligation to pay damages. As far as the protection of competitors is concerned, the principles developed by court decisions on the basis of Article 1382 of the French Civil Code are still the main bases for relief against unfair competition in France. For the protection of consumers, a law on fraud in connection with products was enacted as early as 1905, and has since been complemented by numerous statutes and decrees, including the so-called Loi Royer of 1973, which prohibits misleading advertising, and the Consumer Information Laws of 1978 and 1989.

In Germany, the situation evolved differently. Since the courts refused to extend the tort provisions of the Civil Code to unfair business practices, it was necessary to enact specific legislation on the subject. Thus the "Law Against Unfair Competition" of 1909 became, and has remained, the main basis for the repression of acts of unfair competition. The Law contains two general provisions on dishonest and deceptive trade practices, around which special provisions, for example, on the protection of trade secrets, are grouped. Furthermore, it relies almost exclusively on private party complaints, granting capacity to sue to competitors, consumers and business organizations. The German courts, relying especially on the two general provisions contained in Articles 1 and 3 of the Law, have developed a comprehensive system for the repression of unfair trade practices, which aims at protecting not only competitors but also consumers and the public at large.

The law of the various jurisdictions that make up the UK (England, Scotland, Wales and Northern Ireland) has taken a different approach, based on common law and equity, and has not developed a separate legal regime for protection against unfair competition. A traditionally liberal approach makes for reluctance to enact general rules that allow subjective opinions to be held on what is "fair" or not. The tort of passing-off, which has been recognized since 1824, is regarded as sufficient protection for competitors. Consequently, civil remedies for competitors are still restricted to isolated cases under uncodified tort principles, in particular the protection against passing-off, claims of injurious falsehood or breach of confidence. However, provisions on consumer protection against misleading acts were already introduced in 1862 and have in the meantime been supplemented by an autonomous set of consumer protection statutes, such as the Trade Descriptions Act of 1968, the Fair Trading Act of 1973, the Unsolicited Goods and Services Acts of 1971 and 1975 and the Consumer Protection Act of 1987. In 1988, the Control of Misleading Advertisements Regulations were enacted pursuant to the EC Directive of 1984. Additionally, a number of self-disciplinary advertising codes are fully recognized.

As in the UK, unfair competition law in the USA developed from judicial decisions, especially from the common law tort of passing-off. And, again as in the UK, there was—and is—no comprehensive common law tort of unfair competition. However, limited statutory relief against false claims about one's own product in interstate commerce has been granted since 1946 under the trademark protection provision of section 43(a) of the trademark law (Lanham Act). In 1988 that provision was extended to cover also false or misleading representations about another's product or service. In addition, a federal agency, the Federal Trade Commission (FTC), was created in 1914, which has broad jurisdiction to pursue any unfair or deceptive act or practice in or affecting interstate commerce. However, section 5(a) of the FTC Act gives no right of action to injured competitors or consumers, whereas the statutes against unfair business practices which all States enacted in the latter half of this century (typically modeled on the FTC Act) often allow legal action to be brought by interested parties.

The above examples show how unfair competition law has developed differently in different countries. In the meantime, many countries have passed special legislation on the subject or have replaced earlier laws on unfair competition. As regards recent legislative activity in this area, Switzerland adopted a Law Against Unfair Competition in 1986 which contains a broad general provision and a detailed regulation of specific market behavior, for example slavish imitation; Hungary adopted a Law on the Prohibition of Unfair Market Practice in 1990 which regulates unfair competition and antitrust law; Spain's Unfair Competition Law of 1991 contains a detailed regulation on practices harmful to consumers and competitors; and in 1991 Belgium adopted a Trade Practices and Consumer Protection Law which emphasizes the idea of consumer protection.

[B] International Protection

*[1] Article 10*bis *of the Paris Convention for the Protection of Industrial Property*

Article 1(2) of the Paris Convention mentions the repression of unfair competition along with patents, utility models, industrial designs, trademarks, trade names, indications of source and AO among the objects of industrial property protection, and Article 10*bis* contains an express provision on the repression of unfair competition. In the more than one hundred States party to the Paris Convention the legal basis for the protection against unfair competition may thus be found not only in national legislation but also at the international level.

Under Article 10*bis*(l) of the Paris Convention, the countries of the Paris Union are bound to ensure effective protection against unfair competition. Article 10*ter*(l) of the Convention further provides for the obligation to ensure "appropriate legal remedies." In particular, measures must be taken to permit federations and associations representing interested industrialists, producers or merchants to take action, provided that this is not contrary to the laws of the country concerned and does not exceed the rights normally granted to national associations.

Article 10*bis*(2) of the Paris Convention defines unfair competition as any act of competition contrary to honest practices in industrial or commercial matters. This definition leaves the determination of the notion of "commercial honesty" to the national courts and administrative authorities. Member States of the Paris Union are also free to grant protection against certain acts even if the parties involved are not competing against each other.

Article 10*bis*(3) of the Paris Convention gives three examples of cases that "in particular" have to be prohibited. These examples must not be seen as exhaustive, but rather as the minimum protection that has to be granted by all Member States. The first two—creating confusion and discrediting—can be regarded as belonging to the "traditional" field of competition law, namely that of competitor protection. The third one—misleading—was added by the 1958 Revision Conference in Lisbon, and takes into account the interests of both competitors and consumers.

Apart from Articles 10*bis* and 10*ter*, the Paris Convention contains several provisions relevant to protection against acts of unfair competition in a broader sense, especially those concerning trademarks and trade names. For example, Articles *6sexies* and 8 provide for the protection of service marks and trade names, respectively. The protection of indications of geographical origin, to the extent that it is not provided by

Article 10*bis*(3), results from Article 10 and Article 9, to which Article 10 refers. Special agreements concluded within the Paris Convention, namely, the Madrid Agreement for the Repression of False or Deceptive Indications of Source on Goods and the Lisbon Agreement for the Protection of Appellations of Origin and their International Registration, along with bilateral treaties, specifically provide for the international protection of GIs.

[2] Article 39 of the TRIPS Agreement

In Diplomatic Conferences on the revision of the Paris Convention, Members of the Paris Union refused to extend the discipline of the repression of unfair competition to the unauthorized reproduction of news (1925, at The Hague, and 1934, in London) and to the false indications of origin (1958, in Lisbon). The TRIPS Agreement, besides incorporating the provisions of the Paris Convention (1967) on the repression of unfair competition (TRIPS Agreement, Article 2.1), to some extent overcame those two objections. In Article 39.3 it extended the repression of unfair competition to acts of parasitic use of confidential test data and other data submitted by data holders as a requirement for the marketing approval of pharmaceutical and chemical products consisting of new chemical entities. Of course, this is not the same as news, but it concerns nevertheless a sort of protection of information. Moreover, in Article 22.2(b) of the TRIPS Agreement, WTO Members accepted to extend the protection against unfair competition, under Article 10*bis* of the Paris Convention in respect of GIs. These two provisions, therefore, overcame the reluctance of Paris Contracting Parties in extending the application of Article 10*bis* of the Paris Convention to the designations of origin and to the protection of information.

Importantly, Article 39.2 of the TRIPS Agreement provides for a definition of trade secrets, as information that:

> (a) is secret in the sense that it is not, as a body or in the precise configuration and assembly of its components, generally known among or readily accessible to persons within the circles that normally deal with the kind of information in question; (b) has commercial value because it is secret; and (c) has been subject to reasonable steps under the circumstances, by the person lawfully in control of the information, to keep it secret.

And footnote 10 to the Agreement added a partial definition of acts "contrary to honest commercial practices"—the standard for distinguishing a fair practice from an unfair one—by stating that the term means, at least, "breach of contract, breach of confidence and inducement to breach, and includes the acquisition of undisclosed information by third parties who knew, or were grossly negligent in failing to know, that such practices were involved in the acquisition."

Article 39 of the TRIPS Agreement does not use the term "trade secrets" but of "undisclosed information." This was an initiative of the European Communities, with a view to overcome the resistance of a number of delegations that feared that the traditional term could acquire a connotation of exclusive or proprietary rights, as it had in a few jurisdictions. More importantly, Article 39 overcame a generalized view expressed by developing countries during the TRIPS negotiations that trade secrets were not part of IP. Article 39 makes it clear they are.

In practical terms, the references in Article 22.2(b) and in Article 39 of the TRIPS Agreement to new subject matter of the repression of unfair competition could be seen as two new examples of unfair trade practices added to those provided by Article 10*bis*(3) of the Paris Convention.

[C] National Protection: Three Main Approaches to Unfair Competition Law

According to Article 10*bis*(l) of the Paris Convention, the Member States of the Paris Union have to provide effective protection against unfair competition. Although they are not obliged to introduce special legislation for the purpose, they must provide—at least on the basis of existing general legislation—effective safeguards against all acts "contrary to honest trade practices" and specifically against the practices referred to in Article 10*bis*(3). In the implementation of these treaty obligations, three main approaches can be distinguished.

[1] Protection Based on Specific Legislation

Several countries have enacted special statutes or specific provisions within broader statutes, which, sometimes combined with provisions in general statutes such as the Civil Code, deal with protection against unfair competition. These statutes provide for civil or criminal sanctions and contain a broad general provision (often modeled on Article 10*bis*(2) of the Paris Convention) which is supplemented by detailed provisions on specific forms of unfair trade practice; they usually provide for civil sanctions and, in respect of specific cases, also for criminal sanctions. Although many of these countries have also enacted additional legislation concerning acts relating to certain products (food, drugs, etc.), the media (television) or marketing practices (gifts, bonuses), the statute against unfair competition remains the main basis for protection. Often the scope of that statute has been made even broader by the assumption that the violation of any other law can be an unfair trade practice because it gives an undue advantage in competition over the law-abiding competitor. In some countries the concept of a special law on competition has evolved toward the adoption of a more general law on market behavior, or the link with antitrust law is stressed by the enactment of statutes that deal with the institution of competition itself as well as with fairness in competition.

[2] Protection Based on General Tort Law and/or on the Law Concerning "Passing-Off" and Trade Secrets

In a group of countries with a civil law tradition, which follow the approach consisting in the protection of the honest businessman, such protection is usually to be found in the general tort law. In another group of countries which follow common law traditions, the actions for passing-off and for violation of trade secrets developed by the courts (at least originally) remain the main basis for the protection of competitors. As for the protection of consumers, a number of the same two groups of countries have, in addition, enacted separate sets of laws regulating specific cases of undesirable market behavior, such as misleading advertising, price comparisons, lotteries, games and bonuses; those laws are essentially independent of the protection of competitors under civil law or common law principles.

[3] Combination of the Two Approaches Above

Most countries party to the Paris Convention—even those that at first attempted to regulate unfair competition by means of general tort law—provide for a combination of general civil code principles, case law and special laws. In many countries with a federal structure, the division of legislative competence between the federal legislature and the legislatures of the federated States has led to an even more complex combination of the various forms of protection. In some of those countries, the federal legislator even has no jurisdiction over unfair competition to the extent that it is considered a State common law tort. Where, in such countries, protection is granted by the States, it is in general better developed than that granted at the federal level. In the USA, in particular, the limited availability of common law remedies against unfair competition was first dealt with in federal law through the establishment of an administrative authority (the FTC), and more recently through the extension of a federal law provision on trademarks (Article 43(a) of the trademark law (Lanham Act)) to a wide variety of misleading representations. Yet the most progressive regulation is to be found in the "business laws," "little FTC Acts," "Consumer Protection Laws" and other legislation adopted by States within the USA.

[4] The Role of Jurisprudence

In spite of the different approaches mentioned above, all countries that have introduced effective safeguards against unfair competition take particular care over the enforcement of the law, and usually allow their courts considerable discretion. The success of an unfair competition law depends largely on what the courts make of it. A few words in a general tort provision may be a sufficient basis on which to develop an efficient system of unfair competition law, while a most impressively drafted statute may give disappointing results. This does not mean, however, that an explicit and detailed regulation of unfair trade practices is not useful: it will at least have some preventive effect on market behavior; but it will remain ineffectual if it is not activated by the courts. In the ever-changing world of competition, even the most perceptive legislator cannot possibly anticipate all future forms of unfair market behavior and must rely on interpretation of the law by the courts. Many countries have therefore supplemented their explicit provisions against certain market practices with a general provision, which allows the courts to include new forms of unfair market practice in the general system.

§13.04 ACTS OF UNFAIR COMPETITION

[A] General Definition

According to Article 10*bis*(2) of the Paris Convention, unfair competition consists in "any act of competition contrary to honest practices." Most countries with special laws on unfair competition have adopted the same or similar definitions for their general provision—using such terms as "honest trade practices" (Belgium and Luxembourg), "the principle of good faith" (Spain and Switzerland), "professional correctness" (Italy) and "good morals" (Germany, Greece and Poland). In the absence of specific legislation, the courts have defined fair competition with phrases like "the principles of honesty and fair dealing" or "the morals of the marketplace" (USA).

It is true that describing unfair competition as acts contrary to "honest trade practices," "good faith" and so on does not make for clear-cut, universally accepted standards of behavior, since the meaning of the terms used is rather fluid. The standard of "fairness" or "honesty" in competition is no more than a reflection of the sociological, economic, moral and ethical concepts of a society, and may therefore differ from country to country (and sometimes even within a country). That standard is also liable to change with time. Furthermore, there are always new acts of unfair competition, since there is ostensibly no limit to inventiveness in the field of competition. Any attempt to encompass all existing and future acts of competition in one sweeping definition—which at the same time defines all prohibited behavior *and* is flexible enough to adapt to new market practices—has so far failed.

This does not mean, however, that unfair competition is incapable of any general definition, and that the best one can do is label concrete examples of market behavior as being unfair. On the contrary, there are some aspects that clearly indicate which practices are to be considered "fair" and which "unfair."

It has been generally recognized that certain acts of commercial behavior are always (or, as Article 10*bis*(3) of the Paris Convention puts it, "in particular") considered to constitute unfair competition. The most notable of those acts are the causing of confusion, discrediting and the use of misleading indications. The common aspect of these most important, but by no means exhaustive, examples of unfair market behavior is the attempt (by an entrepreneur) to succeed in competition without relying on his/her own achievements in terms of quality and price of his/her products and services, but rather by taking undue advantage of the work of another or by influencing consumer demand with false or misleading statements. Practices that involve such methods are therefore doubtful at the outset as to their fairness in competition.

Another reference point could be the subjective element in the unfair act. At first sight, the notion of "honesty" seems to refer to a moral standard, and some sort of legal/ethical standard is indeed involved. This, however, has to be distinguished from the question whether an act of unfair competition can be established in the absence of any fault, bad faith or negligence. Where unfair competition law has been developed on the basis of general tort provisions, the "tort of unfair competition" requires some kind of subjective element such as "fault" or "bad faith." In practice, however, the element of fault or bad faith is often assumed by the courts. Such subjective elements are therefore not essential to the notion of fairness in competition. Indeed, with certain exceptions, rather objective standards are applied for the purposes of establishing an act of unfair competition; of course, subjective conditions may be relevant for the purpose of determining the sanction applicable. Sometimes this objective approach to unfair competition law is expressly stated in the legislation, as in the Spanish law of 1991, which uses the expression "any act against good faith in an objective sense."

The most important factor for determining "unfairness" in the marketplace, however, is derived from the purpose of unfair competition law. In this respect, unfair competition law was initially designed to protect the honest businessman. In the meantime, consumer protection has been recognized as equally important. Moreover, some countries put special emphasis on the protection of the public at large, and especially its interest in the freedom of competition. Modern unfair competition law therefore serves a threefold purpose, namely: the protection of competitors, the protection of consumers and the safeguarding of competition in the interest of the public at large. As stated in the Swiss law of 1986 and the Spanish law of 1991, the purpose of unfair competition law is to ensure fair and undistorted competition in the interest of all concerned. In practice, this means that unfair competition has also to be defined functionally, taking into account particularly the interests of those "concerned" by it, namely the parties involved in the operation of the marketplace.

One party who is always "concerned" is the honest businessman. Since unfair competition law started as a special law for the protection of the honest businessman, a businessman's standard of behavior logically serves as a starting point. A practice that is condemned as improper by all businessmen can, therefore, hardly qualify as a "fair" act of competition.

However, certain practices may be generally accepted within a branch of business but nevertheless considered "improper" by other market participants. In such cases, there has to be some ethical correction of the actual standards of behavior. Ethical standards dictate in particular that the interests of consumers must not be unnecessarily impaired, for example, by disregard for the principle of truthfulness (on which the consumer relies in his/her transactions), by enticement of the consumer into unsocial or even harmful behavior or by invasion of his/her privacy.

Furthermore, there may be practices that at first sight are not prejudicial either to other businessmen or to consumers, but nevertheless may have unwanted effects on the economy at large. For example, selling at dumping prices may in the long run destroy small- and medium-sized businesses, and thus have adverse effects on free competition. Where these economic aspects are incorporated in unfair competition law, such behavior will often be expressly labeled as "unfair."

When determining "honesty" in business dealings, all these factors have to be taken into account. In practice, the concept of unfair competition has increasingly become a balancing of interests. Differences in the evaluation of what is "fair" or "unfair" can generally be explained by the different emphasis placed on the aspects referred to above. For example, a particular kind of market behavior may well be seen differently in countries where the traditional law of unfair competition still focuses on the protection of the honest competitor, as opposed to countries that put special emphasis on the protection of consumers or the public at large.

However, there is broad agreement that at least some acts and practices are always irreconcilable with the notion of fairness in competition. These are discussed in detail below.

[B] Categories of Acts of Unfair Competition

Acts of unfair competition may be categorized in a variety of ways, depending on the criteria applied or the emphasis given to certain aspects of a given act or form of behavior. An act which is found to be "unfair" will often have taken place in circumstances which are complex, and which require scrutiny and judgment on the basis of established or prevailing standards. An act may be found to be unfair on more than one count, depending on the approach adopted to characterize the act. Therefore, one and the same act may fall into two or more categories. Likewise, no systematic categorization or classification of the acts of unfair competition can avoid some degree of overlap among the concepts and categories used.

For the purposes of establishing categories of acts of unfair competition and facilitating their analysis in this study, two broad groups of acts of unfair competition are distinguished, namely acts of the types expressly mentioned in Article 10*bis* of the Paris Convention and acts not expressly mentioned in Article 10*bis*.

Article 10*bis*(3) contains a non-exhaustive list of three types of acts of unfair competition, namely, acts likely to cause confusion, acts that discredit a competitor, and acts that may mislead the public. Because the acts that are likely to cause confusion and those that may mislead the public are akin to one another and sometimes overlap, they are dealt with before the act of discrediting a competitor.

There are a number of acts not mentioned in Article 10*bis* which have been recognized by the courts as unfair practices and which, increasingly, have become the subject of legislative provisions. Of particular interest in this connection is the trend toward explicit protection of trade secrets by express provisions in unfair competition laws, and the continuing evolution of provisions governing the practice of comparative advertising. Moreover, there has been an increasing recognition of the need to grant protection against undue "misappropriation" of, or "free riding" on, the achievements of competitors, regardless of the availability of specific industrial property rights, provided that, under the circumstances of the case, such acts are found to be unfair.

[C] Causing Confusion

[1] General Circumstances under Which Confusion Is Established

Article 10*bis*(3)1 of the Paris Convention obliges Member States to prohibit all acts that are of such a nature as to create confusion, by any means, with the establishment, the goods or the industrial or commercial activities of a competitor. The scope of Article 10&/s(3)l is very broad, as it covers any act in the course of trade involving a mark, sign, label, slogan, packaging, shape or color of goods, or any other distinctive indication used by a businessman. Thus, not only indications used to distinguish goods, services or businesses but also the appearance of goods and the presentation of services are considered relevant for the prohibition of confusion. For example, Article 2598(1) of the Italian Civil Code expressly provides that anyone who uses names or distinctive signs likely to cause confusion with those of another person, or slavishly imitates the product of a competitor, or by whatever other means creates confusion with the names, signs, products or activities of competitors, commits an act of unfair competition. Similarly, under Article 6 of the Spanish Law on Unfair Competition, any acts that are capable of creating confusion with the activities, achievements or business of another, including the likelihood of association by consumers with respect to the commercial source, is deemed unfair. In the countries with a common law tradition, the concept of "passing-off" is broad enough to provide all types of indication, product and other subject matter with protection against confusion.

Under Article 10*bis*(3)l of the Paris Convention, the "intent" to confuse is immaterial for the purposes of determining whether such an act constitutes an act of unfair competition. However, bad faith on the part of the imitator may have a bearing on the sanctions to be applied. Also, it is not usually necessary for confusion actually to have occurred, as the likelihood of confusion is often sufficient for an action based on unfair competition. Finally, protection against confusion is provided without any limitation in time. Protection is available as long as confusion is likely, but sufficient latitude is allowed for the use of non-confusing indications in respect of products, services and businesses, so that competition in the relevant market is not stifled. However, as soon as the marketable creation becomes generic or commonplace, it loses its original or distinctive character, and likelihood of confusion may no longer be assumed to the same degree.

There are two main areas in which confusion frequently occurs. These are indications of commercial origin on the one hand, and the appearance of goods on the other. However, this does not preclude or limit the protection of other attributes or achievements against confusion.

[2] Types of Confusion

Confusion can be established in different ways. The test for the basic type of confusion is whether the similar mark so resembles the protected mark that it is liable to confuse a substantial number of average consumers as to the commercial source of the goods or services. Factors frequently considered in determining confusion are the degree of distinctiveness of the protected mark, the size and reputation of its owner, the sophistication of the consumers concerned and, of course, the similarity of the marks and the goods or services involved. In many countries, confusion is not restricted to basic confusion as to the commercial source, but also includes that which gives the impression of a strong business connection between the two users of the same trademark or similar trademarks, i.e., confusion as to affiliation. However, the use of an identical or similar mark on clearly unrelated or completely different goods usually falls outside the scope of protection, as a large degree of dissimilarity of the goods or services involved will lead consumers to assume that the source of the goods or services is not the same and also that there is no particular business connection between the users.

A third form of confusion that has been referred to, for example, under section 43(a) of the Lanham Act of the USA and under section 53 of the Australian Trade Practices Act, is called confusion as to sponsorship. Under this test for confusion, consumers will assume both that the goods or services do not originate from the same source and that the two enterprises do not entertain business relations so intensive and continuous as to cause confusion as to affiliation. Nevertheless, the consumer will expect, from the similarity of the marks, from the types of product or service that the mark is used for and from the manner of use by the second user, that the use of the protected mark by the second user has been authorized by agreement for a certain period of time. This type of confusion can be relevant, for example, in cases where the third party uses the mark (without authorization) for ornamental purposes on goods. However, unlike confusion as to source or affiliation, this third type of confusion has not the same status as other fully established grounds for relief under statutory trademark laws, as its exact boundaries are still developing.

This concept of confusion may be relevant to so-called publicity rights, relating to well-known artists and media or sports personalities, and to "merchandising" rights, relating to fictional characters in literary or artistic works. These rights concern relatively new marketing techniques whereby enterprises are "licensed," for a certain period of time, to make use of the popularity or fame symbolized by the names or likenesses of certain personalities or characters, as this use is expected to stimulate consumer demand for the product or service of the "licensee." Consumers would generally be misled by the use of the name or likeness of the personality or character in connection with the product or service into believing that the personality or the owner of rights in the character, which could also be a registered mark, had expressly authorized the use of their personality or character.

[3] Confusion with Respect to Indications

An indication can be any sign, symbol or device that conveys to the consumer the message that a product or service on the market comes from a particular commercial source, even if this source is not known by its name. Indications may therefore consist of two-dimensional or three-dimensional signs, labels, slogans, packaging, colors or tunes, but are not limited to these. Protection against confusion with respect to indications is already available under specific legislation on trademarks, service marks and trade names. However, this protection is often limited in several ways. The limitations may concern the applicability of the specific law to certain types of indication, or the exact scope of protection. Thus, protection against confusion under unfair competition law may still be relevant where the specific legislation does not afford overall protection against confusion. This aspect is also relevant to the protection of well-known marks against confusion, as required by Article 6*bis* of the Paris Convention.

The general applicability of trademark law is usually confined to particular indications. Some countries do not, for example, recognize titles of single literary works or films, getup (product appearances), shop interiors, colors or color combinations, or trade dress under statutory trademark law. As regards service marks, although most countries have a system for the registration of such marks in the same way as trademarks, in those that do not, protection under the rules of prevention of unfair competition is needed. Also, even in countries where three-dimensional trademarks are recognized and registrable, particular shapes may nevertheless be excluded. For example, shapes determined solely by the nature of the goods, appearances resulting from some technical or industrial function of the goods and product configurations determining the essential value of the goods are expressly excluded by the EC Directive to Approximate the Laws Relating to Trade Marks. The "functionality" doctrine, particularly developed in the USA, produces similar results.

Apart from this, protection under trademark law can sometimes be invoked only for marks that have been properly registered in the country where protection is sought. In this respect Article 6*bis* of the Paris Convention constitutes an exception in favor of a well-known mark, which does not need to be registered in order to be protected against the potentially confusing use of a mark that is a reproduction or an imitation of the well-known mark and is used for identical or similar articles. It is to be noted that a trademark may be well known in a country before it is registered or even used in that country, as a result of the advertising or reputation of the mark in other countries.

Unfair competition law may provide protection against confusion for indications or signs that are not protectable under trademark law. However, the availability of protection for a sign under unfair competition law will depend partly on the reasons for the lack of protection for unregistered signs under the special laws. If a sign can in principle be covered by the specific legislation but does not meet the substantive requirements of that legislation, it would not seem consistent with a balanced system of protection to grant that sign the same protection under unfair competition law as would be granted to it under the special law. It is therefore argued that protection against confusion should only be available under unfair competition law if the indication or sign to be protected has sufficient distinctiveness to distinguish the products, services or other business activities concerned from the same or similar activities of other traders. Nevertheless, in order to promote the registration of marks, some unfair competition laws require more than just a minimum degree of distinctiveness for the protection of unregistered indications. For example, Article 2(1) of the Unfair Competition Prevention Law of the Republic of Korea requires the indication to be "widely known," which could in some cases restrict actual protection to one particular region.

The degree of distinctiveness of an indication that is not protected under statutory trademark law is assessed in relation to the same factors as apply to registered marks, including the meaning and the appearance of the indication, and its uniqueness compared with other indications for the same or a similar activity. Even if distinctiveness is inherently lacking, for example, owing to the descriptive nature of the indication for particular goods or services, the indication can be protected if it has acquired "distinctiveness by use," or secondary meaning, in the country where protection is sought. Secondary meaning implies that, as a result of continuous and exclusive use of the mark on the market, a substantial number of consumers have become aware of it and will associate the activity carried on under it with a particular commercial source. In Germany, for example, the trademark "4711" for perfume has been considered sufficiently distinctive as a result of public awareness that the goods under that mark come from a particular source. Actually, the degree of secondary meaning depends on the market for the goods or services involved and the degree of descriptiveness of the indication in relation to those goods or services. The degree of secondary meaning (or percentage of consumers) necessary to achieve sufficient distinctiveness varies according to the practices of the court concerned. In some countries, opinion polls or market surveys on consumer reactions often provide empirical data with which to determine the degree of secondary meaning, whereas in other countries the courts themselves will judge whether an indication has acquired sufficient distinctiveness.

Secondary meaning analysis also applies to indications that have been expressly excluded from statutory trademark protection. For example, the configurations or shapes of goods that are deemed to be excluded from statutory protection under trademark law by the EC Directive to Approximate Laws Relating to Trade Marks may still acquire secondary meaning among consumers in a particular market. Under those circumstances, protection against confusion is justified if consumers could be led to believe mistakenly that other goods using the configuration come from the first user. It may not always be easy, however, to establish the necessary degree of secondary meaning, since the particular configuration of the goods must be recognized by the relevant consumers as indicating a particular source. If the exclusion in the specific legislation is clearly intended to dismiss the indication as not worth protecting at all, for example, in the case of purely descriptive words, protection is likely to be denied also under unfair competition law.

Limitations on the scope of protection afforded by trademark law may also have the effect of allowing indications to be protected against confusion under unfair competition law. Although trademark laws usually grant protection against any potentially confusing use of a registered trademark, there may still be differences with respect to the exact scope of the protection against confusion. For example, protection against the use of the same or a similar mark might be restricted to those goods or services for which the mark is registered. If a mark identical or similar to the registered trademark is used for other goods or services and that use is likely to cause confusion, such protection might only be available under unfair competition law or passing-off principles. Generally, trademarks are protected against the use of identical or similar signs not only in respect of identical goods or services but also in respect of similar goods or services. This type of protection derives from what is sometimes called the "principle of specialty," as the protection is related to the trademark's primary function of distinguishing the goods of one enterprise from those of competitors and other market participants. Thus if trademark protection is not available because the goods or services involved are held to be dissimilar (although confusion as to source may in fact be possible), protection against confusion can be sought under unfair competition law. However, there are also trademark laws that consider the likelihood of confusion to be the sole criterion for protection, regarding the similarity of the goods or services involved as not decisive in itself, but only as one of several determining factors. This kind of statutory protection would encompass all types of confusion.

The criteria used to judge the similarity of indications are, with some minor differences, the same throughout the world. The determining factors include the common elements of appearance, pronunciation and meaning or verbal translation of the marks involved, but the decisive factor is the overall impression on the average consumer of the goods or services involved. Particularly if the goods are for mass consumption, the individual elements of the marks involved are less carefully examined by the average consumer. Since the two marks are as a rule not closely examined side by side, in practice the similarities between the indications are more important than the differences. The similarity of the goods or services depends largely on the question whether consumers would generally expect the goods or services to originate from the same source. However, they do not need to be either functionally interchangeable or competitive.

Protection against confusion may be too limited for so-called well-known marks and, in particular, for marks with an even higher reputation. Article 6*bis* of the Paris Convention requires Member States to protect trademarks that are well known in their country against any potentially confusing use of similar trademarks, but that obligation is only relevant for identical or similar goods. In certain cases, the unauthorized use of well-known marks for different goods or services may nevertheless cause confusion among consumers. For example, if the mark has been used for a broad range of products and has been extensively advertised or is well known for the particular "image" of its proprietor, consumers might associate such a mark with a certain origin and quality consistency rather than with goods or services of a specific kind. Such associations can also cause confusion. The Member States are not obliged under Article 6*bis* to grant this extended protection, but unfair competition law may be relevant. The question whether a trademark is "well known" in a given country for the purposes of Article 6*bis* of the Paris Convention has to be decided in each case on the basis of the facts. Usually, the factual determination of the notoriety of a trademark is based on its reputation and image in the mind of the trade circles and consumer groups concerned at the place and time relevant in the particular case. Factors such as the mark's inherent distinguishing power, the length of time that it has been used in the given country, the amount of advertising and other publicity given to it in various media and its established association with particular goods or services are often taken into consideration.

Statutory trademark law frequently requires that the use of a similar mark must be a form of trademark use, that is, use as an indication of the commercial source of the products or services. Thus, ornamental use, such as use on advertising material or as a mere decoration on goods, for instance, on ballpoint pens or ashtrays, or even as the configuration of an actual product such as an earring in the shape of the mark, is not always regarded as falling within the scope of statutory trademark protection. Protection against this type of use could, however, be sought under unfair competition law. One example of a trademark law that is very extensive in the above respects is the Uniform Benelux Trademark Law of 1971, which provides a broad definition of registrable marks and protection against any use of an identical or similar trademark by others without proper justification that is likely to cause prejudice to the trademark proprietor.

Similar limitations on protection against the unauthorized use of traders' or businesses' indications are to be found in the protection of trade names. Trade names serve to identify and to distinguish an enterprise and its business activities from those of other enterprises. Article 8 of the Paris Convention imposes the obligation to protect trade names in all countries of the Paris Union, without specifying what kind of protection should be granted or how it should be given. Nevertheless, trade names must be protected without any obligation of filing or registration. Most countries already protect trade names against the risk of confusion. This protection applies not only where trade names are covered by a special law, but also where they are protected under special provisions of unfair competition law, civil law, company law or commercial law. As a general rule, a direct competitive relationship between the enterprises concerned is not decisive, but remains relevant in determining whether the use of the same or similar trade names might confuse consumers regarding the identity of enterprises or the relationship between them. The protection may extend beyond the particular field in which the prior trade name is used, as trade practice or the likelihood of expansion and diversification of the activities of the enterprise is frequently taken into account by the courts. Thus the scope of protection of trade names against confusion may sometimes be a little wider than the scope of protection of trademarks under trademark law.

[4] Confusion with Respect to Product Shapes

The actual shape of a product could also lead to confusion among consumers. If the shape is so well known that consumers will relate the product with a particular commercial source (as in the case of the "Coca-Cola" bottle), then the shape can be regarded as a protectable indication.

It must also be noted that specific legislation is available in many countries for the protection of industrial designs, either to complement or to replace copyright protection for works of so-called applied art. Such legislation usually prohibits the use of identical or similar product appearances for identical or similar goods. However, as with trademark legislation, protection under special laws on industrial designs is also limited in several ways, which vary significantly from country to country. In a manner similar to the specific protection under trademark laws, such limitations may concern the general applicability of the designs law to certain product appearances and also the exact scope of the protection granted by the specific legislation. For example, if the design protection of a surface decoration is limited to the use of the decoration on products for which the design is registered, protection against copying of the design for the decoration of other products may be obtained under unfair competition law, if the copied design is misleading or causes confusion as to the commercial source.

For protection against confusion concerning the products only, most requirements under unfair competition law are established by case law, frequently with reference to the practice of "slavish imitation." Within this particular field of unfair competition law, it has often been stated that, as a principle inherent in the free market system, market participants are free to imitate designs or other shapes, appearances or visual characteristics of products that are not protected by specific laws such as patent, copyright, design or possibly trademark laws. Some of those specific laws even expressly preclude protection under unfair competition law for acts that are covered by the specific legislation if the design involved could be protected under that legislation. For example, Article 14(5) of the Uniform Benelux Designs Law of 1975 precludes actions to protect registrable designs under unfair competition law if protection could have been granted had the design been properly registered. Therefore, the mere risk of confusion as to the shape of the products will be insufficient to constitute unfair competition if the design would have been protectable under a specific law and product imitation would have been covered by that specific legislation. However, the risk of confusion as to the products may be sufficient to obtain protection under unfair competition if the design involved reveals a certain degree of originality but cannot be registered as a design owing to other requirements of the specific legislation, or if registration has been applied for but not yet secured.

If the design, shape or other characteristic non-functional features of the product are associated to a substantial degree by consumers with a certain source or origin, potential confusion as to the source of the product will usually constitute an act of unfair competition. Whether such potential confusion occurs in cases of imitation will be determined by the same factors as outlined above with respect to indications, that is, after examination of the question whether the characteristic features of a product have acquired a sufficient degree of secondary meaning, and the product designs involved will be judged on their similarities. In some countries it is accepted that the risk of confusion as to source can be reduced by the use of disclaimers, like a clearly visible statement ruling out the possible assumption that the product or service comes from a particular source. However, such disclaimers are only seldom recognized as sufficiently reducing the risk of confusion.

Protection against confusion as to the commercial source of a product may also be available under specific trademark law if the applicable trademark legislation provides for the protection of three-dimensional marks or the "getup" of products. However, if the product's appearance is not registered as a trademark, or if particular forms are possibly excluded from statutory trademark protection, the same principles as outlined above will apply to the protection against confusion between product shapes under unfair competition law.

[D] Misleading

[1] General

Misleading can roughly be defined as creating a false impression of a competitor's own products or services. It may well be the single most prevalent form of unfair competition, and it is by no means harmless. On the contrary, misleading can have quite serious consequences: the consumer, relying on incorrect information, may suffer financial (or more harmful) prejudice. The honest competitor loses clients. The transparency of the market diminishes, with adverse consequences for the economy as a whole and economic welfare.

Since truthfulness is rightly considered to be one of the main principles of honest trade practice, it is generally agreed that the prohibition of deception is essential to the concept of fairness in competition. Or, as Article 10*bis*(3) of the Paris Convention states, any indication or allegation that is likely to mislead, has "in particular" to be regarded as being contrary to honest practice.

Consequently, most Member States of the Paris Union have included the prohibition of misleading acts or practices in their legal systems (or have even passed specific laws on the subject). In addition, the courts have developed a particularly abundant case law on misleading. Even in countries where in the past protection against deception has been less strong than in others, recent developments indicate a move toward greater strictness. In the search for effective legal solutions, however, countries have chosen quite divergent methods. A significant factor of this divergence is that misleading acts are primarily directed to the consumer and not directly to competitors. Where consumer protection is primarily looked upon as a matter of criminal law, enforcement is left to the State enforcement authorities. However, most of the countries that have specific legislation on unfair competition have included a provision against deception into the relevant laws, thus adopting a civil law approach.

While, on the whole, the regulation of misleading makes a many-faceted picture, most countries share the distinction between "normal" misleading, which may be done in good faith, and special cases of misleading, which may have particularly severe consequences. For the most serious cases of misleading, such as malicious misleading or deception in the health and drug field, several countries have introduced criminal sanctions in addition to civil law remedies. Moreover, special cases of potential deception such as bonuses, gifts, clearance sales and travelling sales are often regulated in detail. Even tighter restrictions are frequently imposed by self-regulatory institutions, which in some countries have reached a particularly advanced state of development as regards protection against misleading.

In some countries the existing protection against misleading practices is to some extent a result of international harmonization. Because of the internationalization of commerce and communication media such as television, misleading acts and practices, especially in advertising, seldom stop at the border of a given country. Different national laws not only result in different and thus at least to some extent inadequate levels of consumer protection, but also affect the free circulation of goods and services.

Countries that are economically bound in a common market have a particular need for harmonization of diverging national laws on misleading. Thus the EC issued a Directive on Misleading Advertising in 1984 in order to set up a minimum objective criterion for determining whether advertising is misleading. A certain degree of harmonization has also been reached among the Nordic and the African countries.

[2] The Concept of Misleading

There is a consensus according to which the concept of misleading is restricted neither to inherently false statements nor to statements that have actually led to a false impression on the part of the consumer. Instead, it is considered sufficient (as it is by Article 10*bis*(3)3 of the Paris Convention) that the indications in question are likely to have a misleading effect. Even statements that are literally correct can be deceptive. If, for example, chemical ingredients are generally forbidden in bread, the courts of most countries would consider an advertising claim that a certain bread "was without chemical ingredients" to be deceptive, because, though literally true, it gives the misleading impression that the advertised fact is something out of the ordinary.

It is likewise not necessary for the product in question to be inferior, in an objective sense, so long as the indication or allegation has some enticing effect on the consumer. For example, if the public prefers domestic goods to foreign goods, a false declaration to the effect that imported goods are domestic is misleading even if the imported goods are of superior quality.

It is generally agreed that the question whether or not there is deception must be determined by the reaction of the addressee to the statement and not by the intention of its maker. However, the actual determination and evaluation of this reaction may differ from country to country and may also depend on the kind of addressee (consumers or traders) and the type of goods or services. The Paris Convention leaves this question to Member States (as does the EC Directive on Misleading Advertising). The different opinions as to what standards have to be applied are the result of different answers to the following questions:

(1) Is the prohibition of misleading meant to protect the average or (also) the less educated, less critical consumer?
(2) How is the public reaction determined? Empirically or by an overall estimation by the judge him/herself?
(3) How many of the addressees must be likely to be misled for a statement to be considered misleading?

In a number of countries the relevant standards are set on the basis of the notion of the average consumer. Where the courts base their assessments on the judges' own experience, there is a tendency to assume that the average consumer is generally well informed and intelligent enough to be immunized against most of the dangers of deception. In those countries the threshold is also considerably higher. Although it is frequently stressed that it is sufficient if a "not unsubstantial proportion of the addressees" are likely to be misled, the tendency is to favor an average deception rate.

However, in Germany the emphasis is clearly on the less educated, less critically prepared consumer, who is easily influenced by false statements. Misleading is frequently proven by empirical methods, mainly consumer surveys, and the interference threshold is set very low, at 10% to 15% of the consumers.

[3] Communication of Misleading Statements

Since the main area of misleading in commerce is to be found in advertising, most countries with special legislation have focused on misleading advertising. Other countries have chosen, as Article 10*bis*(3) of the Paris Convention has, the broader notion of "indication or allegation." In countries that have a general provision on unfair competition this difference is minimal, however, since there is basic agreement that deceptions other than those in advertising are irreconcilable with "honest trade practice" and can therefore be judged under the general provision.

It is further agreed that the exact way in which the allegation, indication or presentation is made is immaterial. So is the form of the message. All methods of communication—written, oral or even symbolic—have to be taken into account. Communications may be in the form of trademarks, labels, brochures, radio commercials, television publicity spots, posters and so on. In general, misleading is concerned only with the effect a statement has on the addressee and not with the way in which the statement is communicated.

The communication need not contain "information" in a neutral, objective sense in order to be considered under the heading of misleading practices. However, the concept of misleading is restricted to those indications that might cause misconceptions on the part of the consumer. The allegation, indication or presentation must therefore be able to create some sort of concrete impression which can be shown to be true or untrue. "Unobjective" or suggestive advertising which does no more than create vague positive feelings about a product is therefore outside the scope of misleading. If in some countries certain kinds of suggestion are forbidden, this is not done under the provisions on misleading, but rather under the general provision concerning honest trade practices.

A misleading communication does not necessarily have to be a positive one: a half-truth is always also a half-lie. For example, if it is claimed that a particular slice of bread has fewer calories than others, while this is solely due to the fact that it is thinner, the omission of this information can create as strong an incorrect impression as an express statement would have done. Consequently, some countries have expressly mentioned the omission of relevant facts in their lists of misleading practices, or alternatively the courts have recognized that such omission can be a misleading practice. An omission cannot always be equated with a positive statement, however. Since no businessman has the general duty to reveal adverse features of the product that he/she is offering, there can only be deception if the public, in the absence of express information, expects a certain characteristic to be present.

[4] Exaggerations

The consequences of the different concepts of misleading can best be seen in the treatment of exaggerations. Although in all countries obvious exaggerations (even if literally inaccurate) are not considered deceptive because they can easily be recognized as "sales talk," the question of what is mere "hot air" or "puffing" and what is to be taken seriously is answered differently in different countries. In some countries (such as Germany), it is assumed that the public basically believes all advertising statements, and especially those that claim uniqueness ("the best, the first," etc.); consequently, an especially strict standard is applied. Other countries (such as Italy and the USA) take the exact opposite position and tolerate generally formulated indications, in particular those in the form of claims of uniqueness. Thus, in the USA the courts have generally only intervened if the product advertised as the best is in reality inferior.

[5] The Subject Matter of Misleading

Deceptive statements can be made on all relevant aspects of business matters. However, in principle, the prohibition of deception should be broad enough to cover those new forms of misleading that the legislator has not thought of. Nevertheless, a statutory provision must give guidance to the courts. In countries with a predominantly civil law approach, this is often achieved by expressly naming those forms that "in particular" must be regarded as misleading, leaving the courts free to take other forms of deception into account. Usually at least the examples given in Article 10*bis*(3)(3) of the Paris Convention are included, namely, "the nature, the manufacturing process, the characteristics, the suitability for their purpose, or the quantity, of the goods." Often services and indications of geographical origin are also included. Recent legislation on unfair competition also mentions some "modern" examples of misleading. The Greek Decree on Misleading Advertising, for example, expressly refers to misleading statements in the endorsement of products or the passing-off of an advertisement as a press article. The same applies in Belgium. In Hungary, any misleading references to the environment, among other things, are expressly forbidden. Still other countries (and the EC Directive on Misleading Advertising) prohibit any deception with respect to the identity of the advertiser. This is interesting inasmuch as there seems to be basic agreement that these specific errors of identity (while they do, of course, involve deception) are rather dealt with under the heading of confusion (or passing-off), which is largely covered by specific laws on trademarks and trade names. However, the express inclusion of errors as to commercial origin under the heading of deception is significant in that the special procedure provisions of unfair competition law may be applied. For example, consumer associations may bring an action in a case of misleading involving trademarks, whereas trademark law itself would restrict the right of action to the trademark owner.

A list of examples of misleading practices supplemented with a general provision is only possible, however, if the sanctions against misleading are predominantly those of civil law. Criminal law usually requires a relatively narrowly worded, enumerative prohibition, although in practice this difference is mitigated by the fact that usually the list of expressly named practices is fairly comprehensive.

[6] Subjective Requirements

Even the most careful businessman can issue a statement that the public misunderstands in a way not foreseen by him. Misleading statements, especially in advertising, are therefore not always made in bad faith. However, even in the absence of any fault on the part of the advertiser, deception in competition has to be stopped in the interest of the consumer and of other competitors. The EC Directive on Misleading Advertising, for example, obliges Member States to ensure the cessation of misleading "even without proof of actual loss or damage or of intention or negligence on the part of the advertiser." Countries that favor a civil law approach in the repression of unfair competition usually have few problems in doing so, but where the law against misleading conduct is essentially part of criminal law, at least in theory some subjective element is required. Because of the difficulty of furnishing such evidence, this "subjective" concept has proved a hindrance. Thus, in practice, the courts have gradually reduced the requirement of intent. This can best be seen in France, where the (criminal) prohibition of misleading advertising in Article 44 of the Loi Royer in theory still requires "bad faith," but where the courts have first reduced this requirement to mere knowledge of facts, and have later even assumed such knowledge.

This primarily objective approach to the repression of misleading statements is, of course, restricted to a cease-and-desist action (and possibly to the remedy of publication). In all countries, an action for damages will only be successful if there is at least negligence. Intent, or even malicious behavior, is required in cases that can be described as real criminal offenses, for example in the food and drug field.

[7] Burden of Proof

The question of who has to furnish evidence of the accuracy of a statement or the likelihood of deception can be of paramount importance in misleading advertising cases. According to general principles of procedural law in most countries, it is the plaintiff (or the public prosecutor or administrative authority) who bears the burden of proof. In the field of misleading, especially misleading advertising, however, some exceptions to this rule are made. The EC Directive on Misleading Advertising, for example, obliges Member States to require the advertiser to furnish evidence of the accuracy of factual claims if "such a requirement appears appropriate on the basis of the circumstances of the particular case." Some countries have gone even further by implementing a general reversal of the burden of proof or by placing the advertiser under the obligation to "reasonably substantiate" all advertising claims.

[E] Discrediting Competitors

[1] General

Discrediting (or disparagement) is usually defined as any false allegation concerning a competitor that is likely to harm his/her commercial goodwill. Like misleading, discrediting tries to entice customers with incorrect information. Unlike misleading, however, this is not done by false or deceptive statements about one's own product, but rather by casting untruthful aspersions on a competitor, his/her products or his/her services. Discrediting, therefore, always involves a direct attach on a particular businessman or a particular category of businessmen, but its consequences go beyond that aim: since the information on the competitor or his/her products is incorrect, the consumer is liable to suffer also.

Article 10*bis*(3)(2) of the Paris Convention obliges Member States to prohibit all "false allegations in the course of trade of such a nature as to discredit the establishment, the goods, or the industrial or commercial activities, of a competitor." A similar provision can be found in most national laws on unfair competition. But even without such an express prohibition, it is generally agreed that discrediting is irreconcilable with the notion of "fairness" in competition. Where unfair competition law has been developed on the basis of general tort provisions, it is considered one of the "classical" forms of unfair competition. In all common law countries a (common law) tort of disparagement or discrediting is recognized; additionally some of those countries have recently granted statutory relief. Since it is primarily the individual businessman who suffers from disparaging remarks, civil law sanctions (injunctive relief or damages) are preferred. However, in the most serious cases, especially those involving intentional or malicious defamation, criminal sanctions are also provided, often under the general criminal code.

[2] Reference to an Individual Competitor

As mentioned above, it is in the very nature of discrediting to be directed against a particular businessman or a particular category of businessmen. The target need not necessarily be named, however: easy identification by the addressee of the statement is sufficient. This can be achieved by references like "a certain enterprise in X" or may even be the result of a special market situation, for example if there is only one relevant competitor.

Frequently, the person attacked will be a competitor. As in Article 10*bis*(3)2 of the Paris Convention, most countries restrict unfair competition law protection against disparagement to cases where there is at least some sort of competitive relationship between the plaintiff and the defendant. In some countries, however, the requirement of a competitive relationship has been totally abandoned, and this has led to a considerably broader concept of discrediting: not only competitors but also consumer associations or the media can be held liable under unfair competition law if they make derogatory statements about an individual businessman.

[3] The Subject Matter of the Attack

As to the subject matter of the attack, Article 106*bis*(3)2 of the Paris Convention names the establishment, the goods and the industrial or commercial activities (of a competitor). However, any kind of disparaging remark that is likely to harm the goodwill of an entrepreneur should be forbidden. The way in which the harm is done should be irrelevant. Harm to a business reputation can be caused by all forms of reference to the enterprise or to its goods, prices, employees, credit rating, qualifications and so on. It can also be caused by references to an entrepreneur's personal status, for example, his/her race, his/her nationality, his/her religion or his/her political position. These so-called personal references which have nothing to do with commercial activities are in some countries expressly forbidden as disparaging; in others they are considered illegal under the general provisions on protection against unfair competition.

[4] Intent or Actual Damage

References to a competitor that affect his/her commercial goodwill can be made in good faith, for example if the maker of the statement believes it to be true. Effective protection against discrediting is therefore typically independent of any proof of actual damage or intent. In some countries (such as the USA), however, the common law tort of disparagement in theory requires proof of malice and damage. Although the courts in the USA have gradually eased that requirement, the concept still has proved to be too narrow, and that has led to the enactment of legislative provisions for the grant of statutory relief against disparagement without any evidence of damage or intent (*see* section 43(a) of the Lanham Act).

[5] Statements of Fact

Opinions differ on whether discrediting should be restricted to statements of fact. In some countries, the statutory notion of discrediting is broad enough to cover also statements of opinion. In other countries, it has at least been recognized by the courts that such statements are within the scope of the general provision against dishonest trade practices. In still other countries, disparagement is concerned mainly with statements of fact.

[6] False Statements

The question whether statements of opinion can be discrediting has to be considered in connection with another question, namely, whether protection should be extended to the case of accurate statements. Article 10*bis*(3)(2) of the Paris Convention speaks of false allegations. Many countries go further, however, recognizing that true, but nevertheless discrediting remarks are either directly within the scope of the express prohibition of discrediting, or at least a violation of the general provisions on honest trade practices. Thus, a literally truthful remark about a competitor may be considered unfair competition if the "attack" is blown up out of proportion, or if the words used are needlessly injurious. However, some countries expressly restrict the notion of discrediting to inaccurate or at least misleading statements. In the USA, for example, true but nevertheless disparaging statements are neither within the scope of the common law tort of disparagement nor within that of the statutory relief granted by section 43(a) of the Lanham Act or—at State level—the statutes on business practices.

An explanation of this difference in attitudes can be found in the diverging assessment of "commercial honor." Where unfair competition law has its roots in the protection of the commercial reputation of the individual businessman—as it does in the continental European countries—a "special tort of business disparagement" has emerged, to which, in principle, much stricter rules apply than to defamatory statements outside the bounds of competition, where constitutional considerations such as freedom of speech have to be taken into account. In other countries, especially those that have not developed a comprehensive system of protection against unfair competition, the attitude is exactly the opposite: it is assumed that, in the interest of competition, attacks on individual competitors are unavoidable, that they must be widely tolerated and that a line should only be drawn where the attack is based on false facts. In those countries, the plaintiff usually also bears the burden of proof as to the falseness of the statement (which can sometimes make an action impossible).

[F] Violation of Trade Secrets

[1] General

Competitive strength usually depends on innovative techniques and accompanying know-how in the industrial and/or commercial field. However, such techniques and know-how are not always protectable by patent law. First, patents are available only for inventions in the field of technology and not for innovative achievements concerning the conduct of business, etc. Moreover, some technical discoveries or information, while providing a valuable commercial advantage for a particular trader, may lack the novelty or inventive step required to make them patentable. Furthermore, during the pendency of a patent application, as long as the information has not been disclosed to the public, the owner of the information to be patented ought to be protected against any wrongful disclosure of the information by others, regardless of whether or not the application eventually leads to the grant of a patent. Although the Paris Convention does not mention trade secrets, the need for their protection against wrongful disclosure is generally recognized. The unauthorized use of valuable secret information by persons other than the holder of the secret is regarded as a misappropriation of business values that have been developed by the holder, who loses his/her competitive and economic advantage over competitors as soon as the information is used or disclosed by another.

Trade secrets are protected against unauthorized use and disclosure by various statutory means. Some countries have special provisions for the protection of trade secrets either under specific legislation on unfair competition or as part of another law. Other countries treat trade secrets as an aspect of tort law. Still other countries have enacted criminal, administrative, commercial or civil law provisions prohibiting the unauthorized use or disclosure of business secrets. The criminal provisions are less important in practice, however, since normally knowledge of the secrecy, as well as malicious or fraudulent intent, have to be proved. Yet if the disclosure of a trade secret constitutes a criminal offense, it will normally constitute an act of unfair competition as well. Furthermore, since employees, consultants, independent contractors and joint venturers are often privy to trade secrets, several aspects of civil law concerning employment contracts and general contract law are also relevant, depending on the circumstances of the case. Finally, it is not unusual to have combinations of the above means available. For example, violation of trade secrets could result in unfair competition or tort liability, as well as in criminal sanctions. However, in situations where non-competitors have intimidated or influenced agents or employees, or have otherwise induced them or other persons bound to secrecy to disclose the secret information, only civil tort law might be applicable.

[2] What Information Can Be a Trade Secret?

Although a legal definition of a trade secret rarely exists, several countries (following the example of France) differentiate between manufacturing (or industrial) secrets and commercial secrets, which could have consequences for the applicability of criminal law. The first category of trade secrets is related to information of purely technical character, like production methods, chemical formulae, blueprints or prototypes. Such information could constitute a patentable invention but, generally, patentability of the information in question, in particular, novelty in a patent law sense, is not required for the secret to be protectable. Commercial secrets include sales methods, distribution methods, contract forms, business schedules, details of price agreements, consumer profiles, advertising strategies and lists of suppliers or clients. Usually, the subject matter of trade secrets is rather broadly defined, and the final determination of what information can be a trade secret will depend on the specific circumstances of each individual case. For example, in the Unfair Competition Prevention Act of Japan, a trade secret is defined as any information relating to a production method, a sales method or any other information on technology or business that is unknown to the public. A similar definition is contained in the Uniform Trade Secrets Act of the USA, which has been adopted by about twenty States.

There are several lines of inquiry that serve to determine what information constitutes a trade secret: the extent to which the information is known to the public or within a particular trade or industry, the amount of effort and money expended by the trader in developing the secret information, the value of that information to the trader and to his/her competitors, the extent of measures taken by the trader to guard the secrecy of the information and the ease or difficulty with which the information could be properly acquired by others. From a subjective point of view, the trader involved must have a considerable interest in keeping certain information as a trade secret.

Although contractual obligations are not necessary, the trader must have shown the intention to have the information treated as a secret. Frequently, specific measures to maintain the secrecy of the particular information are also required. The fact that the information has been supplied confidentially will not always be sufficient. In some countries (e.g., the USA and Japan), the efforts made by the owner of the information to keep it secret are considered by courts to be of primary importance in determining whether the information constitutes a trade secret at all.

From an objective point of view, the information must, in order to qualify as a trade secret, be known to a limited group of persons only, that is, it must not be generally known to experts or to competitors in the field. Even patent applications may be regarded as trade secrets as long as they are not published by the patent office. Therefore, external publications or other information that is readily available will not be considered secret. For example, the use or disclosure of a trade secret by a person who has acquired it in a legitimate business transaction and without any negligence is not deemed unfair. However, absolute secrecy is not a requirement, for the information might also be discovered independently by others. Also, business partners can be informed without loss of secrecy if it is obvious that the information has to remain secret. Factors that indicate whether the information has the necessary degree of confidentiality to constitute a protectable trade secret are whether it contains material that is not confidential if looked at in isolation, whether it has necessarily to be acquired by employees if they are to work efficiently and whether it is restricted to senior management or is also known at the junior level. Still, the most solid proof is the strict confidentiality of the information and the contractual duty to keep it secret.

A definition of trade secrets is provided by Article 39.2 of the TRIPS Agreement. They are information that:

(a) is secret in the sense that it is not, as a body or in the precise configuration and assembly of its components, generally known among or readily accessible to persons within the circles that normally deal with the kind of information in question;
(b) has commercial value because it is secret; and
(c) has been subject to reasonable steps under the circumstances, by the person lawfully in control of the information, to keep it secret.

[3] Use and Disclosure by (Former) Employees

Even in countries where specific provisions on wrongful or unfair disclosure apply, employment contracts may serve to reinforce and supplement the protection afforded to trade secrets under the law of unfair competition or tort law. It is generally accepted that employees have a basic right to use and exploit, for the purpose of earning their living, all skills, experience and knowledge that they may have acquired in the course of previous periods of employment, even with the help of trade secrets. Yet, an employee does have the duty, during the period of employment, to act with good faith toward his/her employer and, after the employment has come to an end, not to use or disclose any confidential information about his/her employer's affairs that may have come to his/her notice during his/her employment. Thus, in many cases the use or disclosure of information will constitute a breach of the employment contract by the (former) employee if the information in question must remain secret. However, the distinction between using the skills, knowledge and experience legitimately acquired during employment and the prohibition on the use or disclosure of the former employer's industrial or commercial secrets is often difficult to make. Clearly, in cases where the behavior of the employee is equivalent to theft, embezzlement, industrial espionage or conspiracy with a competitor, a willful breach of confidence will be presumed.

Frequently, employment contracts incorporate specific provisions prohibiting the disclosure of business or trade secrets, but such provisions, like undertakings not to compete, must not be so restrictive of the professional abilities of the employee in the future that they constitute an undue restraint of trade. Criminal law, as well as civil and labor law, could create relevant duties in employment relations. For example, according to Article 237 of the Criminal Code of the Netherlands, the disclosure of trade secrets by a person employed by a trader is an offense, and Article 2622 of the Italian Civil Code forbids the disclosure of secret business information by directors, general managers and legal auditors of any type of company. Such provisions may be very important in situations where the employee is not bound by contractual clauses, or where the use of such information by former employees is not related to a competitive action. If the former employee can be regarded as a competitor of the former employer, for example if he/she has set up a company on his/her own in the same sector, a breach of confidence by the former employee will normally be an act of unfair competition. For example, the inducement of customers of the former employer to become clients of the employee in his/her new position will probably be deemed unfair, particularly if the employee misuses lists of customers or internal business details in order to make better offers. However, there can also be wrongful misuse of confidential information if special knowledge of the employer's activities in relation to clients' affairs is made use of to persuade those clients to transfer their business to another.

[4] Use and Disclosure by Competitors

Competitors are usually very interested in acquiring the trade secrets of others. However, as trade secrets themselves are not fully equivalent to exclusive rights under industrial property law, the determination of the unfairness of competitors who use or disclose the trade secrets of others is based on the means of acquiring the information. For example, it is expressly stated in the Unfair Competition Prevention Law of Japan that the rules concerning the protection of trade secrets will not apply where a trade secret is obtained in the course of a legitimate trade activity, provided that the person obtaining the secret did not use dishonest means to do so, or did not negligently disregard the dishonesty of such means. Thus competitors who have not used any influence to bring about the disclosure of the secret information, but have merely taken advantage of the breach of contract of a former employee or partner of the competitor, will seldom be held liable. The competitor's awareness that the disclosure of the trade secret by the former employee or partner would be a breach of contract is regarded as a minimum level of intent for determining liability. The Mexican law, for example, makes it an offense to use a trade secret which has been disclosed by a third party where the person to whom the secret was disclosed knew that the third party was not authorized to disclose the secret. In any case, competitors are not allowed to interfere recklessly with the contractual relations of others. For example, if a competitor has bribed or otherwise unlawfully persuaded a (former) employee to disclose a competitor's trade secret, he/she will be liable for unfair competition.

There are many situations that will depend on the specific circumstances of the case. For example, where the use of trade secrets was part of a former business relationship between the competitors, the fact that the know-how was to be kept secret does not in itself imply that use by the competitor would always be deemed unfair. However, the possible lack of a contractual clause concerning the use of trade secrets does not preclude unfairness. If the disclosure of trade secrets by a (former) employee is willfully induced by a competitor, the competitor is committing an actionable offense, provided he/she should reasonably have known or suspected that disclosure of the information was a breach of contract at the time of receiving the information. Frequently, the inducement of employees to disclose trade secrets is combined with a (separate) act of unduly enticing employees away, which is consistently deemed to be a violation of unfair competition law.

Article 39.2 of the TRIPS Agreement adopted a broad approach and, instead of identifying the possible authors of trade secret violations, preferred to define those violations in terms of their substance. A violation occurs when the secret information is lawfully within control of the victim; when the information is susceptible of being disclosed, acquired by, or used by others; lack of consent for these practices given by the person in lawful possession of the information; and when the manner of disclosure, acquisition, and use of that information is contrary to honest commercial practices. These practices are defined by note 10 of the TRIPS Agreement in a similar, but broader manner as Article 10*bis*(2) of the Paris Convention.

[G] Taking Undue Advantage of Another's Achievement ("Free Riding")

[1] General

In addition to the likelihood of confusion, there are other circumstances that may be held relevant under various doctrines with respect to the imitation of indications, products or other marketable creations. Such circumstances involve the act of taking undue advantage of, or free riding on, another person's achievement recognized by consumers and other market participants like dealers, traders and suppliers. Frequently such achievements concern a certain indication or product but they could also be of purely technical character.

Protection in such cases depends on a number of requirements which vary from country to country. The unfairness of the competitive act is regarded as resulting not only from the obvious exploitation of the notoriety of the indication, commercial success of the product or technical achievement of the competitor without any proper effort being made to depart substantially from the characteristic features of that particular achievement, but also from the risk of damage to the reputation of the existing business. As a minimum prerequisite, the indication or the product must have a certain distinctiveness (which may be of a level not sufficient for protection under specific legislation). As the scope of protection may depend on the degree of distinctiveness, completely banal indications or products will not usually qualify for protection against mere imitation.

From a purely systematic point of view, the notion of "free riding" has a number of common features with the notions of causing confusion and misleading. Free riding on another person's market achievements can be defined as any act that a competitor or another market participant undertakes with the intention of directly exploiting another person's industrial or commercial achievement for his/her own business purposes without substantially departing from the original achievement. In that sense, free riding is the broadest form of competition by imitation. Under the principles of a free market, however, the exploitation or "appropriation" of another person's achievements is unfair only under specific circumstances. However, acts that cause confusion or mislead normally imply free riding on another person's achievements, but are generally recognized as forms of free riding that are always unfair.

When assessing the availability of protection against unfair competition for market achievements of others in the absence of confusion, it has often been stated that the mere exploitation of another's achievement is consistent with the principles of a free market system. Thus protection under the rules concerning unfair competition cannot simply be regarded as an alternative route to the securing of protection which would be available without the obligation to comply with the various requirements of protection imposed by specific industrial property legislation. As a certain balance of interests on the relevant market has been achieved by adopting specific legislation on patents, industrial designs, trademarks and so on, that balance must also be taken into consideration in the application of unfair competition law. As a general rule, protection under unfair competition law will be denied if the achievement that has been copied or appropriated is covered by specific industrial property legislation and the type of protection sought by resorting to unfair competition law could have been obtained, at least for a certain period of time, under that specific legislation (principle of "preemption").

As indicated above, protection as such may be invoked if the subject matter of specific legislation does not cover the achievement involved, for example, if the law is not applicable to achievements made before a certain date, or if the protection granted by the special law is not broad enough to give the relief sought in the specific case. Some industrial property laws expressly provide that protection under unfair competition provisions may be invoked for achievements that are not protectable under the specific law. Some industrial property laws expressly exclude additional protection under unfair competition law for inventions, indications, signs or product shapes that are protectable under those laws. Still, it is not always clear what interests the legislation has in fact balanced by adopting the special law. Even legislative commentaries do not comprehensively clarify that question. Thus, a common approach to the grant of protection against free riding under unfair competition law is to make such protection available only under specific circumstances, which must differ in some respects from the circumstances under which protection is granted by the specific legislation. The definition of those circumstances is often possible only under some sort of "catch-air" provision, and thus usually is established by case law. For the following types of free riding, specific circumstances resulting in an act of unfair competition are already recognized in many countries: dilution of the distinctive quality or advertising value of a mark, misappropriation of a reputation, slavish imitation and so-called parasitic acts. These are dealt with in the following paragraphs.

[2] Dilution of the Distinctive Quality or Advertising Value of a Mark

Generally, where the unauthorized use of a mark for different goods or services is not likely to cause confusion, there is neither trademark or service mark infringement nor an act of unfair competition. This follows from the "specialty principle" in trademark law, which is a consequence of the distinguishing function of trademarks and service marks. In some countries, however, such as Canada, the EC Member States under the EC Directive to Approximate National Laws on Trade Marks and several States of the USA, marks that have acquired a certain renown are given additional protection against the so-called dilution of their distinctive quality or advertising value. The concept of "dilution" is understood as the watering down or gradual lessening of the ability of a mark to be immediately associated by consumers or the general public with a particular source. As some dilution can be regarded as being an inherent result of the use of identical or similar marks for totally different goods or services, the main rationale behind the notion of dilution is that marks that have acquired a certain renown should be protected against the obvious desire of other market participants to take advantage of the essential "uniqueness" of a mark. The likelihood of substantial damage to the proprietor of the mark is assumed from the fact that the mark may lose its established association with certain products. The required degree of renown of the mark involved is determined by the relevant public or consumer groups. If it is a trademark for goods that appeal only to a selected group of consumers, it will have a better chance of reaching the required degree of renown than if it is one for mass-consumption goods. However, the required degree may still vary considerably from country to country.

Under Article 16.3 of the TRIPS Agreement, well-known trademarks are protected against dilution, provided that the interests of the trademark owner are likely to be damaged. WTO Members are free to limit protection against dilution to registered well-known trademarks.

[3] Exploitation of Another's Reputation

Another type of misappropriation that has been recognized in recent years as being contrary to honest business practice is that of unfairly taking advantage of the reputation or "prestige" of the market achievements of other industrial or commercial enterprises. This doctrine has been particularly relevant in the appropriation of well-known indications. For example, if the quality of the genuinely marked product or service has led consumers to associate the mark with a certain origin or consistency of product quality, its unauthorized use for other goods or services, while not causing confusion as to their source, might still be considered unfair appropriation of a reputation. The doctrine may equally apply to product appearances, but in such a case the appearance must be recognized as indicating a certain degree of quality, image or prestige. Countries have different approaches to this kind of misappropriation, however. For example, whereas in France the appropriation of the prestige of another's mark or product is usually assumed to be unfair, in Spain that type of misappropriation is expressly prohibited without any further prerequisites in Article 12 of the Law Against Unfair Competition of 1991. In Germany it is required, for the appropriation by a third person to be allowed, that a secondary exploitation of the mark could not reasonably be expected. In the USA there is in principle no objection to appropriation unless a likelihood of confusion, for example as to "sponsorship," is established, for which purpose the prestige of the mark is taken into account.

Taking advantage of another's trademark or service mark may occur as a more or less veiled form of appropriation. For example, a competitor may use a generally similar, but noticeably different mark, nevertheless consciously drawing closely on the characteristic and well-known features of another's mark. Alternatively, he/she may use the mark in advertising his/her own trademarked goods with the aim of transferring the image of the well-known mark to his/her own goods, or again he/she may use another's mark with qualifying terms like "model," "type," "style," and so on (however, in some countries the term "suitable for" or other similar terms may be permissible in connection with spare parts and accessories). In this respect, it is not necessary that the market participant be a direct competitor of the proprietor of the mark, as long as there is a likelihood of damage to the exclusive image or reputation of the mark or the business involved.

[4] Slavish Imitation

The concept of slavish imitation as a separate act of unfair competition has been developed in several countries of Europe. This kind of unfair free riding is usually regarded as an exception to the general rule of free appropriation in the area of products or indications that are not protectable or for which protection has lapsed under specific legislation, or where there is no likelihood of confusion as to the source of the products. In the absence of likelihood of confusion, the specific circumstances of the case must reveal some exceptional character for the act to be deemed unfair. Usually, the unfairness is seen in the lack of research, investment, creativeness and expense on the part of the imitator, who has merely copied the achievement of another, despite the fact that alternative ways of competing effectively were available. The imitated products or indications would still have to possess a particular distinctiveness, which must not merely derive from technical features necessary for the product to function properly, but must concern aesthetic or decorative features that leave sufficient room for alternative shapes and designs.

Not all prerequisites of slavish imitation are equivalent in all countries, however. Apart from that, the qualifying circumstances may sometimes be combined with the concepts of dilution, misappropriation of reputation or "parasitic competition." Frequently, there has to be a marked contrast between the efforts made by the competitor to develop his/her achievement, to introduce it on the market and to win some success or recognition and the efforts made by the imitator to copy and exploit that achievement for the act to be deemed unfair. One statutory example of a provision against this kind of unfair misappropriation is to be found in Article 5(c) of the Swiss Law Against Unfair Competition, which specifically treats as unfair any act which, by means of technical reproduction processes and without any corresponding effort, takes the marketable results of the work of another person and exploits them as such. There is a similar provision in Article 11(2) of the Spanish Law on Unfair Competition, which considers imitation of the achievements of another to be unfair if undue advantage is taken of the other's goodwill or efforts.

Acts of slavish imitation should be distinguished from acts of so-called reverse engineering. The latter is generally understood to consist in examining or analyzing, by taking apart or decomposing, a product or substance in order to understand its structure, composition or operation and find out how it was made or constructed, and subsequently producing an improved version of the product or substance. The practice of reverse engineering is commonly practiced in industry in connection with the products of competitors, with the purpose of learning the technology they embody, and eventually producing a competing (improved or different but equivalent) product. In fact, it is part of the normal exercise of competition in a free market environment which, in turn, is based on broader public policy considerations. The practice of reverse engineering is, therefore, not in and of itself unfair; nevertheless, the product or other result obtained through reverse engineering may, under certain circumstances, constitute an infringement of an industrial property right. For example, if a product made after reverse engineering of a competitor's product falls under the claims of a valid patent (where appropriate, taking into account the doctrine of equivalence), that would constitute patent infringement. If a patent is not infringed, but the manner in which the original product was copied is found to be dishonest or unfair (regardless of whether reverse engineering took place), the relevant acts might still be actionable on grounds of unfair competition.

[5] Parasitic Acts

Another variety of unfair free riding recognized in some countries is the concept of "parasitic acts." This concept has many features in common with the concept of slavish imitation. Here the mere imitation of the achievements of others is still considered inherent in a free market system, but exceptional circumstances may make the imitation unfair. For example, the imitation of one product which is not particularly new or original could possibly be allowed, but, as soon as the achievement involved is recognized as innovative or strongly appealing to consumers, the imitator has less reason to claim the fairness of his/her action. What tips the balance definitely against the imitator is his/her systematic and methodical appropriation of the characteristic achievements of one particular competitor in a routine manner. Moreover, circumstances relating to the modus operandi of a competitor may denote unfairness: for example, ordering samples from a competitor for the purpose of imitating his/her products more easily and systematically may be found to be unfair parasitic behavior. Some countries adopt a flexible approach in these cases, in particular, by adapting the scope of injunctions and also the time limits of protection to the particular circumstances. For example, the amortization of the innovation costs could be considered a relevant factor in determining whether or not a particular imitation is fair. As a result, protection could be restricted to identical imitations, and only for a period of time that is much shorter than under specific industrial property legislation. It is to be noted, however, that in some countries (e.g., the USA) just copying the product of another person (even if done systematically, or in respect of one particular competitor) will not be recognized as unfair competition unless there is copying of non-functional features which are distinctive or have acquired secondary meaning.

[H] Comparative Advertising

[1] Definition

The different attitudes toward true but nevertheless discrediting statements can best be seen in the examination of comparative advertising. Comparative advertising may take two forms: a positive reference to another's product (claiming that one's own product is as good as the other) or a negative reference (claiming that one's own product is better than the other). In the first instance, where the competitor's product is usually well known, the crucial question relates to the possibility of misappropriation of another's goodwill. In the second case, where the competitor's product is criticized, it is the question of disparagement that arises. However, both forms of comparison involve an (unauthorized) reference to a competitor, who is either mentioned by name or implicitly identifiable as such by the public.

[2] The General Restrictions: "Misleading" and "Discrediting" Comparisons

It goes without saying that comparative advertising has to respect the restrictions applicable to all advertisements. In particular, it must not be misleading or disparaging. Comparison based on false or misleading statements about one's own product or involving false statements about the competitor's product is forbidden in all countries.

It must be remembered, however, that there are differences in the evaluation of the notion of "misleading" and especially in that of "discrediting." As mentioned above, some countries, consider statements claiming superiority or uniqueness (like "the best," etc.) misleading unless they can be proved correct, while others consider them harmless exaggerations. Different assessments of the notions of "discrediting" and "misappropriation" are of even greater importance. In countries with a rather permissive attitude toward true but nevertheless disparaging statements, comparative advertising is generally tolerated. As long as what is said is true, the courts will not interfere, even if the reference to the competitor or his/her product is clearly disparaging or exploits his/her goodwill. In countries that traditionally put special emphasis on the protection of the "honest" businessman and his/her reputation, comparative advertising is either forbidden or at least severely restricted. Sometimes the mere fact that a competitor is named against his/her will is considered discrediting and therefore unfair competition. According to the rule that "the honest businessman has a right not to be spoken of, even if the truth is spoken," the legislation of some countries has even expressly forbidden all comparisons that needlessly identify a competitor. The same argument has led the courts of other countries to find comparative advertising more or less automatically against honest trade practice (and therefore against the general provision on unfair competition law). Although it has sometimes been stressed that true comparisons might be in the interest of consumers, doctrine and case law have in practice allowed comparisons only under very special circumstances, for example, if they have been expressly required by a customer, if they have been made to counter an illegal attack on the advertiser, or if the comparison is necessary to explain a certain system or new technical developments in general.

[3] The Trend Toward Admission of True Comparisons

In recent years, however, this negative attitude toward comparative advertising has changed. It has been increasingly recognized that true comparisons of relevant facts can not only reduce the consumer's information search costs, but also have positive effects on the economy by improving market transparency. The courts of those countries that traditionally view comparative advertising as disparaging have gradually relaxed the strict prohibition on all statements identifying a competitor. In France, for example, price comparisons, if based on true, relevant and ample material, are allowed. More important, recent statutes on unfair competition at least indirectly allow comparative advertising. At the EC level, a new Directive has been proposed that would oblige Member States of the EC to allow truthful comparative advertising. On the whole, there seems to be a clear trend toward the admission of truthful comparative advertising. This trend was confirmed by Article 17 of the TRIPS Agreement, which allows WTO Members to implement exceptions to trademark rights, under certain conditions, such as "fair use of descriptive terms" by third parties (including, naturally, trademark owner's competitors).

[4] Special Dangers of Comparative Advertising

However, it cannot be denied that comparative advertising can more easily be misleading or disparaging than most other forms of advertising, for example if the comparison is based on irrelevant (or not really comparable) aspects, or if the overall impression is misleading. These potential dangers require special safeguards against abuse. Countries that allow comparisons place special emphasis on the fact that even true statements must not be unnecessarily disparaging or that irrelevant facts must not be compared. The 1991 EC proposal for a Directive on Comparative Advertising goes even further by expressly requiring that only relevant, objective and verifiable characteristics be compared, that the overall impression be not misleading, that there be no risk of confusion between the products compared and that the competitor and his/her product be in no way disparaged or discredited. Furthermore, the advertiser can be required to prove any claims made in surveys used to support the comparison.

[5] Comparative Advertising and Trademark Law

Comparison is often impossible without reference to a certain mark which refers to a particular product, service or business. In these cases, not only unfair competition law, but also trademark law has to be taken into account.

In countries where trademarks are protected solely as indications of the source of a product or service, the use of a trademark in comparative advertising may not be within the scope of trademark law. However, there are countries where the use of another's trademark in comparative advertising may be considered trademark infringement. Article 13A of the Uniform Benelux Trademark Law, for example, protects the "advertising value" of trademarks against any use in potentially adverse circumstances (which can also take the form of an unwanted reference in comparative advertising). Canadian trademark law generally protects the goodwill of a trademark, while the current UK trademark law in principle forbids any reference to another's trademark. Even in the USA, where comparative advertising is generally allowed, the so-called antidilution statutes enacted by many States are in theory applicable to the use of another person's marks in comparative advertising, since they grant—regardless of confusion—trademark protection against all acts that are liable to injure the business reputation or that dilute the distinctive quality of a mark. However, the statutes so far have not been applied in cases of truthful comparative advertising, and there may be constitutional reasons for such an exception in cases of comparative advertising. It is noteworthy that the proposal for a EC Directive on Comparative Advertising would allow such advertising provided, in particular, that it does not cause confusion between the marks of the advertiser and those of a competitor, and that it does not discredit, denigrate or indicate contempt for a competitor's marks.

[6] Comparisons Made by Third Parties

In many countries product testing is done by consumer organizations and/or private or public institutions like the press, television and other media. Usually two questions will arise here: are the organizations liable under unfair competition law, and may the results of their testing be used in advertising?

In those countries that have given up the requirement of a competitive link between plaintiff and defendant, unfair competition law is applicable to these organizations too. In other countries, "unfair" product tests, which have an adverse effect on a business reputation, are primarily dealt with under general civil law tort provisions.

There seems to be no general agreement on the question whether and under what conditions such test results may be used by advertisers. In some countries (such as Germany) that in general do not accept comparative advertising, this kind of indirect comparison is basically considered legal. In other countries (such as Belgium), it is expressly forbidden for a competitor to refer to tests conducted by consumer organizations, and in still others (such as Switzerland), such references are severely restricted. In the proposal for an EC Directive on Comparative Advertising, tests by third parties may be used only with the express consent of the person who conducted them, apart from which the advertiser would be held responsible for any advertising claim based on such surveys.

[I] Other Acts of Unfair Competition

[1] General

As mentioned earlier, unfair competition law particularly reflects the sociological, economic and ethical conceptions of a society. Apart from the specific categories of acts already discussed which are generally considered unfair competition, there is a wide range of acts and practices that may be dealt with under unfair competition law in one country but not necessarily in another. The discussion that follows is therefore restricted to those aspects that most countries appear to consider (although perhaps with different emphasis) contrary to "honest trade practice," either in the form of an express prohibition in the specific law or, more frequently, under the general provisions on unfair competition, or in specific other laws, decrees and the like. It is to be noted that the following explanations only give examples, not an exhaustive list of these other unfair practices.

[2] Nuisance Advertising, Exploitation of Fear, Undue Psychological Pressure, Etc.

Modern competition law aims to protect all those concerned by unfair market practices. Consequently, practices that "unduly" influence the consumer (or try to do so) may be considered contrary to honesty in competition. In practice, however, it is difficult to determine what requirements have to be met before a practice is deemed to be "undue" in relation to the consumer. Since the very purpose of all marketing or advertising practice is to influence consumers favorably, a certain borderline of influence has to be crossed. This is often asserted in cases where the privacy of the consumer has been invaded or where he/she has been manipulated by means of advertising techniques.

For example, in many countries the delivery of unsolicited goods to a person who is required to pay for them unless he/she expressly refuses or returns them is considered unfair competition, because it plays on the fact that many consumers either tend to forget to return the goods or even feel under an obligation to keep them. However, many countries tolerate unsolicited home visits ("door-to-door sales") as long as they do not involve any deception or impose undue psychological pressure on the consumer. Opinions may vary on the question of unsolicited telephone calls: while some countries consider them per se an intrusion into the privacy of the consumer, most other countries tolerate them as long as the consumer's lack of experience and his/her privacy are not exploited. The same is true of the unsolicited sending of advertising material.

It is further considered unfair in many countries to abuse the consumer's superstitions, credulity, fears or feelings of charity. For example, an advertisement that exploits elderly people's fears of ending up in a nursing home, or causes unnecessary anxiety over death or health problems can be considered contrary to "honest" trade practice. The same is true if a special situation in which the consumer is especially vulnerable is exploited for commercial purposes, for example, if victims of car accidents are pestered with offers of towing services, or if the recently bereaved are offered funeral services. Most countries, moreover, take special precautions against any abuse of children's lack of experience.

Apart from these special cases, often regulated in specific laws, the courts of some countries have identified a group of cases under the general clause against unfair competition which can be described as "psychological pressure to purchase" or "exaggerated enticement." These cases are mainly seen in connection with special marketing practices, however, like the offering of free goods or discounts and lotteries.

[3] Sales Promotion: Bonuses, Gifts, Lotteries, Etc.

A frequent marketing technique to attract new customers consists in the offering of bonuses, gifts and other inducements, and in the organization of competitions, lotteries or games. Such sales promotion can be a new and efficient channel of distribution and may thus stimulate competition. However, it may distract consumers from the merits of the principal goods or services and thereby entice them to buy something that is either not worth its price or not really needed. This is particularly true of marketing techniques like games, lotteries and other competitions, which exploit for advertising purposes a consumer's predisposition to gambling. Most of these are therefore regulated in one way or another, and sometimes even expressly forbidden. Additionally, they are subject to self-regulation measures. There is, however, little agreement (and little consistency) on the question of what specific practices should be considered unfair competition. For example, bonuses, or any discount or other advantage dependent on the purchase of a product, are forbidden in principle in some countries, allowed in principle in others and more or less strictly regulated in others. Lotteries, where the winning of prizes is a matter of pure chance, are generally forbidden if they are linked to the purchase of a product, and otherwise are severely restricted. Contests in which the outcome can be influenced to a certain extent by the participant's own skill are generally viewed more favorably, provided that no deception is involved and that the consumer is not put under any pressure to buy. However, "pyramid" ("snowball") sales and other such methods are often considered potentially misleading and consequently forbidden (sometimes even on pain of criminal sanctions), or are at least severely restricted, whereas sweepstakes are often considered legal.

On the whole, the courts of most countries, even those that allow the sales promotion techniques mentioned above, pay special attention to the actual conditions under which these sales practices take place: if the consumer is put under any psychological or other pressure to buy, if the prizes are extremely valuable and so all the more enticing, an otherwise accepted marketing practice may well be considered contrary to "honest trade practice."

[4] Impeding of Market Activities

Finally, there are several acts which may hinder or obstruct a competitor in his/her business activities, either directly or indirectly. An example of a direct obstruction would be the actual obstruction of trading on a particular market location, which would normally be considered unfair. Another example would be the deliberate destruction of bottles destined to be recycled and refilled by a producer of soft drinks in order to lessen his/her ability to supply the market. Other (indirect) impediments are often controlled by antitrust law but, under certain circumstances, unfair competition law may offer some additional protection. Impediments that are traditionally covered by antitrust law are discrimination, boycotting and dumping, but that does not preclude the application of unfair competition law, at least if the acts are perpetrated on an individual scale. For example, unreasonable interference with the business activities of competitors, sales at unreasonably low prices, like below-cost prices, or the imposition of fixed retail prices are practices that have been designated by the Fair Trade Commission of Japan as being prohibited by the Japanese Anti-Monopoly Act, but which might also be regarded, in theory, as forms of unfair competition. In some countries, selling below cost or at an "exceptionally low profit margin" is expressly prohibited under unfair competition law. In the UK, the USA and other countries, "predatory pricing" with a view to damaging a competitor may be prohibited under competition law.

Other such unfair practices consist in enticing away from competitors, or in inducing the personnel or agents of competitors to terminate their employment or agency contracts. As indicated earlier, these acts of unfair competition are frequently accompanied by the violation of trade secrets but may, nevertheless, constitute separate unfair acts. Merely inducing the clients or employees of competitors to change suppliers or employers by offering better conditions is inherent in free competition and cannot therefore be regarded as unfair. However, means such as bribery or deception of clients, agents or employees, or inducement to breach a valid undertaking not to compete, will be deemed unfair, as will the systematic enticing away of personnel with a view to damaging one particular competitor.

§13.05 UNFAIR COMPETITION AND COMPETITION (ANTITRUST) LAW

[A] Introduction

In very broad terms, antitrust law is the branch of law that seeks to ensure that markets are competitive, this meaning that they operate under the pressure of forces of competition. Antitrust laws protect the competitive process, not individual competitors. It is therefore the public interest that is at the basis of the protection of the competitive process. Generally speaking, unfair competition law also seeks to ensure the freedom of market through competition, but its enforcement is triggered only when free competition is jeopardized by some sort of socially blameful act and is directed toward the protection of the interests of individual companies or IP right holders. At least, this is the traditional distinction between those two branches of law, which is based on a qualitative notion. When practices are anticompetitive but do not entail the social blamefulness that makes them unlawful, such as fraud, deceit and, in more general terms, dishonesty, traditionally they do not qualify as acts of unfair competition.

Antitrust law, as a consistent body of law, emerged for the first time in the end of the nineteenth century, in Canada, through the Anti-Combines Act (May, 1889). It was then followed by the US, when the Sherman Act was passed in 1890. The two main provisions of the Sherman Act represent an evolution of previous case law. Section 1, which deals with anticompetitive concerted practices, has emerged from case law on restraints of trade, as construed by UK and US courts. Section 2, which prohibits private monopolization as well as the attempt to privately monopolize, represents an advance over previous statutes and court decisions that addressed public or quasi-public monopolies, which had fallen in disgrace since the Statute of Monopolies, of 1624.

In parallel to antitrust law, the repression of unfair competition also acquired the status of a consistent body of law in the nineteenth century, first by means of court opinions in France, proffered on the basis of a provision of the Civil Code, of 1804, as well as in the UK and the US, and later by the enacting of dedicated statutes, such as those of Portugal, of 1895, and Germany, of 1909.

When they emerged, in spite of their evident similarities, antitrust law and unfair competition law were different bodies of law, governed by different principles, and seeking different goals. In a large number of countries, the two branches of law remained apart, until a relatively recent and consistent movement toward approaching them started, by gradually expanding the scope and the nature of the practices repressed by unfair competition rules. The reason for such a movement was the idea that the traditional notion of unfair competition, strictly linked to actual or potential diversion of clientele by dishonest means, was no longer enough to handle a growing number of practices that would not fall under the purview of antitrust law, and yet would have some anticompetitive impact and would cause harm to consumers. The clear insufficiency in the design of statutes and their interpretation by courts would leave many anticompetitive practices out of reach of judicial sanction. We can detect the beginning of this trend in the 1960s and 1970s. However, in the US, a movement toward the merger of antitrust and unfair competition laws, albeit in limited terms and circumstances, started earlier. The expression of that merger was the language of section 5 of the FTC Act, of 1914 (15 U.S.C. §§ 41-58).

As a matter of course, the evolution of law is rarely, if ever, linear. Law evolves along with society, and it is not rare that it changes by way of experiments, in which society tests new approaches, which may succeed and be kept until new perspectives gain dominance, or fail and be abandoned. This is particularly true for unfair competition, which has social rather than economic values in its core. Some of those values may be fleeting and may vary from society to society. What constitutes a dishonest practice for one society may not be so for another. Therefore, it is not possible to identify precise moments and precise places where a specific understanding of commercial honesty changes by expanding or contracting. However, it is possible to find large movements or social waves that at some point are expressed in the form of statutory language.

[B] The Meaning and the Evolution of the Repression of Unfair Competition

At the outset, it should be noted that neither antitrust nor unfair competition admits a precise definition. As the US Supreme Court said in *FTC v. Raladam*, 283 U.S. 643, 648 (1931):

> [The phrase "unfair methods of competition"] belongs to that class of phrases which do not admit of precise definition, but the meaning and application of which must be arrived at by what this court elsewhere has called "the gradual process of judicial inclusion and exclusion."

In the same sense, the Supreme Court of California, in *Weinstock, Lubin & Co. v. H. Marks*, 109 Cal. 529, 541 (1895), said:

> The foregoing principles of law do not apply alone to the protection of parties having trademarks and trade names. They reach away beyond that, and apply to all cases where fraud is practiced by one in securing the trade of a rival dealer; and these ways are as many and as various as the ingenuity of the dishonest schemer can invent.

The same impossibility of framing antitrust violations in a single concept was stated by US Congress when it was discussing the Clayton and the FTC Acts:

> It is impossible to frame definitions which embrace all unfair practices. There is no limit to human inventiveness in this field. ... If Congress were to adopt the method of definition, it would undertake an endless task.

Therefore, if we want to understand what an act of unfair competition is, we have to look at its constitutive elements. Today, the repression of unfair competition seeks two objectives, comprises four types of practices, and is grounded on two constitutive elements.

[C] Objectives

The enforcement of the law of unfair competition seeks two objectives: repressing those acts that (a) deceive consumers (thus diverting competitors' clients or preventing customers from switching to competitors) and (b) repressing those dishonest acts that harm competitors' ability to keep customers or attract new customers. The first of these objectives seeks to protect consumers directly and competitors, indirectly. The second objective seeks to protect competitors directly and consumers, indirectly.

[D] Types of Unfair Competition Acts

Unfair competition acts, which were described in detail in the previous sections, may be classified under four broad types, which correspond to the emphasis put by statutes on specific elements that trigger repression. It is not uncommon that national laws repress several of these types. Actually, repression of both the first and the second types is mandatory under the TRIPS Agreement.

[1] Dishonest Practices

The first type is perhaps the more traditional one: acquisition of a competitive advantage as a result of a *dishonest practice*. This type corresponds to the basic notion of unfair competition as set by Article 10*bis* of the Paris Convention. The Convention language that, in very broad terms, defines unfair competition ("Any act of competition contrary to honest practices in industrial or commercial matters") was introduced in 1925, during the Diplomatic Conference for the Revision of the Paris Convention held at The Hague. This language has a moralistic tone and corresponds to an idea that free competition is a useful social tool but only if it is built on ethically acceptable business conduct. The moralistic tone of the Paris Convention has been endorsed by the TRIPS Agreement, not only indirectly, by means of the incorporation of the substantive provisions of the Paris Convention (TRIPS, Article 2.1), but also directly, by means of an explicit repetition of Paris Convention language in Article 39.2 and its corresponding note 10.

As a consequence of the language of these two treaties, the association of unfairness in business rivalry with dishonesty has been transposed to many national statutes. The moralistic tone of that language has also persuaded a significant number of lawmakers to treat unfair trade practices as crimes. This aspect ensures a more severe repression of dishonesty in business competition even if it limits the spectrum of sanctionable practices, given the mandatory principle of *numerus clausus* required by criminal law. This shortcoming has been compensated in a number of civil code jurisdictions by introducing the notion of *unlawful* competition practices as opposed to *unfair* competition practices. According to this approach, whereas *unfair competition practices* involve dishonesty and fraud, *unlawful competition practices* only require negligence. Therefore, competition practices are unlawful and sanctioned as civil torts when courts say so, and are unfair and treated as crimes when statutes say so.

[2] Parasitism

The second type corresponds to the acquisition of a competitive advantage as a result of acts of *parasitism*. We can detect this type in the provisions of paragraphs 1 and 3 of the TRIPS Agreement. Paragraph 3 of Article 39 establishes two cumulative layers of protection to those confidential data, including test data, which pharmaceutical and agrochemical companies are obliged to submit to governmental agencies as a requirement for obtaining marketing approval of new chemical entities. The first layer corresponds to protection against *unfair commercial use* of the data. The second layer consists of protection against disclosure (except in the circumstances mentioned in the end of the paragraph). The two layers, as said, are cumulative. This notion results from the specific language of Article 39.3, which, after defining the substantive obligation of Members in the first sentence, says: "*In addition*, Members shall protect such data against disclosure." (emphasis added). It follows that a WTO Member cannot discharge itself from Article 39.3 obligations if it only protects the data against disclosure, and fails to protect them against unfair commercial use.

Because Article 39.3 does not provide for a definition of "unfair commercial use," under Article 1.1 it is up to each Member to find a way to give that protection a practical expression. Most of those WTO Members that have implemented Article 39.3 have adopted a regime of exclusive protection for a limited period. During that period, the authority in question will not grant marketing approval to any other substitute product submitted by a competitor of the first registrant unless the second registrant submits its own data or obtains authorization from the first registrant that the authority may rely on its data. A few international trade agreements make reference to an alternative mechanism of substantive protection of test data, which is the right to remuneration. Under this mechanism, the authority may use information extracted from the data submitted by the first registrant in order to register a substitute product, but only if the second registrant pays reasonable compensation.

The protection of confidential information against unfair commercial use represents a departure from the traditional notion of unfair competition, to the extent that the manufacturer of generic products does not engage, in a strict sense, in a dishonest practice when it asks a governmental agency that it relies on data submitted by another company. Nor is the governmental agency that accepts such a request, as matter of course, involved in unfair competition. In the first case, that is an act of competition (or with a competitive effect), but it is not dishonest. In the second case, the act is unfair—to the extent that the government only requires the submission of costly data from the first registrant, but not from the subsequent registrants—but it is not an act of competition.

To rely on data acquired by competitors is an act of parasitism, and it is in this sense that the TRIPS Agreement deems it an act of unfair competition. In other words, the TRIPS Agreement has expanded the notion of unfairness of trade practices from dishonesty, as set in the Paris Convention, to parasitism. Actually, paragraphs 1 and 3 of Article 39 may be read as if WTO members had agreed to add another example to the list of three examples of unfair competition practices that Article 10*bis* provides.

In addition to the repression of parasitism in connection to pharmaceutical and agrochemical test data, a number of countries—in particular those that have hosted major sports events—have adopted or amended trademark protection statutes with the aim of preventing and/or repressing certain modalities of commercial parasitism known as "ambush marketing," either by association or by intrusion—for example, the "Cup Act," Law nr. 12,663/2012 (Brazil), the Major Events Management Act 2007 (New Zealand), and the Merchandise Marks Act of 1941, as amended in 2002 (South Africa). Under the statutes against ambush marketing, competitive gains acquired by entrepreneurs who somehow draw prestige from big sports events so as to promote their goods and services without having contributed financially or otherwise to the organization of those events are made unlawful.

[3] Violation of Statutory Duties

The third type of unfair competition acts that some national laws repress concerns those acts that, consisting in violations of statutory duties, generate competitive advantages. In some countries, such violation relates to specific statutes (e.g., Australia and the sixteen West African countries that are members of the OAPI, which are bound by the Bangui Agreement, of 1977 and as revised in 1999 (breach of rules on business activities), Germany and Spain (breach of rules on market behavior), Spain (breach of laws on immigrant workers), the State of Louisiana (US) (breach of rules on property rights, including software), the State of Washington (US) (breach of rules on property in information technology), and Switzerland (breach of labor laws)). But in other countries, the breach concerns any statutory provision by which the competitors accused of unfair competition are bound (e.g., Colombia, Ecuador and Peru).

This type of unfair competition raises two important issues. First, any element of subjectivism that unfair competition could have is completely eliminated. Unfair competition becomes the sum of two objective components: the direct or indirect acquisition of a competitive advantage and the breach of a statute—including an IP statute. Second, and taking this last observation into account, whereas unfair competition rules were traditionally evoked in the event of injury caused by a competitor to unregistered industrial property assets, under this approach unfair competition can also be enforced in the case of an infringement of a formally recognized IP asset. This means that, in those countries that have included the breach of statutes in the scope of the repression of unfair competition, unfair competition may be enforced in addition (or alternatively, as the IPR holder sees fit) to the enforcement of IP.

[4] Acts That Harm Competition Without Entailing Superior Efficiency

The fourth type of unfair competition acts is not explicitly defined in any national statute, but it results from the language of a number of national laws. One example is the federal law of the US. In the US, unfair competition law emerged in the course of the nineteenth century with the goal of protecting unregistered trademarks and trade names. To this extent, nineteenth century US unfair competition law emerged as complementary to trademark law. But courts, deciding both on law and on equity, gradually expanded the notion of unlawful competition to a growing number of business practices, even if they were not explicitly characterized as unfair competition. In 1914 the abovementioned FTC Act was passed with specific language on unfair competition. Section 5(1) of the Act reads:

> Unfair methods of competition in or affecting commerce, and unfair or deceptive acts or practices in or affecting commerce, are hereby declared unlawful.

This provision establishes a dichotomy between "unfair methods of competition," on the one hand, and "unfair or deceptive acts or practices," on the other. The second term is closer to the traditional notion of repression of unfair competition (based on deception or dishonesty), while the first term is closer to antitrust laws. The same dichotomy can be found in section 337(a) of the US Tariffs Act of 1930 (19 U.S.C. §1337).

The exact meaning of the expression "unfair methods of competition" has been the subject of debate. In the already cited opinion of *FTC v. Raladam* (1931), the US Supreme Court said that:

> All three statutes [the Sherman Act, the Clayton Act, and the FTC Act] seek to protect the public from abuses arising in the course of competitive interstate and foreign trade. In a case arising under the Trade Commission Act, the fundamental questions are, whether the methods complained of are "unfair," and whether, as in cases under the Sherman Act, they tend to the substantial injury of the public by restricting competition in interstate trade and "the common liberty to engage therein." The paramount aim of the act is the protection of the public from the evils likely to result from the destruction of competition or the restriction of it in a substantial degree, and this presupposes the existence of some substantial competition to be affected, since the public is not concerned in the maintenance of competition which itself is without real substance. [...]

The *Raladam* opinion, therefore, links the FTC Act (hence, the repression of unfair methods of competition) to antitrust enforcement. Both sets of laws seek to protect "the public from the evils likely to result from the destruction of competition or the restriction of it in a substantial degree." Besides, both presuppose "the existence of some substantial competition to be affected." But, in spite of being a provision clearly related to antitrust law and its principles, §5(1) of the FTC is not an antitrust law provision. The Supreme Court said so in unequivocal terms in *FTC v. Sperry*, 405 U.S. 233, 244 (1972). After a thorough discussion on the legislative history and the case law around the exact meaning of §5(1) of the FTC Act, the Supreme Court concluded that:

> Thus, legislative and judicial authorities alike convince us that the Federal Trade Commission does not arrogate excessive power to itself if, in measuring a practice against the elusive, but congressionally mandated standard of fairness, it, like a court of equity, considers public values beyond simply those enshrined in the letter or encompassed in the spirit of the antitrust laws.

Without entering the complex discussion of what is the real meaning and scope of the term "unfair methods of competition" under the FTC Act, it is possible to conclude that they do not encompass dishonest and unfair acts, but rather acts that substantially harm competition (and yet do not reach the level of an antitrust violation). One of the proponents of the FTC Act, George Rublee (an advisor to President Theodore Roosevelt), characterized unfair methods of competition as those acts that lead to a (significant) competitive advantage and that are not grounded on superior efficiency:

> Fair competition is competition which is successful through superior efficiency. Competition is unfair when it resorts to methods which shut out competitors who, by reason of their efficiency, might otherwise be able to continue in business and prosper. Without the use of unfair methods no corporation can grow beyond the limits imposed upon it by the necessity of being as efficient as any competitor. *Apud* Marc Winerman, *The Origins of the FTC: Concentration, Cooperation, Control, and Competition*, 71 Antitrust L.J. 1, 67 (2003), available on the website of the Federal Trade Commission (www.ftc.gov).

In a nutshell, the FTC Act has brought unfair competition to the door of antitrust (or vice versa), the threshold for moving from one body of law to the other being the existence of the factors that trigger the enforcement of antitrust. There is a common ground in the two bodies of law, however: the occurrence of substantial harm to competition. In this manner, unfair competition law goes beyond repressing acts of deceit and dishonesty and also represses acts that harm competition. To put it in more suggestive terms, unfair competition law becomes, under the FTC Act, part of *free competition law*. However, in general, it is possible to distinguish acts of unfair competition from antitrust practices based on one single criterion: while an act of unfair competition harms or is aimed at harming *one or more competitors*, antitrust violations are aimed at (or have the effect of) harming *competition*. That is why for an antitrust violation to take place, also in general, the presence of market power is required. A small competitor is not usually able to harm *competition* as a whole.

[E] Constitutive Elements

Regardless of the specific types of acts of unfair competition national statutes embrace, all four types present two constitutive elements:

(1) First, there must be a social perception of unfairness or blamefulness in the practice. This element makes unfair competition a somewhat inconstant or fleeting concept, because social perceptions keep changing. At most, it is possible to say that as far as unfair competition moves closer to antitrust law, the seriousness of the blame is reduced, and a conduct to be deemed unfair does not need to be seen as dishonest or even parasitic to be unfair—the present of certain malice, even if in a modicum, could suffice. Such malice would permit a less efficient competitor to gain a competitive advantage over more efficient competitors. For an expanded concept of unfair competition, malice is enough to bring the method of competition within the reach of unfair competition law.

(2) Second, unfair competition is only found in situations of actual or potential competition. This may sound tautological, but here and there, the idea of unfair competition without competition has been voiced. Of course, such an idea does not make any sense. However, the fact that unfair competition only occurs in the face of competition does not mean that unfair competition acts are only practiced by competitors. Indeed, protection against unfair competition may be invoked by an injured non-competitor when the practice in question has a negative impact on his/her ability to compete against his/her own competitors—this is the case, for example, of protection of well-known trademarks against dilution (*see* TRIPS Agreement, Article 16.3), under which, even if the trademark infringer does not compete with the well-known trademark owner, he/she gains a competitive advantage for his/her own goods or services and harms the competitive position of the trademark owner to the extent it dilutes its prestige and ability to attract clients. The same is true, for example, as regards deceptive advertisement. After all, as a Circuit Court once said, in the expression "unfair competition" there should be no fetish in the word "competition." *Vogue Co. v. Thompson-Hudson Co.*, 300 F. 509, 512 (6th Cir. 1924). But for an offense to constitute unfair competition, it must have an impact, no matter whether direct or indirect, on the ability of the offended party to compete, either with the offender or with other firms. In a nutshell, without a competition element involved, be it directly or indirectly, there is no unfair competition.

§13.06 TRENDS AND CONSEQUENCES OF THE EXPANSION OF PROTECTION AGAINST UNFAIR COMPETITION

Along with the expansion of the scope of the repression of unfair competition that brings it closer to antitrust laws, two major trends in the way that national statutes handle unfair competition can be identified. The first trend is revealed by the increasing number of national competition authorities that receive a mandate to repress unfair competition acts, ex officio—as in the case of the US FTC—or per request of private parties. This trend can be detected in, e.g., the recent statutes of Vietnam, Ecuador, and the Dominican Republic.

The second trend is the inclusion of the same practices in lists of unlawful acts under unfair competition and antitrust laws. For example, the Unfair Competition Law of Chile defines the anticompetitive abuse of the judicial process (sometimes referred to as "sham litigation") as an act of unfair competition. By contrast, the competition laws of Ecuador and Peru define the same practice as an anticompetitive practice.

These trends, which are associated with, if not a consequence of, the expansion of the concept of unfair competition, may have a positive side, in the sense that they put emphasis on the need to promote and protect free competition. By putting moralistic tones aside—but without ignoring them, because there may be no unfair competition without unfairness—the expanded notion of unfair competition increases the tools of the competent authorities in pursuing that meritorious goal. However, there are also some risks, which may be more acute in regard of some of the specific types of unfair competition acts mentioned above.

For example, repressing any act that leads to the gain of competitive advantage without entailing superior efficiency may lead to unwarranted proliferation of unfair competition cases, especially if there is no requirement that the harm to competition be substantial. Litigation grounded on frivolous motivation or on *de minimis* injury naturally gives rise to legal insecurity, and transforms the repression of unfair competition law into a social burden. Moreover, if not tied to a threshold of injury, making breaches of law a constitutive factor of unfair competition may impose on unfair competition law-enforcement governmental agencies and courts the burden of looking into minor violations. For example, if two competitors haul fashion apparel from the city in which their businesses are based to a neighboring city where a fashion fair is taking place, and one of the competitors drives the truck at speeds over the legal limit, whereas the other abides by that limit, the consequence will be that the speeding competitor will arrive first at the event and will be in a better position to sell his/her merchandise. Strictly speaking, in those countries that would be an act of unfair competition. But whether unfair competition law-enforcement authorities should be involved with this breach of a statute rather than, or in complement of traffic-law-enforcement authorities, it would be a debatable matter. Therefore, where countries wish to use the repression of unfair competition as an instrument to promote free competition, i.e., as a complementary tool of antitrust laws, the laws may adopt an objective approach by accepting a looser notion of dishonesty or unfairness, but they should also put emphasis on the requirement for a substantial harm to competition as a result of the unfair trade practice. This requirement would reduce the risk of excessive or frivolous litigation, and yet could keep the possibility of harmed competitors to launch lawsuits, in addition to governmental ex officio enforcement.

A second risk arises from the third type of unfair trade practices above mentioned: violation of statutory duties. No one could seriously argue against the proposition that the acquisition of a competitive advantage—expressed in injury caused directly to a competitor or in the deceit of consumers—resulting from the breach of a statutory duty is an act of unfair competition. As much as objective this notion may be, by contrast with the vague and moralistic concept of dishonesty, to gain competitive advantages by infringing statutes is unfair vis-à-vis law-abiding competitors, regardless of whether compliance with the law is costly (as it happens with environmental and labor statutes) or not.

However, where the laws that qualify competitive gains that result from breaches of statutory duties as acts of unfair competition fail to clearly identify those statutes, problems of territoriality may arise. Indeed, when a firm is accused of engaging in unfair competition because of an act of infringement of an IPR, for example, one may ask where that act has taken place. If the patent infringement occurred in the territory of another country, that firm is undoubtedly an unfair competitor vis-à-vis other importers, and, indirectly, vis-à-vis the patent owner, but one may wonder how the courts or the administrative authorities of a country can find a patent infringement in another country. Of course, the argument in contrary could be that what matters is the place where the infringement has an impact—and that place is the importing territory, not the exporting one. So, an element of connection would be formed between the two laws. However, in spite of the relative harmonization of national legal standards of protection of IP introduced by the TRIPS Agreement, full harmonization is still a distant mirage and the acquisition of IPRs may be grounded on considerably different requirements in different jurisdictions. One therefore may wonder what would happen if the authority of the importing country decided that imported goods had infringed the IP laws of that country when their manufacturer/merchant in the country of origin had benefitted from an exclusion from protection admitted by the TRIPS Agreement. This same debate could be extended to other areas of law, such as labor and environment laws, where the standards are stricter in some countries than in others.

Another risk to which the expansion of the notion of unfair competition may give rise has to do with problems of inter-institutionalism—this term meaning that the attribution of the power to enforce unfair competition laws to competition authorities may generate tensions with national IPOs and courts, whose decisions may be called into question. This is not a theoretical possibility, but a reality. More than once national competition authorities have been requested to investigate and sanction allegedly anticompetitive abuses of process (both administrative and judicial) that were grounded on titles granted by national IPOs or on court findings. This sort of embarrassing situation can only be avoided by carefully calibrated statutory language, which should reserve to courts the enforcement of unfair competition law concerning those practices that imply the risk of inter-institutionalism. One example that immediately springs to mind is, of course, sham litigation.

Another consequence of making the repression of unfair competition as an auxiliary tool of antitrust law with the aim of promoting free competition is the possibility of extending to its enforcement some sanctions that so far are exclusive of antitrust, such as divestiture and compulsory licenses. Indeed, certain violations of unfair competition laws may be not adequately remedied with injunctions and damages, particularly when they result from the inappropriate use of IPRs.

Even though unfair competition has evolved on the multilateral level (from the Paris Convention to the TRIPS Agreement), its fundamentals and objectives have been set at the national level. The reason is obvious. Because unfair competition corresponds to the social values of ethics in business, and those values are essentially of a national nature insofar as they are related to cultural norms and even religious beliefs, it is natural that national concerns and experiences dictate changes in the treatment of unfair competition. This explains the large diversity of national views on the repression of unfair competition. This also explains the absence of proposals on the harmonization of unfair competition law. But, in view of the globalization of markets and the constant territorial expansion of the struggle for the preference of consumers, predominantly national approaches entail the risks of international inconsistencies. At some point it might be useful for WIPO Member States to revisit this matter with the objectives of better understanding the differences in the repression of unfair competition in various jurisdictions and of finding common grounds that would avoid the various risks that were mentioned above.

However, it is undeniable that, in spite of its risks—which may be overcome by using appropriate statutory language—the expansion of unfair competition from a subjective to a more objective approach gives national governments a useful tool to protect the freedom of markets by ensuring that competition is kept under ethical constraints thereby giving consumers the possibility of free and reasonably informed choices. This point alone should give food for thought to those countries that keep unfair competition constrained by the straightjacket of a more traditional approach of only sanctioning competitive gains derived from strictly dishonest acts.

CHAPTER 14
Enforcement of IPRs

§14.01 SECTION I: JUDICIAL ENFORCEMENT

[A] Introduction

[1] Enforcement Measures as the Necessary Correlatives of IPRs

Black's Law Dictionary defines enforcement as *"the act or process of compelling compliance with a law, mandate, command, decree, or agreement."* In the area of IP, enforcement aims at safeguarding compliance with the various IPRs granted by a given legal system. As a matter of course, it will only then become relevant where these rights are not respected. IP enforcement can thus be understood as all the procedures and remedies that a legal system provides to address the infringement.

As for any other right, IPRs are credible and effective only insofar as they can be enforced. If there were no sound and reliable system of enforcement of IPRs, such rights would be empty shells. The absence of effective IP enforcement would undermine the credibility of IP rights and hence be detrimental to the whole purpose of IP rights, i.e., the promotion of innovation and creativity and their impact on economic growth and development. The enforcement of IPRs is therefore quintessential in its contribution to a sound system of valorization of creativity and innovation and of IP protection. That explains also why, at international level, the TRIPS Agreement devotes no less than twenty-one of its seventy-three articles to the enforcement of IPRs.

The enforcement of IPRs is all the more important since such infringements, particularly trademark counterfeiting and copyright piracy, are an unwelcome worldwide phenomenon, rendered wider and more difficult to detect and fight with the development of new technologies such as the internet. Figures on the scope and impact of infringements of IPRs exist, though the determination of methodologies to obtain reliable figures measuring activities which are clandestine (given their illegal nature) is a serious challenge. Nevertheless, there is little doubt as to the existence and quantitative importance of IP infringements and, particularly, of trademark counterfeiting and copyright piracy. Having sound and reliable systems of enforcement of IPRs is therefore a core condition of a well-performing system of IP protection.

[2] IP Enforcement in the Wider Context of Building Respect for IP

WIPO activities related to IP enforcement fall within its work toward Strategic Goal VI: International Cooperation on Building Respect for IP. Respect for IP is a fundamental principle shared by all WIPO Member States and its promotion a broad and cross-cutting goal. To build respect for IP may be understood as being to help create an environment in which IP can, in a sustainable manner, fulfill its functions in the interest of right holders and the general public at large. At the national level, this presupposes, first of all, a legal framework that adequately protects the various forms of IP and guarantees compliance. It is equally important to create an institutional structure, both at administrative and judicial level, which possesses the necessary capacities to put such IP laws into practical effect. In addition, for the IP system to provide maximum benefits, everybody in society should be encouraged to make active use of it. To that end, it is crucial to emphasize the benefits that a fully functioning IP system provides for any WIPO Member State and to demonstrate the potential negative impact of goods and services that violate IP rights.

Where IP rights are infringed and such infringements are not appropriately remedied, the IP system cannot work properly. In that sense, the availability of adequately operating national civil, administrative, and criminal procedures to enforce IP holders' rights is an important element for building respect for IP. Yet, the concept of building respect for IP is much broader than enforcement alone. It equally encompasses mechanisms to prevent infringements before they happen rather than to cure them. Raising awareness of the functioning and the benefits of IP plays an important role in this regard. To lead to positive results, awareness-raising strategies, in turn, must be based on solid knowledge of the attitude and perceptions of those consumers who currently buy counterfeit and pirated goods and the socioeconomic reality in which they live. Other mechanisms aim to strengthen the supply chain security of trademarked products to prevent infiltration by counterfeit components. Moreover, voluntary engagements put into place by internet service providers to discourage infringements can be seen as one example of such preventive action. This list of possible avenues for building respect for IP is by no means exclusive and, as a concept, building respect for IP goes beyond pre-established categorization. On the contrary, the array of pertinent issues evolves as all relevant stakeholders continue to discuss, elaborate and try creative solutions for establishing an environment in which IP can thrive.

Building respect for IP is a development-oriented approach and at WIPO finds its theoretical underpinning in Recommendation 45 of the WIPO Development Agenda, which encourages WIPO "to approach intellectual property enforcement in the context of broader societal interests and especially development-oriented concerns, with a view that 'the protection and enforcement of intellectual property rights should contribute to the promotion of technological innovation and to the transfer and dissemination of technology, to the mutual advantage of producers and users of technological knowledge and in a manner conducive to social and economic welfare, and to a balance of rights and obligations', in accordance with Article 7 of the TRIPS Agreement." The fundamental notion underlying Development Agenda Recommendation 45 and Article 7 of the TRIPS Agreement is that of a balance between the private interests of the holders of IP rights and the interests of the public at large. The texts call for a renewed affirmation of the fact that the grant of exclusive rights over IP not only aims to benefit the holders of these rights but finds an additional, and arguably more important, rationale in the benefits it achieves for the general public. Where IP protection and enforcement does not appropriately conciliate both objectives, the overall goal of social and economic development through increased innovation and creation cannot be reached.

Locating IP enforcement in the development-oriented concept of building respect for IP has a number of consequences. First of all, it implies that balance between private and public interests have to be established in both national legal IP frameworks as well as their day-to-day application. As far as IP legislation is concerned, Part III of the TRIPS Agreement, representing multilateral consensus in relation to enforcement, contains certain minimum standards applicable to WTO members. Yet, it also provides for options and flexibilities, allowing WTO members to make conscious decisions as to how best they should be implemented to achieve the necessary balance. In the administration of IP laws, the competent authorities typically have a considerable degree of discretion when deciding whether and how to carry out enforcement mechanisms and hence an opportunity to conciliate private and public interests. At the same time, it is clear that the societal interests and development-oriented concerns mentioned in Development Agenda Recommendation 45 differ from one country to another. As a consequence, where to strike the balance can only be assessed in light and full knowledge of all national specificities.

[3] The WIPO ACE

The Advisory Committee on Enforcement (ACE) is WIPO's forum for policy dialogue on questions of IP enforcement and building respect for IP. When the WIPO General Assembly created the Committee in 2002, it gave the Committee the mandate for technical assistance and coordination in global enforcement issues while specifically excluding any norm-setting remit. Covering both industrial property rights as well as copyright and related rights, the Committee provides WIPO Member States with the opportunity to share experiences and lessons learned, among each other and with interested observers, on how to enhance national capacities for and deal with the challenges of implementing systems of IP protection and compliance that respond to the practical needs of society and reflect the realities in the respective countries. In addition, the ACE allows its participants and observers to exchange information with other stakeholders, such as the private sector, on topical developments against counterfeiting and piracy. As such, the ACE sessions have been characterized as a "market place of ideas" in which all participants and observers find at least one good idea to take home and reflect upon.

The working method of the Committee is thematic in that it identifies topics of particular interest for further examination and discussion at future meetings. Experts in the field of enforcement and building respect for IP prepare written documents on various aspects of the respective chosen theme and present their work while the Committee is in session. In turn, these presentations instigate discussions and debate among the ACE participants and observers.

Over the years, the choice of topics that the Committee adopted as its work program has broadened. The ACE has looked at core elements of effective IP enforcement, such as the role of the judiciary, quasi-judiciary and prosecution; enforcement coordination at the national, regional and international level (in particular in relation to criminal measures); and the role of right holders in enforcement. In addition, and especially after the adoption of the WIPO Development Agenda, the Committee conducted considerable work to understand the economic and social variables that influence whether people consume counterfeited and pirated goods. It looked at the motivations of IP infringements, at methodologies that measure the social, economic and commercial impact of counterfeiting and piracy and explored non-punitive measures to address counterfeiting and piracy. More recently, the ACE addressed IP dispute resolution, effective preventive measures, awareness raising, and institutional arrangements concerning IP enforcement, as well as WIPO's capacity building in the area of building respect for IP.

[B] The Enforcement of IP Rights under the TRIPS Agreement

[1] Relevance of Part III of the TRIPS Agreement in a Multilateral Context

The TRIPS Agreement has a specific Part dedicated to the enforcement of IPRs: Part III of the TRIPS Agreement, entitled "Enforcement of Intellectual Property Rights" contains twenty-one provisions divided into 5 sections (section 1 "General Obligations"—Article 41; section 2 "Civil and Administrative Procedures and Remedies"—Articles 42-49; section 3 "Provisional Measures"—Article 50; section 4 "Special Requirements Related to Border Measures"—Articles 51-60; and section 5 "Criminal Procedures"—Article 61). The relevance of Part III of the TRIPS Agreement cannot be overestimated: it provides for minimum compulsory standards and options for implementation by the WTO Member States in their legislative framework. In addition, as of today, Part III of the TRIPS Agreement is the only reasonably complete set of provisions on the enforcement of IP rights having been adopted at the multilateral level.

When implementing the TRIPS Agreement, WTO Member States are free to provide for IP enforcement provisions which go beyond what is required by the Agreement, provided that such measures are not inconsistent with its other provisions. In other words, Member States have the option of only implementing the minimum requirements of Part III of the TRIPS Agreement or deciding to provide for enforcement provisions going beyond those minimum requirements. In making such a decision, it is important to take into consideration the prevailing socioeconomic circumstances, as well as financial and human resources constraints. In this regard, Article 7 and Article 8 of the TRIPS Agreement establish references to broader socioeconomic, public health and development-oriented concerns. Article 7 of the TRIPS Agreement provides that the protection and enforcement of IPRs should promote social and economic welfare and achieve a balance of rights and obligations to the mutual advantage of both producers and users of technological knowledge. Article 8 of the TRIPS Agreement allows for the adoption of measures "necessary to protect public health and nutrition, and to promote the public interest in sectors of vital importance to their socio-economic and technological development."

[2] Enforcement under Part III of the TRIPS Agreement: Preliminary Considerations

As indicated, IP rights can only have a social or economic effect to the extent that they are perceived, at least, to be enforceable. As these rights are intangible, methods of self-help, such as, for example, the physical retaking of misappropriated property, are inapplicable. Only legal obligations imposed by the state, such as a liability to pay compensation or a criminal sanction, can assist the holder of IP rights which have been infringed.

The inclusion of IP enforcement within the politics of global trade under the TRIPS Agreement marked a change in the approach to IP in international public law. In the past, international conventions, such as those of Paris (*see* Article 9 (on seizure of infringing goods) and Article 10*ter*(2) (on the standing of federations and associations)) or Berne (*see* Articles 13, 16 (on seizure of infringing copies) and Article 15 (on presumption of authorship)), contained limited obligations as to enforcement beyond the requirement of national treatment. These obligations were satisfied by the enactment of suitable legislation, and no mechanism for securing compliance with those commitments was provided for.

Article 41 of the TRIPS Agreement, however, consistently with the WTO system as a whole, introduced a requirement of substantive effectiveness. Thus, states bound by the Agreement are required to ensure that enforcement procedures are available "so as to permit effective action against any act of infringement of intellectual property rights covered by [the] Agreement." In other words, Member States must not only as a matter of legislation provide for the enforcement tools specified in the Agreement, these must also be such as to permit enforcement to be undertaken as a practical matter.

The TRIPS Agreement recognizes that the protection of IP rights must take its place among the other priorities and necessities of government. Article 41(5) hence acknowledges that the enforcement provisions of the Agreement do not create any obligation to put in place a special judicial system for the enforcement of IPRs. The

TRIPS Agreement does not require that more resources are applied in the enforcement of IP rights than in the enforcement of the law in general.

Conventionally, legal enforcement can be implemented by means of civil or criminal judicial procedures or administrative measures undertaken by some non-judicial organ of the state. The TRIPS Agreement requires that civil enforcement procedures, at least, be provided concerning the enforcement of any IP right covered by the Agreement. Articles 43-48 and Article 50 provide detailed requirements as to the procedures and remedies that must be available in civil cases. Article 49 provides that to the extent that any civil remedy can be ordered as a result of administrative procedures on the merits of a case, such procedures shall conform to principles equivalent in substance to those required by the Agreement in respect of civil proceedings. Article 61 provides for criminal penalties and procedures.

The TRIPS Agreement sets out the main enforcement measures developed by courts around the world. The legal systems of countries which are not bound by the enforcement provisions of the Agreement typically include the minimum final remedies for which it provides, namely injunctions and damages. At the date of the enactment of the Agreement, however, not all countries provided for pre-trial relief to the extent required and some adjustments were necessary.

[3] Definitions of Concepts Relating to the Enforcement of IPRs

The bulk of Part III of the TRIPS Agreement aims at enforcing the IPRs that are being infringed. However, WTO Member States may limit the border measures contemplated under Articles 51 et seq. to the importation of goods suspected to be "counterfeit trademark or copyright pirated goods." Similarly, in accordance with Article 61 of the TRIPS Agreement, WTO Member States may limit criminal procedures and penalties applicable to IP infringements to cases of "willful trademark counterfeiting or copyright piracy on a commercial scale." Therefore, it is important to understand and define further these concepts of "counterfeit trademark goods" and "trademark counterfeiting," on the one hand, and of "copyright pirated goods" and "copyright piracy," on the other hand, as indicative of specific cases of infringements to IP rights.

There is a link between the concepts of "counterfeit trademark goods" and "trademark counterfeiting," just as there is a link between the concepts of "copyright pirated goods" and "copyright piracy." This has been explicitly confirmed by the WTO Panel in the case *China—Measures Affecting the Protection and Enforcement of Intellectual Property Rights* (WT/DS/362R, paragraph 7.520), stating that "[t]he terms 'trademark counterfeiting' and 'copyright piracy' are not defined in the TRIPS Agreement. [...] They are *similar* to the terms 'counterfeit trademark goods' and 'pirated copyright goods' which are defined for the purposes of the TRIPS Agreement in footnote 14 [...]" (emphasis added).

Footnote 14 to the TRIPS Agreement provides:

> For the purposes of this Agreement:
>
> (a) "counterfeit trademark goods" shall mean any goods, including packaging, bearing without authorization a trademark which is identical to the trademark

validly registered in respect of such goods, or which cannot be distinguished in its essential aspects from such a trademark, and which thereby infringes the rights of the owner of the trademark in question under the law of the country of importation;

(b) "pirated copyright goods" shall mean any goods which are copies made without the consent of the right holder or person duly authorized by the right holder in the country of production and which are made directly or indirectly from an article where the making of that copy would have constituted an infringement of a copyright or a related right under the law of the country of importation.

Because of the similarity underlined by the WTO panel, it can be concluded that: (i) "trademark counterfeiting" means the unauthorized use of a sign which is identical to a validly registered trademark or which cannot be distinguished in its essential aspects from such a trademark, when that sign is used for goods or services for which the trademark has been registered; (ii) "copyright piracy" means the unauthorized copy of a copyrighted work. However, the similarity between the concepts of "counterfeit trademark goods" and "trademark counterfeiting" cannot be construed as meaning that trademark counterfeiting would relate to the unauthorized use of a sign for goods only. There would be no justification to exclude the qualification of trademark counterfeiting in case of unauthorized use of a sign identical to an earlier registered trademark for the services for which the trademark has been registered.

Given these definitions, it is relevant to note that the terms "trademark counterfeiting" and "copyright piracy" are distinct from the concepts of "trademark infringement" and "copyright infringement" (WT/DS/362R, paragraph 7.520). Any trademark counterfeiting constitutes a trademark infringement, just as any copyright piracy constitutes an infringement to copyright. But the converse is not true: not all trademark infringements are acts of trademark counterfeiting, and not all copyright infringements can be qualified as acts of copyright piracy. For example, the unauthorized use of a sign which is similar to—though not identical to or essentially undistinguishable from—an earlier registered trademark for the same goods can constitute a trademark infringement if there is a likelihood of confusion. But then, such trademark infringement would not be qualified as an act of trademark counterfeiting. Adapting a copyrighted novel without the consent of the copyright holder would constitute an act of copyright infringement, though that would not be qualified as copyright piracy. The delineation between these various concepts is important in the cases where border measures or criminal procedures and sanctions, in national law, apply only to acts of "trademark counterfeiting" or "copyright piracy."

[4] Procedural Justice and Efficiency

The TRIPS Agreement seeks to establish minimum standards of procedural justice and efficiency and a balance between the interests of complainants and defendants. Hence enforcement procedures must be fair and equitable. They may not be unnecessarily complicated or costly, or entail unreasonable time limits or unwarranted delays.

The Agreement establishes certain basic requirements of due process, providing that decisions on the merits of a claim shall preferably be in writing and reasoned, provided to the parties without undue delay, and based on evidence in respect of which parties were offered the opportunity to be heard.

In relation to civil procedures, defendants are entitled to timely, written notice of proceedings. Such notice must contain sufficient detail, including the basis of the claims asserted by the complainant. Parties are to be allowed to be represented by independent legal counsel, and procedures shall not impose overly burdensome requirements requiring the parties to attend in person at hearings. All parties to civil enforcement procedures shall be duly entitled to substantiate their claims and to present all relevant evidence. The procedure shall provide a means to identify and protect confidential information, unless this would be contrary to existing constitutional requirements.

Parties to enforcement proceedings must have an opportunity for review by a judicial authority of final administrative decisions. Subject to jurisdictional provisions in a Member's law concerning the importance of a case, such judicial review must be also available at least in respect of the legal aspects of initial judicial decisions on the merits of a case. Similarly, the Agreement provides that where pre-trial relief ("provisional measures") has been granted by the court, the parties affected are entitled to notice and to judicial review of the decision. Where enforcement measures have been granted and are subsequently found to be unjustified, the responsible authorities, whether judicial or administrative, must be empowered to order the claimant to pay compensation to the defendant.

The TRIPS Agreement lays down similar procedural requirements in relation to Customs action against the movement of infringing goods across national borders ("border measures").

[5] Border Measures

Part III section 4 of the TRIPS Agreement contains rules on particular enforcement measures to be taken by WTO members at their borders with a view to preventing the importation of IP infringing goods into their markets. More specifically, Article 51 of the TRIPS Agreement requires WTO Members to establish procedures allowing their national customs authorities to suspend the release into free circulation of goods suspected of infringing IP rights.

[a] Applicability of the Suspension of the Release of Allegedly Infringing Goods

Article 51 of the TRIPS Agreement clarifies that WTO members are obliged to put into place procedures for the suspension of goods that are suspected to be "counterfeit trademark or pirated copyright goods," but free to apply these procedures also to goods involving other types of IP infringements (provided that Article 1.1 is complied with) or goods destined for exportation. According to footnote 13, the obligation to establish border measures does not extend to parallel imports ("goods put on the market in another country by or with the consent of the right holder") or goods in transit. Moreover, pursuant to Article 60 of the TRIPS Agreement, WTO members are free not to apply border measure to so-called *de minimis* imports, namely "small quantities of goods of a non-commercial nature contained in travelers' personal luggage or sent in small consignments."

[b] Procedure to Suspend the Release of Goods

According to Article 51 of the TRIPS Agreement, the procedure to be established by WTO members must enable right holders to file an application in writing for the suspension of the release of the allegedly infringing goods. The application must be lodged "with the competent authorities, administrative or judicial," a wording which indicates that WTO members are free to determine which authority would be competent to receive such a request and that this authority may be different from the custom authorities eventually executing the suspension of release.

Further details on the applicable procedure can be found in Article 52 of the TRIPS Agreement. Notably, the applicant must provide "adequate evidence" of a prima facie infringement as well as a "sufficiently detailed description of the goods" allowing the customs authorities to recognize them. In practice, such an application is to be made on a specific form. Moreover, technical tools have been established at the European (such as the Enforcement Database of the European Union Intellectual Property Office) and international level (such as the Interface Public-Members tool developed by the World Customs Organization) to allow for secure and electronic collaboration between right holders and enforcement authorities. Once an application has been received by the competent authority, the applicant shall be informed within a reasonable period whether his/her application has been accepted and notified of the "period for which the customs authorities will take action," where the competent authority makes such a determination under national law.

Once the release of allegedly infringing goods has been suspended by the customs authorities, both the importer of the goods and the applicant shall be promptly notified (Article 54 of the TRIPS Agreement). In addition, customs authorities shall have the power to provide both the right holder and the importer with an opportunity to inspect the detained goods, provided that any confidential information is protected (first and second sentence of Article 57 of the TRIPS Agreement). Such inspections allow them to determine whether the detained goods are genuine or counterfeit, to prepare future proceedings, and to secure evidence.

How long the release of the goods remains suspended, depends on the right holder (Article 55 of the TRIPS Agreement). After a period of no more than ten working days after the applicant has received the notification of the suspension of release, the goods will be released unless the customs authorities have been informed that a provisional measure has been granted to prolong the suspension or that the right holder has initiated proceedings on the merits of the case. Where the suspension of release or its prolongation has been ordered by way of provisional measure, the general rule applies that the defendant may request this measure to be revoked if no proceedings on the merits of the case are initiated within the applicable time limit. Where proceedings on the merits have been initiated, the defendant may request a review to have the order of suspension modified, revoked or confirmed.

[c] Remedies

According to Article 59 of the TRIPS Agreement, WTO Members must endow the competent authorities with the power to order that the detained goods be destroyed or disposed of outside the channels of commerce. This provision largely echoes the principle set out in Article 46 of the TRIPS Agreement, discussed below. Suffice it to emphasize that this power is without prejudice to any measures that may be ordered in a decision on the merits and subject to the defendant's right to seek judicial review. The power to order destruction or disposal may also be made subject to conditions or limitations. Finally, WTO members may also give their competent authorities the discretion to order additional remedies other than destruction or disposal (WT/DS362R, paragraphs 7.239 and 7.240).

A supplementary remedy is contained in the third sentence of Article 57 of the TRIPS Agreement for cases in which the decision on the merits of the case has determined that the suspended goods are infringing. In such instances, WTO members have the option to provide the competent authorities with the power to inform the right holder of the names and addresses of the consignor, the importer and the consignee and of the quantity of the goods in question. For the right holder this information is valuable as it allows for assessing the scope of the infringement and potentially the enforcement of his/her rights against the different participants in the supply chain for the infringing goods.

[d] Safeguards

The suspension of the release of import goods is a powerful tool in the enforcement of IP rights. To prevent abuse of the procedure by right holders, the TRIPS Agreement provides for certain safeguards. Under Article 53.1, the competent authorities must have the power to require any applicant for the suspension of release of allegedly infringing goods to provide security or equivalent assurance. Where competent authorities demand this as a precondition for border measures, they need to strike a balance in the interest of proportionality. On the one hand, such security must be sufficient to protect the defendant and the competent authority and to prevent abuse but, on the other hand, it shall not unreasonably deter recourse to border measures.

In addition, Article 56 of the TRIPS Agreement provides for an indemnification of the importer, the consignee and the owner of the goods against right holders that unduly initiate a suspension procedure. WTO Members must endow a relevant authority with the power to order the right holder to pay appropriate compensation for any injury that was caused to them in case the detention of the goods was wrongful or the goods had to be released pursuant to Article 55 due to the right holder's inaction.

[e] Ex Officio Action

While WTO members are obliged to establish application-based procedures for the suspension of release of (at least) allegedly counterfeit trademark or pirated copyright goods, no such obligation exists to provide for procedures that allow the competent authorities to act ex officio, that is upon their own initiative. However, as Article 58 of the TRIPS Agreement shows, WTO members may allow ex officio action, where there is prima facie evidence that an IPR is being infringed. Where WTO member choose to do so, the provision contains certain qualifications. Notably, competent authorities may seek information from the right holder. Furthermore, the importer and the right holder shall be promptly notified of the suspension. Following this notification, the importer has the right to lodge an appeal with the competent authority. In this case, the conditions of Article 55 of the TRIPS Agreement apply *mutatis mutandis* and the goods will be released if the right holder remains inactive during the applicable time period. Finally, WTO members may not exempt public authorities and officials from liability to appropriate remedial measures unless their actions are taken or intended in good faith.

[f] Simplified Border Procedures

Where the release of suspicious goods has been suspended by the competent authorities, the conditions foreseen by Article 55 of the TRIPS Agreement mean that a right holder must ultimately initiate proceedings on the merits of the case (very often with a court) so as to keep the goods suspended. To wait until a decision has been taken confirming the infringement and ordering the appropriate remedies, however, may be time-consuming and costly for the right holder. This is why some countries or groups of countries have adopted, in addition to the border measures mechanism specifically foreseen in the TRIPS Agreement, what is often referred to as a "simplified procedure." Under such a "simplified procedure" the allegedly infringing goods may be destroyed or disposed of without the need for a decision on the merits from the competent authority, under specific conditions, notably the agreement to the destruction of the goods by both (i) the right holder and (ii) the person in whose name the customs declaration for the goods has been made or the holder of the goods (i.e., the importer or the owner to whom the goods are destined). In addition, even where the latter did not declare his/her agreement, customs authorities may deem such an agreement to exist if he/she did not, in due time, oppose to the destruction. An explicit example of the "simplified procedure" can be found in the EU legal framework (Article 23 of Regulation (EU) No. 608/2013 concerning customs enforcement of IPRs, OJEU, 2013, L181/15; another comparable procedure for goods in small consignment is to be found under Article 26 of this Regulation). According to the official statistics, 85% of the goods whose release into the EU was suspended in 2014 were destroyed via the simplified procedure.

[6] Provisional Measures

The TRIPS Agreement establishes guidelines—to be further implemented and detailed in the national laws of the Member States—concerning provisional measures. These are, by definition, temporary, at the latest until a final decision on the merits as to the alleged infringement. Such provisional measures can even be requested and ordered before any action on the merits has been lodged.

Provisional measures can have two purposes. The first is to prevent an infringement of any IPR from occurring, and in particular to prevent the entry of goods into the channels of commerce in the jurisdiction, including imported goods immediately after customs clearance (Article 50(1), *litt.* (a)). The second one aims at preserving relevant evidence with regard to the alleged infringement (Article 50(1), *litt.* (b)): the provisional measures are then used to collect evidence as regards the existence of the infringement, its scope and its origin. In many common law countries, these provisional measures aimed at gathering evidence are known as "*Anton Piller*" orders, so called after the name of a case in which the use of such kind of provisional measures was approved by a Court of Appeal in the UK (*Anton Piller K.G. v. Manufacturing Processes Ltd. [1976] RPC 719)*. In many francophone countries (with civil law tradition), these provisional measures are known as "*saisie-contrefaçon.*"

Articles 50(3) and 50(5) of the TRIPS Agreement provide for obligations that the applicant requesting the provisional measure may have to meet. He may be ordered to submit reasonable, prima facie, evidence to satisfy with a sufficient degree of certainty that he/she is indeed the right holder and that his/her right is being infringed or that the infringement is imminent. He may also be ordered to provide a security or equivalent assurance to protect the defendant or to prevent abuse later on, if need be. And he/she may be requested to supply additional information relating to the identification of the goods with which the provisional measures are concerned.

The provisional measures may be taken *inaudita altera parte*, where necessary (Article 50(2)). This ex parte characteristic of provisional measures is of great relevance in practice, particularly in the case of measures requested for obtaining evidence of infringement, as a way to preserve the evidence.

The defendant's rights against possible abuses are safeguarded under Article 50(4) of the TRIPS Agreement, which provides that notice of the provisional measure ordered shall be given to the parties affected without delay, at the latest immediately after the execution of the measure. Once notified, the party affected shall have the opportunity to ask the competent authority to review the provisional measure, and shall be granted a right to be heard. This may lead to the revocation, modification or confirmation of the provisional measure at stake. A further safeguard against the abuse of provisional measures is set out under Article 50(6) of the TRIPS Agreement, according to which provisional measures shall be revoked or cease to have effect, upon request of the party affected, if an action on the merits is not lodged within a reasonable time frame (this time frame is to be determined by the judicial authority ordering the provisional measure; if there is no such determination, the time frame cannot exceed twenty working days or thirty-one calendar days, whichever is the longer). In addition, according to Article 50(7) of the TRIPS Agreement, the defendant may be entitled to appropriate compensation, in case provisional measures are revoked or lapse due to any act or omission by the applicant or in case it would later appear that there was no infringement or threat of infringement of an IPR.

The principles laid out above also apply in case national law provides for provisional measures to be ordered as a result of administrative procedures, rather than judicial ones.

[7] Civil Procedures and Remedies

[a] Injunctions

Article 44 of the TRIPS Agreement relates to the issuance of a specific injunction. WTO Member States must ensure that the courts have the power to issue an injunction ordering a party to desist from an infringement of an IPR; *inter alia*, to prevent that infringing imported goods enter into the channels of commerce. The order "to desist from an infringement" shall be available "immediately after customs clearance." The article thus applies to existing infringements only, and not to mere threats of infringements, contrary to provisional measures aimed at preventing infringements to occur, dealt with under Article 50 (*see* above).

Article 44 of the TRIPS Agreement adds that Member States are not obliged to accord such power to the courts "in respect of protected subject matter acquired or ordered by a person prior to knowing or having reasonable grounds to know that dealing in such subject matter would entail the infringement of an intellectual property right." In other words, Member States may decide to exclude injunctions in case the infringers were acting in good faith (innocent infringement) in relation to goods previously acquired or ordered by them. The applicable national law will determine whether courts may issue injunctions or not in cases of "innocent infringements."

[b] Evidence

In order to be able to enforce his/her IPRs, the right holder must first prove that his/her IPRs have been infringed. In that respect, there is nothing distinguishing the management of IP-related cases in the judicial process from other non-IP-related claims. However, and because the question of the evidence in IP cases can be arduous, it is not surprising that several provisions deal with this issue.

Article 42 of the TRIPS Agreement, which requires that fair and equitable civil judicial procedures be available in all WTO Member States, provides that "(a)ll parties [...] shall be duly entitled to substantiate their claims and to present relevant evidence." In principle, the burden of proof lies on the plaintiff claiming remedies for the alleged infringement of his/her IPR. However, some issues, such as the proof of invalidity of a registered IP right, may lie on the defendant.

To uncover evidence, one key tool already consists of the provisional measures discussed above (Article 50(1)(b), TRIPS), including the Anton Piller orders and "*saisie-contrefaçon*" mechanisms. Reference is made to paragraphs 36 et seq. above in this regard.

Article 43(1) of the TRIPS Agreement, under the heading "Evidence," provides that the courts "shall have the authority, where a party has presented reasonably available evidence sufficient to support its claims and has specified evidence relevant to substantiation of its claims which lies in the control of the opposing party, to order that this evidence be produced by the opposing party, subject in appropriate cases to conditions which ensure the protection of confidential information." The condition that the party requesting such measure has first presented reasonably available evidence to support his/her claim and specified the evidence in the possession of the other party which disclosure he/she requests to substantiate his/her claim is aimed at preventing any abuse such as a blind "fishing expedition." Also prominent is the role of the courts in ensuring that the order for disclosure of the evidence, if granted, is strictly limited to what is necessary for the prosecution of the case and does not harm the protection of confidential information such as trade secrets. For example, depending on the circumstances at stake, the court may order that the document will be disclosed to the attorneys of the requesting party but not to the requesting party him/herself. Another example: if some confidential elements contained in the document are not necessary for the evidence the requesting party tries to bring out while others are, the court can order that only a copy of the document will be disclosed, with the non-essential elements being omitted.

Article 43(2) of the TRIPS Agreement ensures the efficiency of the disclosure of evidence under Article 43(1) by providing that, if a party refuses without good reason (as determined by the court) to provide access to the evidence in his/her possession, fails to provide the necessary information within a reasonable period or significantly impedes a procedure relating to an enforcement action, then courts are not prevented from "mak[ing] preliminary and final determinations, affirmative or negative, on the basis of the information presented to them, including the complaint or the allegation presented by the party adversely affected by the denial of access to information, subject to providing the parties an opportunity to be heard on the allegations or evidence." The purpose of this provision is to ensure that the lack of cooperation of a party to disclose evidence does not unduly hinder the judicial process. Beyond this optional provision of the TRIPS Agreement, national laws may provide for mechanisms to ensure the cooperation of a party requested to disclose evidence, such as the payment of a daily penalty for the delay in bringing out the requested evidence or, in common law countries, the application of sanctions relating to "contempt of court."

If the burden of proof lies on the claimant's shoulders, as indicated, Article 43 of the TRIPS Agreement qualifies this principle, in that it allows the claimant to request the court to order the other party to produce evidence which is deemed to be favorable to the claimant. There is another, more substantial, nuance to the principle relating to the burden of proof, though limited to the specific case of process patents. Article 34 ("Process Patents: Burden of Proof") of the TRIPS Agreement provides that, in case of a civil procedure for alleged infringement of a process patent, the competent courts "shall have the authority to order the defendant to prove that the process to obtain an identical product is different from the patented process." Article 34 further adds:

> Therefore, [WTO Member States] shall provide, in at least one of the following circumstances, that any identical product when produced without the consent of the patent owner shall, in the absence of proof to the contrary, be deemed to have been obtained by the patented process:
>
> (a) if the product obtained by the patented process is new;
> (b) if there is a substantial likelihood that the identical product was made by the process and the owner of the patent has been unable through reasonable efforts to determine the process actually used.

Article 34, hence, establishes a rebuttable presumption. The joint reading of paragraphs 1 and 2 of Article 34 clarifies that Member States have three possibilities to implement the presumption in their legislation. The national lawmaker has discretion to decide whether such presumption should apply:

- only where condition (a) is met;
- only where condition (b) is met;
- where either condition (a) or condition (b) is met.

Article 47 ("Right of Information") of the TRIPS Agreement empowers the WTO Member States to provide that courts "shall have the authority, unless this would be out of proportion to the seriousness of the infringement, to order the infringer to inform the right holder of the identity of third persons involved in the production and distribution of the infringing goods or services and of their channels of distribution." Though Member States are not obliged to implement Article 47 and provide for such "right of information," practice has shown how useful and beneficial such mechanism is, where it exists. If the infringer is a retailer, for example, it is useful that the court can order him to disclose information about his/her supplier, allowing the right holder to "climb up" the chain of distribution and find the wholesaler and the manufacturer of the infringing goods. Conversely, if the infringer is the manufacturer of the infringing goods, it is useful to know who distributed the infringing goods in order to be able to stop further distribution of goods still in stock.

By its nature, the request for information can only be granted if the court has considered that there is an infringement in fact, which distinguishes it from the information that could be obtained through a provisional measure within the scope of Article 50(1)(b), of the TRIPS Agreement (*see* above).

Because of the utility of the right of information in practice, some countries or groups of countries go even further: (i) as to the scope of the information to be provided (not only the identity of third parties, but also information on the quantities manufactured and sold, prices, etc.); and (ii) as to the person liable to disclose the information (someone other than the infringer). A good example is to be found in Article 8 of EU Directive No. 2004/48/EC on the enforcement of IPRs.

[c] Damages

The TRIPS Agreement requires the Member States to provide for the recovery of damages in case of an infringement to an IPR. Article 45 stipulates that:

- Courts must be able to order the infringer to pay the right holder damages "adequate to compensate for the injury the right holder has suffered because of that person's IPR by an infringer who knowingly, or with reasonable grounds to know, engaged in infringing activity" (Article 45(1) TRIPS).
- Courts must also have the authority to order the infringer to pay the right holder "expenses, which may include appropriate attorney's fees" (Article 45(2), *in limine*, TRIPS).
- "In appropriate cases, [Member States] may authorize the [courts] to order recovery of profits and/or payment of pre-established damages even where the infringer did not knowingly, or with reasonable grounds to know, engage in infringing activity" (Article 45(2), in fine, TRIPS).

The rules applicable to the allocation and determination of damages—which are key issues in many IP litigation cases—are often to be found in the relevant IP laws and statutes or in the ordinary rules of law applicable to the determination of damages for statutory wrongs. Article 45 of the TRIPS Agreement provides for the framework applicable to damages. Since the TRIPS obligations are minimum obligations, the laws of Member States may go beyond this framework. As a matter of example, a law may provide that damages will also be payable by the infringer even though he/she did not engage knowingly or with reasonable grounds to know in the infringing activity.

The rationale of an award of damages is to serve as compensation to the right holder for the prejudice suffered by reason of the infringement of his/her IPR. The issue, however, is how to quantify the damages due to the right holder, and parties and courts often struggle to determine the right compensation for the infringement of IP rights. Not surprisingly, the issue of the calculation of damages may be the subject of separate hearings or necessitate the appointment of an expert.

The general rule is that the measure of the prejudice of the right holder to be compensated is typically his/her loss of profits. This loss of profits is usually calculated in respect of the sales of the goods protected by the IP right at stake that would have been made if the infringement had not taken place. The loss of profits is usually due to the fact that the right holder, because of the infringement, sells fewer products, charges lower prices in order to compete with the infringer or must bear increased production costs. The right holder will typically have to prove the extent of the infringement (generally the quantity of infringing goods sold), the proportion of genuine goods that the right holder could and would have sold but for the infringement, and the profit the right holder would then have made on those goods. In addition to this loss of profits, the right holder is entitled to recover the costs of detecting, countering (e.g., the costs of additional advertising to compete with the infringing products) and terminating the infringement, including the judicial costs, which may include appropriate attorney's fees.

Providing evidence of the lost profits deriving directly from the infringement is particularly difficult. In many jurisdictions, an alternative to the loss of profits may be used, in the form of notional royalty. This way of calculating damages is also more appropriate if the right holder is not him/herself active in the market at stake (because he/she refrains from any activity in the market in question or because he/she has granted a license to a market actor/actress instead of exploiting the right him/herself).

This approach consists in allowing the right holder to claim a notional royalty from the infringer, i.e., the royalty the infringer should have paid to the right holder in the first place, had he/she requested the consent of the right holder to use the IP right instead of infringing it. The right holder will have to prove the usual royalty rate in his/her license agreements or, alternatively, what in commercial practice a reasonable royalty is in the market at stake.

A third way of allocating damages is the account of profits, i.e., the allocation to the right holder of the gains made by the infringer by committing the infringement. Those gains made by the infringer are seldom equivalent to the actual loss of the right holder: they can be lower or higher, depending on the circumstances of the case.

Although the account of profits is contemplated as an option in Article 45(2) TRIPS, it exists in many jurisdictions, either as an alternative or in (partial) addition to the actual loss of profits.

The good or bad faith of the infringer can be of tremendous importance in national law. In some jurisdictions, the absence of bad faith in the infringer (i.e., the fact that the infringer did not know and had no reasonable grounds to know he/she was committing an infringement) will exonerate him/her from having to pay damages to the right holder. In others, the good faith of the infringer does not exonerate him for the obligation to compensate the right holder.

The forms of damages contemplated above, in line with Article 45 of the TRIPS Agreement, aim at indemnifying the right holder for the prejudice suffered because of the infringement. The rationale of such damages is not to punish the infringer. However, in some jurisdictions, punitive damages are available against a deliberate infringer who has behaved in a particularly appalling manner.

[d] Other Remedies

Article 46 of the TRIPS Agreement provides for further remedies, in addition to the payment of damages, such as the authority to order the disposal outside the channels of commerce or destruction of infringing goods "in such a manner as to avoid any harm to the right holder," as well as the disposal of materials and implements predominantly used in the creation of infringing goods "in such a manner as to minimize the risks of further infringements."

It is appreciated that the destruction of goods is a form of disposal outside the channels of commerce, though "disposal" is broader than destruction only. For example, the donation of trademark counterfeit goods to charities (insofar as these goods are not sub-standard, defective, dangerous or hazardous) may constitute another kind of disposal outside the channels of commerce: the donation to charities as a way of disposal has been confirmed in WT/DS/362R without prejudice to submitting the donation to charities to conditions in order to ensure that the infringing goods do not reappear on the market and that such donation does not harm the right holder.

The authority to order the disposal of goods is qualified in that goods are to be disposed outside the channels of commerce in such a manner as to avoid any harm caused to the right holder. It is in this context that, in countries where donation to charities is possible, such measure is often ordered with the consent of the right holder. This constitutes a way for a court to ensure that this form of disposal of the infringing goods does not harm the right holder.

Further, competent authorities must have the power to order the destruction or disposal without compensation of any sort for the infringer.

The rationale of Article 46 of the TRIPS Agreement is to ensure that the infringement does not continue or is not repeated. However, before ordering such remedies, the court must ensure that they are reasonable and proportionate: Article 46 of the TRIPS Agreement provides expressly that, "[in] considering such requests, the need for proportionality between the seriousness of the infringement and the remedies ordered as well as the interests of third parties shall be taken into account." For example, depending on the circumstances of the case, a court may decline to order the infringer to proceed to a recall of trademark counterfeit goods that were already sold among end users, taking into account the interests of the end users who acquired the goods in good faith.

Particular rules apply to counterfeit trademark goods, since Article 46 of the TRIPS Agreement provides that "in regard to counterfeit trademark goods, the simple removal of the trademark unlawfully affixed shall not be sufficient, other than in exceptional cases, to permit release of the goods into the channel of commerce." The rationale lies in the heightened risk that such goods may infringe again, as trademarks identical to the one removed can be produced, imported separately and unlawfully reaffixed, often with relative ease. As a general rule, counterfeit trademark goods would need to be altered in a way that effectively deters further infringement, going beyond just taking off the trademark, in order to be allowed into the market. It is only in exceptional cases that the simple removal may be sufficient, as the wording of the fourth sentence of Article 46 of the TRIPS Agreement itself notes. Such cases would have to be narrowly circumscribed and the application of the exception would have to be rare in order not to become ordinary or even the rule.

The destruction or disposal of infringing goods is not as straightforward a measure as it can seem. Current disposal options include recycling, open air burning, shredding, crushing, burying in landfill sites and donation to charities. The methods adopted, however, depend on the nature of the goods requiring disposal as well as the appropriate disposal facilities, taking into account the social and environmental impact of the chosen method. By way of illustration, the disposal of counterfeit chemicals and pesticides that present serious environmental and health risks can be costly and technically complex. While high temperature incineration is common for disposing of these toxic substances, this could generate air pollution and hazardous wastes. Moreover, many countries do not have the necessary infrastructure or technical know-how to dispose of these substances safely. While transporting hazardous IP infringing goods to countries with appropriate disposal facilities might seem an obvious solution, this can be impeded or prevented by national or regional legislation, and needs to be compliant with multilateral environment agreements such as the Montreal Protocol on Substances that Deplete the Ozone Layer and the Basel Convention on the Control of Transboundary Movements of Hazardous Wastes and their Disposal. The technical difficulties associated with the environmentally sound disposal of infringing goods containing harmful substances and hazardous wastes underline the importance of greater public-private cooperation and a broad sharing of technical information and experiences regarding disposal, as well as close cooperation between law-enforcement and environmental agencies.

[8] Criminal Procedures

[a] Preliminary Considerations

The modern law of registered IP rights, as developed in the nineteenth century, has long included the availability of criminal remedies, at least for trademark counterfeiting. Similarly, the use of explicitly criminal sanctions to enforce copyright is found as early as the Napoleonic decree on the book trade of 1810 and the Prussian Copyright Act of 1837. Before that, penalties recoverable by action, analogous to fines, were provided for in the British Statute of Anne of 1710 and the first US Copyright Act of 1790, to be shared between the right holder and the state.

Although the extent to which criminal sanctions should be available for IP enforcement has provoked debate, the protection of IP, whether by civil or criminal means, is an expression of the coercive force of the State. Disobedience to an injunction or a willful failure to pay compensation for infringement following civil proceedings will usually result in enforcement measures more or less indistinguishable in character from criminal penalties. This said, a criminal conviction may carry a greater moral sanction than a civil judgment. Although IP rights are, like all property rights, private in character, their violation may engage the interests of society. It is widely accepted that in such cases, it is appropriate for criminal sanctions to be available.

The public interest is of course a matter for each jurisdiction, be it local, national or supra-national, to determine. Such issues as the protection of public health, the prevention of organized crime, compliance with international legal obligations, the protection of the economy and respect for culture and its practitioners may be regarded as justifying the use of criminal proceedings in the enforcement of IP rights.

[b] Definition of IP Crimes

Criminal offenses are typically defined by reference to the objective conduct which is prohibited, on the one hand, and the mental state of the offender in relation to that conduct, on the other. Thus, a statute may criminalize a particular act (e.g., the sale of an infringing copy of a copyright work in the course of a business), but require the prosecution to prove also a particular state of intention or knowledge on the part of the alleged infringer (e.g., knowledge that the copy is infringing). The mental state may be defined by reference to the facts which would have been apparent to a reasonable person in the position of the infringer, rather than his/her actual mental state. For example, criminal liability may arise where the accused did the prohibited conduct when he/she had objective reasons to believe that the article offered for sale was an infringing copy, whether he/she subjectively had that belief or not. Countries of the common law tradition tend in their statutes to define IP offenses in a specific manner, both as to the prohibited conduct and the mental state required for conviction. Countries of the civil law tradition tend, more succinctly, to criminalize any willful infringement of IP.

The criminal process can be divided into three stages: investigation, trial and sentencing. The investigation of IP offenses in accordance with national rules of criminal procedure displays few distinctive features. The usual police powers are employed to secure evidence and bring suspected persons before the courts. The investigation of IP crime, increasingly a category of cybercrime, requires law-enforcement agencies to be familiar with technical aspects of modern communications technologies and to have the skills necessary for the analysis of computers and digital media. Like other sorts of cybercrime, internet-based IP crime is characterized by geographical dispersion. The tools used to commit offenses (typically computer equipment) and the perpetrators may be situated in several different jurisdictions, throwing up problems of practical cooperation between different national agencies.

The evolving understanding of the substantive nature of IP rights in the digital environment raises particularly complicated questions of jurisdiction and applicable law. These are not specific to criminal proceedings. However, some evolution of existing criminal enforcement tools can be observed. In particular, some jurisdictions permit the preventive seizure of domain names used by criminals for web sites facilitating copyright or trademark infringements. In the case of a domain name registered outside the jurisdiction, this may take the form of a general order to internet service providers to block access by their local subscribers within the jurisdiction to infringing websites abroad.

[c] Criminal Proceedings

The general principles set out in Article 41 of the TRIPS Agreement are applicable in criminal proceedings as in civil. Thus, criminal procedures must be fair and equitable. They may not be unnecessarily complicated or costly, nor may they entail unreasonable time limits or unwarranted delays. Decisions on the merits of a case shall preferably be in writing and reasoned and should be made available to the parties without undue delay. Decisions on the merits of a case should be based only on evidence in respect of which parties were offered the opportunity to be heard.

The trial of IP offenses may engage other areas of criminal liability, such as offenses against laws concerning consumer protection, food, medicines or fraud. Jurisdictions differ, however, as to the duties of the public authorities in relation to complaints of criminal conduct, including IP crime. In some instances, the police may proceed with an investigation ex officio, that is to say, of their own motion; in others, the injured party must make a complaint before the public authorities may take action.

The prosecution of IP crimes as such requires proof that the IP rights in question subsisted at the time of the conduct complained of and that this conduct took place without the license of the right holder. Where the subject matter of the offense is a registered right, the proof of the right is straightforwardly based on the production of a valid certificate or extract from the register.

Proof of the subsistence of unregistered rights, such as (in most cases) copyright or performers' rights, may present problems for prosecutors, if the defendant declines to make a suitable admission. Some kinds of copyright work, such as software, are the result of the efforts of numerous authors or performers, often located outside the jurisdiction. Hence, the production of relevant witnesses to prove such matters may be difficult, even if in reality there is no realistic dispute as to the subsistence, ownership or licensing of rights.

In this context, the registration of copyright can play a useful role. Notwithstanding the fact that the Berne Convention has since 1908 prohibited the requirement of copyright registration as a *condition* of protection, some countries retain the facility of the voluntary registration of copyright. Where a copyright owner has gone to the trouble of registering his/her rights, the law in these countries provides a presumption that the registrant is the holder of a valid right in the work in question.

In some countries, rebuttable presumptions assist the prosecutor in establishing a prima facie case. However, more normally such presumptions are limited to civil cases. Similarly, although in criminal cases the burden of proof generally lies with the prosecution, in some jurisdictions the defendant carries the burden of disproving the relevant guilty state of mind. Further, the copyright statute may provide for the admissibility of an affidavit to prove facts relating to subsistence of copyright, ownership and the absence of license.

[d] International Norms

The Berne and Paris Conventions do not specifically address enforcement, save for providing for the seizure of infringing goods. The TRIPS Agreement, however, deals with criminal sanctions in Article 61, providing that criminal procedures and penalties shall be applied "at least in cases of willful trademark counterfeiting or copyright piracy on a commercial scale." The remedies available "shall include imprisonment and/or monetary fines sufficient to provide a deterrent, consistently with the level of penalties applied for crimes of a corresponding gravity." States bound by the TRIPS Agreement may provide for criminal sanctions in other types of IP infringement, but are not obliged to do so.

The minimum obligation under the TRIPS Agreement is hence to penalize certain infringements of copyright and registered trademarks. In relation to trademarks, the infringements in question are those falling within the category of "counterfeiting"; in relation to copyright, "piracy."

[e] Sanctions

Article 61 of the TRIPS Agreement requires that potential sanctions for counterfeiting and piracy shall include "imprisonment and/or monetary fines sufficient to provide a deterrent, consistently with the level of penalties applied for crimes of a corresponding gravity." It is for each jurisdiction to decide the maximum penalty for counterfeiting and piracy, subject to this TRIPS obligation.

The wording of this requirement is rather compressed: penalties must be sufficient to provide a deterrent, but at the same time they must be consistent with sanctions provided for crimes of a "corresponding gravity." Article 41 of the Agreement assists in interpretation, providing as it does that enforcement procedures are to be such as to permit effective action against any act of infringement, and must include "remedies which constitute a deterrent to further infringements." Deterrence is a primary objective of Part III of the TRIPS Agreement. Thus, the requirement that criminal sanctions be deterrent is not diluted by the qualification that penalties should be consistent with those applicable to crimes of equivalent gravity. The penalties for IP crime within the scope of Article 61 of the Agreement must be such as to deter future infringements and in addition consistent with penalties available in the case of crimes of comparable seriousness.

Article 61 of the TRIPS Agreement also addresses the issue of orders ancillary to sentence, providing that: "In appropriate cases, remedies available shall also include the seizure, forfeiture and destruction of the infringing goods and of any materials and implements the predominant use of which has been in the commission of the offence." It is a matter for the judgment of the courts to decide whether in any particular case an order for the destruction or disposal of infringing goods should issue.

Although as a matter of positive law Article 61 does not stipulate the criteria by reference to which a court is to decide the appropriateness of orders for the seizure of infringing goods, the policy of the TRIPS Agreement is evident from Articles 46 and 59 of the Agreement, which Article 61 echoes. These provide that goods found to be infringing may be disposed of outside the channels of commerce, without compensation for the infringer, in such a manner as to avoid any harm caused to the right holder. Reference is made to the considerations pertaining to Article 46 of the TRIPS Agreement.

§14.02 ADR OF IP AND TECHNOLOGY DISPUTES

Over the last years, the number of IP and technology disputes has increased with the multiplication of international IP transactions. Although an IP dispute can be brought before a court, litigation is not always well equipped to take account of the distinctive elements of this type of dispute. In this context, ADR procedures can be particularly advantageous in resolving IP disputes, especially IP and technology-related disputes involving parties from different jurisdictions.

[A] The WIPO Arbitration and Mediation Center

The WIPO Arbitration and Mediation Center (WIPO Center) was established in 1994 as a neutral, international and nonprofit dispute resolution provider specialized in IP and technology that offers ADR options to enable private parties to efficiently settle their domestic or cross-border disputes. The WIPO Center has its primary office at WIPO Headquarters in Geneva, Switzerland and furthermore maintains an office in Singapore.

The WIPO Center offers clauses, rules and neutrals for the following ADR options:

- Mediation: an informal consensual process in which a neutral intermediary, the mediator, assists the parties in reaching a settlement of their dispute, based on the parties' respective interests. The mediator cannot impose a decision. The settlement agreement has force of contract. Mediation leaves open available court or agreed arbitration options.
- Arbitration: a consensual procedure in which the parties submit their dispute to one or more chosen arbitrators, for a binding and final decision (award) based on the parties' rights and obligations and enforceable internationally. Arbitration normally forecloses court options.
- Expedited Arbitration: an arbitration procedure that is carried out in a short time and at a reduced cost.
- Expert Determination: a consensual procedure in which the parties submit a specific matter (e.g., technical question) to one or more experts who make a determination on the matter, which can be binding unless the parties have agreed otherwise.

[1] WIPO Rules and Neutrals

WIPO Mediation, Arbitration, Expedited Arbitration and Expert Determination Rules (WIPO Rules)[34] are generally suitable for all commercial disputes, and additionally feature provisions to address specific needs in IP disputes, notably provisions on confidentiality and technical evidence. In assisting parties in finding a suitable neutral, the WIPO Center draws upon a database of over 2,200 independent WIPO arbitrators, mediators and experts globally.

The WIPO Rules, first promulgated in 1999 (with the exception of the more recently introduced WIPO Expert Determination Rules), have proven a well-functioning framework for the WIPO Center's rapidly growing caseload, including in complex procedural circumstances. In 2014, selected provisions of the Arbitration Rules were updated in line with external developments in arbitration law, including taking account of the 2010 revision of the UNCITRAL Arbitration Rules. In addition,

34. WIPO Rules are available at www.wipo.int/amc/en/rules.

with a view to offering additional guidance to parties and neutrals, the 2014 WIPO Rules formalize certain WIPO Center practice that has emerged over the years.

As of January 1, 2016, a party that wishes to propose referring a dispute to WIPO Mediation can unilaterally submit a Request for Mediation to the WIPO Center. Article 4(a) of the updated WIPO Mediation Rules facilitates submission of a dispute to mediation in cases where there is no mediation agreement between the parties. This can also be helpful in a court environment that encourages mediation. Also, upon request by a party, the WIPO Center may appoint an external neutral to help parties considering submission of the dispute to WIPO Mediation (Article 4(b)); provided the parties agree, such neutral may subsequently be appointed as mediator. Similar options are now also available under Article 6 of the WIPO Expert Determination Rules.

On January 1, 2020, revised version of the WIPO Rules came into effect. The revised WIPO Mediation Rules facilitate party production of settlement agreements as may be required for enforcement purposes under the 2018 United Nations Convention on International Settlement Agreements Resulting from Mediation. To clarify the availability of mediation in connection with pending arbitration proceedings, the revised WIPO Arbitration and Expedited Arbitration Rules make express reference to mediation, adding to the existing settlement incentives in WIPO cases.

The most recent update of the WIPO Rules came into effect on July 1, 2021. The updated WIPO Rules expressly permit, and foresee as default option, the electronic filing of new WIPO ADR cases, as well as the electronic submission of any case communication. Remote WIPO mediation and arbitration meetings and hearings are expressly permitted and encouraged by the updated WIPO Rules, including the preparatory conference, emergency arbitrator proceedings, mediation meetings, and arbitration hearings. The updated Arbitration Rules and Expedited Arbitration Rules further introduce certain disclosure requirements concerning the identity of third-party funders, at an early stage of the proceedings. The updated Schedule of Fees and Costs introduces a 25% reduction on the WIPO Center's fees that applies if one or both parties to a dispute is a SME.

The revisions to the WIPO Rules were conducted by the WIPO Center in consultation with a group of selected IP mediation and arbitration experts, including WIPO Neutrals and party representatives.

[2] Types of Disputes

As of January 2023, the WIPO Center has administered some 1,350 mediation, arbitration and expert determination cases under the applicable WIPO Rules, as well as cases co-administered by the WIPO Center under other rules.[35] These cases were filed by large companies, SMEs, including start-ups, creators and innovators, collecting management organizations, research organizations and universities. It is important to

35. WIPO caseload summary is available at https://www.wipo.int/amc/en/center/caseload.html.

highlight here that in some 30% of mediation, arbitration and expedited arbitration cases filed with the WIPO Center under WIPO Rules, the parties used an escalation clause providing for WIPO mediation followed, in the absence of settlement, by WIPO expedited arbitration or WIPO arbitration. In addition, the WIPO Center regularly provides procedural guidance to parties in order to facilitate their direct settlement, or the submission of a dispute to WIPO ADR. The WIPO Center has assisted parties based in different jurisdictions form all regions of the world in over 850 "Good Offices" requests.

The WIPO Center has administered mediations, arbitrations and expedited arbitrations involving a range of issues, such as patent, trademark and copyright infringement, patent licenses, patent pools, appropriate patent licensing terms, including the determination of fair, reasonable and non-discriminatory (FRAND) terms, information technology transactions (including telecommunications), distribution agreements for pharmaceutical and consumer products, copyright issues, including copyright licensing and removal of content from online platforms, research and development agreements, trademark coexistence agreements, franchising agreements, art marketing, artistic production, media-related agreements, joint venture agreements and cases arising out of agreements in settlement of prior multi-jurisdictional IP litigation.

As of January 2023, 29% of cases filed with the WIPO Center under the applicable WIPO Rules involve patent-related issues, followed by copyright disputes (24%), trademarks disputes (20%), IT and telecommunication disputes (14%) and various commercial disputes (12%). Table 14.1 shows the distribution of WIPO cases in accordance with their legal and business areas.

Table 14.1 Dispute Areas in WIPO Mediation and Arbitration Cases

Patents 29%	*Copyright* 24%	*Trademarks* 20%	*ICT* 14%	*Commercial* 12%
Cross-licensing Infringements Licenses Ownership Patent Pools R&D / Tech Transfer Royalty Payment F/RAND Disputes	Art Broadcasting Collective Management Entertainment Film and Media Infringements TV Formats	Coexistence Infringements Licenses Oppositions Revocations	Mobile Apps Outsourcing Systems Integration Software Development Software Licensing Telecommunications	Design Distribution Energy Merchandising Marketing Sports

Parties to WIPO ADR cases have included large-sized companies, SMEs and start-ups across industries and sectors, artists and inventors, R&D centers, universities, producers and collecting societies based in some eighty different jurisdictions.

[3] Settlement Rates

WIPO ADR procedures are organized to stimulate positive opportunities for party settlement. As of January 2023, 70% of the mediation procedures administered by the WIPO Center have been settled. Even in arbitration, some 33% of WIPO cases settle before any tribunal award is issued.

In the WIPO Center's experience, most settlement agreements resulting from WIPO mediation are complied with voluntarily by the parties. Typically, a mediation settlement takes the form of a legally binding agreement, so that its enforcement would effectively be the enforcement of the contractual obligations of the parties. Under the laws of some jurisdictions, mediation settlement agreements can be enforced as court judgments, which provide a further measure of finality. In addition, the Singapore Mediation Convention[36] facilitates the enforcement of cross-border commercial mediation settlement agreements.

[4] WIPO Model Clauses

Referral to WIPO dispute resolution procedures is consensual and to facilitate party agreement, the WIPO Center provides recommended contract clauses (for the submission of future disputes under a particular contract) and submission agreements (for existing disputes).[37] While WIPO ADR cases are predominately based on contract clauses, a growing number of cases are being submitted to WIPO ADR procedures as a result of a submission agreement concluded after a dispute has arisen (e.g., non-contractual infringement of IP rights).

Parties may combine mediation with (expedited) arbitration and expert determination in different manners. The most commonly used WIPO ADR clause is "Mediation Followed, in the Absence of a Settlement, by [Expedited] Arbitration," which provides that:

> Any dispute, controversy or claim arising under, out of or relating to this contract and any subsequent amendments of this contract, including, without limitation, its formation, validity, binding effect, interpretation, performance, breach or termination, as well as non-contractual claims, shall be submitted to mediation in accordance with the WIPO Mediation Rules. The place of mediation shall be [specify place]. The language to be used in the mediation shall be [specify language].
>
> "If, and to the extent that, any such dispute, controversy or claim has not been settled pursuant to the mediation within [60][90] days of the commencement of the mediation, it shall, upon the filing of a Request for Arbitration by either party, be referred to and finally determined by arbitration in accordance with the WIPO [Expedited] Arbitration Rules. Alternatively, if, before the expiration of the

36. United Nations Convention on International Settlement Agreements Resulting from Mediation, *see* https://uncitral.un.org/en/texts/mediation/conventions/international_settlement_agreements.
37. Recommended WIPO contract clauses and submission agreements are available at https://www.wipo.int/amc/en/clauses/index.html.

> said period of [60][90] days, either party fails to participate or to continue to participate in the mediation, the dispute, controversy or claim shall, upon the filing of a Request for Arbitration by the other party, be referred to and finally determined by arbitration in accordance with the WIPO [Expedited] Arbitration Rules. [The arbitral tribunal shall consist of [a sole arbitrator] [three arbitrators].][38] The place of arbitration shall be [specify place]. The language to be used in the arbitral proceedings shall be [specify language]. The dispute, controversy or claim referred to arbitration shall be decided in accordance with the law of [specify jurisdiction]."

[5] *Clause Generator*

To facilitate the referral of a dispute to WIPO ADR procedures, the WIPO Center makes available an online clause generator. This user-friendly tool enables parties to develop tailored clauses and submission agreements by selecting WIPO ADR procedures, core elements, such as place and language of proceedings and applicable law, and, if desired, additional elements such as specific qualifications of neutral. The new clause generator works on the basis of the WIPO model clauses and submission agreements.

[6] *WIPO Case Examples*

To give a practical expression of the type of IP and technology disputes lending themselves to the use of ADR, the WIPO Center makes available on its website a range of anonymized summaries of cases administered by the WIPO Center. Set out below is a selection; further examples, always anonymized to preserve the confidentiality of WIPO proceedings, are available on the WIPO Center's website.

[7] *WIPO Mediation Case Examples*

Example 1: WIPO Mediation in the Area of Research and Development

A major European research institute and a French company entered into a license agreement. The agreement related to a technology in the area of building materials with an application for patent filed with the EPO. The parties included in their contract a multi-tier dispute resolution clause providing for WIPO mediation, followed by court litigation.

Three years after the conclusion of the agreement the company alleged the invalidity of the license agreement and requested a refund of royalty payments in light of the rejection of the patent application by the EPO. The research institute commenced mediation proceedings requesting payment of the royalty rates. The parties invited the

38. The WIPO Expedited Arbitration Rules provide that the arbitral tribunal shall consist of a sole arbitrator.

WIPO Center to provide them with a list of mediator candidates experienced in mediation, drafting licensing agreements and specialized in patent law.

One of those mediators was selected by the parties. The mediator conducted a preparatory telephone conference with the parties including an explanation of mediation principles, the submission of documents as well as details of the mediation meeting, such as the timetable, venue and party representation. Following a dinner which proved useful to restore communication between the parties, a one-day mediation session took place in Munich, Germany. At the end of the mediation session the parties were able to conclude a settlement agreement. This settlement agreement included options for the amendment of the license agreement and payment of royalty rates, based on future decisions on the patent application, and the additional option to conclude a research and development agreement between the parties. Thus, the mediation settled within less than three months after its commencement and enabled further extended collaboration between the parties.

Example 2: WIPO Mediation of a Trademark Coexistence Dispute

After a dispute arose between them, a North American company requested mediation with two Italian companies and one Spanish company on the basis of an agreement which the parties had reached for mediation under the WIPO Mediation Rules. The goal of the mediation was to help the parties avoid confusion and misappropriation of their similar trademarks and to regulate future use of their marks. Although Italian was agreed as the language of proceedings, any settlement agreement would be recorded in both Italian and English.

The WIPO Center suggested to the parties potential mediators with specific expertise in European trademark law and fluency in Italian and English. The parties selected an Italian mediator with a trademark practice. The mediator conducted an initial telephone conference with the lawyers of the parties in which he/she scheduled the mediation timing, and agreed on the procedure.

Two months later, the mediator met with the parties in a two-day session in Milan. The meeting was held in joint session with the exception of two brief caucuses. At the end of the second day the parties—with the assistance of the mediator—were able to draft and sign a settlement agreement covering all of the pending issues in dispute.

Example 3: WIPO Online Mediation of a Software Dispute

A European software developer entered into a software licensing agreement with a European customer which included a contract clause providing for WIPO Mediation followed by court litigation.

In a dispute regarding non-execution of the agreement and related damages claims, the parties initiated mediation and the WIPO Center appointed a mediator with experience in technology contracts. The mediation sessions took place entirely online, with live interpretation, and a settlement agreement was concluded within six months after the commencement of the mediation.

[8] WIPO Arbitration Case Examples

Example 1: WIPO Expedited Arbitration Relating to a Banking Software Dispute

A US company providing data processing software and services and an Asian bank concluded an agreement regarding the provision of account processing services. The parties agreed that the US company was to be the exclusive service provider for certain of the bank's affiliates in North America and Europe. The agreement stated that any dispute arising out of or in connection with the agreement would be resolved under the WIPO Expedited Arbitration Rules and that the sole arbitrator will be selected from a panel of persons having experience of information technology.

Four years after the conclusion of their agreement, the US company alleged that the bank had violated the agreement by using processing services offered by third parties in the countries covered by the agreement. When the parties failed to settle the dispute, the US service provider commenced WIPO expedited arbitration proceedings claiming infringement of the agreement and substantial consequential damages.

The parties agreed upon a sole arbitrator who held a two-day hearing in New York City. Three months after the request for expedited arbitration, the arbitrator rendered a final award finding partial infringement of the agreement and granting damages to the US service provider.

Example 2: WIPO Patent License Arbitration

A European inventor holding patents in Australia, Canada, Europe and the US licensed patent rights and know-how to an Asian company. The license contained a WIPO arbitration clause providing for a three-member tribunal.

The parties disagreed on who should pay the renewal fees of the patents. Eventually the Asian company terminated the license whereupon the European inventor filed a request for arbitration, claiming damages and requesting a declaration that he/she was free to use the patents.

The three arbitrators appointed possessed substantial IP expertise and the necessary language skills allowing them to consider evidence in different languages.

Following a series of evidentiary exchanges, the tribunal rendered an award fourteen months after commencement of the arbitration. Finding that the Asian company had not been entitled to terminate the contract as it did, the tribunal ordered it to pay damages and to return to the inventor the prototypes, plans and documents that had been communicated in the context of the license.

Example 3: Patent Infringement Dispute Submitted to WIPO Arbitration

Following litigation in several jurisdictions, two American companies agreed to submit to WIPO Arbitration a dispute related to the alleged infringement of a European patent concerning consumer goods. The submission agreement provided that the national patent law of a particular European country would apply and that the patent litigation timelines of that country should be followed. The three-member tribunal was asked to decide whether the manufacture and sale of certain products infringed the patent.

The submission agreement, and compliance with the procedural timetable in the subsequent arbitration process, reflected the parties' mutual interest to resolve the dispute in a time- and cost-efficient manner. The parties accepted the WIPO Center's recommendation to appoint three arbitrators with substantial expertise in arbitration and in the relevant national patent law. Further to the exchange of written submissions, the arbitral tribunal held a one-day hearing in Geneva for further statements and for the examination of expert witnesses. In accordance with the time schedule agreed by the parties, the final award was rendered within five months of the commencement of the arbitration.

[9] WIPO ADR Services for Specific Sectors

Most WIPO cases are based on parties' inclusion in their contract of ADR clauses referring to the WIPO Rules. However, specific areas of IP and technology transactions may benefit from targeted adaptations to the standard WIPO ADR framework, for example in relation to rules, fees and clauses or separate panels of mediators and arbitrators specialized in the relevant subject. As a resource center, the WIPO Center develops, in collaboration with relevant stakeholders and international experts in the respective sectors, operational and legal frameworks for such tailored dispute resolution procedures.

The WIPO Center's ADR services for specific sectors[39] currently cover various areas including:

- Art and Cultural Heritage
- B2B Data Disputes
- Digital Copyright and Content
- Energy
- Fashion
- Film and Media and Entertainment
- Franchising
- Green Technology and Sustainability
- Information and Communication Technology
- Intellectual Property Offices
- Life Sciences
- Patents in Standards
- Research and Development/TT
- SMEs
- Sports
- Trade Fairs
- Video Games and eSports.

39. Information on WIPO ADR for specific sectors in available at https://www.wipo.int/amc/en/center/specific-sectors.

In the area of life sciences, for example, in 2022, the WIPO Center developed and launched, in consultation with leading international life sciences and ADR experts, the publication WIPO ADR for Life Sciences Disputes Management and Resolution. It presents new WIPO ADR options and model clauses tailored to life sciences disputes, notably WIPO Mediation to facilitate contract negotiation (deal mediation), which may be particularly useful in the context of medical innovation and collaborations across regions and types of entities.

Another example of WIPO Center's ADR services for specific sectors, are services for disputes concerning FRAND terms for standard-essential patents (SEPs). To date, the WIPO Center has administered some eighty SEP-related mediations involving SMEs, patent pools and large companies, with parties from over twenty jurisdictions. Reflecting this growing case experience, including cases pending before multiple courts, the WIPO Center published in 2022 updated guidance to further facilitate referral to WIPO mediation and arbitration.

The WIPO Center also provides ADR procedures to help parties resolve disputes related to copyright and content in the digital environment. Noting the increase in digital copyright disputes filed to WIPO ADR, the WIPO Center with the support of the Ministry of Culture, Sports and Tourism of the Republic of Korea conducted the Survey on the Use of ADR Mechanisms for Business to Business (B2B) Digital Copyright- and Content-related Disputes, which attracted over thousand participants. The WIPO Center's survey report provides insight into such disputes across industries internationally, including current use of mediation and arbitration instead of court litigation to resolve such disputes. The survey and report have helped to inform the development of best ADR practices for digital copyright- and content-related disputes, taking into account relevant legislation and existing contractual practices.

One further area of WIPO Center activity is collaboration with IP and Copyright Offices globally. Such collaboration, which may include establishment of optional ADR frameworks, training programs, promotional activities and case administration, aims to provide cost-effective and flexible options for parties to resolve their disputes before IPOs in relation to pending applications or granted rights. The WIPO Center also collaborates with a growing number of courts to facilitate the referral to WIPO mediation of cases where parties are willing to explore settlement, including training for members of the judiciaries and mediators. On this topic, the WIPO Center has published the "WIPO Guide on Alternative Dispute Resolution Options for IP Offices and Courts."[40]

[10] Domain Name Dispute Resolution

The Domain Name System (DNS) raises challenges for the use and protection of IP. In particular because the Internet is global, solutions to these challenges call for an

40. The WIPO Center now collaborates with IP and Copyright Offices and Courts in more than eighty jurisdictions. Full list of current collaborations is available at https://www.wipo.int/amc/en/center/specific-sectors/ipoffices.

international approach. WIPO addressed the challenge of "cybersquatting" by developing the Uniform Domain Name Dispute Resolution Policy (UDRP) to allow brand owners to reclaim infringing domain names. Since WIPO's creation of the UDRP in 1999, more than sixty thousand UDRP-based cases have been filed with WIPO by brand owners the world over (case parties have come from 185 countries).[41]

Showcasing WIPO's case experience and policy expertise, in 2017 WIPO published the Third edition of its "Jurisprudential Overview" of UDRP cases. The WIPO Overview provides jurisprudential guidance on a wide range of substantive and procedural questions faced by parties to UDRP cases. WIPO also provides a subject matter-searchable Legal Index of UDRP decisions. WIPO also provides a Model Complaint and Response to assist parties in preparing their cases.

The UDRP applies to all domain names registered in generic top-level domains (gTLDs), such as ".com" and more recently introduced new gTLDs.

Many country-code top-level domain (ccTLD) registries have also adopted the UDRP or sometimes a variation tailored according to local law, for example allowing holders of not only trademark rights, but other rights such as personal names or GIs to file a case. WIPO provides free policy assistance to ccTLD operators in creating registration terms and conditions and dispute resolution procedures to address cybersquatting. WIPO also provides UDRP-like domain name dispute resolution services for over eighty ccTLDs at present (Figure 14.1).[42]

Figure 14.1 WIPO ccTLD Program

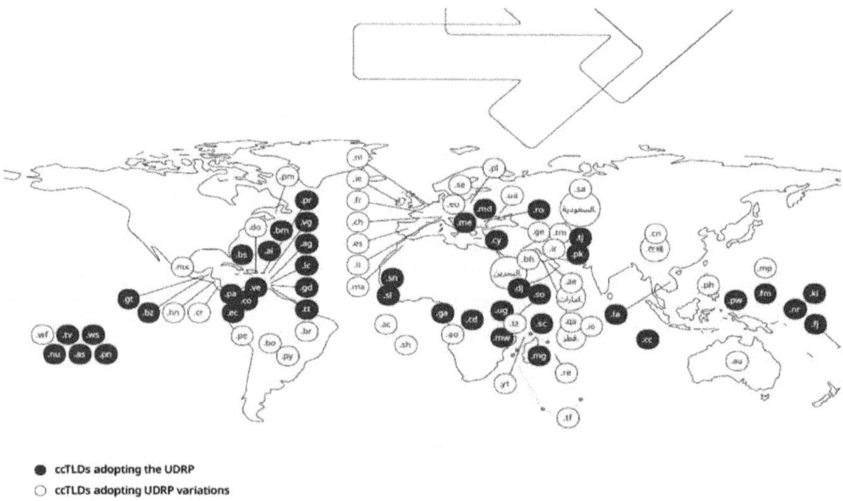

41. WIPO domain name dispute resolution statistics are available at https://www.wipo.int/amc/en/domains.
42. Information on WIPO domain name dispute resolution services for ccTLDs is available at https://www.wipo.int/amc/en/domains/cctld.

PART II Global Protection

CHAPTER 15
The Paris Convention for the Protection of Industrial Property

§15.01 HISTORY

During the last century, before the existence of any international convention in the field of industrial property, it was rather difficult to obtain protection for industrial property rights in the various countries of the world because the laws were very different. Moreover, patent applications had to be made roughly at the same time in all countries in order to avoid a publication in one country destroying the novelty of the invention in the other countries. These practical problems created a strong desire to overcome such difficulties.

In addition to those practical considerations, there was, as more and more countries developed a system for the protection of inventions during the second half of the last century, a general desire, as in other fields of law, for the harmonization of the laws of industrial property on an international, and even worldwide, basis. This was due to the development of a more internationally oriented flow of technology and to the increase of international trade, which made such harmonization urgent in both the patent and the trademark field.

The lack of adequate protection of foreign inventions became particularly apparent when the Government of the Empire of Austria-Hungary invited the other countries to participate in an international exhibition of inventions held in 1873 at Vienna. Participation was hampered by the fact that many foreign visitors were not willing to exhibit their inventions at that exhibition in view of the inadequate legal protection offered to exhibited inventions.

This led to two developments: first, a special Austrian law secured temporary protection to all foreigners participating in the exhibition for their inventions, trademarks and industrial designs. Second, the Congress of Vienna for Patent Reform was convened during the same year 1873. The Congress for Patent Reform passed several resolutions, setting forth a number of principles on which an effective and useful patent system should be based, and urging governments "to bring about an international understanding upon patent protection as soon as possible."

As a follow-up to the Vienna Congress, an International Congress on Industrial Property was convened at Paris in 1878. The main result of that second Congress was a decision that one of the governments should be asked to convene an international (diplomatic) conference "with the task of determining the basis of uniform legislation" in the field of industrial property.

Following that Congress, a final draft proposing an international "union" for the protection of industrial property was prepared in France. That draft was sent by the French Government to a number of other countries, together with an invitation to attend the International Conference in Paris of 1880. That Conference adopted a draft convention which contained in essence those substantive provisions which are still today the main features of the Paris Convention.

A new Diplomatic Conference was convened in Paris in 1883, which ended with final approval and signature of the Paris Convention for the Protection of Industrial Property. The Paris Convention was signed by eleven States: Belgium, Brazil, El Salvador, France, Guatemala, Italy, the Netherlands, Portugal, Serbia, Spain and Switzerland. When the Paris Convention came into effect on July 7, 1884, Great Britain, Tunis and Ecuador had adhered as well, bringing the initial number of member countries to fourteen. At the end of the nineteenth century, the number of member countries had risen to nineteen. It was only during the first quarter of this century and then in particular after the Second World War that the Paris Convention increased its membership more significantly.

The Paris Convention has been revised from time to time after its signature in 1883. Revision Conferences were held in Rome in 1886, in Madrid in 1890 and 1891, in Brussels in 1897 and 1900, in Washington in 1911, in The Hague in 1925, in London in 1934, in Lisbon in 1958 and in Stockholm in 1967. The last Revision Conference held its first session in Geneva in 1980, its second session in Nairobi in 1981, its third session in Geneva in 1982 and its fourth session in Geneva in February-March 1984.

Each of the revision conferences, starting with the Brussels Conference in 1900, ended with the adoption of a revised Act of the Paris Convention. With the exception of the Acts concluded at the revision conferences of Brussels and Washington, which are no longer in force, all those earlier Acts are still of significance, although the great majority of the countries are now party to the latest Act, that of Stockholm of 1967. It was this last Act that the TRIPS Agreement incorporated (in Article 2.1). This means that the Stockholm Act of Paris Convention has become mandatory to WTO Members, even if they are not members of the Paris Union, or if they are, even if they are bound by earlier versions of the Paris Convention.

§15.02 PRINCIPAL PROVISIONS

The provisions of the Paris Convention may be subdivided into four main categories:

- A first category of provisions contains rules of substantive law which guarantee a basic right known as the right to national treatment in each of the member countries.
- A second category of provisions establishes another basic right known as the right of priority.
- A third category of provisions defines a certain number of common rules in the field of substantive law which contain either rules establishing rights and obligations of natural persons and legal entities or rules requiring or permitting the member countries to enact legislation following those rules.
- A fourth category of provisions deals with the administrative framework, which has been set up to implement the Convention, and includes the final clauses of the Convention.

[A] National Treatment Principle

The provisions concerning national treatment are contained in Articles 2 and 3 of the Convention.

National treatment means that, as regards the protection of industrial property, each country party to the Paris Convention must grant the same protection to nationals of the other member countries as it grants to its own nationals.

The same national treatment must be granted to nationals of countries which are not party to the Paris Convention if they are domiciled in a member country or if they have a "real and effective" industrial or commercial establishment in such a country. However, no requirement as to domicile or establishment in the country where protection is claimed may be imposed upon nationals of member countries as a condition for benefitting from an industrial property right.

This national treatment rule is one of the cornerstones of the system of international protection established under the Paris Convention. It guarantees not only that foreigners will be protected, but also that they will not be discriminated against in any way. Without that rule, it would frequently be very difficult and sometimes even impossible to obtain adequate protection in foreign countries for inventions, trademarks and other subjects of industrial property.

The national treatment rule applies first of all to the "nationals" of the member countries. The term "national" includes both natural persons and legal entities. With respect to legal entities, the quality of being a national of a particular country may be difficult to determine. Generally, no nationality as such is granted to legal entities by the various national laws. There is of course no doubt that State-owned enterprises of a member country or other entities created under the public law of such country are to be considered as nationals of the member country concerned. Legal entities created under the private law of a member country will usually be considered a national of that country. If they have their actual headquarters in another member country, they may also be considered a national of the headquarters country.

According to Article 2(1), the national treatment rule applies to all advantages that the various national laws grant to nationals. This means that the national law, as it is applied to the nationals of a particular member country, must also be applied to the nationals of other member countries. In this respect, the national treatment rule excludes any possibility of discrimination to the detriment of nationals of other member countries.

This means furthermore, that any requirement of reciprocity of protection is excluded. Suppose that a given member country has a longer term of patent protection than another member country: the former country will not have the right to provide that nationals of the latter country will enjoy a term of protection of the same length as the term of protection is in the law of the latter country. This principle applies not only to codified law, but also to the practice of the courts (jurisprudence) and to the practice of the Patent Office or other administrative governmental institutions, as it is applied to the nationals of the country.

The application of the national law to the national of another member country does not, however, prevent him from invoking more beneficial rights specially provided in the Paris Convention. These rights are expressly reserved. The national treatment principle must be applied without prejudice to such rights.

Article 2(3) states an exception to the national treatment rule. The national law relating to judicial and administrative procedure, to jurisdiction and to requirements of representation is expressly "reserved." This means that certain requirements of a mere procedural nature which impose special conditions on foreigners for purposes of judicial and administrative procedure, may also validly be invoked against foreigners who are nationals of member countries. An example is a requirement for foreigners to deposit a certain sum as security or bail for the costs of litigation. Another example is expressly stated: the requirement on foreigners to either designate an address for service or to appoint an agent in the country in which protection is requested. This latter is perhaps the most common special requirement imposed on foreigners, and is a permitted exception from the national treatment rule.

As indicated initially, the application of the national treatment rule extends also to nationals of non-member countries, provided they are *domiciled* or have an industrial or commercial establishment in a member country. This provision is contained in Article 3.

The term "domiciled" is generally interpreted not to require a domicile in the strict legal sense of the term. A person is also "domiciled" in the sense of Article 3 if he/she lives more or less permanently in a particular place, without having his/her legal residence there. In other words, a mere residence, as distinct from a legal domicile, is sufficient. Legal entities are domiciled at the place of their actual headquarters.

If there is no domicile, there may still be an industrial or commercial establishment which gives a person the right to national treatment. The notion of the industrial or commercial establishment in a member country of a national of a non-member country is further qualified by the text of the Convention itself. It requires that the establishment be real and effective. This means that there must be actual industrial or commercial activity. A mere letter box or the renting of a small office with no real activity is not sufficient.

[B] The Right of Priority

The provisions concerning the right of priority are contained in Article 4 of the Convention. The right of priority means that, on the basis of a regular application for an industrial property right filed by a given applicant in one of the member countries, the same applicant (his/her successor in title) may, within a specified period of time (six or twelve months), apply for protection in all the other member countries. These later applications will then be regarded as if they had been filed on the same day as the first (or earlier) application. In other words, these later applications enjoy a priority status with respect to all applications relating to the same invention filed after the date of the first application. They also enjoy a priority status with respect to all acts accomplished after that date which would normally be apt to destroy the rights of the applicant or the patentability of his/her invention.

The right of priority offers great practical advantages to the applicant desiring protection in several countries. The applicant is not required to present all applications at home and in foreign countries at the same time, since he/she has six or twelve months at his/her disposal to decide in which countries to request protection. The applicant can use that period to organize with due care the steps to be taken to secure protection in the various countries of interest in this case.

The beneficiary of the right of priority is any person entitled to benefit from the national treatment rule who has duly filed an application for a patent for invention or another industrial property right in one of the member countries.

The right of priority can be based only on *the first* application for the same industrial property right which must have been filed in a member country. It is therefore not possible to follow a first application by a second, possibly improved application and then to use that second application as a basis of priority. The reason for this rule is obvious: one cannot permit an endless chain of successive claims of priority for the same subject, as this could, in fact, considerably prolong the term of protection for that subject.

Article 4A(1) of the Paris Convention recognizes expressly that the right of priority may also be invoked by the successor in title of the first applicant. The right of priority may be transferred to a successor in title without transferring at the same time the first application itself. This allows in particular also the transfer of the right of priority to different persons for different countries, a practice which is quite common.

The later application must concern the same subject as the first application the priority of which is claimed. In other words, the same invention, utility model, trademark or industrial design must be the subject of both applications. It is, however, possible to use a first application for a patent for invention as priority basis for a registration of a utility model and vice versa. The same change of form of protection in both directions is also possible between utility models and industrial designs.

The first application must be "duly filed" in order to give rise to the right of priority. Any filing, which is equivalent to a regular national filing, is a valid basis for the right of priority. A regular national filing means any filing that is adequate to establish the date on which the application was filed in the country concerned. The notion of "national" filing is qualified by including also applications filed under bilateral or multilateral treaties concluded between member countries.

Withdrawal, abandonment or rejection of the first application does not destroy its capacity to serve as a priority basis. The right of priority subsists even where the first application generating that right is no longer existent.

The effect of the right of priority is regulated in Article 4B. One can summarize this effect by saying that, as a consequence of the priority claim, the later application must be treated as if it had been filed already at the time of the filing, in another member country, of the first application the priority of which is claimed. By virtue of the right of priority, all the acts accomplished during the time between the filing dates of the first and the later applications, the so-called priority period, cannot destroy the rights which are the subject of the later application.

In terms of concrete examples, this means that a patent application for the same invention filed by a third party during the priority period will not give a prior right, although it was filed before the later application. Likewise, a publication or public use of the invention, which is the subject of the later application, during the priority period would not destroy the novelty or inventive character of that invention. It is insignificant for that purpose whether that publication is made by the applicant or the inventor him/herself or by a third party.

The length of the priority period is different according to the various kinds of industrial property rights. For patents for invention and utility models the priority period is twelve months, for industrial designs and trademarks it is six months. In determining the length of the priority period, the Paris Convention had to take into account the conflicting interests of the applicant and of third parties. The priority periods now prescribed by the Paris Convention seem to strike an adequate balance between these conflicting interests.

The right of priority as recognized by the Convention permits the claiming of "multiple priorities" and of "partial priorities." Therefore, the later application may not only claim the priority of one earlier application, but it may also combine the priority of several earlier applications, each of which pertaining to different features of the subject matter of the later application. Furthermore, in the later application, elements for which priority is claimed may be combined with elements for which no priority is claimed. In all these cases, the later application must of course comply with the requirement of unity of invention.

These possibilities correspond to a practical need. Frequently after a first filing further improvements and additions to the invention are the subject of further applications in the country of origin. In such cases, it is very practical to be able to combine these various earlier applications into one later application, when filing before the end of the priority year in another member country. This combination is even possible if the multiple priorities come from different member countries.

[C] Provisions Concerning Patents

[1] Independence of Patents

The rule concerning the "independence" of patents for invention is contained in Article 4*bis*. This rule means that patents for invention granted in member countries to nationals or residents of member countries must be treated as independent of patents for invention obtained for the same invention in other countries, including non-member countries.

This principle is to be understood in its broadest sense. It means that the grant of a patent for invention in one country for a given invention does not oblige any other member country to grant a patent for invention for the same invention. Furthermore, the principle means that a patent for invention cannot be refused, invalidated or otherwise terminated in any member country on the ground that a patent for invention for the same invention has been refused or invalidated, or that it is no longer maintained or has terminated, in any other country. In this respect, the fate of a particular patent for invention in any given country has no influence whatsoever on the fate of a patent for the same invention in any of the other countries.

The underlying reason and main argument in favor of the principle of independence of patents for invention is that the national laws and administrative practices are usually quite different from country to country. A decision not to grant or to invalidate a patent for invention in a particular country on the basis of its law will frequently not have any bearing on the different legal situation in the other countries. It would not be justified to make the owner lose the patent for invention in other countries on the ground that he/she or she lost a patent in a given country as a consequence of not having paid an annual fee in that country or as a consequence of the patent's invalidation in that country on a ground which does not exist in the laws of the other countries. Moreover, a system where patents are dependent from foreign patents would not be in conformity with the national treatment rule. Another matter that is closely linked to the independence of patents is the so-called international exhaustion of patents, under which, putting it simple, once a patented product is sold (or otherwise transferred) by the patent owner or a licensee on the market of one country, the patentee loses the right to oppose its importation and/or commercialization in the territory of any other country where he/she or she may have a patent on the same invention. In a strict sense, international exhaustion—which is implicitly permitted under Article 6 of the TRIPS Agreement—is in breach of the principle of independence, given that not only the titles in inventions are to be independent, but also the rights that flow from them. Therefore, it can be said that the principle of independence of patents implies an obligation for Paris Contracting Parties to adhere to national exhaustion. In other words, the principle that Article 4*bis* establishes is not just one of independence of *patent letters*, but rather of independence of *patent rights*.

A special feature of the principle of independence of patents for invention is contained in Article 4*bis*(5). This provision requires that a patent granted on an application which claimed the priority of one or more foreign applications must be given the same duration which it would have according to the national law if no priority had been claimed. In other words, it is not permitted to deduct the priority period from the term of a patent invoking the priority of a first application. For instance, a provision in a national law starting the term of the patent for invention from the (foreign) priority date, and not from the filing date of the application in the country, would be in violation of this rule.

[2] The Right of the Inventor to Be Mentioned

Another important common rule is Article 4*ter* which deals with the mentioning of the inventor. The Paris Convention provides for this question only a general rule. It states that the inventor must have the right to be mentioned as such in the patent for invention. National laws have implemented this provision in several ways. Some give the inventor only the right for civil action against the applicant or owner in order to obtain the inclusion of his/her name in the patent for invention. Others—and that tendency seems to be increasing—enforce the naming of the inventor during the procedure for the grant of a patent for invention on an ex officio basis. In some countries, for instance, the USA, it is even required that the applicant for a patent be the inventor him/herself.

At this juncture it should be noted that:

- Article 4*ter* gives individual inventors a right to be mentioned, but it does not bestow on national governments a corresponding obligation. In practical terms, this means that inventors may waive their right. However, national laws should request the presentation of a reasonable justification for such a waiver to be accepted, in view of the possible implications, such as losing the right to financial compensation from the patent assignees.
- The legal consequences of Article 4*ter* bifurcate into two. One is the setting of inventors' *moral rights*—the right to be designated as the originator of a specific invention. As noted above, in general this right is not set as an absolute one, and therefore it may be waived from. The other is the entitlement of inventors to financial compensation in the case of work for hire, either as employees or as contractors. This is an area which international law has not yet entered.

[3] Importation; Failure to Work and Compulsory Licenses

The Convention deals in Article 5A with the questions of failure to work the patented invention, of importation of articles covered by patents, and of compulsory licenses.

With respect to importation the provision states that importation by the patentee, into the country where the patent has been granted, of articles covered by the patent and manufactured in any of the countries of the Union will not entail forfeiture of the patent. This provision is quite narrowly worded, and hence only applies when several conditions are met. Consequently the countries of the Union have considerable leeway to legislate with respect to importation of patented goods under any of the circumstances which are different to those foreseen in this provision.

This article applies to patentees which are entitled to benefit from the Paris Convention ad who, having a patent in one of the countries of the Paris Union, import to this country goods (covered by the patent) which were manufactured in another country of the Union. In such a case, the patent granted in the country of importation may not be forfeited as a sanction for such importation.

In this context, the term "patentee" would also cover the representative of the patentee, or any person who effects the importation in the name of such patentee.

With respect to the goods that are imported, it suffices that they be manufactured in a country of the Union. The fact that the goods, having been manufactured in a country of the Union, are thereafter circulated through other countries and eventually imported from a country which is not a member of the Union, would not prevent this article from being applicable.

Finally, it may be mentioned that the term "forfeiture" in Article 5A(1) includes any measure which has the effect of definitively terminating the patent. Therefore it would cover the concepts of invalidation, revocation, annulment, repeal, etc. Whether "forfeiture" may, in light of the purpose of this article or the spirit of the Paris Convention, be construed as covering also other measures that would have the effect of preventing importation (fines, suspension of rights, etc.) is left for the national legislation and courts to decide.

With respect to the working of patents and compulsory licenses, the essence of the provisions contained in Article 5A is that each country may take legislative measures providing for the grant of compulsory licenses. These compulsory licenses are intended to prevent the abuses which might result from the exclusive rights conferred by a patent for invention, for example failure to work or insufficient working.

Compulsory licenses on the ground of failure to work or insufficient working are the most common kind of coercive measure against the patent owner to prevent abuses of the rights conferred by the patent for invention. They are expressly dealt with by Article 5A.

The main argument for enforcing working of the invention in a particular country is the consideration that, in order to promote the industrialization of the country, patents for invention should not be used merely to block the working of the invention in the country or to monopolize importation of the patented article by the patent owner. They should rather be used to introduce the use of the new technology into the country. Whether the patent owner can really be expected to do so, is first of all an economic consideration and then also a question of time. Working in all countries is generally not economical. Moreover, it is generally recognized that immediate working in all countries is impossible. Article 5A therefore tries to strike a balance between these conflicting interests. Anyway, for those Contracting Parties that have joined the WTO, this aspect of the Paris Convention is incompatible with the provisions of Article 27.1 of the TRIPS Agreement as well as with the principle of national treatment of goods of the GATT, of 1947. Both provide that, where it is necessary to prove the working of patents, imported goods may not be discriminated in favor of locally made goods. If all

WTO Members adopted the so-called local exploitation requirement, all trade of goods bearing or incorporating patented inventions would cease.

Anyway, Paris Union members should be careful in transposing these provisions, in the sense that they should not consider the mere absence of work as abuse, hence as ground for a compulsory license, and, ultimately, of forfeiture. This recommendation results not only from the legislative history of Article 5(A)(2), which was introduced at The Hague, in 1925, as a measure against the abuse of monopolies, but also from the way the provision is drafted. Failure to work is set as an example of an abuse that results from "the exercise of the exclusive rights conferred by the patent." Because the exercise of patent rights consists of their being enforced against third parties (*see*, in this sense, Article 28.1 of the TRIPS Agreement), and, as a corollary, of their being licensed, the mere omission or suppression of the exploitation of the invention may not constitute an abuse. Therefore, the abuse is the enforcement of the rights in a patent that is not worked—and only in the case the patent owner does not have legitimate reasons to justify his/her omission. But even in that case, as far as Paris Union members that are WTO Members are concerned, a compulsory license is to be granted only if the third party seeks a voluntary license from the patent owner and offers "reasonable commercial terms and conditions" (Article 31(b) of the TRIPS Agreement).

Compulsory licenses for failure to work or insufficient working of the invention may not be requested before a certain period of time of non-working or insufficient working has elapsed. This time limit expires either four years from the date of filing of the patent application or three years from the date of the grant of the patent for invention. The applicable time is the one which, in the individual case, expires last.

The time limit of three or four years is a minimum time limit. The patent owner must be given a longer time limit, if he/she can give legitimate reasons for his/her inaction. In other words, the patent owner can produce evidence that legal, economic or technical obstacles prevent working, or working more intensively, the invention in the country. If that is proven, the request for a compulsory license must be rejected, at least for the time being. The time limit of three or four years is a minimum time limit also in that sense that national law can provide for a longer time limit.

The compulsory license for non-working or insufficient working must be a non-exclusive license and can only be transferred together with the part of the enterprise benefitting from the compulsory license. The patent owner must retain the right to grant other non-exclusive licenses and to work the invention himself. Moreover, as the compulsory license has been granted to a particular enterprise on the basis of its known capacities, it is bound to that enterprise and cannot be transferred separately from that enterprise. These limitations are intended to prevent that a compulsory licensee obtains a stronger position on the market than is warranted by the purpose of the compulsory license, namely, to ensure sufficient working of the invention in the country.

All these special provisions for compulsory licenses in Article 5A(4) are only applicable to compulsory licenses for non-working or insufficient working. They are not applicable to the other types of compulsory licenses which the national law is free to provide for. Such other types of compulsory licenses may be granted to prevent abuses other than non-working or insufficient working. Such abuses may be, for example, excessive prices or unreasonable terms for contractual licenses or other restrictive measures which hamper industrial development.

Compulsory licenses may also be granted, by considerations of public interest, in cases where there is no abuse by the patent owner of his/her rights. These are in particular cases where a patent for invention affects a vital public interest, for example, in the fields of military security or public health.

There are also cases where a compulsory license is provided for to protect the public interest in unhampered technological progress. This is the case of the compulsory license in favor of the so-called *dependent patents*. If a patented invention cannot be worked without using an earlier patent for invention granted to another person, then the owner of the dependent patent, under certain circumstances, may have the right to request a compulsory license to enable the use of that invention. If the owner of the dependent patent for invention obtains the compulsory license, he/she may in turn be obliged to grant a license to the owner of the earlier patent for invention. Article 31(l) of the TRIPS Agreement sets specific conditions for these compulsory licenses to be granted.

All these other types of compulsory licenses can be grouped together under the general heading of compulsory licenses *in the public interest*. The national laws are not prevented by the Paris Convention to provide for such compulsory licenses, and they are not subject to the restrictions provided for in Article 5A. This means in particular that compulsory licenses in the public interest can be granted without waiting for the expiration of the time limits provided for compulsory licenses that relate to failure to work or insufficient working.

[4] Grace Period for the Payment of Maintenance Fees

Article 5*bis* provides for a grace period for the payment of maintenance fees for industrial property rights and deals with the restoration of patents for invention in case of non-payment of fees. In most countries the maintenance of certain industrial property rights, mainly the rights in patents for invention and trademarks, is subject to the periodic payment of fees. For patents, the maintenance fees must generally be paid annually, and in that case are also called annuities. Immediate loss of the patent for invention in the event that one annuity is not paid at the due date would be too harsh a sanction. Therefore, the Paris Convention provides for a period of grace, during which the payment can still be made after the due date with the effect to maintain the patent. That period is six months, and is established as a minimum period so that countries are free to accord a longer period.

The delayed payment of the annuity may be subjected to the payment of a surcharge. In that case, both the delayed fee and the surcharge must be paid within the grace period. During the grace period, the patent for invention remains provisionally in force. If the payment is not made during the grace period, the patent for invention will lapse retroactively, that is, as of the original due date of the annuity.

[5] Patents in International Traffic

Another common rule of substantive importance, containing a limitation of the rights of the patent owner under special circumstances, is contained in Article 5*ter*. It deals with the transit of devices on ships, aircraft or land vehicles through a member country in which such device is patented.

The effect of this provision is essentially the following. Where ships, aircraft or land vehicles of other member countries enter temporarily or accidentally a given member country and have on board devices patented in that country, the owner of the means of transportation is not required to obtain prior approval or a license from the patent owner. Temporary or accidental entry of the patented device into the country in such cases constitutes no infringement of the patent for invention.

The device on board the ship, aircraft or vehicle must be in the body, in the machinery, tackle, gear or other accessories of the conveyance, and must be used exclusively for operational needs.

The provision covers only the use of patented devices. It does not allow the making of patented devices on board a means of transportation, nor the sale to the public of patented products or of products obtained under a patented process.

[6] Inventions Shown at International Exhibitions

A further common rule of a substantive nature is the provision concerning the temporary protection in respect of goods exhibited at international exhibitions, contained in Article 11 of the Convention.

The principle stated in Article 11 is that the member countries are obliged to grant, in conformity with their domestic legislation, temporary protection to patentable inventions, utility models, industrial designs and trademarks in respect of goods exhibited at official or officially recognized international exhibitions held in the territory of any member country.

The temporary protection may be provided by various means. One is to grant a special right of priority, similar to that provided for in Article 4. This priority right would start from the date of the opening of the exhibition or from the date of the introduction of the object at the exhibition. It would be maintained for a certain period, say twelve months, from that date, and would expire if the application for protection does not follow the exhibition within that period.

Another means of temporary protection, which is found in a number of national laws, in particular with respect to patents for invention, is that of prescribing that, during a certain period of, say, twelve months before the filing or priority date of a patent application, a display of the invention at an international exhibition will not destroy the novelty of the invention. When choosing that solution, it is important to protect the inventor or other owner of the invention during the same period also against abusive acts of third parties. This means in particular that the person exhibiting the invention must be protected against any copying or usurpation of the invention for purposes of a patent application by a third party. The owner of the invention must also be protected against disclosure by third parties based on the exhibition.

Article 11 applies only to official or officially recognized exhibitions. The interpretation of that term is left to the member country where protection is sought. An interpretation corresponding to the spirit of Article 11 is to consider an exhibition as "official," if it is organized by a State or other public authority, to consider it as "officially recognized," if it is not official but has at least been recognized as official by a State or other public authority, and to consider it as "international," if goods from various countries are exhibited.

[D] Provisions Concerning Trademarks

[1] Use of Trademarks

The Convention touches on the issue of the use of marks in Article 5C(1), (2) and (3). Article 5C(1) relates to the compulsory use of registered trademarks. Some of the countries which provide for the registration of trademarks also require that the trademark, once registered, be used within a certain period. If this use is not complied with, the trademark may be expunged from the register. For this purpose, "use" is generally understood as meaning the sale of goods bearing the trademark, although national legislation may regulate more broadly the manner in which use of the trademark is to be complied with. The said Article states that where compulsory use is required, the trademark's registration may be cancelled for failure to use the trademark only after a reasonable period has elapsed, and then only if the owner does not justify such failure.

It is important to emphasize that Article 5C(1), in admitting the possibility of the compulsory use of trademarks, does not imply the existence of a right to use trademarks. Trademark rights, like all IPRs, are negative in nature, in the sense that they are exercised by means of excluding third parties from their use (and, as a corollary of the right to say "no," also by means of authorizing third parties to use them). IP laws do not have a saying on the use of the protected intangible assets—this is a matter left for national laws that deal with economic regulation. When IP laws refer to the use of the protected assets—as opposed to the use of the rights in those assets—they go exactly in the opposite direction, i.e., they imply that there is no right to use them. One of those provisions is exactly Article 5C(1) and its acceptance of the compulsory use of trademarks: in doing so, it rejects the idea that trademark owners may have a choice as to use or not their signs. To use or not trademarks in a free economy is, in principle, a prerogative of businesses, not a right enforceable against governments. In certain fields, policymakers may wish to ensure differentiation of products as a matter of public security and thus they oblige manufacturers and merchants to use registered signs (i.e., signs that have been subject to a prior analysis of distinctiveness). Another provision is Article 20 of the TRIPS Agreement, which authorizes WTO Members to impose encumbrances of the use of trademarks, provided those encumbrances are justifiable—such as those based on public health concerns.

Both provisions mean that, as a matter of the organization of national economies, lawmakers wish and expect that businesses acquire and use differentiating assets, for these are the very foundation of competitive markets, hence of better and cheaper products and services. But IP owners are not necessarily entitled to use their protected differentiating assets: the use of patented inventions may be prohibited on grounds of concerns with *ordre public* and morality (TRIPS Agreement, Article 27.2); the circulation, presentation and exhibition of copyrighted works may be controlled or prohibited where governments deem it necessary (Berne Convention, Article 17); the use of registered trademarks may be encumbered when policymakers decide it is justifiable (TRIPS Agreement, Article 20). Interestingly, Article 17 of the Berne Convention goes even further when it refers to the right of Governments to permit the circulation of copyrighted works, which means that such right is not in the private hands of copyright owners, but in the Government's.

The definition of what is meant by "reasonable period" is left to the national legislation of the countries concerned, or otherwise to the authorities competent for resolving such cases. This reasonable period is intended to permit the owner of the mark enough time and opportunity to arrange for its proper use, considering that in many cases the owner has to use his/her mark in several countries. This is a matter covered by Article 19 of the TRIPS Agreement, which set a period of three years.

Cancellation of a mark's registration may only be decided if the owner does not justify the failure to use his/her trademark. Such justification would be acceptable if it were based on legal or economic circumstances beyond the owner's control, for example if importation of the marked goods had been prohibited or delayed by governmental regulations.

The Convention also establishes in Article 5C(2) that the use of a trademark by its proprietor in a form differing in elements which do not alter the distinctive character of the mark in the form in which it was registered in one of the countries of the Union shall not entail invalidation of the registration nor diminish the protection granted to the mark. The purpose of this provision is to allow for unessential differences between the form of the mark as it is registered and the form in which it is used, for example in cases of adaptation or translation of certain elements for such use. This rule applies also to similar differences in the form of the mark as used in the country of its original registration.

Whether in a given case the differences between the mark as registered and the mark as actually used alter the distinctive character is a matter to be decided by the competent national authorities.

[2] Concurrent Use of the Same Trademark by Different Enterprises

Article 5C(3) of the Convention deals with the case where the same mark is used for identical or similar goods by two or more establishments considered as co-proprietors of the trademark. It is provided that such concurrent use will not impede the registration of the trademark nor diminish the protection in any country of the Union, except where the said use results in misleading the public or is contrary to the public interest. Such cases could occur if the concurrent use misleads the public as to the origin or source of the goods sold under the same trademark, or if the quality of such goods differs to the point where it may be contrary to the public interest to allow the continuation of such inconsistency.

This provision does not, however, cover the case of concurrent use of the mark by enterprises which are not co-proprietors of the mark, for instance, when use is made concurrently by the owner and a licensee or a franchisee. These cases are left for the national legislation of the various countries to regulate.

[3] Grace Period for the Payment of Renewal Fees

Article 5*bis* requires that a period of grace be allowed for the payment of fees due for the maintenance of industrial property rights. In the case of trademarks this provision concerns primarily the payment of renewal fees, since it is by renewal that trademark registrations (and hence the rights that depend on such registrations) may be maintained. A failure to renew the registration will normally entail the lapse of the registration, and in some cases the expiration of the right to the mark. The period of grace provided by the Convention is intended to diminish the risks of a mark being lost by an involuntary delay in the payment of the renewal fees.

The countries of the Paris Union are obliged to accord a period of grace of at least six months for the payment of the renewal fees, but are free to provide for the payment of a surcharge when such renewal fees are paid within the period of grace. Moreover, the countries are free to provide for a period of grace longer than the minimum six months prescribed by the Convention.

During the period of grace, the registration remains provisionally in force. If the payment of the renewal fees (and surcharge where appropriate) is not made during the period of grace, the registration will lapse retroactively as of the original date of expiration.

[4] Independence of Trademarks

Article 6 of the Convention establishes the important principle of the independence of trademarks in the different countries of the Union, and in particular the independence of trademarks filed or registered in the country of origin from those filed or registered in other countries of the Union.

The first part of Article 6 states the application of the basic principle of national treatment to the filing and registration of marks in the countries of the Union. Regardless of the origin of the mark whose registration is sought, a country of the Union may apply only its domestic legislation when determining the conditions for the filing and registration of the mark. The application of the principle of national treatment asserts the rule of independence of marks, since their registration and maintenance will depend only on each domestic law.

This article also provides that an application for the registration of a mark, filed in any country of the Union by a person who is entitled to the benefits of the

Convention, may not be refused, nor may a registration be cancelled, on the ground that filing, registration or renewal of the mark has not been effected in the country of origin. This provision lays down the express rule that obtaining and maintaining a trademark registration in any country of the Union may not be made dependent on the application, registration or renewal of the same mark in the country of origin of the mark. Therefore, no action with respect to the mark in the country of origin may be required as a prerequisite for obtaining a registration of the mark in that country.

Finally, Article 6 states that a mark duly registered in a country of the Union shall be regarded as independent of marks registered in the other countries of the Union, including the country of origin. This means that a mark once registered will not be automatically affected by any decision taken with respect to similar registrations for the same marks in other countries. In this respect, the fact that one or more such similar registrations are, for example, renounced, cancelled or abandoned, will not *eo ipso* affect the registrations of the mark in other countries. The validity of these registrations will depend only on the provisions applicable in accordance with the legislation of each of the countries concerned. The observation made above concerning the incompatibility of international exhaustion of patent rights under the principle of independence can be extended to trademarks.

[5] Well-Known Trademarks

The Convention deals with well-known trademarks in Article 6*bis*. This article obliges a member country to refuse or cancel the registration and to prohibit the use of a trademark that is liable to create confusion with another trademark already well known in that member country. The effect of this article is to extend protection to a trademark that is well known in a member country even though it is not registered or used in that country. The protection of the well-known trademark results not from its registration, which prevents the registration or use of a conflicting trademark, but from the mere fact of its reputation.

The protection of well-known trademarks is deemed justified on the grounds that a trademark that has acquired goodwill and a reputation in a member country ought to give rise to a right for its owner and because the registration or use of a confusingly similar trademark would, in most cases, amount to an act of unfair competition and be prejudicial to the interests of the public who would be misled by the use of a conflicting trademark for the same or identical goods than those in connection with which the well-known trademark is registered.

The trademark that is protected by Article 6*bis* must be a "well-known" trademark. Whether a trademark is well known in a member country will be determined by its competent administrative or judicial authorities. A trademark may not have been used in a country, in the sense that goods bearing that trademark have not been sold there, yet that trademark may be well known in the country because of publicity there or the repercussions in that country of advertising in other countries. In 1999 the Assembly of the Paris Union for the Protection of Industrial Property and the WIPO

General Assembly adopted the Joint Recommendation Concerning Provisions on the Protection of Well-Known Marks, which, besides setting a number of conditions for the protection of well-known trademarks, lists some elements for the assessment of notoriety.

The protection of a well-known trademark under Article 6*bis* exists only where the conflicting trademark has been filed, registered or used for identical or similar goods. Whether the condition is fulfilled will be determined by the administrative or judicial authorities of the country in which protection is claimed.

The protection of a well-known trademark under Article 6*bis* results from the obligation of a member country to take ex officio where its legislation so permits, or at the request of an interested party, the following type of action:

(1) a member country must refuse the application for registration of the conflicting trademark;
(2) the member country must cancel the registration of a conflicting trademark. A member country is required to allow at least a period of five years from the date of registration within which a request for cancellation of the conflicting trademark may be made, unless that trademark was registered in bad faith, in which event no time limit may be fixed;
(3) the member country must prohibit the use of the conflicting trademark. A member country is free to prescribe a period within which that request must be made; however, no time limit may be fixed for such a request in the case of a conflicting trademark used in bad faith.

Article 16 of the TRIPS Agreement completes Article 6*bis* in three aspects: it extends protection to well-known service marks; it defines one mandatory condition for the determination of notoriety of trademarks ("In determining whether a trademark is well-known, Members shall take account of the knowledge of the trademark in the relevant sector of the public, including knowledge in the Member concerned which has been obtained as a result of the promotion of the trademark."); and it extends protection to well-known trademarks used to designate "goods or services which are not similar to those in respect of which a trademark is registered, provided that use of that trademark in relation to those goods or services would indicate a connection between those goods or services and the owner of the registered trademark and provided that the interests of the owner of the registered trademark are likely to be damaged by such use." This last aspect is known as protection against dilution.

[6] State Emblems, Official Hallmarks and Emblems of IGOs

The Convention deals with distinctive signs of States and international IGOs in Article 6*ter*. This article obliges a member country, in certain circumstances, to refuse or invalidate the registration and to prohibit the use, either as trademarks or as elements of trademarks, of the distinctive signs specified in that Article of member countries and certain international IGOs.

The purpose of Article *6ter* is not to create an industrial property right in favor of the State or the IGO in respect of the distinctive signs concerned, but simply to prevent the use of those signs as trademarks in industrial or commercial activities.

The provisions of Article *6ter* do not apply if the competent authorities of the member country allow the use of its distinctive signs as trademarks. Similarly, the competent authorities of an IGO may allow others to use its distinctive signs as trademarks. Moreover, in the case of the distinctive signs of a member country, nationals of any member country that are authorized to use the distinctive signs of their country may do so even if those signs are similar to those of another member country.

The distinctive signs of States that are referred to in Article *6ter* are the following: armorial bearings, flags and other emblems, official signs and hallmarks indicating control and warranty and any imitation of those signs from a heraldic point of view.

The objective of the provisions of Article *6ter*, insofar as the distinctive signs of States are concerned, is to exclude the registration and use of trademarks that are identical or present a certain similarity to the armorial bearings, flags or other emblems of *States*. The reasons for this are that such registration would violate the right of the State to control distinctive signs of its sovereignty and, further, might mislead the public with respect to the origin of the goods to which such marks would be applied.

To give effect to the provisions of Article *6ter*, a procedure is established pursuant to that Article whereby the distinctive signs of the member countries and IGOs concerned are communicated to the International Bureau of WIPO, which in turn transmits those communications to all the member countries. The 1995 Agreement between WIPO and the WTO applied these same procedures to notifications to be made by WTO Members that are not WIPO Member States.

[7] Assignment of Trademarks

Article *6quater* of the Convention deals with the assignment of trademarks. The rule of Article *6quater* arises because of the situation where a trademark is used by an enterprise in various countries and it is desired to make a transfer of the right to the trademark in one or more of those countries.

Some national legislations allow an assignment without a simultaneous or corresponding transfer of the enterprise to which the trademark belongs. Others make the validity of the assignment depend on the simultaneous or corresponding transfer of the enterprise.

Article *6quater* states that it shall suffice for the recognition of the validity of the assignment of a trademark in a member country that the portion of the business or goodwill located in that country be transferred to the assignee, together with the exclusive right to manufacture in the said country, or to sell therein, the goods bearing the trademark assigned. Thus, a member country is free to require, for the validity of the assignment of the trademark, the simultaneous transfer of the enterprise to which the trademark belongs, but such a requirement must not extend to parts of the enterprise that are located in other countries. This freedom, however, has been eliminated for those States that are Members of the WTO, under Article 21 of the TRIPS

Agreement: "the owner of a registered trademark shall have the right to assign the trademark with or without the transfer of the business to which the trademark belongs."

It should be noted that Article *6quater* leaves a member country free not to regard as valid the assignment of a trademark with the relevant part of the enterprise, if the use of that trademark by the assignee would be of such a nature as to mislead the public, particularly as regards important features of the goods to which the trademark is applied. This freedom may be exercised, for example, if a trademark is assigned for part only of the goods to which it is applied, and if these goods are similar to other goods for which the trademark is not assigned. In such cases, the public may be misled as to the origin or essential qualities of similar goods to which the assignor and assignee will apply the same trademark independently.

[8] Protection of Trademarks Registered in One Country of the Union in Other Countries of the Union

Parallel to the principle of independence of marks which is embodied in the provisions of Article 6, the Convention establishes a special rule for the benefit of owners of trademarks registered in their country of origin. This exceptional rule is governed by Article *6quinquies* of the Convention.

The provisions of Article *6quinquies* come into operation in the case where a registration in the country of origin is invoked in the country where protection is sought. Whereas the principle of national treatment of applications calls for the normal rule of complete independence of trademarks (as recognized in Article 6), in the exceptional situation regulated by Article *6quinquies* the opposite rule prevails, providing for extraterritorial effects of the registration in the country of origin.

There are two main reasons for this special rule. On the one hand, it is in the interest of both owners of trademarks and the public to have the *same* trademark apply to the *same* goods in various countries. On the other hand, there are some important differences in the domestic legislation of the member countries regarding the registration of trademarks. As a consequence, the differences in domestic legislation could prevent this uniform use of the same trademark.

In order to diminish the impact of those differences on the registration of trademarks in respect of goods in international trade, Article *6quinquies* of the Paris Convention establishes certain effects where registration in the country of origin has taken place and is invoked in another member country where registration and protection is sought. This provision has the effect of bringing about certain uniformity of the law of the various countries as to the concept of trademarks.

For Article *6quinquies* to apply it is necessary that the trademark concerned should be duly registered in the country of origin. A mere filing or use of the trademark in that country is not sufficient. Moreover, the country of origin must be a country of the Union in which the applicant has a real and effective industrial or commercial establishment or, alternatively, in which he/she has his/her domicile, or otherwise, the country of the Union of which he/she is a national.

The rule established by Article *6quinquies* provides that a trademark which fulfills the required conditions must be accepted for filing and protected—*as is* (to use the expression found in the English version) or *telle quelle* (to use the expression adopted in the authentic French text)—in the other member countries, subject to certain exceptions. This rule is often called the *"telle quelle"* principle.

It is to be noted that the rule only concerns the *form* of the trademark. In this respect, the rule in this article does not affect the questions relating to the nature or the function of the trademarks as conceived in the countries where protection is sought. Thus a member country is not obliged to register and extend protection to a subject that does not fall within the meaning of a trademark as defined in the law of that country. If, for example, under the law of a member country, a three-dimensional object or musical notes indicating tunes is not considered a "trademark" in that country, it is not obliged to accept that subject matter for registration and protection.

Article *6quinquies,* section B, contains certain exceptions to the obligation of accepting a registered trademark "as is" for registration in the other countries of the Union. That list of exceptions is exhaustive so that no other grounds may be invoked to refuse or invalidate the registration of the trademark. However, the list does not exclude any ground for refusal of protection for which there is a need in national legislation.

The first permitted ground for refusal or invalidation of a trademark exists where the trademark infringes rights of third parties acquired in the country where protection is claimed. These rights can be either rights in trademarks already protected in the country concerned or other rights, such as the right to a trade name or a copyright.

The second permitted ground for refusal or invalidation is when the trademark is devoid of distinctive character, or is purely descriptive, or consists of a generic name.

The third permissible ground for refusal or invalidation exists where the trademark is contrary to morality or public order, as considered in the country where protection is claimed. This ground includes, as a special category, trademarks which are of such a nature as to deceive the public.

A fourth permissible ground for refusal or invalidation exists if the registration of the trademark would constitute an act of unfair competition.

A fifth and last permissible ground for refusal or invalidation exists where the trademark is used by the owner in a form which is essentially different from that in which it has been registered in the country of origin. Unessential differences may not be used as grounds for refusal or invalidation.

[9] Service Marks

A service mark is a sign used by enterprises offering services, for example, hotels, restaurants, airlines, tourist agencies, car-rental agencies, employment agencies, laundries and cleaners, etc., in order to distinguish their services from those of other enterprises. Thus service marks have the same function as trademarks, the only difference being that they apply to services instead of products (or goods).

Article *6sexies* was introduced into the Paris Convention in 1958 to deal specifically with service marks, but the revision Conference did not accept a more ambitious proposal to entirely assimilate service marks to trademarks. However, a member country is free to apply the same rules it applies for trademarks also to service marks in analogous situations or circumstances. That assimilation has been introduced by Article 15.1 of the TRIPS Agreement.

By virtue of Article *6sexies,* member countries undertake to protect service marks, but are not required to provide for the registration of such marks. This provision does not oblige a member country to legislate expressly on the subject of service marks. A member country may comply with the provision not only by introducing special legislation for the protection of service marks, but also by granting such protection by other means, for example, in its laws against unfair competition. Registration of service marks has become mandatory (for those countries or territories that make protection available on the basis of registration) under Article 15 of the TRIPS Agreement.

[10] Registration in the Name of the Agent Without the Proprietor's Authorization

Article *6septies* of the Convention deals with the relationship between the owner of a trademark and his/her agent or representative regarding registration or use of the trademark by the latter.

This article regulates those cases where the agent or representative of the person who is the owner of a trademark applies for or obtains the registration of a trademark in his/her own name or uses a trademark without the owner's authorization.

In such cases, Article *6septies* confers upon the owner of the trademark the right to oppose the registration or to demand cancellation of the registration or, if the national law so allows, to demand an assignment of the registration in his/her favor. In addition, Article *6septies* confers upon the owner of a trademark the right to oppose the unauthorized use of the trademark by his/her agent or representative, whether or not application for registration of the trademark has been made or its registration has been granted.

[11] Nature of the Goods to Which a Trademark Is Applied

Article 7 of the Convention stipulates that the nature of the goods to which a trademark is to be applied shall in no case be an obstacle to the registration of the mark. Article 15.4 of the TRIPS Agreement has extended that same rule to service marks.

The purpose of this rule, and also the comparable rule in Article *4quater* regarding patents for invention, is to make the protection of industrial property independent of the question whether goods in respect of which such protection would apply may or may not be sold in the country concerned.

It sometimes occurs that a trademark concerns goods which, for example, do not conform to the safety requirements of the law of a particular country. For instance, the food and drug laws of a country may prescribe requirements concerning the ingredients of a food product or the effects of a pharmaceutical product and allow its sale only after approval of the competent authorities on the basis of an examination of the food product or of clinical trials as to the effect of the use of the pharmaceutical product on human beings or animals.

In all such cases, it would be unjust to refuse registration of a trademark concerning such goods. The safety or quality regulations may change and the product may be permitted for sale later on. In those cases where no such change is contemplated but the approval of the competent authorities of the country concerned is still pending, such approval, if imposed as a condition to filing or registration in that country, may be prejudicial to an applicant who wishes to make a timely filing for protection in another member country. In other words, Article 7 of the Paris Convention (as well as Article 15.4 of the TRIPS Agreement, which extends the scope of Article 7 to services) does not concern those prohibitions of commercialization that are based on social permanent values, like religion. For example, it is admissible that Muslim countries exclude trademarks for alcoholic beverages from registration. The reason is that such a prohibition is not expected to change.

[12] Collective Marks

A collective mark may be defined as a sign which serves to distinguish the geographical origin, material, mode of manufacture, quality or other common characteristics of goods or services of different enterprises that simultaneously use the collective mark under the control of its owner. The owner may be either an association of which those enterprises are members or any other entity, including a public body.

Article 7*bis* of the Convention deals with collective marks. It obliges a member country to accept for filing and to protect, in accordance with the particular conditions set by that country, collective marks belonging to "associations." These will generally be associations of producers, manufacturers, distributors, sellers or other merchants, of goods that are produced or manufactured in a certain country, region or locality or that have other common characteristics. Collective marks of States or other public bodies are not covered by the provision.

In order that Article 7*bis* be applicable, the existence of the association to which the collective mark belongs must not be contrary to the law of the country of origin. The association does not have to prove that it conforms to the legislation of its country of origin, but registration and protection of its collective mark may be refused if the existence of that association is found to be contrary to that legislation.

Refusal of registration and protection of the collective mark is not possible on the ground that the association is not established in the country where protection is sought, or is not constituted according to the law of that country. Article 7*bis* adds a further stipulation that the association may not even be required to possess an industrial or commercial establishment anywhere. In other words, an association, without possessing any industrial or commercial establishment itself, may be one that simply controls the use of a collective mark by others.

[13] *Trademarks Shown at International Exhibitions*

The provision concerning marks shown at international exhibitions is contained in Article 11 of the Convention, which also applies to other titles of industrial property.

The principle stated in Article 11 is that the member countries are obliged to grant, in conformity with their domestic legislation, temporary protection to trademarks in respect of goods exhibited at official or officially recognized international exhibitions held in the territory of any member country.

The temporary protection may be provided by various means. One is to grant a special right of priority, similar to that provided for in Article 4. Another possibility for protection, which is found in certain national laws, consists in the recognition of a right of prior use in favor of the exhibitor of the goods bearing the trademark as against possible rights acquired by third parties.

In order to apply its national legislation regarding temporary protection, the competent authorities of the country may require proof, both as to the identity of the goods exhibited and as to the date of their introduction at the exhibition, in whatever form of documentary evidence they consider necessary.

[E] Provisions Concerning Industrial Designs, Trade Names, AO and Indications of Source, and Unfair Competition

[1] *Industrial Designs*

The Paris Convention deals with industrial designs in Article 5*quinquies*.

This provision merely states the obligation of all member countries to protect industrial designs. Nothing is said about the way in which this protection must be provided.

Member countries can therefore comply with this obligation through the enactment of special legislation for the protection of industrial designs. They can, however, also comply with this obligation through the grant of such protection under the law on copyright or the law against unfair competition.

The normal solution, chosen by a great number of countries for compliance with the obligations under Article 5*quinquies* is, however, to provide for a special system of protection of industrial designs by registration or by the grant of patents for industrial designs.

There is a special provision dealing with forfeiture in the case of industrial designs. It is contained in Article 5B, and states that the protection of industrial designs may not under any circumstance be subject to any measure of forfeiture as sanction in cases of failure to work or where articles corresponding to those protected are imported. "Forfeiture" in this provision includes equivalent measures, such as cancellation, invalidation or revocation. Member countries could, however, provide other sanctions for those cases, such as compulsory licenses in order to ensure working in case of non-working or insufficient working. "Working" means here the manufacture of products representing or incorporating the industrial design.

[2] Trade Names

Trade names are dealt with by the Convention in Article 8. This article states that trade names shall be protected in all the countries of the Union without the obligation of filing or of registration, whether or not they form part of a trademark.

The definition of a trade name for the purposes of protection, and the manner in which such protection is to be afforded, are both matters left to the national legislation of the countries concerned. Therefore, protection may result from special legislation on trade names or from more general legislation on unfair competition or the rights of personality.

In no case can protection be made conditional upon filing or registration of the trade name. However, if in a member country protection of trade names were dependent on the use of the name and to the extent that another trade name may cause confusion or prejudice with respect to the first trade name, such requirement and criterion could be applied by that member country.

[3] AO and Indications of Source

AO and indications of source are included among the various objects of protection of industrial property under the Paris Convention (Article 1(2)).

Both these objects can be referred to under the broader concept of GIs, although traditionally, and for the purposes of certain special treaties (e.g., the Madrid Agreement for the Repression of False or Deceptive Indications of Source on Goods, and the Lisbon Agreement for the Protection of Appellations of Origin and their International Registration), both concepts have been distinguished.

Indications of source include any name, designation, sign or other indication which refers to a given country or to a place located therein, which has the effect of conveying the notion that the goods bearing the indication originate in that country or place. Examples of indications of source are the names of countries (e.g., Germany, Japan, etc.) or of cities (e.g., Hong Kong, Paris, etc.) when used on or in connection with goods in order to indicate their place of manufacture or their provenance.

AO have a more limited meaning, and may be considered a special type of indication of source. An AO is the geographical name of a country, region or locality which serves to designate a product originating therein, the quality and characteristics of which are due exclusively or essentially to the geographical environment, including natural and human factors.

The Paris Convention contains in Articles 10 and 10*bis* provisions on the protection of indications of source. These provisions cover in general any direct or indirect use of a false indication of the source (including, where applicable, the AO) of the goods or the identity of the producer, manufacturer or merchant, as well as any act of unfair competition by the use of indications or allegations which are liable to mislead the public as to the nature or the characteristics of the goods for which they are applied.

The Convention requires the countries to seize the goods bearing false indications or, to prohibit their importation, or otherwise to apply any other measures that may be available in order to prevent or stop the use of such indications. However, the obligation to seize goods on importation only applies to the extent that such a sanction is provided for under the national law.

The Convention provides that action may be taken not only by the public prosecutor but also by any interested party. In this connection, Article 10(2) states that any producer, manufacturer or merchant, whether a natural person or a legal entity, engaged in the production, manufacture or trade in such goods established in the locality, region or country falsely indicated as the source or in the country where such false indications used, is in any case deemed to be an interested party. Moreover, in accordance with Article 10*ter,* states that the countries are required to provide measures to permit federations and associations representing interested industrialists, producers and merchants to take action before the competent authorities with a view to the repression of the acts referred to above.

[4] Unfair Competition

The Convention provides in Article 10*bis* that the countries of the Union are bound to assure to persons entitled to benefit from the Convention effective protection against unfair competition. The Convention does not specify the manner in which such protection should be granted, leaving this to the laws existing in each of the member countries.

Article 10*bis* defines acts of unfair competition as those acts of competition which are contrary to honest practices in industrial or commercial matters. Further, the article gives some typical examples of acts of unfair competition which should be prohibited in particular.

The first example refers to all acts of such a nature as to create confusion by any means whatever with the establishment, the goods or the industrial or commercial activities of a competitor. These acts cover not only the use of identical or similar marks or names, which could be attacked as an infringement of proprietary rights, but also the use of other means which can create confusion. Such could be the form of packages, the getup or style used on products and on their corresponding outlets or points of distribution, titles of publicity, etc.

The second example relates to false allegations in the course of trade of such a nature as to discredit the establishment, the goods or the industrial or commercial activities, of a competitor. It has been left to the domestic legislation or case law of each country to decide whether, and under what circumstances, discrediting allegations which are not strictly untrue may also be considered acts of unfair competition.

The third example of acts of unfair competition concerns indications and allegations which are liable to mislead the public as to the nature, the manufacturing process, the characteristics, the suitability for their purpose or the quality of their goods. This provision may be distinguished from the previous cases to the extent that it is concerned with the interests and well-being of the public and is one of the provisions in the Convention that is more directly related to the consumer protection role of industrial property.

§15.03 ADMINISTRATIVE AND FINANCIAL PROVISIONS

[A] Organs of the Paris Union

The countries party to the Paris Convention constitute a "Union" for the Protection of Industrial Property. In creating a Union, the Paris Convention goes beyond a mere treaty establishing rights and obligations. It also establishes a legal entity in international law with the necessary organs to carry out certain tasks. The Union forms a single administrative entity, and an administrative link among the various Acts of the Paris Convention.

Under this concept of the Union, a state which becomes a member of the Union by acceding to the most recent (the Stockholm) Act of the Paris Convention becomes bound with respect to all member countries, even those not yet party to the Stockholm Act. Article 27(3) of the Convention says that such a country must apply the Stockholm Act also to member countries of the Union not yet party to that Act, and must recognize that member countries not yet bound by the substantive provisions of the Stockholm Act may apply, in their relations with it, that earlier Act which is the most recent of the Acts to which they are party.

The Union has three administrative organs, the Assembly, the Executive Committee and the International Bureau of WIPO, headed by the Director General of the WIPO.

The Assembly is dealt with in Article 13. It consists of all member countries bound at least by the administrative provisions of the Stockholm Act. The Assembly is the chief governing body of the Union in which all policymaking and controlling powers are vested. It deals with all matters concerning the maintenance and development of the Union and the implementation of the Paris Convention. In particular, it gives directions for the preparation of conferences of revision of the Convention. It reviews and approves the reports and activities of the Director General of WIPO concerning the Union and gives him instructions concerning matters within the competence of the Union. It determines the program, adopts the biennial budget of the Union, and approves its final accounts. The Assembly meets once in every second calendar year in ordinary session, together with the General Assembly of WIPO.

The Assembly has an Executive Committee, which is dealt with in Article 14. It consists of one-fourth of the country members of the Assembly, and is elected by the Assembly for the period between two ordinary sessions with due regard to an equitable geographical distribution. The Executive Committee meets once a year in ordinary session, together with the Coordination Committee of WIPO.

The Executive Committee is the smaller governing body of the Union. It deals with all the functions which have to be carried out during the period between the ordinary sessions of the Assembly and for which the Assembly is too big a body. It prepares the meetings of the Assembly and takes all necessary measures to ensure the execution of the program.

The provisions concerning the International Bureau are contained in Article 15. The International Bureau of WIPO is the administrative organ of the Union. It performs all administrative tasks concerning the Union. It provides the secretariat of the various organs of the Union. Its head, the Director General of WIPO, is the chief executive of the Union.

[B] Finances

The financial provisions are contained in Article 16. The Union has its own budget which is mainly financed by mandatory contributions from member countries. The contributions are calculated in applying a class and unit system to the total sum of contributions needed for a given budgetary year. The highest class I corresponds to a share of twenty-five units, the lowest class VII to a share of one unit. Each member country determines freely the class to which it wishes to belong, but it may also change class afterward.

[C] Amendments and Revision

Article 18 contains the principle of periodic revision of the Paris Convention. The Convention must be submitted to revision with a view to the introduction of amendments designed to improve the system of the Union. These revisions are dealt with by diplomatic conferences of revision in which delegations appointed by the governments of the member countries participate. According to Article 18(2), such conferences must be held successively in one of the member countries.

The preparations for the conferences of revision of the Paris Convention are carried out by the International Bureau of WIPO in accordance with the directions of the Assembly and in cooperation with the Executive Committee. In performing it, the International Bureau of WIPO may also consult with other intergovernmental and with international NGOs.

[D] Special Agreements

An important provision among the administrative clauses of the Paris Convention is Article 19, dealing with special agreements.

According to that provision, the member countries have the right to make separately among themselves special agreements for the protection of industrial property. These agreements must, however, comply with the condition that they do not contravene the provisions of the Paris Convention.

Such special agreements may take the form of bilateral agreements or multilateral treaties. Special agreements in the form of multilateral treaties may be agreements prepared and administered by the International Bureau of WIPO, or agreements prepared and administered by other IGOs.

[E] Becoming Party to the Convention

Accession to the Paris Convention is effected by the deposit of an instrument of accession with the Director General of WIPO, as provided in Article 21. The Convention enters into force, with respect to a country so adhering, three months after the accession has been notified by the Director General of WIPO to all Governments of the member countries. Accession therefore needs only unilateral action by the interested country and does not require any decision by the competent bodies of the Union.

Accession to the Convention automatically entails acceptance of all the clauses in the Convention, as well as admission to all the advantages thereof, as is indicated in Article 22.

Provisions concerning denunciation are contained in Article 26 of the Convention. Any member country may denounce the Convention by addressing a notification to the Director General of WIPO. In that case, the denunciation takes effect one year after the day on which the Director General receives the notification to that effect.

It is provided, however, that the right of denunciation may not be exercised by any country before the expiration of five years from the date on which it became a member of the Union.

[F] Disputes

The matter of disputes is dealt with in Article 28 of the Convention. Any dispute between two or more countries of the Union concerning the interpretation or application of the Convention, which has not been settled by negotiation, may be brought, by any of the countries concerned, before the International Court of Justice. However, the countries concerned may agree on any other method for settling their dispute, for example, by international arbitration. In any case, it should be noted that the International Bureau of WIPO may not take a position in controversies concerning the interpretation or application of the Paris Convention among member countries.

Any country acceding to the Convention may declare upon accession that it does not consider itself bound by the preceding provisions concerning the solving of disputes before the International Court of Justice.

[G] Membership

As of November 30, 2023, 179 States were party to the Paris Convention for the Protection of Industrial Property.

CHAPTER 16
The Berne Convention for the Protection of Literary and Artistic Works

§16.01 HISTORY

Copyright protection on the international level began by about the middle of the nineteenth century on the basis of bilateral treaties. A number of such treaties providing for mutual recognition of rights were concluded but they were neither comprehensive enough nor of a uniform pattern.

The need for a uniform system led to the formulation and adoption on September 9, 1886, of the Berne Convention for the Protection of Literary and Artistic Works. The Berne Convention is the oldest multilateral international treaty in the field of copyright. It is open to all States. Instruments of accession or ratification are deposited with the Director General of the WIPO.

The original text of the Convention has undergone revision since. The Berne Convention has been revised several times in order to improve the international system of protection which the Convention provides. Changes have been effected in order to cope with the challenges of accelerating development of technologies in the field of utilization of authors' works; in order to recognize new rights as also to allow for appropriate revisions of established ones. The first major revision took place in Berlin in 1908, twenty-two years after the initial formulation of the Berne Convention in 1886. This was followed by the revisions in Rome in 1928, in Brussels in 1948, in Stockholm in 1967 and in Paris in 1971.

The purpose of the Stockholm revision was to respond to rapid technological developments as well as the needs of several newly independent developing countries, and to introduce administrative and structural changes. As for the preferential provisions for developing countries worked out in Stockholm, these were further taken up at the Paris Revision Conference in 1971, where new compromises were worked out. The substantive provisions of the Stockholm Act which had also never entered into force were, however, adopted by the Paris Revision Conference in fact as they had been worked out and included in the Stockholm Act.

The aim of the Berne Convention as indicated in its preamble is "to protect, in as effective and uniform a manner as possible, the rights of authors in their literary and artistic works." Article 1 lays down that the countries to which the Convention applies constitute a Union for the protection of the rights of authors in their literary and artistic works.

Chapter 31 describes a number of provisions established in the TRIPS Agreement that complement and/or clarify those of the Berne Convention and which were deemed by GATT Contracting Parties as of particular importance in the context of international trade. In addition, Chapter 28 explains how certain provisions in the WCT complement and clarify several provisions of the Berne Convention in the context of digital technology and the Internet.

§16.02 PRINCIPAL PROVISIONS

[A] Basic Principles

The Convention relies on three basic principles: First, that of national treatment, according to which works originating in one of the Member States are to be given the same protection in each of the Member States as the latter grant to works of their own nationals (subject to five exceptions set out in the Convention, in particular regarding duration—Article 7(8)); second, that of minimum protection, according to which eligible authors must enjoy also the rights and protection established as a minimum in the Berne Convention, even where national law of the country for which protection is claimed does not provide such standard; and third, that of automatic protection, according to which national treatment and minimum protection is not dependent on any formality; in other words protection is granted automatically and is not subject to the formality of registration, deposit, or the like. The application of these principles is clarified by the rule on independence of protection, according to which enjoyment and exercise of the rights granted is independent of the existence of protection in the country of origin of the work.

[B] Works Protected

Article 2 contains a non-exhaustive list of such works, which include any original production in the literary, scientific and artistic domain, whatever may be the mode or form of its expression. The works explicitly contained in the list are part of the minimum protection of the Convention. Derivative works, that is those based on other pre-existing works, such as translations, adaptations, arrangements of music and other alterations of a literary or artistic work, receive the same protection as original works (Article 2(3)). Also, collections of works, which by reason of the selection or arrangement of their contents, constitute intellectual creations, are protected as works without prejudice to the works contained in the collections (Article 2(5)). The protection of some categories of works is optional; thus, every State party to the Berne Convention may decide to what extent it wishes to protect official texts of a legislative, administrative and legal nature (Article 2(4)), works of applied art (Article 2(7)), and political speeches and speeches delivered in the course of legal proceedings (Article 2*bis*(1)). Furthermore, Article 2(2) provides for the possibility of making the protection of works or any specified categories thereof subject to their being fixed in some material form. For instance, protection of choreographic works may be dependent on their being fixed in some form. Article 2(8) clarifies that the Convention does not apply to news of the day, or miscellaneous facts or mere items of press information; they are not considered "works."

One of the historically important provisions is Article 15(4), aiming to protect expressions of what is called "folklore" or "TCEs." Without using these terms, the Convention provides that any member country may give protection to unpublished works where the identity of the author is unknown, but where there is every ground to presume that the author is a national of that country, by designating, through the national legislation, the competent authority which should represent the author of unknown identity and protect and enforce the author's rights in the countries party to the Convention (*see* §16.05 below).

[C] Owners of Rights

Article 2(6) lays down that protection under the Convention is to operate for the benefit of the author and his/her successors in title. For some categories of works, however, such as cinematographic works (Article 14*bis*), ownership of copyright is a matter for legislation in the country where protection is claimed.

[D] Persons Protected

Authors of works are protected, in respect of both their unpublished or published works if, according to Article 3, they are nationals or residents of a member country; alternatively, if, not being nationals or residents of a member country, they first publish their works in a member country or simultaneously in a non-member and a member country.

[E] Minimum Standards of Protection

Certain minimum standards of protection have been set out relating to the rights of authors, works (those categories explicitly listed in Article 2), and the duration of protection. Authors may enjoy them if the conditions of the principle of minimum protection set out in Article 5(1) are fulfilled.

[F] Rights Protected

The exclusive rights granted to authors under the Convention include the right of translation (Article 8), the right of reproduction in any manner or form (which includes any sound or visual recording, and any digital reproduction) (Article 9), the right to perform dramatic, dramatico-musical and musical works and to have the performance communicated to the public (Article 11), the right to broadcasting and other wireless communication of the work, the right of communicating to the public by wire and by rebroadcasting (if done by another organization) and the right of communication by loudspeaker or any other analogous instrument of the broadcast of the work (Article 11*bis),* the right of public recitation and communication thereof to the public (Article 11*ter*), the right of making adaptations, arrangements or other alterations of a work (Article 12), and the right of making and distributing the cinematographic adaptation and reproduction of a work (Article 14), which shall be treated as an original work (Article 14*bis* (1)). The so-called *droit de suite* provided for in Article 14*ter* (concerning original works of art and original manuscripts) is optional and applicable only if legislation in the country to which the author belongs so permits.

Independently of the author's economic rights, Article 6*bis* provides for the right of the author to claim authorship of his or her work (which includes using a pseudonym or staying anonymous) and to object to any distortion, mutilation or other modification of, or other derogatory action in relation to, the work which would be prejudicial to the author's honor or reputation ("moral rights").

[G] Limitations

As a sort of counterbalance to the minimum standards of protection there are also other provisions in the Berne Convention allowing Member States to limit the strict application of the rules regarding exclusive rights. It provides for the possibility of using protected works in particular cases without having to obtain the authorization of the owner of the copyright and without having to pay any remuneration for such use. Such exceptions which are commonly referred to as free use of protected works are included in Articles 9(2) (reproduction in certain special cases), 10 (quotations and use of works by way of illustration for teaching purposes), 10*bis* (reproduction of newspaper or similar articles and use or works for the purpose of reporting current events), 11*bis*(3) (ephemeral recordings).

There are two cases where the Berne Convention provides the possibility of compulsory licenses: in Article 11*bis*(2) for the rights of broadcasting or wireless communication of the work and communication to the public by wire, by rebroadcasting, or by loudspeaker or any other analogous instrument of the broadcast of the work, and in Article 13(1) for the right of recording musical works after an initial authorization by the author.

In so far as the exclusive right of translation is concerned, the Berne Convention offers a choice. A developing country may, when acceding to the Convention, make a reservation under the so-called ten-year rule (Article 30(2)(b)) or avail itself of the provisions in the Berne Appendix (Special Provisions Regarding Developing Countries) related to translation (Article II) (*see* §16.05 below).

[H] Duration of Protection

The minimum standards of protection provided for in the Berne Convention also relate to the duration of protection. Article 7 lays down a minimum term of protection. According to this, the term shall be the life of the author and fifty years after his/her death.

There are, however, exceptions to this basic rule for certain categories of works. For example, for cinematographic works, the term is at least fifty years after the work has been made available to the public, or, if not made available, then fifty years after the making of such a work. For photographic works and works of applied art, the minimum term of protection is twenty-five years from the making of the work (Article 7(4)). For photographic works, the WCT in 1996 has, for its Members, adapted the minimum duration to the general one of fifty years.

A majority of countries in the world have legislated for life plus a fifty-year term of protection since it is felt fair and right that the lifetime of the author and the lifetime of the author's children should be covered; this could also provide the incentive necessary to stimulate creativity, and constitute a fair balance between the interests of the authors and the needs of society. As the life span has expanded in many countries, a growing number of countries have adopted a life plus seventy-year term.

The term of protection for moral rights extends at least until the expiry of the economic rights.

§16.03 THE LATEST (PARIS) ACT OF THE CONVENTION

The Berne Convention was developed initially according to the standards and requirements of the industrialized countries in Europe. Later, when the system of the Berne Convention extended to other areas of the globe, it started acquiring new dimensions. Particularly in the wake of the Second World War, when the political map of the world changed considerably, the Berne Convention also had to face new political developments. Several territories previously having colonial or similar status, and in that capacity being bound by the provisions of the Berne Convention, progressively became independent and other States were newly created. These countries had to face the question of possible accession to the international system of copyright protection as contained in the Convention. They were free to join or not to join it or, where they were already members, to withdraw from the Convention.

While it was almost universally recognized that authors and other creators should be afforded the necessary protection for their intellectual creations, there was also a consciousness that the newly independent developing countries had genuine problems in gaining greater and easier access to works protected by copyright, particularly for their technological and educational needs, from the developed countries, both in respect of formal as well as non-formal educational programs. Solutions had to be found for meeting the immense and urgent needs of educational material in developing countries. The necessity for setting up of an international arrangement for permitting developing countries a greater degree of access to protected works while respecting the rights of authors, seemed to gather momentum. Meanwhile, the advance of technology made the extension of the geographical scope of the international conventions and multilateral agreements to an increasingly larger number of countries, more attractive.

In view of these new facts and circumstances, it was felt by many that the systems of international protection of copyright required adaptation or modification to suit the new concepts and the new needs. Deliberations at the more recent revision conferences were, therefore, directed to adapting the systems of international protection of literary and artistic works to the needs of these newly independent countries.

The question of incorporating into the Convention special provisions for the newly independent developing countries was initially mooted at an African Copyright Meeting in Brazzaville in 1963. This matter was pursued at the Conference called in Stockholm in 1967 for revision of the Berne Convention where a "protocol regarding developing countries" known as the Stockholm Protocol was added to the Convention.

However, it soon became clear that the solution (the Stockholm Protocol) proposed was unlikely to gain much acceptance among Union countries, particularly those whose works were likely to be made use of under the provisions of the Protocol. If the needs of the developing countries were to be met without too much delay, it seemed necessary to take a second look at conditions under which translation and reproduction of the works of other countries might be made for purposes of education and scientific research.

The Revision Conference convened in Paris in 1971 was predominantly concerned with finding solutions in order to support the universal effect of the Convention and to establish an appropriate basis for its operation, particularly in relation to the increasing number of newly independent States which had to face serious problems in the nascent stage of their economic, social and cultural development as independent nations. After the Second World War, with the break-up of colonial structures, the lurking question was whether it was fair and workable to ask these newly developing countries to take on obligations under the Convention that were agreed upon by developed countries, without taking into consideration the special situations in the developing ones. There was certainly a challenge then posed to international copyright itself and this was, in a manner, sorted out through the give and take that culminated in the special provisions concerning developing countries that were incorporated in an Appendix which now forms an integral part of the Convention (*see* §16.05 below).

§16.04 ADMINISTRATION

[A] Administrative Provisions

The provisions of the Berne Convention fall into two categories viz. those of substance covering the material law and the administrative and final clauses covering matters of administration and structure. In the latest text of the Convention as revised at Paris in 1971, Articles 1-21 and the Appendix contain the substantive provisions and Articles 22-38 the administrative and final clauses.

The Berne Convention is administered by WIPO. The administrative tasks performed by WIPO include assembling and publishing information concerning the protection of copyright, including information on national copyright laws included in the WIPO Lex database. WIPO conducts studies and provides services designed to facilitate protection of copyright; as the Secretariat, it participates in all meetings of the Assembly, the Executive Committee or any other Committee of Experts or Working Groups; in accordance with the directions of the Assembly and in cooperation with the Executive Committee, it shall also, when required, make preparations for the conferences to revise the Convention.

The administrative provisions provide for an Assembly in which the Government of each Member State shall be represented by one delegate. The Assembly determines the program, adopts the budget and controls the finances of the Union. It also elects members of the Executive Committee of the Assembly. One-fourth of the number of member countries are to be elected to the Executive Committee. The Executive Committee meets yearly during the WIPO Assemblies.

[B] Becoming Party to the Convention

In order to become a party to the Berne Convention, an instrument of accession has to be deposited with the Director General of WIPO (Article 29(1)). Accession to the Berne Convention and membership of the Berne Union becomes effective three months after the date on which the Director General of WIPO has notified the deposit of the abovementioned instrument of accession (Article 29(2)(a)). In accordance with Article I of the Appendix, a developing country has to specifically declare, at the time of its ratification of or accession to the Paris Act, that it will avail itself of the provisions in the Appendix concerning the compulsory licenses for translation and/or reproduction.

In becoming party to the Berne Convention, the State concerned becomes a member of the Berne Union. It would therefore be entitled to:

(1) full membership (right to vote) in the Berne Union Assembly (Article 22(3)(a));
(2) the right to vote in elections of or to be elected to the Executive Committee of the Berne Union (Article 23(2)(a));
(3) automatic membership in the WIPO Coordination Committee during the period of its membership in the Executive Committee of the Berne Union (Convention establishing WIPO, Article 8(l)(a)).

To become a member of the Berne Union is in the interest of every country that wants to establish healthy conditions for the development of its culture and economy, and it is particularly in the interest of every developing country.

§16.05 DEVELOPING COUNTRIES AND THE BERNE CONVENTION

[A] Protection for TCEs

The predominant concern at the last revision of the Berne Convention was to find solutions in order to support the universal effect of the Convention and to establish an appropriate basis for its operation, particularly in relation to the increasing number of newly independent States which had to face serious problems in the nascent stage of their economic, social and cultural development as independent nations. The lurking question was whether it was fair and workable to ask these newly developing countries to take on obligations under the Convention that were agreed upon by developed countries without taking into consideration the special situations in the developing ones. The latest (1971) Paris Act of the Berne Convention thus recognizes a special right in favor of developing countries. It provides that in case of unpublished works, where the identity of the author is unknown, but where there is every ground to presume that the author is a national of a country of the Union, the rights in such a work are to be acknowledged in all countries of the Union. By this provision the Berne Convention has rendered it possible for the developing countries to protect their TCEs abroad. It was made a matter for legislation in the country of origin of such works to designate the competent authority which should represent the unknown author, and protect and enforce the author's rights in the countries of the Union. By providing for the bringing of actions by authorities designated by the State, the Berne Convention offers to developing countries whose TCEs are a part of their heritage, a possibility of exploiting it. More recently, there are ongoing discussions at WIPO about achieving a separate instrument of protection for TCEs. Chapters 12 and 35 cover this matter.

[B] The Berne Appendix

The Appendix to the Paris (1971) Act of the Berne Convention provides for special faculties open to developing countries concerning translation and reproduction of works of foreign origin. The Appendix augments the Convention's existing exceptions to the author's exclusive rights including those of reproduction and translation (Articles 2*bis*, 9(2), 10(2), 10*bis*) and the ten-year rule (Article 30(2)(b)).

According to this Appendix, countries which are regarded as developing countries in conformity with the established practice of the General Assembly of the UN may, under certain conditions, depart from the minimum standards of protection provided for in the Convention. This exceptional regime concerns two rights: the right of translation and the right of reproduction.

The Berne Convention provides, in respect of developing countries, for the possibility of granting non-exclusive and non-transferable compulsory licenses in respect of (i) translation for the purpose of teaching, scholarship or research, and (ii) reproduction for use in connection with systematic instructional activities, of works protected under the Convention; the term "systematic instructional activities" including systematic out-of-school or non-formal education. These licenses could be granted under certain conditions to any national of a developing country which has duly availed itself of one or both of the faculties provided for in the Appendix for grant of such compulsory licenses in respect of translation and/or reproduction of works of foreign origin.

These licenses may be granted, after the expiry of certain time limits and after compliance with certain procedural steps, by the competent authority of the developing country concerned. They have to be applied for from the authority designated in the developing country as being competent to grant such licenses. They must provide for just compensation in favor of the owner of the right. In other words, the payment to be made by the compulsory licensee must be consistent with standards of royalties normally operating in respect of licenses freely negotiated between persons in the two countries concerned.

Provision has also to be made in the legislation to ensure a correct translation or an accurate reproduction of the work, as the case may be, and to indicate the name of the author on all copies of such translations or reproductions. Copies of translations or reproductions made and publication under such licenses are not, however, allowed to be exported. In other words, such copies may be distributed only in the country in which the compulsory license was granted.

Since the license is non-exclusive, the copyright owner is entitled to bring out and place on the market his/her own equivalent copies upon which the power of the licensee to continue making copies under the license would cease. However, in that event, the compulsory licensee's stock can be disposed of.

Compulsory license for translations can be granted for languages generally spoken in the developing country concerned. There is a distinction between languages in general use also in one or more developed countries (particularly English, French and Spanish) and those not in general use there (largely local languages of developing countries). In the case of a language in general use in one or more developed countries, a period of three years, starting on the date of the first publication of the work, has to elapse before a license can be applied for, whereas for a language not in general use in a developed country, the period is one year.

In respect of reproduction, the period after which compulsory licenses may be obtained may vary according to the nature of the work to be reproduced. Generally, it is five years from the first publication. However, for works connected with the natural and physical sciences and with technology (and this includes mathematical works), the period is three years; and for works of fiction, poetry and drama, the period is seven years.

In accordance with Article I of the Appendix, a developing country has to declare specifically, at the time of its ratification of or accession to the Paris Act, that it will avail itself of the provisions in the Appendix concerning the compulsory licenses for translation and/or reproduction.

§16.06 MEMBERSHIP

As of December 9, 2023, 181 States were Contracting Parties to the Berne Convention.

CHAPTER 17

The Patent Cooperation Treaty

§17.01 INTRODUCTION

[A] The Traditional Patent System

The traditional patent system requires the filing of individual patent applications for each country for which patent protection is sought, with the exception of the regional patent systems such as the OAPI system established by the Bangui Agreement, the system established by the Harare Protocol in the framework of the African Regional Intellectual Property Organization (ARIPO), the system established by the EPC in the framework of the European Patent Organization (EPO), the Gulf Cooperation Council (GCC) patent system and the system established by the Eurasian Patent Convention of the Eurasian Patent Organization (EAPO).

Under the traditional "Paris Convention route," the priority of an earlier application can be claimed for applications filed subsequently in foreign countries, but such later applications must be filed within twelve months of the filing date of the earlier application. Within this twelve-month period the applicant must prepare and file patent applications for all countries in which he/she is seeking protection. This means expenses for translation, patent attorneys in the various countries and payment of fees to the patent Offices before the applicant knows whether he/she is likely to meet the patentability criteria.

Filing patent applications under the traditional system means also that every national or regional patent Office with which an application is filed has to carry out at least a formal examination of each application against the country's applicable national requirements. In addition, where patent Offices examine patent applications as to substance, each Office has to carry out a search to determine the state of the art in the technical field of the invention, and has to carry out an examination as to patentability (i.e., is the invention new considering the state of the art, does it involve an inventive step (non-obviousness), and is it susceptible of industrial application?).

The principal difference between the traditional national patent system and the regional patent systems, such as those mentioned above, is that a regional patent or a bundle of national patents are granted by one patent Office for several States. Otherwise, the procedure is the same, and the explanations given in the preceding paragraphs are equally valid which means that the regional patent systems are only partially alleviating the burden of seeking patent protection internationally under the traditional system.

[B] History of the PCT

In order to overcome some of the inconveniences inherent in the traditional patent system, the Executive Committee of the International (Paris) Union for the Protection of Industrial Property invited, in September 1966, BIRPI (the predecessor of WIPO) to urgently undertake a study of solutions to reduce the duplication of the effort both for applicants and national patent Offices. In 1967, a draft international treaty was prepared by BIRPI and presented to a Committee of Experts. In the following years, a number of meetings prepared revised drafts and a Diplomatic Conference held in Washington in June 1970 adopted a treaty called the PCT. The "PCT" entered into force on January 24, 1978, and became operational on June 1, 1978, with an initial eighteen Contracting States. As of August 1, 2023, 157 Contracting States had joined the PCT.

The filing of international applications under the PCT commenced on June 1, 1978. In the first year 459 international applications were received and with slow but constant growth rates filings accumulated to more than 3 million in total by 2017, and more than 5 million in total by 2023. Approximately 278,100 international applications were received in 2022 from applicants in 134 countries, an increase of 0.3% over 2021. With regard to the national phase, there were 715,200 national phase entries in 2022. Interestingly, more than half (58.9%) of worldwide non-resident filings in 2021 used the PCT in order to seek patents abroad.

These brief indications of growth in use of the PCT demonstrate the maturity of the system.

[C] Objectives of the PCT

As its name suggests, the PCT is an agreement for international cooperation in the field of patents. It is often spoken of as being the most significant advance in international cooperation in this field since the adoption of the Paris Convention itself. It is, however, largely a treaty for rationalization and cooperation with regard to the filing, searching and examination of patent applications and the dissemination of the technical information contained therein. The PCT does not provide for the grant of "international patents": the task of and responsibility for granting patents remains exclusively in the hands of the patent Offices of, or acting for, the countries where protection is sought (the "designated Offices"). The PCT does not compete with but, in fact, complements the Paris Convention. Indeed, it is a special agreement under the Paris Convention open only to States which are also party to the Paris Convention.

The principal objective of the PCT is to simplify and to render more effective and more economical—in the interests of the users of the patent system and the Offices which have responsibility for administering it—the previously established means of applying in several countries, for patent protection for inventions.

To achieve its objective of providing an opportunity to avoid the need to file a separate application in each country, each being dealt with in isolation and involving repetition of the work for filing and examination, the PCT:

(1) establishes an international system which enables the filing, with a single patent Office (the "receiving Office"), of a single application (the "international application") in one language, having legal effect in each of the countries party to the PCT and provides for the formal examination of the international application by the receiving Office against a single, binding set of formal requirements, and for several procedural safeguards;
(2) subjects each international application to an international search which results in a report citing the relevant prior art (mainly published patent documents relating to previous inventions) and a preliminary patentability opinion both of which should be taken into account in deciding whether the invention is patentable; these are made available first to the applicant and are later published as well as made available to the designated Offices;
(3) provides for centralized international publication of international applications with the related ISRs on PATENTSCOPE;
(4) provides an option to request a supplementary international search to be carried out by an International Searching Authority (ISA) other than the ISA which performed the main international search; that has the potential of reducing the risk of new patent documents and other technical literature being discovered in the national phase since, by requesting supplementary search the applicant can enlarge the linguistic and technical scope of the documentation searched; and
(5) provides an option for an international preliminary examination of the international application which gives to the Offices that have to decide whether or not to grant a patent (the Offices "elected" by the applicant), and to the applicant, a report containing an additional opinion as to whether the claimed invention (typically, an amended version of the application by this point) meets the internationally accepted criteria for patentability. The international preliminary examination provides the applicant with an even stronger basis on which to evaluate the chances of obtaining patents and, if the report is favorable, a stronger basis on which to continue with the application before the national and regional patent Offices.

The procedure described in the preceding paragraph is commonly called the "international phase" of the PCT procedure, whereas one speaks of the "national phase" to describe the last part of the patent granting procedure which is the task of the designated Offices, i.e., the national and regional Offices of or acting for the countries which have been designated in the international application.

In most countries, patent Offices struggle with heavy workloads (leading to delays) and with questions of how best to allocate resources so as to ensure that the patent system yields the greatest return from the available manpower. Under the PCT system, by the time the international application reaches the national Office, it has already been examined as to form by the receiving Office, been searched by the ISA and possibly examined by an International Preliminary Examining Authority, thus providing the national patent Offices with the important benefits of "work sharing" and potentially reducing their workloads since they have the benefit of this information as produced during the international phase using centralized procedures and thus need not duplicate those efforts. Further, the formalities check, the international search and the optional supplementary international search and the likewise optional preliminary examination carried out during the international phase, give the applicant more time and a better basis for deciding whether and in which countries to further pursue the application.

Further main objectives of the PCT are to ensure that more robust patents are granted by the patent Offices of the PCT Contracting States, to facilitate and accelerate access by industries and other interested sectors to technical information related to inventions and to assist developing countries in gaining access to technology. The third-party observation system introduced in 2013 provides the possibility for third parties to submit prior art relevant to the invention disclosed in the published international patent application in order to further contribute to the purpose of granting robust patents by the national patent Offices after the international phase.

§17.02 THE FUNCTIONING OF THE PCT SYSTEM

[A] Filing an International Application

Any national or resident of a PCT Contracting State can file an international application. International applications can be filed in most cases with the national Office, which will act as a PCT receiving Office.[43] Nationals and residents of some countries can only file international applications with the International Bureau of WIPO, which acts as receiving Office for them. In addition, the International Bureau acts as a receiving Office at the option of nationals and residents of all PCT Contracting States.

An international application has the legal effect, as of the international filing date, of a national application in each PCT Contracting State. In addition, it has the effect of

43. Nationals and residents of States which are party to the PCT and to the ARIPO Harare Protocol, the Eurasian Patent Convention, the EPC or the OAPI Bangui Agreement generally also have the option of filing an international application with the ARIPO Office, the Eurasian Patent Office, the EPO or the OAPI Office, respectively.

a regional patent application in those PCT Contracting States which are party to a regional patent treaty.[44]

The international application has the second main effect of automatic deferral of the processing or examination of the international application to thirty months from the priority date by the national or regional Offices, eighteen months more than applicants have under the Paris Convention route. This effect is also referred to as the effect of "delaying" the examination and granting procedure before the Offices.

The PCT prescribes certain formality standards for international applications. An international application which is prepared in accordance with these standards will be acceptable, so far as the form and contents of the application are concerned, to all the PCT Contracting States. No national law may require compliance with requirements relating to the form or contents of the international application different from or additional to those which are provided for by the PCT. The international application must contain a request, a description, one or more claims, one or more drawings (where required) and an abstract; it must comply with the prescribed physical requirements; it must be in one of the prescribed languages and finally, the required fees must be paid.

Only a single set of fees is payable for the filing of the international application, and they should be paid in one currency and at one Office (the receiving Office). Payment of national fees to the designated Offices is delayed until the national phase is entered.

The fees payable to the receiving Office for an international application consist of three main elements:

(1) the transmittal fee—to cover the work of the receiving Office;
(2) the search fee—to cover the work of the ISA; and
(3) the international filing fee—to cover the work of the International Bureau.

Applicants from certain countries are entitled to a reduction of 90% of certain PCT fees, including the international filing fee.

In the majority of cases, applicants file PCT applications electronically with their competent receiving Office. The language in which an international application can be filed depends upon the requirements of the receiving Office with which the application is filed. It is usually the national language. At the receiving Office of the International Bureau, international applications can be filed in any language.

44. For the States party to the OAPI agreement, only regional OAPI patents can be obtained via the PCT; national patents are not available in those States. States party to the regional patent systems established by the Harare Protocol and by the EPC have the possibility of "closing the national route" for obtaining patent protection, whereby an international application designating such a State will automatically be treated as an application for a regional (ARIPO or European) patent and will thus be handled by the respective regional Patent Office.

[B] International Search

The receiving Office, after having made a formal check and accorded an international filing date, sends a copy of the international application to the International Bureau of WIPO (the "record copy") and another copy (the "search copy") to the ISA. It keeps a third copy (the "home copy"). The receiving Office also collects all the PCT fees and transfers the search fee to the ISA and the international filing fee to the International Bureau. Certain ISAs offer substantial reductions in search fees to specific categories of applicants, such as small or micro entities, in accordance with their respective national laws.

Every international application is subjected to an international search, that is, a high-quality search of the patent documents and related technical literature made available worldwide The high quality of the international search is assured by the standards prescribed in the PCT for the documentation, staff qualifications and search methods of the ISAs, which are experienced patent Offices that have been specially appointed to carry out international searches by the Assembly of the PCT Union (the highest administrative body created under the PCT which is composed of all PCT Member States) on the basis of an agreement to observe PCT standards and time limits.

The following twenty-five Offices have been appointed to act as ISAs: the national Offices of Australia, Austria, Brazil, Canada, Chile, China, Egypt, Finland, India, Israel, Japan, the Republic of Korea, Philippines, the Russian Federation, Saudi Arabia, Singapore, Spain, Sweden, Türkiye, Ukraine and the USA, and the following regional Offices, the EPO, the EAPO, the Nordic Patent Institute and the Visegrad Patent Institute. Which ISA is competent will depend on the receiving Office and respectively the nationality and residence of the applicant or applicants; in case of several competent ISAs, the applicant has the choice but may select only one.

Each ISA is required to have at least the prescribed PCT minimum documentation, properly arranged for search purposes, which can be described in general as comprising the patent documents, as from 1920, of the major industrialized countries, together with agreed items of non-patent literature, contained in approximately 135 technical periodicals. The ISA, in making the search, must make use of its full facilities, the minimum documentation and any additional documentation it may possess. The obligation to consult at least the PCT minimum documentation guarantees a high level of international search. Moreover, the PCT minimum documentation is updated to reflect new realities in the means of publication of technical patent and non-patent literature. Further, if the applicant wishes, the ISA can take into account the results of earlier searches under certain conditions.

The results of the international search are provided in an ISR, which is made available to the applicant generally by the fourth or fifth month after the application is filed. The ISR contains no comment on the value of an invention but lists prior art documents relevant to the claims contained in the international application and makes an indication of the possible relevance of the citations to the questions of novelty and inventive step (non-obviousness). The citations of relevant prior art in the ISR enable the applicant to gauge the chances of obtaining a patent in or for the countries in which he/she may later seek protection. Together with the search report, the ISA prepares a written opinion on patentability, applying the identified prior art to the generally accepted patentability criteria, which gives a first detailed analysis of the potential patentability of the invention.

A search report and the written opinion assist the applicant in the subsequent prosecution of the application before the designated Offices. The high quality of the international search assures the applicant that any patent granted is a "robust" patent, one which is less likely to be successfully challenged based on prior art, and thus provides a sound basis for investment or licensing actions.

The ISR assists designated Offices, in particular Offices which do not have technically qualified staff and an extensive collection of patent documents arranged in a manner suitable for search purposes, in examining applications and otherwise evaluating the inventions described.

The ISR assists the applicant in deciding whether it is worthwhile, in light of the state of the art evidenced by the documents cited in the search report, to continue to seek protection for this invention in the designated States or whether to continue only after the claims in the international application have been amended to better distinguish the invention from the identified prior art.

The ISA sends the ISR and the written opinion to the applicant and to the International Bureau. The International Bureau includes the search report in the international publication of the international application and makes a copy available to the designated Offices.

In addition to this, an applicant may wish to request a supplementary international search to be carried out by an ISA other than the ISA which performed the main international search. Supplementary international search can therefore enhance the linguistic and technical scope of the documentation searched in the international phase and may reveal new patent documents and other relevant technical literature.

For applications not filed under the PCT system, the PCT also provides a feature to strengthen national patent systems and to assist national Offices in the processing and granting of national patents. The national patent law can include provisions for an "international-type search" (provided for in Article 15(5) of the PCT) of purely national applications. This search is the same as an international search and is carried out by the ISA which the national Office specifies for carrying out international searches. Adoption of an international-type search mechanism has a twofold benefit for the country. First, it means that all patents would have been subjected to the same kind of search whether or not the corresponding applications took the PCT route. Second, national enterprises and inventors could have the benefits of an international-type search report even without filing an application under the PCT.

[C] International Publication

International publication under the PCT serves two main purposes: to disclose to the public the invention (i.e., in general, the technological advance made by the inventor) and to set out the scope of the protection which may ultimately be obtained.

Following the international search, the International Bureau of WIPO performs the task of international publication of the international application as filed, along with the ISR established by the ISA, exclusively in electronic format online in its searchable database, PATENTSCOPE. The publication of the application disseminates important technological and legal information for the benefit of applicants, patent Offices and interested third parties. Each publication also contains a Classification Index, allowing the selection of the published international applications by technical fields.

The international application is published in the language of the international application as filed, if that language is Arabic, Chinese, English, French, German, Japanese, Korean, Portuguese, Russian or Spanish. Regardless of the publication language of the international application, the title of the invention and the abstract are additionally published in English and French, and the ISR is also published in English. If the international application has been filed in a language that is not one of the publication languages, a translation must be furnished by the applicant for publication in one of those languages.

Applicants, after receipt of the ISR and the accompanying written opinion, have the opportunity to enhance the application's quality through additional, yet optional, steps. One such step involves amending the claims that describe the invention. These amendment of the claims will subsequently be included in the international publication, which could provide a better indication of the patent protection that the applicant might obtain for the invention. Additionally, applicants may submit comments on the written opinion on an informal basis to the International Bureau which will be made publicly available together with the written opinion at international publication. Until international publication (eighteen months after the priority date—unless the applicants request early publication), no third party is allowed access to the international application unless the applicant requests or authorizes it. However, when international publication occurs, most other documents in the international application file are made publicly available on PATENTSCOPE together with the published international application, for example, the written opinion of the ISA and any informal comments on the written opinion. Copies of the international application as published will also be made available to designated Offices.

[D] International Preliminary Examination

Once the applicant has received the ISR, he/she has the possibility to request an international preliminary examination, which is provided for in Chapter II of the PCT, in order to obtain an opinion as to whether the claimed invention meets the patentability criteria. The international preliminary examination also provides the opportunity for the applicant to submit amendments to the international application or arguments relating to opinion of the examiner on these criteria. Proceeding with an international preliminary examination is not automatic but only upon a specific "demand" by the applicant in which he/she states the wish to use the results of such examination in the national phase. A fee for international preliminary examination is due when a demand is filed with the International Preliminary Examining Authority, together with a handling fee (to cover the work of the International Bureau).

All ISAs are International Preliminary Examining Authorities.

The results of the international preliminary examination are set out in a report which is made available to the applicant and the national offices by the International Bureau, which is also responsible for translating the report into English, if required by any Office. The opinion on the patentability of the invention, on the basis of the international criteria mentioned above, provides the applicant with an even stronger basis for calculating the chances of obtaining patents, and the Offices have an even better basis for their decision whether to grant a patent. In countries where patents are granted without examination as to substance, the international preliminary examination report will provide a solid basis for parties interested in the invention (e.g., for licensing purposes) to evaluate the validity of such patents. In addition, the International Preliminary Examining Authority normally carries out a "top-up" search, to discover any documents which have been published or have become available to the International Preliminary Examining Authority subsequent to the date of establishment of the ISR.

[E] Prosecution Before the Designated (or Elected) Offices (the "National Phase")

The processing of an international application in the national phase may not start prior to the expiration of generally thirty months from the priority date of the international application, unless the applicant requests an earlier start.

After having received an ISR and, where requested, an international preliminary examination report, and after having had the possibility of amending the application, the applicant is now in a good position to decide whether he/she has a chance of obtaining patents in the designated States. If he/she sees no likelihood, he/she can either withdraw the application or do nothing; in the latter case, the international application will lose the effect of a national application and the procedure will automatically come to an end.

Where the applicant decides to continue the procedure, and only in that event, he/she must pay the prescribed national fees to the Offices before which he/she intends to enter the national phase and, if required, furnish to these Offices translations of the international application into their official language; a local agent may also have to be appointed. The furnishing of the translation and the payment of the national fees must be effected within generally thirty months from the priority date. Once national processing starts, the normal national procedures apply, subject to specific exceptions arising out of the PCT procedure (e.g., matters of form and contents of the international application, and the provision of copies of the priority document). The applicant also has the choice to enter the national phase at any time before the expiration of thirty months, as well as separately and independently at each national Office.

WIPO has published a "*PCT Applicant's Guide*" (updated weekly). This Guide is available online and offers general information for users of the PCT (relating to the international phase)as well as the procedure before the designated and elected Offices (national phase). Further information is regularly published in the *PCT Newsletter*, a monthly publication which contains up-to-date news about the PCT, *PCT Highlights*, a high-level summary of recent and future developments in the PCT, with hyperlinks to more detailed information, databases, videos, etc. and the *PCT Gazette*, Notices and Information of a General Character. The *PCT Web page* also includes the PCT Treaty and Regulations, the PCT Administrative Instructions, the Guidelines for receiving Offices and International Authorities, and the *PCT Newsletter* as well as other information of a general nature on the PCT.

§17.03 ADVANTAGES OF THE PCT SYSTEM

[A] Advantages for Patent Offices

More and more patent Offices are having to consider how to employ their available manpower to greatest advantage. This is true not only because of the number of patent applications which they must handle (in a country in the process of development, the number must surely rise considerably in the future as a consequence of an increase in the country's industrial activity) but also because of the expanding role that patent Offices are being required to fulfill in providing technical advisory services to local industry (because of available patent documentation and technically trained staff), either in terms of advising on available technologies or in connection with national research and development activities.

PCT applications can contribute to national and regional patent Offices being able to reduce their workloads in connection with the handling of patent applications since the work of verification as to compliance with formal requirements becomes practically negligible.

The PCT also contributes in that the patent Offices can save part of the cost of publishing. If the international application has been published in an official language of the country, and not amended subsequently or upon national phase entry, they can forego publication altogether. Countries having a different official language may limit themselves to publishing only a translation of the abstract that accompanies an international application or the claims. Copies of the full text of the international application could be supplied upon request to interested parties.

The PCT does not affect the revenue of designated Offices unless they decide voluntarily to reduce national fees in view of the savings they make through the PCT and in order to make the use of the international application route more attractive to the applicant. In any case, the most profitable source of revenue for most Offices is from maintenance or renewal fees which are generally collected after the grant of the patent, and thus which are not affected by the Treaty.

Both examining and non-examining patent Offices can likewise benefit from the PCT system, in respect of most applications, from an ISR and an international preliminary report on patentability (IPRP) (Chapter I) and, in some cases, from an IPRP (Chapter II).

Patent Offices of States party to the ARIPO Harare Protocol, to the Eurasian Patent Convention or to the EPC which opt to close the national route are not involved in the processing of international applications designating such States. Choosing this option is therefore particularly advisable if the national Patent Office is less well equipped than the regional Office and is not prepared to receive and process increasing numbers of applications.

[B] Advantages for the Applicant

Applicants may file their application in their own country (or, where applicable, with the competent regional Office, or with the International Bureau as receiving Office) with effect in foreign countries and have more time to make up their minds as to the countries in which they wish to seek protection. In a typical case using the PCT system, applicants will have spent less money in the stage prior to grant than otherwise.

If the applicant does not use the international procedure offered by the PCT, he/she must start preparations for filing abroad three to nine months before the expiration of the priority period. He/she must prepare translations of the application and must have them put into a different form for each country. Under the PCT, the applicant, within the priority year, files only one application (the international application).

The cost of further translation has to be met eventually (if the national phase is entered), but not until generally eighteen months later than under a procedure which does not use the PCT and only if the applicant, having evaluated the ISR, the written opinion of the ISA and, where available, the IPRP (Chapter I) or the IPRP (Chapter II), is still interested in the countries concerned.

In summary, the PCT System has many advantages for an applicant:

(1) the applicant has up to eighteen months more to reflect on the desirability of seeking protection in foreign countries, to appoint local patent agents in each foreign country, to prepare the necessary translations and to pay the national fees;
(2) if the international application is in the form prescribed by the PCT, it cannot be rejected on formal grounds by a patent Office during the national phase of the processing of the application;
(3) the ISR and written opinion contain important information about the potential patentability of the invention, providing a useful basis for making business decisions;
(4) the applicant has the possibility during the optional international preliminary examination to amend the international application, enter into dialogue with the examiner and put the application in order before processing by the various national patent Offices;
(5) the search and examination work of patent Offices in the national phase can in some cases be reduced thanks to the ISR, the written opinion and,

where applicable, the IPRP (Chapter II) that accompany the international application;

(6) the applicant may be able to apply for fast-track examination procedures in the national phase in Contracting States that have PCT-PPH) agreements or similar arrangements;

(7) since each international application is published together with an ISR, third parties are in a better position to evaluate the potential patentability of the claimed invention, contributing to the granting of more robust patents;

(8) for any applicant, international publication provides a worldwide online notice of the invention. The applicant may also highlight any interest in concluding licensing agreements on PATENTSCOPE, which can be an effective means of advertising and looking for potential licensees;

(9) savings in document preparation, communication and translations are achieved because the work done during the international processing is generally not repeated before each Office (e.g., the applicant must submit only one copy of the priority document instead of having to submit several copies); and

(10) if the invention appears to not be patentable at the end of the international phase, it may be abandoned, saving the costs which would otherwise have been incurred by processing the application at each office, appointing local patent agents in each foreign country, preparing the necessary translations and paying the national fees.

[C] Advantages for the National Economy and for Industry

In most countries (even developed countries), the majority of patent applications are filed by foreigners. This is a consequence of the need of the owner of new technology to obtain patent protection separately in or for each of several countries in which he/she is economically interested. Foreign filings are a basis for the inflow of technology. By facilitating the filing of patent applications, the PCT contributes to a country's acquisition of new technology.

By being able to offer the PCT route to foreign entrepreneurs owning patentable technology, a country may find them more willing to transfer (sell or license) their technology and will, in general, attract more foreign investment. The industrialization of the country is thus further promoted.

Of course, care needs to be taken to ensure that the freedom of the market is not hampered by unjustified (weak) patents. The PCT system helps to prevent this. Although it facilitates the filing of patent applications, the PCT also contains mechanisms which assist the national and regional patent systems in avoiding the grant of patents where it is not justified. Applications filed under the PCT first pass through the central processing mechanism of the international phase of the PCT procedure. They are examined as to form, searched as to novelty and inventive step (non-obviousness), centrally published and, where applicable, examined as to patentability. When the PCT application reaches the national phase of the procedure for the grant of a patent, it is almost always formally in order, publicly available in one of the most important languages (with an English-language abstract, when not in English) and accompanied by an ISR, patentability opinion and possibly an international preliminary examination report.

By adding to national law the requirement that each national patent application must be accompanied by an international-type search report (*see* above), a national patent office can extend the advantages of the PCT to national applications. Such a requirement contributes to the elimination of low-quality patents and duplication of effort by providing a basis for assessing patentability, and thus results in a net gain for the national economy.

[D] Technological Information

A further important advantage of the PCT for developing countries lies in its information effect. It is always difficult to obtain a complete picture of all the patent documents published in many countries and many languages and of the most recent state of the art resulting therefrom. Since many important inventions are the subject of PCT applications, developing countries have, through the international publication of these applications, early and easier access to modern technological information. The access will be early, because international applications are published eighteen months after the priority date of the application. It will be easier, because the application will be published in one of the most important languages and, where not in English, with an English-language abstract, and because the ISR, published together with the application, will make it easier to evaluate the technology disclosed in the application.

Technological progress is an essential factor of national economic development. It is now generally recognized that real technological progress cannot be achieved or continue in a country, even a highly industrialized country, without constant stimulation of domestic inventive activities and at the same time importation (via licenses) of advanced technologies from foreign countries. Since the PCT system greatly facilitates the seeking of patent protection on a multinational level, allowing for patents granted through the PCT route to be subjected to high-quality international search and optionally to an international preliminary examination, more and more applicants are seeking patent protection through the PCT, thus paving the way for TT and licensing agreements. WIPO provides a licensing information feature within the PCT itself that allows PCT applicants to highlight their interest to license their inventions contained in their international applications.

With an increase in licensed technology, foreign investment will be stimulated. In addition, more advanced technologies and investment will lead to increased levels of local employment and the technical skills of the local workforce will be enhanced. As the level of economic and technological development rises, an increasing number of nationals will use and greatly benefit from the PCT system when they seek patent protection abroad for their inventions, thus aiding in the penetration of export markets by local industry and the promotion of economic cooperation with foreign countries. It is thus important for a nation to adapt its economy to international standards, including those in the patent field.

Accession to the PCT can make a country's patent system more attractive for the filing of patent applications, thus potentially stimulating investment and TT as well as promoting domestic inventive activities. It is undoubtedly a useful tool which, if effectively used, can contribute to reducing the technological gap between the developing and industrialized countries.

The PCT system is self-supporting since the fees paid by the applicants cover the costs incurred by WIPO in administering the system. No financial contributions are required from the Contracting States under the PCT.

§17.04 FUTURE DEVELOPMENTS OF THE PCT

In relation to the future development of the PCT, Contracting States in the PCT Working Group discuss ongoing initiatives and future proposals that aim to improve the functioning of the PCT system, thereby increasing the benefits that the Treaty can offer for all interested parties. In this regard, the PCT Working Group endorsed a series of recommendations in 2010, referred to as the PCT Roadmap. These recommendations cover a variety of actions for the International Bureau, applicants, Contracting States and national Offices, such as improving quality and timeliness of international search and preliminary examination in the international phase, cost and accessibility to the PCT system, technical assistance and PCT information and TT. In 2018, the PCT Working Group, reviewed the implementation of the PCT Roadmap recommendations and discussed a Memorandum entitled "The PCT System: Overview and Possible Future Directions and Priorities," which was drafted by the WIPO Director General in 2017, intended to build on and complement the PCT Roadmap recommendations, which largely remain relevant. The Memorandum sets out key areas for further work in the coming years in four areas: legal and institutional issues, the technical (IT) environment, financial issues and quality. Work continued in the PCT Working Group to develop proposals in these areas with a view to making further improvements to the PCT system for the benefit of Offices and applicants, but also taking into account the experiences from the COVID-19 pandemic.

§17.05 MEMBERSHIP

As of August 1, 2023, one hundred fifty-seven States were party to the PCT. The recently joined countries include Jamaica (became bound by the PCT on February 10, 2022), Iraq (became bound by the PCT on April 30, 2022), Cabo Verde (became bound by the PCT on July 6, 2022) and Mauritius (became bound by the PCT on March 15, 2023).

CHAPTER 18

Budapest Treaty on the International Recognition of the Deposit of Microorganisms for the Purposes of Patent Procedure

§18.01 BACKGROUND TO THE TREATY

The Budapest Treaty on the International Recognition of the Deposit of Microorganisms for the Purposes of Patent Procedure (the Budapest Treaty) which is a special agreement under the Paris Convention, entered into force on August 19, 1980.

Disclosure of the invention is a generally recognized requirement for the grant of patents. Normally, an invention is disclosed by means of a written description. Where an invention involves a microorganism, or the use of a microorganism, which is not available to the public, such a description is not sufficient for disclosure. That is why in the patent procedure of an increasing number of countries it is necessary not only to file a written description but also to deposit, with a specialized institution, a sample of the microorganism. Patent offices are not equipped to handle microorganisms, whose preservation requires special expertise and equipment to keep them viable, to protect them from contamination and to protect health or the environment from contamination. Such preservation is costly. The furnishing of samples also requires specialized expertise and equipment.

When protection is sought in several countries for an invention involving a microorganism or the use of a microorganism, the complex and costly procedures of the deposit of the microorganism might have to be repeated in each of those countries. It was in order to eliminate or reduce such multiplication, in order to enable one deposit to serve the purpose of all the deposits which would otherwise be necessary, that the Treaty was concluded.

§18.02 MAIN FEATURES OF THE TREATY

[A] Recognition of the Deposit of a Microorganism with any "International Depositary Authority" for the Purposes of the Patent Procedure

The main feature of the Treaty is that a Contracting State which allows or requires the deposit of microorganisms for the purposes of patent procedure must recognize, for such purposes, the deposit of a microorganism with any "international depositary authority" (Article 3(1)(a)), irrespective of whether such authority is on or outside the territory of the said State. In other words, one deposit, with one international depositary authority, will suffice for the purposes of patent procedure before the national patent offices (called "industrial property offices" in the Treaty) of all of the Contracting States and before any regional patent office if such a regional organization declares that it recognizes the effects of the Treaty (Article 9(1)) (as of September 1, 2023, this is the case of the ARIPO, OAPI, EAPO and EPO).

What the Treaty calls an "international depositary authority" is a scientific institution—typically a "culture collection"—which is capable of storing microorganisms. Such an institution acquires the status of "international depositary authority" through the furnishing, by one of the Contracting States on the territory of which it is located, of assurances to the Director General of WIPO to the effect that the said institution complies, and will continue to comply, with certain requirements (Article 6(1)), including, in particular, that it will be available, for the purposes of the deposit of microorganisms, to any "depositor" (person, firm, etc.) under the same conditions, that it will accept and store the deposited microorganisms and that it will furnish samples thereof to anyone entitled to such samples but to no one else. The said assurances may be furnished also by certain intergovernmental industrial property organizations (Article 9(1)(a)). There is no "international depositary authority" on the territory of each Contracting State. However, some Contracting States have given their assurances for more than one "international depositary authority."

The Treaty and the Regulations also contain provisions permitting the termination or limitation of the status of international depositary authority at the will of the Contracting States where the said authority does not, or does not fully comply with its assumed duties (Article 8). For example, if an "international depositary authority" is about to cease to serve as such an authority, all microorganisms that have been deposited and stored with them shall be transferred to another international depositary authority (Rule 5.1).

[B] Deposit of Microorganisms and Furnishing of Samples

The Regulations under the Budapest Treaty lay down the procedures which depositors and "international depositary authorities" must follow for the deposit of microorganisms and the duration of storage of deposited microorganisms. For instance, they include the content of the receipt that each international depositary authority is required to give to the depositor for the deposited microorganism (Rule 7), testing of the viability of the deposited microorganisms and issuance of viability statements by the international depositary authority (Rule 10), and the kinds of fees that the international depositary authority are allowed to charge (Rule 12). The fee for the storage of the deposited microorganisms shall cover the entire duration of the mandatory storage period (Rule 12). In addition, the Regulations contain detailed provisions (Rule 11) on who is entitled—and when—to receive samples of the deposited microorganism. The depositor him/herself has a right to a sample at any time (Rule 11.2(i)). He may authorize any third party (authority, natural person, legal entity) to ask for a sample and such a third party will receive a sample upon producing such an authorization (Rule 11.2(ii)). Any "interested" industrial property office to which the Treaty applies may ask for a sample and will receive one; an industrial property office will mainly be regarded as "interested" where the microorganism is needed for the purposes of patent procedure before the said office (Rule 11.1). Any other party may obtain a sample if, roughly stated, an industrial property office to which the Treaty applies certifies that, under the applicable law, such a party has the right to a sample of the given microorganism; the elements of the certification are provided for in detail to ensure that the maximum extent of caution will be exercised by the industrial property office before it issues a certification (Rule 11.3(a)).

The Treaty and the Regulations also contain provisions allowing for what is called a "new" deposit where no samples of the originally deposited microorganism can be furnished (Article 4).

The Regulations do not address, however, the timing of deposit (i.e., the time limit applicable for depositing, with an international depositary authority, a microorganism which is the subject of a patent application) and the conditions for the furnishing of samples, that are left to the relevant national patent laws.

§18.03 MAIN ADVANTAGES OF THE TREATY

The Treaty is primarily advantageous to the depositor who is an applicant for patents in several countries; the deposit of a microorganism under the procedures provided for in the Treaty will save him money and strengthen his/her security. It will save him money because, instead of depositing the microorganism in each and every country in which he/she files a patent application referring to that microorganism, he/she can deposit it only once, with one depositary, with the consequence that in all but one of the countries in which he/she seeks protection he/she will save the fees and costs that deposits would have otherwise entailed. In most cases, there will be at least one international depositary authority in the country of the depositor, which means that he/she will deal with an authority which is close to him, with which he/she can deal in his/her own language, to which he/she can pay the fees in his/her own currency and which he/she may even know from personal experience; in other words, he/she will be able to avoid dealing with distant authorities, in foreign currencies and in foreign languages. He will probably have a natural trust in the authority carefully preserving the viability of the deposited microorganism and furnishing samples only to those to whom it is supposed to furnish them.

The security of the depositor is increased by the fact that, for an institution to become an international depositary authority, solemn assurances as to the seriousness and continued existence of that institution must be given; such assurances must be given by a State or by an IGO, and they are addressed to all the Member States of the Budapest Union. Consequently, it may be expected that the assurances will be strictly respected, all the more so since, if they are not so respected, the Member States may take away from the defaulting institution the status of international depositary authority.

Finally, it is to be noted that adherence to the Treaty entails no financial burden or obligation for any Government.

§18.04 MEMBERSHIP

As of September 1, 2023, eighty-eight States were party to the Budapest Treaty. On the same date, forty-nine Authorities were recognized as International Depositary Authorities under Article 7 of the Treaty.

CHAPTER 19
Patent Law Treaty

§19.01 OBJECTIVES AND SUMMARY OF THE TREATY

The aim of the PLT is to harmonize and streamline formal procedures in respect of national and regional patent applications and patents and, thus, to make such procedures more user-friendly. With the significant exception of filing date requirements, the PLT provides the maximum sets of requirements the office of a Contracting Party may apply. This means that a Contracting Party is free to provide for requirements that are more generous from the viewpoint of applicants and owners, but that the requirements under the PLT are mandatory as to the maximum an office can require from applicants or owners.

The Treaty contains, in particular, provisions on a number of issues that are seen as essential to the international harmonization of procedures.

[A] Requirements for Obtaining a Filing Date

Requirements for obtaining a filing date were standardized in order to minimize the risks that applicants could inadvertently lose the filing date, which is of utmost importance in the patent procedure. The PLT requires that the office of any Contracting Party must accord a filing date to an application upon compliance with three simple formal requirements:

(1) an indication that the elements received by the office are intended to be an application for a patent for an invention;
(2) indications that would allow the office to identify or to contact the applicant (however, a Contracting Party is allowed to require indications on both); and
(3) a part which appears to be a description of the invention. No additional elements can be required for according a filing date.

In particular, a Contracting Party cannot include one or more claims or a filing fee in a filing date requirement. As mentioned above, these requirements are not maximum requirements but constitute absolute requirements, so that a Contracting Party would not be allowed to accord a filing date unless all those requirements are complied with.

[B] Requirements for National and Regional Applications

A set of formal requirements for national and regional applications was standardized by incorporating into the PLT the requirements relating to form or content of international applications under the PCT, including the contents of the PCT request Form and the use of that request Form accompanied by an indication that the application is to be treated as a national application. This eliminates or reduces procedural gaps between national, regional and international patent systems.

[C] Model International Forms

The standardized Model International Forms that have to be accepted by the offices of all Contracting Parties were established.

[D] Simplification of Procedures

A number of procedures before patent offices were simplified, which contributes to a reduction in costs for applicants as well as for offices. Examples of such procedures are exceptions from mandatory representation, the restriction on requiring evidence on a systematic basis, the requirement that offices accept a single communication covering more than one application or patent in certain cases (e.g., a single power of attorney) or the restriction on the requirement to submit a copy of an earlier application and a translation thereof.

[E] Avoiding the Unintentional Loss of Rights

The PLT provides procedures for avoiding the unintentional loss of substantive rights resulting from failure to comply with formality requirements or time limits. These include the obligation that offices notify the applicant or other concerned person, extensions of time limits, continued processing, reinstatement of rights, and restrictions on revocation/invalidation of a patent for formal defects, where they were not noticed by the office during the application stage.

[F] Electronic Filing

The implementation of electronic filing is facilitated, while ensuring the coexistence of both paper and electronic communications. The PLT provides that Contracting Parties were allowed to exclude paper communications and to fully switch to electronic communications as of June 2, 2005. However, even after that date, they have to accept paper communications for the purpose of obtaining a filing date and for meeting a time limit. In this connection, the Agreed Statements adopted with the PLT stipulate that industrialized countries will continue to furnish support to developing countries and countries in transition in relation to the introduction of electronic filing.

§19.02 MEMBERSHIP

The PLT was concluded in 2000, and entered into force in 2005. The Treaty is open to States members of WIPO and/or States party to the Paris Convention for the Protection of Industrial Property. It is also open to certain IGOs. Instruments of ratification or accession must be deposited with the Director General of WIPO. As of August 1, 2023, forty-three States were party to the PLT.

CHAPTER 20
Protocol Relating to the Madrid Agreement Concerning the International Registration of Marks

§20.01 INTRODUCTION

The Madrid Agreement Concerning the International Registration of Marks (hereinafter referred to as "the Madrid Agreement") is an international treaty that was adopted in April 1891. It has since undergone a number of revisions. The last revision took place in Stockholm in 1967. A Protocol Relating to the Madrid Agreement Concerning the International Registration of Marks (hereinafter referred to as "the Protocol") was adopted in Madrid on June 27, 1989, entered into force on December 1, 1995, and came into operation on April 1, 1996. Following a decision by the Madrid Union Assembly in October 2016, the Madrid Agreement is no longer in operation and the Protocol is the prevailing treaty.[45]

Both treaties were concluded on the basis of the same principles. The Protocol introduced a series of options making the system of the international registration of marks (hereinafter referred to as "the Madrid System") more accessible to new Contracting Parties. This significantly contributed to enlarging the geographic coverage and the use the System.

The main changes introduced by the Protocol to the Madrid System include the following:

(1) introducing English as a working language, in addition to French, which was the only language used in the Agreement. However, now the Madrid System has trilingual coverage, with English, French and Spanish;

45. *See* Information Notice No 34/2016 at www.wipo.int/edocs/madrdocs/en/2016/madrid_2016_34.pdf.

(2) the applicant may base the application for international registration on an application filed with the Office of origin; under the Agreement, an international application had to be based on a registration in the Office of origin;
(3) each Contracting Party may declare that the time limit for issuing provisional refusals shall be eighteen months (instead of one year), with the possibility of an even longer period in the case of oppositions;
(4) each Contracting Party may declare that it wishes to receive individual fees which are higher than the standard fees applicable under the Madrid System, i.e., the amount that it charges for national (or regional) registration or renewal; the said amount being diminished by the savings resulting from the international procedure;
(5) where the basic mark ceases to have effect within a period of five years counted from the date of the international registration, the international registration will, upon the request by the Office of origin, be cancelled to the same extent. Such cancellation may also take place after the five-year period, as long as the action, leading to the final decision of ceasing of effect was initiated with the period. Where the international registration is cancelled the holder may transform the international registration into national (or regional) applications in the respective Contracting Parties in which the international registration had effect (or in which protection was sought), in each case benefitting from the date of the international registration and, where applicable, its priority date. This possibility did not exist under the Madrid Agreement.

The Protocol also established a link between the Madrid System and the regional systems of trademark registration providing that not only States but also certain IGOs can become party to the Protocol. The EU and the OAPI are such IGOs.

The Contracting Parties to the Protocol constitute the Madrid Union, which is a special Union under Article 19 of the Paris Convention. As of September 1, 2023, the Madrid Union includes 114 members (covering 130 countries), of which 112 are Contracting States and 2 are Contracting Organizations.

§20.02 APPLICABLE TREATY

Following the decision by the Madrid Union Assembly in October 2016, the Madrid Agreement is no longer in operation. All the members of the Madrid System are members of the Protocol, which is now the prevailing treaty.

§20.03 THE PRINCIPLES OF INTERNATIONAL REGISTRATION

The trader or manufacturer wishing to obtain protection for his/her trademark in a number of States must normally comply with the trademark registration formalities of the national Offices of each individual State (differing procedures, need to file the application in different languages, varying terms of protection resulting in different renewal dates, and the need, in some cases, to appoint a local agent). Moreover, the need to file national applications in each country leads to very considerable costs (national fees, fees of the various agents and the costs of translation to be paid in each country). The purpose of the Madrid Protocol is to avoid all these complications. To file an application for international registration having effect in the Contracting Parties of the Madrid System, the applicant need only comply with one set of formalities with the International Bureau of WIPO. The application is submitted in one language (English, French or Spanish) and fees are paid once only to the International Bureau, in one currency (Swiss francs).

The subsequent management of the international registration is also made much easier. There is only one registration to renew, and changes such as a change in ownership or in the name or address of the holder, or a limitation of the list of goods and services, can be recorded in the International Register through a single simple procedural step. If it is desired to transfer the registration for only some of the designated Contracting Parties, or for only some of the goods or services, or to limit the list of goods and services with respect to only some of the designated Contracting Parties, the system is flexible enough to also accommodate this.

§20.04 WHO MAY APPLY FOR INTERNATIONAL REGISTRATION

An international application may be filed only by a natural person or a legal entity which is a national of, is domiciled, or has a real and effective industrial or commercial establishment in a country which is party to the Protocol, or who is a national of a State member of a Contracting Organization, is domiciled, or has such an establishment in the territory of that Contracting organization. Actually, the listing of entitlements follow Article 2 of the Protocol, and it is up to the applicant to freely choose the entitlement.

The Madrid System cannot be used by a person or legal entity which does not have the necessary connection, through establishment, domicile or nationality, with a member of the Madrid Union. Nor can it be used to protect a mark outside the Madrid Union.

§20.05 REGISTRATION PROCEDURE

[A] Basic Application or Registration

The Madrid System is founded on the requirement of a basic mark, meaning a national or regional application or registration in the Trademark Office of the Contracting Party with which the applicant has the necessary connection, as described in §20.04, above, to be able to file an international application. This Office is referred to as the Office of origin.

Under the Protocol, an international application may be based on either a registration with the Office of origin (basic registration) or on an application for registration filed with that Office (basic application). The international application may relate only to goods and services covered by the basic mark.

[B] Submission of the Application for International Registration

The applicant must submit the international application to the International Bureau of WIPO through the Office of origin. An international application which is presented direct to the International Bureau by the applicant is not be considered as such and will be returned to the sender.

An international application can be filed in any one of the three languages of the Madrid System, namely, English, French or Spanish. The Office of origin may, however, restrict the applicant's choice to only one language, or to two languages, or may permit the applicant to choose between any of the three languages.

Before forwarding the application to the International Bureau, the Office of origin checks and certifies that the particulars of the international application correspond to the particulars of the basic mark, meaning that it concerns the same mark, the same applicant and that the goods and/or services listed in the international application are covered by the scope of the basic mark.

[C] Fees Accompanying the Application

The applicant must pay the required fees, namely:

(1) the basic fee whose amount depends on whether the representation of the mark is in black/white or in color. Where the representation of the mark is in color, a higher fee is payable. For international applications filed by applicants whose country of origin is an least-developed country (LDC), in accordance with the list established by the UN, the basic fee is reduced to 10% of the prescribed amount;

(2) an individual fee for each designated Contracting Party that has made the relevant declaration and is designated under the Protocol. However, in the mutual relations between Contracting Parties bound by both the Madrid Agreement and the Protocol, the declaration of individual fees does not apply. For a designation of a Contracting Party which is a State bound also by the Madrid Agreement and the Office of origin is the Office of a State bound also by the Madrid Agreement, a complementary fee is payable (Article 9*sexies* of the Protocol);

(3) where any of the designated Contracting Parties have not made declaration of individual fees, a complementary fee for each designated Contracting Party and a supplementary fee for each class of goods and services in excess of three.

A number of Contracting Parties acting as Office of origin also require the applicant to pay a handling fee for the processing and certification of the international application. This fee must be paid directly to the concerned Office.

A Contracting Party that requires an individual fee may also require that the fee comprises two parts, one part to be paid at the time of filing the international application and the second part to be paid at a later date determined in accordance with the law of the Contracting Party concerned. In practice, the second part will be payable when the Office concerned is satisfied that the mark qualifies for protection. In other words, payment of the second part of the individual fee is analogous to payment of a registration fee in the case of a national application. At the stage of filing the international application, the only practical effect of this requirement is that the amount to be paid corresponds to the first part of the individual fee. The holder will be notified by the International Bureau when the second part of the fee becomes due.[46] For more information on the applicable fees to pay for an international application, *see* the Fee Calculator on WIPO's website (https://madrid.wipo.int/feecalcapp/).

[D] Right of Priority

Priority of an earlier filing may be claimed in the international application under Article 4 of the Paris Convention. That earlier filing will normally be the basic application or the application which resulted in the basic registration. However, it may also be:

(1) another application made either in a country party to the Paris Convention or in a member of the WTO even if the latter is not a party to the Paris Convention; or
(2) an application which, under a bilateral or multilateral treaty concluded between countries of the Paris Union, is equivalent to a regular national filing. On this basis, the International Bureau of WIPO records claims to priority from applications for CTMs filed with the Office for Harmonization in the Internal Market.

[E] Examination by the International Bureau; Registration, Notification and Publication

Upon receipt of the international application, the International Bureau checks whether it complies with the provisions of the Protocol and the Regulations under the Protocol Relating to the Madrid Agreement Concerning the International Registration of Marks (the Regulations under the Protocol).

When the International Bureau is in possession of a correct and complete international application (i.e., which complies with requirements of the Protocol and the Regulations under the Protocol), it proceeds with the registration of the mark in the International Register, its notification to the Contracting Parties in which protection has

46. For more information on the applicable fees to pay for an international application, *see* the Fee Calculator on WIPO's website (madrid.wipo.int/feecalcapp/).

been requested and its publication in the periodical "WIPO Gazette of International Marks." The International Bureau also informs the Office of origin and sends a certificate to the holder.

[1] Irregularities in General

Where the International Bureau considers that there is an irregularity in an international application, it will communicate this fact both to the Office of origin and to the applicant. Whether the responsibility for remedying it lies with the Office or with the applicant will depend on its nature.

The irregularity may be remedied within three months from the date of the notification. If it is not remedied within three months, the international application is considered abandoned. In that case, the International Bureau will refund the fees paid, after deducting an amount corresponding to one half of the basic fee for a mark in black and white.

While the Protocol does not have any provision on *restitutio in integrum*, the Regulations under the Protocol have two provisions that would allow the applicant to request the application to be revived, provided certain conditions are met. It may be possible to request continued processing of an international application where the applicant failed to comply with a time limit in an action before the International Bureau. *See* more on this in Rule 5*bis* in the Regulations under the Protocol. Furthermore, where the failure to meet the time limit in an action before the International Bureau is due to force majeure event, the applicant may be excused under Rule 5 of the Regulations under the Protocol.

[2] Classification of Goods and Services

If the International Bureau considers that, in the application, the goods and services are not grouped in the appropriate class or classes, or if they are not preceded by the number of the class or classes, or if that number is not correct, it will make its own proposal, which it notifies to the Office of origin and copies to the applicant.

If the International Bureau considers that the goods and services indicated in the international application belong to more classes of the International Classification than indicated in the international application, additional supplementary and/or individual fees may be payable to cover the additional classes.

The procedure following the notification of the irregularity is entirely the responsibility of the International Bureau and of the Office of origin which may communicate its opinion on the proposed classification and grouping to the International Bureau. This opinion may originate from or be influenced by the applicant who, following the information which he/she received from the International Bureau, may have intervened with the Office of origin or may have been invited to give their opinion. The Office of origin is, however, not obliged to give an opinion on the proposal.

If the Office of origin gives an opinion on the proposal of the International Bureau, the latter may, having considered this opinion, either withdraw, modify or confirm its proposal. It will notify the Office of origin accordingly and, at the same time, inform the applicant. Where the International Bureau decides to modify its proposal, the communication to that effect will also indicate any change in the amount of any fees due. Where the International Bureau withdraws its proposal, any additional amount previously claimed will not be due and, if already paid, will be reimbursed to the party having paid it.

Any additional fees that may have to be paid as a consequence of the proposed reclassification must be paid:

(1) where the Office of origin has communicated no opinion on the proposal of the International Bureau, within a period of four months from the date of the notification of that proposal; or
(2) where the Office of origin has communicated an opinion, within a period of three months from the date on which the International Bureau notified its decision to modify or confirm its proposal.

If these fees are not paid within the period prescribed, the international application will be considered abandoned. In that case, the International Bureau will notify the Office of origin and inform the applicant accordingly. If the applicant decides to withdraw one or more classes from the international application instead of paying additional fees, such decision should be communicated to the International Bureau by the Office of origin.

Where the International Bureau has made a proposal for the classification and grouping of the goods and services, it will, whether or not an opinion on the proposal has been communicated by the Office of origin, register the mark with the classification and grouping that it considers to be correct.

[3] List of Goods and Services Containing Too Vague, Incomprehensible or Linguistically Incorrect Terms

If the International Bureau considers that a term used in the list of goods and services is too vague for the purposes of classification, is incomprehensible, or is linguistically incorrect, it will notify the Office of origin and inform the applicant at the same time. It may suggest either a substitute term or the deletion of the term.

The Office of origin may, within three months of the notification, make a proposal for remedying the irregularity. The applicant may communicate their views to the Office, or the Office may seek the views of the applicant. If this proposal by the Office is acceptable, or if the Office agrees to accept any suggestion which the International Bureau may have made, the International Bureau will change the term accordingly. If the proposal made by the Office is acceptable but irregular with respect to the classification of goods and services, the procedure described in §20.05[E][2], above, applies.

Where no proposal acceptable to the International Bureau is made within the time limit, there are two possibilities. If the Office of origin has specified the class in which it considers that the term should be classified, the International Bureau will include the term in the international registration just as it appears in the international application, but the international registration will contain an indication to the effect that, in the opinion of the International Bureau, the term is too vague for the purposes of classification, or is incomprehensible, or is linguistically incorrect, as the case may be. If, however, no class has been indicated, the International Bureau will delete the term and will notify the Office of origin and inform the applicant accordingly.

§20.06 THE EFFECTS OF INTERNATIONAL REGISTRATION

[A] Territorial Effect

The international registration has no effect, and cannot have any effect at any time, in the Contracting Party whose Office is the Office of origin. The trademark is protected in that territory under the national or regional application or registration that constitutes the basis for the international registration.

As regards the other Contracting Parties to the Protocol, the effects of the international registration extend to those expressly designated by the applicant in the international application or a subsequent designation, as described in §20.08, below.

[B] Legal Effect

If no refusal is notified to the International Bureau by the designated Contracting Party within the prescribed time limit, or a refusal so notified is not regarded as such or is subsequently withdrawn, the protection of the mark in the Contracting Party concerned is the same, as from the date of the international registration, or the date of the subsequent designation, as if the mark had been registered by the Office of that Contracting Party.

An international registration is therefore equivalent to a bundle of national or regional registrations. Although it is a single registration, protection may be refused by some of the designated Contracting Parties, or the protection may be limited or renounced with respect to some of the designated Contracting Parties. Likewise, an international registration may be transferred to a new owner with respect to only some of the designated Contracting Parties. An international registration may also be invalidated (e.g., for non-use) with respect to one or more of the designated Contracting Parties. Moreover, any action for infringement of an international registration must be brought separately in each of the Contracting Parties concerned.

This is in contrast to a unitary regional right such as the CTM, which cannot be refused, limited or transferred with effect for only a part of the territory covered by the right, and which may be enforced by a single legal action covering infringement occurring anywhere in that territory.

[C] Date of International Registration

The international registration resulting from an international application will, as a rule, bear the date on which the international application was received by the Office of origin. Where, however, the international application is not received by the International Bureau within a period of two months from the date on which it was received by the Office of origin, the international registration will instead bear the date on which the application was actually received by the International Bureau. Certain irregularities may also impact the date of the international registration.

[D] Validity of International Registration

Under the Protocol, registration of the mark is effected for ten years from the date of international registration, with the possibility of renewal for further periods of ten years.

[E] Link Between the International Registration and the Basic Mark

For a period of five years from the date of the international registration, the protection resulting from the international registration remains dependent on the basic mark. The protection resulting from the international registration may no longer be invoked if, or to the extent that, the basic registration, or the registration resulting from the basic application is canceled, renounced, revoked, invalidated or has lapsed, or if the basic application is the subject of a final decision of rejection or is withdrawn, either within that five-year period or as a result of an action commenced within that period. This dependence is absolute, and is effective regardless of the reasons why the basic application is rejected or is withdrawn or the basic registration ceases to enjoy, in whole or in part, legal protection.

Under the Protocol, there is an increased risk of the holder who chooses to base the international registration on an application with the Office of origin losing their protection as a result of the basic application ceasing to have effect. The basic application may be refused protection, totally or partially, on absolute grounds or because of the existence of a prior right cited ex officio in the examination procedure, or as a result of an opposition by the holder of such earlier right in that territory. In all these cases, and provided the decision in respect of the basic application is final (i.e., no longer subject to review or appeal), the Office of origin is required to request the International Bureau to cancel the international registration, either totally or partially.

In order to soften the consequences of the five-year dependency feature of the Madrid System, the Protocol provides for the holder of an international registration which is canceled as a result of the ceasing of effect of the basic mark, within three months of the date of the cancellation of the international registration in the International Register, for registration of the same mark with the Offices of all Contracting Parties where the international registration had effect. The national or regional applications resulting from this so-called transformation are treated as if they had been filed on the date of the l international registration, or the date of the subsequent designation.

On the expiration of the period of five years from the date of the international registration, the latter becomes independent of the basic mark, and the protection resulting from the international registration is therefore no longer affected, in other Contracting Parties, by loss of protection in the Contracting Party of origin.

§20.07 EXAMINATION BY THE OFFICE OF A DESIGNATED CONTRACTING PARTY; REFUSAL AND GRANT OF PROTECTION

The Office of a designated Contracting Party examines the international registration in exactly the same way as an application filed directly with that Office. If grounds for objection are found during the ex officio examination, or if an opposition is filed, the Office has the right to refuse protection of the mark in that Contracting Party, in accordance with its national or regional legislation.

[A] Grounds for Refusal

The refusal may be based on any grounds that are supported by a provision of the Paris Convention, or that are not prohibited by a provision of the Convention, and any such refusal will generally be subject to review or appeal, depending upon the laws and practice of the Contracting Party concerned.

At the same time, a Contracting Party may not refuse protection of an international registration, even partially, on the ground that the applicable legislation permits registration only in a limited number of classes or for a limited number of goods or services. Even if that legislation requires that an application made directly to that Office must be in one class only, the Office must accept that an international registration may be protected in that Contracting Party where it relates to several (or even all) classes of goods and services.

Moreover, since the International Bureau will already have established, before notifying the designation to the Contracting Party, that all applicable formal requirements of the Protocol and the Regulations under the Protocol have been complied with, an Office should therefore never have occasion to raise objections on formal or presentational grounds.

Nor is it appropriate for an Office to object to the classification of the goods and services in the international registration. Even if an Office disagrees with the classification (which will have been approved by the International Bureau), an objection on such grounds would have no effect, since the classification in the International Register remains unchanged. An Office may use its own interpretation of the classification, for example, in order to carry out a search for earlier conflicting marks. Furthermore, it is explicitly provided that the indication of the classes does not bind Contracting Parties with regard to the determination of the scope of the protection of the mark.

An Office may object if it considers that a term is too broad or too vague; such objection might take the form of a partial refusal, resulting in the replacement of the broad or vague term by a more narrow or precise term in the entry in the International Register as it applies to that Contracting Party—in effect, a limitation of protection for that Contracting Party.

[B] Time Limit for Refusal

Any provisional refusal must be notified to the International Bureau by the Office of the Contracting Party concerned within the time limit specified in the Protocol. This standard time limit is one year. A Contracting Party may however declare that, when it is designated under the Protocol, this time limit shall be replaced by eighteen months. A Contracting Party that has made this declaration may further declare that a provisional refusal based on an opposition may be notified even after the expiry of this eighteen-month period.

Notwithstanding the general principle that the Protocol is the applicable treaty, a declaration extending the refusal period to eighteen months or more is rendered inoperative in the mutual relations between States bound by both treaties. What this means, in effect, is that in the case of an international registration where the Office of the Contracting Party of the holder is bound by both treaties, a designation of a Contracting Party bound by both treaties will, be subject to the standard refusal regime—that is, the time limit of one year for the notification of a provisional refusal, notwithstanding that the designated Contracting Party in question may have declared an extended period for notifying a provisional refusal.

[C] Procedure for Refusal of Protection

The notification of refusal of protection must be sent by the Office concerned to the International Bureau, together with all the grounds on which the provisional refusal is based and with a reference to the corresponding essential provisions of the national law.

The provisional refusal is recorded in the International Register and published in the Gazette, and a copy is transmitted to the holder of the international registration.

Where the holder of an international registration receives, through the International Bureau, a notification of refusal, he/she has the same rights and remedies as if the mark had been deposited directly with the Office that issued the notification of refusal. The international registration is, therefore, with respect to the Contracting Party concerned, subject to the same procedures as would apply to an application for registration filed with the Office of that Contracting Party. Any procedure subsequent to the refusal, such as review, appeal or response to an opposition, is carried out directly between the holder and the Office concerned, without any involvement on the part of the International Bureau.

However, once all the procedures before that Office have been completed, the Office must send to the International Bureau a final statement. Depending upon the outcome of the case, such statement will confirm either that protection for the mark has been totally refused, or that protection has been partially or totally granted to the mark, as the case may be.

Where, before the expiry of the refusal period, all the procedures before an Office have been completed and the Office has found no grounds to refuse protection, the Office shall, as soon as possible (and before the expiry of the refusal period), send to the International Bureau a statement to the effect that protection is granted to the mark.

The statements mentioned above, are recorded in the International Register and published in the Gazette. The copies thereof are transmitted by the International Bureau to the holder of the international registration.

§20.08 SUBSEQUENT DESIGNATION

The effects of an international registration can be extended to any Contracting Party by filing a subsequent designation, unless the Contracting Party has made the declaration under Article 14(5). Thus, the holder of an international registration can expand the geographical scope of the protection of their mark in line with their business needs. Moreover, a subsequent designation may be made in order to extend the protection of the mark to a Contracting Party which was not a party to the Protocol at the time of the filing of the international application.

Where protection has initially been refused, it is possible to later make a subsequent designation if the ground for refusal no longer applies.

The recording of a subsequent designation has the same effect as the international registration in those Contracting Parties for which it is requested. The grant or refusal of protection, by a designated Contracting Party, of a subsequent designation follows the same procedures as for the grant or refusal of protection of a designation contained in the international application. The time limit for a Contracting Party to notify a refusal of protection starts from the date on which the International Bureau has notified the subsequent designation to the Office of that Contracting Party.

§20.09 CHANGES AFFECTING THE INTERNATIONAL REGISTRATION

Various changes may be recorded in the International Register during the validity of the international registration: total or partial change in ownership of the registration, limitation of the list of goods and services for one or more Contracting Parties, renunciation of protection in one or more Contracting Parties, change of name or address of the holder or his/her representative, partial or total cancellation of the registration, recording of a license, etc. Information concerning such changes is published in the Gazette and notified to the designated Contracting Parties.

At the same time, some types of requests for recording of a change cannot be accepted. Such is the case, for example, of a request for a change in the reproduction of the mark as registered or for the addition of new goods or services to the list of goods and services entered in the International Register. In such cases, a new international application has to be submitted.

As for the correction of errors affecting an international registration, this can be done at any time if the error is attributable to the International Bureau. Where an error is attributable to a national or regional Office, there are two separate cases. Correction can be made at any time if it would not affect the rights deriving from the international registration. However, where the correction would affect the rights deriving from the international registration, the request for correction must reach the International Bureau, at the latest, within nine months after the publication containing the error.

§20.10 RENEWAL

An international registration is effective for ten years, as described above. It may be renewed for further periods of ten years on payment of the prescribed fees.

If a provisional refusal is recorded in the International Register with respect to a particular Contracting Party for all the goods and services covered by the international registration, the holder may nevertheless request the renewal of this international registration with respect to that Contracting Party. Such renewal must then be for all the classes covered by that designation concerned. The holder may wish to renew such designation that has been initially refused because at the time of renewal there may still be pending a judicial or administrative procedure in respect of such refusal. The rights of the holder need to be preserved where the refusal was the subject of an appeal and no final decision had been taken by the date on which the renewal was due.

As from February 1, 2020, international registrations will be renewed in respect of a designated Contracting Party for all the goods and services not affected by limitation, partial invalidation or partial cancellation. However, for Contracting Parties that have declared for an individual fee per class, the renewal fee will be calculated taking into account only the number of classes for which protection has been granted in a statement recorded under Rule 18*ter* of the Regulations under the Protocol (final or further decision).

Upon renewal, holders of international registrations who have been granted partial protection in a statement under Rule 18*ter* of the Regulations under the Protocol and are appealing such decision will no longer be required to pay individual fees for classes that are not protected. Where a designated Contracting Party that has declared for an individual fee per class informs in a further statement under Rule 18*ter* of a change in the goods and services protected, the next renewal fee in respect of that Contracting Party will be calculated in accordance with this further statement.

Changes to the goods and services for which protection has been granted in a designated Contracting Party will not have retroactive effect on renewal fees that have already been paid in accordance with Rule 34(6)(a) of the Regulations under the Protocol.

Holders will continue to have the options of not renewing an international registration in respect of some of the designated Contracting Parties, or renewing it in respect of designated Contracting Parties that have refused protection for all goods and services in a statement under Rule 18*ter* of the Regulations under the Protocol. In the latter case, an amendment to Rule 30(2)(b) clarifies that the international registration must be renewed in respect of that designated Contracting Party for all the goods and services concerned.

The situation is different with respect to an invalidation, since the recording of an invalidation in the International Register means that the invalidation is no longer subject to appeal. The international registration therefore may not be renewed with respect to a Contracting Party for which a total invalidation has been recorded. Nor may it be renewed with respect to a Contracting Party for which a renunciation of protection has been recorded. In the case of a partial invalidation, a limitation of the list of goods and services with respect to a particular Contracting Party, or a partial cancellation with respect to all designated Contracting Parties, renewal may not be effected with respect to those goods and services to which the invalidation, limitation or cancellation relate.

[A] Unofficial Reminders

Six months before the expiry of the ten-year term of protection, the International Bureau, by sending an unofficial notice, reminds the holder of the international registration of the exact date of expiry. If the holder does not receive such unofficial notice, this does not constitute an excuse for failure to comply with any time limit for payment of the fees due. The unofficial notice will list all the designated Contracting Parties in respect of which no total refusal or invalidation is recorded in the International Register, or which have not been renounced.

[B] Renewal and Fees

Renewal is effected by simple payment of the required fees. The latter are the same as those for the international registration.

As from November 1, 2022, amendments to Rule 30(1)(b) of the Regulations under the Protocol will allow holders to renew their international registrations as early as six months before the expiry date, up from three months. In addition, the International Bureau of WIPO will inscribe the renewal of the international registration, issue the corresponding renewal certificate and notify the designated Contracting Parties as soon as it confirms that the holder has paid the required fees, instead of waiting until the expiry date to inscribe the said renewal.

The amendments and change in practice described above, will not affect the new period of validity of the international registration. The new period of validity of the international registration will continue to be ten years counted from the expiry of the preceding period, as prescribed in Article 7(1) of the Protocol.

Changes recorded after the renewal of the international registration has been inscribed cannot be taken into account retroactively. For example, a cancellation or an invalidation recorded after the renewal of the international registration has been inscribed will not result in a retroactive recalculation of the renewal fees.

Holders who request the recording of a subsequent designation between the date on which the renewal has been inscribed and the date of expiry of the current period of validity must request a complementary renewal and pay the corresponding renewal fees for the newly subsequently designated Contracting Parties. In accordance with Rule 24(3)(c)(ii) of the Regulations under the Protocol, holders will continue to have the option to request that the subsequent designation take effect at the start of the new period of validity of the international registration to avoid paying renewal fees for the newly subsequently designated Contracting Parties.

The fees should be paid to the International Bureau by, at the latest, the date of expiry of the international registration concerned. The payment can still be made up to six months after the date on which the renewal was due, provided that a surcharge (which amounts to 50% of the basic fee for renewal) is paid at the same time.

[C] Nature and Effect of Renewal

Since renewal is considered to be a simple prolongation of the period of protection of the international registration against payment of the necessary fees, it may not include any change in relation to the international registration in its latest form, that is at the expiry of the current period of protection. Therefore, no change in the name or address of the holder or in the list of goods and services may be made as part of the renewal procedure. Any such changes which the holder wishes to have recorded in the International Register when the registration is renewed must be communicated separately to the International Bureau according to the applicable procedures. They will be included in the data recorded at renewal provided they are recorded in the International Register no later than the date of expiry of the international registration.

§20.11 PUBLIC INFORMATION ABOUT INTERNATIONAL APPLICATIONS AND REGISTRATIONS

New international registrations, renewals, subsequent designations and modifications affecting existing registrations, as well as grants of protection, refusals and invalidations are published every week in the WIPO Gazette which is available online. The Gazette also contains information of general interest such as declarations and notifications made by Contracting Parties under the Protocol or the Regulations under the Protocol regarding particular requirements, or the amounts of individual fees under the Protocol.

The current status of all international registrations in force, including data relating to international applications and subsequent designations under examination by the International Bureau, is published by the International Bureau online on the Madrid Monitor (which has replaced ROMARIN). Madrid Monitor is a new service provided by WIPO combining the search, WIPO Gazette, Madrid E-alert, Designation status, Madrid Realtime status tools into a single, simple tool. The "designation status" tab in Madrid Monitor allows you to easily check the status of protection of an international registration in designated Contracting Parties, you can download unofficial certificates of protection and more. *See* more https://www3.wipo.int/madrid/monitor/en/.

The only official publication remains the Gazette and the only official statements by the International Bureau regarding the contents of the International Register for a given international registration remain the certified extracts from the Register established on request by the International Bureau.

§20.12 MEMBERSHIP

As of September 1, 2023, 55 States were party to the Madrid Agreement; as of that same date, 112 States and two IGOs (the OAPI and the EU) were party to the Protocol.[47]

47. For more information on which Contracting Parties are also members of the Madrid Agreement, *see* www.wipo.int/export/sites/www/treaties/en/docs/pdf/madrid_marks.pdf.

CHAPTER 21

The Hague Agreement Concerning the International Registration of Industrial Designs

§21.01 INTRODUCTION

On November 6, 1925, the Hague Agreement Concerning the International Deposit of Industrial Designs was adopted within the framework of the Paris Convention for the Protection of Industrial Property. This agreement, which entered into force on June 1, 1928, has been revised and supplemented several times. It is now referred to as the Hague Agreement Concerning the International Registration of Industrial Designs (hereinafter "the Hague Agreement"). Taking into account the freeze of the application of the London (1934) Act of the Hague Agreement Concerning the International Deposit of Industrial Designs (hereinafter referred to as "the 1934 Act"), two Acts of the Hague Agreement are currently in force: the Hague (1960) Act and the Geneva (1999) Act (hereinafter referred to as "the 1960 Act" and "the 1999 Act," respectively). These two Acts are autonomous and totally independent of each other. In other words, each of them in itself constitutes a fully fledged international treaty.

The 1999 Act was adopted on July 2, 1999, by the Diplomatic Conference for the Adoption of a New Act of the Hague Agreement Concerning the International Deposit of Industrial Designs, which was convened by WIPO and held in Geneva from June 16-July 16, 1999. The 1999 Act aims at making the system more responsive to the needs of users and facilitating the accession of Contracting Parties whose industrial design laws do not permit them to accede to the 1960 Act, in particular Contracting Parties with substantive examination systems and IGOs. The Hague System is expected to become a single treaty system in the near future that is solely governed by the 1999 Act.

§21.02 THE PRINCIPLE OF INTERNATIONAL REGISTRATION

The Hague Agreement offers the possibility of obtaining protection for one or more industrial designs in a number of States and/or IGOs (both referred to as "Contracting Parties") through a single application filed with the International Bureau of WIPO.

The registration that ensues from the international application can be centrally managed at WIPO, as far as changes and renewals are concerned, which constitutes an advantage for the user.

The applicant is thus relieved of the need to make a separate national application in each of the territories in which protection is sought, thus avoiding the inherent complication of procedures that vary from one State or IGO to another. The ability to centrally manage international registrations represents a long-term advantage for users.

§21.03 MAIN PROVISIONS OF THE HAGUE AGREEMENT

An international application may be filed by any natural or legal person being a national of a Contracting Party or a Member State of an IGO, or having a domicile or a real and effective industrial or commercial establishment in the territory of a Contracting Party. In addition, but only under the 1999 Act, any natural or legal person having a habitual residence in the territory of a Contracting Party may file an international application.

An international application does not require any prior national application or registration. It can be made directly with the International Bureau of WIPO by the applicant or the applicant's representative on the official application form provided by the International Bureau or through the electronic filing interface ("eHague") available on the website of WIPO. A few Contracting Parties, however, offer the possibility for their users to file indirectly through their Office.

The applicant enjoys the priority right afforded under Article 4 of the Paris Convention for the Protection of Industrial Property if the applicant claims this right and if the international application is made within six months of the first national, regional or international application made in, or having effect in, a State party to the Paris Convention or, under the 1999 Act only, any Member of the WTO. Conversely, a Hague application may serve as a priority application in jurisdictions not covered by the application.

A single international application may comprise several designs, up to a maximum of hundred. All designs must, however, belong to the same class of the International Classification of Industrial Designs (the Locarno Classification). However, under the 1999 Act, Contracting Parties may notify, in a declaration to the Director General of WIPO, that their domestic law has special requirements concerning unity of design. If a Contracting Party with such a requirement is designated and this requirement is not complied with, the Office concerned may refuse protection in its territory pending compliance through a procedure before that Office.

The international application is subject to the payment of fees, in Swiss francs. Three types of fees must be paid: a basic fee, a publication fee and, for each designated Contracting Party, either a standard fee or an individual fee.

The working languages of the Hague Agreement are English, French and Spanish. An international application may be filed in either of these languages, at the choice of the applicant. The recording in the International Register and the publication in the International Designs Bulletin ("the Bulletin") of the international registrations and of any changes affecting them is in English, French and Spanish. Any communication addressed by the International Bureau of WIPO to the applicant or holder is in the language in which the international application was filed (unless the applicant or holder has expressed the wish that all such communications be in English, or be in French or be in Spanish).

The international registration shall, from the date of the international registration, have at least the same effect in each Contracting Party, designated by the applicant, as a regularly filed application for the grant of protection of the industrial design under the law of the Contracting Party. If no refusal is notified by a given designated Contracting Party within the prescribed time limit (or if such refusal has subsequently been withdrawn), the international registration shall have the same effect as a grant of protection for the industrial design, under the law of that Contracting Party.

International registrations are published in the Bulletin which is published electronically on the website of WIPO. Relevant data concerning international registrations, such as the reproductions of the industrial designs, are notably published in the Bulletin.

In terms of timing of the publication of an international registration, the applicant may choose between different options. An international registration is by default published twelve months after the date of the international registration. The applicant may, however, request that the international registration be published immediately after the registration or at any time before the standard publication period of twelve months. The applicant may also request that publication of the international registration be deferred beyond the standard publication period of twelve months. Under the 1999 Act, the general principle is that each Contracting Party is assumed to permit the prescribed period of deferment of thirty months from the filing date or, where priority is claimed, from the priority date, unless it has notified, in a declaration to the Director General of WIPO, that it authorizes only a shorter period, or that it does not authorize deferment at all. If a Contracting Party that made such a declaration is designated, the applicant cannot request deferred publication beyond the period indicated in that declaration. The possible maximum deferment period that the applicant may request depends therefore on the Contracting Parties designated in the international application. Moreover, unless immediate publication was requested at the time of filing, the holder has the possibility to request the publication of the international registration at any time before the expiration of the publication period initially specified in the international application.

The Hague Agreement offers the possibility for the Office of each designated Contracting Party to refuse protection, in its territory, to an industrial design which does not fulfill the substantive conditions of protection provided for by its domestic law. Refusals may be based on an objection resulting from the ex officio examination carried out by the Office or an opposition lodged by a third party. Refusals may only be issued on the grounds provided for by the domestic law other than formal requirements, since such requirements are to be considered as already been satisfied following the formal examination carried out by the International Bureau.

A refusal of protection must be notified to the International Bureau of WIPO within six months from the date of publication of the international registration in the Bulletin. Under the 1999 Act only, any Contracting Party whose Office is an Examining Office, or whose law provides for opposition proceedings, may declare that the refusal period of six months is replaced by a period of twelve months. A refusal of protection is notified to the International Bureau of WIPO by the Office of the designated Contracting Party concerned. The International Bureau records the refusal in the International Register, publishes it in the Bulletin and transmits a copy of the notification of refusal to the holder of the international registration concerned. The latter has the same rights and remedies (such as review of, or appeal against, the refusal) as if the industrial design had been filed directly with the Office that issued the notification of refusal. If no refusal is notified by the Office of a designated Contracting Party within the prescribed time limit (or if such refusal has subsequently been withdrawn), the international registration has the same effect as a grant of protection for the industrial design under the law of that Contracting Party.

The international registration is effected for an initial term of five years from the date of the international registration. The international registration may be renewed for at least one additional five-year period under the 1960 Act (ten years in total) or two additional five-year periods under the 1999 Act (fifteen years in total). In both cases, however, and provided that the law of a designated Contracting Party provides for a duration of more than the minimum period of ten or fifteen years for an industrial design for which protection has been granted under that law, the duration of protection shall, provided that the international registration is renewed, be the same as that provided for by the law of that Contracting Party.

§21.04 BENEFITS OF ACCESSION TO THE HAGUE AGREEMENT

Through the Hague Agreement, industrial designs contained in a single international application can be protected in a number of Contracting Parties with a minimum of formalities and expenses. In particular, one of the main features of the Hague Agreement is to relieve applicants of the need to file separate national or regional applications in each of the countries or IGOs where they seek protection and therefore to avoid complications that may arise from different procedures in different jurisdictions. In addition, changes concerning the international registration and renewals of it are centrally managed so that holders do not have to deal with different procedures with different Offices or to monitor different deadlines.

The simplification of the formalities and the reduction of the cost of obtaining protection abroad favorably influence the development of foreign trade. Domestic manufacturers and traders are encouraged to apply for protection of their industrial designs in Contracting Parties to the Hague Agreement, and to export their products to those Contracting Parties.

The manufacturers and traders in other Contracting Parties to the Hague Agreement are, in turn, able to protect their industrial designs more easily in Contracting Parties to the Hague Agreement and thus have more incentive to export their products to those Contracting Parties. The result is growth in trade and an increased likelihood of new industrial and commercial activities being set up on the territory of any Contracting Party, thus promoting its economic development.

A part of the fees paid by the applicants is distributed each year, by the International Bureau, to the competent authorities of the Contracting Parties to the Hague Agreement. To improve access to the Hague Agreement for applicants whose sole entitlement is a connection with an LDC or with an IGO the majority of whose Member States are LDCs, the fees have been reduced to 10% of the amounts prescribed in the Schedule of Fees.

The Offices of the Contracting Parties have no specific tasks in the implementation of the Hague Agreement, except those whose domestic or regional legislation permits the international application to be filed through them or lays down an examination procedure for industrial designs when they are designated. Under the 1999 Act, international applications are in general filed directly with the International Bureau of WIPO, and primarily through eHague.

A list of Contracting Parties to the Hague Agreement is to be found in the appropriate document inserted in the back flap of this volume. Further information concerning the system of international registration of industrial designs, including helpful user guidance, an updated list of Contracting Parties and the fees, the last annual statistics and the full texts of the 1960 Act, the 1999 Act, the Common Regulations Under the 1999 Act and the 1960 Act of the Hague Agreement and the Administrative Instructions for the Application of the Hague Agreement, is also available on the website of WIPO (www.wipo.int/hague).

§21.05 FREEZE AND TERMINATION OF THE 1934 ACT

The Contracting States to the 1934 Act have decided to freeze the application of the 1934 Act, with effect from January 1, 2010. By consequence, it is no longer possible to file international deposits or to record new designations in the International Register under this Act. While this freeze was without prejudice to the continuation in force of designations recorded in the International Register before the effective date of the freeze, the last designations governed by the 1934 Act will expire at the end of 2024. In addition, the Contracting Parties to the 1934 Act decided to terminate the 1934 Act, which became effective on October 18, 2016.

§21.06 MEMBERSHIP

As of August 1, 2023, seventy-seven States and two IGOs (OAPI and the EU) were party to the Hague Agreement. The Hague System thus covers ninety-six countries.

CHAPTER 22

The Trademark Law Treaty

§22.01 INTRODUCTION

The TLT was adopted on October 27, 1994, at a Diplomatic Conference in Geneva. The purpose of the TLT is to simplify and harmonize the administrative procedures in respect of national applications and the protection of marks. Individual countries may become party to the Treaty as well as IGOs which maintain an office for the registration of trademarks with effects in the territory of its Member States such as the EU and the OAPI. The provisions of the Treaty are supplemented by the Regulations and Model International Forms. The Treaty does not deal with the substantive parts of trademark law covering the registration of marks.

§22.02 PROVISIONS OF THE TREATY

[A] Marks to Which the Treaty Applies

According to Article 2, the Treaty applies only to marks consisting of visible signs. Sound marks, olfactory marks and holographic marks are explicitly excluded. As for three-dimensional marks, the Treaty applies to them only if a Contracting Party accepted those marks for registration at the time of joining the TLT.

The Treaty is applicable to trademarks and service marks, but not to collective marks, certification marks or guarantee marks: such marks can be subject to special conditions that are not provided for in the Treaty. As for associated marks, defensive marks and derivative marks, Article 21 of the Treaty provides that any State or IGO may, by means of a reservation, declare that the provisions of certain articles of the Treaty are not applicable to such marks.

[B] Applications

Article 3 of the Treaty contains an exhaustive list of information and elements which may be required by an Office in respect of an application for the registration of a trademark. Such indications are, for example, the name and address of the applicant and of the representative, if any, a declaration of priority if priority of an earlier application is claimed, one or more reproductions of the mark depending on the colors or dimensions of the mark, names of the goods or services for which registration is sought grouped according to the classes of the Nice Classification, or a declaration of intention to use the mark or of actual use. No Office may require other information than that referred to in the Treaty, such as an extract from a Commercial Register, an indication that the applicant is carrying on an industrial or commercial activity or that the applicant is carrying on an activity corresponding to the goods or services listed in the application.

The same application may relate to several goods or services. According to Article 6 of Treaty, the Office must accept the application irrespective of whether the goods or services belong to several classes of the Nice Classification. In this case the application must lead to a single registration.

An Office cannot refuse an application in writing on paper if it is on a form corresponding to the model application form contained in the Regulations.

[C] Representation

Article 4 of the Treaty allows a Contracting Party to require that the representative of an applicant or a holder is a representative admitted to practice before its Office and that a person who has neither a domicile nor a real and effective industrial or commercial establishment on its territory be represented by a representative. According to this provision the power of attorney may relate to several existing or future applications or registrations.

[D] Filing Date

The according of a filing date is essential in view of the rights which come into existence on that date and in view of the possibility of claiming a right of priority effective from the said date in respect of successive applications in other countries. Article 5 of the Treaty provides for the maximum information that an Office may require for the according of a filing date. These include the identification of the applicant, information sufficient to contact the applicant or his/her representative, a reproduction of the mark, a list of the goods and services for which registration is sought, etc. In addition, for according a filing date, an Office may require the payment of a fee if the national trademark law applied this condition before the country adhered to the Treaty.

If registration of a trademark is refused in respect of certain goods or services, Article 7 of the Treaty provides that the applicant can divide the application in order to avoid any delay in obtaining registration for the trademark on the goods or services that have not been refused and still keep the filing date of the initial application or the priority date, if any. At the same time the applicant may proceed with an appeal regarding the application concerning the goods or services which have been refused.

[E] Signature

Article 8 of the TLT contains provisions in respect of the signature and other means allowing the identification of the source of a communication such as the filing of an application to the Office, in particular where the transmission of the communication is by electronic means. Instead of a handwritten signature, the Office may accept a printed or stamped signature or the use of a seal. Of special importance is the prohibition of requirements for the attestation, notarization, authentication, legalization or other certification of the signature, except where the signature concerns the surrender of a registration, if such an exception is prescribed in the national law.

[F] Changes and Corrections Concerning Applications and Registrations

The TLT sets forth in Articles 10 and 11 the requirements that apply to a request for the recordal of change in names, addresses and ownership. Article 12 contains the maximum requirements that an Office may request for the correction of mistakes made by an applicant or holder in any communication to the Office, which is reflected in the register. The provisions in Articles 10-12 apply equally to changes or corrections in respect of applications and registrations. These provisions provide that a single request is sufficient even where the changes or corrections relate to several applications or registrations of the same parties. The request must clearly identify the present relevant information held by the Office and the changes or corrections requested. The Office may not ask for further information than that mentioned in the Treaty, except where the Office may reasonably doubt the veracity of the information received, for example if it suspects that a change in name and address is in fact a change in ownership. In particular, the Office is not allowed to require the furnishing of any certificate concerning the change of a name or address, indications to the effect that the new owner carries on an activity corresponding to the goods or services affected by the change in ownership, or that the holder transferred his/her business to the new owner.

In case of a request of the recordal of change in ownership the Office may, according to Article 11, require a certified copy or extract of the contract, a certificate of transfer and a document of transfer. Where the change in ownership results from a merger or from an operation of law or a court decision, for example in case of inheritance or bankruptcy, the Office may require that the request be accompanied by a certified copy of a document evidencing the change in ownership.

A mistake made by the Office must be corrected ex officio or upon request.

[G] Duration and Renewal of Registration

Article 13 of the TLT provides for a duration of ten years for the initial period of registration of the trademark with a possibility of renewal for further ten-year periods. With respect to renewal, the provision enumerates the maximum requirements that an Office can impose. In particular, the Office may not, for the purposes of effecting the renewal, examine the registration as to the substance or request a reproduction of the mark or the furnishing of evidence concerning use of the mark.

[H] Other Provisions in the Treaty

In case of the intention to refuse a request for the recordal of a change in names, addresses and ownership or a request for the correction of a mistake or for renewal, the Office must, according to Article 14, give the requesting part an opportunity to make observations on the intended refusal within a reasonable time limit.

In general, where the Treaty sets forth the maximum requirements that an Office may request in respect of the application, power of attorney, requests for changes, correction and renewal, the Office is entitled to require evidence or further evidence if it may reasonably doubt the veracity of any indication contained in the request or in any document accompanying it.

The Treaty further allows a Contracting Party to require that any application or request filed with its Office must be submitted in the language, or in one of the languages, admitted by it.

[I] Compliance with Other Conventions

The TLT contains no obligations for a Contracting Party to be party to other international conventions. However, it provides in Article 15 that Contracting Parties must comply with the provisions in the Paris Convention which concern marks. Article 9 obliges Contracting Parties to refer by name to the goods and services specified in the registration of the mark and in any publication of an application or registration relating to a mark. It also requires that the relevant class number(s), as established by the Nice Classification, be indicated, and that the goods and services belonging to the same class be grouped together under the corresponding class number.

[J] Regulations and Model International Forms

The provisions of the TLT are supplemented by the Regulations, which provide rules concerning details useful in the implementation of the provisions on administrative requirements and procedures according to the Treaty. The rules apply to the requirements in respect of applications, representation, filing date, signature, duration, renewal, the manner of indicating names and addresses, and the identification of an application without its application number. The rules prescribe, for example, the number of reproductions of the mark that should accompany the application, time limits concerning the payment of fees and other communications to the Office such as the filing of the power of attorney, invitation to make corrections in case of noncompliance.

The Regulations also contain eight Model International Forms which concern the filing of an application, the requests for renewal, recordal of change in names, addresses and ownership, correction of mistakes, appointment of representative, certificates of transfer and transfer documents. Some of the elements contained in these forms cannot or de facto are not required under the national or regional law applicable by the Office concerned. Where this is the case, the national or regional Office should prepare an "Individualized International Form" where reference to inapplicable elements should be omitted. This form must not contain mandatory requirements additional to or contrary to the Treaty or the Regulations. By using the Model International Forms or the Individualized International Forms, applicants and other parties are assured that no Office of a Contracting Party can refuse an application or a request in accordance with the forms.

[K] Transitional Provisions

Article 22 provided a number of transitional provisions allowing Contracting Parties to declare that some of the obligations deriving from the Treaty will not be applicable to them. Such declarations concerned, for example, the multiple class application system, prohibition of requirements concerning certification of signature of an application and a power of attorney, furnishing of a declaration and/or evidence concerning use on the occasion of renewal of a trademark registration and substantive examination on the occasion of the renewal. Article 22 contained a clause in accordance with which any such declaration would lose its effect on October 28, 2004.

[L] Membership

As of August 1, 2023, fifty-four States were party to the TLT.[48]

48. Regularly updated information on TLT membership can be found at www.wipo.int/treaties/en/ip/tlt/.

CHAPTER 23
The Singapore Treaty on the Law of Trademarks

§23.01 OBJECTIVE AND SCOPE OF THE SINGAPORE TREATY

The objective of the Singapore Treaty on the Law of Trademarks (hereinafter the "Singapore Treaty") is to create a modern and dynamic international framework for the harmonization of administrative trademark registration procedures. Building on the TLT of 1994, the Singapore Treaty has a wider scope of application and addresses more recent developments in the field of communication technologies.

The Singapore Treaty is applicable to all types of marks registrable under the law of a given Contracting Party.

Contracting Parties are free to choose the means of communication with their offices (including communications in electronic form or by electronic means of transmittal).

Relief measures in respect of time limits as well as provisions on the recording of trademark licenses were introduced, and an Assembly of the Contracting Parties established.

However, other provisions of the Singapore Treaty (such as the requirements to provide for multiclass applications and registrations and the use of the International ("Nice") Classification) closely follow the TLT.

§23.02 ADVANCES OF THE SINGAPORE TREATY AS COMPARED TO THE TLT

The two treaties are separate and may be ratified or adhered to independently.

Unlike the TLT, the Singapore Treaty applies generally to all marks that can be registered under the law of a Contracting Party. Most significantly, it is the first international instrument dealing with trademark law to explicitly recognize non-traditional marks. The Treaty is applicable to all types of marks, including non-traditional visible marks, such as holograms, three-dimensional marks, color, position and movement marks, as well as non-visible marks such as sound, olfactory or taste and feel marks. It should be noted that the STLT does not provide the form of representation of these types of marks.

Rule 3 of the Singapore Treaty provides for the mode of representation of all visible marks as well as sound marks. The details concerning the representation of other non-visible marks are prescribed by the law of the Contracting Party concerned.

§23.03 COMMUNICATION

The Singapore Treaty leaves Contracting Parties the freedom to choose the form and means of transmittal of communications and whether to accept communications on paper, in electronic form or in another form. This has consequences on formal requirements for applications and requests, such as the signature on communications with the office. The Treaty maintains a very important provision of the TLT, namely that the authentication, certification or attestation of any signature on paper communications cannot be required. However, Contracting Parties are free to determine whether and how they wish to implement a system of authentication of electronic communications.

§23.04 RELIEF MEASURES

The Treaty provides for relief measures when an applicant or holder has missed a time limit in an action for a procedure before an office. Contracting Parties must make available, at their choice, at least one of the following relief measures after the expiration of the time limit concerned:

- extension of the time limit;
- continued processing; and
- reinstatement of rights in so far as the failure to meet the time limit was unintentional or occurred in spite of due care required by the circumstances.

§23.05 OTHER PROVISIONS

The Singapore Treaty includes provisions on the recording of trademark licenses, and establishes maximum requirements for requests for recordal, amendment or cancellation of the recordal of a license.

The creation of an Assembly of the Contracting Parties introduced a degree of flexibility in defining the details of administrative procedures to be implemented by national trademark offices, where it is anticipated that future developments in trademark registration procedures and practices will warrant amendments to those details. The Assembly is endowed with powers to modify the Regulations and the Model

International Forms, where necessary, and can also address—at a preliminary level—questions relating to the future development of the Treaty.

Furthermore, the Diplomatic Conference adopted a Resolution Supplementary to the Singapore Treaty and the Regulations thereunder, with a view to declaring an understanding by the Contracting Parties on several areas covered by the Treaty, namely, that the Treaty does not impose any obligations on Contracting Parties to:

(i) register new types of marks; or
(ii) implement electronic filing systems or other automation systems.

The Resolution also contains special provisions to provide developing and least-developed countries with additional technical assistance and technological support to enable them to take full advantage of the provisions of the Treaty. It was recognized that LDCs shall be the primary and main beneficiaries of technical assistance by Contracting Parties. The Assembly monitors and evaluates, at every ordinary session, the progress of the assistance granted.

§23.06 DISPUTES

Any dispute arising in relation to the interpretation or application of the Treaty is to be settled amicably through consultation and mediation under the auspices of the Director General of WIPO.

§23.07 MEMBERSHIP

The Singapore Treaty was concluded in 2006 and entered into force in 2009. As of August 1, 2023, fifty-four States and two IGOs (OAPI and the Benelux Organization for Intellectual Property (BOIP)) were party to the Singapore Treaty.[49]

49. Regularly updated information about membership of the Singapore Treaty can be found at www.wipo.int/treaties/en/ip/singapore/.

CHAPTER 24
The Lisbon Agreement for the Protection of Appellations of Origin and Their International Registration and the Geneva Act of the Lisbon Agreement on Appellations of Origin and Geographical Indications (The "Lisbon System")

§24.01 THE LISBON AGREEMENT FOR THE PROTECTION OF APPELLATIONS OF ORIGIN AND THEIR INTERNATIONAL REGISTRATION

The Lisbon Agreement for the Protection of Appellations of Origin and their International Registration (hereinafter "the Lisbon Agreement"), concluded in 1958, revised at Stockholm in 1967, and amended in 1979, was established to facilitate the protection of AOs at the international level. It offers a means of obtaining protection for an AO originating in one Member State in the territories of all other members through a single registration called "an international registration."

Only an AO that is recognized and protected in its country of origin may be the subject of an application for international registration. The "country of origin" is defined as "the country whose name, or the country in which is situated the region or locality whose name, constitutes the AO which has given the product its reputation."

The Lisbon Agreement provides for the protection of AO, that is, the "geographical denomination of a country, region, or locality, which serves to designate a product originating therein, the quality or characteristics of which are due exclusively or essentially to the geographic environment, including natural and human factors."

Such denominations are registered by the International Bureau of WIPO in Geneva upon the request of the competent authority of a Contracting State, usually the national IPO. The International Bureau keeps the International Register of Appellations of Origin and formally notifies the other Contracting States of the international registrations. It also publishes them in the Lisbon System's official bulletin.

§24.02 THE GENEVA ACT OF THE LISBON AGREEMENT ON APPELLATIONS OF ORIGIN AND GEOGRAPHICAL INDICATIONS

The Geneva Act of the Lisbon Agreement on Appellations of Origin and Geographical Indications (hereinafter referred to as "the Geneva Act of the Lisbon Agreement") that was adopted on May 20, 2015, entered into force on February 26, 2020.

The Geneva Act of the Lisbon Agreement updates and enhances the existing international registration system established by the Lisbon Agreement for the Protection of Appellations of Origin and their International Registration of 1958, while introducing several flexibilities to take into account the varieties of legal means existing to recognize and protect GIs at domestic level.

While the Lisbon Agreement only applies to AOs—a special kind of GIs for products that have a particularly strong link with their place of origin—the Geneva Act of the Lisbon Agreement extends that protection to GIs alongside AOs, to better take into account existing national or regional systems for the protection of distinctive designations in respect of origin-based quality products. In addition, it introduces maximum flexibility with respect to how the protection standard of the Act may be implemented at domestic level (i.e., through a sui generis (specific) AO or GI system or through the trademark system).

The Geneva Act of the Lisbon Agreement also allows certain IGOs to accede, making the international system of protection more inclusive.

As a complementary flexibility to the Lisbon Agreement, under the Geneva Act, the beneficiaries of the right to use the AO or GI, or their representatives, as well as natural person or legal entity having legal standing to assert the rights of the beneficiaries or other rights in the AO or GI, may submit individual applications directly to the International Bureau, if such direct applications are permitted by their domestic legislation.

In addition, the Geneva Act covers trans-border AOs and GIs—those that originate from a geographical area which extends over the territory of two adjacent Contracting Parties. These may file joint or separate applications in respect of such AOs or GIs.

The other main changes introduced by the Geneva Act of the Lisbon Agreement concern: (i) the possibility for newly acceding Contracting Parties to make a certain number of declarations (e.g., to request payment of an individual fee or to request additional information on the link between the quality, characteristics and/or reputation of the AO/GI for which protection is sought and its geographical area of origin); (ii) the clarification of the scope of protection with respect to goods of the same kind or goods of a different kind or services; and (iii) the introduction of safeguards with respect to prior rights and prior uses, such as prior trademark rights, prior use of generic terms, personal names used in business and rights based on a plant variety or animal breed denomination.

Together, the Lisbon Agreement and the Geneva Act of the Lisbon Agreement form the Lisbon System, offering more comprehensive and effective international protection for the names of origin-based quality products.

§24.03 SCOPE OF PROTECTION

Under the Lisbon System, once an AO or a GI has been internationally registered, it is protected without any limitation in time, and without any need for renewal, for as long as the AO or GI is protected in the country of origin.

GI or AO producers in a given Lisbon member will thus acquire the right to prevent third parties from using their internationally registered AO or GI commercially, in the other Lisbon members, for products which do not come from a specific geographical area or do not comply with the product's requirements for using the AO or GI.

The Lisbon System clearly defines the minimum level of protection to be granted to internationally registered AOs and GIs. Contracting parties are required to protect registered AOs and GIs in their territories against any usurpation and imitation (in respect of both goods of the same kind or goods of a different kind, or services, as specified by the Geneva Act of the Lisbon Agreement), even if the true origin of the product is stated, or if the AO or GI is used in translated form, or accompanied by terms such as "kind," "type," "make," "imitation" or the like. The Lisbon System also protects registered AOs and GIs against any other misleading practice as to the true origin or nature of the goods. Once registered under the Lisbon System, AOs and GIs can no longer be considered to have become generic terms serving to designate a type of product in those contracting parties that have not refused their protection.

The Lisbon System establishes the only legally binding international register for AOs and GIs, directly enforceable in multiple jurisdictions. This makes the protection particularly effective and considerably eases the burden of proof when AO or GI operators seek to enforce protection of their AOs or GIs abroad.

§24.04 COMMON IMPLEMENTATION PROCEDURES UNDER THE LISBON SYSTEM: THE COMMON REGULATIONS

In order to streamline the legal framework of the Lisbon System, for the benefit of the users of the System and the International Bureau, a single set of regulations governing international registrations under the Lisbon Agreement and the Geneva Act of the Lisbon Agreement was adopted in February 2017, namely the Common Regulations under the Lisbon Agreement and the Geneva Act of the Lisbon Agreement. These entered into force on February 26, 2020.

[A] Application for Registration and Examination

To qualify for international protection under the Lisbon System, AOs and GIs must be already protected as such in their Contracting Party of Origin, by means of either legislative or administrative provisions, judicial decision or any form of registration.

After conducting a formal examination of the application, WIPO notifies the other Contracting Parties to the Lisbon Agreement or the Geneva Act of the Lisbon Agreement, as applicable, of any new international registration. Each Contracting Party is then free to decide whether to protect a newly registered AO or GI or to refuse protection in its territory.

[B] Refusal

Competent Authorities of the Lisbon members have one year from the date of receiving a notification of an international registration to determine whether they may recognize and protect the international registration in their respective territory.

Should protection be refused, a declaration of refusal must be communicated to WIPO within the one-year time limit, otherwise protection of the AO or GI takes effect as of the date of the international registration.

[C] Grant of Protection

Contracting Parties may also issue statements of grant of protection when they know, well before the expiry of the one-year refusal period, that they will not issue a declaration of refusal of protection with respect to a particular AO or GI international registration.

§24.05 MEMBERSHIP

On January 1, 2024, thirty States were Party to the Lisbon Agreement, while nineteen States and two IGOs (the EU and the OAPI) were Party to the Geneva Act of the Lisbon Agreement. Thus, the Lisbon System as a whole currently extends over the territory of seventy-two countries.

CHAPTER 25
Conventions on Classification

§25.01 THE NICE AGREEMENT CONCERNING THE INTERNATIONAL CLASSIFICATION OF GOODS AND SERVICES FOR THE PURPOSES OF THE REGISTRATION OF MARKS

[A] Introduction

The Nice Agreement Concerning the International Classification of Goods and Services for the Purposes of the Registration of Marks is a multilateral international treaty signed on June 15, 1957. It entered into force on April 8, 1961, was revised in Stockholm on July 14, 1967, and in Geneva on May 13, 1977 (the text resulting from this latter revision is referred to hereinafter as "the Geneva Act"). This note is based on the provisions of the Geneva Act.

The International Classification Under the Nice Agreement Comprises:

(1) a List of Classes, accompanied, where appropriate, by explanatory notes; the list comprises thirty-four classes of goods and eleven classes of services;
(2) an Alphabetical List of Goods and Services (hereinafter referred to as "the Alphabetical List"), giving the class in which each product or service is classified.

The Nice Classification exists in both English and French authentic texts. It is also translated in many other languages, for example, in Arabic, Chinese, Dutch, French, German, Hebrew, Italian, Japanese, Korean, Norwegian, Portuguese, Russian, Serbian, Spanish, Turkish and Ukrainian.

[B] Legal Scope and Application of the Nice Classification

Under Article 2(3) of the Nice Agreement, the countries of the Nice Union are required to include in the official documents and publications concerning the registrations of marks the numbers of the classes of the Classification to which the goods or services for which the mark is registered belong.

The effect of the Nice Classification is that given to it by each Nice Union country. For example, the Classification does not bind the Nice Union countries either as regards evaluation of the extent of protection of a mark or the recognition of service marks (Article 2(1)).

Furthermore, Article 2(2) of the Nice Agreement provides that each of the Nice Union countries will reserve the right to use the Nice Classification either as a principal system or as a subsidiary system, meaning that the Nice Union countries are free to adopt the Nice Classification of Goods and Services as the sole classification to be used for the purposes of registration of marks or to keep an existing national system of classification of goods and services and to use the Nice Classification as a supplementary classification which will also be shown in the official publications of marks.

Finally, Article 2(4) of the Nice Agreement stipulates that the fact that a term is included in the Alphabetical List of Goods and Services of the Nice Classification in no way affects any rights which may subsist in that term.

[C] The Nice Union Assembly and the Committee of Experts

On becoming party to the Nice Agreement, a country automatically becomes a member of the Nice Union Assembly.

The Assembly meets in ordinary session once every two years; usually, such ordinary sessions are held during the same period and at the same place as the ordinary sessions of the Paris Union Assembly and the Conference and General Assembly of WIPO. The Assembly deals with all matters concerning the maintenance and development of the Special Union and the implementation of the Nice Agreement.

Each country party to the Nice Agreement is also represented in the Committee of Experts set up by the Agreement. The Committee of Experts:

(1) decides on any changes to be made to the Classification;
(2) addresses recommendations to the countries of the Special Union for the purpose of facilitating use of the Classification and promoting its uniform application;
(3) takes any other measures which, without financial implication for the budget of the Organization, are such as to facilitate the application of the Classification by developing countries;
(4) is empowered to set up subcommittees and working groups.

In practice, the proposed changes to the Nice Classification are examined and adopted by the Committee of Experts for incorporation in the Classification.

Membership of the Nice Union therefore enables countries to participate actively in the periodical reviews of the Nice Classification and to adapt it as far as possible to technical developments and to national interests.

[D] Utilization and Updating of the Nice Classification

Currently, in addition to the countries party to the Nice Agreement, over 60 other countries use the Nice Classification. In all, therefore, more than 150 countries use the Classification.

The Nice Classification has to be kept constantly up to date. It must be borne in mind that the first full draft of the Alphabetical List was produced in 1935. An amended draft was adopted at the Nice Diplomatic Conference in 1957. This means that the Nice Classification has been in force for more than sixty-five years. During those sixty-five years, numerous products shown in the first Alphabetical List have disappeared from the market and were therefore deleted from the Alphabetical List, whereas numerous other products have appeared and had to be incorporated.

The updating of the Nice Classification is carried out by the Committee of Experts composed of representatives of the countries party to the Nice Agreement.

The Committee of Experts meets regularly every year at the invitation of the Director General of WIPO. The Committee of Experts decides on the changes and amendments to be made to the Alphabetical List, on the wording of the class headings and the relevant explanatory notes and on the general remarks preceding the list of classes.

The changes and amendments to the Alphabetical List may take the following forms:

(1) deletion of an item shown in the Alphabetical List;
(2) addition of a product or service to the Alphabetical List;
(3) modification of the wording of an item in the Alphabetical List;
(4) transfer of an item from one class to another.

The wording of the class headings and of the explanatory notes is also constantly reviewed in order to improve the definition of the content of each class and to adapt it to changes in trade and industry.

Countries that are not party to the Nice Agreement, IGOs that specialize in marks and also representatives of international NGOs may be invited by the Director General of WIPO to send observers to meetings of the Committee of Experts.

In practice, the updating of the Nice Classification takes place as follows: to begin with, the International Bureau invites the member countries of the Nice Union to submit any proposed changes to the Classification that they would like the Committee of Experts to look at; subsequently, the proposals are subject to an initial round of comments from Member States. Based on these comments, the proposing office might withdraw or amend the initial proposal and submit a consolidated proposal. The consolidated proposals serve as a basis for discussions during the annual meeting of the Committee of Experts. The Committee of Experts is therefore able to work on proposals for modifications that have already been pre-discussed and which should not lead to protracted debate. As a result, the Committee of Experts can work under optimum conditions and take decisions more rapidly.

[E] Membership

As of September 1, 2023, ninety-three States were party to the Nice Agreement Concerning the International Classification of Goods and Services for the Purposes of the Registration of Marks.

§25.02 THE VIENNA AGREEMENT ESTABLISHING AN INTERNATIONAL CLASSIFICATION OF THE FIGURATIVE ELEMENTS OF MARKS

[A] Introduction

The Vienna Agreement Establishing an International Classification of the Figurative Elements of Marks was adopted on June 12, 1973, by a Diplomatic Conference held in Vienna, Austria. The Agreement entered into force on August 9, 1985, and was amended on October 1, 1985.

The International Classification under the Vienna Agreement comprises a list of categories, divisions and sections in which the figurative elements of marks are classified, accompanied, where appropriate, by explanatory notes.

The Classification itself constitutes a hierarchical system that proceeds from the general to the particular. It currently comprises twenty-nine categories, further divided into divisions and sections.

The Vienna Classification exists in the English and French languages, both texts being equally authentic.

[B] Legal Scope and Application of the Vienna Classification

Under Article 4(3) of the Vienna Agreement, the competent Offices of the countries of the Vienna Union are required to include in the official documents and publications relating to registrations and renewals of marks the numbers of the categories, divisions and sections in which the figurative elements of those marks are to be placed. However, this requirement is not retroactive to the extent that the Offices of the countries party to the Vienna Agreement are not required to classify figurative marks registered prior to entry into force of the Agreement for their territory; nevertheless, they have to be classified as and when the registration of such marks is renewed. Moreover, Article 4(4) indicates that the said numbers are to be preceded by the words "Classification of Figurative Elements" or the abbreviation CFE.

The main aim of the Vienna Classification is to facilitate anticipation searching, making it possible to identify marks that are composed of elements that are alike or similar. The effect of the Vienna Classification is that attributed to it by each Vienna Union country. For example, the Classification of Figurative Elements does not bind the Vienna Union countries in respect of the extent of protection of a mark (Article 4(1)).

Furthermore, Article 4(2) of the Vienna Agreement provides that each of the Vienna Union countries will reserve the right to use the Vienna Classification either as a principal system or as a subsidiary system. In other words, they are free to consider

the Vienna Classification as the sole classification to be used or to use it at the same time as a national classification.

The Vienna Agreement allows its member countries, at the time of their accession, the possibility of not including the numbers of all or some of the sections in official documents and publications relating to registrations and renewals of marks (Article 4(5)). This provision is of importance particularly for those Offices that only register a small number of marks. The Vienna Classification contains not only the sections required to place all figurative elements. It also contains auxiliary sections intended for figurative elements that are already covered by (main) sections, but which it is considered useful to group according to a particular criterion in order to facilitate searching.

Otherwise, the countries party to the Agreement are required to apply the Vienna Classification as it stands. They may not, for example, change the content or number of categories, divisions or sections, group together varying sections to form a single one or create new sections, whether main or auxiliary.

Finally, since it is not possible to directly place obligations on IGOs, the Vienna Agreement provides that, if a country of the Vienna Union entrusts the registration of marks to an intergovernmental authority, it must take all possible measures to ensure that such authority uses the Vienna Classification in accordance with the Agreement.

[C] The Vienna Union Assembly and the Committee of Experts

On becoming party to the Vienna Agreement, a country automatically becomes a member of the Vienna Union Assembly.

The Assembly meets in ordinary session once every two years; usually, such ordinary sessions are held during the same period and at the same place as the ordinary sessions of the Paris Union Assembly and the Conference and General Assembly of WIPO. The Assembly deals with all matters concerning the maintenance and development of the Special Union and the implementation of the Vienna Agreement.

Each country party to the Vienna Agreement is also represented in the Committee of Experts set up by the Agreement. The Committee of Experts:

(1) makes amendments and additions to the Classification;
(2) addresses recommendations to the countries of the Special Union for the purpose of facilitating use of the Classification and promoting its uniform application;
(3) takes any other measures which, without financial implication for the budget of the Organization, are such as to facilitate the application of the Classification by developing countries;
(4) is empowered to set up subcommittees and working groups.

In practice, the proposed changes to the Vienna Classification are examined and adopted by the Committee of Experts for incorporation in the Classification.

Membership of the Vienna Union therefore enables countries to participate actively in the periodical reviews of the Vienna Classification and to adapt it as far as possible to technical developments and to national interests.

[D] Utilization and Updating of the Vienna Classification

In order to keep the Vienna Classification up to date, it is continuously revised by the Committee of Experts composed of representatives of the countries party to the Vienna Agreement.

The revision period, which is determined by the Committee of Experts, is currently every three years. The Committee decides on the changes and amendments to be made to the list of categories, divisions and sections.

In practice, the updating of the Vienna Classification takes place as follows: to begin with, the International Bureau invites the member countries of the Vienna Union to submit any proposed changes to the Classification that they would like the Committee of Experts to look at; subsequently, the proposals are subject to an initial round of comments from Member States. Based on those comments, the proposing office may choose to withdraw or amend its initial proposal. The consolidated proposals serve as a basis for discussions during the regular meeting of the Committee of Experts.

The amendments and additions made by the Committee of Experts, together with its recommendations, are notified by the International Bureau of WIPO to the competent Offices of the Vienna Union countries and enter into force six months after notification. Additionally, the International Bureau of WIPO incorporates the amendments and additions in the Vienna Classification and publishes them in the periodicals designated by the Assembly of the Vienna Union.

[E] Advantages of the International Classifications Relating to Marks

The internationalization of industrial, technical and commercial relations demands the creation of uniform tools of work in the industrial property field. Such is the case of the international classifications produced by cooperation between States and by means of which the national Offices are provided with tools, which each of them would otherwise have been obliged to establish and maintain. When documents are exchanged, there is no need to reclassify them.

These advantages are particularly telling for developing countries that do not always have the necessary staff to undertake such tasks and which permit them to make noticeable savings in means and time so that they can devote themselves to other priorities.

In the specific field of marks, there already exists an International Classification of Goods and Services established by the Nice Agreement on June 15, 1957. That Classification constitutes for the Offices responsible for anticipation searching a working tool whose usefulness and effectiveness has long since been proved.

However, in carrying out those searches, it is also necessary to classify the figurative elements of marks. Thus, a uniform classification facilitates the anticipation searching work of the national Offices. For its part, the International Bureau of WIPO uses the International Classification of the Figurative Elements of Marks for coding the figurative marks that are internationally registered under the Madrid System.

[F] Membership

On September 1, 2023, thirty-eight States were party to the Vienna Agreement Establishing an International Classification of the Figurative Elements of Marks.

§25.03 THE LOCARNO AGREEMENT ESTABLISHING AN INTERNATIONAL CLASSIFICATION FOR INDUSTRIAL DESIGNS

[A] Introduction

The Locarno Agreement Establishing an International Classification for Industrial Designs is a multilateral international treaty, which was signed on October 8, 1968. It entered into force on April 27, 1971, and was amended on September 28, 1979.

The Locarno Classification comprises three parts:

(1) a list of Classes and Subclasses;
(2) an Alphabetical List of Goods in which industrial designs are incorporated;
(3) Explanatory Notes.

The Locarno Classification exists in the English and French languages, both texts being equally authentic.

[B] Legal Scope and Application of the Locarno Classification

According to Article 2(3) of the Locarno Agreement, the industrial property Offices of the countries of the Locarno Union must include in the official documents for the deposit or registration of designs, and if they are officially published, in the publications in question, the numbers of the classes and subclasses of the Locarno Classification into which the goods incorporating the designs belong.

Each country may attribute to such classification the legal consequences, if any, which it considers appropriate. In particular, the Locarno Classification does not bind the countries of the Locarno Union as regards the nature and the scope of protection afforded to the design in those countries (Article 2(1)).

Further, Article 2(2) of the Locarno Agreement provides that each of the countries of the Locarno Union reserves the right to use the Locarno Classification either as a principal or as a subsidiary system, which means that the countries of the Locarno Union are free to adopt the Locarno Classification as the only classification to be used for industrial designs, or to maintain an existing national classification system for industrial designs and to use the Locarno Classification as a supplementary classification, also to be included in official documents and publications concerning the deposit or registration of designs.

Finally, Article 2(4) of the Locarno Agreement provides that the inclusion of any word in the Alphabetical List of Goods is not an expression of opinion of the Committee of Experts on whether or not such a word is subject to exclusive rights.

[C] The Locarno Union Assembly and the Committee of Experts

On becoming party to the Locarno Agreement, a country automatically becomes a member of the Locarno Union Assembly.

The Assembly meets in ordinary session once every two years; usually, such ordinary sessions are held during the same period and at the same place as the ordinary sessions of the Paris Union Assembly and the Conference and General Assembly of WIPO. The Assembly deals with all matters concerning the maintenance and development of the Special Union and the implementation of the Locarno Agreement.

Each country party to the Locarno Agreement is also represented in the Committee of Experts set up by the Agreement. The Committee of Experts is entrusted with the revision of the Locarno Classification.

In practice, the proposed changes to the Locarno Classification are examined and adopted by the Committee of Experts for incorporation in the Classification.

Membership of the Locarno Union therefore enables countries to participate actively in the periodical reviews of the Locarno Classification and to adapt it as far as possible to technical developments and to national interests.

[D] Utilization and Updating of the Locarno Classification

In order to keep the Locarno Classification up to date, it is continuously revised by the Committee of Experts composed of representatives of the countries party to the Locarno Agreement.

The revision period, which is determined by the Committee of Experts, is currently every two years. The Committee decides on the amendments and additions to be made to the alphabetical list and explanatory notes.

In practice, the updating of the Locarno Classification takes place as follows: to begin with, the International Bureau invites the member countries of the Locarno Union to submit any proposed changes to the Classification that they would like the Committee of Experts to look at; subsequently, the proposals are subject to an initial round of comments from Member States. Based on those comments, the proposing office may choose to withdraw or amend its initial proposal. The consolidated proposals serve as a basis for discussions during the regular meeting of the Committee of Experts.

The amendments and additions made by the Committee of Experts are notified by the International Bureau of WIPO to the competent Offices of the Locarno Union countries and enter into force six months after notification. Additionally, the International Bureau of WIPO incorporates the amendments and additions in the Locarno Classification and publishes them in the periodicals designated by the Assembly of the Locarno Union.

[E] Membership

As of September 1, 2023, sixty-two States were party to the Locarno Agreement Establishing an International Classification for Industrial Designs.

§25.04 THE STRASBOURG AGREEMENT CONCERNING THE IPC

[A] Introduction

The industrial property Offices, which have to handle such enormous numbers of patent documents, are faced with two different problems, namely, the administrative processing of the patent applications and the maintenance of the search files containing the published patent documents. The search files are established for the purposes of carrying out documentary searches necessary for the examination of patent applications and for retrieving the patent documents relevant to specific technical fields. Special systems for arranging the patent documents are required to permit the economical handling of patent applications and patent documents within the offices, and the greater the number of patent documents, the better the system has to be.

On the one hand, patent applications have to be provided with a symbol or number for administrative purposes, that is, for registration and handling within an industrial property Office. For this purpose, a serial number is usually used. On the other hand, patent applications also have to be provided with special symbols, which relate to the technical field or fields to which the patent application relates. These symbols are required to assist the public concerned, e.g., industry, and to facilitate the orderly and classified arrangement of patent documents in order to permit the efficient search and, thus, the retrieval of documents relating to distinct technical subject matter. Industrial property Offices have, therefore, been forced to develop systems for the classification of patents, in other words, to develop systems specially adapted for the filing and fast and reliable retrieval of patent documents for the purposes of search. The development of such special Classification systems for patent documents became necessary because existing Classifications systems, as used in libraries, for instance, proved unsuitable for the classification of patent documents. Different national Classification systems were thus elaborated in different Offices.

National Classification systems were established as early as 1831 at the Patent Office of the USA, 1877 at the German Patent Office and 1880 at the UK Patent Office. The initial system of mere registration of patent applications was gradually abandoned and replaced by examination of patent applications, in the course of which the patent applications were compared with existing national patent documents. The next step was the inclusion of the universal state of the art in the area covered by the examination of patent applications, in other words, the inclusion also of patent documents published by other countries. For the purpose of this type of examination procedure, the industrial property Offices were obliged to search for distinct patent documents dealing with specific technical subjects, and to locate them among a great number of foreign patent documents bearing the symbols of other national Classification systems.

One means of overcoming this problem was to establish concordance tables between two different national Classification systems, in other words, to devise tables, which cited, for each entry in one national Classification system, the corresponding entry in the other national Classification system. Because of the different underlying classification principles, however, national classifications are so different that the value of such concordance tables is more than questionable. Moreover, different concordance tables would have to be set up between, on the one hand, a country's own national Classification and, on the other hand, each of the other national Classifications that are of interest. This method, therefore, did not offer an acceptable solution.

Another possibility for overcoming this problem was for each country to reclassify the foreign patent documents according to its own national Classification. This also proved to be an unacceptable solution because of the high number of documents, which would have to be reclassified, the specialists required for such high-level technical work and the linguistic knowledge required for work with patent documents in foreign languages. Thus, the need for an international Classification system to solve these problems became more and more apparent.

Many years of international cooperation, which started in 1956 under the auspices of the Council of Europe and the WIPO, resulted in 1971 in the Strasbourg Agreement Concerning the IPC, amended in 1979 and provided for a worldwide forum for the IPC. It is open to States party to the Paris Convention for the Protection of Industrial Property (1883). As of August 1, 2023, sixty-five States were party to the Strasbourg Agreement.

[B] Legal Scope and Application of the IPC

The IPC is based on an international multilateral treaty (the said Strasbourg Agreement) administered by the International Bureau of WIPO.

Under Article 4(2) of the Strasbourg Agreement, each country of the IPC Union has the right to use the Classification either as a principal or as a subsidiary system.

The IPC provides for a hierarchical system of language independent symbols for the classification of patents and utility models, etc., according to the different areas of technology to which they pertain. It divides technology into eight sections with approximately eighty thousand subdivisions. Each subdivision has a symbol consisting of Arabic numerals and letters of the Latin alphabet. Each of the sections, classes, subclasses, groups and subgroups has a title and a symbol, and each of the subsections has a title. The symbol or symbols of at least the subclass or subclasses to which the technical invention described in any patent document belongs are indicated generally on the patent document by the industrial property office of the country where the application was filed. Thus, the document will be retrievable according to its subject matter, with the help of the IPC. The appropriate IPC symbols are indicated on each patent document, of which more than three hundred thousand were issued each year in the last ten years. The IPC symbols are allotted by the national or regional industrial property Office that publishes the patent document. For PCT documents, IPC symbols are allotted by the ISA.

The IPC exists in English and French languages, both texts being equally authentic, which are published by the International Bureau of WIPO. Translations of the IPC are also prepared and published in other languages by the Offices concerned. For example, the IPC is available in the following languages through the "bridge" function of the Internet publication: Chinese, Czech, Dutch, German, Japanese, Polish, Portuguese (Brazil), Russian, Serbian, Slovak, Spanish and Ukrainian.

[C] The IPC Union Assembly and the Committee of Experts

On becoming party to the Strasbourg Agreement, a country automatically becomes a member of the IPC Union Assembly.

The Assembly meets in ordinary session once in every second calendar year; usually, such ordinary sessions are held during the same period and at the same place as the General Assembly of WIPO. The Assembly deals with all matters concerning the maintenance and development of the Special Union and the implementation of this Agreement.

Each country party to the Strasbourg Agreement is also represented in the Committee of Experts established by the Agreement. The Committee of Experts:

(1) amends the Classification;
(2) addresses recommendations to the countries of the Special Union for the purpose of facilitating the use of the Classification and promoting its uniform application;
(3) assists in the promotion of international cooperation in the reclassification of documentation used for the examination of inventions, taking in particular the needs of developing countries into account;
(4) takes all other measures which, without entailing financial implications for the budget of the Special Union or for the Organization, contribute toward facilitating the application of the Classification by developing countries;
(5) has the right to establish subcommittees and working groups.

In practice, the proposals for amendments to the Classification are considered and adopted by the Committee of Experts for incorporation in the Classification.

Those amendments adopted by the Committee of Experts are notified by the International Bureau of WIPO to the competent Offices of the IPC Union countries and enter into force six months after notification. Additionally, the International Bureau of WIPO incorporates the amendments in the IPC and publishes them in the periodicals designated by the Assembly of the IPC Union.

[D] Advantages of the IPC

The Committee of Experts, taking note of the fact that the IPC is a means for obtaining an internationally uniform classification of patent documents, has agreed that:

(a) as the primary purpose, the IPC is to be an effective search tool for the retrieval of relevant patent documents by industrial property Offices, potential inventors, research and development units and other users in order to establish the novelty and evaluate the inventive step (including the assessment of technical advance and useful results or utility) of patent applications;
(b) as other purposes (equally important to developing and developed countries) the IPC is to serve as:
   (i) an instrument for the orderly arrangement of patent documents in order to facilitate access to the information contained therein;
   (ii) the basis for selective dissemination of information to all users of patent information;
   (iii) a basis for investigating the state of the art in given fields of technology; and
   (iv) a basis for the preparation of industrial property statistics, which in turn permit the assessment of technological development in various areas.

[E] Membership

As of August 1, 2023, sixty-five States were party to the Strasbourg Agreement Concerning the IPC.

CHAPTER 26
The International Convention for the Protection of Performers, Producers of Phonograms and Broadcasting Organizations (The "Rome Convention")

§26.01 GENESIS OF THE ROME CONVENTION

Related rights are primarily an offshoot of technological development. At the national level, it was first the phonogram industry that looked for protection against unauthorized duplication of sound recordings of musical performances. In the UK, the Copyright Act recognized in 1911 a copyright for the benefit of the producers of sound recordings, and this copyright approach has been followed in several countries which have adopted the Anglo-Saxon concept of copyright, despite the different implications of the protection of authors' works, on the one hand, and phonogram products, on the other. It was in that context also that the question of protecting performers emerged in some countries. For example, performers in Germany obtained through case law protection a so-called right of adaptation—authorship. At the international level, it was likewise the development of the phonogram industry that promoted the establishment of special protection for the so-called related or neighboring rights.

As in the case of some national laws, the first proposals aiming at the protection of producers of phonograms and performers at the international level were also based on copyright protection. The rights involved were discussed by the Berne Union for the Protection of Literary and Artistic Works at its Diplomatic Conference in Rome in 1928, where it was proposed that "when a musical work has been adapted to a mechanical instrument by the contribution of performing artists these latter should also benefit from the protection granted to that adaptation." Corresponding to this approach, a resolution was passed asking governments to consider the possibility of adopting measures to safeguard the interests of performers.

Later on, in 1934, CISAC, the International Confederation of Societies of Authors and Composers, signed an agreement in Stresa with the International Federation of the Gramophone Industry according to which during the forthcoming revision of the Berne Convention: (i) the protection of phonograms against unauthorized duplication; and (ii) the right of producers of phonograms to equitable remuneration for communication to the public of their phonograms by broadcasting or cinematography should be proposed by means of an annex to be added to the Berne Convention. However, the ILO had maintained since 1926 a continuing interest in the protection of performers, and the problem was considered at a meeting in Samaden, Switzerland, in 1939. Drafts were prepared in cooperation with the Bureau of the Berne Union but all progress was stopped for several years by the outbreak of World War II.

After the war, the matter was taken up again, on the occasion of the revision of the Berne Convention in Brussels in 1948, but the attempts to secure at the international level a kind of copyright for performers and producers of phonograms were of no avail. However, wishes were expressed that governments should continue their efforts toward providing some sort of adequate protection. Different committees of experts prepared drafts of conventions also including protection of the interests of broadcasting organizations: the so-called Rome Draft (1951), a draft produced under the sponsorship of the International Labour Office (1957) and the Monaco Draft (1957) prepared by experts convened by the International Bureau of the Berne Union and by UNESCO. Finally, in 1960, a committee of experts convened jointly by WIPO, UNESCO and the International Labour Office, met at the Hague and drew up the draft convention which served as a basis for the deliberations in Rome, where a Diplomatic Conference agreed upon the final text of the International Convention for the Protection of Performers, Producers of Phonograms and Broadcasting Organizations, the so-called Rome Convention of October 26, 1961.

§26.02 RELATION BETWEEN THE PROTECTION OF RELATED RIGHTS AND COPYRIGHT

Considering that the use of literary and artistic works was usually implied in the work of performers, recorders and broadcasters, the Diplomatic Conference at Rome established a link with copyright protection. The first article of the Rome Convention provides that the protection granted under the Convention shall leave intact and shall in no way affect the protection of copyright in literary and artistic works. Consequently, no provision of the Rome Convention may be interpreted as prejudicing such protection. Under the text of Article 1 it is clear that whenever, by virtue of the copyright law, the authorization of the author is necessary for the use of his/her work, the need for this authorization is not affected by the Rome Convention.

The majority of the Conference at Rome decided to go even further. They considered the possibility that the performers, producers of phonograms and broadcasting organizations of a country would enjoy international protection even when the literary and artistic works they used might be denied protection in that country because it was not a party to at least one of the major international copyright conventions. The

Rome Convention therefore provides that in order to become a party to the Convention a State must not only be a member of the UN, but also a member of the Berne Union or a party to the Universal Copyright Convention (UCC) (Article 24(2)). Accordingly, a Contracting State shall cease to be a party to the Rome Convention as from that time when it is not party to either the Berne or the UCC (Article 28(4)). Because of this link with the copyright conventions, the Rome Convention is sometimes referred to as a "closed" convention from the point of view of the circle of States which may adhere to it. However, given the large number of countries that are Member States of the Berne Convention (181 in 2024), the impact of this limitation seems negligible.

§26.03 THE BASIC PRINCIPLE OF PROTECTION UNDER THE ROME CONVENTION: NATIONAL TREATMENT

Similar to the Berne Convention, the protection accorded by the Rome Convention consists basically of the national treatment that a State grants under its domestic law to domestic performances, phonograms and broadcasts (Article 2(1)). National treatment is, however, subject to the minimum level of protection specifically guaranteed by the Convention, and also to the limitations specifically provided for in the Convention (Article 2(2)). That means that, apart from the rights guaranteed by the Convention itself as constituting that minimum level of protection, and subject to specific exceptions or reservations allowed for by the Convention, performers, producers of phonograms and broadcasting organizations to which the Convention applies, enjoy in Contracting States the same rights as those countries grant to their nationals. In addition, formalities may only be required for protection under specified conditions (Article 11). This provision may be seen as a solution between automatic protection (as it exists under the Berne Convention) and full choice to require any desired formalities (*see also* §26.09 below).

§26.04 ELIGIBILITY FOR PROTECTION

One of the most important questions to be answered unequivocally by each international convention is to whom and in what cases does it apply? The Rome Convention provides for its application by determining criteria of eligibility for national treatment and minimum protection.

National treatment and minimum protection shall be granted to performers if the performance takes place in another Contracting State (irrespective of the country to which the performer belongs) or if it is incorporated in a phonogram protected under the Convention (irrespective of the country to which the performer belongs or where the performance actually took place) or if it is transmitted "live" (not from a phonogram) in a broadcast protected by the Convention (irrespective again of the country to which the performer belongs) (Article 4). These alternative criteria of eligibility for protection allow for the application of the Rome Convention to the widest possible circle of performances.

National treatment and minimum protection shall be granted to producers of phonograms if the producer is a national of another Contracting State (criterion of nationality) or the first fixation was made in another Contracting State (criterion of fixation) or the phonogram was first or simultaneously published in another Contracting State (criterion of publication) (Article 5).

The Convention allows reservations in respect of these alternative criteria. By means of a notification deposited with the Secretary-General of the UN, any Contracting State may at any time declare that it will not apply the criterion of publication or, alternatively, the criterion of fixation. Any State which, on the day the Convention was signed at Rome, granted protection to producers of phonograms solely on the basis of the criterion of fixation, can exclude both the criteria of nationality and publication. This possibility has been provided for mainly in view of the contemporary Nordic legislation. Thus, the implementation of the Rome Convention can easily be adapted to conditions of protection already existing under different national laws.

National treatment and minimum protection have to be granted to broadcasting organizations if their headquarters is situated in another Contracting State (principle of nationality) or the broadcast was transmitted from a transmitter situated in another Contracting State, irrespective of whether the initiating broadcasting organization was situated in a Contracting State (principle of territoriality). Contracting States may declare that they will protect broadcasts only if both the condition of nationality and of territoriality are met in respect of the same Contracting State (Article 6).

§26.05 THE MINIMUM RIGHTS REQUIRED BY THE CONVENTION

The minimum rights guaranteed by the Convention to performers are provided by "the possibility of preventing certain acts" done without their consent. Instead of enumerating the minimum rights in the form of exclusive rights of performers, this expression was used in order to allow countries like the UK to continue to protect performers by virtue of penal statutes, determining offenses and penal sanctions under public law. It was agreed, however, that the enumerated acts that may be prevented by the performer require consent in advance. In fact, the possibility of preventing certain acts as defined in the Convention amounts to a distinct bundle of rights granted to performers.

The restricted acts comprise: (i) broadcasting or communication to the public of a "live" performance; (ii) recording an unfixed performance; (iii) reproducing a fixation of the performance, provided that the original fixation was made without the consent of the performer or the reproduction is made for purposes not permitted by the Convention or the performer (Article 7).

Producers of phonograms have the right to authorize or prohibit the direct or indirect reproduction of their phonograms (Article 10). The Rome Convention does not provide for any right to authorize performances of the phonogram and does not explicitly prohibit distribution or importation of unauthorized duplicates of phonograms.

Article 12 also provides an option for contracting parties to provide a statutory remuneration right for performers or phonogram producers for use of commercial phonograms for broadcasting and communication to the public, subject to possible reservations. *See* §26.06 below.

Broadcasting organizations have the right to authorize or prohibit:

(i) the simultaneous rebroadcasting of their broadcasts;
(ii) the fixation of their broadcasts;
(iii) the reproduction of unauthorized fixations of their broadcasts or reproduction of lawful fixations for illicit purposes; and
(iv) the communication to the public of their television broadcasts by means of receivers in places accessible to the public against payment. It should be noted, however, that this right does not extend to communication to the public of merely sound broadcasts, and that it is a matter for domestic legislation to determine the conditions under which such a right may be exercised.

It should also be observed that the Rome Convention does not protect against retransmission of broadcasts by cable. This is a matter that has been on the agenda of the WIPO SCCR as part of the discussion of a proposed treaty to update broadcasters' rights for the Internet era. Detailed information on the various proposals and the status of work is available at www.wipo.int/copyright/en/activities/broadcast.html. *See also* Chapter 36 below.

§26.06 PROVISIONS FOR DISCRETIONARY REGULATION OF THE EXERCISE OF RIGHTS

The Rome Convention, over and above the minimum requirements of protection, also contains provisions allowing national laws to regulate certain aspects of the protection at their discretion.

As regards the protection of performers, it is a matter for domestic legislation to regulate the protection against rebroadcasting of the performance and fixation thereof for broadcasting purposes, where the broadcasting of the performance was consented to by the performer. The principle of preeminence of contractual arrangements was embodied in a provision requiring that domestic laws shall not operate to deprive performers of the ability to control by contract their relations with broadcasting organizations (Article 7(2)); whereas it was understood that the meaning of contract in this context includes collective agreements and also decisions of an arbitration board if involved.

If several performers participate in the same performance, the manner in which they should be represented in connection with the exercise of their rights may be specified by each Contracting State (Article 8).

Concerning both the protection of performers and producers of phonograms, Article 12 (perhaps initially the most controversial part of the Convention) provides that if a phonogram published for commercial purposes is used directly for broadcasting or any communication to the public, an equitable remuneration shall be paid by the user to the performers, or to the producers of the phonogram, or to both. This article does not grant any right to either the performers or producers of phonograms to authorize or to prohibit the secondary use of a phonogram. By guaranteeing a single remuneration for the use of the phonogram it seems to establish a sort of nonvoluntary license. It does not, however, specify the beneficiary or beneficiaries of the remuneration for the secondary use of the performance and the phonogram embodying it. Article 12 only says that at least one of the interested parties should be paid for the use; nevertheless, it provides that in the absence of agreement between these parties, domestic law may (if considered appropriate) lay down the conditions for the sharing of this remuneration.

The implementation of these provisions, however, can be excluded or restricted by the Contracting States at any time by an appropriate notification (Article 16(1)(a)). A State may declare that it will not apply the provisions of Article 12 at all. A Contracting State may declare that it will not apply this article in respect of certain uses, for instance, as regards communications to the public other than broadcasting, or broadcasting of phonograms acquired before the date of the Convention. It is also possible to apply this article only as regards phonograms for which the producer is a national of another Contracting State. Furthermore, as regards phonograms for which the producer is a national of another Contracting State, the extent and term of protection can be limited so as to correspond to the protection granted by the other State concerned. The fact, however, that the protection in both countries concerned is not granted to the same beneficiary, cannot be considered as justifying the restriction of the protection provided for in Article 12.

§26.07 LIMITATIONS

The Rome Convention allows for certain limitations of the rights granted and, as regards the performers, also imposes limitations on rights itself.

Any Contracting State may provide for exceptions as regards private use, use of short excerpts in connection with reporting current events, ephemeral fixation by a broadcasting organization by means of its own facilities and for its own broadcasts, and for all kinds of uses solely for the purpose of teaching or scientific research (Article 15(1)). This latter possibility of introducing exceptions may be of special benefit to developing countries.

Besides the exceptions specified by the Convention, any Contracting State may also provide for the same kind of limitations with regard to the protection of performers, producers of phonograms and broadcasting organizations as it provides for in connection with copyright protection. There is, however, an important difference: compulsory licenses may be provided for only to the extent to which they are compatible with the Rome Convention (Article 15(2)).

In view of the film industry's interest in exclusively exploiting the contributions made to their productions, Article 19 of the Rome Convention provides that once a performer has consented to the incorporation of a performance in a visual or audiovisual fixation, the performer shall have no further minimum rights under Article 7 of the

Rome Convention as regards the performance concerned. These rights for performers have now been addressed in the BTAP (*see* Chapter 29).

§26.08 DURATION OF PROTECTION

The minimum term of protection under the Rome Convention is a period of twenty years to be computed from the end of the year in which:

(i) the fixation was made, as far as phonograms and performances incorporated therein are concerned; or
(ii) the performance took place, as regards performances not incorporated in phonograms; or
(iii) the broadcast took place, for broadcasts (Article 14).

§26.09 RESTRICTION OF FORMALITIES

If a country requires compliance with formalities as a condition for protecting related rights in relation to phonograms, these should be considered as fulfilled if all copies in commerce of the published phonogram or their containers bear a notice consisting of the symbol P in a circle ("circle P"), accompanied by the year of first publication. If the copies or their containers do not identify the producer or the licensee, the notice shall also include the name of the owner of the rights of the producer and, if the copies or their containers do not identify the principal performers, the notice shall also include the name of the person who owns the rights of such performers (Article 11). It should be emphasized that this provision is *not* a formality requirement; it is a restriction of the formalities that may be required by some national laws.

§26.10 THE ROME CONVENTION AND DEVELOPING COUNTRIES

A significant proposition of the membership of the Rome Convention consists of developing countries. This is quite natural since most developing countries attach great importance to music, dance and other creations in their national heritage. The value of the Rome Convention to such countries stems in part from the fact that it affords the protection of those who contribute to the dissemination of that heritage abroad.

The Convention is particularly interesting for those countries whose civilization and tradition are oral and where the author is often the performer as well. In this context, the place occupied by expressions of folklore, now referred to as "TCEs" must be borne in mind and the interests of the artists constantly performing, and thus perpetuating them, must be safeguarded when use is made of their performances. While the possibilities of protecting creations of TCEs by copyright may be limited, and the establishment of a sui generis protection is still under discussion at the multilateral level, expressions of TCEs can efficiently be protected indirectly by protecting recordings and broadcasts of them. However, since the Rome Convention only protects performers of "works" (Article 3(a)), performers of TCEs are not protected; this gap has been filled in the WPPT (*see* Chapter 28 below) and BTAP (*see* Chapter 29 below).

By also protecting the producers of phonograms, the Rome Convention promotes, particularly in developing countries, the setting up of an industry in the tertiary sector of the economy whose dynamic activity needs no proving. Such an industry, while guaranteeing the dissemination of national culture, both within the country and throughout the world, can additionally constitute a substantial source of revenue for the country's economy and, in those cases where its activities extend beyond the frontiers, can represent an inflow of foreign currency.

By giving performers and phonogram producers the possibility of benefiting from their performances and productions, the Rome Convention is instrumental in promoting the artistic heritage and represents an important incentive to creativity. It is also certain that, where the interests of performers and producers of phonograms are safeguarded by law, works will enjoy greater development and that those works will suffer less from the competition of unprotected performances of foreign works. Where performances and phonograms are exported, there is one reason more to protect them internationally, that is to say, by accepting the relevant international conventions.

Finally, the part played by the broadcasting organizations in the developing countries should not be forgotten either, since they also have an interest in the protection of their costly programming against rebroadcasting, reproduction and communication to the public of their broadcasts. The rebroadcasting of television broadcasts in public places can be very profitable, especially when the subject of the original broadcast is an exceptional event. Frequently, the organizers of such events only allow broadcasting for certain territories or on the condition that no public communication close to the place of the event drains away potential spectators. The broadcasting organization must therefore be able to prohibit rebroadcasting. The same refers to broadcasting of performances or recordings of expressions of national TCEs: the broadcasting organization should be entitled internationally to prevent rebroadcasting or fixation for reproduction of its own broadcast of expressions of TCEs or works of national heritage.

§26.11 MEMBERSHIP

As of June 2, 2024, ninety-seven States were party to the Rome Convention.

CHAPTER 27
Other Special Conventions in the Field of Related Rights

§27.01 THE SPECIAL CONVENTIONS

The Rome Convention of 1961, discussed in the previous chapter, protects at the international level three categories of beneficiaries of related rights: performers, producers of phonograms and broadcasting organizations. Besides this basic Convention, and the treaties designed to update its provisions—the TRIPS Agreement (1994), the WPPT (1996), and the BTAP (2012)—two other international instruments have been drawn up with regard to certain related rights. These are the Convention for the Protection of Producers of Phonograms Against Unauthorized Duplication of Their Phonograms, concluded in Geneva in October 1971 and generally referred to as "the Phonograms Convention," and the Convention Relating to the Distribution of Programme-Carrying Signals Transmitted by Satellite; concluded in Brussels in May 1974 and known as "the Satellites Convention" or "the Brussels Convention." These two Conventions are also within the area of related rights, and their purpose is to protect producers of phonograms and broadcasting organizations, respectively, against certain prejudicial acts that have been widely recognized as infringements or acts of piracy. As the newer related rights treaties like the WPPT address infringement as well as broader protection, the rate of countries joining the Conventions has slowed considerably.

From the point of view of the Rome Convention, the Phonograms Convention and the Satellites Convention may be regarded as special agreements, the conclusion of which is reserved for Contracting States insofar as the agreements grant to performers, producers of phonograms or broadcasting organizations more extensive rights than those granted by the Rome Convention or contain other provisions not contrary to the Convention (Article 22 of the Rome Convention).

§27.02 REASONS FOR AND PURPOSES OF THE SPECIAL CONVENTIONS

As of December 9, 2023, the Phonograms Convention had eighty-one ratifications or accessions to its credit. At the time of its adoption this Convention was rapidly accepted due, on the one hand, to the accelerating increase in international piracy during the decades preceding the Convention, and, on the other hand, to the legal characteristics of the Convention itself.

While a number of countries were preparing new legislation in the field of related rights in view of the standards set by the Rome Convention, international piracy of sound recordings (phonograms), referred to at the time as "records" (although some copies were distributed in formats other than vinyl), was growing. The dramatic development of record piracy led to the view by the early 1970s that it was necessary to establish without delay a special convention intended solely for the international protection of the basic interests of producers of phonograms and taking into consideration all measures already available under various national laws. The subject was raised in May 1970 in the Preparatory Committee for the revision of the two major copyright conventions, and the new Convention was signed in less than eighteen months in Geneva.

As far as the legal characteristics of the Phonograms Convention are concerned, it takes into account all the measures that had already been adopted in various national laws, and allows for the application of all of them instead of requiring a uniform solution for the same purpose, as is the case under the Rome Convention, which provides for the granting to producers of phonograms the right to authorize or prohibit the reproduction of their phonograms. Thus, amendments of existing national laws became largely unnecessary to States which already protected producers of phonograms by some other means and also wanted to extend this kind of protection at the international level. In addition, States interested in focusing on protection of phonograms saw an advantage in this Convention.

The adoption of the Satellites Convention is due to the fact that the use of satellites in international telecommunications had, since about 1965, been presenting a new problem for the protection of broadcasting organizations, and it was considered unclear whether the Rome Convention could be interpreted as covering forms of satellite broadcasting.

At the time, some programs were transmitted by satellite in order to reach areas that were difficult to reach by antenna, and the use of satellites for program placement prior to distribution to the public (e.g., to a cable headend) continues today. Electronic signal carrying broadcast programs that are passed on by satellite cannot be picked up directly by conventional receivers generally used by the public at large. They have first to be picked up by ground stations, which make them accessible and bring them to the public using various transmission platforms including over-the-air broadcast radio and television, cable radio and television, satellite radio and television, and webcasting.

In the case of direct broadcasting by satellite (sometimes referred to as "DBS"), which is an everyday occurrence, the signals sent to the satellite are demodulated by the satellite itself; as a result, the signals transmitted down to earth can be received directly from space by ordinary receivers, without the intervention of ground receiving stations. However, the signals transmitted upwards to the satellite remain inaccessible to the public even with this mode of transmission.

The legal problem addressed by the Satellites Convention stems from the wording of Article 3 of the Rome Convention, under which broadcasting means the transmission by wireless means for public reception of sounds or of images and sounds. The difficulties with regard to satellite transmission are twofold: on the one hand, the signals emitted by the originating organization are not suitable for public reception; on the other hand, the derived signals, generally obtained by means of ground stations, are frequently transmitted to the public by wire (e.g., through cable transmission) and not by wireless means.

The Satellites Convention provides a solution by requiring Contracting States to take adequate measures to prevent the "distribution" of any program-carrying signals by any "distributor" for whom the signal emitted to or passing through the satellite is not intended. "Distribution" is defined by the Convention as the operation by which a distributor transmits derived signals to the public, and therefore also encompasses cable distribution. To avoid confusions, it should be noted that the term "distribution" in copyright, such as in the WCT and national laws, is regularly used for the making available of tangible copies to the public, rather than for forms of (intangible) transmission. Advances in telecommunication have made it possible for individual users to capture the signal that is intended only for the distributor. In addition, illegal retransmission of broadcasting signals through the Internet has led to discussion of the need for further protection of the program-carrying signal. For example, this topic is on the agenda of the WIPO Standing Committee for Copyright and Related Rights (*see also* Chapter 36 below).

§27.03 MAIN FEATURES OF THE SPECIAL CONVENTIONS

While it can be said that the Phonograms Convention and the Satellites Convention supplement the Rome Convention to a certain extent, it should nevertheless be mentioned that their philosophy is different, in three main respects.

First, the Rome Convention gives the beneficiaries of related rights essentially a right to authorization or prohibition, without of course overlooking the safeguarding of the rights of authors. The Phonograms and Satellites Conventions, however, do not introduce rights but rather leave the Contracting States free to choose the legal means of preventing or repressing acts of piracy.

Second, the Rome Convention is based on the "national treatment" principle. That means that the protection prescribed by the Rome Convention is only minimum protection and that, apart from the rights guaranteed by that Convention itself as constituting that minimum of protection, and within the limits of reservations conceded by it, performers, producers of phonograms and broadcasting organizations enjoy the same rights in countries party to the Convention as those countries grant their nationals. The Phonograms Convention does not speak of the system of "national treatment," but defines expressly the unlawful acts against which Contracting States have to provide effective protection; consequently, the States are not bound to grant foreigners protection against all acts prohibited by their national legislation for the protection of their own nationals. For instance, countries whose national legislation provides protection against the public performance of phonograms are not obliged to make this form of protection available to the producers of phonograms of other Contracting States, because the Phonograms Convention does not itself guarantee any protection against the use in public of lawfully reproduced and distributed phonograms. It should be mentioned, however, that the Phonograms Convention should not be interpreted as limiting the protection available to foreigners under any domestic law or international agreement (Article 7(1)). As a general rule the question of national treatment does not arise in the Satellites Convention either. This Convention places Contracting States under the obligation to take the necessary steps to prevent just one type of activity, namely the distribution of program-carrying signals by any distributor for whom the signals emitted to or passing through the satellite are not intended.

Third, it was in the interests of combating piracy over the widest possible area that the new international agreements were made open to all Member States of the UN or any of the specialized organizations brought into relationship with the UN, or parties to the Statute of the International Court of Justice (virtually all States of the world); whereas the Rome Convention is a so-called closed Convention, its acceptance being reserved for States party to at least one of the two major international copyright conventions.

§27.04 SUBSTANTIVE PROVISIONS OF THE PHONOGRAMS CONVENTION

As far as the substantive provisions are concerned, the Phonograms Convention differs from the Rome Convention mainly as regards: (i) the criteria of eligibility for protection; (ii) the scope of protection; and (iii) the means of ensuring the protection that is provided.

The Phonograms Convention requires only the criterion of nationality as a condition of granting protection. Any Contracting State, however, which on October 29, 1971, afforded protection solely on the basis of the place of first fixation may, by a declaration deposited with the Director General of WIPO, declare that it will apply this criterion.

Protection is granted not only against making duplicates of the phonogram, but also against the distribution of illicit duplicates and importation of such duplicates for distribution (Article 2). However, the scope of protection does not extend to claiming remuneration for secondary uses of the phonogram.

The means by which the Phonograms Convention is to be implemented are a matter for domestic legislation. They may include protection by granting copyright in the phonogram, by granting other specific (related or neighboring) rights, by the law relating to unfair competition, or by penal sanctions (Article 3).

The Phonograms Convention permits the same limitations as those accepted in relation to the protection of authors. The Convention also permits compulsory licenses if reproduction is intended exclusively for teaching or scientific research, limited to the territory of the State whose authorities give the license, and is made in return for equitable remuneration.

Regarding the term of protection, the same minimum duration is required by the Phonograms Convention as by the Rome Convention: if the domestic law prescribes a specific duration for the protection, that duration shall not be less than twenty years from the end either of the year in which the sounds embodied in the phonogram were first fixed or of the year in which the phonogram was first published.

It should be noted that the Phonograms Convention also contains a provision concerning performers. Under its Article 7, the national legislation of each Contracting State may lay down, where necessary, the scope of protection afforded to performers whose performance is fixed on a phonogram and the conditions of enjoying such protection.

§27.05 SUBSTANTIVE PROVISIONS OF THE SATELLITES CONVENTION

The Satellites Convention enlarges the scope of the protection of broadcasting organizations by suppressing the unlawful distribution of program-carrying signals transmitted by satellite irrespective of the fact that such signals (except in the case of DBS) are not suited to reception by the public, and, consequently, their emission does not constitute broadcasting according to the definition of this notion under the Rome Convention. Furthermore, the protection provided for by the Satellites Convention also applies when the derived signals are distributed by cable and not by wireless means, a kind of communication to the public of broadcasts not covered by the Rome Convention. Formally, however, the Convention gives no new right to broadcasting organizations. It obliges the Contracting States to prevent the distribution of program-carrying signals by any distributor from whom the signals passing through the satellite are not intended.

It should be noted that the Satellites Convention, like the Rome Convention, does not protect the transmitted program, because the subject of the protection is the signals emitted by the originating organization. As regards the rights related to the programs, the Convention simply states that it may not be interpreted in any way as limiting or prejudicing the protection afforded to authors, performers, phonogram producers, and broadcasting organizations.

The Satellites Convention permits the distribution of program-carrying signals by non-authorized persons if those signals carry short excerpts containing reports of current events or, as quotations, short excerpts of the program carried by the emitted signals, or, in the case of developing countries, if the program carried by the emitted signals is distributed solely for the purposes of teaching, including adult teaching or scientific research.

With regard to the duration of the protection, the Satellites Convention refers to national legislation in this special context. In any State in which the application of the above measures is limited in time, the duration is to be fixed by its domestic law.

The Satellites Convention does not apply when the signals emitted by the originating organization are intended for direct reception from a satellite by the public (Article 3). In such cases the signals emitted are not intended for any intervening distributor of derived signals; they are directly accessible to the public at large.

§27.06 THE PHONOGRAMS AND SATELLITES CONVENTIONS AND DEVELOPING COUNTRIES

It is significant that the States that joined the Phonograms and Satellites Conventions, similar to the countries party to the Rome Convention, are not necessarily highly industrialized market-economy States. To the contrary many are developing countries. This may be explained by the role that protection of related rights is capable of playing in the development of those countries. In more recent years, the rate of joining these Conventions has slowed, as many developing countries have become parties to the TRIPS Agreement (1994) and the WPPT (1996).

By protecting the phonogram producers, the Phonograms Convention promotes the creation, particularly in developing countries, of an industry in the tertiary sector of the economy whose vitality needs no demonstrating. Such an industry, while ensuring that national culture is propagated both throughout the country itself and throughout the world, can also constitute a source of substantial revenue for the national economy and, where its activities extend beyond the frontiers, lead to an inflow of foreign currency. The international protection of phonogram producers also promotes the protection of TCEs incorporated in phonograms against unlawful reproduction abroad.

By giving phonogram producers the possibility of deriving profit from their productions internationally, the Phonograms Convention becomes an instrument promoting artistic heritage and an indisputable encouragement to creativity. It is also certain that if the interests of foreign performers and phonogram producers are equally safeguarded, national productions will enjoy greater dissemination, and it will therefore be national works, and not above all foreign works, that will increasingly be used by the mass media and the public. Further, if the results of this type of activity are exported, it becomes necessary for these interests concerned to be protected on an international scale, and that can be done by acceding to the relevant international conventions.

Finally, broadcasting organizations play an important role in developing countries, and they also have an interest in protecting their costly programs against reproduction, rebroadcast, and other communication to the public of their broadcasts, including broadcasting via satellites. Frequently, the broadcasting of a particular program, concert or other event is permitted only for given territories and on condition that no televised presentation is made outside that territory. The broadcasting organization therefore needs to be able to prohibit the rebroadcasting and presentation to the public of television shows. The same principle applies to the broadcasting of performances and recordings of expressions of national folklore, now referred to as TCEs. The broadcasting organization should have the possibility at the international level of preventing illicit distribution or fixation for the purpose of reproduction of its own broadcast programs in respect of creations belonging to the national heritage.

The recognition and international protection of the rights of performers, producers of phonograms and broadcasting organizations, in conjunction with copyright, quite definitely contribute to the development of nations, as does protection of IP as a whole. Thus it is desirable that more and more countries recognize the necessity of establishing legal protection of authors, performers, producers of phonograms and broadcasting organizations as an interdependent system, both at the national and international levels.

§27.07 MEMBERSHIP OF THE PHONOGRAMS AND SATELLITES CONVENTIONS

As of June 2, 2024, eighty-one States were party to the Convention for the Protection of Producers and Phonograms Against Unauthorized Duplication of Their Phonograms.

As of June 2, 2024, forty States were party to the Brussels Convention Relating to the Distribution of Programme-Carrying Signals Transmitted by Satellite.

CHAPTER 28
The WIPO Internet Treaties: The WCT and the WPPT

§28.01 THE WCT

[A] Background

After the last revision of the Berne Convention in 1971, a number of important new technological developments took place—reprography, video technology, compact cassette systems facilitating "home taping," satellite broadcasting, cable television, the increase of the importance of computer programs, computer storage of works and electronic databases, etc.

For a while, the international copyright community followed the strategy of "guided development" by study and discussion, rather than trying to establish new international norms. The recommendations, guiding principles and model provisions worked out by experts in various WIPO bodies (in the beginning, sometimes in cooperation with UNESCO) offered guidance to governments on how to respond to the challenges of new technologies. Those recommendations, guiding principles and model provisions were based, in general, on the exchange of national experiences and the interpretation of existing international norms, particularly the Berne Convention (e.g., concerning computer programs, databases, "home taping," satellite broadcasting and cable television). But they also included some new standards (e.g., concerning distribution and rental of copies). The guidance thus offered in the "guided development" period had an important impact on national legislation, contributing to the development of copyright all over the world. At the end of the 1980s, however, it was recognized that mere guidance would no longer suffice, but the work undertaken by the various group of experts was important to prepare for discussion regarding a binding instrument.

While the WIPO "guided development" led to discussion about a possible protocol to the Berne Convention in 1991, discussion of international norms of IP was included in the agenda of the 1986 Uruguay Round of the GATT.

After the adoption of the TRIPS Agreement in 1994 under the auspices of GATT, the preparatory work on new copyright and related rights norms in the WIPO committees was intensified to deal with problems not addressed by the TRIPS Agreement. The discussions held at WIPO coincided with the fact that policymakers around the world were looking at the challenges imposed by network communications and digital technologies such as the Internet. To this end, in 1996 the WIPO Diplomatic Conference on Certain Copyright and Related Rights Questions adopted two treaties, the WCT and the WPPT, which are also collectively referred to as the "Internet Treaties."

[B] Legal Nature and Relationship with Other Treaties

The Treaty was one of the two Treaties that were adopted by the Diplomatic Conference to address the issues raised by the advances in technology especially in the digital environment. The Treaty is deemed to be a special agreement within the meaning of Article 20 of the Berne Convention for the Protection of Literary and Artistic Works, as regards Contracting Parties that are countries of the Union established by that Convention. Article 1(1) of the WCT makes it clear that no interpretation of the WCT is acceptable which may result in any lowering of the level of protection granted by the Berne Convention.

In implementing the provisions of the Treaty, Contracting States are expected to ensure that they comply with the substantive provisions of the Berne Convention, namely Articles 1-21. The Treaty seeks to fill some gaps regarding issues not addressed by the Berne Convention and to clarify some of the existing provisions in light of the new technologies that had emerged in the digital environment. It is also important to note that many of these issues had not been addressed by the time the WTO TRIPS Agreement was discussed and concluded in 1994. Other than the Berne Convention, the Treaty has no formal relationship with other conventions or treaties and shall not in any way be construed to prejudice any rights or obligations under other treaties, for example the TRIPS Agreement or the UCC.

It should also be pointed out that although both the WCT and the WPPT were concluded in the same diplomatic conference in 1996, no formal relationship exists between the treaties. Nevertheless, several provisions of the WCT and WPPT are either identical or very similar.

[C] Provisions Relating to the Digital Environment

During the preparatory work, it became clear that the most important and most urgent task was to clarify existing norms and, where necessary, create new norms to respond to the problems raised by digital technology, and particularly by the Internet. The issues addressed in this context were referred to as the "digital agenda," although the scope of potential digital issues is much broader. The digital agenda included the rights applicable to the storage and transmission of works in digital systems, the limitations on and exceptions to rights in a digital environment, technological measures of protection and RMI, and the right of making available or distribution in respect of transmissions in digital networks.

In June 1982, a WIPO/UNESCO Committee of Governmental Experts clarified that storage of works in an electronic medium is reproduction. The Diplomatic Conference adopted an agreed statement which reads as follows: "The reproduction right, as set out in Article 9 of the Berne Convention, and the exceptions permitted thereunder, fully apply in the digital environment, in particular to the use of works in digital form. It is understood that the storage of a protected work in digital form in an electronic medium constitutes a reproduction within the meaning of Article 9 of the Berne Convention."

It follows from this first sentence that Article 9(1) of the Berne Convention continued to be fully applicable in the digital environment. This means that the concept of reproduction under Article 9(1) of the Convention, which extends to reproduction "in any manner or form" irrespective of the duration of the reproduction, must not be restricted merely because a reproduction is in digital form through storage in an electronic memory, and just because a reproduction is of a temporary nature. Similarly, the issue of the transient and incidental reproductions would be left for national legislation according to the first sentence of Article 9(2) of the Convention: "It shall be a matter for legislation in the countries of the Union." Thus Article 9(2) continued to offer an appropriate basis to introduce into national legislation any justified exceptions such as transient and incidental reproductions, in harmony with the "three-step test" provided for in that provision of the Convention.

During the preparatory work, an agreement emerged that the transmission of works on the Internet and in similar networks should be the object of an exclusive right of authorization of the author or other copyright owner, with appropriate exceptions. There was, however, no agreement concerning the right or rights that should actually be applied, although the rights of communication to the public and distribution were identified as the two major possibilities. It was also noted, however, that the Berne Convention does not offer full coverage for those rights; the former does not extend to certain categories of works, while explicit recognition of the latter covers only one category, namely that of cinematographic works.

Differences in the legal characterization of digital transmissions were partly due to the fact that such transmissions are of a complex nature, and that the various experts considered one aspect more relevant than another. However, the most fundamental reason was that coverage of the abovementioned two rights differs to a great extent in national laws. It became evident that it would be difficult to reach consensus on a solution based on one right over the other. A specific solution was therefore adopted, which provided that the act of digital transmission should be described in a neutral way, free from specific legal characterization; that such a description should not be excessively technical and, at the same time, should convey the interactive nature of digital transmissions; that, in respect of legal characterization of the exclusive right—that is, in respect of the actual choice of the right or rights to be applied—sufficient freedom should be left to national legislation; and, finally, that the gaps in the Berne Convention in the coverage of the relevant rights—the right of communication to the public and the right of distribution—should be covered. This solution was referred to as the "umbrella solution."

The WCT applies this "umbrella solution" by extending applicability of the right of communication to the public to all categories of works, and clarifies that the right also covers transmissions in interactive systems described in a manner free of legal characterization. It was stated in the Diplomatic Conference that Contracting Parties are also free to implement the obligation to grant an exclusive right to authorize such "making available to the public" through the application of a right other than the right of communication to the public or through the combination of different rights. This only applies to the right chosen; however, since Article 8 of the WCT does not provide for any exhaustion of the right, implementing national laws that choose the right of distribution may not apply any rule of exhaustion. It is also worth noting that the right of communication including making available to the public to be respected as minimum protection does not include any restriction to for-profit acts or acts directed to a "new public," but fully applies to any acts of communication to any public.

The WCT does not list specific limitations or exceptions as the Berne Convention does; however, the Berne limitations and exceptions have to be complied with under Article 1(4) of the WCT. In addition, the WCT follows the approach found in the TRIPS Agreement of expanding the three-step test, found in Article 9(2) of the Berne Convention with respect only to the right of reproduction, to cover all rights recognized in that Convention. It also applies a similar version of the three-step test as a condition for national legislation creating exemptions to any of the rights recognized by the WCT.

Digital technologies facilitate the ability of any user to undertake acts such as the reproduction of a work in very easy and inexpensive manner. Against that possibility, right holders started to make use of technological tools to control some of the acts and information with respect to their works. The WCT text followed that new reality in the protection of copyrighted works and included provisions regarding technological protection measures (TPMs) and RMI. It does not require the use of TPMs or RMI by the right holder, but does provide an obligation to provide protection against the circumvention of such tools and related acts once they are in place.

[D] Other Substantive Provisions

[1] Eligibility for Protection, Scope and Subject Matter of Protection

The WCT did not aim to repeat what was already stated in the Berne Convention. Therefore, it settles certain issues regarding the principles of protection (national treatment, minimum protection and formality-free protection) and rules for their application (e.g., country of origin, eligibility for protection, possible restriction of ("backdoor") protection in respect of works of nationals of certain countries not party to the Treaty) in a simple way; in Article 3, it provides for the *mutatis mutandis* application of Articles 2-6 of the Berne Convention. In addition, exceptions to national treatment also have to be complied with on the basis of Article 1(4) of the WCT. The WCT also clarifies the protection extending to computer programs and original databases, and thereby makes them part of the minimum protection. It further clarifies that protection of copyright is restricted to the expression and not to "ideas, procedures, methods of operation or mathematical concepts as such." This is virtually the same as the clarification included in Article 9.2 of the TRIPS Agreement. Nor is this principle reflected in Article 2 new in the context of the Berne Convention, since countries party to the Convention have always understood the scope of protection under the Convention in that way.

[a] Rights Protected

Under the Berne Convention, it is only in respect of cinematographic works that the right of distribution is granted explicitly. Such a right, surviving at least until the first sale of copies, may be deduced as an indispensable corollary to the right of reproduction, and, in some legal systems, the right of distribution is in fact recognized on this basis. Article 6(1) of the WCT provides an exclusive right to authorize the making available to the public of originals and copies of works through sale or other transfer of ownership, that is, an exclusive right of distribution. Article 6(1) should be considered at least a useful clarification of the obligations under the Berne Convention (and also under the TRIPS Agreement, which includes by reference the relevant provisions of the Convention), and perhaps as an addition to those obligations.

Article 6(2) of the WCT addresses the issue of the exhaustion of the right of distribution. It does not oblige Contracting States to regulate the issue of exhaustion or to choose among the national, regional or international exhaustion regimes for the right of distribution after the first sale or other first transfer of ownership of the original or a copy of the work, with the authorization of the author. An important agreed statement clarifies that the distribution right and its possible exhaustion (as well as the rental right) exclusively applies to fixed copies that can be put into circulation as tangible objects, and thus not to transmission of works in intangible form, such as via the internet.

Article 7 of the WCT provides an exclusive right of authorizing commercial rental to the public in respect of the same categories of works—computer programs, cinematographic works and works embodied in phonograms, as determined in the national laws of Contracting Parties—as those covered by Articles 11 and 14.4 of the TRIPS Agreement, and with the same exceptions. The exceptions are in respect of computer programs that are not themselves the essential objects of the rental, in respect of cinematographic works unless commercial rental leads to widespread copying of such works, materially impairing the exclusive right of reproduction, and in respect of a Contracting Party which, on April 15, 1994, had and still has in force a system of equitable remuneration for rental of copies of works included in phonograms, instead of an exclusive right. In the case of the exclusive right, the Contracting

Party may maintain that system provided that commercial rental does not give rise to the material impairment of the exclusive right of authorization.

Beyond addressing the making available of works on the Internet (*see* [C] above), Article 8 of the WCT also complements the fragmentary provisions of the Berne Convention on the communication right.

[b] Duration of Protection for Photographic Works

While the duration of protection for photographic works under the Berne Convention is a minimum of twenty-five years, Article 9 of the WCT has the effect of extending that term of protection in order to apply the same minimum term of protection that applies to other protected works. The duration for all other works is governed by the provisions of the Berne Convention (Article 1(4) of the WCT), under which in general the minimum term is the life of the author plus fifty years.

[c] Limitations and Exceptions

Article 10(1) and (2) set out the criteria for the application of limitations and exceptions to all the exclusive rights covered in the WCT and the Berne Convention, in addition to those Berne limitations and exceptions referred to under Article 1(4) WCT. They are subject to the three-step test as per Article 9(2) of the Berne Convention. While Article 9(2) only covers the right of reproduction, Article 10 of the WCT covers all exclusive rights granted in the Convention as well as the WCT.

[d] Other Provisions

Article 13 of the WCT refers simply to Article 18 of the Berne Convention to determine the works to which the Treaty applies at the moment of its entry into force for a given Contracting State, and stipulates that the provisions of that Article must also be applied to the Treaty. Article 14 is similar to Article 36(1) of the Berne Convention, which requires the Contracting Parties to ensure that they have within their legal systems measures that facilitate enforcement of the rights. It is also in line with Article 41.1 of the TRIPS Agreement.

[E] Administrative Provisions

The administrative provisions and final clauses, in general, are the same as or similar to the provisions of other WIPO treaties on the same issues. Recent WIPO treaties no longer have a deadline for countries to accede as was the case in the first acts of the Berne Convention.

Article 17 of the WCT provides that any WIPO Member State is eligible to become a party to the Treaty. It also states that "The Assembly may decide to admit any IGO to become party to this Treaty which declares that it is competent in respect of, and has its own legislation binding on all its Member States on, matters covered by this Treaty and that it has been duly authorized, in accordance with its internal procedures, to become party to this Treaty." Paragraph (3) adds the following: "The European Community, having made the declaration referred to in the preceding paragraph in the Diplomatic Conference that has adopted this Treaty, may become party to this Treaty."

The number of instruments of ratification or accession needed for the entry into force of the WCT was fixed at thirty. The WCT entered into force on March 6, 2002.

[F] Implementation of the WCT

It is important to note that the implementation of the Treaty in national law does not change the fundamental policy structure of copyright norms at the international level. Implementation needs to take into account the rapid technological changes that led to the adoption of the WCT, and should include the consideration of several related features in national legislation, including adequate exceptions and limitations in the digital environment, as highlighted in the agreed statement to Article 10 of the WCT.

The WCT was an early reaction to digital technologies and a new reality shaped by the Internet where copyright would play a central role in protecting content. It raised significantly the international minimum standard of protection from that of the Berne Convention, which at the time was reflected in many national laws. The implementation of the WCT into national legislation has been noticeable, especially considering that before its adoption many countries had not established provisions regarding TPMs, RMI or the right of making available. Some of the innovations first brought by the TRIPS agreement and later repeated by the WCT have influenced many national laws. These include the protection of computer programs and original databases, as well as the clarification regarding the non-protection of mere ideas. Many countries are still seeking to adapt their national legislation to the WCT, sometimes in conjunction with joining the WTO including the TRIPS Agreement. However, several countries have yet to ratify or accede to the WCT even in cases where they have already domesticated its provisions.

The WCT came into force in 2002.

[G] Membership of the WCT

116 Contracting Parties were party to the WCT as of June 4, 2024.

§28.02 THE WPPT

[A] History

The preparation of the WCT and the WPPT took place in two Committees of Experts. The Committee of Experts on the Possible Protocol to the Berne Convention was established first in 1991 and prepared what eventually became the WCT. The original terms of reference of the Committee also included the rights of producers of phonograms. However, in 1992, those rights were carved out, and the Committee of Experts on the Possible Instrument for the Rights of the Performers and Producers of Phonograms was established. Its terms of reference extended to all aspects of protection of the rights of performers and producers of phonograms where the clarification of existing international norms or the establishment of new norms seemed desirable.

In respect of those rights, the existing international standards were included in the Rome Convention of 1961. At the time of its adoption, the Rome Convention was recognized as a "pioneer convention," as it had established norms concerning what are known as related or neighboring rights, which existed neither in the international legal framework nor in most of the WIPO Member States.

In the 1970s and 1980s, however, a great number of important new technological developments took place, and these were discussed in the Intergovernmental Committee of the Rome Convention as well as in various other WIPO meetings together with the so-called neighboring rights. As a result, guidance was offered to governments and legislators in the form of recommendations, guiding principles and model provisions. At the end of the 1980s, it was recognized that mere guidance would no longer suffice; binding norms were indispensable.

The preparation of the new norms began in two forums: at WIPO in the abovementioned committees of experts and at GATT, in the framework of the Uruguay Round of negotiations. After the adoption of the TRIPS Agreement, the work on new copyright and neighboring rights norms in the WIPO Committees was accelerated.

The WIPO Diplomatic Conference on Certain Copyright and Neighbouring Rights Questions, held in Geneva in December 1996, adopted two treaties: the WCT and the WPPT.

[B] Legal Nature of the WPPT and Its Relationship with Other International Treaties

In the early preparatory work on the WPPT, there was a proposal to have a provision that would provide a special relationship with the Rome Convention as was with the case between WCT and the Berne Convention. This idea did not get sufficient support. However, the WPPT clearly has a thematic relationship with the Rome Convention, which has been regulated in a way similar to the relationship between the TRIPS Agreement and the Rome Convention. This means that: (i) in general, application of the substantive provisions of the Rome Convention is not an obligation of the Contracting Parties; (ii) only a few provisions of the Rome Convention are included by reference (those relating to the criteria of eligibility for protection); and (iii) Article 1(2) of the Treaty contains, *mutatis mutandis*, practically the same provision as Article 2.2 of the TRIPS Agreement, stating that nothing in the Treaty derogates from obligations that Contracting Parties have to each other under the Rome Convention.

The WPPT has no connection with other treaties. It shall not in any way prejudice the rights and obligations afforded under any other treaties, and shall not affect their provisions as they relate to the underlying copyright.

[C] Provisions Relating to the Digital Environment

The provisions of the WPPT relating to the "digital agenda" cover certain definitions, rights applicable to storage and transmission of performances and phonograms in digital systems, limitations on and exceptions to rights in a digital environment, TPMs and RMI. The definitions are structured in the same way as under the Rome Convention. The definitions take into account the impact of digital technology as it affects the performers and producers of sound recordings.

The specific provisions that were meant to address the reproduction and storage of performances and phonograms were not included in the final text, but are contained in an agreed statement, which interprets the text on the reproduction right. It corresponds to the agreed statement (to Article 1(4)) on the reproduction right in the WCT discussed above. In June 1982, a WIPO/UNESCO Committee of Governmental Experts clarified that storage of works and objects of related rights in an electronic medium is reproduction. The right of reproduction as well as other rights is subject to exceptions and limitations in line with the three-step test.

Performers and producers of sound recordings under Articles 10 and 14 of the Treaty have the exclusive right of making available to the public their performances fixed in phonograms and their phonograms respectively. The limitations and exceptions to the use of these works in the digital environment are also subject to the three-step test (Article 16(2)).

The provisions in Articles 18 and 19 of the WPPT concerning TPMs and RMI and infringement correspond to the similar provisions of the WCT as discussed above.

[D] Other Substantive Provisions

[1] Criteria for Eligibility and National Treatment

The criteria for application is as per the Rome Convention (Articles 4, 5, 17 and 18), to be applied by analogy (Article 3 of the WPPT). National Treatment applies just as in the TRIPS Agreement, but only extends to exclusive rights granted under the Treaty (and thus not to statutory remuneration rights that may exist under national laws, except for that provided under Article 15 of the WPPT). Still, in this context, only the updated definitions of the WPPT have to be applied.

[2] Rights of Performers

It is important to address the issue as to what performances are covered by the Treaty. One aspect to be highlighted is the inclusion, for the first time in an international treaty, of performances made by performers of expressions of folklore, now referred to as TCEs (Article 2(a) of the WPPT), in addition to performances of works. One other particularity of the WPPT is that although it is almost entirely dedicated to aural performances, it recognizes the right of broadcasting of live (unfixed) performances for all performances. In a similar way, Article 14.1 of the TRIPS Agreement recognizes the right of broadcasting of audiovisual performances but also grants the right of communication to the public of such performances. In the WPPT, all the remaining rights recognized in the WCT, besides the right of broadcasting of live performances, are provided exclusively with respect to aural performances. One important aspect is that, for the first time in an international instrument, protection of the moral rights of the performer is recognized. Although this provision is modelled on Article *6bis* of the Berne Convention, the level of protection is slightly lower.

The economic rights granted to performers in the WPPT are similar to those listed in the WCT for authors. These include the right of broadcasting and communication to the public of unfixed performances except where the performance is already broadcast (Article 6(ii)), right of reproduction, and right of rental (Articles 6, 7 and 9). Other rights include the right of making available as discussed above, and the right of distribution. However, as regards communication to the public beyond these rights, performers (as well as phonogram producers) only enjoy a statutory right to remuneration (*see* [4] below).

[3] Rights of Producers of Phonograms

The rights discussed above in the digital agenda apply to the producers of phonograms in addition to other rights, namely the right of reproduction, distribution and rental (Articles 11, 12 and 13).

[4] Right to Remuneration for Broadcasting and Communication to the Public

The equitable right to remuneration for broadcasting and communication to the public is economically among the most important rights of performers and phonogram producers, and is regularly administered by CMOs. This provision requires the payment of a single equitable remuneration where performances fixed in phonograms and phonograms are broadcast or communicated to the public. Article 15 of the WPPT provides for almost the same kind of right of remuneration to performers and producers of phonograms as Article 12 of the Rome Convention; however, it is broader because it includes indirect uses (in particular, rebroadcasting and communication of the relevant broadcast) and in principle acknowledges the right for both performers and phonogram producers. In addition, it also applies to phonograms that exclusively have been made available over the Internet or similar networks, rather than having been published in the traditional way. Contracting Parties can make a notification if they choose not to apply the right or to do so only in certain ways.

[5] Limitations and Exceptions

Under Article 16(1) of the WPPT, Contracting Parties may "provide for the same kinds of limitations or exceptions with regard to the protection of performers and producers of phonograms as they provide for, in their national legislation, in connection with the protection of copyright in literary and artistic works." This provision corresponds in substance to Article 15.2 of the Rome Convention. However, the Rome Convention, in Article 15.1, also provides for specific limitations independent of those provided in a given domestic law concerning copyright protection for use of short excerpts for private use, reporting current events, ephemeral fixations by broadcasting organizations, and uses for teaching and research. The WPPT does not contain such a list.

Article 16(2) of the WPPT requires the application of the "three-step test" for any limitations and exceptions to the rights provided for in the WPPT.

[6] Transferability of Rights

The WPPT, like the Berne Convention and the WCT, generally permits the transfer of economic rights. It contains no limitation on the transferability of economic rights, and the transferability is confirmed by the introductory phrase of Article 5(1) on moral rights of performers which reads: "Independently of a performer's economic rights and *even after the transfer of those rights ....*" (emphasis added).

[7] Duration of Protection

Like the TRIPS Agreement, the WPPT provides a fifty-year term of protection. However, the calculation of the term of protection of phonograms under the WPPT differs from the method provided for in the TRIPS Agreement, which may result in substantive differences in the term of protection. Under Article 14.5 of the TRIPS Agreement, the fifty-year term is always computed from the end of the year in which the fixation was made, while under Article 17(2) of the WPPT, the term is calculated from the end of the year in which the phonogram was published, and it is only in the case of absence of publication that it is calculated as under the TRIPS Agreement. Since publication normally takes place after fixation, in general the term under the Treaty is slightly longer.

[8] Formalities and Application in Time

The enjoyment and exercise of rights provided for in the Treaty must not be subject to any formality, as clearly stated in Article 20 of the WPPT. Article 22(1) of the WPPT, in general, provides for the *mutatis mutandis* application of Article 18 of the Berne Convention regarding application to works in existence at the time of its entry into force. Article 22(2), however, allows Contracting Parties to limit the application of Article 5 on moral rights to performances that take place after the Treaty enters into force for them.

[a] *Enforcement of Rights*

The provisions on enforcement in Article 20 of the WPPT correspond to the similar provisions in Article 14 of the WCT.

[E] Administrative Provisions

The administrative provisions in the WPPT are, in general, the same as, or similar to, the provisions of other WIPO treaties on the same issues, and they correspond to the similar provisions of the WCT.

The number of instruments of ratification or accession needed for the entry into force of the WPPT was fixed at thirty.

[F] Implementation of the Treaty

The WPPT came into force in 2002. Many countries are still seeking to adapt their national legislation to the WPPT. However, several countries have yet to ratify or accede to the WPPT even in cases where they have already domesticated its provisions.

[G] Membership of the WPPT

112 Contracting Parties were party to the WPPT as of June 4, 2024.

§28.03 SECTION III: BENEFITS OF ADHERENCE TO THE WCT AND WPPT

[A] Updating Protections for the Digital Era

In the era of digital networks and the proliferation of high-speed Internet coupled with affordability of different digital media, it is important to ensure that protected works and subject matter of related rights are protected. This need is highlighted by the "borderless" nature of digital networks. The WCT and WPPT offer copyright and related rights protection beyond national borders. The Treaties also promote electronic commerce within and outside national borders. It is essential to update and "future proof" the international normative framework to take into account the ever-changing technologies to facilitate the dissemination and use of copyright-protected works over the Internet. The WCT and WPPT provide important incentives for creators and authors, especially in the digital environment. This in turn will contribute to the national economy due to the growth of copyright-based industries which have become a major source of intellectual capital, especially for developing countries.

It is important to note that the Treaties do not create new categories of rights as such, but seek to clarify the use of works and ensure that they get protection from the application of existing rights in the digital environment. The Treaties do not create a new right of access or control of access as these already exist within the copyright law. The TPM and RMI provisions seek to address the issues of access and control in the digital environment. It is important to note that it is still possible to apply limitations and exceptions, or what some national systems call "exemptions," to the TPM and RMI provisions, subject to the three-step test.

[B] Advantages for Developing Countries

It is crucial that developing countries, countries in transition and LDCs update their laws to ensure that they take into account the various developments in the digital environment and international law. Trade in copyright-protected works is a major element in global electronic commerce. Proper protection encourages rights holders to securely sell and license their works online and over other digital networks. The appropriate limitations and exceptions will continue to safeguard public interest uses.

Another important element is the increased contribution to the national economy through e-commerce. The economic importance of copyright industries has over the last few years been well documented in studies covering developing countries. The knowledge-based sector in developing countries is growing, and the market for products and services protected by copyright and related rights will increase online. Thus. to compete in the global marketplace, it is necessary to have a supportive legal framework both at the national and regional level.

For developing countries, countries in transition and the LDCs, the implementation of the WCT and WPPT has various advantages. The first is the increased protection of performers at the international level. This takes into account that the Internet is global and is deemed to be "borderless"; thus. the need to have rights protected beyond national borders. The protection covers both the digital and non-digital environment. Second, joining the Treaties is likely to encourage FDI due to the legal framework that is put in place upon ratification and domestication of the Treaties. These provisions will enable competition on a level playing field once the threshold of initial access to digital networks is passed. It is important to note that with the proliferation of affordable high-speed Internet connectivity and mobile telephones, there is increased use and dissemination of works, including local works, offering more opportunities to the creators and rights holders of works.

CHAPTER 29
The Beijing Treaty on Audiovisual Performances

§29.01 BACKGROUND

The international protection of audiovisual performances is clearly recognized by the Rome Convention for the Protection of Performers, Producers of Phonograms and Broadcasting Organizations (the Rome Convention), although in a very limited manner. In this respect, the Rome Convention grants rights to prevent broadcasting, communication to the public and fixation of live performances, and rights to prevent reproduction of a performance which was fixed without the consent of the performer (Article 7.1). Nonetheless, Article 19 of the Rome Convention provides that the economic minimum rights of performers in fixed performances end once a film performer has consented to incorporation of his or her performance in an audiovisual fixation. As a consequence of this so-called *cut-off provision*, performers in those performances fixed in audiovisual media were deprived of any meaningful international protection.

The WIPO Diplomatic Conference on Certain Copyright and Neighbouring Rights Questions, which took place from December 2 to 20, 1996, represented a serious attempt to overcome the exclusion of audiovisual performances from the international standard of protection. During the discussions leading to the WCT and WPPT, some countries preferred to focus on sound performances while others were ready also to consider the protection of audiovisual performances.

The WPPT only focuses on the exploitation of performances fixed on phonograms, and not in audiovisual media. Many of the issues on the protection of actors were already debated in the December 1996 Diplomatic Conference, including the transfer of rights from the performer to the producer, moral rights of audiovisual performers, and so-called flexible implementation, according to which Treaty obligations could be implemented by means of collective bargaining instead of legal statute. Already at that time the difficulties were described as related to the international compatibility of two systems; related (or neighboring) rights and collective bargaining based on labor law, each of which functioned in a satisfactory manner at national level according to the groups of Member States concerned.

The definitions of the terms "phonogram," "fixation" and "communication to the public" in Article 2(b) and (c) of the WPPT limit the application of that Treaty to the sounds of a performance. As regards audiovisual use of performances (use through moving images, with or without sound) the WPPT only grants protection against live broadcasting (Article 6(i)). The 1996 Diplomatic Conference that adopted the WPPT also discussed a possible extension of the scope of protection to cover such audiovisual use, but agreement was not reached at the time. In accordance with a Resolution adopted by the Diplomatic Conference, work on the issue continued in the WIPO SCCR. The Conference also adopted a resolution calling for the convening the following year of a Diplomatic Conference on the protection of audiovisual performances. Such a Diplomatic Conference did not take place until December 2000.

At the Diplomatic Conference on the Protection of Audiovisual Performances, which was held in Geneva in December 2000, agreement was reached on all issues, except for the question of international recognition of statutory provisions on the transfer of rights from performers to producers. Thus, nineteen out of twenty substantive articles were agreed.

After ten years, the WIPO General Assembly decided to reconvene the Diplomatic Conference in June 2012. Informal discussions, first between US performers and producers and later among the WIPO Member States, resulted in a formal agreement in the SCCR on the new article regarding the transfer of rights. However, in June 2011, during the SCCR, another issue was raised as to the status of the provisionally agreed nineteen Articles of the proposed treaty and the possibility of adding new provisions. Most Member States were of the considered opinion that the discussion on the nineteen Articles should not be reopened. A compromise was reached to include a new recital to the preamble taking into account the WIPO Development Agenda, and to undertake negotiations during the proposed Diplomatic Conference on three additional Agreed Statements to address other issues, including the relationship of the proposed treaty with TRIPS and the WPPT.

The WIPO Diplomatic Conference on the Protection of Audiovisual Performances was reconvened in June 2012. It adopted the BTAP, which included the nineteen articles that were provisionally agreed upon during the 2000 Diplomatic Conference, Article 12 with the language that had been agreed to regarding the transfer of rights, and the additional preambular and agreed statements that had been the subject of the compromise agreement.

§29.02 LEGAL NATURE OF THE BTAP AND RELATIONSHIP WITH OTHER INTERNATIONAL TREATIES

The WIPO BTAP in a very general manner recognizes its connection with the WPPT in Article 1. Nonetheless, Contracting Parties under the BTAP are not obliged to apply the substantive provisions of the Rome Convention or the WPPT. This is similar to the regulation of the relationship between the Rome Convention and the TRIPS Agreement as well as between the WPPT and the Rome Convention. The protection granted under the Treaty shall not in any way affect the protection of copyright in literary and artistic works and no provision in the treaty shall in any way prejudice such protection. Thus it sets the limits of protection in relation to copyright in literary and artistic works.

§29.03 PROVISIONS RELATING TO THE DIGITAL ENVIRONMENT

There are several provisions in the BTAP that relate to the digital environment. These include some of the definitions and provisions on reproduction, including storage as well as transmission of audiovisual performances, TPMs, RMI, and limitations and exceptions. The digital environment is ever evolving especially with increased Internet bandwidth and availability of various media for transmission, and the Treaty attempts to address these issues in a future-proof manner.

§29.04 OTHER SUBSTANTIVE PROVISIONS

[A] National Treatment and Definitions

Like in the WPPT, national treatment is restricted to the exclusive rights provided under the Treaty and the remuneration right under its Article 11. The BTAP however allows for further-reaching restrictions of national treatment (Article 4 of the BTAP). The criteria for eligibility for national treatment and minimum protection do not follow the rules of the Rome Convention and the WPPT; instead, nationality or habitual residence are the criteria under the BTAP (Article 3).

The definitions in the BTAP are different from the definitions found in the WPPT in the sense that they focus on audiovisual rather than aural performances. An "audiovisual fixation" is defined as "an embodiment of moving images whether or not accompanied by sounds or by the representations thereof, from which they can be perceived, reproduced or communicated through a device." The Agreed Statement to this article clarifies that this definition shall not in any way prejudice the definition of "fixation" under Article 2(c) of the WPPT, in order to avoid a possible overlap between the BTAP and the WPPT prejudicing the rights of performers recognized in the WPPT.

Under Article 2(d) "broadcasting" is defined to cover wireless transmission, including satellite transmission. This approach follows the definitions from the Rome Convention and the WPPT regarding broadcasting as a wireless form of transmission that is differentiated from other types of "communication to the public." Transmission in any medium other than broadcasting is defined as "communication to the public" and covers both unfixed and fixed audiovisual performances. For purposes of Article 11, communication to the public also includes making a performance fixed in an audiovisual fixation audible or visible or audible and visible to the public.

As under the WPPT, performers are defined to include those who perform expressions of folklore, now usually referred to as "TCEs," rather than only works.

[B] Transfer of Rights

The regime of transfer of rights is of great relevance for performers when exercising rights granted under the BTAP, and it was one of the major points of contention throughout the negotiations. In production of audiovisual works, the transfer of rights from the performers to the producers is crucial for the negotiation of commercial deals by the producers. It negates the need for the producers to seek authority from the performers every time they have to negotiate a deal. The issue of transfer of rights prevented the Member States from reaching a final agreement in the 2000 Diplomatic Conference, as there was no reconciliation between different approaches on the issue, especially those of the USA and the EU. The different positions can be explained by the fact that in the USA, performers' rights are automatically transferred to producers, while actors' remuneration is negotiated by a trade union with strong collective bargaining power, the Screen Actors Guild. This is different from the situation in Europe, where the practice varies. In some European countries, especially the civil law countries, transfer is presumed by law, while in others it is a legal presumption but an agreement to the contrary is possible. Countries such as the UK and a number of developing countries that followed the common law tradition have no statutory rules on transfer of rights in audiovisual fixations, leaving the issue completely to contractual agreements. In addition, moral rights also play a relevant role in the negotiations of audiovisual productions and while they do not apply in "works for hire" or are considered transferable in the US, and may be waived in a few countries, they are inalienable in most countries. The Beijing Treaty addresses these diverging practices as regards exclusive rights of authorization under the Treaty (though not regarding moral rights) by offering a level of flexibility in the transfer of rights once the performer has consented to the transfer in writing.

[C] Rights Granted

Audiovisual performers are guaranteed for the first time in an international instrument a number of exclusive rights, as well as moral rights, which were already recognized for other performers. The moral rights recognized include the right of the performer to claim identification as the performer of the performances and to object to modifications prejudicial to his or her reputation. Such rights are not infringed when the fixed performance is modified in an insubstantial way and in the normal course of exploitation due to the nature of audiovisual works, which are frequently edited and distributed in different formats (as specified in the agreed statement to Article 5 of the BTAP). The economic rights in the Beijing Treaty are similar to those granted to performers under the WPPT and include the exclusive rights of broadcasting and communication to the public of their unfixed performances excluding those that have been broadcast, fixation of their unfixed performances, reproduction, distribution, rental and making available. In addition, exclusive rights of broadcasting and communication to the public are also provided, though subject to possible reservations.

Also following the approach first used in the WCT and WPPT, the Agreed Statement to Article 7 of the BTAP states that the reproduction right applies in the digital environment and in particular that the storage of audiovisual performances in digital formats and any other electronic formats is also covered. Like the WPPT, the BTAP recognizes the "right of making available" in Article 10, differentiating it from communication to the public by the fact that members of the public can access the fixed performances at their convenience, at a time and location of their choosing. The right of making available is increasingly important as streaming and online services offering audiovisual content increase in number and reach more consumers around the globe.

[D] Duration of Protection

The rights granted by the BTAP last for fifty years from the fixation of the performance.

[E] Technological Measures

The BTAP reaffirms in a broad sense the protection against the circumvention of technological measures, which have become a relevant tool against illegal uses of protected content, especially online. The Agreed Statement concerning Article 15, however, states that Contracting Parties may provide for measures to enable beneficiaries of limitations and exceptions to enjoy them, despite the technological measures applied, under further conditions, in particular that there is legal access to the performances and that right holders have not themselves enabled access to the performances.

[F] Limitations and Exceptions

The BTAP, like the Rome Convention and the WPPT, allows adoption of limitations and exceptions that already exist for literary and artistic works, and imposes the three-step test on the adoption of any limitations and exceptions by the Contracting Parties with regard to any of the rights recognized in the BTAP.

[G] Administrative Provisions

The Administrative provisions are found in Articles 21 to 30 of the Treaty. Like the WCT and the WPPT, the BTAP is also administered by WIPO and provides for an Assembly of the Member States. The Assembly determines the program, adopts the budget and controls the finances of the Union. The other functions of the Assembly are set out in Article 21 of the Treaty.

In addition to WIPO Member States eligible to become party to the Treaty, Article 23(2) provides that any IGO may become eligible to become party to the treaty by making a declaration that it is competent in respect of the matters covered by the Treaty, has its own legislation binding on all its Member States, and is authorized by its internal procedures to become party to the Treaty. Article 23(3) states that the EU made the required declaration and may become a party to the Treaty.

§29.05 IMPLEMENTATION

The implementation of the rights of performers in audiovisual works in many countries, including those of the civil law system, may not require any significant change in national legislation, because those laws traditionally have protected performers of all kinds alike. In countries where protection has traditionally relied on contractual agreements at the national and international level, more changes could be required.

§29.06 IMPORTANCE OF THE BTAP

The protection of audiovisual performances at the international level is essential for the growth and development of the audiovisual sector, especially in developing countries and countries in transition. In the last twenty-five years, the audiovisual sector has emerged and grown in Latin America, Asia, and Africa, for example with the growth of *Bollywood* in India and *Nollywood* in Nigeria. Access to high-speed Internet and the proliferation of mobile telephony as well as affordability of the equipment essential to the industry has led to the increased opportunities for the production and dissemination of audiovisual works. However national laws may not have kept up with these developments to ensure that the rights of performers are well protected.

In this era where audiovisual content is consumed globally and simultaneously through the Internet, the BTAP incentivizes global recognition of performers' rights. It also raises the level of protection of performers in audiovisual fixations to a standard that other performers already enjoy and closes the gap between performers in terms of protection of their performances.

At the same time, the BTAP also allows Contracting Parties to opt for the most appropriate system of transfer of rights in order to better equip their national laws in a way that fosters the local audiovisual industry and neither imposes further obstacles to the lawful exploitation of audiovisual content nor deprives performers of their well-deserved revenues. To accomplish these goals, some countries have considered using the option of granting performers in audiovisual fixations an equitable remuneration for the use of their performances. They seek to encourage digital commerce as film producers will feel confident having their films exploited over the Internet and other digital platforms, while performers will be fairly remunerated for their performances.

§29.07 MEMBERSHIP OF THE BTAP

The BTAP came into force on April 28, 2020, three months after thirty eligible parties had deposited their instruments of ratification or accession. As of June 4, 2024, the BTAP had forty-seven Contracting Parties.

CHAPTER 30

Marrakesh Treaty to Facilitate Access to Published Works for Persons Who Are Blind, Visually Impaired or Otherwise Print Disabled ("MVT" or "Marrakesh Treaty")

§30.01 BACKGROUND

Copyright law at the international level has always provided for the balance of grants of exclusive rights and the public interest through the provision of limitations and exceptions to exclusive rights. This practice can be traced back to the Berne Convention for the Protection of Literary and Artistic Works of 1886, which allows Contracting Parties to provide specific limitations and exceptions. These include exemptions for short quotations, news reporting, and teaching. Article 9(2) of the Berne Convention sets out what is known as the three-step test, which determines the scope of limitations and exceptions in relation to the right of reproduction. Limitations and exceptions are permissible in certain special cases, provided that they do not conflict with the normal exploitation of the work and do not unreasonably prejudice the legitimate interests of the author. The subsequent international copyright and related rights treaties and agreements (WCT, WPPT, BTAP, MVT, and copyright provisions of the TRIPS Agreement) incorporated the three-step test, albeit with slight variations in wording, extending its application to all the exclusive rights granted under those instruments.

Most countries provide for limitations and exceptions in their national copyright laws, but the scope and number of limitations and exceptions vary greatly. While most copyright laws include specific limitations or exceptions formulated in various degrees of detail, some countries including many following the Common Law tradition also have broader exceptions for fair dealing or fair use, which are generally interpreted by an important body of case law. In 2008 only about one-third of the WIPO Member

States had chosen to provide for specific exceptions for the benefit of persons who are blind, visually impaired, or otherwise print disabled (referred to going forward as "persons who are print disabled"). The existing limitations and exceptions were frequently limited in their scope, permitted uses, and types of accessible formats covered. In addition, given the territorial nature of limitations and exceptions, these provisions did not provide clear authorization to import accessible format works from another country. In a later study commissioned by WIPO, well less than half of the WIPO Member States had some type of limitation or exception to benefit persons who are print disabled, and there were very few in developing countries.

In 2004, the WIPO SCCR started discussing the harmonization of exceptions and limitations at the international level. With the adoption of the United Nations Convention on the Rights of Persons with Disabilities (UNCRPD) and the advances in the discussions on limitations and exceptions for persons with print disabilities, this topic was given priority at the SCCR. The work of the SCCR was complemented by discussions related to other WIPO initiatives regarding access to works by people with print disabilities, such as the Stakeholder's Platform established in 2009. In 2014 it was newly launched with additional involvement from organizations representing persons with print disabilities as the WIPO Accessible Books Consortium (ABC), which continues to undertake useful work to implement the Marrakesh Treaty objectives, such as encouraging the production of "born-accessible books," capacity building in developing countries to help produce and distribute books in accessible formats, a list of websites with sources for accessible books, and an online catalogue for libraries for the blind as a basis for an international inter-library service (the ABC Global Book Service).

In December 2012, the Member States agreed to convene a Diplomatic Conference in June 2013. Provisional agreement had been reached on several issues in the proposed draft treaty text, including some of the key definitions. After intensive negotiations, the text of the Marrakesh Treaty to Facilitate Access to Published Works for Persons Who are Blind, Visually Impaired or Otherwise Print Disabled (MVT or Marrakesh Treaty) was adopted at the Diplomatic Conference in Marrakesh in June 2013. It entered into force on September 30, 2016. This relatively short period between adoption and entry into force indicates the eagerness with which it was welcomed by Member States.

§30.02 LEGAL NATURE AND RELATIONSHIP WITH OTHER TREATIES

The MVT became part of the international legal framework in a way that differentiates it from previous copyright treaties. The Treaty sets out limitations and exceptions to the exclusive rights already granted under the international copyright regime. Other treaties have recognized exclusive rights and established a minimum standard of protection, while retaining the possibility of limiting such rights in some cases. The MVT establishes mandatory limitations and exceptions to exclusive rights for the benefit of persons with print disabilities under certain conditions. It also recognizes the importance of the international copyright system and seeks to harmonize the limitations and exceptions to ensure access to and use of copyright-protected works by persons with print disabilities. Article 1 provides that it does not prejudice the rights that a Contracting Party has in respect of other treaties.

§30.03 SUBSTANTIVE PROVISIONS

[A] Definitions

The Treaty reaffirms the definition of copyright-protected works within the meaning of Article 2(1) of the Berne Convention, but it limits the works that are the subject of the Treaty to a subsection of the works covered by Article 2(1)—those that cannot be accessed by people with print disabilities, that is to say printed works. It does not include, for example, audiovisual works. The MVT also defines the formats into which the material can be transformed when enjoying the limitations and exceptions that it provides. The Treaty refers to "accessible format copy," which covers any copy in an alternative manner or form that makes the work accessible to beneficiary persons without constraints. The Treaty also refers to the role of intermediary organizations or entities that provide services including creating accessible format copies of works and distributing them to the beneficiary population. These organizations or entities, referred to as "authorized entities" have a broad scope and can include institutions such as libraries, schools, or government agencies.

[B] Beneficiary Persons

The Treaty is meant to provide access to accessible format copies of works for persons who are blind, or who have a visual impairment or perceptual or reading disability, or who through physical disability cannot hold or manipulate a book to read. It covers a broad range of persons who are print disabled or visually impaired to ensure that they have access to printed works.

[C] National Limitations and Exceptions

Article 4(1) clearly states that the Contracting States shall in their national laws provide for a limitation or exception to the rights of reproduction, distribution and making available in the sense of the WCT, and should permit the changes needed to make the work available in an accessible or alternative format. An exception to the right of public performance is optional. It also sets out the circumstances in which an authorized entity may perform the abovementioned acts without obtaining the authorization of the rights holder. This may only be done if the authorized entity has legitimate access to a copy of the work, it has been converted to an accessible format copy to be used exclusively by beneficiary persons, and it is done on a nonprofit making basis.

Article 4 gives the Contracting Party leeway to confine the exceptions under Article 4 to accessible format copies that cannot be accessed commercially under reasonable terms in the market. This takes into account cases where the works have been made available commercially at reasonable terms, which may implicate the three-step test. The available work must be in the specific format that is needed for the beneficiary person. This optional provision was advocated mainly by Member States that already had commercial availability provisions and did not want to change their laws. A number of these Member States have authorized entities that also produce significant numbers of accessible format copies.

The MVT reaffirms the existing scope of limitations and exceptions present in the Berne Convention, the TRIPS Agreement, and the WCT, and also states that Member States may opt to utilize other limitations and exceptions (besides those set out in the MVT) when implementing the MVT. Such provisions would need to observe the international obligations assumed by that Contracting Party, especially with regard to the three-step test.

Article 7 provides that the legal protection accorded to TPMs in national laws should not prevent beneficiary persons from enjoying the limitations and exceptions provided under the Treaty. Member States should thus take "appropriate measures, as necessary" to ensure that the laws on anti-circumvention of TPMs do not block access for persons who are print disabled.

[D] Cross-Border Exchange of Accessible Format Copies

Many organizations that produce and have a number of copies of works available in accessible formats have had their activity circumscribed to their national borders. This usually occurs because their agreement with right holders has only a national scope or because they make accessible format copies based on a limitation or exception from the national copyright law that does not apply outside the territorial borders. Thus accessible format copies of works rarely were exchanged across borders and governments, intermediary organizations and beneficiaries undertook the costly effort of producing accessible format copies of the same work in parallel due to the impossibility of obtaining an existing copy from another country. To address this inefficiency, Article 5 allows the cross-border exchange of accessible format copies between authorized entities in MVT Contracting Parties. The use of the copies exchanged across borders is limited to beneficiary persons. The authorized entities in such cases do not require the authorization of the rights holder to distribute or make available the accessible format copies within the provisions of Article 5 of the Treaty.

Nonetheless, in a limited number of cases, an authorized entity may not be authorized to export an accessible format copy if the Contracting Party where that exporting organization is located is not a Contracting Party to the Berne Convention. The cross-border exchange may also be limited if the Contracting Party has no obligation consistent with the three-step test with regard to its limitations and exceptions to the rights of distribution and making available. These limits and other references to the three-step test provide assurance to authors and publishers that the implementation of the Treaty will not expose their works to abuse and misuse by non-beneficiaries, as the limitations and exceptions must be exercised within the provisions of the three-step test.

Under the Treaty, national laws should provide that a beneficiary person or authorized entity is permitted to make available an accessible format copy by importing it into the country. This will not require the authorization of the rights holder, but the use of the work is restricted to the beneficiary person.

The Treaty also encourages exchange of information among WIPO, Contracting Parties and authorized entities in order to foster cross-border exchange of accessible format copies. This information should make it easier to identify the corresponding entities from other Member States and help to avoid the risk of the parties falling outside the provisions on limitations and exceptions.

§30.04 ADMINISTRATIVE PROVISIONS

The administrative provisions are found in Articles 13 to 22 of the Treaty. They follow other WIPO treaties and are very similar to those in the WCT, WPPT and BTAP, allowing, for example, the EU to be a Contracting Party to the instrument. Unlike other recent WIPO copyright treaties that require thirty members to enter into force, the number of parties required to bring the MVT into force was twenty. The lower number of ratifications or accessions required was designed to speed the entry into force of the Treaty due to its human rights focus. The Treaty became effective once it entered into force (on September 30, 2016). Only Contracting Parties benefit from the cross-border provisions of the Treaty as they relate to print disabled persons.

§30.05 IMPLEMENTATION OF THE TREATY

Article 10 expressly recognizes that Contracting Parties are free to implement the Treaty within their own legal systems. The Treaty includes a number of alternatives for Contracting Parties with regard to the nature of the specific limitations and exceptions used to achieve the Treaty requirements. Member States may refine at the national level concepts such as beneficiary, authorized entity and accessible format copies, within the provisions of the MVT. In addition, Article 4(4) allows Contracting Parties to limit Treaty application to situations in which the necessary accessible format of the work is not available in the marketplace, and Article 4(5) allows Contracting Parties to provide for remuneration to the right owner for accessible format copies of works produced pursuant to the limitation or exception. Considering that when the Treaty was adopted a large number of countries did not have a limitation or exception for persons with print disabilities, many countries amended their national legislation in order to implement the Treaty. Even those countries with a limitation or exception in place prior to Treaty adoption may need to amend their legislation to provide for the possibility of exchanging works across borders.

§30.06 IMPORTANCE OF THE MVT FOR HUMAN RIGHTS AND DEVELOPMENT

The MVT is also a tool for the fulfillment of fundamental rights set forth in other international instruments. The preamble refers to the UNCRPD, in which Article 30 provides that the laws protecting IP must not pose a discriminatory or unreasonable barrier limiting access to cultural materials. The essence of the MVT, which is to facilitate access to published works for persons who are blind, visually impaired, or otherwise print disabled, will also provide a mechanism to meet this human rights obligation.

According to the WHO and the World Blind Union, as of 2016, at the time the MVT came into force, 285 million people were visually impaired with 90% of them living in developing countries. It was estimated that less than 7% of published works (including public domain works) were then available in accessible formats in developed countries, and the percentage in developing countries was below 1%. And due to the "territorial" nature of copyright, the operation of any limitations and exceptions designed to address this situation before the adoption of the MVT was limited to the national level and (absent right holder permission) could not be applied across borders. This had resulted in what is known as the "book famine" for persons with print disabilities. The Treaty was drafted to address the book famine by, among other things, increasing the number of works prepared in accessible formats by freeing up resources through exchanging copies of works across borders.

Contracting Parties may now also address the "book famine" by facilitating the making available of accessible format copies in real time to persons who are print disabled. In some instances, the issue is not money but the time needed to prepare the accessible format copy, for example for university students required to read certain works for their courses. If such copies of works are available from another jurisdiction the students may be able to obtain access much more quickly.

Developing countries may benefit from the provisions of the MVT first by ratifying or acceding to the Treaty, and then by ensuring that the provisions are domesticated within their national laws. As quite a number of countries already have collections of works converted into accessible formats, countries joining the MVT stand to benefit through the cross-border exchange and importation of the works in accessible formats by beneficiary persons and authorized entities. This is also a cost saving measure as authorized entities can focus on making accessible format copies of works that are not otherwise available, such as works in local languages.

Cluster A of the WIPO Development Agenda offers the necessary technical assistance and capacity building for the Member States to join WIPO treaties. Developing countries and LDCs can take advantage of this and get the necessary assistance to help in implementing the MVT at the national level. The process of ratification or accession is unique to each WIPO Member State, but there is a need to understand the overall potential of the Treaty to increase access to published works, and many of the Treaty's greatest benefits for countries within the same language groups can be realized through regional cooperation and coordination during the implementation process.

§30.07 MEMBERSHIP OF THE MVT

The MVT came into force on September 30, 2016, three months after twenty eligible parties had deposited their instruments of ratification or accession. It is the fastest-growing WIPO treaty body in the modern era. As of June 4, 2024, the MVT had 95 Contracting Parties, covering 121 countries (the 26 EU Member States joined as a bloc).

CHAPTER 31
The Agreement on Trade-Related Aspects of Intellectual Property Rights

§31.01 INTRODUCTION

[A] The GATT, the WTO and the TRIPS Agreement

The Uruguay Round of multilateral trade negotiations held under the framework of the "GATT" was concluded on December 15, 1993. The agreement embodying the results of those negotiations, the Agreement Establishing the World Trade Organization ("WTO Agreement"), was adopted on April 15, 1994, in Marrakesh. Those negotiations included, for the first time within the GATT, discussions on aspects of IPRs which impacted on international trade. The result of those negotiations, contained in an Annex to the WTO Agreement, was the "TRIPS Agreement."

It is generally said that the TRIPS Agreement was adopted to solve certain shortcomings in the international protection of IP, in the framework of the Paris and Berne Conventions. Indeed, there was an issue that caused a major impact on the international trade of goods bearing or incorporating IP: the significant asymmetries in the protection of pharmaceutical-related inventions by a number of large developing countries. The trading partners that host major research-based pharmaceutical companies saw those asymmetries as opportunistic parasitism and used the GATT negotiations to eliminate them. As a consequence, a provision prohibiting discriminatory treatment of patents as regards the field of technology was included in the TRIPS Agreement. In return, developing countries obtained concessions aiming at facilitating access of their products to markets in developed countries. In this way, those developing countries accepted to use IP protection as a tool of access to markets. Both the Paris and the Berne Convention had naturally provisions concerning international trade—after all, it is international trade that explains the trend toward international harmonization of the protection of intangible assets. But because those Conventions did not imply direct trade-offs in various areas of trade, the link of IP with access to foreign markets was not as clear as it is under the WTO Agreement. However, what explains international protection of IP is not always the need to increase its level of protection in trading partners. Sometimes trade interests may impose lowering the levels of protection. Actually, when a product is manufactured in a country where it is protected by IP (any of its branches), the absence of protection in another country may negatively affect the opportunities of exporting it. The first paragraph of the Preamble of the TRIPS Agreement reflects this perspective when it refers to the "need to promote effective [...] protection of intellectual property" as a way of reducing "distortions and impediments to international trade." But the reverse is also true. When a product is made in a country without the coverage of IP, its exportation to another country where the same product is protected by IP may prove impossible or very costly. Article XX(d) of the GATT speaks in this sense, to the extent that it sets the application of IP rules as an exception to free trade. In other words, it is not necessarily less protection in other countries that motivates international harmonization of IP, but the very existence of differences in the levels of protection that may constitute non-tariff barriers to trade. The TRIPS Agreement reflects both sides of the equation: it is *mostly* an Agreement that raises the levels of protection above those that existed under international conventions, but in at least two places it reduces those same levels: Article 9.1 exempts WTO Members from complying with Article 6*bis* of the Berne Convention (protection of authors' moral rights) and Article 24 sets a number of exceptions to the protection of GIs that would be unacceptable under the Lisbon Agreement, of 1958. Both aspects correspond to specific issues of US law. The reason is that US negotiators in the GATT understood that higher levels of protection in those two specific areas created obstacles to exports of US products to the European Communities.

[B] The TRIPS Agreement and the Paris and Berne Conventions

The TRIPS Agreement belongs in a confined jurisdiction, that of the WTO, and therefore does not have the power to modify commitments taken by the Contracting Parties of Paris and Berne. TRIPS commitments are enforceable in the jurisdiction of the WTO only. Of course, those Paris and Berne Contracting Parties that have joined the WTO are bound by them, but only under the WTO jurisdiction.

The TRIPS Agreement, for those Berne and Paris Contracting Parties that have joined the WTO, interacts with those two conventions in at least four different manners:

- the TRIPS Agreement, in Articles 2.1 and 9.1, incorporated the commitments taken by Contracting Parties of the two Conventions; they have become, therefore, commitments under the TRIPS Agreement, and therefore they are covered by the WTO Dispute Settlement Mechanism;
- the TRIPS Agreement has, for its large measure, increased the standards of protection that existed under Berne and Paris Conventions; Contracting Parties are, in the context of the WTO, bound by those higher standards; however, in

the specific context of the two Conventions, the higher standards of the TRIPS Agreement does not apply to them;

- conversely, the TRIPS Agreement has reduced some rights to which IP owners were entitled under Paris and Berne Conventions; one case is the protection of moral rights, as already mentioned (TRIPS, Article 9.1); another case is the eventual impingement on the rule of independence of patents and trademarks caused by the adoption of international exhaustion, which is not imposed, but it is implicitly admitted (Article 6); another case is the right to assign a trademark with or without the transfer of the business to which the trademark belongs (TRIPS, Article 21); in these cases, Paris and Berne Contracting Parties are still bound by the commitments taken under the respective Conventions, but not under the jurisdiction of the WTO (which means, in practice, that they may not resort to the WTO Dispute Settlement Mechanism to enforce those TRIPS *plus* commitments);
- the TRIPS Agreement requires that WTO Members comply with the obligations adopted under the last Acts of Paris (1967) and Berne (1971) Conventions, but under those Conventions, Contracting Parties may be bound (and some are, indeed) by previous Acts.

The WTO Agreement, including the TRIPS Agreement (which is binding on all WTO Members), entered into force on January 1, 1995. The former agreement established a new organization, the "WTO," which began its work on January 1, 1995.

[C] Transitional Arrangements and Technical Cooperation (Part VI)

No Member of WTO was obliged to apply the provisions of the TRIPS Agreement before the expiry of a general period of one year following the date of entry into force of the Agreement Establishing the WTO (i.e., before January 1, 1996) (Article 65.1). However, additional transitional periods were (and some still are) available for certain countries. The date on which the relevant transitional period expires for a Member is referred to as the date of application of the Agreement for that Member.

Developing countries which were members of WTO, and also countries which were in the process of transformation into a market, free-enterprise economy and which were undertaking structural reform of their IP systems and facing special problems in the preparation and implementation of IP laws and regulations, were entitled to delay for a further period of four years (i.e., until January 1, 2000) the date of application of the Agreement, except for obligations concerning national treatment and most-favored-nation (MFN) treatment (Article 65.2 and 65.3).

Developing countries which were obliged by the Agreement to extend product patent protection to types of products not previously patentable in that country were allowed to avail themselves of an additional five years (i.e., until January 1, 2005) before applying the provisions of the Agreement to such products (Article 65.4).

LDC Members are not required to apply the provisions of the Agreement, other than those concerning national treatment and MFN treatment, for a period of ten years from the general date of application of the Agreement (i.e., until January 1, 2006). The WETO General Council, in 2021, extended this period until July 1, 2034—or when a particular country ceases to be an LDC if that happens before 2034. That period will be extended upon duly motivated request (Article 66.1). LDCs also enjoy from an additional transitional period concerning the protection of pharmaceutical products as regards patents and undisclosed information until January 1, 2033, or when they cease to be an LDC, the earlier date prevailing. The same waiver has been extended to the application of mailbox and exclusive marketing rights provisions (Article 70.8 and 70.9).

The TRIPS Agreement also requires developed country Members to provide, on request and on mutually agreed terms and conditions, technical and financial cooperation in favor of developing country and LDC Members, including assistance in preparation of laws and support regarding establishment or reinforcement of domestic offices and agencies, including training of personnel (Article 67).

[D] Institutional Arrangements (Part VII)

The WTO Agreement creates a three-tiered organizational structure for the WTO. The highest tier is the Ministerial Conference, which meets at least once every two years (Article IV.1). It has the authority to take decisions on all matters under the WTO Agreement. The second tier is the General Council, consisting of representatives of all the Members, which is to meet "as appropriate" to carry out its own duties as well as those of the Ministerial Conference in the intervals between meetings of the latter body (Article IV.2). The General Council also serves as the Dispute Settlement Body and the Trade Policy Review Body (Article IV.3 and IV.4).

The WTO Agreement (Article IV.5) also establishes a Council for Trade-Related Aspects of Intellectual Property Rights (the "TRIPS Council") which, under the general guidance of the General Council, is to oversee the functioning of the TRIPS Agreement (Article IV.5). Membership in the TRIPS Council is open to representatives of all Members. Under the provisions of the TRIPS Agreement (Part VII, Article 68), the TRIPS Council is charged with monitoring the operation of the TRIPS Agreement and Members' compliance with the obligations under that Agreement. The TRIPS Council shall also review the implementation of the TRIPS Agreement after the expiration of the transitional period for developing countries (i.e., after January 1, 2000), and every two years thereafter (or when amendment or modification is warranted by new developments) (Article 71.1). The first meeting of the TRIPS Council was held on March 9, 1995.

[E] Arrangements for Cooperation with WIPO

Consultations to establish arrangements for cooperation and a mutually supportive relationship between the WTO and WIPO concerning IP are required by the TRIPS

Agreement. The Preamble of the Agreement contains the following statement: "Desiring to establish a mutually supportive relationship between the WTO and the World Intellectual Property Organization as well as other relevant international organizations; [...]."

The TRIPS Agreement further states that the TRIPS Council, in carrying out its functions, may consult with and seek information from any source it deems appropriate and that, in consultation with WIPO, the Council is to seek to establish, within one year of its first meeting, appropriate arrangements for cooperation with bodies of WIPO (Article 68).

Consultations for specific areas of cooperation between WIPO and WTO are also required by the Agreement. In particular, Article 63.2, which concerns notification of laws and regulations by Members to the TRIPS Council, states that: "The Council shall attempt to minimize the burden on Members in carrying out this obligation and may decide to waive the obligation to notify such laws and regulations directly to the Council if consultations with WIPO on the establishment of a common register containing these laws and regulations are successful. The Council shall also consider in this connection any action required regarding notifications pursuant to the obligations under this Agreement stemming from the provisions of Article 6ter of the Paris Convention (1967)."

§31.02 GENERAL PROVISIONS, BASIC PRINCIPLES AND FINAL PROVISIONS (PARTS I AND VII)

A basic principle concerning the nature and scope of obligations under the TRIPS Agreement is that Members must give effect to the provisions of the Agreement and accord the treatment provided for in the Agreement to the nationals of other Members. A "national" is understood as meaning those natural or legal persons who would be eligible for protection if all Members of WTO were also bound by the Paris, Berne and Rome Conventions and by the Washington Treaty on the "IPIC Treaty."

Members are free to determine the appropriate method of implementing the provisions of the TRIPS Agreement within their own legal system and practice, and may implement more extensive protection than is required, provided that such additional protection does not contravene other provisions of the Agreement (Article 1.1 and 1.3).

[A] Definition of IP

The TRIPS Agreement states that, for the purposes of the Agreement, the term "intellectual property" refers to all categories of IP that are the subject of sections 1-7 of Part II of the TRIPS Agreement, namely, copyright and related rights, trademarks, GIs, industrial designs, patents, layout-designs (topographies) of integrated circuits, and undisclosed information (Article 1.2).

[B] Incorporation-by-Reference of the Paris and Berne Conventions

The TRIPS Agreement is built on the century-old principles embodied in the Paris and the Berne Conventions. In fact, almost all the substantive provisions of these two Conventions are incorporated by reference directly into the TRIPS Agreement.

Concerning industrial property, the TRIPS Agreement requires that Members comply with Articles 1-12, and Article 19, of the Paris Convention, in respect of Parts II, III and IV of the Agreement (Article 2.1). This includes all of the substantive provisions of the Paris Convention.

In the field of copyright, Members are required to comply with Articles 1-21 of the Berne Convention and its Appendix. However, Members do not have rights or obligations in respect of Article 6*bis* of the Berne Convention concerning moral rights, or of the rights derived therefrom (Article 9.1).

The TRIPS Agreement, however, stipulates that nothing in Parts I-IV of the Agreement shall derogate from existing obligations that Members may have to each other under the Paris or Berne Conventions (Article 2.2).

[C] The Principle of National Treatment

The TRIPS Agreement provides for the principle of national treatment, requiring that Members accord the treatment provided for in the Agreement to the nationals of other Members, the latter defined in terms, for the corresponding rights, of the relevant provisions of the Paris, Berne and Rome Conventions, and the IPIC Treaty. Exceptions provided for under the relevant conventions are respected within the context of the TRIPS Agreement. As regards industrial property and copyright, this principle applies to all rights. As regards rights in respect of performers, producers of phonograms and broadcasting organizations, the obligation only applies in respect of the rights provided under the Agreement (Article 3). Also exempted from this principle are procedures provided in multilateral agreements concluded under the auspices of WIPO relating to the acquisition or maintenance of IPRs (Article 5).

But it is worth noticing that the formulation of Article 3 of the TRIPS Agreement is made in a manner that is entirely different of the way that Article 2 of the Paris Convention states the same right. While Article 2 of the Paris Convention reads "(1) Nationals of any country of the Union shall ... enjoy in all the other countries of the Union the advantages that their respective laws now grant, or may hereafter grant, to nationals," Article 3.1 of the TRIPS Agreement reads: "Each Member shall accord to the nationals of other Members treatment *no less favourable* than that it accords to its own nationals ..." (emphasis added).

These different formulations mean a different notion of national treatment. While the Paris Agreement requires that foreign nationals (of Union Members) be treated *in the same manner* as nationals (and residents) of the country in question, the TRIPS Agreement requires that foreigners will *not receive less protection* than nationals—but they may receive more, when the protection granted to nationals is inferior to those minimum levels required by the Agreement.

[D] The MFN Treatment Principle

The TRIPS Agreement contains a principle, the MFN principle, which has not traditionally been provided for in the context of IPRs, at least on the multilateral level.[50] This principle provides that any advantage, favor, privilege or immunity granted by a Member to the nationals of any other country (whether a Member or not) shall be accorded immediately and unconditionally to the nationals of all other Members, with certain specified exemptions (Article 4). As is the case for national treatment, procedures provided in multilateral agreements concluded under the auspices of WIPO relating to the acquisition or maintenance of IPRs are exempted from this principle (Article 5).

[E] Protection of Existing Subject Matter: Transitional Arrangements

The TRIPS Agreement contains specific provisions regarding the effect of the Agreement on the subject matter of IPRs that exists on the date of application of the Agreement in a Member. While the Agreement does not give rise to obligations in respect of acts which occurred before the date of application of the Agreement for the Member in question (Article 70.1), the Agreement does give rise to obligations in respect of all subject matter existing and protected at the date of application of the Agreement, or which meets or comes subsequently to meet the criteria for protection under the terms of the Agreement (Article 70.2). However, copyright obligations with respect to existing works and obligations with respect to the rights of producers of phonograms and performers in existing phonograms are determined solely under Article 18 of the Berne Convention (Article 70.2). The difference in scope of paragraphs 1 and 2 of Article 70 is that the former concerns the non-retroactivity of enforcement of higher standards of protection ("acts" meaning acts of infringement) whereas the latter refers to the expansion of the subject matter of protection.

A member may provide for limited remedies for acts which become infringing as a result of the implementation of the Agreement and which were commenced, or in respect of which a significant investment was made, before the date of acceptance of the Agreement. These must include at least the payment of equitable remuneration (Article 70.4).

There are certain exceptions to these general rules. In particular, there is no obligation to restore protection to subject matter which has fallen into the public domain (Article 70.3). In addition, certain obligations concerning computer programs, cinematographic works and phonograms (Articles 11 and 14(4)) need not be applied with respect to originals or copies purchased prior to the date of application of this Agreement (Article 70.5). Further, provisions concerning guidelines for use without

50. Actually, in the nineteenth century, the UK celebrated some bilateral agreements on trademarks and designs with certain countries in which an MFN clause was included.

authorization (Article 31) and non-discrimination as to the field of technology (Article 27.1) need not be applied to use without the authorization of the right holder where authorization for such use had been granted by the government before the date the Agreement became known (Article 70.6) (this date is deemed to be December 21, 1991, when the preliminary results of the Uruguay Round were made public by the then Secretary-General of the GATT, Arthur Dunkel).

Applications for protection of IPRs which are pending on the date of application of the Agreement may be amended to claim any enhanced protection provided under the Agreement, but such amendments may not include new matter (Article 70.7).

These provisions were provisional and have lost their efficacy as regards most of the Members of the WTO, except as those LDCs that have not anticipated the implement of TRIPS obligations.

[F] Reservations

Reservations may not be entered in respect of any of the provisions of the Agreement without the consent of the other Members (Article 72).

[G] Security Exceptions

The Agreement provides a general exception for matters which are deemed to be essential to national security interests. In particular, a Member is not required to furnish any information if it considers disclosure to be contrary to its essential security interests. In addition, it may take any action which it considers necessary for the protection of its essential security interests relating to fissionable materials or the materials from which they are derived, relating to traffic in arms, ammunition and implements of war and to such traffic in other goods and materials as is carried on directly or indirectly for the purpose of supplying a military establishment, or taken in time of war or other emergency in international relations. It may also take any action in pursuance of its obligations under the UN Charter for the maintenance of international peace and security (Article 73).

§31.03 STANDARDS CONCERNING THE AVAILABILITY, SCOPE AND USE OF IPRS (PART II)

Part II of the TRIPS Agreement provides minimum standards concerning the availability, scope and use of IPRs. This Part contains eight sections relating, respectively, to copyright and related rights, trademarks, GIs, industrial designs, patents, layout-designs (topographies) of integrated circuits, protection of undisclosed information and control of anticompetitive practices in contractual licenses (the latter subject is not contained in the definition of IP of Article 1.2).

[A] Copyright and Related Rights (Section 1)

The essential elements of the standards concerning the availability, scope and use of copyright and related rights include the following:

(1) members must comply with Articles 1-21 of the 1971 Paris Act of the Berne Convention and, where applicable, with the Appendix to that Act (containing special provisions for developing countries). However, Members do not have rights or obligations under the Agreement concerning the subject matter of Article 6*bis* of the Berne Convention (concerning moral rights), or of the rights derived therefrom (Article 9.1);

(2) copyright protection shall extend to the expression and not to ideas, procedures, methods of operation or mathematical concepts as such (Article 9.2);

(3) computer programs, whether in source or object code, must be protected as literary works under the Berne Convention (Article 10.1);

(4) compilations of data or other material, whether in machine-readable or other form, which by reason of the selection or arrangement of their contents constitute intellectual creations shall be protected "as such"; the protection does not extend to, but is without prejudice to any copyright subsisting in, the data or material itself (Article 10.2);

(5) a commercial rental right is provided in respect of at least computer programs except where the program itself is not the essential object of the rental, and to cinematographic works; however, Members are excepted from the latter obligation unless such rental has led to widespread copying which materially impairs the exclusive right of reproduction in a Member (Article 11);

(6) the term of protection for works other than photographic works or works of applied art, where the term is calculated on a basis other than the life of a natural person, shall be no less than fifty years from the end of the calendar year of authorized publication or, if publication has not taken place within fifty years from the making of the work, fifty years from the end of the calendar year of the making of the work (Article 12);

(7) limitations or exceptions to exclusive rights are confined to cases which do not conflict with normal exploitation of the work and do not unreasonably prejudice the legitimate interests of the right holder (Article 13);

(8) with respect to related rights, performing artists shall have the right to prevent the fixation and reproduction of their unfixed performances on phonograms, and the wireless broadcasting and communication to the public of their live performances (Article 14.1);

(9) producers of phonograms shall have the right to authorize or prohibit the direct or indirect reproduction of their phonograms (Article 14.2);

(10) broadcasting organizations (or, if such rights are not granted to broadcasting organizations, the owners of copyright in the subject matter of broadcasts) shall have the right to prohibit the fixation, reproduction, wireless rebroadcasting and communication to the public by television broadcast (Article 14.3);
(11) a rental right is provided for producers of, and certain other right holders in, phonograms; Members may maintain systems, in existence on April 15, 1994, of equitable remuneration in respect of the rental of phonograms, provided such system does not materially impair exclusive rights of reproduction (Article 14.4);
(12) the term of protection for performers and producers of phonograms is at least fifty years from the end of the calendar year of fixation or performance, and for broadcasters at least twenty years from the end of the calendar year of broadcast (Article 14.5);
(13) the conditions, limitations, exceptions and reservations permitted by the Rome Convention may be applied to certain related rights (under paragraphs 14.1-14.3) granted in the Agreement; however, the provisions of Article 18 of the Berne Convention apply, *mutatis mutandis,* to the rights of performers and producers of phonograms in phonograms (Article 14.6).

[B] Trademarks (Section 2)

The essential elements of the standards concerning the availability, scope and use of trademark rights include the following:

(1) any sign capable of distinguishing the goods or services of one undertaking from those of other undertakings (thus including service marks) shall be eligible for registration as a trademark (Article 15.1);
(2) registrability may be conditional upon visual perceptibility and, for signs which are not inherently distinctive, on distinctiveness acquired through use (Article 15.1);
(3) registrability may be conditional upon use (Article 15.2), but use may not be a condition for filing, and an application may not be refused solely on the ground that intended use has not taken place within three years of the filing date (Article 15.3);
(4) the nature of the goods or services to which a trademark is to be applied may not be an obstacle to the registration of the mark (Article 15.4);
(5) members shall publish each trademark and afford a reasonable opportunity for petitions to cancel the registration, and may afford an opportunity to oppose the registration (Article 15.5);
(6) the rights conferred by registration shall include the exclusive right to prevent third parties from using identical or similar signs for identical or similar goods or services, where such use would result in a likelihood of confusion, the latter to be presumed where the goods or services are

identical (Article 16.1), subject to certain allowable exceptions such as the fair use of descriptive terms (Article 17);

(7) certain rights are provided for the owners of well-known trademarks and service marks (Article 16.2 and 16.3);

(8) the term of initial registration and renewals shall be no less than seven years, renewable indefinitely (Article 18);

(9) if a showing of use is required for the maintenance of a registration, the registration may be cancelled only after an uninterrupted period of at least three years of non-use, unless valid reasons for non-use are shown (Article 19.1);

(10) certain restrictions on use are not permitted (Article 20);

(11) compulsory licensing of trademarks is not permitted (Article 21);

(12) trademarks may be assigned with or without the transfer of the business to which the trademark belongs (Article 21).

[C] GIs (Section 3)

The essential elements of the standards concerning the availability, scope and use of rights involving GIs include the following:

(1) "GIs" are defined as indications which identify a good as originating in the territory of a Member, or a region or locality in that territory, where a given quality, reputation or other characteristic of the good is essentially attributable to its geographical origin (Article 22.1).

(2) Members must provide the legal means for interested parties to prevent the use of indications that misleadingly indicate or suggest that a good originates in a geographical area other than the true place of origin (Article 22.2(a)).

(3) Members shall refuse or invalidate the registration of a trademark which consists of a misleading indication (Article 22.3), and provide means to prevent any use which constitutes an act of unfair competition within the meaning of Article 10*bis* of the Paris Convention (Article 22.2(b)).

(4) Protection shall be applicable against a GI which is literally true but misleading (Article 22.4) and, in the case of wines or spirits, even where the true origin of the goods is indicated or the GI is used in translation or accompanied by expressions such as "kind," "type," or "style," "imitation" or the like (Article 23.1).

(5) Protection is not required in respect of a GI of another Member which is identical with the common name for goods or services, or, for products of the vine, which is identical with the customary name of a grape variety existing in the territory of that Member as of the date of entry into force of the WTO Agreement (Article 24.6).

(6) There is no obligation to protect GIs which are not or cease to be protected in their country of origin, or which have fallen into disuse in that country (Article 24.9).
(7) Guidelines are provided for additional protection for GIs for wines and spirits (Article 23), including concurrent protection of homonymous GIs for wines (Article 23.3), certain exceptions to substantive rights such as prior rights (Article 24.4) and the right to use personal names (Article 24.8), and time limits for registration in certain cases (Article 24.7).
(8) In order to facilitate the protection of GIs for wines, negotiations are to be undertaken in the TRIPS Council concerning the establishment of a multilateral system of notification and registration of GIs for wines which would be effective for those Members participating in the system (Article 23.4).

[D] Industrial Designs (Section 4)

The essential elements of the standards concerning the availability, scope and use of industrial design rights include the following:

(1) Members shall provide protection for independently created industrial designs that are original or new, certain standards for determining protectability being allowed (Article 25.1).
(2) Requirements for protection of textile designs, which may be provided through industrial design or copyright law, shall not unreasonably impair the opportunity to obtain protection, particularly in regard to any cost, examination or publication (Article 25.2).
(3) Exclusive rights shall include the right to prevent third parties from making, selling or importing, for commercial purposes, articles bearing or embodying a protected industrial design (Article 26.1), subject to certain allowable exceptions (Article 26.2).
(4) The duration of protection shall amount to at least ten years (Article 26.3).

[E] Patents (Section 5)

The essential elements of the standards concerning the availability, scope and use of patent rights include the following:

(1) Patents shall be available for products and processes in all fields of technology, provided they are new, involve an inventive step and are capable of industrial application (Article 27.1), except that Members may exclude inventions, the prevention within their territory of the commercial exploitation of which is necessary to protect *ordre public* or morality, including to protect human, animal or plant life or health or to avoid serious prejudice to the environment, provided that such exclusion is not made merely because

the exploitation is prohibited by their law (Article 27.2); and Members may further exclude diagnostic, therapeutic and surgical methods for the treatment of humans or animals, plants and animals other than microorganisms, and essentially biological processes for the production of plants or animals other than non-biological and microbiological processes (Article 27.3); however, Members shall provide for the protection of plant varieties either by patents or by an effective sui generis system or by any combination thereof (Article 27.3).

(2) Patents shall be available and patent rights enjoyable without discrimination as to the place of invention, the field of technology and whether products are imported or locally produced (Article 27.1).

(3) Exclusive rights shall include, for products, the right to prevent third parties from making, using, offering for sale, selling or importing the patented product, and for processes, the right to prevent third parties from using the process and from using, offering for sale, selling or importing for those purposes the product obtained directly by that process (Article 28.1), subject to certain allowable exceptions (Article 30).

(4) Patents shall be assignable, transferable and shall be available for licensing (Article 28.2).

(5) Certain conditions are imposed concerning the disclosure of the invention in a patent application (Article 29).

(6) Any use allowed without the authorization of the right owner (commonly known as a compulsory license), and such use by the government, is made subject to certain enumerated conditions (Article 31); such use in the case of semiconductor technology is limited to certain enumerated purposes (Article 31(c)); a waiver from the rights granted to patent holders under Article 31(f) and Article 31(h), under some circumstances, has been introduced by Article 31*bis*, which entered into force in January 2017 (compulsory licenses predominantly aimed at exporting pharmaceutical products to countries facing public health problems and without or with insufficient production capacity);[51] this waiver was introduced under the frame work of the Doha Declaration on the TRIPS Agreement and Public Health, of 2001.[52]

51. For those WTO Members who have not yet accepted the amendment to the TRIPS Agreement, an interim waiver (introduced by a Decision of the General Council, in 2003) continues applying.

52. An additional waiver was approved by the WTO Ministerial Conference in June 2022, which, for the purpose of permitting the production and supply of COVID-19 vaccines "to the extent necessary to address the COVID-19 pandemic," to issue compulsory licenses of patents even if the Member has not adopted (formally) a system of compulsory licenses under a statute. This means that such a license can be granted through ministerial decisions, court orders, etc. The WTO decision adds that such compulsory license may be granted: (a) without the need for the prospect licensee to seek previously a voluntary license; (b) the compulsory license may be granted with the primary goal of exporting the products but, reciprocally, Members shall avoid their re-exportation; and (c) the determination "of adequate remuneration under Article 31(h) may take account of the humanitarian and not-for-profit purpose of specific vaccine distribution programs aimed at providing equitable access to COVID-19 vaccines in order to support manufacturers in eligible Members to produce and supply these vaccines at affordable prices for eligible Members." Interestingly, the Ministerial Decision (found in document WT/MIN(22)/30;

(7) Judicial review shall be available for any decision to revoke or forfeit a patent (Article 32).
(8) The term of protection shall be at least twenty years from the date of the filing of the application (Article 33).
(9) The burden of proof concerning whether a product was made by a patented process shall in certain cases be placed on the alleged infringer (Article 34).

In addition to the foregoing obligations, where a Member had not made available, as of the date of entry into force of the WTO Agreement (i.e., January 1, 1995), patent protection for pharmaceutical and agricultural chemical products commensurate with its obligations under Article 27, that Member must provide as from that date a means by which applications for patents for such inventions can be filed. The Member must, as of the date of application of the Agreement, apply to such applications the criteria for patentability as if those criteria were being applied on the filing date or priority date of the application. If the subject matter of the application meets the criteria for protection, the Member must provide patent protection for the remainder of the patent term counted from the filing date (Article 70.8).

Where such an application is filed, exclusive marketing rights must be granted for a period of five years after the obtaining of marketing approval or until a product patent is granted or rejected in that Member, whichever period is shorter, provided that, subsequent to the entry into force of the WTO Agreement, a patent application has been filed and a patent granted for that product in another Member and marketing approval obtained in that other Member (Article 70.9).

The measures contained in Article 70.8 and 70.9 were part of the Transitional Arrangements, and therefore, are no longer applicable to WTO Members, whose right to a transitional period has ceased. Nor are they applicable to LDCs, in accordance with a waiver decided by the WTO's General Council.

WT/L/1141, of June 22, 2022) adds that "Recognizing the importance of the timely availability of and access to COVID-19 vaccines, it is understood that Article 39.3 of the Agreement does not prevent an eligible Member from enabling the rapid approval for use of a COVID-19 vaccine produced under this Decision." This seems to imply that a sanitary authority may rely on test data submitted by a patent owner in order to approve the commercialization of the products manufactured under the compulsory license. This includes the possibility of the authority to not only waive from the obligation of the licensee to submit its own data (which that licensee will not have, as a matter of course) but also to disclose the data or parts of the data, which contain teachings on the best way to manufacture the product. The Ministerial Decision does not refer to remuneration in the case of the compulsory license of test data, but the language of the fourth paragraph of the Preamble of the TRIPS Agreement ("intellectual property rights are private rights") suggests that WTO Members in 1994 agreed that in such cases the national rules on expropriation (or taking, as per the language of the Fifth Amendment to the US Constitution) should apply. Because the Decision has limited its own scope to measures necessary to fight the COVID-19 pandemic, its purpose and opportunity seem to have disappeared. If a new pandemic emerges, some Members may feel tempted to resort to the rules set in the 2022 Ministerial Decision, but it is not clear whether other WTO Members would accept such application of legal analogy to situations that may be factually very different.

[F] Layout-Designs (Topographies) of Integrated Circuits (Section 6)

The TRIPS Agreement incorporates nearly all of the substantive provisions, with a few exceptions, of the IPIC Treaty (which was approved in 1989, but never entered into force). The IPIC Treaty provides for a regime of legal protection for layout-designs (topographies) of integrated circuits, and includes provisions on, *inter alia,* protectable subject matter, the legal form of protection, national treatment, scope of protection, exploitation, registration, disclosure and duration of protection. The requirements of the TRIPS Agreement are as follows:

(1) Members must provide protection for the layout-designs (topographies) of integrated circuits in accordance with Articles 2-7 (other than Article 6(3), which contains provisions on compulsory licenses), Article 12 and Article 16(3) of the IPIC Treaty (Article 35).
(2) The TRIPS Agreement has kept the large flexibility provided by the IPIC as regards the form of protection of layout-designs, which can take the shape of a sui generis system, or of copyright, patents, utility models, industrial designs, unfair competition or any other system, or a combination of any of those mechanisms (Article 4 of the IPIC Treaty).
(3) The TRIPS Agreement substitutes a minimum term of ten to fifteen years for the minimum term of eight years provided in Article 8 of the IPIC Treaty (Article 38).
(4) The TRIPS Agreement contains an additional prohibited act to those listed in the IPIC Treaty, namely any act relating to an article incorporating an integrated circuit, but only in so far as it continues to contain an unlawfully reproduced layout-design (Article 36).
(5) The TRIPS Agreement provides that certain acts engaged in unknowingly will not constitute infringement (Article 6(4) of the IPIC Treaty explicitly allows such exclusions), but that a reasonable royalty shall be payable with respect to stock on hand after notice is given (Article 37.1).
(6) The TRIPS Agreement extends to layout-designs the application of subparagraphs (a)–(k) of Article 31 (concerning compulsory licenses of patents) (Article 37.2); the need for an express reference to Article 31 in the context of layout-designs—as opposed to the silence in respect of compulsory licenses of industrial designs—is explained by the opposition of several signatories to the IPIC Treaty to its provisions on compulsory licenses.

[G] Protection of Undisclosed Information (Section 7)

The TRIPS Agreement provides that, in the course of ensuring effective protection against unfair competition as provided in Article 10*bis* of the Paris Convention, Members shall protect undisclosed information and data submitted to governments or governmental agencies in accordance with the following provisions (Article 39.1):

(1) natural and legal persons shall have the possibility of preventing information lawfully within their control from being disclosed to, acquired by, or used by others without their consent in a manner contrary to honest commercial practices (Article 39.2);
(2) such protection is required for information which is secret (i.e., not generally known among or readily accessible within the circles that normally deal with such information), which has commercial value because it is secret, and which has been subject to reasonable steps to keep it secret (Article 39.2);
(3) certain undisclosed test or other data submitted as a condition of approving the marketing of pharmaceutical or agricultural chemical products which utilize new chemical entities, shall be protected against unfair commercial use and, under certain circumstances, against disclosure (Article 39.3).

It is worth noticing that the negotiators of the TRIPS Agreement accepted that, under Article 10 of the Paris Convention, the Members of the Paris Union were obliged of protecting trade secrets. But during the Uruguay Round of negotiations a number of those Members disagreed. So, eventually, we may have here an instance of interpretation of the Paris Convention by WTO Members, which does not necessarily coincide with the views of Paris Union Members.

[H] Control of Anticompetitive Practices in Contractual Licenses (Section 8)

Recognizing that some licensing practices or conditions pertaining to IPRs which restrain competition may have adverse effects on trade and may impede the transfer and dissemination of technology (Article 39.1), the TRIPS Agreement provides that Members may specify in their national laws licensing practices or conditions which may, in particular cases,[53] constitute an abuse of IPRs having an adverse effect on the competition in the relevant market, and that they may adopt appropriate measures to control or prevent such practices (Article 40.2).

Members agree to enter into consultations with each other, upon request, to secure compliance with laws in this regard (Article 40.3) or where their nationals are subject to such proceedings in other Members (Article 40.4).

§31.04 ENFORCEMENT OF IPRs (PART III)

[A] General Obligations (Section 1)

The TRIPS Agreement requires that specified enforcement procedures be available to permit effective action against any act of infringement of IPRs covered by the

53. Article 40.2 provides for three examples of such cases: exclusive grantback conditions, conditions preventing challenges to validity of the licenses right, and coercive package licensing. The reference to these cases does not mean that WTO Members are in the obligation of treating them as per se abuses. Members can apply the *rule of reason* to those (and other) sorts of abusive practices. That is a matter left to Members.

Agreement, including expeditious remedies to prevent infringements and remedies which constitute a deterrent to further infringements. The procedures must be applied in such a manner as to avoid the creation of barriers to legitimate trade and to provide for safeguards against their abuse (Article 41.1).

Enforcement procedures are to be fair and equitable, not be unnecessarily complicated or costly, nor entail unreasonable time limits or unwarranted delays (Article 41.2). Decisions on the merits of a case shall preferably be in writing and reasoned, shall be made available at least to the parties to the proceeding without undue delay, and shall be based only on evidence in respect of which parties were offered the opportunity to be heard (Article 41.3). Parties to a proceeding shall have an opportunity for review of final administrative decisions and of at least the legal aspects of initial judicial decisions on the merits of a case (except for acquittals in criminal cases) (Article 41.4).

However, Members have no obligation to put in place a judicial system for IP enforcement distinct from that for the enforcement of law in general, nor with respect to the distribution of resources as between enforcement of IPRs and the enforcement of law in general (Article 41.5).

[B] Civil and Administrative Procedures and Remedies (Section 2)

The TRIPS Agreement establishes guidelines concerning civil and administrative procedures which must be followed with respect to enforcement of IPRs, including provisions on fair and equitable procedures (Article 42), evidence (Article 43), injunctions (Article 44), damages (Article 45), other remedies such as the authority to order that infringing goods or that materials and implements used in the creation of infringing goods be disposed of (Article 46), right of information, for example the authority to order that the infringer inform the right owner of the identity of third persons involved in the production and distribution of infringing goods or services and of their channels of distribution (Article 47), indemnification of the defendant (Article 48), and application of the above guidelines to administrative procedures (Article 49).

[C] Provisional Measures (Section 3)

The TRIPS Agreement establishes guidelines concerning provisional measures to prevent an infringement of any IPR from occurring, and in particular to prevent the entry into the channels of commerce in their jurisdiction of goods, including imported goods immediately after customs clearance, and to preserve relevant evidence in regard to the alleged infringement, and to adopt provisional measures *inaudita altera parte* where delay is likely to cause irreparable harm or where there is a risk of evidence being destroyed (Article 50).

[D] Special Requirements Related to Border Measures (Section 4) and Criminal Procedures (Section 5)

The TRIPS Agreement provides for certain procedures concerning enforcement related to border measures to enable a right holder who has valid grounds for suspecting that the importation of counterfeit trademark or pirated copyright goods may take place to lodge an application for the suspension by the customs authorities of the release into free circulation of such goods. Guidelines are established with respect to suspension of release by customs authorities (Article 51), application for such procedures (Article 42), security or equivalent assurance (Article 53), notice of suspension (Article 54), duration of suspension (Article 55), indemnification of the importer and of the owner of the goods (Article 56), right of inspection and information (Article 57), ex officio action (Article 58), remedies (Article 59) and *de minimis* imports (Article 60). The TRIPS Agreement requires that Members provide for criminal procedures and penalties to be applied at least in cases of willful trademark counterfeiting or copyright piracy on a commercial scale, and that they make available remedies such as imprisonment, monetary fines, and seizure, forfeiture and destruction of the infringing goods and of any materials and implements the predominant use of which has been in the commission of the offense.

More detailed information about enforcement rules and procedures under the TRIPS Agreement can be found in Chapter 14, above.

§31.05 ACQUISITION AND MAINTENANCE OF IPRs AND RELATED PROCEDURES (PART IV)

The TRIPS Agreement provides general language relating to principles concerning procedures for acquisition and maintenance of industrial property rights. Members may require, as a condition of the acquisition or maintenance of the industrial property rights covered by the Agreement (except protection of undisclosed information), compliance with reasonable procedures and formalities consistent with the Agreement (Article 62.1). Any procedures for grant or registration must permit the granting or registration of the right within a reasonable period of time so as to avoid unwarranted curtailment of the period of protection (Article 62.2).[54] Procedures concerning acquisition, maintenance, administrative revocation and *inter partes* procedures are to be governed by the guidelines applicable to enforcement (Article 62.4, referring to Article 41.2 and 41.3), and most final administrative decisions are subject to judicial or quasi-judicial review (Article 62.5).

54. This provision was accepted in a moment (1994) when national IP offices were not under the pressure of the *backlogs* in patent applications that today are almost normal and that result from the significant increase in patent applications around the world. Such an increase has resulted from the wave of invention and innovation generated by the latest technological advances in almost all technical fields, but with a particular emphasis in telecommunications and electronics. Eventually, resorting to collaborative patent examination among patent offices and the use of Artificial Intelligence will help patent offices to overcome the backlogs, and give expression to the provisions of Art. 62.2 of the TRIPS Agreement.

The Agreement also stipulates that Article 4 of the Paris Convention concerning the right of priority shall apply, *mutatis mutandis,* to service marks.

§31.06 DISPUTE PREVENTION AND SETTLEMENT (PART V)

[A] Transparency

The TRIPS Agreement requires that laws and regulations, final judicial decisions, administrative rulings of general application and bilateral agreements pertaining to the subject matter of the Agreement be published or made publicly available by Members (Article 63.1).

Members are further required to notify such laws and regulations to the TRIPS Council. The Council, in turn, is to attempt to minimize this burden on Members by engaging in consultations with WIPO on the possible establishment of a common register containing these laws and regulations (Article 63.2).

The TRIPS Council will also consider, in this connection, any action required regarding notifications pursuant to the obligations under the Agreement stemming from the provisions of Article 6*ter* of the Paris Convention.

[B] Dispute Settlement

A particularly important element of the TRIPS Agreement is the system of dispute settlement established under the WTO Agreement. The TRIPS Agreement itself invokes the provisions of Article XXII and XXIII of GATT 1994 (the WTO Agreement), as elaborated by the WTO Understanding on Rules and Procedures Governing the Settlement of Disputes (included as an Annex to the WTO Agreement), which applies to consultations and the settlement of disputes under the TRIPS Agreement (Article 64.1).

However, subparagraphs 1(b) and 1(c) of Article XXIII of GATT 1994, which refer to so-called non-violation dispute settlement cases, are not to apply to the settlement of disputes under the TRIPS Agreement for at least five years from the date of entry into force of the WTO Agreement (i.e., at least until January 1, 2000). Any extensions of that period are to be decided in the Ministerial Conference by consensus (Article 64.2 and 64.3).

"Non-violation and situation" disputes have been in the agenda of the TRIPS Council since 2000, but WTO Members are far from reaching a consensus. A large number of Members oppose the applicability of those grounds to disputes. Some Members fear that their application of TRIPS flexibilities could be jeopardized by a loose notion of impairment of obligations, under Article XXIII of the GATT. Other Members are wary of the difficulties in assessing or quantifying levels of noncompliance. However, Article 64 is unequivocal about the applicability of non-violations to TRIPS-related disputes, unless provided otherwise (such as in Article 6). Therefore, the application of non-violation disputes, in principle, should depend only on a matter of time, not of consensus, given that consensus on their application was reached on April 15, 1994. It is foreseeable, however, that this topic will be kept pending for many years to come.

Part III Reframing International IP? New Challenges and Negotiating Processes at WIPO

CHAPTER 32
The Role of Intellectual Property in Innovation Ecosystems

§32.01 SUMMARY

This chapter addresses the relationship between IP and the dynamic world of innovation ecosystems. The chapter begins by shedding light on the fundamental role of government policies in shaping the innovation landscape, and highlights how these policies act as a cornerstone, laying the groundwork for subsequent developments. We then turn to the role of intellectual property creators and look at the strategies employed to effectively disseminate their knowledge and bring their products to market.

We analyze some innovation spaces, where large corporations, SMEs and start-ups are at the center of the action and in particular, how these various entities actively contribute to and profit from intellectual property, thus fueling innovation.

The chapter then takes a legal perspective, focusing on aspects such as IP protection, and the role of the courts and/or ADR mechanisms. In the midst of these discussions, we address initiatives aimed at fostering a culture of innovation. In addition, we highlighted actions to promote a more inclusive innovation ecosystem, for example, by closing gender gaps and supporting under-resourced inventors.

The second part of this chapter focuses on data and economic analysis, emphasizing their crucial role in making informed innovation decisions. We explore how data-driven insights contribute to strategic planning and the development of intellectual property assets.

In essence, this chapter offers a holistic exploration of the multifaceted relationship between IP and innovation. It navigates the realms of policy, creativity, creators and firms, legal frameworks, and data-driven decision-making, while offering a practical perspective through which readers can understand the real-world impact of these concepts. This chapter serves as a resource for anyone wishing to navigate the intricate landscape in which intellectual property and innovation converge.

The IP and Innovation Ecosystem Sector (IES), established in 2020 by WIPO Members States, designs it works around this concept of an ecosystem approach.

§32.02 INTRODUCTION

[A] Definition of the Innovation Ecosystem

Innovation has boomed exponentially in the last century, driven by a diverse range of technological catalysts. In the early decades of the last century, the innovation landscape was dominated by technologies associated with combustion engines, transportation and mechanical machinery. In the 1930s, a burgeoning biopharmaceutical sector emerged through advances in pharmaceuticals, and since the 1990s, biotechnologies have further fueled its growth. As we approached the end of the twentieth century, there was a notable shift toward information and communication technologies (ICTs) and semiconductors, which accounted for a quarter of all patent applications between 1990 and 2010.[55]

An innovation ecosystem can be defined as the sum of all stakeholders, who make decisions and influence the direction of innovation. The choices and interactions that occur within the ecosystem are based on two elements: First, knowledge flows define the interaction between stakeholders in the innovation ecosystem. They provide potential innovation opportunities available to stakeholders, which in turn set the direction of innovation. Second, based on predictions, companies, entrepreneurs and governments identify innovation opportunities that can potentially generate private and social returns, i.e., the potential benefit to a company or society.[56]

The direction of innovation is not determined by a single entity, but is the result of dynamic interactions involving entrepreneurs, researchers, consumers and policymakers. This direction changes constantly, shaped by the choices and commitments of stakeholders, both public and private, who seek to reap the benefits of innovation. It is in this innovation ecosystem that the direction of innovation is set.

Curiosity is the guiding force behind researchers exploring new scientific frontiers and innovators experimenting with emerging technologies. Businesses, entrepreneurs and governments alike identify innovation opportunities based on predictions of potential benefits, both in private and societal terms. Private actors tend to take advantage of innovation opportunities more readily when the expected benefits are easily predictable and quantifiable in monetary terms. They are also inclined toward shorter-term innovation projects with lower risk of failure. However, it should be noted that riskier, longer-term opportunities tend to have the greatest potential for generating social benefits. Consequently, numerous governments undertake the responsibility of investing in long-term opportunities with the aim of benefiting the public. A prime illustration of this is the development of the aerospace industry. Taken the example of the US ecosystem, from the very beginning about 80% of the NASA's funding has been

55. WIPO, World Intellectual Property Report: *The Direction of Innovation*, Geneva, 2022, at 8.
56. *Ibid.*, at 10.

spent in contracts with the industry, however, it is until recently that private companies have begun to invest in and rely on space systems. It is in early twenty-first century that private investment has increased drastically, but even now some of these companies will not survive without sales to government.

Governments play a key role in promoting innovation. Governments have a dual objective, on the one hand, to enhance societal benefits and, on the other, individual goals. One of the main approaches they employ is the centralization of efforts and resources in areas where innovation has a profound impact on the common good, encompassing goods and services accessible to all, such as national defense and public health. In addition, governments are often the main drivers of the adoption of innovative technologies. They formulate policies aimed at shaping the provision of public goods in areas such as healthcare, security, environmental protection and education.

At the same time a significant part of the innovation trajectory is influenced by the wealth of knowledge accumulated by industries through their operational experiences and supply chains. The sharing of knowledge and innovation across fields and industries provides scientists, engineers and entrepreneurs with strong incentives to venture into new areas. They leverage their existing technological expertise, reconfigure the allocation of resources and ultimately exert a substantial influence on the course of innovation.

A country's innovative capacity depends on the strength of its innovation ecosystem, its stakeholders and the institutions that influence that environment. In this context, IP and specifically intangible assets play an increasingly important role in the global economy.

Estimates of the global sum of value of intangible assets show a tenfold increase over the past twenty-five years. Global intangible assets held by companies worldwide were worth USD 74 trillion in 2021, a growth of more than 25% from 2019, up from an estimated USD 6 trillion in 1996.[57]

The financing of intangible assets has emerged as a topic of great interest among WIPO Member States, international financial institutions and companies. WIPO reports highlight that the contribution of IP and other intangible assets is twice that of tangible capital to the value of products. Thus, one-third of the value of the products we buy comes from intangibles.[58]

WIPO's work on this regard, includes *Global INTAN-Invest Database and* an annual publication with Luiss Business School (LBS), the *WIPO-LBS World Intangible Investment Highlights*. The *World Intangible Investment Highlights* and the underlying *Global INTAN-Invest Database* offer novel, up-to-date cross-country, quarterly, and annual measures of investment in intangible assets, including those not included in

57. Brown, A., Gregory, J., Wunsch-Vincent, S. & WIPO website (2021), "Intangible Assets Owned by All Listed Companies Grew to USD 74 trillion in 2021," WIPO.
58. WIPO, World Intellectual Property Report: *Intangible Capital in Global Value Chains*, Geneva, 2017, p. 20.

official statistics. These estimates cover a range of high-income and emerging economies (starting with India), representing a significant advancement for evidence-based policymaking (hyperlink)

Putting this into a broader context, the 2030 Agenda for Sustainable Development, with its seventeen SDGs, has set out an ambitious agenda. SDG 9 focuses specifically on innovation-related targets, including increasing R&D spending as a share of GDP and the number of researchers per million population. WIPO has earned recognition for its role in gauging and fostering the development of intellectual property and innovation ecosystems, thereby playing a pivotal role in advancing the SDGs.

Figure 32.1 shows the knowledge and economic flows between the main actors in the innovation ecosystem.

Figure 32.1 Conceptual Summary of the Interactions in the Innovation Ecosystem[59]

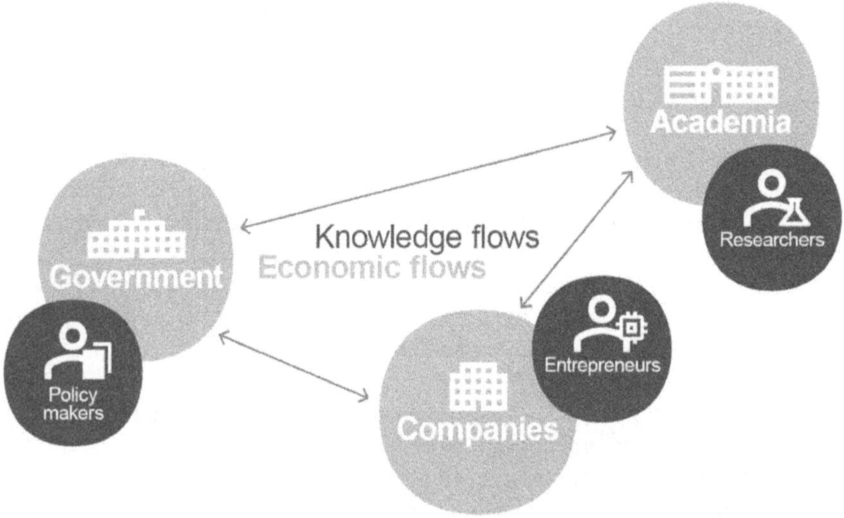

[B] IP and Global Innovation Trends

The Global Innovation Index (GII) in recent reports highlights two "waves of innovation" that it considers important to drive growth and return to productivity-enhancing levels: The wave of digital-age innovation—supercomputing, AI and automation, and a wave of Deep Science innovation—biotechnology, nanotechnology and new materials. These advances are likely to have a particular impact in areas such as health, food, environment and mobility.[60] The wave of the digital age, driven by supercomputing, AI

59. WIPO, World Intellectual Property Report: *The Direction of Innovation*, Geneva, 2022, at 10.
60. WIPO, Innovation Index 2022: *What is the future of innovation-led growth*, Geneva, 2022, at 21.

and automation, would impact productivity in all sectors, including services, and will facilitate scientific breakthroughs. The wave of deep science, characterized by advances in biotechnology, nanotechnology, new materials and other sciences, will revolutionize key areas such as health, food, environment and mobility. However, the report recognizes that realizing the positive impacts of these waves will take time due to barriers to technology adoption and diffusion. Overall, if these waves are effectively harnessed, with strong government intervention on critical issues, productivity and welfare are expected to improve substantially.

The GII 2024 Report shows mixed results in innovation investments. Regarding science and innovation investment, following a boom between 2020 and 2022, we witness a slowdown of R&D expenditures and a decline of some science and innovation investment metrics, namely, scientific publications dropped by 5% in 2023 (following growth rates above 8% annually in 2020 and 2021, and a slowdown in 2022); the value of VC investments has been falling with a 36% drop in 2022 followed by a further 39% drop in 2023; international patent filings—which had stagnated since 2021—saw a decline of 1.8% 2023, marking the first such decline since 2009 and global R&D grew at a rate of 5% in 2022 (slightly down from 2021).

In contrast, technological progress and adoption continued strong, i.e., technology continues to progress rapidly, particularly in health-related fields and computing power. Technology adoption is also growing, particularly in 5G, robotics, and electric vehicles (EVs)—where the global stock of EVs increased by 54% in 2022.

Scientific publications, R&D spending, total VC deal transactions and patents continued to increase (grew by only 0.3%, the slowest pace since 2009). However, the value of venture capital investments declined (falling significantly in 2022).

The 2024 GII report shows important changes in the geography of global innovation:

- For the fourteenth consecutive year, Switzerland ranks first in the GII 2024.
- Sweden and the US maintain 2nd and 3rd positions, respectively.
- Singapore (4th) moves further into the top 5, followed by the UK (5th).
- The Republic of Korea moves up to the 6th position.
- China—still the only middle-income economy within the GII top 30—moves up the ranking to edge closer to the top 10 again, reaching 11th position.

Emerging economies show uneven progress, with Indonesia rising rapidly, the Philippines and Vietnam progressing, and China, Turkey and Iran falling back, partly due to COVID-19. India, Moldova and Vietnam are among the twenty most innovative countries. India, Moldova and Vietnam consistently outperform in innovation development, as do Indonesia, Uzbekistan, Pakistan and Brazil. Positive innovation performance is observed in the Middle East, including the UAE, Saudi Arabia, Qatar, Bahrain and Oman. Mauritius and South Africa lead Sub-Saharan Africa, with Rwanda always above. Many middle- and low-income economies could benefit from systematic improvements in the innovation ecosystem.

In terms of technological progress, there have been notable advances in the information technology, health and energy sectors, with improvements in supercomputers, genome sequencing costs and renewable energy technologies. However, the cost of electric batteries increased in 2022. Technology adoption is generally positive, with improvements in safe sanitation, connectivity, robots and EVs. Still, some technologies, such as EVs, have relatively low adoption rates. The socioeconomic impact of innovation continues to show significant global challenges; for the second year in a row, labor productivity is stagnant, life expectancy has fallen, and carbon dioxide emissions continue to rise.

The World Intellectual Property Indicators Report for 2023 reveals a record-breaking surge in global patent applications in 2022, with India and China leading the charge despite concerns over economic uncertainties.[61] While trademark and industrial design filings experienced a decrease, patent applications reached 3.46 million, marking three consecutive years of growth. Notably, China, the US, Japan, Republic of Korea, and Germany topped the list of countries with the highest patent filings, though China's growth rate showed a slight dip. India stood out with a remarkable 31.6% increase in patent applications. The report highlights the vital role of governments in fostering innovation and stresses the significance of intellectual property amidst geopolitical instability. Despite trademark application declines, trademark filing trends still indicate positivity, particularly in the research and technology sector. Additionally, industrial design filings saw a slight decrease, predominantly driven by Asia. Plant variety applications and protected GIs demonstrate growth and geographical diversity, signifying a thriving global intellectual property landscape.

Overall, the outlook for innovation investments in 2024 appears uncertain, due to venture capital funding problems and the socioeconomic impact of the COVID-19 pandemic. Technological progress is continuous, but its impact on society and the environment remains a concern. That said, the positive effects of the two new waves of innovation, while reflected in patent applications and other IP rights, will take time to materialize and other obstacles will have to be overcome, particularly in the area of technology adoption and diffusion.

§32.03 GOVERNMENTS SHAPE THE IP AND INNOVATION LANDSCAPE

[A] Policies That Set the Course for Innovation

Governments can influence the direction of innovation by allocating human and financial resources through a wide range of public policy instruments, as well as by implementing a number of different public support or incentive policies.

In shaping the direction of innovation, public policy plays a crucial role in influencing the allocation of resources and priorities in various scientific fields and industries. Innovation policies aim to induce and guide innovation in specific directions.

61. WIPO, World Intellectual Property Indicators, Geneva, 2023.

These policies may serve different objectives, among others:[62]

Discovery-inducing policies. These policies stimulate scientific and technological discoveries, especially when the uncertainty and risks of innovation are high. Examples include publicly funded research in academic institutions and public research organizations. Governments can prioritize certain fields over others through such policies.

Risk mitigation and early adoption policies. These policies aim to reduce the risks associated with innovation and encourage the early adoption of new technologies. Examples include R&D subsidies, soft loans and R&D tax incentives. Governments can also promote adoption by subsidizing production, offering tax incentives or supporting workforce training.

Diffusion policies. These policies focus on the widespread adoption of technologies and converting them into industry standards. Governments can influence diffusion through workforce training, grants, loans, tax credits and outright purchases. Technologies that are successful in their home industry tend to face lower risks and costs of adoption. Governments influence IP and innovation standards through legislation, international treaties, promotion of best practices, support for R&D, standardization organizations, enforcement of IP rights, access to knowledge and global cooperation.

Demand-driven or mission-oriented policies. These policies involve centralized decision-making and the concentration of resources on specific objectives set by the government. The government becomes the main source of demand for specific innovations. Examples are programs such as NASA space exploration or wartime medical research.

In conclusion, public policies are instrumental in directing innovation by influencing resource allocation and research priorities. These policies, spanning from discovery-inducing initiatives to demand-driven strategies, aim to mitigate risks, foster early adoption, and facilitate widespread diffusion of new technologies toward public and societal goals.

[B] The Particular Challenges of Developing Economies

Developing economies have two main avenues for innovation, either adapting foreign technologies or creating technologies locally.

In many developing economies, especially the less innovative ones, innovation usually consists of adapting foreign technologies to local needs. However, this adaptation tends to be incremental and ad hoc, with limited improvements to the original technology. It is essential to recognize that not all innovations from more advanced economies are directly applicable to the needs of developing economies. Innovations from highly industrialized nations are often designed for capital-intensive industries, highly skilled labor, and consumers with greater purchasing power. These innovations

62. WIPO, World Intellectual Property Report: *The Direction of Innovation*, Geneva, 2022, p. 28.

may not fit the characteristics of developing economies, which tend to have less skilled labor, inadequate infrastructure and consumers with less purchasing power. Adapting foreign technologies to local conditions often means making them more affordable, which requires a deep understanding of local needs and the ability to reduce costs.

Some developing economies, especially middle-income ones, can take advantage of their scientific and technological capabilities to bridge the technological gap with advanced economies, thus creating technologies locally. These economies can become sources of innovation in various fields and actively participate in global innovation networks by contributing knowledge, technologies and advanced goods and services.

In both approaches, solutions must be tailored to local conditions, which may include limited access to finance, inadequate infrastructure (such as energy and transportation) and shortages of skilled labor. Successful innovation in developing economies often requires collaboration between various stakeholders, such as research institutions, government agencies and NGOs. Local adaptation of foreign technologies can lead to innovations that are valuable not only for the local market, but also for industrialized economies.

In addition, developing economies often contain a diverse range of regions, from fast-growing emerging economies to less developed areas. Successful TT depends on matching the needs and competencies of the destination economy with those of the source economy. Successful innovation in developing economies does not always conform to traditional indicators of innovation, such as R&D investment, skilled labor force or patent filings, making them "off the radar" innovations.

In short, the direction of innovation is determined by a complex interplay of policy choices, local contexts and global networks. The ability to harness innovation for societal progress depends on thoughtful design and implementation of innovation policies, especially in developing economies where challenges and opportunities abound.

[C] The Role of International Agreements in Shaping IP and Innovation

The absence of a multilateral regulatory framework made it difficult to protect invention, trademark and design rights, among other categories. The main reason for this difficulty was that national legislations were very different from each other—and still are, despite their progressive harmonization—and, however, applications had to be filed in other countries in short periods of time, if not at the same time, in order to avoid risks.

As, during the second half of the nineteenth century, more and more countries developed a system of protection for inventions and trademarks, there was a general desire to harmonize industrial property laws on an international basis. The increase in trade and technological flows between countries made such harmonization more and more necessary. This process led to the adoption of important intellectual property treaties, which are mentioned and explained throughout this book.

This important progress in the adoption of industrial property treaties continued throughout the twentieth century. Needless to say that the vast majority of these treaties have been subject to successive modifications in order to incorporate new elements or to adjust them to new trends or realities, with the result that there are different treaties in the same treaty.

WIPO[63] administers twenty-eight treaties, of which fourteen are dedicated to the protection of intellectual property, among which it is worth mentioning the Paris Union Treaty on industrial property and the Berne Union Convention on copyright.

This complex normative framework ensures inventors, creators and entrepreneurs the mechanisms to seek adequate protection of their interests at the international level, and its implementation in domestic law, in the different WIPO Member Countries, guarantees that the Treaties are incorporated bearing in mind the level of development of each country and in particular the specific interests of their public policies.

[D] Conceptualization of National IP Strategies in the Innovation Ecosystem

A national IP strategy is a comprehensive set of policy measures developed and implemented by a government to promote a coordinated approach to creating, developing, managing and protecting economically valuable IP assets at the national level.

This strategy is designed to align intellectual property with the economic, social, cultural, technological, legal and institutional context of a country. It helps the government establish and manage intellectual property policies and regulatory frameworks that enhance the nation's development.

Intellectual property is recognized as a cross-cutting issue relevant to various industries, services and public policy areas. It influences critical policy issues such as climate change, access to medicines, cultural development and food security. It also plays a crucial role in a country's innovation policy, contributing to economic performance. Therefore, forging strong connections between IP and these areas (social, cultural, health, economic, ecological, etc.) is essential to harnessing the national IP system in support of a country's development goals.

The value of a national IP strategy lies in its ability to harness the potential impact of intellectual property on a country's economic, cultural, social and technological development. A balanced Intellectual property system contributes to economic competitiveness and innovative capacity. It also plays a role in achieving broader development objectives. Various industries depend on national and international intellectual property systems to be competitive, and cultural industries can benefit from the appropriate use of intellectual property.

A national intellectual property strategy aims to create functional linkages by integrating intellectual property issues into relevant public policies within a national

63. In 1967, the Stockholm Diplomatic Conference led to the creation of WIPO, a specialized agency of the United Nations. WIPO has served as a permanent structure for both industrial property and copyright Unions.

development framework. It enables the strategic use of intellectual property in all economic sectors, fosters an environment for generating valuable intellectual property assets, promotes intellectual property as an engine of economic growth, balances intellectual property protection with innovation and competitiveness, and ensures better alignment with national policies.

Ultimately, a national IP strategy provides a roadmap for a country to effectively manage and use the IP system to contribute to its development priorities, policies and economic objectives. It provides a structured approach for the government to systematically deploy and implement national IP policies, facilitating collaboration among stakeholders in the creation, protection, management, promotion and commercialization of intellectual property assets derived from innovations and creative works.

WIPO assists its Member Countries, but particularly transition, developing and least-developed countries (LDCs), throughout the national intellectual property strategy development process, which have a positive impact on economic development, innovative and creative capacity and business vitality. WIPO draws on its unique global experience to help countries develop their national IP strategies in line with their social, cultural and economic development objectives and priorities. WIPO provides customized assistance throughout the entire national IP strategy development process in support of Member States' objectives, needs and priorities. Drawing on its unique global experience, WIPO offers policy advice, data and analysis, best practices and other customized guidance.

§32.04 ACADEMIA, INNOVATORS AND PIONEERING ENTREPRENEURS IN IP CREATION

[A] Technology Transfer

Academic institutions, innovators and entrepreneurs have increasingly recognized the potential of intellectual property as a means of fostering innovation, transferring knowledge from the laboratory to the marketplace and driving economic development. Academic institutions have long been at the forefront of IP creation, generating a wealth of novel ideas, discoveries and inventions. Faculty, researchers and students at these institutions play a key role in advancing knowledge, knowledge transfer and innovation.

TT is a collaborative process that allows scientific findings, knowledge and intellectual property to flow from creators, such as universities and research institutions, to public and private users. Its goal is to transform inventions and scientific outcomes into new products and services that benefit society. TT is closely related to knowledge transfer.

To bridge the gap between academia and industry, many universities have established Technology Transfer Offices (TTOs). These offices specialize in managing intellectual property assets, facilitating licensing agreements and fostering entrepreneurship among faculty and students. TTOs are often created within universities to manage intellectual property assets and facilitate the transfer of knowledge and technology to industry. These offices may go by various names, such as Technology Licensing Office (TLO), Technology Management Office, etc. The main functions of these offices are to transfer laboratory innovations to society and the marketplace and ultimately to enhance the impact of research results. TTO/TLOs usually require financial support from the government and relevant institutions for an initial period before becoming financially self-sufficient. From an IP management perspective, TTO/TLOs are responsible for IP promotion, filing IP protection applications, commercialization (marketing, negotiation, licensing and spin-off creation), maintenance of IP assets, enforcement of IP rights, management of revenue sharing, and management of conflicts of interest and commitments.

They may also engage in other revenue-generating activities, such as management of consulting services, marketing of training programs and short courses, management of contract research and related projects, marketing of laboratory services, and other identified revenue-generating activities. Their performance is usually assessed using benchmark indicators, such as the number of IP disclosures, IP applications, grants, licensing contracts, licensing revenues, start-up companies created and joint ventures formed.

TTOs can adopt a variety of organizational structures, such as internal university offices, wholly owned subsidiary companies, private IP service providers, IP management consortia, and government offices acting as TTOs. The choice of structure depends on local needs and resources.

WIPO provides support to many TTOs/TLOs through different services ranging from the definition of IP policies to the training and coaching of their staff on IP and TT issues. Moreover, these structures are often located in the same space as the TISCs,[64] a WIPO project to support innovators in accessing patent information, scientific and technical literature and databases to promote innovation, TT, commercialization and utilization of technology.

In conclusion, TT involves a multifaceted collaboration between researchers and TT entities, each of which plays a crucial role in translating academic research into real-world applications and driving innovation for the benefit of society.

[B] Promoting the Commercialization of Intellectual Property

The commercialization of intellectual property consists of obtaining additional economic benefits from the exploitation of intangibles. Prototypes and implemented processes lead to the development of products and services by entrepreneurs, start-ups, existing companies and governments, generating economic, cultural and social benefits. The commercialization of technologies and the work of companies to bring these products to market—supported by intellectual property rights—requires a continuous series of activities to further refine, test and improve these inventions. The

64. WIPO has a network of 1,500 TISCs distributed in different regions of the world. In 2022, they received two million requests for information on topics as diverse as general guidance, state-of-the-art studies to define innovation strategies or to establish free spaces for new developments or patent-based opportunity studies.

results of the research help guide the appropriate path to a license, a new venture or a spin-off company.

The commercialization of intellectual property usually involves steps such as filing, evaluation, protection, business planning, marketing, licensing, product development and market dissemination.

The benefits of commercialization of research results are shared among various stakeholders, such as universities, research institutions, inventors, investors and the private sector. Institutions often establish knowledge transfer offices and implement policies and programs to support IP commercialization, such as incubators, accelerators, research parks and participation in networks focused on IP commercialization.

Academic asset management for TT involves identifying and leveraging tangible or intangible resources owned or controlled by academic institutions to create public and economic value. These assets can be broadly classified into intellectual assets and non-intellectual assets.

Intellectual assets encompass intellectual property, such as patents, trademarks, industrial designs and copyrights, as well as knowledge assets, including trade secrets, know-how, experience and others. Non-intellectual assets include collections (e.g., libraries), research infrastructure and capacity (e.g., laboratories and equipment), financial assets (e.g., spin-offs and private fund managers), operational assets (e.g., TTOs) and strategic assets (e.g., reputation and access to customers).

To maximize the potential value of academic assets, universities and research institutions must effectively map their intellectual and non-intellectual assets. IPR management is a crucial aspect of academic institutions' efforts to leverage their intellectual assets. Effective IPR management involves a strategic approach, including steps such as identifying potential assets, assessing their advantages, deciding on forms of protection (e.g., patents, trade secrets), determining commercialization and TT strategies, and identifying suitable partners. IPR management is essential for the success of TT and the long-term impact of research results on society.

The legal framework for IPR management policies in academic institutions operates at multiple levels, including the international, national, institutional and professional association levels. Clear IP management principles and guidelines are needed to ensure effective outcomes in the complex process of managing academic assets for TT.

In order to maximize the socioeconomic impact of publicly funded research results, universities and research institutions need to ensure that they are disseminated effectively. That means considering all types of diffusion and transfer mechanisms (e.g., open access publication, licensing, spin-offs, start-ups and collaboration in R&D) and all possible commercialization partners (such as spin-offs, existing companies, investors, SMEs, other nonprofit organizations, innovation support agencies, even governments), and selecting the most appropriate ones.

Innovators and entrepreneurs, who often come from academia or work closely with academic institutions, are crucial catalysts in the pioneering creation of intellectual property. These individuals and organizations play a critical role in transforming academic research and innovative ideas into practical applications and marketable products. Often, innovators and entrepreneurs create new companies or spin-offs to commercialize intellectual property derived from academic research. These companies bridge the gap between academia and the marketplace, ensuring that promising innovations reach consumers.

In addition, IP-driven start-ups need financial resources for R&D, product development and market entry. Innovators and entrepreneurs seek funding from venture capitalists, business angels and public grants to support the creation and development of intellectual property.

Thriving entrepreneurial ecosystems, linked to academic centers, provide an environment conducive to the creation of intellectual property. These ecosystems offer mentorship, networking opportunities and access to resources that empower innovators and entrepreneurs. Collaborative open innovation models allow innovators to leverage external expertise and resources for the creation of intellectual property. Partnerships with academic institutions, research centers and other innovators amplify the potential for breakthrough discoveries.

[C] Challenges in Pioneering IP Creation

One of the main challenges arises from the different objectives of the stakeholders in the innovation ecosystem. Academic institutions focus on research dissemination and social impact, while market players are primarily motivated by profit. This difference in objectives can complicate negotiations. Academic institutions, being nonprofit entities, emphasize primarily the dissemination of research results. This mission-oriented approach often diverges from the for-profit perspective of market players, such as venture capitalists, industrial partners or technology brokers.

In addition, academic institutions may face problems related to asymmetric information. In emerging economies, where IP markets may be underdeveloped, there is often a lack of transparency regarding IP valuation mechanisms and tools. This lack of information can lead to unequal bargaining positions with trading partners.

In addition, one of the main obstacles is the significant funding required for research, development and legal protection of intellectual property. Innovators and entrepreneurs must devote resources for filing patents, trademarks and copyrights, which can be costly.

Furthermore, market uncertainty affects "early adopters" the most. Predicting consumer demand and market dynamics for breakthrough inventions is inherently uncertain, making it difficult to attract investment and plan for the long term. However, those who successfully overcome these challenges have the potential to revolutionize industries and leave a lasting mark on the world of innovation.

The synergy between academia, innovators and entrepreneurs in pioneering IP creation has far-reaching implications for society, the economy and technological progress. By enhancing academic research, fostering entrepreneurship and protecting intellectual property, this ecosystem contributes to economic growth, job creation and improved quality of life.

§32.05 COMPANIES AT THE HEART OF THE ECOSYSTEM

[A] Innovation Hotspots

From Beijing to Frankfurt to the Silicon Valley, companies are working on their next innovations. The private sector has been playing a very important role in driving innovation. Entrepreneurial ecosystems represent a dynamic perspective on entrepreneurial activity, focusing on high-growth companies and the complex interplay of factors that foster their development and success.

These ecosystems are shaped by a combination of location-specific advantages, the presence of established businesses, the active participation of experienced entrepreneurs, cultural elements, and access to financial and information resources.

The geography of innovation presents a paradox in which scientific knowledge and innovation are increasingly global and, at the same time, more concentrated in specific centers. New players, particularly Asian countries, are contributing significantly to scientific research and innovation, challenging the historical dominance of higher-income economies. At the same time, there is a growing concentration of innovative activities in densely populated urban areas, such as Silicon Valley and China's Shenzhen-Hong Kong region.[65] However, this paradox is more apparent than real. The world's most innovative urban areas are also the most open to international collaboration, and often have stronger global connections than national ones. These urban areas form global innovation networks, driven by skilled individuals and innovative companies.

Collaboration among researchers and the proximity of knowledge within these urban centers drive innovation. We see an extension of knowledge creation to more countries, with China and South Korea playing significant roles in global innovation. High-income economies are experiencing an increase in international collaboration in academia and business, except in East Asia, where Japan, South Korea and China have experienced a decline in international collaboration rates. Most international collaboration occurs among a selected group of countries, mainly the US and Western Europe, with emerging economies collaborating more with established ones.[66] Global innovation hubs and specialized clusters are at the center of global innovation networks and foster national and international collaboration. Multinational companies are at the center of these networks and increasingly include foreign inventors in their patent applications.

Patent data shed light on the corporate R&D networks at the center of global innovation networks. Multinational companies around the world increasingly include foreign inventors in their patent applications, and those foreign inventors come from an expanding set of countries. In the 1970s and 1980s, only 9% of patents filed by US companies had foreign inventors; by the 2010s, this percentage had risen to 38%.

65. WIPO, World Intellectual Property Report: The Geography of Innovation—*Local Hotspots, Global Networks*, Geneva, 2019, p. 9.
66. *Ibid.*, p. 10.

Western European companies experienced a similar increase, from 9% to 27% over the same period.

The importance of openness and international collaboration for innovation is key. Policies that promote openness to innovation and collaboration can boost knowledge production, especially in the face of declining R&D productivity. International cooperation is crucial for incentivizing investment in innovation, facilitating international business and financing large-scale scientific projects. However, growing national regional disparities within countries require specific regional support and development policies to address the concentration of innovation in already wealthy countries and metropolitan areas.

[B] Start-Ups and SMEs as Agile Contributors to and Beneficiaries of IP and Innovation

Start-ups and SMEs are critical to both developed and developing economies, contributing significantly to GDP and driving innovation. This has been the case even during crises such as the COVID-19 pandemic. Intellectual property plays a crucial role in the success of SMEs.

SMEs and entrepreneurship are instrumental in driving innovation in various dimensions, contributing substantially to economic progress. Their involvement in innovation encompasses the introduction of improvements in products, processes, organizational methodologies and marketing strategies into the economic landscape. These innovations manifest themselves at two fundamental levels: the creation of breakthrough innovations that push technological frontiers and the adoption of incremental innovations that push the economy closer to its technological limits. These innovative ideas may originate within SMEs or start-ups, or they may be sought from external sources.

In addition, SMEs and entrepreneurship serve as a repository of ideas and vital inputs to the innovation process, benefiting large corporations, universities, research institutions and other small businesses. There are multiple perspectives on the intricate relationship between entrepreneurship and innovation.[67] These functions are not mutually exclusive, but represent distinct facets of the multifaceted innovation process. The concept of entrepreneurship encompasses individuals who seek to generate value through economic activities by identifying and exploiting novel products, processes or market opportunities. Entrepreneurial activities can manifest themselves in start-ups, SMEs, large corporations or public-sector organizations, underlining the importance of entrepreneurs in driving innovation. Here we focus primarily on start-ups and SMEs, highlighting their role in fostering innovation-driven entrepreneurship. This innovation-driven role serves as a catalyst for economic growth and a means to address societal challenges.

The creation of new companies and the expansion of SMEs stimulate "creative destruction," forcing established competitors to modernize or exit the market. This

67. OECD, Study on SMEs, Entrepreneurship and Innovation, 2010, p. 32.

process increases overall productivity and boosts economic growth, especially during economic downturns and recoveries.

SMEs and start-ups play a crucial role in the commercialization of knowledge generated in universities, research institutions and large companies. They actively contribute to the dissemination of knowledge, which is a cornerstone of economic progress.

Although debate persists about the relative roles of SMEs and large firms in innovation, empirical evidence suggests that SMEs stand out as pioneers of breakthrough innovations.[68] Synergy between these entities remains critical.

Two distinct modes of innovation coexist: the Science, Technology and Innovation (STI) mode and the Do, Use and Interact (DUI) mode. SMEs play different roles in these modes: STI emphasizes research and development and DUI emphasizes experiential and user-based learning. A comprehensive approach to innovation recognizes the importance of both modes and addresses the various barriers affecting SMEs and start-ups. Policy initiatives should tailor support measures to the specific needs of these entities to foster innovation and drive economic growth.

In addition, studies reveal that SMEs thrive when they prioritize IP, which benefits ambitious high-growth SMEs, start-ups and established companies. However, SMEs face challenges related to IP, such as the perception that patent costs are high.[69] However, the value of IP far outweighs these expenses, as intangible assets increasingly dominate a company's core assets. In the 1970s, tangible assets accounted for more than 80% of the value of the S&P 500. The Titans of this time—from Exxon Mobile, to Procter & Gamble, to General Electric—were full of physical, quantifiable and easily insurable assets. Today we live in a substantially different world, with a very different global economy, where intangible assets account for over 90% of a company's business value (S&P 500 2020). It is estimated that the total value of global intangible assets today stands at USD 65 trillion, greater than the value of the US and Chinese economies combined.

A well-crafted IP strategy can help maximize the potential of businesses. Using and understanding IP rights can help businesses secure competitive advantage, generate revenue streams, serve as a source of competitive intelligence, reduce tax liability, attract investors and partners, and facilitate access to financing.

[C] Leveraging Intellectual Property for Competitive Advantage

Intellectual property rights can be used to secure financing, either by pledging them or by transferring rights to the cash flows derived from these assets. Alternatively, a company's intellectual property can provide an indicator of the company's value and support financing decisions. For some companies, intangible assets represent only a small part of the company's value. For others, the majority of their value may come

68. *Ibid.*, p. 35.
69. Tietze, F. & WIPO Magazine (2021), "Empowering SMEs to Leverage IP for Innovation," University of Cambridge, UK.

from their intellectual property. These companies must communicate the value of their intellectual property and other intangible assets to lenders and investors. Collateral-based financing of intangible assets is growing, but is still in its infancy. Commercial actors and governments are conducting experiments to improve access to IPR-based financing.

A key aspect is the valuation of intellectual property, which involves identifying and assessing the potential benefits and risks associated with intangible assets. Being able to estimate the value of intangibles is crucial in business planning, licensing, acquisitions, mergers, investments, joint ventures and lending.

The difference between intellectual property evaluation and valuation lies in their approach. Appraisal estimates the value of the technology based on its technical merits, its applicability in the marketplace and its freedom to operate, whereas valuation projects the potential value that the technology can generate in a specific market context, taking into account risk and changes in the value of money over time.

TTO/TLOs evaluate technologies during the decision-making process for IP protection and commercialization. They tend to focus on inventions with the greatest market potential, which often represent only a fraction of research disclosures. IP valuation is complex and subject to a number of challenges, especially in the context of universities and research institutions working with early-stage technologies. The projection of future benefits can be uncertain, given the risks associated with TT and the difficulty of defining potential areas of use and appropriate markets.

There are two main approaches to IP valuation: qualitative and quantitative. Qualitative IP valuation evaluates an invention based on predefined criteria in the pre-commercialization phase. Quantitative IP valuation involves measuring potential benefits and risks using methodologies such as the Cost Method, the Market Method and the Income Method, which estimate the monetary value of IP. The choice of the most appropriate IP valuation method depends on the context, the maturity of the market, the industry and the specific partners involved. The subjective nature of valuation, combined with contextual variability, often results in a range of estimated values.

In the area of access to credit, it is common practice for lenders to require borrowers to pledge their assets as collateral. This serves as security for lenders, allowing them to reclaim and liquidate these assets in the event of a borrower's default, thus mitigating their losses. Traditionally, tangible assets, such as company equipment and condominium property, have been the preferred options as collateral. However, there is a growing trend to use specific intellectual property assets, such as copyrights, designs, patents or the revenue streams generated by them, to secure loans. When intellectual property is used as collateral, the borrower usually retains ownership. However, lenders may impose certain restrictions on how the intellectual property may be used in the future, which may affect the ability to license or transfer it to third parties. In the event that the borrower defaults on the loan, lenders often register their rights in the intellectual property, known as a security interest. Depending on the laws of the jurisdiction, this registration may be done through an IP office or a security interest registry. If a lender uses IP as security in multiple countries, this registration process may need to be repeated in each jurisdiction.[70]

§32.06 PROMOTE AND SAFEGUARD INTELLECTUAL PROPERTY AND INNOVATIONS IN THE ECOSYSTEM

[A] IP and the Gender Gap in Innovation

Innovation and creativity are key drivers of economic growth. Policies that foster creativity and innovation can address today's challenges and raise global living standards; however, when we analyze the demographics of those involved in IP protection systems, a pronounced gender disparity becomes apparent.

Despite women's considerable progress in the labor market and in education, their participation in the field of intellectual property is unequal and they obtain fewer benefits, resulting in a gender gap in the field of intellectual property. It is imperative to eliminate this gap, as the underutilization of women's potential contribution to the economy hinders global economic progress. Closing gender gaps in labor force participation alone could potentially inject the sum of USD 12 trillion into global GDP by 2025.[71]

Research on the gender gap in intellectual property transcends the realm of patents, broadening its scope to assess women's participation in all sectors related to innovation and creativity. Although the proportion of women inventors has increased, they still constitute a low percentage of inventors in PCT applications. According to a WIPO report published in 2023 on PCT patent applications filed by women, women participated in 31% of PCT applications and represent 16% of the total number of inventors listed in patent applications. According to the report, the estimated contribution of women in applications is equivalent to 14% of PCT applications.[72] This discrepancy amounts to missed opportunities for progress and economic prosperity around the world.

Moreover, this imbalance can overshadow innovation and economic productivity, potentially hindering the wealth and growth of economies. Correcting this gender participation gap aligns deeply with the UN's SDG #5, which strives to achieve gender equality and empower all women and girls.

To address this pressing problem, economic researchers and policymakers can embark on two fundamental tasks. The first is to identify women inventors and creators, establishing a baseline to gauge the magnitude of the problem. Current data on women's participation in innovation and intellectual property provide a starting

70. Examples of various national approaches to IP-backed financing can be found in WIPO series of publications "Unlocking IP-backed Financing," available at www.wipo.int/publications/en/series/index.jsp?id = 241 (accessed December 2024).
71. WIPO, Action Plan on Intellectual Property and Gender: *The Role of IP in Supporting Women and Girls*, Geneva, 2023, p. 3.
72. WIPO, The Global Gender Gap in Innovation and Creativity: *An International Comparison of the Gender Gap in Global Patenting over Two Decades*, Geneva, 2023, p. 10.

point for assessing the gender gap, in line with UN SDG #5. Intellectual property data, covering patents, utility models, industrial designs and registered copyrights, contain a wealth of information on inventors, designers and creators.

The second step is to promote quantitative research at the intersection of gender participation, innovation and creativity. By combining data on innovation and intellectual property with complementary information related to economic activities, researchers can obtain information on women's contribution to socioeconomic development and economic growth. Crucial issues to be addressed include the extent of women's participation in innovation and IP creation, the challenges they face during the initiation and innovation phases, and policies that favor gender balance.

Encouragingly, the global gender gap in patenting has seen a gradual narrowing over the past two decades, with the most rapid progress in the past five years. However, at the current rate, the world expects to reach gender parity in patent applications by 2061. Nevertheless, regional disparities persist, with North America leading the way in 2055, followed by Asia in 2056. Latin America and the Caribbean plan to bridge the gender gap by 2068, while Europe and Oceania face a longer timetable, with convergence estimated in 2088.

Women inventors tend to gravitate toward specific industries such as biotechnology, food chemistry and pharmaceuticals, with limited representation in fields such as mechanical engineering. Academic institutions tend to host a higher concentration of women inventors than the private sector. The increase in women's participation in patenting is often due to collaboration in mixed teams, while teams of female inventors led exclusively by women remain rare.

In summary, the imperative to address the gender gap in innovation and IP participation transcends mere equality and equity; it is a strategic necessity to drive economic growth and overcome global challenges. It must be accompanied by overall efforts to improve diversity, equity and inclusion in the IP and innovation ecosystem. Rigorous measurement, an understanding of the challenges faced by women and other groups, and the implementation of supportive bottom-up policies collectively represent the path to achieving gender parity and greater equity in the fields of innovation and creativity.

[B] Intellectual Property Awareness and Education

Promoting respect for intellectual property requires a strategy that encompasses both awareness-raising efforts and practical measures. Various elements come into play in this framework, such as the revision of educational programs, the promotion of the legitimate consumption of IP-protected products through commercial strategies, the implementation of technical measures to prevent access to infringing content, the existence of enforcement measures and a judicial system with jurisdiction in the matter.

To begin with, it is essential to examine consumer perceptions and awareness of IP, as well as to understand the legal and social ramifications. Once this assessment phase is complete, the next step is to establish clear objectives for the strategy. Defining precisely the behavioral changes being pursued, such as curbing the purchase of counterfeit products, is of vital importance. The main target groups that should adopt or contribute to the desired behavioral changes are then identified. These groups cover a broad spectrum, including consumers, law-enforcement authorities, the media and distributors of IP-protected goods. The messages conveyed through these activities may highlight the accessibility of authentic products, highlight the injustices associated with counterfeiting and piracy, or shed light on the adverse impact on employment, culture or public health. The temporal scope of the strategy is then determined, with a breakdown into phases that are synchronized with the established objectives, target groups and activities. Finally, a continuous monitoring and evaluation process is carried out. The aim is to periodically review each activity in relation to the initial objectives.

To facilitate awareness and support innovation, a number of tools can be used. These tools can be developed by IP offices or in collaboration with government agencies. They include publications and case studies that highlight how innovators use IPRs, educational programs that highlight the importance of IP protection and enforcement, guidance for developing IP strategies, online resources related to IP in the context of green technology solutions, webinars and various events. These activities are often part of a broader national strategy, such as a country's innovation strategy that emphasizes innovation-led growth.

In addition, such initiatives can improve public perception of the IP system as a crucial element in achieving objectives. Collaborating with partners such as NGOs, think tanks, industry groups or businesses can help reduce the resource burden on IP offices while increasing their impact. Integrating awareness-raising activities into broader IP education strategies or government programs aimed at promoting IP can be an effective approach.

[C] The Role of the Judiciary in the IP and Innovation Ecosystem

The judiciary plays a crucial role in the intellectual property and innovation ecosystem. Its main function is to interpret and apply the laws and regulations governing intellectual property rights, while balancing the interests of the parties.

Indeed, for the instrumental goal of the IP system to foster innovation and creativity to be fully realized, a sound IP legal framework must be accompanied by a fair and effective dispute resolution system that provides predictability to market structures and contributes to the broad balance of public considerations provided for in the IP system. Courts take on the task of interpreting and applying intellectual property laws to the real-life disputes that come before them, integrating the static legal framework into the dynamic fabric of our societies. In doing so, courts uphold rights and provide fair resolution to disputes, and render judgments that can have legal, economic, and social consequences beyond the disputing parties and ultimately impact the public. Ultimately, the effectiveness of the intellectual property system will depend critically on the foundation of a strong and effective justice system for intellectual property disputes.

The current intellectual property system is the result of multiple court decisions and rulings that shaped the course of the history of intellectual property law. In the patent area, the contours of patentability have been defined through a series of court verdicts over the past two centuries, including more recently on genetically modified (GM) organisms,[73] business methods[74] or computer-implemented inventions.[75] In the field of copyright, it was the courts that defined the scope of protection when disputes arose over whether a photograph is protected when the law does not explicitly mention them,[76] considered that advertisements are also expressive, even if they are commercial,[77] and that a creative element the work incorporated into a useful and manufactured article may be protected by copyright[78]

However, the current rapid pace of technological advances is unprecedented. Our lives are being transformed by an explosion of cutting-edge technologies including digital technologies such as the Internet of Things (IoT), blockchain, the metaverse, AI, big data and cloud computing; physical technologies, such as autonomous driving, 3D printing and hardware innovations; as well as biological technologies, such as genetic engineering, human augmentation and brain-computer interface.

While the law changes and adapts in response to evolving technologies and the economy, the breakneck speed of today's technological transformations results in situations where legislatures are unable to keep up and create policy backlogs. In such cases, courts are increasingly on the front lines to provide clear and effective answers to questions that have not yet received a legislative policy response, establishing important precedents that shape intellectual property laws, affect market participants, and may involve broader social, economic, and societal issues. scientific and ethical consequences.

A prominent example, in the last few months alone, a new wave of powerful "generative" AI chatbots, such as OpenAI's ChatGPT and Google's Bard, which produce plausible text and images in response to conversational prompts, has come to the forefront. This is just one small example of the application of AI, and AI is predicted to change nearly every industry and impact society in ways we are just beginning to understand. The prevalence of AI is seen in patent application data, where patent applications in the AI field increased by 718% between 2016 and 2022, and the AI market is expected to grow to USD 191 billion by 2024.[79]

The explosive growth of AI technology and convergence with other technologies such as blockchain, 5G and quantum computing gives new urgency to questions in the intellectual property sphere, such as: should an AI system be considered an inventor or author and granted a patent for its use? Invention or a copyright for its work? When the AI system has been trained on existing intellectual property, how do you determine

73. *Diamond v. Chakrabarty*, 447 US 303 (1980).
74. *Bilski v. Kappos*, 561 US 593 (2010).
75. *O'Reilly v. Morse* (telegraph patent case), 56 US 62 (1854).
76. *Burrow-Giles Lithographic Co. v. Sarony*, 111 US 53 (1884).
77. *Bleistein v. Donaldson Lithographing Co*, 188 US 239 (1903).
78. *Mazer v. Stein*, 347 US 201 (1954).
79. WIPO, Conversation at WIPO: *Intellectual Property and AI Technologies Inventions*, Geneva, 2023.

whether an invention is truly novel and non-obvious? What standard of disclosure is sufficient? Does the use of copyrighted works as data in training AI systems constitute copyright infringement?

Intellectual property law was created to protect the innovative and creative activity of humans and does not explicitly recognize non-human creators. With the increasing sophistication of AI systems, pressure is being added to the current intellectual property legal framework. And until a consensus emerges on how IP laws might be reformed, it is the courts that need to step in to provide some clarity amidst the high degree of uncertainty. Moreover, the broader economic and even geopolitical impact of court rulings should not be underestimated. There is geographic and political competition as countries strive to position themselves as the best place to build, test and use AI. Will countries whose courts provide more favorable protection for AI-generated inventions incentivize investment from innovative industries?

These questions are not purely hypothetical, as AI disputes are increasing in number and some litigants are testing and experimenting with courts in different countries to identify forums that are more favorable to their interests. This was blatant when Steven Thaler, a computer scientist, filed patent applications in several countries, naming DABUS (Device for Autonomous Bootstrapping of Unified Sentience), an AI machine, as the inventor of the patent. He subsequently litigated in courts in Australia, Germany, New Zealand, the Republic of Korea, the UK and the US, raising the same question: can an AI machine be designated as an inventor for the purposes of patent prosecution? All the courts in these countries have denied the possibility of naming an AI machine as inventor for patent purposes, but not without differences of opinion and instances of appeal overturning first instance decisions (for a discussion on AI and patents, see *infra* §37.05).

Equally difficult questions arise regarding the protection of intellectual property rights in the metaverse, a virtual space in which users can interact and connect with each other in myriad ways: playing games, collaborating, shopping and exploring. Some say the metaverse is the next big breakthrough, a transformative revolution in the way we interact with technology and live our lives. While it remains to be seen whether this is hype or fact, what is certain is that the metaverse is giving rise to a number of legal issues in the field of intellectual property. Who has the right to mint a non-fungible token (NFT) containing an intellectual property right? How to deal with preemptive and bad faith trademark applications in the metaverse? These are again questions that are currently before the courts for determination.

An additional challenge may be the jurisdictional reach of the court in the metaverse, characterized by inherent anonymity and decentralization. These virtual spaces employ cutting-edge technologies for companies to "privately" manage the space. Governance is through private contractual frameworks, in the form of terms of service. Local laws and courts sometimes find themselves powerless when operators of these platforms do not cooperate with the enforcement of national laws and verdicts. In such a case, where and how should an aggrieved party in the metaverse turn to enforce your intellectual property rights?

In the context of the challenges just described and given the unique aspects of intellectual property litigation, judicial authorities in many countries are working to streamline intellectual property proceedings with the overall goal of delivering justice quickly, at reasonable costs and ensuring that parties, particularly SMEs, can present their arguments and participate in proceedings efficiently and fairly. Failure to recognize these challenges and respond effectively risks a diminished legitimacy and role of the judiciary, where parties will seek and opt for forums, judicial or otherwise, that are capable of providing the desired resolution of disputes.

Efforts to modernize and specialize the judiciary in intellectual property disputes prioritize the reduction of the cost and time of intellectual property litigation and the adoption of specific procedural rules and case management elements. They may refer to the examination and preservation of evidence, calculation of damages, early and active case management, constitution of confidentiality clubs, summary adjudication, technical experts, consolidation of cases and adoption of ADR mechanisms. The modernization of judicial administration, leaving behind obsolete and slow working methods, plays a central role.

The fruits of these deliberations and efforts are seen in different parts of the world, including the recent establishment of the Intellectual Property Division in the Delhi High Court in India, the new Supreme Court of Judicature (Intellectual Property) Rules 2022 in Singapore, which aim to make the dispute resolution system more accessible to individuals and businesses, particularly SMEs and, of course, the launch of the Unified Patent Court in Europe earlier this year.

But these developments are not limited to recent times, as we can see in the important role played by the Andean Court of Justice, whose caseload is mostly related to intellectual property issues. And we do not need to go very far: the competence in contentious-administrative litigation in Intellectual Property matters changed in Colombia since January 2022, being the competent entity in first instance now the Administrative Court of Cundinamarca and in second instance, the Council of State.

These changes have inherent challenges. Jurisdictional reforms will bring new realities for both court judges and users of the justice system. Judges will have to become familiar with new types of disputes and, at times, handle a significant volume of actions that they had not been handling. They will have to respond to the specific needs of litigants faced with new procedures and still unpredictable interpretation by a new court.

A recurring concern relates to the considerable variation in the levels of experience and expertise of judges in intellectual property disputes, which affects the consistency, uniformity and predictability of judicial practice. These challenges are particularly acute for non-specialized courts, where the specificity of the technical and legal issues presented in IP litigation presents a challenge for judges who are ill-equipped to understand the technical issues presented. At the same time, specialized courts may not be appropriate in all circumstances and require consideration in the event that judges adopt a narrow focus and place too much importance on the IP dimension over other interests; accessibility for parties if a specialized court is located in a single fixed location; and significant human and budgetary resources.

The WIPO Judicial Institute works with national and regional judicial authorities to provide a comprehensive set of support tailored to the legal traditions and economic and social circumstances of WIPO Member States, enabling judges to play their vital role in ensuring that Member States' IP, innovation and creativity ecosystems are balanced and effective.

The WIPO Judicial Institute has established itself as a global convener of intellectual property judges, providing a forum for the exchange of information and practices. We believe this is a particularly important function in a globalized but also culturally, politically and socially diverse world. We therefore promote international exchange and comity, while fully respecting the independent decision-making of each court and judge. I must stress that WIPO's objective in this role is not harmonization but rather informed and strengthened judicial decision-making.[80]

In general, the legal and judicial system provides a framework that helps build trust in the innovation ecosystem so that its actors interact with each other effectively and fairly.

[D] ADR Methods for Intellectual Property Disputes

There is growing recognition of the importance of ADR in the management of intellectual property and technology-related litigation, especially in the context of international disputes.

There is an upward trend in IP litigation, attributed to the growth of entrepreneurial operations and their increased international presence. Litigation in front of the Courts is often a lengthy procedure and unsatisfactory to address the unique complexities of IP disputes in complex technology fields. ADR methods are considered more effective in resolving these issues.

The WIPO Arbitration and Mediation Center presents itself as an impartial, international, not-for-profit provider of dispute resolution services, specializing in intellectual property, technology and entertainment disputes. It offers a range of ADR options tailored to intellectual property and technology matters. The WIPO Center is based in Geneva, Switzerland, with an additional office in Singapore.

In collaboration with dispute resolution and intellectual property experts, the WIPO Center has developed specific rules for mediation, arbitration, expedited arbitration and expert determination to effectively manage intellectual property and technology disputes. WIPO's ADR procedures are designed to facilitate settlement, and approximately 70% of mediated cases are settled.[81]

Parties may include ADR clauses in their contracts, specifying the use of mediation, arbitration or expedited arbitration in case of disputes. The most common

80. A flagship activity in this role is the annual WIPO IP Judges' Forum, where the judicial community gathers to learn from the experiences of their judicial peers in addressing the most pressing challenges in the resolution of intellectual property cases, developed in the context of their respective legal, economic and social environment. In its 2022 edition we have 360 judges from ninety-four national and regional jurisdictions.
81. WIPO, Resolving IP and Technology Disputes Through WIPO ADR, Geneva, 2016, p. 5.

clause combines mediation with expedited arbitration. The WIPO Center tailors its ADR services to specific sectors within technology and IP transactions, addressing unique needs through tailored rules, fees and clauses. WIPO plays a key role in resolving domain name disputes through the UDRP, especially favored by trademark owners. In addition, WIPO assists country-code Top-Level Domains (ccTLDs) in establishing intellectual property protection mechanisms.

§32.07 IP DATA AND ECONOMIC ANALYSIS: THE IMPORTANCE OF EVIDENCE-BASED DECISION-MAKING

Evidence-based decision-making entails data and economic analysis, which are critical to understanding a country's IP landscape. Developing comprehensive national innovation and IP policies require a thorough understanding of the connections between a country's IP and innovation system and its economic, social, technological and creative sectors. The concept is defined as making decisions based on credible evidence rather than ideology or political opinion.

For instance, a country's authority that adopts this approach might rely on scientific evidence to shape the creation of an innovation policy, rather than ideological convictions.

Fundamentally, evidence-based policy and practice aim for unbiased decisions that address the needs of communities or countries, rather than solely aiming to secure voter support. Policymakers adhering to this methodology may leverage existing evidence to underpin policy formation or conduct fresh research to strengthen their positions.

Data collection and analysis are essential in this process. This data-driven approach involves two main steps: First, detailed research is carried out to gather information on various aspects of the country, such as its economic, social, cultural and institutional context, national development plans, core and emerging economic sectors, innovation and research systems, IP-related legal frameworks, IP statistics and related regulations.

Second, while desk research lays the groundwork, in-depth stakeholder consultations are essential. This phase involves engaging a wide range of stakeholders to gather opinions, validate information and understand perspectives related to IP and its impact on various sectors. This consultation should be based on the data gathered during the desk research. The data and analysis collected serves as the basis for the development of IP and innovation policies tailored to the specific context.

As a crucial third step, it is essential to institute continuous monitoring and evaluation of these policies. This ensures a thorough examination of whether the proposed policies are achieving their intended effects. If necessary, adjustments to measures and interventions can be made.

Evidence is imperative to address the complex challenges facing policymakers in today's world, which is why WIPO's Department for Economics and Data Analytics oversees the collection and dissemination of global statistics on intellectual property activity, as well as conducting economic analysis on the impact of IP and innovation policies on economic performance. Their activities include conducting annual surveys on IP activity worldwide, presenting IP statistics through various reports and platforms, publishing the GII and the World Intellectual Property Report bi-annually, and providing inputs on innovation performance and the creative economy. WIPO provides a diverse array of global, freely accessible data that serves researchers, policymakers, and decision-makers worldwide.[82]

It has been established that an economy's innovation capabilities are related in part to both its degree of development and size, and partly to the specialization choices that an innovation ecosystem makes to further improve its functioning. But what about the qualities of these capabilities? Assessing the worth of capabilities and their potential impact on a country's ability to innovate involves considering several factors. They include market demand, profitability, entry barriers, scalability, risk and uncertainty.

Economists solve this issue partially by asking "who does what?" and "what is done by how many?" A first step is to assume that ubiquitous capabilities are easy to adopt, and that rare ones are harder. However, this is not always the case. Some capabilities can be rare just because the incentives to develop them are low. Likewise, there may be widespread capabilities whose rewards are so high that countries are motivated to develop them, even at a high cost.

Hence, a second step is to look at how diversified are those countries that have these capabilities. A broad set of capabilities allows innovation ecosystems to create increasingly sophisticated outputs. Therefore, if a rare technology appears exclusively in diversified countries, then it is the result of this process; and for it to be developed, it must be leveraged with other capabilities. Conversely, if this same technology were to appear in non-diverse countries, it would mean that countries do not need extra know-how in order to develop it, making the process simpler.

This discussion is just one of the many aspects of IP-led innovation and it emphasizes the importance that IP-related policymaking decisions are based on exhaustive data search and analysis.

§32.08 CONCLUSION

In conclusion, the exploration of the innovation ecosystem, IP, and its intersection with various stakeholders has illuminated the intricate dynamics shaping our modern innovation economy. From the foundational definitions and global trends to the pivotal roles of governments, academia, entrepreneurs, and corporations, it is evident that IP is not only a legal construct but a cornerstone of innovation and economic growth.

Throughout this chapter, we have witnessed how governments play a crucial role in shaping the IP landscape through policies, international agreements, and national strategies, while also addressing the unique challenges faced by developing economies.

82. WIPO, Department for Economics and Data Analytics, Geneva, 2024, www.wipo.int/about-wipo/en/activities_by_unit/index.jsp?id=48 (accessed December 2024).

Academia, innovators, and entrepreneurs are key actors in IP creation, driving TT, commercialization, and navigating the challenges inherent in pioneering innovation.

Companies, particularly start-ups and SMEs, are at the heart of the innovation ecosystem, leveraging IP for competitive advantage and contributing to its continuous evolution. However, promoting and safeguarding IP necessitates addressing gender disparities, enhancing awareness and education, and ensuring a robust legal framework supported by an effective judiciary and ADR mechanisms.

Moreover, the significance of evidence-based decision-making, as highlighted by IP data and economic analysis, underscores the importance of informed policies and strategies in fostering innovation and economic growth.

As we reflect on the insights gleaned from this exploration, it becomes clear that fostering a balanced environment for IP and innovation is not only imperative for individual stakeholders but essential for the collective prosperity and progress of society as a whole. Embracing collaboration, inclusivity, and forward-thinking approaches will be paramount in navigating the complexities of the innovation landscape and unlocking its full potential for the betterment of humanity.

CHAPTER 33
Intellectual Property and Global Challenges

Introduction

Intellectual property rights and innovation are key elements at the nexus of interconnected global challenges, like global health, climate change and food security. Challenges in these areas are constant and fast evolving, requiring a coordinated global policy response that can account for different countries' needs, priorities and realities. In addressing these challenges, WIPO provides a neutral global forum to Member States to discuss intellectual property and related issues. WIPO also produces reliable and updated information based on empirical evidence and provides technical and policy-oriented resources. Key issues described in this chapter include climate change, food security, global health and the role of women and youth in intellectual property and innovation systems. Effectively responding to global challenges would also assist in realizing the UN SDGs and support the fulfilment of WIPO's mandate.

§33.01 SUSTAINABLE DEVELOPMENT GOALS

Sustainable development, in its many manifestations, is of growing importance globally. Increasingly, governments are setting targets for sustainability improvements ranging from societal inclusiveness to carbon emission reductions. More companies are marketing their products and services by highlighting their "eco" credentials. Consumers are basing purchase decisions on sustainability criteria.

As a UN Specialized Agency, WIPO has a significant role in supporting Member States to achieve the SDGs. WIPO and IPOs worldwide have a role in supporting the achievement of SDG 9 relating to industry, innovation and infrastructure. Intellectual property encourages, incentivizes and supports innovation, resulting in new technical solutions that can help to address sustainability challenges, including, but not limited to, climate change and improved living standards. Examples of WIPO and IPO initiatives related to education, diversity promotion and inclusion, and more efficient use of natural resources support achieving SDG 9.

[A] The Origin of SDGs

The origin of the SDGs can be traced back to the 1992 Rio Summit, which laid the ground for a closer look at environmental issues affecting different species and their livelihood, survival and existence in the sea, on land and the planet. Subsequently, the UN adopted the UN MDGs,[83] which covered eight international development goals to be achieved by the year 2015.[84]

The UN adopted the SDGs in 2015 as a universal call to action to end poverty, protect the planet and ensure that all people can enjoy a better life, in peace and prosperity by 2030. SDGs are not restricted to the UN or governmental organizations. In fact, SDGs have been embraced to a greater extent by the private sector and the youth (Figure 33.1).

Figure 33.1 SDGs Summarized by the UN

[B] The Role of Intellectual Property in Achieving SDGs

The multiple areas of inequality highlighted by the UN SDGs require substantial innovative solutions. In particular, SDGs are essential to address social and economic challenges posed by climate change, the impact of the COVID-19 (severe acute respiratory syndrome *coronavirus 2, SARS-CoV-2*) pandemic on lives and livelihoods,

83. Millennium Summit | United Nations.
84. United Nations Millennium Declaration | OHCHR.

the global food crisis, gender inequality and inclusion, and the rising geopolitical tensions.

Intellectual property supports sustainability, mainly due to its unique characteristics as an intangible asset. More specifically, there are three aspects of intellectual property which are central to supporting the achievement of SDGs: first, intellectual property has a role in promoting innovation. Intellectual property provides inventors and creators legally enforceable mechanisms that enable them to generate returns on their investment and acquire competitive advantages. Without enforceability, it would be highly unlikely that inventors, creators and enterprises would be willing to invest in research and development (R&D).

Second, intellectual property contributes to the innovation ecosystem. More specifically, intellectual property plays an important role in creating and sustaining innovation systems. The key to successful innovation systems is a sustainable circulation of funds, human and natural resources and technologies among industry, government, and academia, as well as non-monetary incentives like recognition and authorship for scientists. In these systems, intellectual property can ensure return of monetary and non-monetary investment, thus incentivizing and facilitating innovation by diverse stakeholders.

Third, and finally, intellectual property has developed a high level of international acceptance and conformity. The intellectual property system is backed by a series of treaties and regulations administered by WIPO, which harmonize rights of protection, provide efficient ways to extend and enforce intellectual property and facilitate considerably the protection of intellectual property rights worldwide, with efficiency and much lower costs. International agreements, such as the Madrid International Registration System for Trademarks (Madrid System), date back to 1891. The Madrid System generates efficiencies that count with sustainability benefits such as simplified procedures, paperless and a centralized filing and registration system for trademarks.

Therefore, WIPO's work has direct relevance for many SDGs. Whilst WIPO considers that SDG 9 (Industry, Innovation and Infrastructure) is at the core of its mission to lead the development of the international intellectual property system for the common good, the reach of its actions related to SDGs is much broader. It extends to other areas such as SDG 2 (Zero Hunger), SDG 3 (Good Health and Well-being), SDG 4 (Quality Education), SDG 5 (Gender Equality), SDG 13 (Climate Action) and SDG 17 (Partnerships).

§33.02 ENVIRONMENTAL ISSUES

With the rapid advancement of climate change, the need for innovation and technology to address current challenges has increased. A well-functioning innovation ecosystem is underpinned by an efficient and fair intellectual property rights system that can stimulate innovation and disseminate relevant technology to global markets.[85] Intellectual property rights are a cornerstone of protection for the rights of inventors and creators and, as such, enables continued innovation and development. A strong intellectual property system can also support inventors in connecting with investors and successfully reaching the market, resulting in faster and wider deployment of technology.[86]

[A] Climate Change, Environmental Degradation and Biodiversity Loss

The rise in climate change, environmental degradation and loss of biodiversity can negatively impact human well-being and health, and planetary health. The intensity of such impacts may be "unpredictable, diverse, and context dependent."[87] According to the Intergovernmental Panel on Climate Change (IPCC), human-induced climate change, for instance, is affecting weather and climate in every region across the globe, resulting in widespread adverse effects and related loss and damage to nature, agriculture, infrastructure (like ports and cities) and lives of people and their livelihoods.[88] Vulnerable communities, who have historically contributed the least to current climate change, are likely to be disproportionately affected by such trends.[89]

[1] Biodiversity

The loss of biodiversity is growing at a rapid rate globally. Estimates indicate that nearly one million species are threatened with the possibility of extinction.[90] Irreplaceable ecosystems, such as the Amazon rainforests, are being transformed into carbon sources from carbon sinks due to high levels of deforestation. Further, approximately 85% of wetlands, including salt marshes and mangrove swamps, which are known to absorb large amounts of carbon, have disappeared.[91]

To reduce and reverse the rate of biodiversity loss, countries adopted the Kunming-Montreal Global Biodiversity Framework (GBF) at the 15th Conference of Parties to the UN CBD in 2022. The GBF includes four overarching goals, to be achieved by 2050, which focus on ecosystem and species health such as halting human-induced species extinction, the sustainable use of biodiversity, and equitable sharing of benefits. A total of twenty-three targets are set out to be achieved by 2030. These include 30% conservation of land, sea, and inland waters; and 30% restoration of degraded ecosystems.[92]

---

85. WIPO Green Technology Book on Adaptation.
86. *Ibid.*
87. *Ibid.*
88. *See* www.ipcc.ch/report/sixth-assessment-report-cycle/.
89. *Ibid.*
90. *See* www.ipbes.net/news/Media-Release-Global-Assessment.
91. *Ibid.*
92. *See* www.unep.org/resources/kunming-montreal-global-biodiversity-framework.

[2] *Climate Change*

'Climate change' has been defined as a change in the state of the climate which is identified by differences in the mean and/or variability of its properties (for e.g., by using statistical tests).[93] The change persists for an extended period, which may typically be decades or longer.[94] The causes for climate change may, individually or collectively, be due to natural processes such as modulations of the solar cycles and volcanic eruptions; or/and by anthropogenic changes, i.e., caused by human activity, in the composition of the atmosphere or land use.[95]

The UN Framework Convention on Climate Change (UNFCCC) defines climate change as: "a change of climate which is attributed directly or indirectly to human activity that alters the composition of the global atmosphere and which is in addition to natural climate variability observed over comparable time periods."[96] Through this definition, the UNFCCC makes a distinction between climate change attributable to human activities which alter the atmospheric composition and climate variability attributable to natural causes.

The Paris Agreement under the UNFCCC was adopted on December 2015 in Paris, France, at the 21st Session of the Conference of the Parties (COP). The primary objective of the Paris Agreement is to limit global temperature increases to "well below 2 degrees Celsius above pre-industrial levels."[97] All Parties to the Paris Agreement have communicated their Nationally Determined Contributions (NDC). Through NDCs, parties to the Paris Agreement outlines their plans for reducing their emissions. Besides this, a growing number of Parties have also communicated long-term low greenhouse gas (GHG) emission development strategies (LT-LEDS). These strategies indicate the difference between the emission levels implied by the NDCs and the average emission levels of global-modelled mitigation pathways, consistent with limiting global warming to 1.5°C or 2°C.[98] Current studies, however, indicate that more ambition is needed in implementing domestic mitigation measures and setting NDC targets in order to reduce global GHG emissions by 43% by 2030, 60% by 2035 (compared with 2019 levels), and reach net zero CO_2 emissions by 2050 globally.[99]

[B] The Role of Intellectual Property in Promoting Green Technology

Achieving net zero CO_2 and GHG emissions would require systems transformations across all sectors including, *inter alia*, scaling up renewable energy, phasing out

93. *See* www.ipcc.ch/site/assets/uploads/sites/2/2022/06/SR15_AnnexI.pdf.
94. *Ibid.*
95. *Ibid.*
96. Article 1, UNFCCC, available at unfccc.int/files/essential_background/background_publications_htmlpdf/application/pdf/conveng.pdf.
97. *Ibid.*
98. UNEP, The Emission Gap Report 2021, available at wedocs.unep.org/bitstream/handle/20.500.11822/36995/EGR21_CH4.pdf.
99. *Ibid.*

unabated fossil fuels, and reducing deforestation.[100] For instance, reversing deforestation and improving agricultural practices can reduce emissions and enhance carbon sinks. Promoting sustainable agriculture without further land expansion could also catalyze sustainable development benefits.[101]

The Paris Agreement recognizes technology as a critical lever for enabling climate action (Article 10).[102] International cooperation on technology development and transfer can enable systems transformations aligned with achieving the goals of the Paris Agreement. IPCC's sixth assessment synthesis report also emphasizes the importance of enhancing technology innovation systems and TT. According to the UNFCCC Global Stocktake report (2023): "Collaborative approaches to climate technology research, development and demonstration are crucial for deploying mature climate technologies and developing emerging technologies on a large scale. Such approaches can include investments in technology development and transfer through joint research and development programmes and capacity-building."[103]

UNFCCC's Technology Mechanism, comprising the United Nations Technology Executive Committee and the United Nations Climate Technology Centre and Network, was established in 2010 with the objective of enhancing climate technology development and transfer. It aims to facilitate international cooperation on technology development and transfer through capacity building, knowledge sharing, and technical and financial support to aid developing countries in their efforts to develop, adopt and deploy climate technologies.[104] R&D in climate technology are essential for implementing existing technologies and developing new technologies. International cooperation, especially with developing countries, can enhance dissemination of knowledge by providing access to these technologies and reducing costs. Such collaborations can also increase local data creation and ownership and promote shared innovation.

Various intellectual property tools support the invention, development, and marketability of green technologies including, *inter alia*, patents, copyrights, trademarks, and trade secrets. However, most discussions on climate change and intellectual property principally relate to patents. Patents facilitate transfer of knowledge and technology, promoting collaboration and partnerships among various stakeholders. It also allows the inventors to choose market strategy and increase accessibility of the inventions. Sophisticated intellectual property strategies and portfolios based on quality patents can help innovative businesses signal the value of their inventions to the market, in particular, to potential partners, as well as investors.[105] Moreover, patents create a repository of relevant technical knowledge and information since the inventor discloses comprehensive details about the invention. Concurrently, patents also may support various technological collaborations and partnerships by providing legal certainty which assist in promoting the sharing and spread of technology. Trade

100. *See* unfccc.int/documents/631600.
101. *See* www.ipcc.ch/srccl/chapter/chapter-4/.
102. *See* unfccc.int/process-and-meetings/the-paris-agreement.
103. *See* unfccc.int/documents/631600.
104. *Ibid.*
105. WIPO, Global Challenges Report, available at tind.wipo.int/record/28856.

secrets, which could comprise any protected business information that is not known and which confers a competitive advantage to the owner, can also be used in this context. Being distinct from patents and other categories of intellectual property, trade secrets may be used in securing channels for exchanges of know-how, thereby creating a safe environment for the diffusion of knowledge.[106]

§33.03 GLOBAL HEALTH

WIPO functions as a neutral forum for dialogue and its work on global health seeks to raise awareness and understanding of the complex linkages between it and intellectual property to different stakeholders. Several WIPO divisions and sectors engage in multidisciplinary activities to support open dialogues and evidence-based legal and policymaking discussions around the globe by treating intellectual property as an instrument to promote and enhance innovation and access to medical technologies. Thus, WIPO provides technical and legal assessments and technical assistance and capacity building on global health challenges connected to intellectual property. It also supports the development of sophisticated views by Member States regarding the multiple tools and strategies—like compulsory license, voluntary licensing, and access clauses in TT agreements—comprised in intellectual property legislations and policies and how and when to use them.

[A] Global Health and Intellectual Property: Challenges and Opportunities

Multiple factors including complex legal and policy intersections in various governance levels and areas influence the achievement of the highest standard of health (World Health Organization. WHO Constitution, Preamble)[107] worldwide. Debates about the role of intellectual property as an incentive or barrier to promote access and innovation in the biomedical sector have been constant in the global health scene and were exacerbated during the COVID-19 pandemic.

The devastating impact of the COVID-19 pandemic in multiple dimensions—from health systems to social and economic development—challenged perceptions on how to promote global health and improve the biomedical innovation ecosystem in a manner that primes access and innovation. Responding to the pandemic required unprecedented global coordination of multiple stakeholders at different levels (internationally, regionally, and locally). A combination of unparalleled financial, technological, infrastructure, and human resources allowed and accelerated the development of new medical technologies to prevent, diagnose and treat people with COVID-19. Even though the development of COVID-19 vaccines relied on existing medical

106. *Ibid.*
107. WHO Constitution, Preamble. Available at www.who.int/about/governance/constitution.

technologies, platforms and networks of scientists, their development and approval can be described as the fastest in history.[108]

From the lens of innovation, the COVID-19 pandemic confirmed the power of collaboration through various schemes like PPP in addressing barriers encountered in the R&D pipeline that could limit innovation and access to medical technologies globally and locally. From product development to clinical trials and regulatory approvals, the level of collaborations among pharmaceutical and biotechnology companies, universities and research institutions (primarily public), and governments across various regions showed strengths and weaknesses of different policy and legal frameworks. It further highlighted the role of diverse stakeholders in the biomedical innovation ecosystem and their nuanced choices about intellectual property protection. Intellectual property issues also raised questions about how to more efficiently engage in scientific and R&D activities and the importance of implementing new and open R&D models and regulating medical technologies for the public good.[109]

Desirable and equal access levels to medical technologies still need to be fully accomplished. The COVID-19 pandemic impacted all countries, resulting in over 6.9 million deaths worldwide as of December 24, 2023.[110] It also led to significant shifts in global health priorities and strategies to ensure access. For instance, the pandemic emphasized the importance of preparedness, response and coordination of actions among countries. COVID-19 also exposed glaring inequities in access to medical technologies. While "70.6% of the global population has received at least one dose of a COVID-19 vaccine," only "32.9% of people in low-income countries have received at least one dose."[111] This crisis has galvanized efforts to address systemic healthcare disparities in terms of research priorities, funding, health systems strengthening, and enabling local production to ensure that essential medical technologies reach those in need. Therefore, the pandemic highlighted existing problems, gaps and fragilities in global health systems and stakeholders' interactions and cooperation modes. It also stressed the urgency for governments to prioritize investments in health systems and R&D and promote universal health coverage as critical foundations for global health protection and security in an interconnected world.

In the post-COVID-19 pandemic world, debates associating intellectual property with access to medical technologies have intensified the need for more transparency about R&D costs by the pharmaceutical industry.[112] Informed debates about the importance of publicly funded R&D in the biomedical innovation ecosystem have also increased.[113] Even though new issues arose during and after the pandemic, old

108. WIPO, Patent Landscape Report, COVID-19 Vaccines and Therapeutics, 2023, at 25.
109. WHO-WIPO-WTO, *An Integrated Health, Trade and IP Approach to Respond to the COVID-19 Pandemic*, second update, May 2023, at 11.
110. *See* data.who.int/dashboards/covid19/deaths.
111. *See* ourworldindata.org/covid-vaccinations.
112. World Health Assembly (WHA), *A72/A/CONF./2 Rev.1. Improving the Transparency of Markets for Medicines, Vaccines, and Other Health Products* (World Health Organization (WHO), 2019).
113. Abbott, F.M. (2023), *Intellectual Property and Technology Transfer for COVID-19 Vaccines: Assessment of the Record*, WIPO Report, Geneva. Available at www.wipo.int/edocs/pubdocs/

problems remained and were exacerbated by the pandemic due to disruptions in healthcare systems and shifting priorities to contain the pandemic.[114] Solving problems related to non-communicable diseases, infectious diseases and neglected diseases, fixing market distortions regarding R&D investments and the dynamic of the pharmaceutical market, addressing the evolving epidemiological profile of different populations and the challenges to provide primary health needs, facing the increase and threat of antimicrobial resistance (AMR) and other emerging infectious diseases, and addressing the rising impact of climate change in human health are part of the list of global health challenges.[115]

Adding to the above context and challenges, the long-waited advancements in the biotechnology sector combined with the rise of personalized medicine, AI, and platform technologies (for instance, mRNA, CRISPR-Cas 9, and monoclonal antibodies) have leapfrogged biomedical science into a new era. On the one hand, these advancements significantly increased the complexity of regulating and managing emerging technologies and their related intellectual property rights and landscapes while also setting up associated strategies.[116] On the other hand, they increased collaboration among the private sector, research and academic communities, and governments and redefined these stakeholders' roles in the biomedical innovation ecosystem. Thus, this multi-stakeholder setting raises challenges related to intellectual property ownership, management, and strategy between multiple stakeholders.

Therefore, how society moves forward to address these challenges, ensuring adequate levels of pandemic preparedness and response, as well as other global health threats, connects with several factors, including intellectual property. Intellectual property is not the only or most important issue to overcome global health challenges, but it plays a critical role in this context. Therefore, a balanced intellectual property system tailored to local needs is vital to jointly promote access (in all its dimensions, including accessibility and affordability) and innovation.

[B] Historical Context of Intellectual Property Law and Global Health

Intellectual property rights have long been part of debates on global health, innovation, and access to medical technologies led by different stakeholders across multiple forums—multilateral, regional, plurilateral, bilateral and national. These multiple

---

en/wipo-pub-rn2023-39-en-intellectual-property-and-technology-transfer-for-covid-19-vaccines-assessment-of-the-record.pdf.

114. *See* generally, WHO, *Strengthening WHO Preparedness for and Response to Health Emergencies*, Report by the Director General, A76/10, May 19, 2023.

115. *See* generally: Promoting Access to Medical Technologies and Innovation—Intersections between Public Health, Intellectual Property and Trade (www.wipo.int), at pp. 33-35, 100, 144-150; WHO-WIPO-WTO. Promoting World Health Organization (WHO), *Neglected Tropical Diseases*, WHO, at www.who.int/neglected_diseases/diseases/en/; Quadripartite launches a new platform to tackle antimicrobial resistance threat to human and animal health and ecosystems (www.who.int).

116. The intellectual property landscape related to COVID-19 vaccines exemplifies this complexity. For more information, *see* www.nature.com/articles/s41587-021-00912-9 and www.wipo.int/publications/en/details.jsp?id=4589.

levels of interaction influence and determine the dynamic relationship between the intellectual property international legal framework and the incorporation of minimum standards of protection, principles, obligations and flexibilities into national legislations by different Member States, as well as these States' abilities to implement and use those rights to achieve their goals.

The Paris Convention for the Protection of Industrial Property of 1883,[117] alongside the Berne Convention for the Protection of Literary and Artistic Works of 1886[118] and other legal instruments, made the international and multilateral life of intellectual property rights official. In 1893, the United International Bureaux for the Protection of Intellectual Property (BIRPI) was established to manage intellectual property rights at the international level and in 1970, the BIRPI became WIPO. Even though legal dispositions to address global health challenges, such as compulsory license (Paris Convention, Article 5A (2)), existed in the Paris Convention, their negotiation does not follow the same purpose of the TRIPS Agreement, given that the national treatment principle as set in the Paris Convention did not oblige Contracting Parties to provide patent protection without discrimination as to the field of technology.[119]

In 1995, discussions regarding enforcement of intellectual property rights and the connection of these rights to international trade led the transition from the GATT (1947) to the creation of the World Trade Organization (WTO) and, consequently, the WTO's TRIPS Agreement.[120] The TRIPS Agreement incorporated legal dispositions from Paris and Berne Conventions, set up minimum standards of protection for intellectual property rights, provided objectives and principles, determined transitional periods for different countries (especially developing and least-developed countries (LDCs)) to adapt national legislations to the agreement, enhanced enforcement, provided a dispute settlement framework to solve issues related to intellectual property rights and set in place various flexibilities to countries to address local needs and priorities, like the protection of public health.[121]

With the advent of the TRIPS Agreement and the intensification of global health challenges, other legal instruments and declarations by the international community developed, highlighting the need of coordinated action and collaboration among countries. They also stressed the importance of legal tools like the TRIPS Agreement flexibilities (such as research exception, compulsory license, and parallel importation) to address those challenges. In 2001, at the Doha WTO Ministerial Conference, the Doha Declaration on TRIPS and Public Health clarified the importance and legitimacy of the use of TRIPS flexibilities by Member States, especially developing countries and

117. *See* www.wipo.int/treaties/en/ip/paris/ and www.wipo.int/treaties/en/ip/berne/.
118. *See* www.wipo.int/treaties/en/ip/berne/ and www.wipo.int/wipolex/en/treaties/textdetails/12214.
119. *See* www.wipo.int/treaties/en/ip/paris/ and www.wipo.int/treaties/en/ip/berne/.
120. *Agreement on Trade-Related Aspects of Intellectual Property Rights (TRIPS Agreement)*, Annex 1C of the Marrakesh Agreement Establishing the World Trade Organization, signed in Marrakesh, Morocco on April 15, 1994 (April 15, 1994).
121. Promoting Access to Medical Technologies and Innovation—Intersections between Public Health, Intellectual Property and Trade (www.wipo.int).

LDCs, to ensure access to medical technologies.[122] However, given disparities (lack or insufficiency) in local pharmaceutical production capacity in different countries, in 2003, during the Cancun WTO Ministerial Conference the WTO General Council declared the need for an additional flexibility: compulsory license for manufacturing and exporting of generic medicines.[123] On December 6, 2005, the Protocol amending the TRIPS Agreement resulted in Article 31*bis* that determines the need for Member States to incorporate into their national legislations and operationalize this later use of compulsory license.[124]

Other instruments compound this intricate international level, informing stakeholders' actions toward global health challenges. In 2000, the UN established the MDGs to reduce extreme poverty by 2015.[125] The SDGs were established in 2015 via the 2030 Agenda for Sustainable Development comprised seventeen SDGs.[126] In 2007, the WIPO Development Agenda set 45 recommendations and determined the establishment of the Committee on Development and Intellectual Property (CDIP).[127] In 2008, the WHO established the WHO Global Strategy and Plan of Action on Public Health, Innovation and Intellectual Property (GSPA-PHI) and, in 2016,[128] "the Report of UN Secretary-General's High-Level Panel on Access to Medicines: WTO members should respect the Doha Declaration and make full use of TRIPS flexibilities" was published.

Finally, the COVID-19 pandemic brought into light the role of intellectual property in addressing global health challenges in several forums at the international level. In December 2021, at the World Health Assembly (WHA), an Intergovernmental Negotiating Body (INB) was established to strengthen pandemic prevention, preparedness, and response.[129] At its first meeting (March and June 2022), the INB was assigned to drafting and negotiating a WHO Convention, Agreement or Other International Instrument on Pandemic Prevention, Preparedness and Response as a biding instrument among Member States. The INB process follows an agreed timeline and deliverables,[130] and it aims to submit its outcomes to the Seventy-seventh WHA in May 2024. The Pandemic instrument and negotiations touch upon several issues related to intellectual property, like equity, TT and innovation. On July 6, 2022, at the TRIPS Council during the 12th Ministerial Conference (MC12), WTO members adopted the

122. 4th Doha Ministerial Round WTO, *Doha Declaration on the TRIPS Agreement and Public Health* (November 14, 2001).
123. General Council, *Implementation of Paragraph 6 of the Doha Declaration on the TRIPS Agreement and Public Health*, WT/L/540 and Corr.1 (September 1, 2003).
124. *Amendment of the TRIPS Agreement*, WT/L/641 (December 6, 2005).
125. United Nations Millennium Development Goals (MDGs). Available at www.un.org/millenniumgoals/.
126. *Transforming Our World: The 2030 Agenda for Sustainable Development*, A/RES/70/1.
127. Development Agenda for WIPO.
128. World Health Assembly, *WHA62.16: Global Strategy and Plan of Action on Public Health, Innovation and Intellectual Property. WHA Resolution; Sixty-second World Health Assembly, 22 May 2009*, World Health Organization (WHO) (2009).
129. *See* inb.who.int/.
130. *See* apps.who.int/gb/inb/pdf_files/inb3/A_INB3_4-en.pdf.

"TRIPS Waiver Decision on COVID-19 vaccines" and started discussions to extend this decision to COVID-19 diagnostics and therapeutics.[131]

[C] The Role of Intellectual Property as a Catalyst to Access to Medical Technologies and Innovation

The justification for granting intellectual property rights largely varies (from rewarding mechanisms to market incentives and strategic assets) and influences how various stakeholders implement, use, and enforce these rights. As a trade-off, intellectual property rewards inventors and creators for their contributions and efforts to advance knowledge and science, allowing them to recover investments in R&D for medical technologies (for instance, vaccines, therapeutics, digital health devices and diagnostics), further equipping them with the confidence and legal certainty to share their inventions and creations with the world. As an exclusive right that prevents others (third parties) from infringing on protected inventions or creations (making, selling, importing, etc.) without authorization, intellectual property grants its holder the right to explore an invention exclusively, which may cause distortions in access and innovation where monopolies are foreseen. These aspects stress the importance of balanced protection and flexibilities to those rights.[132]

Intellectual property is a driving force to enhance innovation and access to medical technologies in addressing global health challenges. Access is about more than just ensuring that medical technologies R&D is successful. It is also bringing these technologies to the market. It is also about getting these technologies to those who need them most in a timely and affordable way. Therefore, intellectual property is not the only determinant of access and innovation. In a complex global biomedical innovation ecosystem, innovation and access rely on other factors that go beyond intellectual property, including regulatory hurdles, market demand, trade restrictions, supply chain disruptions, manufacturing capacity, health systems' financial and infrastructure capacity to incorporate medical technologies into health systems, and misinformation.[133] It is essential that stakeholders use and combine the TRIPS flexibilities and diverse legal and policy tools to enhance access and innovation.

For instance, the unequal distribution of COVID-19 vaccines resulted from several factors, including vaccine nationalism and distortions on Advanced Purchase

131. Council for Trade-Related Aspects of Intellectual Property Rights, *IP/C/W/669/Rev.1. Waiver from certain Provisions of TRIPS Agreement for the Prevention, Containment and Treatment of Covid-19. Revised Decision Text. Communication from the African group, the Plurinational State of Bolivia, Egypt, Eswatini, Fiji, India, Indonesia, Kenya, the LDC Group, Maldives, Mozambique, Namibia, Pakistan, South Africa, Vanuatu, the Bolivarian Republic of Venezuela and Zimbabwe*, World Trade Organization (WTO) (2021). Available at docs.wto.org/dol2fe/Pages/SS/directdoc.aspx?filename=q:/WT/MIN22/30.pdf&Open=True. For further information, *see An Integrated Health, Trade and IP Approach to Respond to the COVID-19 Pandemic*, second update, May 2023. Available online at covid-trilat-second-update-2023.pdf (wipo.int).

132. WIPO, *Report on the International Patent System*, Standing Committee on the Law of Patents, Twelfth Session, SCP/12/3 Rev.2, June 23-27, 2008.

133. *See* generally, WHO-WIPO-WTO, *An Integrated Health, Trade and IP Approach to Respond to the COVID-19 Pandemic*, second update, May 2023, at pp. 8-14.

Agreements (APAs) that widened North-South disparities, with significantly lower access to them in the Global South. Thus, access to medical technologies problems cannot be exclusively credited to imbalances in intellectual property rights. Whether intellectual property played a role, it was not the most critical factor. These access issues are at the core of ongoing multilateral processes at the WTO and WHO, previously mentioned, and Member States are evaluating lessons learned from the pandemic to apply them to other global health challenges, including future pandemic prevention, preparedness, and response.[134]

Another example in which intellectual property plays a role in access to medical technologies and innovation is voluntary licensing practices and policies. Through voluntary licensing and TT, health technologies treating HIV/Aids and Hepatitis C have reached millions of patients in a timely and affordable manner in developing countries and LDCs. Innovative mechanisms and institutions like the Medicines Patent Pool (MPP) have emerged to promote voluntary licensing. Through pooled licensing—i.e., in-licensing from patent holders to MPP and then, MPP provides multiple sublicenses to different stakeholders in various countries under the scope and rules of standard licensing and TT agreements—MPP is a leading example of innovative use of intellectual property to increase access.[135] Since its creation, MPP has signed thirty-four licenses for various medical technologies and facilitated access to thirty billion doses of treatment in developing countries and LDCs since 2010.[136]

[D] Intellectual Property Applied to Different Medical Technologies: Enabling Sophisticated Policies, Practices, and Strategies to Enhance Access and Innovation

The level of sophistication of those engaging in biomedical R&D while developing their intellectual property protection strategy will directly impact their success in managing those rights and commercializing their technologies. Intellectual property rights are territorial rights and, therefore, locally granted; additionally, some categories of these rights, like patents, require local examination by country authorities (IPOs) to be granted. Therefore, the choice of how, where and when to protect intellectual property rights (for instance, in which countries one should file for patent protection) directly affects the success or failure of different stakeholders in building strong intellectual property portfolios and turning intellectual property into a strong intangible asset.[137]

The various possibilities for stakeholders to protect medical technologies by distinctive categories of intellectual property rights and adopt and implement multiple practices, policies, and strategies related to these rights, as well as technology-specific

134. *See* Abbott, F.M., *supra* note 113. *See also* WHO-WIPO-WTO, *An Integrated Health, Trade and IP Approach*, *supra* note 109, at 15-16.
135. MPP (medicinespatentpool.org).
136. *See* statistiscs.teams.cdn.office.net/evergreen-assets/safelinks/1/atp-safelinks.html.
137. WIPO, *Discussion Paper on the Interplay Between Patents and Trade Secrets in Medical Technologies*, available at https://www.wipo.int/edocs/mdocs/scp/en/wipo_ip_covid_ge_2_22/wipo_ip_covid_ge_2_22_paper.pdf.

characteristics, will impact access and innovation. Access and innovation might be compromised if these differences are poorly understood and implemented. Patents, trademarks, copyrights, industrial design, and trade secrets are some of the categories of intellectual property rights that can protect medical technologies, simultaneously or not, depending on the strategy set out by those who will hold the intellectual property protection considering their commercialization goals. Differences in legislation may also result in an invention or creation being protected by diverse intellectual property rights categories in various countries. Knowing the technical and scientific specificities of medical technologies, how each technology differs from each other—like vaccines, drugs, diagnostics, and therapeutics—and how the development and improvement of technologies take place within the different phases of the R&D pipeline while considering the dynamic between stakeholders participating in R&D are critical details to set in place tailored intellectual property protection strategies.[138]

In conclusion, to set comprehensive legal and policy frameworks that enable effective intellectual property protection strategies by different stakeholders, Member States need to effectively balance legal, regulatory, technical, and marketing aspects that impact access to medical technologies and innovation. These aspects highly depend on context and the goals and roles of those engaging in the R&D process and commercialization of inventions, as well as their views on the role of intellectual property in access to medical technologies and innovation. This glimpse of some technical, legal and regulatory details applied to medical technologies shows the importance of having a complete view of the biomedical innovation system and the role of intellectual property in it.

§33.04 COOPERATION TO TACKLE GLOBAL CHALLENGES

Cooperation and coordination of efforts, resources and technical expertise are essential to address global challenges in dynamic and varied policy areas. At the international level, different stakeholders are working to respond to these challenges as they share and, where necessary, contest views, to help identify common grounds which, in turn, could accelerate response. IGOs play a key role in assisting Member States acquire and enhance technical knowledge in varied fields, provide capacity building and technical assistance, as well as serve as neutral forums for discussions among Member States and various stakeholders—private sector, research and academic communities and institutions, and civil society organizations—that locally and globally aim participate in the intellectual property system. Through its work, WIPO has promoted and prioritized cooperation with other organizations.

138. *See* Aplin, T., Liddicoat, J. & Spiewak, B. (October 2023), *Discussion Paper on the Interplay Between Patents and Trade Secrets in Medical Technologies*, WIPO Secretariat, available at www.wipo.int/edocs/mdocs/scp/en/wipo_ip_covid_ge_2_22/wipo_ip_covid_ge_2_22_paper.pdf; Fisher III, W.W. & Oberholzer-Gee, F. (2013), *Strategic Management of Intellectual Property: An Integrated Approach*, available at www.hbs.edu/faculty/Pages/item.aspx?num=45271.

For more than a decade, WIPO, the WHO and the WTO have collaborated in varied activities and policy areas to address challenges at the intersection of public health, intellectual property, and trade.[139] This interaction takes place within a framework titled "WHO, WIPO, WTO Trilateral Cooperation on Public Health, Intellectual Property and Trade."[140] The Trilateral Cooperation has been a forum for discussions and a source of reliable and neutral technical information and resources for different stakeholders, while basing its findings and advise on empirical and factual information to inform law and policymaking. Meeting regularly, the three organizations exchange information on their respective work programs, discuss and plan common activities, within their respective mandates. During the COVID-19 pandemic, its importance became more apparent in responding to the global challenges at the international level through concerted action and cooperation.

[A] Promoting Access to Medical Technologies and Innovation at the Intersection of Public Health, Intellectual Property, and Innovation: The WHO, WIPO and WTO Trilateral Cooperation

Innovation and access to medical technologies issues emerge at the intersection of multiple policy areas and call for a combined approach for effective and long-term response (Figure 33.2). Intellectual property interacts within different systems (innovation, industrial, health, among others) and is at the core of TT and diffusion that are essential to any country's social and economic development and local response to challenges. In this multisystemic interaction, the knowledge of different stakeholders making up the biomedical innovation ecosystems about different categories of intellectual property rights, as well as related practices and policies, integrate a full assessment of challenges combined with the use of tools and instruments developed to correct distortions (like licensing and freedom to operate). The public health sphere highlights the need to enlarge access and strengthen institutions and mechanisms responsible for it. It connects to providing universal healthcare, strengthening health systems, regulating quality, safety, and efficacy of health technologies, and recalling the human right dimension of the problem. International trade guides economic and commercial policy. Agreements, tariffs and non-tariff measures, competition and procurement policies innovation and access transpose borders, entailing different stakeholders interests and medical technologies to reach those in need.

139. There is no agreement among the WIPO, WHO, and WTO formalizing the Trilateral Cooperation. However, the three organizations keep renewing financial and human resources commitments to prioritizing actions that enhance access to medical and innovation from the international level to the ground. For more details on cooperation agreements established bilaterally between WIPO and these organizations and more details on WIPO Technical Assistance work, *see* Delivery of WIPO Technical Assistance; WTO | intellectual property (TRIPS)—WTO-WIPO agreement.

140. For more information, *see* WHO, WIPO, WTO Trilateral Cooperation on Public Health, IP and Trade, at www.who.int/teams/health-product-policy-and-standards/medicines-selection-ip-and-affordability/cooperation; WTO | intellectual property (TRIPS)—Trilateral cooperation on intellectual property, trade and public health.

These intersections and policy domains are dynamically and constantly filled with challenges as society and technology evolves demanding coordination to effective response to new and current threats. As mandates of different organizations may coincide in different degrees their dialogue enables more effective action.

Figure 33.2 Mapping the Policy Intersections: Key Areas of Law and Policy for Innovation and Access

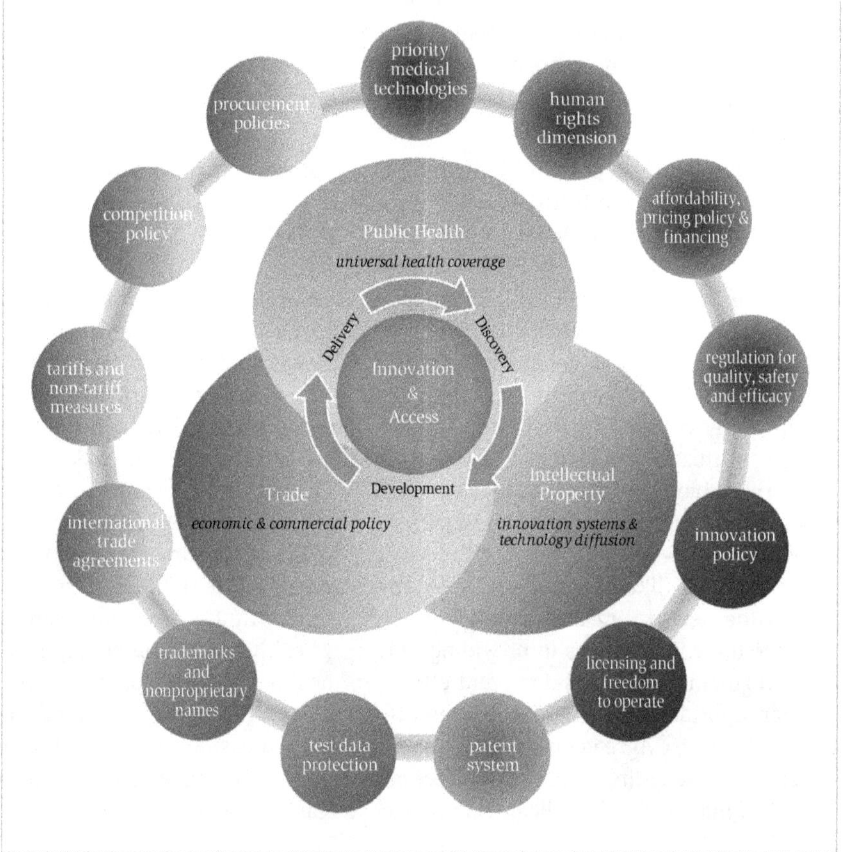

Source: World Health Organization, World Intellectual Property Organization and World Trade Organization, *Promoting Access to Medical Technologies and Innovation: Intersections between public health, intellectual property and trade*, Trilateral Study, 2nd ed., Geneva, Switzerland, 2020.

[B] Challenges and Opportunities to Ensure Access to Medical Technologies and Innovation: From Discussions to Enabling Actions on the Ground

Diversity and tailored approach to Member States' needs, contexts, and problems have guided the WHO, WIPO, WTO Trilateral Cooperation work and activities. These include publications, technical assistance activities, events (Symposium, Seminars, and Workshops), and educational and training activities. Some highlights are the Trilateral Cooperation publications that include "Promoting Access to Medical Technologies and Innovation: Intersections between public health, intellectual property and trade," 2nd edition (2020)[141] and 1st edition (2013),[142] the COVID-19 pandemic specific publications "An integrated health, trade and IP approach to respond to the COVID-19 pandemic" 1st edition (2021)[143] and 2nd edition (2023). The Trilateral Cooperation Symposium that takes place annually and focuses on public health, intellectual property, and trade aspects to address the on-ground challenges. There is also a DL course in collaboration with WIPO Academy (DL 701—Executive Course on Promoting Access to Medical Technologies and Innovation).[144]

During the COVID-19 pandemic, the three organizations provided resources and launched the WHO-WIPO-WTO Technical Assistance Platform to work as a one-stop shop for Member States on issues regarding the interface of public health, intellectual property and trade by jointly leveraging the resources of the three organization.[145] Considering the needs of Member States to go beyond COVID-19, scope and resources related to the Trilateral Cooperation Technical Assistance Platform is being revised to assist Member States in broader issues related to public health, intellectual property and Trade, including the use of TRIPS flexibilities by developing countries and least-developed countries.

§33.05 FOOD SECURITY

Intellectual property is intricately linked to food security. Patent laws, PVP rights (also known as breeder's rights), and GR rights are major intellectual property tools that relate to agriculture and food security. Direct application of intellectual property to agriculture started taking place with the UPOV Convention, catalyzed by associations of horticulturalists and plant breeders for safeguarding plant varieties. With the advent of modern biotechnology, genetic compositions of novel plant varieties have started receiving patents as well, deepening the ties with intellectual property. The interplay

141. Promoting Access to Medical Technologies and Innovation—Intersections between Public Health, Intellectual Property and Trade (wipo.int).
142. *Ibid.*
143. *See* wipo-pub-628e-insert-en-an-integrated-health-trade-and-ip-approach-to-respond-to-the-covid-19-pandemic-update-august-30-2021.pdf.
144. Executive Course on Promoting Access to Medical Technologies and Innovation (DL-701).
145. WHO-WIPO-WTO COVID-19 Technical Assistance Platform (who-wipo-wto-trilateral.org).

between intellectual property, agriculture and food security stresses the need to incentivize innovation while addressing global food security challenges.

[A] Strengthening Food Systems to Overcome Hunger

The global population is projected to reach 9.7 billion in 2050, and 11.2 billion in 2100.[146] To support this increase in population, more food is required. According to the UN FAO, the demand for food output will need to increase by nearly 70% till 2050 to respond to the increase in population.[147]

Food systems—which include, *inter alia*, production, transport, processing, packaging, storage, retail, consumption—are major contributor to the global economy. The economic significance of agriculture varies across regions, accounting for a mean of 4% of global GDP.[148] It also is the second-largest source of employment worldwide, with 27.3% of total global employment (2018).[149]

Current food systems are also linked with vast inequalities, including the persistence of hunger and food insecurity. Despite progress being made in reducing the number of undernourished persons in recent decades, approximately 690-783 million, accounting for approximately 9% of the global population, remain undernourished (based on 2022 estimates).[150] 122 million more people faced hunger in 2022 than in 2019, before the global pandemic, representing an overall upward trend in global hunger.[151] Current diets are resulting in premature mortality and susceptibility to both chronic and infectious diseases. Worldwide, only 19% of children aged 6-23 months eat a minimally acceptable diet.[152] Inadequate nutrition and anemia among women contribute to poor health and development outcomes for both children and mothers.

Global food systems are exceeding some planetary boundaries for key natural resources, generating food loss and waste. Currently, food production occupies 50% of the Earth's habitable land, accounts for 70% of freshwater consumption, and is estimated to produce around 25% of GHG emissions.[153] Food loss and waste amount to between 25-30% of total food production, accounting for between 8% and 10% of GHG emissions.[154] Further, the rise in food supply per capita by 30% (since 1961) is

146. *See* www.un.org/en/desa/world-population-projected-reach-98-billion-2050-and-112-billion-2100#:~:text=COVID%2D19-,World%20population%20projected%20to%20reach%209.8%20billion%20in%202050%2C%20and,Nations%20report%20being%20launched%20today.
147. *See* www.fao.org/fileadmin/templates/wsfs/docs/expert_paper/How_to_Feed_the_World_in_2050.pdf.
148. *See* www.worldbank.org/en/topic/agriculture/overview.
149. *See* www.fao.org/3/cb1366en/cb1366en.pdf.
150. *See* www.fao.org/documents/card/en/c/cc3017en.
151. *Ibid.*
152. *See* data.unicef.org/topic/nutrition/diets/.
153. *See* www.un.org/development/desa/dpad/publication/un-desa-policy-brief-102-population-food-security-nutrition-and-sustainable-development/.
154. IPCC, Food Security (2019), at www.ipcc.ch/site/assets/uploads/2019/08/2f.-Chapter-5_FINAL.pdf.

concomitant with an 800% increase in the use of nitrogen fertilizers, and a rise by over 100% in the consumption of water for irrigation purposes.[155] As a result, food systems can lead to biodiversity loss, pollution (air and water), deforestation, soil degradation, antibiotic-resistant bacteria, and water scarcity.

According to FAO, food security exists when all people, at all times, have physical and economic access to sufficient, safe and nutritious food that meets their dietary needs and food preferences for an active and healthy life.[156] This definition encompasses the dimensions of equitable distribution but also places emphasis on the overarching theme of sustainability and continual accessibility. Notably, the ethical and human rights dimension of food security has also been recognized in the UN Declaration of Human Rights in 1948.[157]

[B] The Role of Intellectual Property in Promoting Technology for Food Security

Technology can play a role in promoting food security by, *inter alia*, increasing crop yields per unit area. Studies indicate that the use hybrid rice technology in China since 1964 have fed over 20% of the world's population using 10% of the world's total arable land. Further, the yield increase has fed an additional-60 million people every year, contributing to food security in the country.[158] GM crops and SMART breeding have also had roles to play in accelerating breeding activities.[159]

The application of technology in agriculture has advanced in recent decades. Some examples of how technology can promote food security by increasing food production, set out in the WIPO Green Technology Book on Adaptation (2022),[160] are: farmers that have traditionally been dependent on irrigation could consider transitioning to water-saving technologies like drip and sprinkler systems. Further, technologies such as Global Positioning Systems (GPS), soil spectroscopy and infrared lighting could provide farmers with insights into factors such as crop health, livestock well-being, and soil conditions. Aerial imagery from satellites and drones, combined with data from connected sensors, could enhance crop productivity outcomes since farmers would be able to assess crop monitoring real time and provide accurate yield predictions. Moreover, as water shortages increase in various parts of the world, innovations such as hydroponics, aeroponics, and aquaponics could address challenges faced in farms.

The international legal frameworks for food security are found in a number of treaties and legal instrument, and intellectual property law treaties indirectly support

155. *Ibid.*
156. *See* generally, www.fao.org/3/al936e/al936e00.pdf.
157. *See* www.un.org/en/about-us/universal-declaration-of-human-rights.
158. *See* ebrary.ifpri.org/utils/getfile/collection/p15738coll2/id/23379/filename/23380.pdf.
159. *See* www.wipo.int/wipo_magazine/en/2011/03/article_0001.html.
160. All examples have been taken from Chapter 3 of the WIPO Green Technology Book on Adaptation 2022. Available at www.wipo.int/edocs/pubdocs/en/wipo-pub-1080-en-green-technology-book.pdf.

food security.[161] Patent law, PVP rights (breeder's rights), and rights over GRs are particularly relevant from the lens of intellectual property law. The UPOV system, for instance, supports food security through, *inter alia*, providing a system that enables plant breeders to protect their innovations and obtain a return on their investment in developing innovative varieties.[162] Intellectual property also supports the safeguarding of GRs, ensuring biodiversity conservation and sustainable farming promotion. More generally, intellectual property may facilitate the transfer of knowledge and technology across different countries and regions, promoting collaboration and partnerships among various stakeholders. Further, the international intellectual property system also amasses vast technical knowledge. By obtaining a patent, an inventor discloses comprehensive details about the innovation, allowing peers to expand on this knowledge and progress in the innovation pathway. At the same time, intellectual property rights could deter unauthorized usage of such innovation.

Intellectual property rights may also potentially create challenges to agriculture. For instance, since protected varieties of plants typically offer higher yields that local varieties, it may result in homogenization of agricultural fields. This may result in loss in diversity and reduce resilience of crops to pests and diseases. Further, when plants have been engineered to increase tolerance to specific biotic stressors like pests of viruses, unintended effects such as interruption of endogenous genes, causing metabolic disruptions in places, resulting in lower fitness of the plants.[163]

§33.06 INNOVATION THROUGH INCLUSIVITY: TAKING INTELLECTUAL PROPERTY TO EVERYONE, EVERYWHERE

In the realm of intellectual property and innovation, inclusivity is not just a goal but a vital strategy for harnessing human potential. WIPO underscores the significance of an inclusive approach, especially as it pertains to populations traditionally underserved by the intellectual property system—notably the youth, women, and marginalized communities. Disparities in gender and other socio-demographic factors reflect deeper systemic barriers and biases that have, for too long, constrained the breadth of innovative contributions. By championing an inclusive intellectual property framework, WIPO aims to open up the world of innovation, ensuring that every voice, regardless of its origin, is heard, valued, and protected.

161. Two main instruments protecting and promoting food security include the International Undertaking for Plant Genetic Resources (1983), and the International Treaty on Plant Genetic Resources for Food and Agriculture (2001).
162. *See* www.wipo.int/wipo_magazine/en/2019/01/article_0007.html.
163. *See* generally, Bauer-Panskus, A. et al. (2020), *Risk Assessment of Genetically Engineered Plants That can Persist and Propagate in the Environment*, Environmental Sciences Europe, 32, available at enveurope.springeropen.com/articles/10.1186/s12302-020-00301-0#:~:text=For%20instance%2C%20native%20plant%20species,the%20fitness%20of%20hybrid%20offspring.

[A] Challenges to Women in Innovation and the Role of Intellectual Property

Despite progress in gender equality, gender disparities persist in patenting and women's capacity to monetize their creativity and innovation. Only around 16% of patent applications filed through the PCT are from women.[164] The underrepresentation of women among inventors has economic costs because the gender gap in patenting represents an inefficient use of female innovative capacity.

WIPO is working to create ecosystems "where innovation and creativity by women anywhere is supported by IP, for the good of everyone,"[165] and in 2022 released the first intellectual property and Gender Action Plan to help address this historical underrepresentation and to support women's increased participation in the intellectual property ecosystem. A literature review conducted in 2019 identified a number of deep-rooted challenges faced by female inventors and innovators.[166]

On a global scale, one key factor is the comparatively lower participation of women in the labor market and their limited involvement in entrepreneurship, which may significantly restrict the pool of potential female innovators.[167] This early disadvantage is often exacerbated by the absence of female role models and their limited presence in science, technology, engineering, and mathematics (STEM) education, which narrows the talent pipeline right from the start.

Even when women enter the STEM fields, they tend to distance themselves from patent-intensive areas and register patents at lower rates than their male counterparts.[168] This could be due to a range of factors, including barriers to career progression, gender discrimination, family related constraints, and unequal access to funding opportunities. These challenges often create a hostile environment for female innovators, hindering their progress in the innovation landscape. Similarly, women often grapple with the limitations of their professional networks and slower career advancement in research, authorship, and academia, which is well documented.[169] These hurdles perpetuate the gender gap in innovation by restricting access to resources and opportunities essential for breaking new ground in various fields.

A further layer of complexity is added by the lack of awareness about intellectual property rights, as well as likely gender bias embedded in intellectual property laws.

---

164. WIPO and Invent Together (2023), *The Global Gender Gap in Innovation and Creativity: An International Comparison of the Gender Gap in Global Patenting over Two Decades*, available at www.wipo.int.
165. IP GAP, available at www.wipo.int/export/sites/www/women-and-ip/en/docs/rn2023-1_ipgap.pdf.
166. Cutura, J. (2019). *Challenges for Women Inventors and Innovators in Using the Intellectual Property System: A Literature Review*, in Development Agenda Project on "Increasing the Role of Women in Innovation and Entrepreneurship, Encouraging Women in Developing Countries to Use the Intellectual Property System."
167. International Labor Organization (ILO) (2018), *World Employment Social Outlook, Trends for Women 2018 Global Snapshot*, ILO, Geneva.
168. Kenny, C. & O'Donnell, M. (2017), *Expanding Women's Role in Developing Technology: Increasing Productivity, Improving Lives*, CGD Notes, Center for Global Development.
169. Sugimoto et al. (2015), "The Academic Advantage," & Milli et al. (2016), "Equity in Innovation."

While intellectual property law is ostensibly gender neutral, it can result in gender-biased outcomes and distinct disadvantages for women in this intricate landscape. Feminist authors have raised concerns about the inherent gender bias within intellectual property laws, highlighting how the legal definitions of "inventor," "author," "works," and "invention" can perpetuate gender disparities in copyright and patent registration.[170] This bias is further exacerbated by the historical underrepresentation of women in patent and copyright ownership, reflecting societal norms that often discourage women from seeking intellectual property protection actively.[171] These issues can compound the challenges women face, particularly in some developing countries, where they may encounter additional obstacles in navigating the intricacies of intellectual property rights and protection. The combination of these factors erects formidable barriers, preventing women from making the impactful contributions they are fully capable of in the world of invention and innovation.

The role of intellectual property is crucial in addressing the multifaceted challenges faced by women in innovation and invention. Understanding the extent of gender disparities in intellectual property applications and patenting through data collection allows for tailored initiatives to be developed. Supporting intellectual property grants, scholarships, and internships designed for girls, women, and educators, alongside academic research funding and investments in female entrepreneurs, establishes a more inclusive pipeline for female innovators. Increasing the number of female STEM professionals and implementing targeted training programs in intellectual property law and administration would not only address the skills gap but would also indirectly enhance the representation of women in these fields. Raising awareness and focusing on capacity-building initiatives can bridge the knowledge gap and empower women with the skills to navigate the intricacies of intellectual property. Additionally, creating an environment that enables women to excel in intellectual property-intensive careers and promotes the commercialization of their inventions through networking and mentoring contributes to a more equitable and inclusive innovation landscape.

[B] Women in STEM and Women Entrepreneurs

The gender gap in innovation and patenting is frequently attributed to the lack of women in STEM disciplines and entrepreneurship. For example, studies have indicated that a rise in the quantity of STEM degrees is linked to a growth in patent-related activities.[172] However, women continue to be inadequately represented in fields of study that are predominant in innovation. While growing numbers of women are

170. Swanson, K. (March/April 2018). "Cat Ladies, Quilters, and Creativity." Landslide, American Bar Association.
171. *Ibid.*
172. Cutura, J. (2019). *Challenges for Women Inventors and Innovators in Using the Intellectual Property System: A Literature Review.* In Development Agenda Project on "Increasing the Role of Women in Innovation and Entrepreneurship, Encouraging Women in Developing Countries to Use the Intellectual Property System."

studying in scientific fields at the tertiary level, they constitute just 30%-46% of the graduates in those fields and are especially underrepresented in engineering, manufacturing, construction, and computer science. In computer science, there has even been a steady decrease in female graduates since 2000, a problem that is especially pronounced in developed countries.[173] An analysis of the results of 2018 Programme for International Student Assessment (PISA), conducted by the OECD, revealed that less than 2% of girls aspired to become engineers or computer scientists.[174]

While there have been significant strides toward gender parity in entrepreneurship, challenges persist. A noticeable gender export gap exists, particularly evident in the limited participation of women-led businesses in foreign markets. Recent research from OECD shows that in 2022, only 11% of women-led SMEs engaged in exporting, compared to 19% of their male-led counterparts.[175] As a result, women-led SMEs face hurdles in fully harnessing the benefits of international trade, underscoring the need for continued efforts to promote gender equality in entrepreneurship.

[C] The Role of Intellectual Property in Addressing Gender Disparities

It is becoming increasingly evident that fostering greater participation of women in STEM and entrepreneurship is pivotal for driving innovation and IP advancements. Intellectual property rights have a direct impact on economic growth at all stages of development. According to one study, intellectual property-backed intangible assets currently account for 90% of total business value.[176] As evidenced in research from the International Monetary Fund (IMF), the unique skills, and perspectives that both men and women bring to the workplace are key drivers of heightened economic growth and productivity.[177] Similarly, the McKinsey Global Institute underscores that achieving full female participation in the labor force has the potential to substantially bolster global GDP by up to 26%, underlining the remarkable impact of gender diversity on the economy.[178] When women, constituting half of the population, do not have equal participation in innovative and economic activity, it results in adverse consequences for the global economy.

Collecting data on the representation of women in the fields of innovation and intellectual property is an important focus, as it can help identify the scale and origins of the challenge, thereby supporting efforts to narrow the gender gap.

173. UNESCO (2015). UNESCO Science Report.
174. Mann, A. et al. (2020), *Dream Jobs? Teenagers' Career Aspirations and the Future of Work*, Organisation for Economic Co-operation and Development, Paris.
175. OECD SME and Entrepreneurship Outlook. Available at OECD SME and Entrepreneurship Outlook 2023 | OECD iLibrary (oecd-ilibrary.org).
176. Ocean Tomo, *Intangible Asset Market Value Study*. Available at www.oceantomo.com/intangible-asset-market-value-study/.
177. IMF (2018), "Economic Gains from Gender Inclusion: New Mechanisms, New Evidence." IMF Staff Discussion Note, SDN/18/06.
178. McKinsey Global Institute, (2015), *The Power of Parity: How Advancing Women's Equality Can Add $12 Trillion to Global Growth*, McKinsey & Co.

Figure 33.3 Women's Inventions in Figures

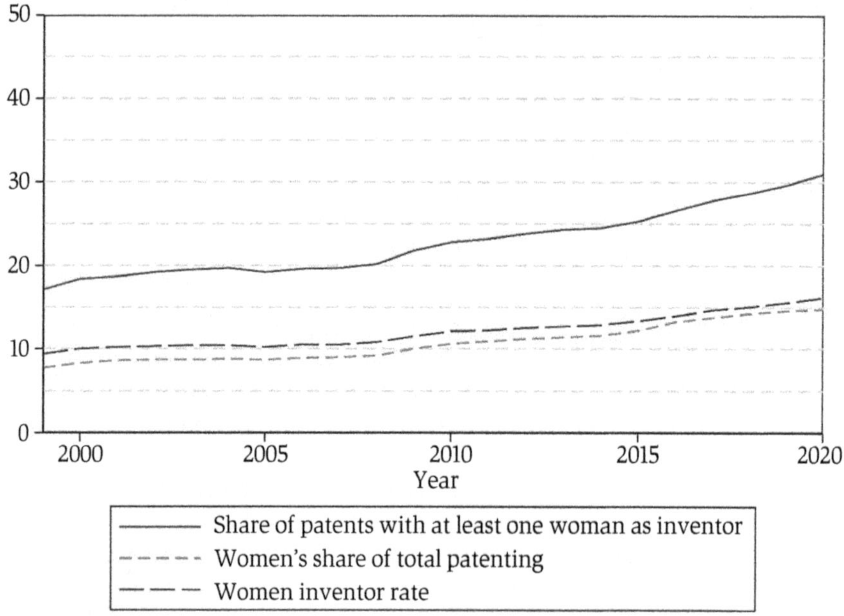

Effective action to address the issue of gender equity in PCT patenting hinges on the collection and comprehensive analysis of relevant data. To tackle this challenge, it is imperative to gather information specifically pertaining to women's participation in patenting activities, establish a baseline measurement, and continuously track and assess trends over time. As illustrated in Figure 33.3, the data not only highlights the current state of female inventors but also reveals a discouraging fact: in the year 2020, a mere 16% of inventors were women.[179]

While there may be a semblance of positive progress, achieving true gender parity in PCT patenting appears to remain an elusive goal, with projections extending anywhere from 33 to 102 years into the future. This contrast between the current situation and the desired outcome underscores the pivotal role that data collection and analysis play in effectively addressing this multifaceted challenge. Therefore, continuous efforts to gather and interpret data are paramount in laying the foundation for evidence-based strategies and policies to address gender disparities effectively.

179. WIPO and Invent Together (2023), *The Global Gender Gap in Innovation and Creativity: An International Comparison of the Gender Gap in Global Patenting over Two Decades*. Available at The Global Gender Gap in Innovation and Creativity: An International Comparison of the Gender Gap in Global Patenting over Two Decades (www.wipo.int).

[D] Preparing Youth for the Future of Intellectual Property and Innovation

As digital natives, young people are uniquely placed to develop novel solutions, leveraging the latest technologies. With advancements in domains like AI, IoT, blockchain, and virtual reality, the nexus between innovation and its legal protection mechanisms through the intellectual property system becomes further intertwined. Understanding intellectual property framework can assist youth in safeguarding their intellectual creations.

One promising avenue in educating youth to intellectual property is use of "edutainment," an educational strategy that integrates entertainment elements. For instance, interactive digital platforms or gamified intellectual property modules can make the complex world of patents, copyrights, and trademarks more digestible and relatable to a younger audience. Such platforms can narrate stories of young inventors who successfully patented their creations, or perhaps highlight the journey of a young artist navigating copyright laws. Infusing intellectual property education within mainstream learning not only equips the youth to safeguard their creative and intellectual endeavors, but also fosters a societal milieu where innovation is both celebrated and protected. This dual focus, on the act of creation and its subsequent protection, could instill a sense of respect and admiration for the processes of creation and invention.

[E] The Importance of Intellectual Property for Young Inventors and Creators

The importance of a targeted approach for young inventors and creators becomes clear when considering the contemporary challenges faced by young innovators. In today's digital era, where ideas are shared globally within seconds, the threat of copying or unauthorized adaptations is apparent. Thus, the diverse tools the intellectual property provides, including, *inter alia*, patents for inventors, copyrights for artists, and trademarks for brands, are instruments that can firm up an innovator's claim to their intellectual creations. This exclusive right, in turn, facilitates economic self-sufficiency. For instance, a young musician can generate revenue through royalty payments every time their copyrighted song is streamed or downloaded. Similarly, a youth-led start-up can leverage its patented technology to attract investors or potential business partners. They ensure that young creators are not only protected against potential infringements but also positioned to capitalize on their innovations, securing both monetary rewards and the invaluable currency of recognition.

[1] Challenges to Young Innovators, Creators and Entrepreneurs

The potential of young innovators is boundless, but unlocking that potential necessitates navigating a complex maze of legal, technical, and economic challenges inherent to the world of intellectual property. While the importance of intellectual property is clear, accessing and leveraging its systems is often riddled with barriers for these budding creators.

A significant challenge lies in intellectual property awareness. At its core, intellectual property is a highly technical field, replete with nuanced legal codes and intricate processes. For a young person with limited or no expertise, this can be especially intimidating. Filing a patent, for instance, requires understanding specific requirements, crafting claims, and conducting prior art searches. Such tasks demand not just an understanding of one's invention but also a grasp of the overarching intellectual property framework. Unfortunately, a lack of educational resources or focused curricula can mean many young inventors remain unaware of their intellectual property rights and the processes involved in securing them.

In addition, intellectual property protections include associated costs. From filing fees to potential costs of hiring intellectual property attorneys or consultants, these financial aspects can be prohibitive for young innovators, especially those who are self-funded or are in the early stages of their entrepreneurial journey.

Beyond the monetary aspect, there's the challenge of accessibility. Many regions lack easily available intellectual property services or offices, making the process of filing or seeking advice logistically challenging. Coupled with this is the issue of intellectual property awareness. The landscape of education often overlooks intellectual property, leading to a generation of innovators who might be brilliant in their creations but remain in the dark about how to safeguard them.

Given the evolving digital landscape and the way young minds engage with information today, there's a pressing need to reframe our intellectual property discourse. It is not enough to merely inform; engagement is essential. The concept of edutainment, which merges education with entertainment, could be a way forward. By discussing intellectual property in a language that resonates with the youth, using platforms they frequent, and integrating interactive and multimedia elements, WIPO stands a better chance of making intellectual property more accessible and less intimidating.

A structured training mechanism, where seasoned professionals mentor young creators, can provide practical insights into the intellectual property world. Such mentorship programs can demystify the complexities and offer a more hands-on approach to understanding intellectual property's intricacies.

In addressing these challenges, it is important to remember that the youth's perspective on intellectual property is shaped by their unique experiences in today's modern digital and interconnected world. Meeting them where they are, understanding their challenges, and tailoring our approach to intellectual property education and services will be essential in fostering a new generation of well-informed, protected, and empowered innovators and creators.

[2] Future Prospects: Encouraging Youth-Led Innovation Through Intellectual Property

Despite the hurdles they face, young individuals are increasingly carving out their niche in the intellectual property sphere. With a 15% rise in patent filings by youth in the past five years, it is evident that when given the right tools and knowledge, young innovators can and will safeguard their creations. Such a trend indicates a shift toward a more informed and proactive youth demographic, understanding the value of intellectual property.

Harnessing this momentum requires a twofold approach: continuing education on intellectual property rights and providing more accessible avenues for intellectual property registration and protection. By doing so, the future of innovation remains secure in the hands of a well-informed, proactive, and intellectual property-conscious youth.

The digital age offers a wide array of opportunities. With modern platforms like GitHub for code, SoundCloud for music, or Kickstarter for entrepreneurial ventures, there's a vast arena of digital terrain for young creators to explore. Platforms like these, while being a space for showcasing talent, also bring forth intellectual property challenges and opportunities. The more adept our youth become at maneuvering through these digital ecosystems with intellectual property awareness, the more secure and prosperous their innovative journey becomes.

In addition, while traditional mechanisms of intellectual property protection are essential, the future calls for an understanding of evolving concepts like open-source, creative commons, and digital rights management. Encouraging youth-led innovation means ensuring they are conversant with both conventional and contemporary intellectual property frameworks.

Moreover, the world is increasingly interconnected. For young innovators, this means collaborating across borders, cultures, and disciplines. Strengthening international intellectual property frameworks and promoting cross-border intellectual property understanding will be pivotal. For instance, understanding how intellectual property functions in the context of joint ventures, multinational research projects, or global start-ups will be indispensable.

Looking forward, the youth may play a role in inspiring change and advancing the intellectual property system. For instance, making intellectual property processes more intuitive and user-friendly can significantly aid young creators. Think of platforms or apps that simplify patent searches, copyright registrations, or trademark queries. Integrating AI and other technologies to simplify and expedite these processes can be a game-changer.

An inclusive approach, where young people from diverse backgrounds, genders, and geographies are equally encouraged and equipped with intellectual property knowledge, can result in a broader innovation landscape as it promotes diversity. In imagining the future, the role of intellectual property is not merely protective but also empowering. As WIPO equips the next generation with the right tools, knowledge, and resources, it is not just safeguarding individual innovations but ensuring a collective, brighter future where creativity knows no bounds, and every idea gets its due recognition and value.

[3] Data and Insight: The Global Landscape of Youth and Intellectual Property

A close analysis of data provides key insights into the dynamics of youth engagement with intellectual property. The World Intellectual Property Report 2022: Direction of Innovation[180] report unveils compelling evidence of the rising engagement of young inventors in the intellectual property world. But beyond sheer numbers, these statistics paint a narrative of aspiration, achievement, and occasional challenges that today's youth encounter in their innovative journeys.

A deep dive into the data reveals interesting geographical trends. While certain regions witness an explosive growth in youth-led patent filings, others may lag. Such discrepancies can be attributed to factors ranging from differential access to resources, the quality of intellectual property education, to regional innovation ecosystems. For instance, countries with robust start-up cultures or heavy investments in STEM education might naturally witness a higher surge in youth-centric intellectual property activities.

The data also unravels sectors where the youth are particularly active. Be it in green technologies, bioinformatics, or digital art platforms, identifying these areas of heightened activity can help stakeholders channel resources and support more effectively.

While the numbers indicate a rising trend, it is equally important to understand potential underreporting or areas where young innovators might be bypassing the traditional intellectual property system, either due to unawareness or alternative intellectual property models like open-source licenses.

Further granularity in data can highlight the involvement of young women, marginalized groups, or other specific demographics in the intellectual property realm. Such insights can guide tailored interventions, ensuring that the canvas of innovation remains diverse and inclusive.

With the power of data, advanced analytics, and AI, one can also forecast trends, helping institutions prepare and adapt. Predicting the rise of specific technologies or identifying potential innovation hubs before they emerge can be invaluable for educators, policymakers and industry leaders alike.

When looking at this kind of data, it becomes evident that numbers are not just cold hard facts; they tell stories. Stories of young people striving to make their mark, of societies evolving to foster creativity, and of an ever-changing world where the lines between innovation and its protection, between dreamers and doers, are continually being redrawn. As different stakeholders interpret and act upon these insights, a cause

180. World Intellectual Property Report 2022: Direction of Innovation, at www.wipo.int/wipr/en/2022/.

reaches championship: to empower every young innovator, everywhere, ensuring their creations are celebrated, protected and thrive in the global arena.

[F] Looking Forward

Policies that promote diversity and evidence-based legal advice need to be implemented to increase the chances of success in addressing the above global challenges. Therefore, integrating different stakeholders' views of the intellectual property system as equal participants and giving them opportunities are essential to the innovation ecosystem and increasing society's chances to overcome global challenges and forecast new ones.

CHAPTER 34
The WIPO Development Agenda

§34.01 INTRODUCTION

The Development Agenda recommendations were adopted by WIPO Member States in 2007. The decision was an important milestone for the Organization. The aim of the Development Agenda is to ensure that development considerations form an integral part of WIPO's work. The effective implementation of the recommendations is a key priority for the Organization, as recognized in its Strategic Pillars.

[A] Background

A proposal for the establishment of a development agenda for WIPO was submitted by Argentina and Brazil at the 2004 WIPO General Assembly. It was supported by twelve other developing countries, namely, Bolivia, Cuba, the Dominican Republic, Ecuador, Egypt, the Islamic Republic of Iran, Kenya, Peru, Sierra Leone, South Africa, the United Republic of Tanzania and the Bolivarian Republic of Venezuela. Following discussions, Member States agreed to hold a series of inter-sessional intergovernmental meetings (IIMs) to examine the proposals originally submitted by Argentina and Brazil, as well as additional proposals put forward by other Member States. Three IIMs were held in 2005 at which eight papers containing a range of proposals were presented. In May 2005, WIPO also hosted an International Seminar on IP and Development in partnership with other multilateral organizations, including the UNCTAD, the United Nations Industrial Development Organization (UNIDO), the WHO and the WTO. It was open to all stakeholders, including NGOs, civil society and academia. The Provisional Committee on Proposals Related to a WIPO Development Agenda (PCDA) was established by the General Assembly in 2005 to accelerate the discussions. It met twice in 2006. 111 proposals, in actionable and operational form, were submitted for consideration. These were based on fourteen proposal papers submitted by various Member States.

In 2006, the General Assembly renewed the mandate of the PCDA for one year. It also decided that two to five-day sessions would be held in 2007 to allow for structured in-depth discussions on the 111 proposals made during the IIMs and PCDA sessions in 2005 and 2006 respectively. For this purpose and to streamline the process for a detailed examination of all proposals in an inclusive manner, the PCDA decided: (i) to narrow down the proposals to ensure that there was no repetition or duplication; (ii) to separate the actionable proposals from those which were declarations of general principles and objectives; and (iii) to note the proposals that related to existing activities in WIPO and those which did not. It was further decided that the PCDA would report to the 2007 General Assembly with recommendations for action on agreed proposals, and on a framework for continuing to address the other proposals following the 2007 General Assembly. In 2007, the PCDA held two sessions, during which Member States, *inter alia*, agreed on a set of forty-five proposals and recommended the establishment of the CDIP. The report was forwarded to the 2007 General Assembly.

Member States at the General Assembly unanimously adopted the forty-five proposals and established the CDIP. The General Assembly also requested Member States, the Secretariat and other relevant WIPO bodies to ensure the immediate and effective implementation of nineteen proposals. It was emphasized that this did not, in any way, imply that these proposals had been accorded a higher priority than the others or that their implementation, or aspects of it, would not be discussed in the CDIP, in coordination with relevant WIPO bodies.

[B] The Contents of the Development Agenda

The proposals adopted by the General Assembly are referred to as the forty-five Development Agenda recommendations. They cover all areas of WIPO's work and are grouped into six clusters:

Cluster A: Technical Assistance and Capacity Building (fourteen recommendations);
Cluster B: Norm-setting, Flexibilities, Public Policy and Public Domain (nine recommendations);
Cluster C: TT, ICTs and Access to Knowledge (nine recommendations);
Cluster D: Assessment, Evaluation and Impact Studies (six recommendations);
Cluster E: Institutional Matters including Mandate and Governance (six recommendations); and
Cluster F: Other Issues (one recommendation).

Although the forty-five recommendations are related to the Development Agenda, it is important to note that Member States have yet to formally discuss and agree on a definition for the term "Development Agenda." The term is not mentioned in the aforementioned decision of the General Assembly in 2007, nor is it referred to in any of the forty-five recommendations. Thus, it is perhaps not surprising that the objectives of the Development Agenda are also not defined in these texts. Nevertheless, it should be noted that the decision of the General Assembly on the Coordination Mechanisms and Monitoring, Assessing and Reporting Modalities in 2010 (discussed in paragraph [] below) includes the following, "The aim of the Development Agenda is to ensure that development considerations form an integral part of WIPO's work." However, the term "Development Agenda" was not defined. In the absence of a definition, it remains uncertain as to whether the Development Agenda is restricted to the forty-five adopted recommendations.

§34.02 DEVELOPMENT AGENDA PRINCIPLES

Member States have also yet to define a comprehensive set of Development Agenda principles. Documents, studies and other literature on the Development Agenda often refer to the principles contained in the adopted recommendations. On this point, it is important to note that Member States have yet to formally agree on whether the principles incorporated in the recommendations are also the overall principles of the Development Agenda. With regard to the principles contained in the forty-five recommendations, it is also essential to note that Member States have yet to discuss and agree on a complete set of principles contained in those recommendations. This is not necessarily a straightforward task as the principles are sometimes not described in the recommendations. For example, although transparency appears to be an underlying principle behind Recommendations 5 and 6, it is not explicitly mentioned in those recommendations. A distinction should also be drawn between the guidelines and underlying principles contained in a particular recommendation.

Furthermore, it is also widely recognized that the recommendations are often ambiguous, with overlaps and shortcomings in drafting that reflect the difficulties and complexities of the negotiations, and the need to achieve consensus on a text acceptable to all Member States. Certain details were left out as they were difficult to negotiate. However, these could be determined by Member States in the course of implementing the recommendations.

All these uncertainties point to the need for Member States to undertake a detailed analysis of all the adopted recommendations. In 2009, a general analysis was undertaken by the Secretariat with the guidance of Member States for the purpose of implementation. It noted, *inter alia,* that many recommendations contained principles. They were primarily included in the list of nineteen recommendations for immediate implementation, although certain principles were contained in some of the other twenty-six recommendations. However, the Secretariat did not describe those identified in its analysis. Although the Secretariat can play a supportive role, the responsibility for resolving uncertainties concerning the recommendations rests with the Member States. They need to identify all the principles that are contained in the forty-five recommendations. Additionally, they need to agree on whether the principles included therein are also the overall principles of the Development Agenda, which as mentioned above, has yet to be formally defined. It is important for all these elements to be discussed and agreed upon as they are central to mainstreaming the Development

Agenda and its recommendations into all areas of the Organization's work. A detailed examination of the recommendations is also required to address other ambiguities in the recommendations. For these reasons, Member States need to conduct a thorough analysis of all the adopted recommendations. The Secretariat is ready to facilitate the task.

§34.03 COMMITTEE ON DEVELOPMENT AND INTELLECTUAL PROPERTY

The CDIP was established by the WIPO General Assembly in 2007 with a mandate to:

(i) develop a work program for implementing the forty-five adopted Development Agenda recommendations;
(ii) monitor, assess, discuss and report on the implementation of all recommendations adopted, and for that purpose, it shall coordinate with relevant WIPO bodies; and
(iii) discuss IP and development-related issues as agreed by the Committee, as well as those decided by the General Assembly.

The CDIP consists of all Member States. WIPO provides financing for the participation of representatives from developing countries, including least-developed countries (LDCs), as well as those from countries with economies in transition, to attend Committee meetings. These are open to the participation, as observers, of all IGOs and NGOs with permanent observer status in WIPO, as well as those admitted by the Committee on an ad hoc basis. As of 2023, 381 organizations were accredited as observers at WIPO meetings.

The Committee meets twice a year. It reports and makes recommendations annually to the General Assembly. The Committee held its first session in March 2008 during which Member States considered and adopted rules of procedure based on the WIPO General Rules of Procedure and began discussions on the implementation of the Development Agenda recommendations based on the working document prepared by the Chair, in consultation with Member States and the Secretariat.

As described above, a key component of the Committee's mandate is to "monitor, assess, discuss and report on the implementation of all recommendations adopted, and for that purpose it shall coordinate with relevant WIPO bodies." In 2009, the Committee began discussions on "Coordination Mechanisms and Monitoring, Assessing and Reporting Modalities" (the "coordination mechanism"). In 2010, a decision on the coordination mechanism was adopted by the General Assembly. The coordination mechanism provides the CDIP with additional tools to ensure that development considerations form an integral part of WIPO's work.

By mid-2023, the CDIP had held thirty sessions. It had agreed on a project-based methodology for the implementation of the Development Agenda recommendations and approved fifty-two projects in this regard. The Committee also considered a wide range of issues and documents, including, *inter alia*:

(i) Director General's Report on the Implementation of the Development Agenda. These annual reports serve as a comprehensive overview of WIPO's initiatives and outline the activities undertaken and achievements made in relation to the implementation and mainstreaming of the Development Agenda recommendations across WIPO Sectors.

(ii) Progress Reports on the implementation of the 45 Development Agenda Recommendations and on ongoing Development Agenda Projects. These annual reports assess the Organization's efforts in incorporating the Development Agenda Recommendations into its policies, projects and activities.

(iii) Proposals for Development Agenda Project. Each project proposal shows how the project contributes to WIPO's Expected Result(s) and how it links to the Development Agenda recommendation(s). It also contains clearly defined objectives, a time frame for implementation, deliverable outcomes, cost estimates and is subject to the Committee's approval.

(iv) Evaluation reports of completed Development Agenda projects. These reports assess the effectiveness of the Development Agenda projects and their alignment with the Development Agenda, as well as with developmental goals of the beneficiary countries. They facilitate informed decision-making for the Committee and promote accountability in resource allocation and project implementation.

(v) External Review of WIPO Technical Assistance in the Area of Cooperation for Development. The first such Review was undertaken by two external evaluators, in the context of the project on Enhancement of WIPO's Results-Based Management (RBM) Framework. The report of the External Review was presented to the Committee at its eighth session in 2011. The Committee had extensive discussions over several sessions and some of the recommendations contained in the report were implemented. The Committee also decided, *inter alia,* to open a new sub-agenda item on "WIPO Technical Assistance in the Area of Cooperation for Development" to continue discussing issues related to WIPO's technical assistance work. At its thirtieth session in 2023, the Committee agreed to undertake a new Independent External Review of WIPO's Technical Assistance and approved the Terms of Reference for such Review.

(vi) Independent Review of the Implementation of the Development Agenda Recommendations. The coordination mechanism, *inter alia,* requested the Committee to undertake an independent review of the implementation of the Development Agenda Recommendations. The Independent review was undertaken by three external evaluators and the report, containing twelve recommendations, was presented to the Committee at its eighteenth session in 2016. After extensive discussions over several sessions, at its twenty-ninth session in 2022, the Committee took a decision on the implementation strategies of most of the Independent Review recommendations and requested WIPO to start the implementation of those strategies.

(vii) WIPO's Contribution to the Implementation of the SDGs and its Associated Targets. At its eighteenth session in 2016, the Committee requested the Secretariat to present an annual report on the Organization's contribution to the implementation of the SDGs and its Associated Targets. The reports provide an update of the SDG-related: (a) activities and initiatives undertaken individually by WIPO; (b) activities undertaken by WIPO as part of the UN System; and (c) assistance provided by WIPO to its Member States at their request.

Furthermore, the WIPO General Assembly, at its forty-ninth session in 2017, took a decision which, *inter alia*, requested to "add new agenda item to the CDIP agenda, named IP and Development to discuss IP and development-related issues as agreed by the Committee, as well as those decided by the General Assembly." Since then, this agenda item has served as a platform for Member States to prompt a dynamic dialogue on IP and development-related issues by sharing experiences on good practices and exchanging lessons learned. A Roster of Topics has been put in place to feature the topics proposed by Member States, indicating the topics already held with respective presentations and relevant materials, the ones scheduled to be held, as well as other proposals that would be kept in the pipeline as received. By year end 2023, the Committee discussed/will discuss the following topics:

- "Addressing Climate Change: IP Helps Achieve the Goals of Carbon Peaking and Carbon Neutrality"—to be discussed at the thirty-first CDIP session.
- "IP and youth: investing in the future" and the revision of the topic "Women and IP"—discussed at the thirtieth CDIP session.
- "IP Commercialization and Technology Transfer"—discussed at the twenty-ninth CDIP session.
- "IP and Innovation: Trademarks and Design Strategies for Entrepreneurs"—discussed at the twenty-eighth CDIP session.
- "The Role of Technology and Innovation Support Centers (TISCs) as a catalyst for Technology Transfer: Opportunities and Challenges"—discussed at the twenty-seventh CDIP session.
- "IP and Creative Economy" and the revision of the topic "Women and IP"—discussed at the twenty-sixth CDIP session.
- "Micro, small and medium-sized enterprises (MSMEs), Innovation and IP"—discussed at the twenty-fourth CDIP session.
- IP and Development in the Digital Environment—discussed at the twenty-third CDIP session.
- "Women and IP"—discussed at the twenty-second CDIP session.

§34.04 IMPLEMENTATION OF THE DEVELOPMENT AGENDA

As discussed earlier, the term "Development Agenda" has not been defined. Thus far, Member States and the Secretariat have approached the implementation of the

Development Agenda in terms of the implementation of the forty-five adopted recommendations. The words "Development Agenda" and "recommendations" are often used together or synonymously in the context of implementation.

The recommendations do not provide details as to how they are to be implemented. In 2009, the CDIP adopted a project-based approach to give impetus to implementation. In addition, efforts have been and are being made by the Secretariat to mainstream development considerations and the recommendations into WIPO's work.

The Director General reports annually to the CDIP on the implementation of the Development Agenda recommendations. The report provides an outline of the work undertaken in this regard by the Organization in a particular year. It includes an overview of the mainstreaming of the Development Agenda recommendations into WIPO's program activities and its various bodies, as well as the implementation of Development Agenda projects.

[A] Mainstreaming the Recommendations into WIPO's Regular Program Activities

WIPO's activities are guided by the Development Agenda recommendations. This is reflected in the WIPO Program and Budget. The design, planning and implementation of activities by each sector is informed and guided by relevant recommendations. Linkages between the Sectors and the Development Agenda recommendations are prominently featured in the Program and Budget document through the use of graphic illustrations. The approach of establishing links between the recommendations and the respective WIPO programs was first introduced in the Revised Program and Budget for 2008/2009. The linkages ensure that Member States and the Secretariat are able to monitor and evaluate progress in the implementation of the recommendations. The WIPO Performance Reports (WPRs) provide details of the role and contribution of each sector to the implementation of the relevant recommendations.

Further, as a result of a decision taken by the Committee in relation to the Independent Review of the Implementation of the Development Agenda Recommendations, Annex I of the Director General's Report on the Implementation of the Development Agenda presents links between the Development Agenda recommendations and WIPO's Expected Results.

Since the adoption of the Development Agenda recommendations in 2007, new WIPO business units and activities that seek to address some of the concerns raised by its recommendations have also been introduced. These include the creation of a Department for Economics and Data Analytics, which focuses, *inter alia*, on empirical economic analysis and impact studies on IP and development for use by policymakers. The Department plays a leading role in the implementation of a number of recommendations under Cluster D. In addition, the Global Challenges Division seeks to enhance WIPO's contribution to addressing a range of global development challenges, including climate change, food security and public health. The WIPO GREEN platform has been established. One of its main objectives is to support the transfer of technology to developing countries. Through its database, network and acceleration projects, it brings together key players to catalyze green technology innovation and diffusion. The WIPO GREEN platform provides opportunities for matchmaking between green technology providers, seekers and partners. The creation of the IP for Innovators Department is central to the implementation of a number of Development Agenda recommendations, including recommendations 8, 30 and 31, through a number of activities and projects that seek to enhance access to, and the capacity to use, technological information that may be of strategic interest to developing countries and LDCs. The Technology Transfer Section within the Department assists in addressing a number of recommendations in Clusters A and C (e.g., recommendations 4, 10, 11, 25, 26 and 28).

[B] Mainstreaming the Recommendations into the Work of WIPO Bodies

The decision of the General Assembly on the coordination mechanism in 2010 instructed the "relevant WIPO bodies to identify the ways in which the Development Agenda Recommendations are being mainstreamed in their work, and urge them to implement the Recommendations accordingly." It also instructed the "relevant WIPO bodies to include in their annual report to the Assemblies, a description of their contribution to the implementation of the respective Development Agenda Recommendations." Accordingly, since 2011, a document entitled, "Description of the contribution of the relevant WIPO Bodies to the implementation of the respective Development Agenda Recommendations" has been compiled and submitted to the General Assembly for discussion. The Director General's annual report on the implementation of the Development Agenda also provides a summary of the developments that took place in various WIPO bodies in the year under review, and their contribution to the implementation of the Development Agenda.

The Secretariat seeks to strictly adhere to the relevant Development Agenda recommendations, notably, those contained under Cluster B, in discharging its duties in relation to the WIPO bodies. It maintains a neutral stance in facilitating the work of the various committees and working groups, and in negotiations among Member States. Norm-setting activities are driven by Member States. They take into account different levels of development and the flexibilities in international IP agreements. Informal, open and balanced consultations are also undertaken prior to norm-setting activities. These promote the participation of experts from developing countries and LDCs.

[C] Implementation of Development Agenda Projects

In 2009, the CDIP agreed that "recommendations that dealt with similar or identical activities would be brought under one theme" in order to enhance efficiency in implementation and avoid overlap or duplication. The Committee also agreed that implementation would be structured in the form of projects and other activities, as appropriate, with the understanding that additional activities may be proposed. In early 2009, implementation began for nine projects based on activities decided by the Committee in 2008. By mid-2023, the Committee had approved fifty-two projects, implementing thirty-four Development Agenda recommendations. Projects are proposed by Member States (twenty-four projects) and the Secretariat (twenty-eight projects). Each project includes clearly defined objectives, a time frame for implementation, deliverable outcomes, cost estimates and is subject to evaluation. A Project Manager is nominated to oversee its implementation. Relevant WIPO sectors are involved in the delivery and implementation of a project. In addition to their involvement through discussions in the CDIP, the engagement of Member States is also essential when projects are implemented in their respective countries and in ensuring the sustainability of results post-implementation.

Projects approved by the CDIP for implementation of the Development Agenda recommendations include the following:

- Conference on Mobilizing Resources for Development (recommendation 2);
- IP Technical Assistance Database (IP-TAD) (recommendation 5);
- Specialized Databases' Access and Support (Phases I and II) (recommendation 8);
- IP Development Matchmaking Database (IP-DMD) (recommendation 9);
- Establishment of "Start-Up" National IP Academies (Phases I and II) (recommendation 10);
- Smart IP Institutions Project (recommendation 10);
- Innovation and Technology Transfer Support Structure for National Institutions (recommendation 10);
- Strengthening the Capacity of National IP Governmental and Stakeholder Institutions to Manage, Monitor and Promote Creative Industries, and to Enhance the Performance and Network of Copyright Collective Management Organizations (recommendation 10);
- Improvement of National, Sub-Regional and Regional IP Institutional and User Capacity (recommendation 10);
- IP and the Public Domain (recommendations 16 and 20);
- IP and Competition Policy (recommendations 7, 23 and 32);
- IP, Information and Communication Technologies (ICTs), the Digital Divide and Access to Knowledge (recommendations 19, 24 and 27);
- Developing Tools for Access to Patent Information (Phases I and II) (recommendations 19, 30 and 31);
- Enhancement of WIPO's Results-Based Management (RBM) Framework to Support the Monitoring and Evaluation of Development Activities (recommendations 33, 38 and 41);
- IP and Product Branding for Business Development in Developing Countries and Least-Developed Countries (LDCs) (recommendations 4 and 10);
- Capacity-Building in the Use of Appropriate Technology-Specific Technical and Scientific Information as a Solution for Identified Development Challenges (Phases I and II) (recommendations 19, 30 and 31);
- IP and Socio-Economic Development (Phases I and II) (recommendations 35 and 37);

- IP and Technology Transfer: Common Challenges—Building Solutions (recommendations 19, 25, 26 and 28);
- Open Collaborative Projects and IP-Based Models (recommendation 36);
- Patents and the Public Domain (recommendations 16 and 20);
- Enhancing South-South Cooperation on IP and Development among Developing Countries and LDCs (recommendations 1, 10, 11, 13, 19, 25 and 32);
- IP and Brain Drain (recommendations 39 and 40);
- IP and the Informal Economy (recommendation 34);
- Strengthening and Development of the Audiovisual Sector in Burkina Faso and Certain African Countries (Phases I and II) (recommendations 1, 2, 4, 10 and 11);
- IP and Design Management for Business Development in Developing and LDCs (recommendations 4 and 10);
- IP, Tourism and Culture: Supporting Development Objectives and Promoting Cultural Heritage in Egypt and Other Developing Countries (recommendations 1, 10 and 12);
- Cooperation on Development and IP Rights Education and Professional Training with Judicial Training Institutions in Developing and LDCs (recommendations 3, 10 and 45);
- The Use of Information in the Public Domain for Economic Development (recommendations 16 and 20);
- IP Management and Transfer of Technology: Promoting the Effective Use of IP in Developing Countries, LDCs and Countries with Economies in Transition (recommendations 1, 10, 12, 19 and 31);
- Enhancing the Use of IP for Mobile Applications in the Software Sector (Phases I and II) (recommendations 4, 11, 23, 24 and 27);
- Increasing the Role of Women in Innovation and Entrepreneurship, Encouraging Women in Developing Countries to Use the IP System (recommendations 1, 10, 12, 23, 25, 31 and 40);
- IP and Gastronomic Tourism in Peru and Other Developing Countries: Promoting the Development of Gastronomic Tourism through IP (Phases I and II) (recommendations 1, 10 and 12);
- Copyright and the Distribution of Content in the Digital Environment (recommendations 1, 3, 4, 10, 11, 16, 25 and 35);
- Development of the Music Sector and New Economic Models of Music in Burkina Faso and in Certain Countries of the West African Economic and Monetary Union (WAEMU) (recommendations 1, 4, 10, 11 and 23);
- Registration of the Collective Marks of Local Enterprises as a Cross-Cutting Economic Development Issue (recommendations 1, 4 and 10);
- Tools for Successful Development Agenda Project Proposals (recommendations 1 and 5);
- Promoting the Use of IP in Developing Countries in Creative Industries in the Digital Era (recommendations 1, 4, 10, 12, 19, 24 and 27);

- Systematization of Statistical Data and the Design and Implementation of a Methodology for Developing Impact Assessments on the Use of the IP System (recommendations 1, 4, 10, 35 and 37);
- Identifying and Using Inventions in the Public Domain (recommendations 16 and 20);
- Empowering Small Businesses Through IP: Developing Strategies for Supporting Geographical Indications or Collective Marks in the Post-registration Period (recommendations 1, 4, 10 and 11);
- Reducing Work-Related Accidents and Occupational Diseases through Innovation and IP (recommendations 1, 10, 19, 30, 31 and 45);
- Empowering Youth (K-12) to Innovate for a Better Future (recommendations 1, 3, 10, 19 and 30);
- Development of Strategies and Tools to Address Online Copyright Piracy in the African Digital Market (recommendations 4, 10, 11 and 45); and
- Text and Data Mining (TDM) to Support Research and Innovation in Universities and Other Research-Oriented Institutions in Africa (recommendations 4, 10, 16, 25 and 27).

The annual progress report to the CDIP on the implementation of the Development Agenda projects provides an overview of the status of Development Agenda projects under implementation in a particular year, as well as their main achievements and outputs. Completion and Evaluation reports of completed Development Agenda projects are also discussed by the Committee. Information on all completed and ongoing projects is available on the online searchable Catalogue that provides structured and detailed information on all Development Agenda projects, reports and outputs, and allows users to filter their search by different criteria, which includes IP rights, IP themes, project status, keywords, etc.

[D] Achievements in the Implementation of the Development Agenda

Some of the achievements in the implementation of the Development Agenda include the following:

- The Intellectual Property Technical Assistance Database (IP-TAD) was developed under the Development Agenda recommendation 5. It provides information on WIPO's technical assistance activities where the beneficiaries included a developing country, LDC or country in transition. Technical assistance activities are searchable by title, beneficiary country, activity type, IP subject area, year, host country and WIPO Sector.
- The Roster of Consultants (ROC) database was developed under the Development Agenda recommendation 6. It contains information on consultants engaged by WIPO to undertake specific IP technical assistance activities at the national level in developing countries, LDCs and countries in transition. The database is regularly updated and used as a tool to identify IP consultants for specific IP tasks and areas. The consultants can be searched by various

criteria, such as name, country of residence, IP field expertise, language and year of assignment.

- The Database on Flexibilities in the IP System was developed under the Development Agenda recommendation 14. It contains data drawn from WIPO documents on Patent Related Flexibilities in the Multilateral Legal Framework and their Legislative Implementation at the National and Regional Levels. The database allows searches for implementation of flexibilities in national IP laws in selected jurisdictions.
- Through the mainstreaming of the project on Specialized Databases' Access and Support, by 2023, 1,400 TISCs were created in ninety countries across the world to facilitate access to technological information in developing countries and LDCs. The ASPI and ARDI databases were also developed for this purpose. The ARDI program provides free or low-cost access for eligible institutions in developing countries to academic and professional peer-reviewed content. The program is also part of the Research4Life partnership, a joint initiative of several United Nations agencies, private sector enterprises, NGOs and academic institutions, which provides researchers in 125 developing countries and LDCs with free or low-cost access to 30,000 journals and up to 203,000 journals, books and other information in the fields of health, food and agriculture, the environment, applied sciences, law and social sciences. Similarly, the ASPI program provides free or low-cost access to 169 registered institutions to commercial patent database services that offer advanced tools and services for retrieving and analyzing patent data.
- Through the mainstreaming of the project on the Establishment of "Start-Up" National IP Academies (currently IP Training Institutions (IPTIs)), the WIPO Academy provides support to countries in developing their own national IP training capacities. By 2023, fourteen IPTIs were established, becoming scalable, cost-effective and self-sustaining structures supporting countries to build the IP skills needed to drive economic growth and development. IPTIs reported the organization of more than 7,600 activities for over 435,000 participants, including underrepresented populations in the innovation ecosystem, such as women, entrepreneurs, children, and people with disabilities.
- The Smart IP Institutions Project aimed at assisting Member States to develop and improve national IP institutional capacity through further development of infrastructure and other facilities. The project was mainstreamed through the WIPO's program of IP Office Business Solutions. By 2023, ninety IP Offices from developing countries in all regions (including twenty LDCs) were actively using WIPO Business Solutions for the administration of their IP rights. Further, fifty-eight IP Offices were participating in one of the online exchange platforms offered by WIPO through the Centralized Access to Search and Examination and the Digital Access Service. A key focus is to upgrade the service level of IP Offices by assisting them to move to online services for filing and for IP information dissemination.

- A methodology and practical tools for the formulation of national IP strategies were developed through the project on Improvement of National, Sub-Regional and Regional IP Institutional and User Capacity. These were mainstreamed for use in national IP strategy formulation processes in developing countries and LDCs. Since 2022, the National IP Strategies team acted as a focal point and center of expertise at WIPO, working hand-in-hand with relevant WIPO business units to provide enhanced support and advice to Member States. In 2023, WIPO adopted a renewed approach to: (i) better align National IP Strategies within the context of Member States' economic development goals and innovation and creative ecosystems; (ii) ensure that WIPO's strategic and substantive advice to Member States produces high-quality Strategies that meet national circumstances, priorities and needs; and (iii) enhance knowledge about the value and impact of National IP Strategies among Member States and policymakers, including through analysis of trends, best practices and effectiveness.
- The studies undertaken in the context of projects, such as IP and the Public Domain; Patents and the Public Domain; IP and the Informal Economy; ICTs, the Digital Divide and Access to Knowledge; IP and Socioeconomic Development; and IP and Brain Drain contribute to greater awareness and enhanced understanding of the respective areas. A few examples of such studies included the Feasibility Study on the Establishment of National Patent Register Databases and Linkage to PATENTSCOPE, as well as the books on the Informal Economy in Developing Nations—Hidden Engine of Innovation? and Global Challenges for Innovation in Mining Industries, both co-published with Cambridge University Press.
- Following the mainstreaming of the project on IP and Competition Policy, WIPO's work program in this area continued to focus on developing the competency to become the reference Organization on the IP and Competition Policy intersection through, *inter alia*: (i) the organization of events with IP and Competition Agencies, also in cooperation with other IGOs; (ii) active presence in the main international fora on competition policy; and (iii) by conducting analysis and research on some of the current policy areas concerning the IP/Competition interface.
- Through the project on Developing Tools for Access to Patent Information, various patent landscape reports were produced with a focus on important areas of public policy, such as health and the environment. The reports also contributed to raising awareness among developing countries, LDCs and the international community of the relevance and utility of PLRs and patent analytics. Since the mainstreaming of the project, WIPO has continued its activities in this area by publishing new patent landscape reports and has built on its experience in this area by publishing a new series of patent analytics-based publications called WIPO Technology Trends (WITT) Reports based not only on patent data, but also other scientific and technical and business

literature to show trends in different technologies, contextualizing them with case studies, insights and perspectives from leading experts and policy considerations.

- The Project on Enhancement of WIPO's RBM Framework to Support the Monitoring and Evaluation of Development Activities focused on strengthening biennial results frameworks and measurement metrics to provide a stronger basis for monitoring and evaluating WIPO's activities, including in the area of cooperation for development. Development has been mainstreamed throughout the Organization's Strategic Pillars, in line with the Development Agenda recommendations. The project also contributed to the institutionalization of an independent evaluation mechanism for all completed Development Agenda projects. Evaluation reports are submitted for discussion in the CDIP to support decision-making. An External Review of WIPO Technical Assistance in the Area of Cooperation for Development was also carried out under the project. At its thirtieth session in 2023, the Committee agreed to undertake a new Independent External Review of WIPO's Technical Assistance and approved the Terms of Reference for such Review.
- Following the mainstreaming of the project on Enhancing South-South Cooperation on IP among Developing Countries and LDCs, the Organization continued to support a number of development-oriented activities requested by Member States, in particular, those that facilitated mutually beneficial exchanges of knowledge and experience among developing countries and LDCs, and aimed at promoting innovation, creativity and the effective use of the IP system for economic, technological, social and cultural development. In addition to the mainstreaming of the abovementioned project, WIPO's 2022-2026 MTSP placed a special focus on South-South and Triangular cooperation initiatives. Work has been undertaken to revitalize the Organization's approach and expand support to such initiatives in the field of innovation and IP at the national, regional and global levels. As a first initiative, WIPO organized two expert-level Roundtables on Fostering South-South and Triangular Cooperation on IP and innovation. The First Roundtable, held on October 14, 2022, explored the matter of South-South, Triangular Cooperation and IP as: (i) a mechanism for enhancing education; (ii) a driver of competitiveness for local businesses; and (iii) a vehicle to implement the Development Agenda of WIPO. The Second Roundtable, held on May 16, 2023, built on the results of the first Roundtable and defined a number of thematic clusters for future initiatives in the field of IP and innovation.
- The project on Capacity-Building in the Use of Appropriate Technology Specific Technical and Scientific Information as a Solution for Identified Development Challenges was mainstreamed into the regular work of WIPO and transformed into the Program on Appropriate Technology. In 2022, a revised, new model "Project on Facilitating Transfer of Appropriate Technology in LDCs for Community Development through Universities and Research

Institutes" was developed. The rationale was to enable more effective delivery for a greater impact on the ground and facilitate the development and deployment of the identified appropriate technologies to the beneficiary communities in LDCs.

- Through the project on Cooperation on Development and IP Rights Education and Professional Training with Judicial Training Institutions in Developing and LDCs, the WIPO Judicial Institute, in collaboration with the WIPO Academy and other relevant WIPO areas of work, developed its range of offerings to support national and regional judiciaries in fulfilling their role in ensuring a balanced and effective IP ecosystem, including in the context of developing countries and LDCs. Specifically, the project was mainstreamed into a Continuing Judicial Education (CJE) program.
- The project on Enhancing the Use of IP for Mobile Applications in the Software Sector improved the understanding of the value of IP protection in mobile applications and empowered application developers, research hubs, and others to better protect their commercial interests. The outputs of the project, including the IP Toolbox for Mobile Application Developers and five educational modules, provide practical guidance on how to protect all or part of the IP at the various stages of the mobile application life cycle.
- The objective of the project on Tools for Successful Development Agenda Project Proposals was to develop and deliver tools that would facilitate the development and implementation of Development Agenda projects and to contribute to a better understanding of the roles of stakeholders in the project implementation and its overall lifecycle. The project delivered the following outputs: (i) a Guidebook for the preparation, implementation and evaluation of Development Agenda projects; (ii) a searchable online Catalogue on all Development Agenda projects and outputs; (iii) a DL course on Development Agenda Project Management (DL-620); and (iv) some informative videos and infographics. During its twenty-ninth session in 2022, the CDIP decided to mainstream the mentioned outputs into the regular work of WIPO and to provide customized trainings on project development and implementation to Member States and other relevant stakeholders.
- The project on Increasing the Role of Women in Innovation and Entrepreneurship, Encouraging Women in Developing Countries to Use the IP System aimed to identify the support required by women inventors and innovators to enable them to access the IP system and use the tools of the system in bringing their innovative products to market. The studies undertaken in the context of the project, such as a Literature Review on Challenges for Women Inventors and Innovators in Using the IP System and a review of existing Policy Approaches to Close the IP Gender Gap, contribute to better understanding of the problems faced by women inventors and innovators in using the IP system. The project also resulted in an easy to understand Guide to IP for Startups. Additionally, an international IP mentorship program was piloted in the

context of the project, bringing together mentors and mentees from four sectors: health, ICT, agriculture, and mechanical engineering.

- The projects on IP, Tourism and Culture; and IP and Gastronomic Tourism in Peru and other Developing Countries focused on how the IP system can create a favorable ecosystem for innovation, entrepreneurship and investment in the tourism sector. The Guide on Boosting Tourism Development through IP, co-published with the World Tourism Organization, provides good practices, features case studies and recommendations for policymakers and other tourism stakeholders on how to ensure that creativity, innovation, traditions and cultural heritage in tourism are properly protected and commercialized and that the benefits are shared by all.

[E] The Development Agenda Coordination Division

The Development Agenda Coordination Division (DACD) is responsible for coordinating the implementation of the Development Agenda recommendations within the Secretariat. The Division's activities include acting as Secretariat of the CDIP; coordinating the implementation of Development Agenda recommendations through activities and projects; ensuring the effective mainstreaming of the Development Agenda into the work of WIPO; and enhancing understanding of the Development Agenda principles by Member States and other interested parties.

Alongside its coordination role, the Division has been entrusted with overseeing various projects and activities concerning IP and development. These responsibilities include the organization of biennial International Conferences on IP and Development, as requested by the Committee. In addition, the Division was managing the development of tools that facilitate the creation, submission, and management of Development Agenda projects by Member States. Notably, as part of its ongoing efforts to mainstream the project on Tools for Successful Development Agenda Project Proposals into its work, the Division initiated customized training programs on Development Agenda project development and implementation.

[F] The Role of Civil Society

Civil society organizations in developed and developing countries across the world were extremely interested in the discussions that led to the adoption of the recommendations. They actively participated in the process, including as observers in IIMs and PCDA meetings. Their contributions to the growing body of literature on the Development Agenda and its recommendations help to enrich the debate within WIPO and beyond. They have continued to take a keen interest in the implementation of the recommendations. As mentioned above, some organizations also participate as observers in CDIP meetings. Their statements are recorded in the reports for the respective sessions.

WIPO continues to identify opportunities and enhance measures that ensure the wide participation of civil society in its activities, in accordance with recommendation

42. The Organization continues to maintain close cooperation and collaboration with its nongovernmental stakeholders, through workshops and seminars in which civil society representatives take part or lend their expertise, and by organizing side events to various committees and information sessions in which valuable exchanges with nongovernmental participants take place. The Director General meets directly with accredited NGO representatives at the WIPO-NGO Stakeholder Dialogue—an annual event that underscores the importance WIPO affords NGOs as critical partners in the Organization's efforts to build of a more inclusive global IP ecosystem that works for everyone, everywhere. WIPO will continue to pursue initiatives that encourage and facilitate active and meaningful participation of civil society in its activities.

[G] Conclusion

Significant progress has been achieved in the implementation of the Development Agenda recommendations since 2007. The recommendations have been integrated into the WIPO Program and Budget, as well as the WPR. Development has been mainstreamed across all the Organization's Strategic Pillars and its relevant sectors. By mid-2023, fifty-two projects had been approved to implement thirty-four Development Agenda recommendations. Thirty-nine projects were completed and evaluated. Development Agenda projects and activities have been carried out in seventy countries across the world. The mainstreaming of completed and evaluated Development Agenda projects into WIPO's regular activities contributes to the integration of the recommendations into the Organization's work. The agenda item on "IP and development," which is driven by topics provided and agreed by Member States, serves as a platform to prompt a dynamic dialogue on IP and development-related issues by sharing experiences on good practices and exchanging lessons learned. The sub-agenda item on "WIPO Technical Assistance in the Area of Cooperation for Development" serves as a platform for Member States to discuss issues related to WIPO's technical assistance work, including External Review of WIPO Technical Assistance in the Area of Cooperation for Development. During its sessions, the Committee also considers the progress of adopted recommendations of the Independent Review of the Implementation of the Development Agenda Recommendations, as well as considers WIPO's annual Contribution to the Implementation of the SDGs and its Associated Targets.

Decisions concerning the Development Agenda and its recommendations are made by Member States. The Secretariat has and will continue to implement the recommendations, in accordance with their collective decisions. As described in this chapter, certain questions remain and it is up to the Member States to resolve them. The course and direction of the Development Agenda are determined by Member States, and the Secretariat will continue to play a supportive role in that regard.

ANNEX

WIPO DEVELOPMENT AGENDA RECOMMENDATIONS

(Recommendations with an asterisk were identified by the 2007 General Assembly for immediate implementation)

Cluster A: Technical Assistance and Capacity Building

*1. WIPO technical assistance shall be, *inter alia*, development-oriented, demand-driven and transparent, taking into account the priorities and the special needs of developing countries, especially LDCs, as well as the different levels of development of Member States and activities should include time frames for completion. In this regard, design, delivery mechanisms and evaluation processes of technical assistance programs should be country specific.

2. Provide additional assistance to WIPO through donor funding, and establish Trust-in-Funds or other voluntary funds within WIPO specifically for LDCs, while continuing to accord high priority to finance activities in Africa through budgetary and extra-budgetary resources, to promote, *inter alia*, the legal, commercial, cultural, and economic exploitation of intellectual property in these countries.

*3. Increase human and financial allocation for technical assistance programs in WIPO for promoting a, *inter alia*, development-oriented intellectual property culture, with an emphasis on introducing intellectual property at different academic levels and on generating greater public awareness on intellectual property.

*4. Place particular emphasis on the needs of small and medium-sized enterprises (SMEs) and institutions dealing with scientific research and cultural industries and assist Member States, at their request, in setting-up appropriate national strategies in the field of intellectual property.

5. WIPO shall display general information on all technical assistance activities on its website, and shall provide, on request from Member States, details of specific activities, with the consent of the Member State(s) and other recipients concerned, for which the activity was implemented.

*6. WIPO's technical assistance staff and consultants shall continue to be neutral and accountable, by paying particular attention to the existing Code of Ethics, and by avoiding potential conflicts of interest. WIPO shall draw up and make widely known to the Member States a roster of consultants for technical assistance available with WIPO.

*7. Promote measures that will help countries deal with intellectual property-related anti-competitive practices, by providing technical cooperation to developing countries, especially LDCs, at their request, in order to better understand the interface between IPRs and competition policies.

8. Request WIPO to develop agreements with research institutions and with private enterprises with a view to facilitating the national offices of developing countries, especially LDCs, as well as their regional and sub-regional intellectual property organizations to access specialized databases for the purposes of patent searches.
9. Request WIPO to create, in coordination with Member States, a database to match specific intellectual property-related development needs with available resources, thereby expanding the scope of its technical assistance programs, aimed at bridging the digital divide.
10. To assist Member States to develop and improve national intellectual property institutional capacity through further development of infrastructure and other facilities with a view to making national intellectual property institutions more efficient and promote fair balance between intellectual property protection and the public interest. This technical assistance should also be extended to sub-regional and regional organizations dealing with intellectual property.

*11. To assist Member States to strengthen national capacity for protection of domestic creations, innovations and inventions and to support development of national scientific and technological infrastructure, where appropriate, in accordance with WIPO's mandate.

*12. To further mainstream development considerations into WIPO's substantive and technical assistance activities and debates, in accordance with its mandate.

*13. WIPO's legislative assistance shall be, *inter alia*, development-oriented and demand-driven, taking into account the priorities and the special needs of developing countries, especially LDCs, as well as the different levels of development of Member States and activities should include time frames for completion.

*14. Within the framework of the agreement between WIPO and the WTO, WIPO shall make available advice to developing countries and LDCs, on the implementation and operation of the rights and obligations and the understanding and use of flexibilities contained in the TRIPS Agreement.

Cluster B: Norm-setting, flexibilities, public policy and public domain

*15. Norm-setting activities shall:
   - be inclusive and member-driven;
   - take into account different levels of development;
   - take into consideration a balance between costs and benefits;
   - be a participatory process, which takes into consideration the interests and priorities of all WIPO Member States and the viewpoints of other stakeholders, including accredited inter-governmental organizations (IGOs) and NGOs; and
   - be in line with the principle of neutrality of the WIPO Secretariat.

*16. Consider the preservation of the public domain within WIPO's normative processes and deepen the analysis of the implications and benefits of a rich and accessible public domain.

*17. In its activities, including norm-setting, WIPO should take into account the flexibilities in international intellectual property agreements, especially those which are of interest to developing countries and LDCs.

*18. To urge the IGC to accelerate the process on the protection of genetic resources, traditional knowledge and folklore, without prejudice to any outcome, including the possible development of an international instrument or instruments.

*19. To initiate discussions on how, within WIPO's mandate, to further facilitate access to knowledge and technology for developing countries and LDCs to foster creativity and innovation and to strengthen such existing activities within WIPO.

20. To promote norm-setting activities related to IP that support a robust public domain in WIPO's Member States, including the possibility of preparing guidelines which could assist interested Member States in identifying subject matters that have fallen into the public domain within their respective jurisdictions.

*21. WIPO shall conduct informal, open and balanced consultations, as appropriate, prior to any new norm-setting activities, through a member-driven process, promoting the participation of experts from Member States, particularly developing countries and LDCs.

22. WIPO's norm-setting activities should be supportive of the development goals agreed within the United Nations system, including those contained in the Millennium Declaration. The WIPO Secretariat, without prejudice to the outcome of Member States considerations, should address in its working documents for norm-setting activities, as appropriate and as directed by Member States, issues such as: (a) safeguarding national implementation of intellectual property rules (b) links between intellectual property and competition (c) intellectual property-related transfer of technology (d) potential flexibilities, exceptions and limitations for Member States and (e) the possibility of additional special provisions for developing countries and LDCs.

23. To consider how to better promote pro-competitive intellectual property licensing practices, particularly with a view to fostering creativity, innovation and the transfer and dissemination of technology to interested countries, in particular developing countries and LDCs.

Cluster C: Technology Transfer, Information and Communication Technologies (ICT) and Access to Knowledge

24. To request WIPO, within its mandate, to expand the scope of its activities aimed at bridging the digital divide, in accordance with the outcomes of the

World Summit on the Information Society (WSIS) also taking into account the significance of the Digital Solidarity Fund (DSF).

25. To explore intellectual property-related policies and initiatives necessary to promote the transfer and dissemination of technology, to the benefit of developing countries and to take appropriate measures to enable developing countries to fully understand and benefit from different provisions, pertaining to flexibilities provided for in international agreements, as appropriate.
26. To encourage Member States, especially developed countries, to urge their research and scientific institutions to enhance cooperation and exchange with research and development institutions in developing countries, especially LDCs.
27. Facilitating intellectual property-related aspects of ICT for growth and development: Provide for, in an appropriate WIPO body, discussions focused on the importance of intellectual property-related aspects of ICT, and its role in economic and cultural development, with specific attention focused on assisting Member States to identify practical intellectual property-related strategies to use ICT for economic, social and cultural development.
28. To explore supportive intellectual property-related policies and measures Member States, especially developed countries, could adopt for promoting transfer and dissemination of technology to developing countries.
29. To include discussions on intellectual property-related technology transfer issues within the mandate of an appropriate WIPO body.
30. WIPO should cooperate with other IGOs to provide to developing countries, including LDCs, upon request, advice on how to gain access to and make use of intellectual property-related information on technology, particularly in areas of special interest to the requesting parties.
31. To undertake initiatives agreed by Member States, which contribute to transfer of technology to developing countries, such as requesting WIPO to facilitate better access to publicly available patent information.
32. To have within WIPO opportunity for exchange of national and regional experiences and information on the links between IPRs and competition policies.

Cluster D: Assessment, Evaluation and Impact Studies

33. To request WIPO to develop an effective yearly review and evaluation mechanism for the assessment of all its development-oriented activities, including those related to technical assistance, establishing for that purpose specific indicators and benchmarks, where appropriate.
34. With a view to assisting Member States in creating substantial national programs, to request WIPO to conduct a study on constraints to intellectual

property protection in the informal economy, including the tangible cost-sand benefits of intellectual property protection in particular in relation to generation of employment.

*35. To request WIPO to undertake, upon request of Member States, new studies to assess the economic, social and cultural impact of the use of intellectual property systems in these States.

36. To exchange experiences on open collaborative projects such as the Human Genome Project as well as on intellectual property models.

*37. Upon request and as directed by Member States, WIPO may conduct studies on the protection of intellectual property, to identify the possible links and impacts between intellectual property and development.

38. To strengthen WIPO's capacity to perform objective assessments of the impact of the organization's activities on development.

Cluster E: Institutional Matters including Mandate and Governance

39. To request WIPO, within its core competence and mission, to assist developing countries, especially African countries, in cooperation with relevant international organizations, by conducting studies on brain drain and make recommendations accordingly.

40. To request WIPO to intensify its cooperation on IP related issues with United Nations agencies, according to Member States' orientation, in particular UNCTAD, UNEP, WHO, UNIDO, UNESCO and other relevant international organizations, especially the WTO in order to strengthen the coordination for maximum efficiency in undertaking development programs.

41. To conduct a review of current WIPO technical assistance activities in the area of cooperation and development.

*42. To enhance measures that ensure wide participation of civil society at large in WIPO activities in accordance with its criteria regarding NGO acceptance and accreditation, keeping the issue under review.

43. To consider how to improve WIPO's role in finding partners to fund and execute projects for intellectual property-related assistance in a transparent and member-driven process and without prejudice to ongoing WIPO activities.

*44. In accordance with WIPO's member-driven nature as a United Nations Specialized Agency, formal and informal meetings or consultations relating to norm-setting activities in WIPO, organized by the Secretariat, upon request of the Member States, should be held primarily in Geneva, in a manner open and transparent to all Members. Where such meetings are to take place outside of Geneva, Member States shall be informed through official channels, well in advance, and consulted on the draft agenda and program.

Cluster F: Other Issues

45. To approach intellectual property enforcement in the context of broader societal interests and especially development-oriented concerns, with a view that "the protection and enforcement of intellectual property rights should contribute to the promotion of technological innovation and to the transfer and dissemination of technology, to the mutual advantage of producers and users of technological knowledge and in a manner conducive to social and economic welfare, and to a balance of rights and obligations," in accordance with Article 7 of the TRIPS Agreement.

CHAPTER 35
The WIPO Intergovernmental Committee on Intellectual Property and Genetic Resources, Traditional Knowledge and Folklore

§35.01 INTRODUCTION

Established in 2000, the WIPO IGC serves as a forum where WIPO Member States can discuss the IP issues that arise in the context of access to GRs and benefit-sharing and the protection of TK and TCEs.

Although the discussions were initially called for and propelled mainly by developing countries, they are not neatly divided along North-South lines. Communities and governments do not necessarily share the same views, and some developed countries, especially those where Indigenous Peoples live, are also active.

In 2010, the IGC began formal negotiations with the objective of reaching agreement on one or more international legal instruments for the effective protection of TCEs and TK, and to address the IP aspects of access and benefit-sharing in GRs. Such an instrument or instruments could range from a recommendation to WIPO members to a formal treaty that would bind countries choosing to ratify it.

In July 2022, the WIPO General Assembly decided to convene a high-level conference to conclude an international legal instrument relating to intellectual property, GRs and TK associated with GRs, to be held no later than 2024. Formally, such a conference is referred to as a "Diplomatic Conference" and it took place from May 13 to 24, 2024. WIPO Member States adopted, by consensus, a historic new WIPO Treaty on Intellectual Property, Genetic Resources and Associated Traditional Knowledge. This is the first WIPO Treaty to address the interface between IP, GRs and associated TK and the first WIPO Treaty to include provisions specifically for Indigenous Peoples as well as local communities (*see* further below).

The IGC's work on one or more international legal instruments on TK more broadly and TCEs will continue in 2024 and 2025.

This chapter describes the origins and rationale of the IGC, the participation of members and observers, its achievements to date, the new Treaty and the state of the negotiations on TK more broadly and TCEs.

§35.02 ORIGINS AND RATIONALE OF THE IGC

Work within the IP community on the protection of TCEs (also known as "expressions of folklore") goes back to the 1960s. The impetus came from a growing sense in developing countries that folklore embodies creativity and is part of the cultural identity of Indigenous Peoples, and also local communities; it is seen as worthy of IP protection, especially since new technologies are making folklore increasingly vulnerable to exploitation and misuse.

However, at first achievements proved rather limited. The 1967 revision of the copyright regime under the Berne Convention for the Protection of Literary and Artistic Works fell short of ensuring adequate protection. The Member States of WIPO and UNESCO nevertheless kept up the momentum, with the development in 1982 of a set of Model Provisions for national laws to serve as a source of inspiration for countries. In 1996, the WPPT succeeded in providing for the protection of the rights of performers of expressions of folklore. The 2012 BTAP extends this protection to audiovisual performers of expressions of folklore.

Work on the relationship between IP, TK and GRs is more recent, and stems from concerns regarding the role that IP protection should play in achieving global policy objectives as varied as the conservation of biodiversity (as enshrined in the CBD, 1992), food security, Indigenous Peoples' rights, free and fair trade, and sustainable development. These linkages have significant implications for the IP system.

In particular, the spread of biotechnology highlighted the potential economic value of GRs and associated TK, which became an important component of patentable inventions. As a result, many began to argue that the patent regime should help to prevent misappropriation and promote fair benefit-sharing between holders of those assets and those with the modern technologies to access and use them. IP issues regarding access to GRs and associated TK came onto the agenda of the WIPO Standing Committee on Patents in the late 1990s, and were raised in the preparatory work leading up to the WIPO Diplomatic Conference for the adoption of a new PLT in 2000.

In parallel, under a new program established in 1998, the WIPO secretariat conducted fact-finding missions and consultations on GRs, TCEs and TK, to ascertain the needs and expectations of Indigenous Peoples as well as local communities as well as representatives of government, industry and civil society around the world. These activities were undertaken by a new WIPO division, the Global Issues Division—which in 2009 was renamed as the Traditional Knowledge Division.

Before and after the 2000 Diplomatic Conference for the adoption of the PLT, the Director General of WIPO held consultations on the question of GRs and associated TK. These led to a proposal that a distinct body be established within WIPO to facilitate discussions. It was also proposed that the discussions should include the results of WIPO's work in the field of TCEs. That same year, this body was established as the IGC.

At roughly the same time, Indigenous Peoples' rights and issues began to command greater attention internationally. In 2000, the UN Permanent Forum on Indigenous Issues was established as an advisory body to the UN Economic and Social Council. Seven years later, the UN Declaration on the Rights of Indigenous Peoples (2007) was adopted by the UN General Assembly. Long-standing claims by Indigenous Peoples for control over their cultural property and IP became more pressing.

In sum, the origins of the IGC and its rationales are varied. First, it was established to address three new themes that shared certain distinct features: GRs, TK and TCEs were becoming regarded less as the "common heritage of humanity" and more as intellectual valuables requiring appropriate forms of IP protection. Second, GRs, TK and TCEs were seen as the intellectual assets of new key players in IP policymaking: developing countries and Indigenous Peoples, as well as local communities. Third, the IGC was conceived as part of a larger and structured endeavor by WIPO to move toward a modern, responsive IP system that could embrace new forms of creativity and innovation, be comprehensive in terms of beneficiaries, and be consistent with developmental and environmental goals.

§35.03 PARTICIPATION IN THE IGC

Each session of the IGC usually lasts for five working days and takes place at WIPO headquarters in Geneva. Participants comprise IGC members (WIPO Member States) and a wide array of observers.

The IGC's intergovernmental character and mandate give it the authority to initiate norm-setting discussions and to propose international rules for adoption by a Diplomatic Conference or other WIPO body as appropriate.

Although representatives from the IPOs of WIPO Member States constitute a substantial part of governmental delegations, the cross-cutting nature of the issues encourages a diverse spectrum of participation, calling for experts specialized in issues related to the environment, agriculture, trade, foreign affairs, food, health and culture, to mention only a few.

Observers include IGOs (notably the secretariats of the CBD, the WTO, UNESCO and the UN FAO) and numerous accredited NGOs.

Indigenous Peoples as well as local communities need to be able to participate, express their views and have their voices heard in the IGC decision-making process, in accordance with the 2007 UN Declaration on the Rights of Indigenous Peoples, as outcomes are likely to affect their rights.

In 2001, a fast-track accreditation procedure was put in place to register observers to the IGC, many of whom represent Indigenous Peoples and local communities. The IGC decided in 2004 that its sessions be preceded by panel presentations chaired and composed of representatives of Indigenous Peoples and local communities, whose participation is funded by WIPO. Among other practical measures to enhance participation, one of the most important was the creation in 2005 of the WIPO Voluntary Fund for accredited Indigenous Peoples and local communities, designed to finance their participation.

Funding is also available for representatives of developing countries and certain countries in Europe and Asia, in order to facilitate their participation.

The IGC elects its chair and vice-chairs every two years. The WIPO secretariat plays a facilitating role and provides administrative support, from preparing documentation to providing briefings, organizing consultations, producing studies on specific subjects, and generally assisting the chair in the performance of his or her functions. Working documents and interpretation of the proceedings are available in the six official UN languages.

§35.04 ACHIEVEMENTS TO DATE

The IGC process has stimulated increased recognition of TK within the patent system. In 2002, certain TK journals were included in the minimum documentation for applications under WIPO's PCT, and TK classification tools were integrated within the IPC in 2003. In 2002, the IGC accepted technical standards for the documentation of TK.

In order to provide guidance on the IP aspects of mutually agreed terms for fair and equitable benefit-sharing related to GRs, WIPO maintains an online database of contractual practices. It has also published a guide on IP clauses in access and benefit-sharing agreements.

The Traditional Knowledge Division has also carried out numerous studies and developed other resources (such as glossaries, surveys of national experiences, a laws database and training programs—for details, *see* Chapter 12). They are the result of a wide exchange of data and views between Member States based on questionnaires and surveys of national experiences and practices, from existing sui generis national or regional protection systems for TK and TCEs to IP-related clauses in contracts framing the access and use of GRs.

These resources illustrate the rich and living cultural traditions that are the subject of the IGC's negotiations and help better identify the policy and legal options available.

Since its first session in 2001, the IGC's achievements also include certain "intangibles" such as:

- the IGC has established new benchmarks for inclusion and consultation;
- age-old IP terms, such as "protection," "originality," "novelty" and the "public domain," are being re-thought;
- the IGC is considering innovative and sui generis approaches to protection of TK and TCEs;
- through coordinating closely with other relevant forums, its work has re-energized WIPO's engagement with the rest of the UN system and other intergovernmental bodies.

Above all, the consensual adoption of the historic new WIPO Treaty on Intellectual Property, Genetic Resources and Associated Traditional Knowledge on May 24, 2024, is a major outcome of the IGC's negotiations.

§35.05 PROGRESS IN ONGOING NEGOTIATIONS

By providing a specialized forum for the structured exchange of information and views within WIPO, the IGC process is trying to build a robust international understanding of the issues. The exploratory "forum" evolved as from 2010 into a true multilateral negotiating body, framed by a mandate and clear work program negotiated and agreed every two years.

[A] GRs and Associated TK

The new WIPO Treaty on Intellectual Property, Genetic Resources and Associated Traditional Knowledge, 2024 is the first WIPO Treaty to address the interface between IP, GRs and associated TK and the first WIPO Treaty to include provisions specifically for Indigenous Peoples as well as local communities.

The Treaty aims to enhance the efficacy, transparency and quality of the patent system with regard to GRs and associated TK, and prevent patents from being granted erroneously for inventions that are not novel or inventive with regard to GRs and associated TK.

The Treaty will come into force three months after there have been fifteen ratifications and accessions.

The new WIPO Treaty establishes a mandatory patent disclosure requirement—this requires patent applicants to disclose the country of origin of the GRs and/or the Indigenous Peoples or local community providing the associated TK, if the claimed inventions are based on GRs and/or associated TK. If such information is unknown, the source of the GRs or associated TK should be disclosed. If none of the above information is known, the patent applicant would be required to declare so. Patent offices should provide certain guidance, though they would have no obligation to verify the authenticity of the disclosure. A failure to disclose the required information would be subject to appropriate, effective, and proportionate measures. Patent applicants would have the opportunity to rectify a failure to disclose the required information unless there has been fraudulent conduct or intent. Where there has been fraudulent intent in regard to the disclosure requirement, post-grant sanctions or remedies may be provided for. Fraud aside, no party to the Treaty should revoke, invalidate, or render unenforceable a patent solely on the basis of an applicant's failure to disclose the required information. The Treaty has no retroactivity, i.e., shall not impose the obligations in relation to patent applications filed prior to the entry into force of the Treaty.

The Treaty allows the establishment of information systems (such as databases) of GRs and associated TK, in consultation, where applicable, with Indigenous Peoples and local communities, and other stakeholders, taking into account their national circumstances. The information systems should be made accessible to patent offices for the search and examination of patent applications, with appropriate safeguards developed in consultation, where applicable, with Indigenous Peoples and local communities, and other stakeholders. One or more technical working groups may be established to address any relevant matters, such as accessibility to patent offices.

A new disclosure option related to TK, TCEs and GRs in applications for industrial design rights has also been adopted as part of the new Riyadh Design Law Treaty, which was discussed and approved in a diplomatic conference held in Riyadh, in November of 2024, as seen above (*see* §9.05).

[B] TK and TCEs

The draft negotiating texts on TK and TCEs owe their origins to "objectives and principles" first published by the WIPO secretariat in 2005. The current drafts reflect the many views and comments of Member States and observers who have participated in the IGC since then, including in Intersessional Working Groups in 2010 and 2011. "Gap Analyses" prepared in 2008 have also contributed to clarifying the issues and options.

An international legal instrument/s would define what is meant by TK and TCEs, who the rights holders would be, how competing claims by communities would be resolved, and what rights and exceptions ought to apply. Working out the details is complex, and there are divergent views, including as to whether IP-type rights are appropriate for protecting traditional forms of innovation and creativity.

The negotiations on TK and TCEs will continue in 2024 and 2025 under the IGC's mandate for that period. WIPO Member States may in due course decide to convene a diplomatic conference for final adoption of one or more international instruments on these subjects.

CHAPTER 36

The Proposed Treaty for the Protection of Broadcasting Organizations

§36.01 INTRODUCTION

Broadcasting organizations had their rights recognized for the first time in an international instrument by the Rome Convention of 1961. Later on, the Satellites (Brussels) Treaty also dealt with the international protection of broadcasting organizations. However, international protection, especially against the unauthorized commercial use of the broadcast signal, has not been updated since. In the meantime, telecommunications have become one of the most advanced fields of technology. The Internet did not exist when the treaties were adopted, and cable technologies were incipient and very limited. With advances in technology, it has become possible for third parties to intercept signals and transmit them via cable or satellite. Perfect copies of the broadcast can be made and distributed via other networks or intercepted and transmitted online without the agreement of the rights holder.

Signal theft is a significant commercial issue for broadcasting organizations around the world. Signal piracy can take physical form, such as unauthorized recordings of broadcasts on video tapes, DVDs or USB drives, or it can be in immaterial form, such as the unauthorized retransmission of signals over the air or online, including the making available of broadcast signals on platforms to the public so that members of the public may access them from a place and at a time chosen by them. Hacking into encrypted pay-TV signals with equipment designed to circumvent the security measures in set-top boxes is another common form of piracy, while live sports broadcasts have been a particular target for unauthorized retransmission on the Internet. Also the interception and further use of pre-broadcast signals represent a major challenge for broadcasting organizations. Broadcasters, including those in developing countries, claim signal piracy of all kinds is costing them millions of dollars in lost pay-TV subscriptions and advertising revenues, affecting investment decisions and competitiveness.

§36.02 PROGRESS OF NEGOTIATIONS

When the Internet Treaties were adopted, the WPPT updated many aspects of the Rome Convention to adapt the rights of performers and producers of phonograms (sound recordings) to the digital era. After WIPO members left the topic of broadcasting for future consideration when they adopted the WPPT, broadcasters have continued to press for updated protection to reflect the new broadcasting technologies.

The process was initiated at the WIPO Worldwide Symposium on Broadcasters' Rights which was held in Manila in 1997. Since the SCCR held its first session in 1998, the updating of the international protection of broadcasting organizations has been discussed at length in the SCCR, and many drafts of the treaty have been prepared. The issue at stake is to update the protection of broadcasting organizations, which are holders of related rights, in response to digital and other new technologies and the growing use of the Internet. The proposed treaty would address important developments in technology and the marketplace that have taken place in the broadcasting sector since the adoption of the Rome Convention in 1961.

At the 2006 WIPO General Assembly, WIPO Member States decided that two special sessions of the SCCR would be convened to clarify the outstanding issues. Those sessions aimed at agreeing and finalizing, on a signal-based approach, the objectives, specific scope and object of protection with a view to submitting a revised basic proposal to a diplomatic conference. The two special sessions took place in Geneva from January 17 to 19 and from June 18 to 22, 2007. The second special session showed a lack of consensus on some key issues.

In 2007, WIPO's General Assembly agreed once again to pursue a "signal-based approach" to drafting a new treaty, to ensure that provisions on signal theft in themselves did not give broadcasters additional rights over program content. But this still left many of the underlying differences of viewpoint in place.

The object of protection under the proposed Treaty is the broadcast signal. Under the Rome Convention, broadcasters have exclusive rights for twenty years to authorize the rebroadcasting, fixation, reproduction and communication to the public of their television broadcasts under certain circumstances. Most broadcasters want the proposed treaty to extend and update these rights in light of new technologies, especially to prevent the unauthorized retransmission of their programs over the internet. It is interesting to note that several countries have these provisions in their national laws, including the EU Member States and India, but due to the territorial nature of copyright and related rights, the provisions do not protect against foreign unauthorized commercial use of works beyond national borders.

Although in general there is broad agreement in principle that broadcasters should have updated international protection from theft of their signals, as of 2024 Members of the SCCR have so far failed to agree on how this should be done and what further rights, if any, broadcasters should be given.

§36.03 OUTSTANDING ISSUES

The outstanding issues include:

- What should be protected? Broadcasters obviously want protection for all means of transmission of their signals ("technology neutral" protection) that would cover newer technologies such as digital program recording devices, on-demand video services and IPTV ("Internet protocol TV" or Internet TV), which can transmit programs not only to televisions but to computers and mobile phones. However, some countries and civil society groups are wary of restrictions affecting Internet transmissions, and some rights holders are concerned about possible interference with their ability to control their content. In 2006, WIPO members agreed to put aside, for discussion on a different and later track, the issue of webcasting (broadcasting over the Internet or video content intended for Internet streaming). The scope of a possible retransmission right over computer networks where it is not simultaneous to a wireless broadcast by the same organization is still open. Likewise, an outstanding issue is whether or to what extent pre-broadcast signals and program-carrying signals embedded in stored programs, such as those to which broadcasters offer access as a service to subscribers (whether giving pre-transmission access or catch-up services), should be protected against certain uses.
- How should broadcast signals be protected? Broadcasters and some Member States want the proposed treaty to contain provisions similar to those in the WIPO Internet Treaties that would outlaw the breaking of anti-piracy "locks" on digital signals, such as encryption and "tagging." As under the WIPO Internet Treaties, these rules would not apply to legal uses of broadcasts, such as recording programs for personal or certain educational uses.
- What further rights should be given to broadcasters? Under the Rome Convention, broadcasters have exclusive rights for twenty years to authorize rebroadcasting, "fixation" (recording), reproduction and communication to the public of their broadcasts under certain circumstances. Most broadcasters want the new treaty to extend and update those rights for the new technologies, especially to prevent unauthorized retransmission of their programs over the Internet. Although some countries have relevant domestic legislation, this does not provide protection from foreign piracy. In much of the world, it is not illegal to retransmit a broadcast over the Internet without permission.
- What limitations and exceptions should there be? The Rome Convention allows the use of transmissions without permission in news broadcasts, for education and scientific research and in other cases, including those provided in national copyright law for authors' works. WIPO Members agree that the proposed treaty should permit some "limitations and exceptions" to the need to seek authorization for the use of broadcasts, similar to those relating to copyright protection in a number of countries (such as personal use, use for parody and certain library uses). But they differ on whether the treaty should

set a general test for individual countries to decide on limitations or exceptions, or whether it should specify certain uses binding on all signatories.
- How long should protection last? Some countries want protection to last for fifty years, the term already granted to performers and producers of sound recordings (and broadcasters in the EU). Others have argued for no more than a twenty-year term (as in the Rome Convention and the WTO's TRIPS Agreement). However, concerns that any rebroadcast would trigger a new term of protection, leading to perpetual protection, appear to be unfounded, since rights on the first broadcast would expire at the end of the term, regardless of any rebroadcast. Another option discussed is not to provide for any particular minimum duration, given that the focus of protection is the signal, which exists for such a short period of time.
- How should protection be implemented? Given different national traditions to protect broadcasters, some countries wish to implement protection in some other way, such as through one or more rights to authorize. Other countries have expressed concern about how national treatment would work for them if protection is implemented in a variety of ways.

Treaty opponents argue that broadcasters do not need strong near-copyright protection for their broadcasts in addition to protection from signal theft. They point out that half WIPO's membership have not joined the Rome Convention. Giving broadcasters a range of exclusive rights would, say the critics, hinder access to copyright-protected material by requiring permission to use it not only from the copyright owner (such as the producer of a TV show or documentary) but also from the broadcaster. This could also diminish the rights of copyright owners by giving broadcasters the power to determine the conditions (and exact a licensing fee) under which a work could be used. By the same token, there are concerns that giving broadcasters exclusive rights over their broadcasts could "privatize" material in the public domain, such as films that are out of copyright or sporting or news events that are not subject to copyright in some jurisdictions (because they are not treated as original, creative works in a particular jurisdiction).

Supporters of giving broadcasters extended international rights say the situation regarding underlying content would not change, because it would always be open to others to broadcast or transmit their own (authorized) versions of the same content. For example, while the broadcast of a concert featuring Beethoven's Fifth Symphony would be protected, the symphony itself would remain in the public domain for others to play, record or broadcast. However, broadcasters argue that they need to protect the broadcast itself, which can involve significant investment in infrastructure as well as the purchase of broadcasting rights.

A related but distinct issue concerns the purchase of exclusive rights to broadcast sporting and other events, which is outside the scope of the proposed treaty but affects how its provisions might work in practice. This is because rights over the broadcast in this case may also restrict access to the underlying content if no other source is available. In a number of countries, including the EU, India and Australia, certain events (e.g., the Football Association Cup Final and the Wimbledon Tennis Final in the

UK) are deemed of sufficient national importance to guarantee coverage by free-to-air broadcasters.

In 2024, according to the Chair's Summary of SCCR/45 and multiple earlier summaries, it is commonly understood that the planned treaty should be limited to signal piracy, not provide protection for post-fixation activities, and enable Member States to implement protection through different, though adequate and effective means. Furthermore, it is understood that the signals protected should be linked to linear transmissions. Some of the main remaining issues include the protection for transmissions over computer networks, such as the Internet; whether and to what extent pre-broadcast signals and signals in stored programs should be covered, and the approach to limitations and exceptions.

CHAPTER 37

Intellectual Property, New Technologies, and New Human Endeavors

§37.01 INTRODUCTION

It is generally understood that IP is technologically neutral, in the sense that its principles and rules do not change regardless of the specific nature of its subject matter. However, even if, in the field of patents, international law speaks in that exact direction, reality is different. Even the TRIPS Agreement has not been able to keep entire coherence with Article 27.1, which prohibits discriminatory treatment against inventions in accordance with their technical field. Indeed, a few of its provisions give explicitly differentiated treatment to certain technologies, in particular pharmaceutical and agrochemical inventions. On the one hand, the so-called mailbox system (Article 70.8) accorded higher protection to inventions on those two technical fields. But, on the other hand, the amendment and waivers added to the Agreement, after its entry into force (namely, Article 31*bis* and the waiver approved by the WTO Ministerial Conference in June 2022, for the purpose of permitting the production and supply of COVID-19 vaccines "to the extent necessary to address the COVID-19 pandemic") reduce the protection of IP in relation to pharmaceutical inventions.

This means that IP, including in the area of patents, is not subject-matter neutral.

Another element that should be added to this discussion is that, even if we could admit the technological neutrality of IP rules, we could not deny the reality of the *use* that IP holders give to their assets. And, to this extent, experience shows that entrepreneurs in various areas of business have used IP in different ways, responding to different pressures either from market forces or from the impact of regulation. This is not the place to examine those matters, but it is undeniable that entrepreneurs in the fashion field, for example, seek to acquire a sort of holistic protection for their intangible differentiating assets that dramatically diverges from the protection that in general designers obtain for their creations. In the same token, indigenous and traditional communities are looking for some sort of legal IP regime that responds to the specific characteristics of their intangible assets, which may be based on inventiveness and creativity, but are also firmly anchored on culture, tradition, and identity.,

Bearing this important aspect in mind, let us have now a brief look at how IP has developed and protects intangible assets created in a few new technical fields and human activities, such as computer programs, biotechnology, space exploration, and AI.

§37.02 APPLICATION OF COPYRIGHT PROTECTION TO EVOLVING DIGITAL TECHNOLOGIES

[A] Computer Software

[1] Introduction

Computers—electronic devices capable of storing and/or processing or transmitting data and works—have become indispensable tools in daily life, especially in connection with Internet uses.

The term "computer software" is generally understood to mean computer programs and other material prepared in connection with the use of computers, such as program descriptions and explanatory material concerning the application of computer programs, for example, problem descriptions and user instructions. In the preparation of a computer program, there are several stages. First, the program is written by its creator (the "programmer," or the team of programmers) in a programming language, i.e., in an artificial language consisting of specific symbols and established for expressing computer programs. This form of computer program is usually called "source code"; it cannot, however, be used by the machine as such, but must be transformed into a set of instructions that can be recognized by the central processing unit of the computer. Those instructions usually consist of only two different elements, symbolized by "0" and "1," which have the effect that the flow of electric current is either barred or permitted. In this machine-readable form of the program, which is usually called "object code," the instructions consist of extremely long combinations of these two digits.

Before a computer program can actually be written by the programmer, the task of the computer (e.g., calculating income tax according to a series of legal rules and exceptions) must be defined, and the logical steps that are to form the basis of the program (the "algorithm") must be formulated. The definition of the task and the algorithm, however, are not considered to be part of the computer program.

[2] Protection of Computer Programs

As regards protection of computer programs by copyright, the first question to be considered was whether computer programs were protectable "works" in the sense of copyright laws implementing the Berne Convention. There may have been doubts as to this, since copyright laws usually contain lists enumerating categories of protected works and such lists normally did not mention computer programs (although many lists were not closed). However, after many years of discussion, global common understanding emerged, according to which computer programs, which are written in a particular computer language, are to be considered a form of literary works in the meaning of the Berne Convention, even if such language may not be understandable to those who are not programmers. This understanding was set out not only in the TRIPS Agreement but also in the WCT. At the same time, it was clarified that mathematical concepts or underlying ideas as such continued to be ineligible for copyright protection.

The second question which had arisen in connection with copyright protection of computer programs concerned the acts against which protection was needed. Once the decision had been taken at international and national level to protect computer programs as literary works, the consequence was that all rights granted to literary works should also apply to computer programs. Detailed and different rules apply at the national level regarding limitations and exceptions, such as for the making of a back-up copy or decompilation of the program in certain cases. It is worth mentioning that, in addition to copyright, protection may be available under patent law (if the program forms an integral part of a process), rules against the violation of trade secrets (also under the relevant conditions) and pursuant to contractual terms, which may provide for protection of computer programs to a limited extent.

[B] Private Copying and Other Reproduction

[1] Reprography and Copyright

Reprography is the generic term used to describe all the kinds of photocopying or similar reproduction on equipment which enables facsimile copies of graphic documents (text, images) of every kind indistinguishable from the original to be made instantly and cheaply on apparatus which is simple to operate and readily available to the public. For example, copying machines, printers, hard drives of computers, USB sticks, smartphones or any other storage media allowing easy reprographic reproduction. Today, in almost all countries, no office, school or library is without such equipment, and nearly everyone has a smartphone or similar device. A very large number of copies of literary, dramatic, musical, and artistic material are churned out through the use of reprographic equipment around the world.

Article 9 of the Berne Convention (Paris Act 1971) stipulates that "authors of literary and artistic works protected by this Convention shall have the exclusive right of authorizing the reproduction of these works, in any manner or form," and all contemporary copyright laws contain provisions implementing this principle. Paragraph (2) of Article 9, however, empowers national copyright laws to permit the reproduction of works in certain special cases, subject to two further conditions:

(1) the permitted reproduction must not conflict with the normal exploitation of the work; and

(2) the reproduction must not unreasonably prejudice the legitimate interests of the author.

Reprography on the scale which exists today has been considered to conflict with the normal exploitation of those works which are copied in such large numbers; and such a volume of copying may unreasonably prejudice the legitimate interests of the author, as well as the publisher.

A variety of solutions to the problem have been adopted in different countries.

In the 1970s, in some Scandinavian countries, a voluntary blanket licensing scheme, initially in respect of national works only, was instituted to cover photocopying in educational establishments. Subsequently, in the 1980s, in some of these countries the copyright law was amended so as to give statutory backing to this blanket licensing approach, and under the statutory provisions the ambit of the blanket license was extended to all copyright works, including foreign works, with a provision for arbitration to deal with disputes arising between the organization administering the blanket licenses and the educational establishments covered by them.

In the (former) Federal Republic of Germany a more advanced and comprehensive system was instituted by amendments to the principal Copyright Act in 1985. These amendments introduced a dual system—of limitations to the exclusive reproduction right combined with statutory rights to remuneration for private and other copying. The statutory remuneration has to be paid by the manufacturers and importers of photocopying and other reprographic equipment, as well as by operators of such equipment, such as copy shops, educational establishments, public libraries or other institutions which make the equipment available to the public on payment of a charge. The remuneration is to be collected and distributed by CMOs. The amount of the payment depends among other factors on the speed of operation of the equipment.

While many countries with such a solution and their CMOs have updated their systems so as to cover also reproduction by digital technologies, such as by computers, external storage discs, USB sticks etc., an outstanding problem to be solved in most countries is the massive copying occurring in the cloud (on servers), which is more and more replacing analog and other traditional ways of copying but has not yet been covered by a remuneration right.

[2] Audio and Audiovisual Recording

Technological advances have made possible the high-quality copying of sound and audiovisual recordings. The copyright implications of this activity are the same as in the case of the copying of literary and other material by reprographic equipment—i.e., it is a potential infringement of the fundamental right protected by Article 9 of the Berne Convention and by the provisions in national laws which implement that Convention requirement.

Home recording has also been the subject of very considerable study at national and international levels; a growing number of countries have enacted or are considering legislation to deal with the matter.

Just as in the case of reprography, the various national solutions adopted are not identical, but they are all based on more or less the same approach which may be summarized as follows:

(1) the basic idea underlining the approach is that in respect of each unit of recording equipment or storage device, such as blank tape, USB stick, smartphone, hard drive of a computer, etc., of a kind likely to be used for home recording, and which is released to the public, an exception to the exclusive reproduction right should be granted, and should be combined with a statutory right to collect remuneration; however, as for reprography, copies in the cloud are mostly not yet covered, although copying there takes place to quite an extent;
(2) the rationale of this approach is that although it is not possible to identify each individual home user, nevertheless it is possible to identify the users as a class because they are those persons who buy the equipment and the blank tapes by means of which home recordings are made; and it is not unreasonable, therefore, that as a class they should make a payment for the right to make home recordings—the payment taking the form of an element in the purchase price of the equipment and blank tape bought for the purpose;
(3) also, as it is the manufacturers and importers of the equipment and blank tapes who, by making those items available to the public, make it possible for the public to use authors' works in this way, it is reasonable to require those manufacturers and importers to collect the statutory remuneration and account for it to the authors and other right owners;
(4) under these schemes the statutory remuneration made—which in some countries is charged on the equipment only, in some on the blank tape only, and in some on both—is paid by the manufacturers and importers to CMOs representing the various categories of right holders entitled to share in the statutory remuneration; and those CMOs are responsible for distributing the amounts so received.

The differences between the various national schemes relate principally to the following matters:

(1) the extent to which the total amount of statutory remuneration is distributed to individual right owners, or is applied to social purposes. In some countries virtually 100% is distributed on an individual basis, whereas in other countries a proportion, which in some cases may be 50%, is applied to general social purposes—e.g., the granting of scholarships to authors and composers;
(2) the extent to which the copyright owners of non-national works (which are protected under the copyright law of the country pursuant to national

treatment) are entitled to participate in the distribution of the statutory remuneration; in some countries all national works from other countries belonging to the same Convention to which the country in question belongs are entitled to participate; in other countries only national authors and other right owners participate.

Since most recently, streaming has become more popular than downloading (copying) audio and audiovisual works on devices, attention has been shifting to rights implicated by streaming.

[C] Broadcasting and Cable Communications Technologies

[1] Introduction

Communication technologies started with the radio and later was followed by television broadcasting through wireless means, first by Hertzian waves, and later also by satellite. After this, cable transmission and retransmission were developed, including simulcasting via the internet and web radio.

[2] Satellites

Satellite broadcasting occurs either via point-to-point satellites for intercontinental communication between one emitting point and one or more receiving points and distribution satellites (for smaller geographical areas) or direct broadcast satellites for direct reception by the general public.

While under the Berne Convention, Article 11*bis*(1) covers direct satellite broadcasting, there has been discussion on which act is to be considered as an act of broadcasting: merely the transmission of signals toward the satellite, or both the upward leg (during which the signals are transported from the place of transmission to the satellite) and the downward leg (during which the signals travel from the satellite toward what is known as the satellite's "footprint," that is to say the area in which the work may normally be received, in particular by individual satellite dishes). Today, there is a broad common understanding in favor of interpreting broadcasting not only as transmission, but also as communication to the public, which would seem in line with Article 11*bis*(1).

Then the question arises as to where the act of broadcasting takes place and thus who is entitled to authorize that broadcast, for example if the person concerned is not the same in the country of the place of transmission and in the country or countries in which the signals may be received. Following Article 5(2) of the Berne Convention, in the case of direct satellite broadcasting, the provisions of at least two legislations have to be complied with, that is to say the legislation of the country of transmission and that of the countries in which signals may normally be received. What happens if the owner of the right of broadcasting is not the same in each of the countries?

Views diverge as regards the applicable legislation and the exercise of rights by the various rights holders in the country of transmission and the countries of reception. The so-called Bosch theory, following the view of the former DG of WIPO, suggested applying the laws of all countries where the broadcast was received by the public (in the footprint). Other variations of this theory exist. The EC Directive 1993 on satellite broadcasting and cable retransmission, instead of regulating the applicable law, adopted a different concept, namely a legal fiction according to which the act of satellite broadcasting is deemed to occur only in the transmitting (uplink) country (subject to more detailed conditions, also for cases when the transmitter is not situated in an EU Member State), but stipulated that the remuneration for this act must take into account among others the actual and potential audience in all receiving countries. The Directive excludes nonvoluntary licenses in the case of satellite broadcasting. Thus, by establishing an exclusive right in all of the Community (EU) Member States, the problem of differences between the law of the country of transmission and that of the country of reception would no longer arise within the EU; it is thus a specific solution suited for closely connected countries with an equivalent level of protection. Other intermediate solutions, where the situation in the country of the footprint (or reception) at least has to be taken into account, for example through collective administration, were also discussed.

In the case of "direct injection," the broadcaster does not itself broadcast to the public, but directly transmits the signal to a signal transmitter, who then transmits the signals to the public. This is in some countries nowadays a widely used method of broadcasting, while in others it is limited to specific cases, such as pay-tv services. The question arises of which of those two companies makes a broadcast. Technically speaking the first broadcaster does not do so, since he/she or she does not directly transmit signals to the public, but to a signal distributor. However, there is a tendency to look at the act as one common act done by both. This solution was notably chosen by the EU in its Directive on Online Satellite Broadcasting and Cable Retransmission of 2019. In many countries, this situation seems to be solved by contracts.

[3] Cable Retransmission

Simultaneously with the development of the use of satellites for broadcasting, the cable retransmission of broadcast programs evolved. It started with small, so-called community antenna. Then it developed into cable retransmission to the public of large numbers of satellite broadcasts, including those from other countries which were received by ground stations by satellite.

Cable retransmission is covered by Article 11*bis*(1)(ii) of the Berne Convention as communication by wire of the broadcast "when this communication is made by an organization other than the original one." Although the Convention does not define the term "wire," it is generally accepted that the word means "cable," which may also include optical fibers and the Internet.

[D] Making Digital Works Available

The making available and transmission of musical, audiovisual, or any other kind of works in digital form to members of the public who can access them at a time and from a place individually chosen by them has become a very widespread method of using works through digital technology. The impact of this type of use of works on copyright and related rights is huge. It has caused a major change in the distribution chains with new business models to accommodate the changes. It has led to a radical transformation of the financial flows since retailers trading in tangible media no longer represent the main source of revenue for producers or, upstream, for authors and performers.

Different platforms offer an enormous amount of works, performances, recordings, etc. via the Internet and other networks, to the public, either for download (reproduction on a device of the user) or via streaming. The user has at his or her disposal practically all creations available anywhere in the world. At least in the case of the possibility of downloads offered, he or she is able to make copies on a digital medium and subsequently reproduce that work an infinite number of times or, with the help of a computer, can manipulate it, transform it and create a derivative work or, at least, a work inspired by the original. The copying can be addressed by national rules, such as rules on exceptions for private copying combined with statutory remuneration rights, as explained above (§36.03), in order to remedy the harm caused by such widespread copying. In this context, authors and other right holders also call for extending such remuneration to copying in the cloud, which is a particularly frequent use. The frequent manipulations and transformations of works done by users of platforms continues to be a challenge, given the right of authors to control adaptations or derivations of their works, and their moral right of integrity of the work. In the case of streaming on legal platforms that have obtained authorization by right owners and offer access and transmission of the works to their subscribers, authors and performers throughout the world have often claimed that they receive very little remuneration, even if their works and performances are being used at high intensity. This question of adequate allocation of revenues under this business model is currently discussed worldwide.

A constant challenge for right holders is the enforcement of their rights against illegal websites, which are still widespread on the internet and other networks and which offer access to huge amounts of works, performances and recordings to the public, without the necessary authorization of right holders. The possibility of effective site blocking is crucial in these cases, with the need to also cover "mirror sites" that often appear once a site has been blocked, offering the same content on the new site. In some countries, as shown for example in the *Newzbin2* case in the UK, the courts permitted dynamic site blocking which also covers mirror sites. The goal of this legal tool is both to combat online piracy and potentially to encourage the relevant internet service providers to transform their offers into legal ones.

Another challenge for authors and other right holders is the platforms offering their users the possibility of uploading works and other protected subject matter, so-called user-generated content or user-uploaded content. Frequently users of such platforms do not have the authorization of music composers, record companies, performers or other right owners to upload those protected works and recordings. Once the content is uploaded (reproduced on a server) for access, it is made available from the platform to the public, also regularly without the necessary authorization of the right owners. Some of this content may be covered by limitations or exceptions in some countries. This can lead to the same digital content being treated differently in different jurisdictions.

Platforms have argued that they only offer these possibilities to users but do not act themselves and thus are not directly liable for infringement. Individual users are liable, but enforcement of rights against them seems hardly possible and unpopular. In a number of countries, rules on secondary liability and systems of notices for take-down (or even stay-down) and obligations of platforms that have been informed of possibly infringing content on their platforms have been introduced, so as to diminish the challenge of this phenomenon for right owners. In some cases, platforms have sometimes introduced systems allowing rights owners to claim their content and decide whether the use can continue. However, right owners have argued that the illegal uses on such platforms considerably diminished their possibilities to gain revenue from the legal exploitation of their works, since users would prefer access without payment rather than legal, subscription-based platforms. The value of their content would shift to the platforms, which earn impressive revenues from advertising while the attractive content uploaded by users is neither authorized nor paid for. To respond to this so-called value gap, the EU in 2019 introduced direct liability for such platform services offering user-generated content, under further conditions. Consequently, such platforms now have to obtain licenses from right owners for making available user-generated content. Such licenses in some areas, such as music, are negotiated with the relevant CMOs. Where licenses are granted to platforms, individual users are no longer liable under the EU rules.

[E] NFTs, Blockchain and Copyright

A recent phenomenon discussed in relation to copyright are NFTs. They are sometimes used by authors in order to monetize their works on NFT platforms. NFTs simply certify the ownership of something which is unique, such as a particular work of an author. NFTs are based on blockchain technology. This technology is based on a database which shows all transactions, such as sales, and is shared in a network of computers. Any verified transaction is represented in a "block" following the previous block in relation to the same item of ownership, thus building a block chain. Since this technique is designed to be secure and to prevent manipulation by third persons, it is best suited to guarantee, for example, the ownership in a work. Transactions are executed on the basis of smart contracts.

An NFT usually does not itself contain a work or other object of transaction. Rather, it usually contains a link to metadata and from there to a particular storage place, where the work has been uploaded. Of course, this upload is a reproduction and requires authorization of the author; mostly, the author himself or herself is doing the uploading in order to sell their work through an NFT. Anyone who buys an NFT on the basis of smart contracts and block chain gets the guarantee of ownership of a particular work, but will not directly receive the underlying work. Also, he or she usually does not acquire the copyright in the work. While there have been misunderstandings around the treatment of copyright in relation to NFTs, this lack of copyright ownership is comparable to the acquisition of an original, analogue art work. Accordingly, smart contracts usually do not provide for any copyright license in the artwork to the buyer. More legal questions may arise, but over time they will likely be addressed in the smart contracts themselves. NFTs are a new business model in particular for authors and creators. The existing copyright law is applicable as shown through legal cases in many jurisdictions.

[F] AI and Copyright[181]

AI has become known in the context of copyright to a broader public, perhaps first through the project "The next Rembrandt" in 2016. In this project, programmers copied selected portraits by the Dutch painter Rembrandt of a Caucasian male with a hat in a certain position into a training database and after application of AI tools generated an image that to some extent resembled the original portraits. Later, different tools were developed to produce images from text, to compose music, or to generate any other products that at first sight may look like the results of human creativity. In fact, AI started to be developed many years earlier, with WIPO and UNESCO hosting some discussions on the copyright implications of machine learning in the 1980s. Practical applications such as translation programs had already been known for some time.

The copyright implications of AI were heightened with the development and rapid dissemination of generative AI. In 2022 ChatGPT and similar services became well known and widely available to everyone, with certain versions available at no cost, and started to be used to produce speeches, novels or any other kinds of text, and the resulting strong publicity finally created general and copyright community awareness of the opportunities and challenges of AI in the creative sector.

The technique making such results possible is, in a nutshell, as follows: online content (including protected texts, photographs, music and other works, performances, recordings) is "scraped," or copied into training database (often called Large Language Models, or LLMs) which constitute the basis for machine learning: an algorithm is applied to these works and other content and uses them to learn through training to establish patterns, trends, and mathematical models and finally to make decisions, when generating new output, that are not explicitly programmed upstream. However, they are based on the models, including the Basic or Foundation Models, which themselves are based on learning from the content in the training databases, but can also "memorize" such content. Nowadays, a user of an AI system often cannot therefore predict the concrete result of such an application of AI. To sum up, artistic and literary production by AI depends and relies on works created by human beings,

181. On artificial intelligence and patents, *see infra* §37.05.

and their qualities have an impact on the AI product. This phase is also called the input phase. Here, the following main issues are discussed:

While the copying of works and other material in training databases represents an act of reproduction that is generally covered by the reproduction right, many national policymakers are currently discussing whether there should be an exception to this right for the purpose of producing AI works, and whether existing limitations and exceptions such as those originally designed for research based on "TDM" apply to this reproduction. Court cases are also pending, including many brought in the USA on the question of whether these uses of copyrighted works are a fair use. In the EU, it is still being debated whether the existing TDM exception covers such copying. If it applies, authors and other right owners may under this TDM rule declare an opt-out and thus prohibit (or license) reproduction in AI-training databases. However, in practice, it is still difficult and in some cases practically impossible to exercise the opt-out, although technological solutions and licensing options are both increasing.

Some countries have introduced wide-reaching TDM exceptions that apply when generating AI outputs, but their application may be limited by the existing copyright legal framework through the conditions of the three-step test. AI companies argue that they need an exception to promote innovation. Authors, creators, and performers see a crucial threat to their possibilities of exploiting their own works in competition with masses of often cheaper products such as texts, images or music that can be generated by anyone, anywhere, very quickly through the use of AI tools. They point to the possibility that they will lose the basis for earning revenues from their creations and thus for being able to continue to create. This could result in major damage for cultures and societies at large. Also, they note that where these uses could be licensed, especially through collective licensing, innovation would not be hindered. A certain amount of licensing is starting to take place, although it does not cover the vast majority of the content being scraped from the web that is finding its way into various LLMs and having an impact on the development of generative AI tools, among others.

In this context, creators also claim that AI companies should reveal what works were used in training databases, and they call for transparency regarding the AI products so as to inform the user whether they were made by means of AI. The EU's 2024 AI Act contains such principles.

Where a work is used to generate AI output that looks like a reproduction or adaptation/derivation of the work used, the further question arises of whether this output itself infringes upon the reproduction or adaptation right of the author of the work used. Given the broad notion of "reproduction" and "adaptation" in the international treaties, and the fact that Basic Models seem to "memorize" content from training databases, legal disputes based on this theory are being brought in various jurisdictions. The question of infringement is also discussed for cases where works of one writer or author are used to generate by AI new texts etc. that "copy" the style (which is usually not protected under copyright) of this author. Also, where the voice or gestures of a performer are used to produce AI-generated performances with this voice and these gestures that were never done by the performer, his or her personality rights may be involved, and concerns may arise based on rules on unfair competition.

The phenomenon of "deep fakes" based on imitation of the voice, image or likeness has also generated concerns, including when the fakes are used for criminal activity and scams. A need for new ways of protection of the used works, performances etc. in these cases is being discussed, to the extent that existing law in a number of areas including copyright does not seem sufficient to protect authors, performers and others against such potentially massive uses.

As regards the status of the AI output, be it text, music, images or the like, the application of existing copyright rules and the requirement for human authorship in most countries of the world leads to the result that such output cannot be protected by copyright or authors rights, as long as the outcome is generated by AI and the human using AI, as is currently the case, cannot predict the concrete outcome of his or her instructions to the AI system. Of course, if the human author, for example, later rewrites, complements or adapts an AI-generated text to such an extent that the results of these activities fulfill the conditions of a protected work, such changes or additions to the AI text (though not the AI text itself) are likely protectable. Discussions on AI output therefore mainly concern the question of whether one should protect such output by a new right (given the lack of human author, it would probably have to be a sort of related or neighboring right, or perhaps a sui generis right). For taking a new kind of object out of the public domain through the establishment of a new related right, based on past practice the legislature needs a particular justification (such as the important investment by sound recording producers in organizing and making sound recordings of protected works or performances, which thereby are more intensively diffused to the public). Major doubts have been expressed as to whether such justification for protection of AI output exists, in particular where AI products are based on exploiting works created by humans, without their consent and adequate payment, and could even stifle or hinder human creativity. In any case, legislatures will have to consider all possible consequences of rules related to copyright and related rights, including for human creativity, cultural diversity and the impact on societies as a whole.

§37.03 BIOTECHNOLOGICAL INVENTIONS

[A] Introduction

The term "biotechnology" means a technological application that uses biological systems, living organisms, or derivatives thereof, such as plants, animals, seeds and microorganisms, as well as biological material, such as enzymes, proteins and plasmids (which are used in "genetic engineering," i.e., processes to modify the genetic composition of living organisms). Biotechnological inventions fall into three categories: processes for the creation or modification of living organisms and biological material; the results of such processes; and the use of such results.

Biotechnology is one of the oldest technologies. For example, the production of wine or beer involves processes using living organisms. Such processes have been known for a long time. Likewise, the selective breeding of plants and animals has an equally long history. Today, modern biotechnology concerns the application of cellular and molecular biology to human needs and the use of cells and biological molecules to solve problems or make useful products. It includes scientific and industrial disciplines directed to understanding and manipulating living or biologically active material at the molecular level. Often it refers to recombinant deoxyribonucleic acid (DNA) techniques and analysis of genetic information.

Modern biotechnology, in particular genetic engineering, may have a very significant effect on our future, particularly having in view significant new technological developments, such as the so-called CRISPR-Cas9. Based on a bacterial defense system named Clustered Regularly Interspaced Short Palindromic Repeats (CRISPR), the technique permits the editing of genomic DNA at a specific target site in a wide variety of cell types and organisms. According to the National Library of Medicine, editing included "insertion, deletion and replacement of DNA, resulting in inactivation of target genes, acquisition of novel genetic traits and correction of pathogenic gene mutations. Due to the advantages of simple design, low cost, high efficiency, good repeatability and short-cycle, CRISPR-Cas systems have become the most widely used genome editing technology in molecular biology laboratories all around the world."[182] Many expect biotechnology to lead to important breakthroughs in medicine which may be effective in combating diseases such as cancer and AIDS. Biotechnology may also lead to new opportunities for obtaining food and energy, and may provide solutions to the problems of pollution of the environment. A recent paper issued by the FAO addresses gene editing in the context of agrifood systems.[183]

The number of modern biotechnology-based drugs has expanded and vaccines have increased. The genomes of a number of organisms have been sequenced, including human, mosquito and the malaria-causing organism, *plasmodia falciparum*. These and related developments are expected to accelerate the pace of drug and vaccine discoveries.

Though regulated from a biosafety point of view, the area of farmland planted with transgenic crops has increased in a number of countries. Biotechnology has also been used to reclaim wasteland through the use of microorganisms and plants that remove or degrade toxic compounds.

The application of patent law to biotechnological inventions has caused a lively debate ever since biotechnological patents have been granted. Traditionally, many circles thought that the grant of patents was limited to the fields of physics and chemistry. For chemistry this was still disputed in the nineteenth and twentieth centuries. However, with the increased ability to control and describe processes and products in the field of biotechnology, it was understood that the concept of invention covered equally biotechnological inventions. If it is possible to influence and control a biotechnological process and to achieve a desired and predefined result through such a controlled process in a previously unknown way then an invention in the field of

182. Detailed and updated information on CRISPR-Cas9 is available at www.ncbi.nlm.nih.gov/pmc/articles/PMC7508700/ (accessed on February 7, 2024).
183. *See* www.fao.org/biotech/biotech-add-edit-section/biotech-add-edit-news/biotech-news-detail/en/c/1630777/.

biotechnology has been made. If such invention fulfils the further patentability criteria, i.e., it has a sufficient level of inventiveness, is useful/industrially applicable and is described in a way that experts in the field can carry out the invention on the basis of the description, a patent grant would be possible.

Biotechnological inventions have been subject of patents since as early as the nineteenth century. For example, the USPTO granted the patent 141,072 to Louis Pasteur on July 22, 1873, claiming yeast, free from organic germs of disease, as an article of manufacture.

But, the appearance of patents in the field of genetic engineering, particularly when inventions related to human or animal genes has posed a number of questions to patent law and even raised strong ethical concerns. Questions have been asked to which extent living things could be subject to IPRs. For example, the microorganisms created by Chakrabarty (an inventor in the USA) were able to break down components of oil pollution in oceans and rivers. The USPTO had rejected the patent application because it found that living things were not patentable. The US Court of Customs and Patent Appeals held that "the fact that micro-organisms are alive is without legal significance for purposes of the patent law." This view was confirmed in a landmark decision by the US Supreme Court in 1980 which recognized modified microorganisms as patentable subject matter. The Court noted that while the laws of nature, physical phenomena and abstract ideas were not patentable, the claimed invention was not directed to an existing natural phenomenon but to new bacteria with markedly different characteristics from any found in nature. The invention therefore resulted from the inventor's ingenuity and effort. According to the Court, statutory subject matter (any new article of manufacture or composition of matter) which is patentable under US patent law includes "anything under the sun that is made by man."

However, subsequently, the Supreme Court has handed over several opinions determining the fine line between invention and nature or, as we can put it, between human-made invention and Nature-made invention. In *Mayo Collaborative Services v. Prometheus Laboratories, Inc.*, 566 U.S. 66 (2012), the Court held that any application for a patent covering an invention that results from a natural phenomenon should consist of something more than must "more than simply state the law of nature while adding the words 'apply it.'" Put in other words, and in accordance with the rule set by the Supreme Court in 1852, there is no invention when a discovered process cannot be alternated by different means. This is what happens when a patent claims an invention made by Nature. The invention becomes unique, not susceptible of being alternated by another (human) inventor, and thus it leads to a monopoly.[184]

---

184. The leading case is *Le Roy v. Tatham*, 55 U.S. 156 (1852), and was invoked subsequently in *O'Reilly v. Morse*, 56 U.S. 62 (1853), and *Corning v. Burden*, 56 U.S. 252 (1854). In *Le Roy*, the Court said:

> "It is admitted that a principle is not patentable. A principle, in the abstract, is a fundamental truth; an original cause; a motive; these cannot be patented, as no one can claim in either of them an exclusive right. Nor can an exclusive right exist to a new power, should one be discovered in addition to those already known. Through the agency of machinery a new steam power may be said to have been generated. But no

[B] Adoption and Dissemination

Developed countries have been the main investors in biotechnology and the principal beneficiaries of its adoption. Developing countries, however, are increasingly adopting this new technology, as illustrated by the uptake of biotechnology in different fields such as the production of medicinal products and the use of GM plants in increasing numbers of developing countries. The FAO-BioDeC database contains information from seventy developing countries, including countries with economies in transition, on the state of the art of crop biotechnology products and techniques, which are in use, or in the pipeline in those countries.[185]

Cuba, India and Malaysia, for instance, conduct health-related biotechnology research, development, production and marketing. Singapore and China have focused on research in biotechnology and development projects in the health and agricultural sectors. Diverse range of other developing countries, for example, Brazil, the Philippines, South Africa and Vietnam have entered the arena of agrobiotechnology by making significant public investments in R&D in that sector.

In the health sector, international PPP for vaccines and drug development have particularly focused on developing drugs and vaccines against diseases, such as malaria, HIV/AIDS and tuberculosis and animal vaccines with the aim of making final products affordable and available to developing countries.

The dominant role of the private sector in biotechnology research has caused concerns about the possible stagnation of technological advancements in certain areas of prime importance to developing countries which have been deemed unattractive in terms of returns on investment (e.g., orphan crops and infectious disease research) where biotechnology can have a particular impact. Questions have been raised as to the additional impact of IP on access to technology and products namely in developing countries. The debate has revealed a need to (i) strengthen the capacity of developing countries to absorb and adapt proprietary technology to their specific needs and (ii) to develop and introduce policy and institutional reforms, conducive to public and private investment and to creating an enabling environment for the application of biotechnology.

> one can appropriate this power exclusively to him/herself, under the patent laws. The same may be said of electricity, and any [the] of other powers in nature, which is alike open to all, and may be applied to useful purposes by the use of machinery.
>
> "In all such cases, the processes used to extract, modify, and concentrate natural agencies, constitute the invention. The elements of the power exist; the invention is not in discovering them, but in applying them to useful objects. Whether the machinery used be novel, or consist of a new combination of parts known, the right of the inventor is secured against all who use the same mechanical power, or one that shall be substantially the same.
>
> "A patent is not good for an effect, or the result of a certain process, as that would prohibit all other persons from making the same thing by any means whatsoever. This, by creating monopolies, would discourage arts and manufactures, against the avowed policy of the patent laws."

Ibid., Le Roy, at 174-175.

185. The database is available at aarhusclearinghouse.unece.org/resources/fao-biodec-biotechnologies-developing-countries.

However, and separately from IP issues, there are still diverging appreciations about the potential benefits and risks of biotechnology. The principal issues of contention among the various stakeholders, range from the potential increase in yield and the decrease in the use of pesticides and herbicides to the impact on the environment (ecology and biodiversity), the health of human beings and animals, the socioeconomic future of small farmers and the ownership and control of GRs. This debate has a strong ethical background and touches upon the basic issue what research is allowed to do and where are the boundaries. It is important to note that this debate is distinct from the discussion on whether IPRs should be granted on biotechnological inventions. However, the debate goes beyond the interpretation of the boundaries imposed by public morality or *ordre public*. What researchers are allowed to do and what can be put on the market is subject to the provisions of the respective substantive law and not an issue of IP.[186] For example: some countries do not allow research with human embryonic stem cells; new pharmaceuticals can be put on the market only where the commercialization has been allowed by a decision of the competent regulatory authority. The decision made by the authority to allow stem cell research or to commercialize new medicine is, at the outset, irrelevant to whether a patent is, or can be granted with respect to stem cells or that new medicine.

A number of countries have introduced specific laws and legal mechanisms to address IP-related biotechnology issues. In general, such provisions clarify questions about what is patentable and whether restrictions to patentability and specific rules regulating the effects of biotechnology patents are indicated.

Modern, flexible IP systems and policies have contributed to fostering investment needed to establish biotechnology industries creating tangible products. Flexible IP policies can play a role in favoring stable legal environments conducive to PPP, investment and other economic activity needed to spread biotechnological innovations to more countries. Enhanced access to biotechnology innovation for public welfare and development will be crucial for the general acceptance of the appropriateness of such laws and policies. Stable, strategic partnerships between developed and developing countries will not only improve TT, but will contribute to the enjoyment of everybody to the benefits of innovation.

[C] Particularities of Legal Protection for Biotechnology

As for all other fields of technology, legal protection is available also in respect of biotechnological inventions. Such protection covers creations of the human mind and protects this intellectual, non-tangible property. Just as much as in any other field of technology, the invention results from substantial research, inventive effort and

186. This is what explains the broad exclusion from patentability of essentially biological processes, these meaning processes that predominantly use naturally biological interactions, or sexual crossing, as opposed to processes that apply predominantly artificial, manipulated actions or steps, or non-sexual crossings. The EPO has developed a set of comprehensive guidelines on the patentability (and the exclusion from patentability) of essentially biological processes for the production of plants and animals. *See* www.epo.org/en/legal/guidelines-epc/2023/g_ii_5_4_2.html.

investment, and is an intellectual result attributable to an inventor in the form of a teaching how to carry out the invention. The legal protection of that invention contributes to creating an environment that makes it interesting for enterprises to invest in research for creation of new and useful products. Hence, as with other inventions, the legal protection of biotechnological inventions is not only in the private interest of inventors and their employers, but also in the public interest in order to promote technological progress through the provision of an appropriate enabling environment.

The grant of legal protection for biotechnological inventions through patents or other titles has to deal with a number of particularities that do not exist in the same way in other areas of technology.

First, it has to be identified whether a claimed invention really is an invention. If, for example, a microorganism as yet unknown is isolated, maybe by a new and innovative process, and if a specific use has been identified, for example the microorganism can be used to produce a medicine, one can argue that the criteria for the grant of a patent are met. However, it may be argued that such a microorganism is not an invention, but a discovery, because, even if it was not known, it existed already in nature. It has been argued that biological materials are unpatentable, because they are "identical" to, or "not markedly different" from material existing in nature, even if they were isolated or purified from the natural state. Some argue that an isolated biological material, such as a gene, is not different from a chemical substance extracted from nature and a chemical substance is patentable subject matter. Others, arguing from a biological point of view, fail to see how a gene could be patentable subject matter. The comparison of biotechnological and chemical inventions has led to the question whether traditional rules applied in the area of chemistry should be applied *mutatis mutandis* in the field of biotechnology.

Second, biotechnology has certain ethical implications that lead to considerations about how to deal with the legal protection of biotechnological inventions from an ethical perspective. Some countries exclude patent protection for specified biotechnological inventions through express legislative provisions, in particular, for reasons of public order and morality. For example, Article 6(2) of the EU Directive on the Legal Protection of Biotechnological Inventions of July 6, 1998, provides a non-exhaustive list of inventions that are considered unpatentable because their commercial exploitation is considered contrary to public order and morality. This list includes processes for cloning human beings, processes for modifying the germ line genetic identity of human beings, uses of human embryos for industrial or commercial purposes and processes for modifying the genetic identity of animals which are likely to cause them suffering, without any substantial medical benefit to man or animal, and also animals resulting from such processes.

Furthermore, a number of typical issues relating to biotechnological inventions result from the fact that biological material is capable of reproducing itself. This specific characteristic requires determination of law if and, if so, to which extent, the legal protection extends to future generations, which is the relationship, and where are overlaps with plant and animal variety protection, whether special exhaustion regimes are required, whether special rules and exemptions are required for plant and animal breeders or farmers, etc.

The development of genetic engineering resulted in the possibility of overlap between plant variety and patent protection even in countries where patent protection for plant varieties is excluded. For example, a plant may have been GM. This modification may not have created a new plant variety. The new plant may have been patented if the criteria for the patent grant were met. A plant breeder may have used this GM and patented plant for developing, with traditional breeding methods that are excluded from patent protection, a new plant variety, which is also not patentable. This example illustrates that, in practice, a patent may have impact on plant varieties even where plant varieties are not patentable. Genetic engineering may lead to interdependencies that did not exist traditionally and this puts the issue of the interface between these two systems at scrutiny. Each of these systems provides a scope of protection and rights as well as limitations that are distinct from each other. For example, the breeder's privilege allows a plant breeder to use a protected variety for the development of a new plant variety through traditional plant breeding. A research exemption under patent law, if a research exemption exists at all, may have a more restricted scope, and may, for instance, not allow the use of the patented plant for commercial purposes. Possible overlaps can be addressed by mutual cross-licenses. The EU Directive on the Legal Protection of Biotechnological Inventions has introduced the possibility of compulsory cross-licenses to address this issue.

Farmers traditionally keep a part of the harvest for propagation purposes and plant and animal reproduction purposes. Such traditionally accepted behavior may no longer be acceptable under patent law. The EU Directive on the Legal Protection of Biotechnological Inventions has resolved that issue through the definition of farmers' rights. The sale of patented plants or animals implies the authorization by the patent holder to the farmer to use the patented plants or animals for reproduction on his/her own farm for agricultural purposes. This derogation from the patentee's rights aims to safeguard the traditional practices of farmers to save and re-use harvested material such as seeds for the next season. It does not allow the farmer to start a plant breeding and animal reproduction business.

Today, patent protection for biotechnological inventions is recognized by many countries and a number of countries have adopted specific laws for biotechnological inventions. This legislation will provide a framework for the patent offices and courts to gain practical experiences and support assessing the appropriateness of patentability rules in this field. For example, DNA patents granted at an early stage of development in the field of genetic engineering were criticized as too broad. It was argued that too broad patents granted on upstream foundational inventions might hamper downstream follow-up research in this area. While, on the one hand, patent grants are naturally broader at early development stages of new technologies, this discussion led, on the other hand, to review and strengthening patent offices' examination procedures, i.e., stringent application of patentability criteria for such inventions. Also, the scope of research exemptions under various patent laws was discussed and its importance in promoting biotechnological research was emphasized.

The importance of clear and complete disclosure of inventions in a patent application applies also to biotechnological inventions. A particular category of biotechnological inventions, namely, inventions concerning microorganisms (either the processes for obtaining a microorganism or the microorganism itself, or the particular use of a microorganism) and living organisms raise a particular challenge in this respect. In view of the fact that it is difficult, if not impossible, to sufficiently describe a new microorganism, a system for depositing of microorganisms has been established in order to meet the legal requirement of sufficient disclosure of inventions in a patent application. Thus, in many countries, applicants for patents may complement a written description of a new microorganism with a deposit of a sample of such microorganism with a recognized depositary authority. In such cases, an applicant must make a reference to such deposit in a patent application.

[D] International Law

Many WIPO Member States are bound by the TRIPS Agreement, as part of their obligations as Members of the WTO. Analysis of the TRIPS Agreement goes beyond the scope of this chapter but, in general, WTO Members are required to implement agreed minimum standards of IP protection.

Article 27.1 of the TRIPS Agreement requires that patents be available in all fields of technology, without discrimination, provided that they are new, involve an inventive step and are capable of industrial application. Article 27.2 enables a Member to exclude from patentability inventions whose commercial exploitation may be contrary to *ordre public* or morality. Further, Article 27.3(b) also allows Members to exclude from patentability certain subject matter, such as diagnostic, therapeutic and surgical methods for the treatment of humans or animals or plants and animals. Protection is not excluded, however, for microorganisms, non-biological and microbiological processes (that are not essentially biological). Concerning protection of plant varieties, Article 27.3(b) of the TRIPS Agreement provides that plant varieties shall be protected either by patents or by an effective sui generis system or by any combination thereof.

Some PVP systems are thought to constitute sui generis systems. Such systems differ from patent protection in the conditions required for protection and the nature of acts that can be prevented. The system established by the UPOV is an internationally recognized sui generis system for the protection of plant varieties.

As provided in the TRIPS Agreement, Article 27.3(b) has been under review at the Council for TRIPS since December 1998.[187] The differences in national laws relating to the protection of biotechnological inventions became evident from the review process, as the positions of Members varied from removing the exclusions from patentability provided for in that provision to clarifying certain terms such as, plants, animals,

187. The reason that led TRIPS negotiators to include in Art. 27.3(b) the clause for review was that, during the negotiations, certain Contracting Parties to the GATT believed that the period accepted (of four years after the entry of the WTO Agreement into force) would be enough to acquire a clearer notion of how the patent system could apply in the biotechnological sector. But when the review started, in 1999, it became clear that such notion had not been acquired.

microorganisms and to amending that provision to prohibit patenting of life forms, including microorganisms. Some Members expressed their interest in leaving Article 27.3(b) as it is, as flexibility provided for in that provision would allow countries to design their national policies regarding the protection of biotechnological inventions in a manner reflecting their specific interests and concerns.

Other topics raised in the discussion at the Council for TRIPS in relation to the revision of Article 27.3(b) include the meaning of effective protection of new plant varieties, how to handle moral and ethical issues, how to deal with the commercial use of TK and genetic material by those other than communities/countries where they originate and how to ensure that the TRIPS Agreement and the UN Convention of Biological Diversity support each other.

Further, the system of a deposit of a sample of microorganisms is also the subject of an international treaty, namely, the Budapest Treaty on the International Recognition of the Deposit of Microorganisms for the Purposes of Patent Procedure, which provides for the setting up of international depositary authorities with which microorganisms can be deposited.

On a final note, it is generally accepted that gene therapies may be excluded from patentability under the broad language of Article 27.3(b) of the TRIPS Agreement. The reason is one of ethics, in the sense that therapeutical methods have been traditionally subject to a peer review as to their efficacy. It is also understood that medical practitioners and surgeons can capture revenue from their inventions by the reputation they gain as inventors, given the individual nature of the practice of their art. But when it comes to gene therapies, things are changing, and not only their development is very costly but their application may take long periods. Thus, the idea of those therapies having their efficacy reviewed by the peers, on an empirical basis, may no longer stand. The patent system could then operate as it does in other fields of technology: as incentives to invent, as tools that ensure the recouping from the market of the sunken costs of inventing, and as instruments that generate legal security and, thus, reduce transaction costs.

§37.04 IP AND SPACE ACTIVITIES[188]

[A] Introduction

Despite the fact that space technology is one of the most advanced technical areas, and outer space activities are, in fact, the fruit of intellectual creations, it is only in recent years that intellectual property protection in connection with outer space activities has raised wider attention. One of the reasons is that the space activities are increasingly

188. This section discusses the legal (and, especially, the international legal) dimension of intellectual property in association with space activities. But for a historical analysis of the technological, political and economic aspects of those activities, it is recommended to go through Hertzfeld, H.R. et al. (April 2022), *Innovations in the Exploration of Outer Space*, Economic Research Working Paper No. 71, WIPO.

shifting from state-owned activities to private and commercial activities. These activities include remote sensing from space, direct broadcasting, research and manufacturing in micro-gravity environments and the launching of touristic initiatives. Not only is the new participation of commercial sector increasing, but the privatization of entities is equally increasing as in the cases of Inmarsat or Intelsat. In general, those nongovernmental entities are more conscious of their "property," both in tangible and intangible forms. Further, due to financial and technical resources that are required to realize space projects, collaboration with the private sector is not alien to many of the state-owned space agencies today. Licensing contracts are concluded between governmental space agencies, between governmental agencies and private companies and between private companies. Such private financing has to be motivated by the expectation that the R&D investment could be recovered in the future. Thus, the acquisition and protection of intellectual property rights would have a positive effect on the participation of the private sector in the development of outer space activities and on further development of space technology in general.

Another reason why intellectual property has become an issue in recent years relates to the globalization of space activities. As it is the case with the International Space Station (ISS), more and more space activities are operated under international cooperation schemes, which include various players under different constituencies from different countries. Consequently, there is a need for a simple, uniform and reliable international legal framework. Although national intellectual property laws are relatively well harmonized, different national laws still apply different principles. Once a dispute arises, each national law regulates questions as to international jurisdiction. Thus, a lack of reliable international legal regime requires parties to negotiate intellectual property clauses in each international cooperation agreement, which may include, for example, issues concerning ownership, rights of use, rights of distribution and licensing of data, information capable of legal protection and confidentiality. Obviously, while such a contractual agreement is valid among the parties concerned, it does not bind third parties.

Yet another reason may be that, due to the advancement of space technology, new business possibilities are emerging. For example, although it is still a dream for the general public, the development of space transportation technology has been clearing the way to space tourism.[189] Up to now, when discussing intellectual property matters in connection with space activities, the primary concerns have related to patent protection of inventions created or used in outer space, or copyright protection of databases using data acquired through space activities. If space tourism becomes reality, the protection of trademarks and industrial designs in outer space may also become an important issue.

The importance of establishing a legal regime that effectively protects intellectual property in space cannot be overemphasized. Lack of legal certainty will influence the advancement of space research and international cooperation. Because of the large

189. For a general, updated overview of recent space tourism developments, *see Space Tourism: The Latest News, Features And Photos*, at www.space.com/tag/space-tourism (accessed on February 8, 2024).

investments involved in space activities, a legal framework that assures a fair and competitive environment is necessary to encourage the private sector's participation in this field. Limited exclusive rights conferred by intellectual property protection would bring competitive benefits to right holders either by concluding a licensing agreement or by excluding competitors from using a given technology. The overall image of the company may be improved by intellectual property rights created in the company. For example, the acquisition of patents may be viewed as a proof of the technical competence of the company. The possibility of licensing intellectual property also has the advantage of allowing to negotiate a cross-license with other parties, particularly where a specific space technology concerned is a consolidation of various high-technologies. Further, legal mechanisms to establish and maintain security interests in intellectual property exists in certain countries.

[B] International Principles Concerning Outer Space

The main body of current international space law is contained in five international agreements:

- Treaty on Principles Governing the Activities of States in the Exploration and Use of Outer Space, including the Moon and other Celestial Bodies (1967 Outer Space Treaty);
- Agreement on the Rescue of Astronauts, the Return of Astronauts and the Return of Objects launched into Outer Space (1968 Rescue Agreement);
- Convention on International Liability for the Damage Caused by Space Objects (1972 Liability Conventions);
- Convention on registration of Objects Launched into Outer Space (1975 Registration Convention); and
- Agreement Governing the Activities of States on the Moon and Other Celestial Bodies (1979 Moon Agreement).

None of those agreements contains a provision expressly dealing with intellectual property.

However, since it may assist in examining whether the general rules on intellectual property protection need adaptation or exceptions for the purposes of outer space activities, the following general principles under international space law are highlighted:

[1] Outer Space Treaty

Article I of the Outer Space Treaty provides the so-called space benefits clause according to which the exploration and use of outer space should be carried out "for the benefit and interests of all countries, irrespective of their degree of economic or scientific development, and shall be the province of all mankind." Further, it states that outer space should be "free for exploration and use by all States without discrimination of any kind, on a basis of equality and in accordance with international law" and that there should be "free access to all areas of celestial bodies." Article II provides for so-called non-appropriation of space, according to which outer space is "not subject to national appropriation by claim of sovereignty, by means of use or occupation, or by any other means."

While non-appropriation of outer space has been agreed, Article VIII of the Outer Space Treaty establishes the principle that the State of registration has jurisdiction and control over space objects as well as personnel launched into outer space. It states that:

> A State to the Treaty on whose registry an object launched into outer space is carried shall retain jurisdiction and control over such object, and over any personnel thereof, while in outer space or on a celestial body. Ownership of objects launched into outer space, including objects landed or constructed on a celestial body, and of their component parts, is not affected by their presence in outer space or on a celestial body or by their return to the Earth. Such objects or component parts found beyond the limits of the State party to the Treaty on whose registry they are carried shall be returned to that State Party, which shall, upon request, furnish identifying data prior to their return.

[2] Registration Convention

Article II of the Registration Convention provides that the launching State shall register the space object by means of an entry in an appropriate registry which it should maintain. The term "launching State" is defined in Article I(a) as "a State which launches or procures the launching of a space object" or "a State from whose territory or facility a space object is launched." According to Article I(b), the term "space object" includes component parts of a space object as well as its launch vehicle and parts thereof. Further, where there are two or more launching States in respect of a space object, they should jointly determine which one of them should register bearing in mind the provisions of Article VIII of the Outer Space Treaty, and without prejudice to appropriate agreements among the launching States on jurisdiction and control over the space object and over any personnel thereof. Article VII of the Registration Convention provides the possibility of an international IGO registering its space objects under certain conditions.

[3] Declaration by the UN Committee on the Peaceful Uses of Outer Space on International Cooperation in the Exploration and Use of the Outer Space for the Benefit and the Interest of All States, Taking into Particular Account the Needs of Developing Countries

An explicit reference to intellectual property rights is made in the Declaration by the UN Committee on the Peaceful Uses of Outer Space on International Cooperation in the Exploration and Use of the Outer Space for the Benefit and the Interest of All States, Taking into Particular Account the Needs of Developing Countries, which was adopted in 1996. Its second paragraph states:

> States are free to determine all aspects of their participation in international cooperation in the exploration and use of outer space on an equitable and mutually acceptable basis. Contractual terms in such cooperative ventures should be fair and reasonable and they should be in full compliance with the legitimate rights and interests of the parties concerned as, for example, with intellectual property rights.

This specific language makes it clear that the principles setting international cooperation as regards outer space, namely the goal of ensuring that space exploration shall be undertaken "for the benefit and in the interests of all countries and shall be the province of all mankind" do not preempt the acquisition and the claim of intellectual property either by private companies or by governmental agencies. Actually, the idea above mentioned that IP owners should handle their exclusive rights in a cooperative manner, through fair licensing and cross-licensing, implies the assertion of the right of inventors and creators in outer space to acquiring or claiming IP rights in such domain.

[C] Activities Relating to Outer Space and Intellectual Property

In 1997, WIPO conducted a study, with the help of consultants from Europe, Japan and the USA, on the possible need for rules and/or principles for the protection of industrial property, in particular inventions, which are created or used in outer space. The discussion focused exclusively on international industrial property law questions.

More general international law issues, for example, the question of territory and jurisdiction, the legal issues relating to the cooperation activities between space faring nations, and the legal questions arising between a regional space agency and its Member States, were not examined.

The consultants raised, in particular, the following issues:

(a) clarification on the principle of Article 5*ter* of the Paris Convention;
(b) whether Member States of WIPO should clarify that the laws applicable to inventions in the territory of a country will also apply in the spacecraft registered by (under jurisdiction of) the said country;
(c) standardization of contractual clauses on the protection of inventions and confidential information, which are created or used in international cooperative agreements between the space faring nations.

However, the study came to the conclusion that, for the time being, there was no need for special international legislative provisions concerning the protection of inventions created or used in outer space, but that it is desirable that the International Bureau of WIPO give information on the existing protection of such inventions to interested States and organizations.

In July 1999, a Workshop on Intellectual Property Rights in Space was held in conjunction with the Third United Nations Conference on the Exploration and Peaceful Uses of Outer Space (UNISPACE III), which was a major intergovernmental conference for the purposes of creating a blueprint for the peaceful use of outer space in the twenty-first century. The recommendations made by the Workshop were amended and adopted by the plenary of the Conference, and included in the Report of the Conference as follows:

"(a) More attention should be paid to the protection of intellectual property rights, in view of the growth in the commercialization and privatization of space-related activities. However, the protection and enforcement of intellectual property rights should be considered together with the international legal principles developed by the United Nations in the form of treaties and declarations, such as those relating to the principle of non-appropriation of outer space, as well as other relevant international conventions;

"(b) The feasibility of harmonizing international intellectual property standards and legislation relating to intellectual property rights in outer space should be further explored with a view to enhancing international coordination and cooperation at the level of both the State and the private sector. In particular, the possible need for rules or principles covering issues such as the following could be examined and clarified: applicability of national legislation in outer space; ownership and use of intellectual property rights developed in space activities; and contract and licensing rules;

"(c) All States should provide appropriate protection of intellectual property rights involving space-related technology, while encouraging and facilitating the free flow of basic science information;

"(d) Educational activities concerning intellectual property rights in relation to outer space activities should be encouraged."

Following the UNISPACE III, at the Legal Subcommittee of the Committee on the Peaceful Uses of Outer Space (COPUOS), some delegations proposed that intellectual property issues be included on the agenda to be considered by the Subcommittee. Such a proposal, however, did not find enough support by the Subcommittee Members. Although priority has been given to other activities due to the absence of any proposal by the Member States concerning intellectual property in outer space, the International Bureau of WIPO has attended meetings and provided lectures on this topic on an ad hoc basis.

[D] Issues

In view of the general legal principles under international intellectual property law and international space law as described above, various issues have been addressed in the context of intellectual property created or used in outer space in the past by scholars and practitioners.

On the basis of the results of the study referred above and the latest developments in this field, this section describes some of the issues which might be relevant to the future development of space activities.

[1] Applicability of National/Regional Intellectual Property Law in Outer Space

As described above, national (and regional) laws on the protection of intellectual property in general apply only to the territory of the relevant country (or region). Thus, the acquisition and enforcement of intellectual property in a particular territory are governed by the applicable national (regional) intellectual property law. In other words, protection of intellectual property is subject to the applicable territorial legal framework. The treaties under the auspices of WIPO as well as the TRIPS Agreement have achieved a certain level of harmonization among national/regional laws. There still remain considerable differences among national/regional intellectual property laws which lead to a different level of intellectual property protection in the territory of each country (region).

One of the most important principles under international space law is the non-appropriation of outer space by any country (Article II of the Outer Space Treaty).

The Outer Space Treaty, however, makes a distinction between "outer space *as such*" and "an object launched into outer space." As far as an object launched into outer space is concerned, in accordance with Article VIII of the Outer Space Treaty, the State on whose registry such an object is carried shall retain jurisdiction and control over that object, and over any personnel thereof. Further, the Registration Convention introduces a rule regarding who should register a space object. According to that Convention, a "launching State," which is a State that launches or procures the launching of a space object or a State from whose territory or facility a space object is launched, should register the space object with an appropriate registry.

Where there are two or more launching States, they should determine among themselves which one of them should register the object, without prejudice to appropriate agreements concluded among the launching States on jurisdiction and control over the space object and over any personnel thereof. Therefore, according to international space law, the country of registry retains jurisdiction and control over the space object and over any personnel thereof unless otherwise agreed among the launching States. In other words, jurisdiction and control over the space object and its personnel is determined by the nationality (registering State) of the space object.

The question arises whether the territorial jurisdiction under intellectual property law permits the extension of each national (and regional) law to the objects which the respective country has registered and launched into outer space. In this respect, a distinction, however, should be made between activities carried out in outer space and activities relating to outer space which are carried out on the territory of a country or on the territories of several countries. Following the general principle of territoriality of intellectual property rights, the acquisition and enforcement of intellectual property rights related to intellectual creations which were made in outer space but which are used in one or more territories on Earth are, in general, governed by the national (or regional) intellectual property law of the country or countries concerned. Therefore, a separate consideration as to the applicability of general intellectual property rules may be needed only in so far as activities are carried out in outer space, regardless of the place where the invention was made.

The USA is the only country that has enacted an explicit provision establishing a link between the three key elements: inventions, jurisdiction and territory.

Section 105 of 35 U.S.C. (Inventions in outer space) reads as follows:

"(a) Any invention made, used, or sold in outer space on a space object or component thereof under the jurisdiction or control of the United States shall be considered to be made, used or sold within the United States for the purposes of this title, except with respect to any space object or component thereof that is specifically identified and otherwise provided for by an international agreement to which the United States is a party, or with respect to any space object or component thereof that is carried on the registry of a foreign state in accordance with the Convention on Registration of Objects Launched into Outer Space.

"(b) Any invention made, used or sold in outer space on a space object or component thereof that is carried out on the registry of a foreign state in accordance with the Convention on Registration of Objects Launched into Outer Space, shall be considered to be made, used or sold within the United States for the purposes of this title if specifically so agreed in an international agreement between the United States and the state of registry."

Therefore, the patent law of the USA provides quasi-territorial effect on a space object that is carried on the registry of the USA, unless otherwise agreed by an international agreement.

In other countries, there is no explicit statutory provision of this kind, except that, by virtue of the ratification of the 1988 Intergovernmental Agreement, German intellectual property law is applicable to the European Space Agency (ESA)-registered elements. Some argue that, in the absence of an explicit legal provision, the applicability of national intellectual property law on space objects registered by that State is doubtful. Some others are of the opinion that in consideration of the broad concept of territoriality according to which national patent law may be applicable on ships which fly that State's flag on the high seas and on aircrafts which are registered by that State, the national patent law might be applicable by way of analogy to space objects registered in that State, even if the national patent law does not.[190]

For example, according to Article 27.1 of the TRIPS Agreement, patents should be available and patents rights enjoyable without discrimination as to the place of invention. Therefore, the same principles should apply to inventions created in outer space and used in the territory of a given country. That is, in order to enforce a patent for an invention created in outer space in a territory of a certain country, an application for a patent shall be filed, and a patent shall be granted, in, or with effect for, that country in accordance with the applicable law of that country.

It should be noted that, in order to clarify this uncertainty in Europe, the Proposal for the Council Regulation on the Community Patent, issued by the European Commission (document COM(2000) 412), provides that the Regulation should apply to inventions created in outer space, which are under the jurisdiction and control of one

190. For a broad analysis of this matter, *see* Maria Balsano, A. (August 28 to September 5, 1992), *Industrial Property Rights in Outer Space in the International Governmental Agreement (IGA) on the Space Station and the European Partner*, 35th Colloquium on the Law of Outer Space, Washington D.C.; Reynolds, G.H. (1990).

or more Member States in accordance with international law. However, EU Regulation 1257/2012, on unitary patent protection, has not retained that provision.

But legal vacuum has not prevented the ESA from issuing Rules on Information, Data and Intellectual Property, of April 23, 2014. Of special relevance to this analysis is Chapter III, on *Information and Data Relating to Payloads flown in the Framework of an Agency Programme*. Section III provides, in part:

> "(a) In the framework of an Agency programme, any Information, Data and Intellectual Property produced by the Agency based on and after analysis of the data resulting from the payload shall be the property of the Agency.
>
> "The access, use and dissemination of the data shall be decided by the Participating States to the programme concerned within a clear and coherent policy.
>
> "The commercial use of the data delivered by the payload may be allocated by the Agency to third parties, on conditions to be approved by the Participating States to the programme concerned. Such conditions shall take account of any investment made or to be made by a third party and shall afford the necessary protection to any Intellectual Property created by the third party at its own expense."

As the ESA explains in its website, "In general, ESA prefers that any IPR generated during the course of an ESA contract shall vest with the contractor as the Agency considers that the originator of said work is best placed to exploit it. Only when the creation lies with an ESA staff member does the IPR belong to ESA outright."[191]

A similar approach is envisaged by the Canadian Space Agency (CSA), as stated on its website.[192] Among other IP-related initiatives, CSA offers to the private sector a number of licensing opportunities.

A similar kind of legal uncertainty also exists in the field of trademarks and industrial designs.

As regards copyright protection, the determination of jurisdiction of a spacecraft is less important, because it is the author's nationality which, in the first place, determines the status of the work as regards its protection. According to Article 3(1)(a) and (2) of the Berne Convention, the Convention applies to authors who are nationals of one of the countries of the Berne Union or who have habitual residence in one of those countries. Only in the case of non-protected authors, the place of the first publication is of importance (Article 3(1)(b) of the Berne Convention). However, since publication normally involves a significant number of copies, it is not likely to occur in outer space, at least in a near future. This would mean, for example, that if a database is created on a spacecraft, its status as regards protection under the Berne Convention will depend on the nationality of its creator.

The determination of the jurisdiction as far as intellectual property is concerned should be clearly defined, particularly where more than one country is involved in the launching of the elements of a space station. A good example of how a joint

191. *See* www.esa.int/About_Us/Business_with_ESA/How_to_do/ESA_Industry_and_Intellectual_Property (accessed on February 8, 2024).
192. *See* www.asc-csa.gc.ca/eng/industry/intellectual-property-technology-transfer/.

government administration can lead to a specific agreement on jurisdiction and control over the elements of an ISS is the Agreement on Cooperation in the Detailed Design, Development and Operation and Utilization of the Permanently Manned Civil Space Station among the governments of the USA, the Member States of the ESA, Japan and Canada (the International Space Station Intergovernmental Agreement (IGA)), concluded in 1988. Although the 1988 IGA was upgraded by the Agreement Concerning Cooperation on Civil ISS, concluded in 1998, which included the participation of the Russian Federation to the cooperation project, both Agreements contain, in Article 21, a provision establishing an intellectual property regime for the ISS.

In principle, Article 21.2 of the IGA stipulates that, for the purposes of intellectual property law, an activity occurring in or on a Space Station flight element should be deemed to have occurred only in the territory of the Partner State of that element's registry. As regards the European Partner States, a separate rule is necessary, since the European Partner States delegate to the ESA the responsibility to register the ESA flight elements. Article 21.2 of the IGA provides that, for the purposes of intellectual property law, any European Partner State may deem the activity to have occurred within its territory for ESA-registered elements.

Thus, with respect to all types of intellectual property law, the principle of quasi-territoriality is implemented on the Space Station, though ESA-registered elements could be considered as a "common territory" of the European Partner States.[193]

The prerequisite for the applicability of the principle of quasi-territoriality is the registration of "all" the space objects which might have a connection with intellectual property, that is, not only the spacecraft and the elements of the space station, but also, for example, an advertisement panel in outer space which might bare a trademark. It was reported that the current Registration Convention raised some practical difficulties, such as a different interpretation of the definition of the term "space object" and the accuracy of the registration carried out by the Contracting States. Further, the Registration Convention does not contain a provision regarding changes of ownership of the registered space object, which was probably not foreseen at the time the Convention was concluded.[194]

Although the maritime law also applies the quasi-territorial principle to ships and to ships on the high sea, in the case of the ISS, each segment, to which the intellectual property law of each registered State applies, is located in proximity. Such a physical proximity might highlight the differences among national intellectual property laws.

For example, the use of a certain invention, or a certain mark, could be considered as an infringement of a patent, or a trademark, in one segment while no problem would arise in the neighboring segment.

193. *See* Vahrenwald, A. (1993) at footnote 22 referring to Beier and Stauder (1985), *Weltraumstationen und das Recht des geistgen Eigentums* [*Space Stations and Intellectual Property Law*], GRUR Int.

194. *See* Lála, P. (2013), *The United Nations Register of Objects Launched into Outer Space*, in Proceedings, United Nations/International Institute of Air and Space Law Workshop on Capacity Building in Space Law, ST/SPACE/14, at 36, available at www.unoosa.org/pdf/publications/st_space_14E.pdf (accessed on February 8, 2024).

[2] Enforcement of Intellectual Property Rights in Outer Space

As described above, enforcement of intellectual property rights relating to intellectual creations which were made in outer space but which are used in one or more territories on Earth is, in general, governed by the national (or regional) law of the country or countries concerned. As regards satellite broadcasting, inasmuch as a satellite transmitting signal is merely a conduit for Earth-based receivers, this would seem to constitute use on Earth, not in outer space.

Adopting the quasi-territoriality principle to a space object would mean that matters of jurisdiction as well as questions of applicable law with respect to such a space object are subject to the national law of the registry country of the space object. Provided that any intellectual property infringed in outer space is treated as if infringement had occurred within the territory of the particular country, the same level of enforcement in that country should be available in respect of inventions, signs and creations used in outer space. At least within a foreseeable future, activities of human beings in outer space would be confined to activities in a space station or physically connected to the space station. Therefore, the primary concerns about the enforcement of intellectual property in outer space may relate to the manufacturing and use of patented inventions as well as the use of copyrighted products, such as software, in outer space. As regards registered signs such as trademarks, in the future, it is not excluded that those signs would be unlawfully used on an advertisement panel setup in outer space or, once space tourism becomes a reality, that space souvenirs sold in outer space might carry those signs.

For disputes arising within the boundaries of a country, it is a national law that will determine which court is competent to decide intellectual property disputes, including intellectual property infringement cases and validity of registered intellectual property rights.

In case of cross-border litigation, the situation is more complicated. Generally, matters of jurisdiction, applicable law and recognition and enforcement of foreign judgments are subject to a country's national rules of private international law. Since harmonization in this respect is still limited, a whole set of national private international laws coexist, and cross-border litigation often requires a complex analysis of questions of jurisdiction.

Nevertheless, in general, a number of jurisdiction laws set forth the complementary concepts of "general jurisdiction" and "special jurisdiction." General jurisdiction is based primarily on the "*actor sequitur forum rei*" principle, the idea behind which is that the plaintiff must bring suit against the defendant in the State of his/her domicile, habitual residence or principal place of business. Special jurisdiction rules focus more on the issue at stake, and refer jurisdiction in intellectual property matters, for example, to the place where a registration or deposit has been made, or in cases of intellectual property infringements considered as tort, where the harmful event took place or the damage occurred.

At the international level, a widely accepted multilateral instrument which covers jurisdiction and the enforcement of foreign judgments (including intellectual property disputes) does not yet exist. On a regional scale, in Europe, the fundamental instrument on jurisdiction is the Council Regulation 44/2001 on Jurisdiction and the Recognition and Enforcement of Judgements in Civil and Commercial Matters (Brussels I). As regards intellectual property litigation, Brussels I distinguishes between proceedings concerned with the registration or validity of patents, trademarks, designs and other intellectual property rights which require registration or deposit, and jurisdiction in other disputes involving intellectual property rights. Disputes involving the registration and validity of registered intellectual property rights are under exclusive jurisdiction of the courts of the Member State in which the deposit or registration has been applied for or has taken place. For other types of intellectual property disputes, it provides that the general and special jurisdiction rules of Brussels I apply. According to Brussels I, general jurisdiction is based on the defendant's domicile in a Member State, irrespective of the defendant's nationality. Further, in matters relating to a contract, the courts of the place where the contractual obligation in question was to be performed and, in cases of tort, the courts of the place where the harmful event occurred or may occur have special jurisdiction.

As a part of contractual agreement, parties of a contract may determine, for example, a specific court, or the courts of a specific country, to have jurisdiction over disputes arising between them in connection with that contract. Such "choice of court clauses" are particularly common in international commercial agreements. Despite the prevalence in contracts, national systems vary considerably as to the prerequisites of choice of court clauses.

While a number of countries place strict formalities on the acceptance of such clauses, such as the identification of a particular court, other countries also limit the possibility of choice of court clauses to business-to-business contracts, or provide special requirements and limitations for clauses involving consumers. In order to harmonize at least some of those issues, and to create greater predictability and reliability in this field, a draft Convention on exclusive choice of court agreements has been discussed under the auspices of the Hague Conference on Private International Law. In this context, the discussion on intellectual property matters focuses, in particular, on the question as to which intellectual property rights should be covered by the Convention.[195]

Under the IGA, since the ESA elements are treated as if it were a "common" territory of the European Partner States, each of them could enforce its intellectual property law. In terms of enforcement of intellectual property rights, therefore, it needs certain additional rules regarding the intellectual property which is protected in more than one European Partner State. The question arises whether a single act that occurred in or on an ESA-registered element constitutes infringement of the same intellectual property rights owned by the same owner in more than one European Partner State. Could the right holder be entitled to compensation in accordance with each national law of the European Partner States concerned for a single act that occurred in or on the

195. The Preliminary draft Convention on exclusive choice of court agreements can be found at assets.hcch.net/docs/003aeeea-b175-45e3-a533-46ffd15f6cc2.pdf (accessed on February 8, 2024).

ESA-registered element? According to Article 21(4) of the IGA, where a person or entity owns intellectual property which is protected in more than one European Partner State, that person or entity could bring the proceedings against infringement only in one country.

Another question arises where the intellectual property right was granted with respect to the same subject matter in more than one European Partner State, and was transferred to another party in some, but not all, of those European Partner States. Could each right holder be entitled to compensation in accordance with the national law of the European Partner State concerned for the single act that occurred in or on the ESA-registered element? Article 21(4), second sentence provides that, where the same act of infringement in or on the ESA-registered element gives rise to actions by different intellectual property owners by virtue of more than one European Partner State's deeming the activity to have occurred in its territory, a court may grant a temporary stay of proceedings in a later-filed action pending the outcome of the earlier-filed action. Thus, the court has the discretion of deciding for an order of a temporary stay of the proceedings. However, in accordance with Article 21(4), third sentence, where more than one action is brought by different right owners, satisfaction of a judgment rendered for damages in any of the actions should bar further recovery of damages in any pending or future action of infringement based upon the same act of infringement. Therefore, from the viewpoint of intellectual property owners, much depends on the quick expedition of litigation in the different States.

In addition, enforcement of intellectual property rights in or on the ESA-registered elements may require further adjustment to the traditional "territorial" concept of intellectual property rights as far as licensing agreements are concerned. For example, a licensee x under the national law of European Partner State X in relation to a certain patent in the State X and a licensee y under the national law of another Partner State Y in relation to the same patent registered in the State Y may not be the same party. Do both licensees x and y have a right to use the patented technology in accordance with the terms and conditions of the licensing agreements in or on the ESA-registered elements in outer space? Where a patent with respect to the same subject matter is owned by a third-party z in another European Partner State Z, could the owner z prevent the licensees x and y from using the patented technology in or on the ESA-registered elements by virtue of assuming that the patented technology is used in the territory of the State Z without the owner's consent? In order to answer those questions, Article 21(5) of the IGA provides that no European Partner State may refuse to recognize a license for the exercise of any intellectual property right if that license is enforceable under the law of any European Partner State, and compliance with the conditions of such license should also bar recovery for infringement in any European Partner State. Thus, it seems that a non-exclusive licensee in any of the European Partner States could use the licensed subject matter in or on the ESA-registered elements in accordance with the terms and conditions of the licensing agreement, without being in conflict with other licensees and right holders in other European Partner States.

In sum, as regards the elements registered by the ESA, the IGA intends to provide practical solutions to bridge the "national territory" approach adopted in respect of the enforcement of intellectual property rights on Earth and the assumption that the ESA-registered elements are deemed to be a "common territory" of all European Partner States. In addition to the fact that such an adjustment creates another layer of complexity, some argue that it is not clear how an injunction issued by a national court could be executed on the space station in view of the fact that the ESA and its staff members enjoy the legal privileges and immunities provided for in the ESA Convention. It is also pointed out that, since Article 21(4) of the IGA concerns the same subject matter protected in more than one European Partner State, the identification of the same subject matter may not always be straightforward, in particular with respect to patents with claims drafted differently. Further, in addition to the general difficulties found in the enforcement of intellectual property at the international level, in outer space, it would be more difficult to detect infringing activities and to provide evidence for the alleged infringement.

It should be noted that, in the field of patents, many national laws provide that the rights conferred by a patent should not extend to the use of patented subject matter for the purposes of non-commercial experimentation and research. What constitutes "non-commercial" activities and the definition of the term "experimentation and research" differ from one country to another. The underlying objective of such an exception, however, is to provide a balance between the patentee who obtains exclusive rights and third parties who wish to test the reproducibility and usefulness of the patented invention or who wish to further develop the technology by way of experimenting with the patented subject matter. Since many activities in outer space could be characterized as experimental and research activities, certain uses of patented technology in outer space may fall under the experiment and research exemption, depending on the scope of the experiment and research exemption clause under the national law.

[3] Role of Arbitration and Mediation

By their nature, outer space activities often involve intellectual property rights registered in one or more jurisdictions. Inevitably, the increase in the number of international commercial contracts regarding space activities also increases the likelihood of disputes arising. Considering the origin and nature of such disputes, mediation, arbitration or other ADR procedures may offer advantages that are particularly relevant to space activities.[196]

[4] Synergy with Other International Obligations and Morality

As prescribed in Articles I and II of the Outer Space Treaty, the exploration and use of outer space for the benefit of mankind and the non-appropriation of outer space by any

196. On arbitration and mediation, and WIPO's mandate in that regard, *see* §14.02, *supra*.

nation are fundamental principles under international space law. Although the participation of the private sector in space activities is increasingly visible today, these principles are still valid.

While recognizing the importance of intellectual property for the exploration of outer space and the further development of science and technology, questions have been raised as to whether the protection and enforcement of intellectual property rights may conflict with fundamental principles laid down in the Outer Space Treaty.

One of the issues concerns the access to knowledge and information derived from space activities. In view of Article I, paragraph 1 of the Outer Space Treaty which stipulates that exploration and use of outer space "must be effected for the good and in the interest of all countries, regardless of their state of economic and scientific development, being the attribute of all mankind," it has been argued that the knowledge and information resulting from space activities should be available to all countries, in particular, to developing countries.[197] For example, earth observation data may be useful in the areas which are critically important for all nations, such as agriculture, natural resources, protection of the environment as well as the prevention and intervention in the event of natural disasters.

Another issue concerns the freedom of exploration and use of outer space on the one hand and the possibility of excluding others from accessing to outer space by way of obtaining intellectual property rights on the other. Today, there is general agreement that the notions of propriety rights over space objects and of appropriation of outer space *as such* should be clearly distinguished. However, it is pointed out that, in certain cases, protection of intellectual property may hamper the development of subsequent research, especially in the case of intelligent orbits for which the necessary technology has been patented. Since these orbits are elliptical and quasi-geostationary, but located outside the equatorial zone, their characteristics of not requiring limited frequencies provide significant advantages for the application to telecommunication. It is argued that such a patent that would cover a system or a method of satellite communication using these orbits would have the effect of limiting the access to those orbits by third parties.[198]

The World Commission on the Ethics of Scientific Knowledge and Technology (COMEST), which is an advisory body of UNESCO, looked into the issues relating to the ethical dimension of outer space activities, and adopted Recommendations at its second session, held from December 17 to 19, 2001.[199] The COMEST believes that every space policy must be based on the concept of mutual and reciprocal benefits, while safeguarding fair competition and the principle of return on investment. It emphasizes the importance of the role that ethics must play in the choice of a specific

197. Pompidou, A. (2000), "The Ethics of Space Policy," UNESCO.
198. *Ibid.*
199. *See*, World Commission on the Ethics of Scientific Knowledge and Technology (COMEST), Recommendations on the Ethics of Outer Space, Rapporteur Mr. Alain Pompidou, March 2002, available at unesdoc.unesco.org/ark:/48223/pf0000127026.page=4 (accessed on February 8, 2024).

project and its long-term assessment from the viewpoint of human security and economic criteria.

In connection with the intellectual property issues, the COMEST recommends:

> To take all appropriate measures to provide researchers with free access to scientific data in order to guarantee sharing of knowledge with a view to promote scientific progress; to place scientific outer space data at the disposal of the developing countries; to foster the definition of procedures to permit sharing of the resulting benefits, bearing in mind the legitimate interests of these countries and acting in the most equitable and balanced manner possible.

It further recommends:

> To pursue reflection with a view to reaching an agreement on the management of intellectual property in manned stations and more broadly in the field of outer space industry, notably as to the eligibility for patenting of products or processes produced in orbital stations or associated with on-board materials or vehicles.

It should be noted that many national patent laws take into account the ethical concerns. They contain a provision according to which inventions the commercial exploitation of which is necessary to protect public order or morality are not patentable.[200] Further, with respect to the enforcement of patent rights, in order to prevent the abuses which might result from the exercise of the exclusive rights conferred by a patent, many national laws provide that a nonvoluntary license may be granted to a third party or the government without the owner's consent. The owner, however, should be paid adequate remuneration. A similar nonvoluntary license may be granted in the cases where the nonvoluntary license is deemed necessary due to a national emergency or other circumstances of extreme urgency.

However, national patent laws obviously do not address all the public policy issues. The determination of the patentability of an invention is essentially based on a technical evaluation of the invention in view of existing technical art, such as the determination of novelty, inventive step (non-obviousness) and industrial applicability (utility). It is other laws that regulate and control the commercial exploitation of patented inventions from the viewpoint of public welfare. For example, in order to safeguard the quality and safety of pharmaceutical products and certain chemical products, those products, whether they are patented or not, are subject to strict marketing approval processes before commercial exploitation. Many products, from daily goods to high technology products, should comply with various quality standards and safety standards for their commercial exploitation. Thus, patent law is not deemed to be a major legal instrument to monitor and control issues such as public security and welfare. In any event, a patent does not confer a positive exclusive right to exploit or market the patented invention. Such a consideration is reflected in Article 4*quater* of

200. In Art. 27.2, the TRIPS Agreement provides that "members may exclude from patentability inventions, the prevention within their territory of the commercial exploitation of which is necessary to protect order public morality, including to protect human, animal or plant life or health or to avoid serious prejudice to the environment, provided that such exclusion is not made merely because the exploitation is prohibited by their law."

the Paris Convention, which provides that the grant of a patent should not be refused and a patent should not be invalidated on the ground that the sale of the patented product or of a product obtained by means of a patented process is subject to restrictions or limitations resulting from the domestic law.

Under the national laws on copyright of most countries, databases that constitute an intellectual creation by reason of the selection or arrangement of its contents are protected. It is to be noted, however, that the threshold of originality that is required to qualify for copyright protection differs from country to country. While a particular kind of database might be protected under copyright in some countries, a similar database might not qualify for copyright protection in other countries. This means that copyright protection might not be available for certain databases, depending on the level of originality required under the copyright law of a particular jurisdiction, even if substantial investments have been made to produce them. Databases that contain comprehensive information without selection in a straightforward manner, such as alphabetical or numerical order, may not be protected under copyright in all countries. This is why certain countries have extended intellectual property protection to such databases through a sui generis regime. Other models of protection are also available, such as repression of unfair competition or misappropriation laws.

Copyright protection of original databases is well established and harmonized through international treaties to that effect, such as the Berne Convention, the TRIPS Agreement and the WCT. However, there are no international norms on protection of nonoriginal databases.

At regional level, the Directive 96/9/EC of the European Parliament and of the Council of March 11, 1996, on the legal protection of databases grants a sui generis right to database makers to protect their investment of time, money and effort to establish a database, regardless of whether the database is in itself innovative. At national level, the copyright law of Mexico and the Korean Copyright Act of 2003 contain provisions on protection of nonoriginal databases.

[5] Interpretation of Article 5ter *of the Paris Convention*

As described above, Article 5*ter* of the Paris Convention provides for certain limitations on the exclusive rights conferred by a patent in the public interest in guaranteeing freedom of transport. In principle, if ships, aircraft or land vehicles temporarily visit foreign countries and have patented invention on board, licenses on patents in force in these countries are not required in order to avoid infringing such patents (doctrine of temporary presence).

The question arises whether the doctrine of temporary presence applies to spacecraft. It can be argued that, since Article 5*ter* of the Paris Convention only mentions vessels, aircraft or land vehicles, space objects do not fall under this provision; therefore, the temporary presence of elements of a space station for the purpose of launching or return in a foreign country will not automatically be exempted from patent infringement. According to this argument, in the context of international cooperation, if the transport of payloads or flight elements of country X depends on launchers registered by country Y, the space agency of country X might infringe patents enforced in country Y due to the fact that the nationality of the launchers is country Y.

In order to clarify this question, the IGA shed some light on the temporary presence of an article in relation to outer space activities in Article 21(6). According to that Article, the temporary presence in the territory of a Partner State of any article, including the components of flight elements, in transit between any place on Earth and any flight element of the Space Station registered by another Partner State or ESA should not in itself form the basis for any proceedings in the first Partner State for patent infringement. Thus, the transport of patented articles to or from the Space Station through a launching site would not infringe patents enforceable in the country of the launching site.

[6] Ownership and Entitlement

The principles for determining ownership of intellectual property and entitlement to use objects protected by intellectual property rights are the same for cooperative space efforts as for cooperative projects on the ground. Ownership of technology resulting from joint development is often determined by the terms of the joint agreement itself. Thus, when inventions or other objects of intellectual property are expected to be produced in the execution of the joint activities, it is advisable that the following issues be agreed upon beforehand: (i) the extent to which any inventions or other technology developed during the joint activity will not be published or disclosed before patents are applied for, or before all parties agree to publish or disclose the technology; (ii) the entitlement to rights; and (iii) the entitlement to benefit from any technology developed during that activity. Similarly, the partners to a joint project should agree on a system that suits their interests for the purposes of protecting confidential information shared by them in a cooperative international project.

Further, in general, the development of distinct public-sector intellectual property management skills and policy mechanisms are important for effective deployment of public funds. In particular, since space activities are largely supported by public investment and other public resources, establishing policies for managing intellectual property from public funded research is essential for successful public-private partnership models.

As a separate issue, currently, many national laws require that an inventor should first apply for patent protection in the State of which the inventor is a resident or in the State in which the invention was made. This is due to the concern that, without such a measure, inventions involving national security might be disclosed in foreign countries by way of filing patent applications abroad. If such a requirement is imposed in relation to international cooperation activities in an ISS, it might have a negative effect on the sharing of elements for research and on the collaboration of researchers from different countries. Thus, in Article 21(3), the IGA states that, in respect of an invention made in or on any Space Station flight element by a person who is not its national or resident, a Partner State should not apply its law concerning secrecy of inventions so as to prevent the filing of a patent application (for imposing a delay or requiring prior authorization) in any other Partner State that provides for the protection of the secrecy of patent applications containing information that is classified or otherwise protected for national security purposes. Therefore, despite the general principle in Article 21(2) of the IGA that activities carried out in the Space Station flight element should be deemed to have occurred in the territory of the Partner State of that element's registry, the rule concerning secrecy of inventions for the purposes of national security should not apply to an inventor who is not the national or resident of that State. However, in accordance with Article 21(3), second sentence, once the inventor has filed a patent application with the Office of a particular country, the provisions concerning secrecy of inventions for the purposes of national security of that country may apply to that application.

[E] Conclusion

It can be expected that technical inputs as well as financial contributions from the private sector will become more and more important in the context of future development of outer space activities. Further advances in a wide range of technologies will create more opportunities for the development of new space applications by the private sector. Although a number of public policy tools can be envisaged to attract the participation of the private sector, intellectual property protection will play an important role in developing successful space business models involving public/private collaborations. While it is difficult to forecast the future, it is very likely that intellectual property protection will be one of the key factors for the establishment of the institutional and regulatory environment that supports further development of space business.

In the absence of legal certainty as to how the territorial jurisdiction under intellectual property law could apply to extraterritorial activities on a spacecraft which is subject to nationality jurisdiction, in practice, registered space objects are treated as quasi-territory for the purposes of intellectual property under a number of international agreements concluded with respect to international space projects. This leads to a patchwork of national intellectual property laws each of which could only be applicable on a relevant registered object. It means that, in the case of international cooperation activities, a complex segmentation of the ISS, or any other future international platform, cannot be avoided.

Further, the lack of a global agreement leads to the situation that an agreement would have to be concluded among the parties in each single case of international cooperation.

From a business perspective, one expert considers that the legal certainty is an essential factor for the space industry. He suggests that, while recognizing the difficulties to overcome the existing national and territorial legal framework, the best solution be to declare space and its accessories (e.g., launch sites and vehicles) as a single territory with a single and uniform law and with a single and universal enforcement body.[201] Indeed, it appears that many of the practical difficulties that arise from the commercial application of space technologies stem from the very principle of territoriality and differences among national intellectual property law. To name a few, industrial property rights should be obtained and enforced in each country in which the protection is sought under its applicable law; the same subject matter may not be protected to the same extent in various countries; the requirements concerning the entitlement to the rights, including the employee's entitlement to his/her creation, are different under each national law; the rules concerning licensing contracts and the protection of confidential information vary in each country; and the enforceability of a court judgment in respect of an international dispute may not always be certain.

Such differences among national intellectual property laws, however, affect not only the space business, but also any other business which expands at the international level. The increasing international dimension of trade and business requires protection of intellectual property assets beyond the borders of the home country. The differences among the national laws require an applicant to "customize" the application in accordance with the applicable law. Time and efforts being spent for the customization of the application to accommodate national specificity may be considerable, and often, professional advice by a local expert is indispensable. Facing this challenge, in order to facilitate the access to the patent system internationally, a number of treaties and recommendations have been adopted under the auspices of WIPO, and efforts for further harmonization of intellectual property law and practice have been undertaken in WIPO in all fields of intellectual property.

Although harmonization of national intellectual property law and practice would eliminate some of the difficulties faced by space agencies and space industries at the practical level, the fundamental issue, i.e., the establishment of an appropriate legal framework for identifying and exercising intellectual property rights in connection with extraterritorial activities, remains unresolved. In order to forestall any legal complexity and disputation, and to underpin the cooperative development of space-based industries, a broad debate on the long-term prospects of space activities would contribute to the progressive development of a less ambiguous and better-coordinated international intellectual property framework. A simple and reliable international legal framework would facilitate maximizing the collective utilization of public and private resources in the area of space technology for the benefit of all nations.

§37.05 AI AND PATENTS[202]

[A] Introduction

The notion of AI is very broad and it has been frequently mistaken for computer programs. But AI is much less that computer software: AI is the capacity of machines

201. Bradford Smith, *Matching Space-Related Intellectual Property Rights to Space Industry Needs*, Echanges ASPI-1997, No. 53.
202. The copyright approach to artificial intelligence is discussed in §37.02[F], above.

producing tasks that are (or have been, so far) exclusive to the human brain. In general, those tasks imply two sorts of behavior that, once again, were exclusive of human beings: to learn, and to create (in the sense of using intuition). Three of the best-known examples of AI that are, today, already functional and operational are *Google Translate*,[203] a superb tool (at least as far as the most common languages are concerned) that has been improving significantly in the last years, and that is capable of providing surprisingly accurate translations, even for texts that contain idiomatic expressions and other forms of innuendo; *ChatGPT*,[204] an open innovation model, which in the form of dialogue, responds to almost any questions that one may wish to ask, obtaining and elaborating well-informed and relatively reliable answers by searching the huge Internet database; and IBM's *watsonx*,[205] a platform that assists businesses in modeling, creating, and applying AI to different purposes, namely by creating intelligent Apps and supervising their entire lifecycle. Moreover, computer vision is one of the most popular applications of AI.[206]

AI is becoming pervasive and the sophistication of its logical and mathematical modules is contributing to the improvement of its intelligence. Accordingly:

> traditional chatbots follow scripted responses and rely on pre-defined rules to interact with users, making them suitable only for specific tasks. In contrast, modern GenAI chatbots such as ChatGPT or Google Gemini can generate human-like text, allowing for conversations that can adapt to many topics without being confined to a predetermined script. In addition, these modern chatbots can produce not only text, but also images, music and computer code based on the dataset on which they were trained.[207]

In IBM's words:

> Under the broad umbrella term of AI is supervised and unsupervised learning, machine learning, several different AI mathematical algorithms (e.g., linear regression, decision trees, etc.) and programming concepts, data sets including deep data, validation sets, test sets, training data, and real-time data. AI also includes aspects that are part of a "black box" (i.e., hidden) including trained models, the coefficients embedded in the trained models, algorithms to train the models, parameters for tweaking the models, neural networks and deep neural networks, and the insights gained from output of using a trained model.[208]

AI-related technology is developing fast, which is represented by the significant increase in publications and patent applications. However, that development does not follow the same pace in all areas: in some areas AI is developing faster than in others. Significantly, AI-related technology that is acquired in other sector frequently can be used in other sectors, which makes the impact of AI in industry and services even more

203. Accessible through translate.google.com.
204. Accessible through chat.openai.com.
205. Accessible through www.ibm.com/watsonx.
206. *See* WIPO, Artificial Intelligence, in WIPO Technology Trends 2019, Executive Trends.
207. WIPO, Generative Artificial Intelligence, Patent Landscape Report, 2024, at 3.
208. *See* IBM Corporation Comments in Response to "Request for Comments on Patenting Artificial Intelligence Inventions," 84 Fed. Reg. 44889 (August 27, 2019), available at www.uspto.gov/initiatives/artificial-intelligence/notices-artificial-intelligence.

preeminent. A search through patent data available in 2019 revealed the abundance of cross-references to AI in patent applications:

> These include, in order of magnitude: telecommunications (mentioned in 15 percent of all identified patent documents), transportation (15 percent), life and medical sciences (12 percent), and personal devices, computing and human–computer interaction (HCI) (11 percent). Other sectors featuring in the results include banking; entertainment; security; industry and manufacturing; agriculture; and networks (including social networks, smart cities and the Internet of things).[209]

[B] Issues

The interface of AI with intellectual property gives rise to two different issues: (1) AI while the subject matter of intellectual property, in particular, of patents; and (2) AI as a creator or inventor. This second issue originates two subsets of discussions: (a) the possibility of designating AI as the author of a work or the inventor of an invention; and (b) AI as the owner of intellectual property. Next, we will discuss these topics very briefly.

[1] AI as Subject Matter of Intellectual Property

AI as subject matter of intellectual property may raise some difficult issues concerning the patentability of certain computer programs and business models, i.e., of software that is implemented by computers, as discussed in the first section of this chapter, but, otherwise, begs for a relatively straightforward answer: AI, in its multiple forms, can, indeed, be appropriated, both directly and indirectly, through the various rights that make up intellectual property.

In this token, the programs that lend intelligence to the machines can be copyrighted. In certain circumstances, as discussed, they can also (or, rather, alternatively) be protected by patents. The same goes for the algorithms that are the "soul" of intelligent machines, and permit their self-learning and self-improving.[210]

The machines themselves, or their parts, can be covered by utility patents (or patents for inventions), utility models, and, where they present esthetical features, they can be protected by design patents or certificates for registered designs.

209. WIPO, Artificial Intelligence, 2019, at 5.

210. WIPO research on the trends of patenting generative (i.e., *grosso modo*, creative) AI, concluded that applications in the last decade have concerned twenty-one application areas, including software (the largest application area), life sciences, telecommunications, and agriculture, among others. "Patent families in the other categories are smaller in number, with life sciences in second place (5,346 patent families between 2014 and 2023) and document management and publishing (4,976) in third place (Figure 26). Other notable applications with GenAI patent families ranging from around 2,000 to around 5,000 over the same period are business solutions, industry and manufacturing, transportation, security and telecommunications." *Ibid.*, at 57-58.

The techniques of designing and programming the machines as well as the programs and algorithms themselves can be protected under trade secrets.[211]

It goes without saying that the business and the trading of AI-derived products fit without any problem in trademark, trade name and unfair competition laws.

This means that, as an object, as inanimate matter, AI raises no fundamental concerns or doubts. AI creators can appropriate it or can leave it as open source (as is the case of ChatGPT).

[2] AI as a Creator or Inventor

This discussion stems from the operation of the so-called generative AI, which, as its name says, is able to create content. And here the term "create" is used in a strict sense, meaning the making of obtaining of something (such as an idea) that did not exist previously. In popular language, if we add 2 plus 2, and reach 4 as a result, there is no creation. But if we add 2 and 2, and reach 5 as a result, in a systematic, consistent, and demonstrable manner, there is genuine creation. Such creation may be the result of luck, but where it is based on research and experimenting, the final result must always contain something of intuitive—something that was not there before.

Before AI, only humans were able to produce such sort of results. But at the current stage, AI can indeed create, be it in the form of literary works, music, arts, or inventions. One may discuss the literary taste of the poems that ChatGPT author, but they are undeniably a product of creation—imaginative, not merely a copying and paste from texts found on the Internet.[212]

---

211. It appears that for a certain period the maker of one of the most successful, thus far, generative AI models, the ChatGPT, owned by OpenAi, was more propense to protect its inventions through trade secrets. Only recently, the number of its patent applications has started to rise, eventually following a strategy of defensive patenting. *See Global Patenting and Research in GenAI*, at 2, in Generative Artificial Intelligence, Patent Landscape Report, 2024. Recently, OpenAI confirmed this strategy in a statement to the market. The statement reads (in part):

> We pledge to only use our patents defensively, so long as a party does not threaten or assert a claim, initiate a proceeding, help someone else in such activities against us, or engage in activities that harm us or our users.

See Davis, R. (October 15, 2024), *OpenAI Says It Will Only Use Its Patents "Defensively,"* available at www.law360.com/articles/1890156 (accessed November 2024).

212. OpenAI is being sued by the New York Times on grounds of massive plagiarism of news reports published by the journal. *See* Grynbaum, M.M. & Mac, R. (December 27, 2013), *The Times Sues OpenAI and Microsoft Over A.I. Use of Copyrighted Work: Millions of Articles from The New York Times Were used to Train Chatbots That Now Compete with It, the Lawsuit Said*, available at www.nytimes.com/2023/12/27/business/media/new-york-times-open-ai-microsoft-lawsuit.html. More recently, Asian News International (ANI) also filed a lawsuit in India against OpenAI alleging infringement caused by the reproduction of news as well as the storing of information. *See* Bloomberg (November 19, 2024), *Agência de notícias indiana processa OpenAI por uso indevido de conteúdo* [*Indian News Agency Sues OpenAI for Unauthorized Use of Content*], available at www.infomoney.com.br/business/agencia-de-noticias-indiana-processa-openai-por-uso-indevido-de-conteudo/ (accessed November 2024).

Regardless of the outcome of this dispute, the fact is that ChatGPT is capable of genuine creation.

On inventions, one may suspect that, given the current stage of AI development, AI may not yet be able to make those breakthrough inventions, which are the product of human genius, intuition, and audacity, and break barriers of long-standing techniques and habits. Being part of a machine, AI, as of today, cannot dream—which is the engine of the greatest inventors. But they can, undoubtedly, produce incremental inventions, the patentability of which should not be challenged.

Once this point is accepted—AI can create and invent—the question that ensues is whether AI can be designated as a creator or inventor and whether it can be recognized as a copyright owner or whether it can be attributed a patent or a design certificate.

In addressing this issue, two different approaches are possible: one is the designation of AI as an inventor *as a matter of fact*; the other is the designation of AI as an inventor *as a matter of law*.

Designating AI as an inventor *as a matter of fact*, as said above, raises not doubts. It is true that, at the current stage, AI is not yet capable of self-awareness. Indeed, if we ask ChatGPT to write a poem about a lake in the mountain, under the bright sun, and surrounded by snowy, steep hills, the computer will write it; but if we close the webpage and ten minutes later reopen it and ask ChatGPT who has written that same poem (and quote a few verses or even the whole poem), the answer ChatGPT will give us is that it does not have elements to identify the author.

But self-awareness is not a condition of inventorship, either as a matter of fact or of law. The situation above described may be assimilated to a person who writes a literary piece and several years later has forgotten it, to the point he/she is not able to recognize it. That person continues being the creator of such piece, no matter what.

AI can also invent. One can even devise in the future an android that not only invents but, subsequently, tests the practical operation of the invention. However, if we stay with computer-implemented inventions, then there is no need for their practical experimentation, so as to check their utility: being essentially abstract, the inventions are self-proved by the computer's operation as intended.

However, as a *matter of law*, AI is not an inventor. The reason is straightforward: patent laws have been established having human beings as targets. Those laws discipline the social relations that stem from creativity and inventiveness, and establish the mechanisms of the acquisition, the enforcement, and the loss of the respective rights. The historical substrates of those rights are unequivocally associated with humans: on the one hand, although the conditions of artificiality may have not been clearly identified in the first patent statutes of the fifteenth and seventeenth centuries, privileges were not to be granted to Nature, but to the human applicants. On the other hand, although automats have been developed and used since the days of Alexandria's Museum, no state leader has ever thought of the possibility of their behaving like humans.

In *international law*, we find language that clearly suggests that intellectual property has not been designed in a way that admits that machines can be treated as inventors. One example is found in Article 4*ter* of the Paris Convention, which reads:

> The inventor shall have the right to be mentioned as such in the patent.

This text leads to two consequences. One is that, machines not being recognized as holders of rights, there would be no way possible to acknowledge this "moral right of paternity" to a computer. Second, this provision implies the possibility of the inventor's waiving the right to be designated as such in the patent letter, and opting for anonymity. But, as far a machine is concerned, it is not capable of making that kind of options.

The same conclusion has to be reached as far as *national* law is concerned. To mention one example only, Article I, section 8, Clause 8, of the US Constitution provides:

> "The Congress shall have power: [...]
>
> To promote the Progress of Science and useful Arts, by securing for limited Times to Authors and Inventors the exclusive Right to their respective Writings and Discoveries."

The necessarily human nature of inventors lies in the fact that computers or androids do not respond to incentives. They are not reactive to encouragements. Generative AI operates as a result of pressing a key on a computer. If a computer could be seen as responsive to incentives, these could be the keyboard and electric current.

In the field of patents, this matter has already been discussed. The US owner (Steven Thaler) of a computer that carries generative AI, designated as DABUS, has filed national and international patent applications mentioning DABUS as the inventor. The following table shows the outcome of that mention in nine jurisdictions, revealing that there is practically unanimity in rejecting that idea:[213]

Countries Where DABUS Has Been Designated by the Patent Applicant as an AI Inventor

Country	*Result of the Designation*
Australia	rejected
Brazil	rejected
European Patent Office (EPO)	rejected
Germany	rejected
Japan	rejected
New Zealand	rejected
South Africa	accepted*
Saudi Arabia	rejected
South Korea	rejected

213. *See also* Egbuonu, K. (December 20, 2023), *The Latest News on DABUS Patent Case*, available at www.ipstars.com/NewsAndAnalysis/The-latest-news-on-the-DABUS-patent-case/Index/7366 (accessed on February 10, 2024).

Countries Where DABUS Has Been Designated by the Patent Applicant as an AI Inventor	
Country	*Result of the Designation*
United Kingdom	rejected
United States	rejected

* Patent applications in South Africa are not examined as regards substantive matters, such as inventorship and ownership.

[3] AI as a Patent Owner

It follows from the previous discussion that AI cannot be the owner of patent rights. The reason is that those rights belong originally in the true inventor, who keeps or assigns them. Because a machine cannot be designated as author or inventor, there is nothing that machine could subsequently assign to its owner (or *employer*?). Moreover, even if we were willing to admit the possibility of a machine to be designated as the inventor, such machine would not have the ability to assign the right to (or of) ownership. Machines are not legal entities, so they cannot hold, enforce, or assign rights.

[C] Conclusion

Although AI is an old concept, and since Antiquity humans have attempted to ease and simply tasks by resorting to intelligent machines, this is an area of technology that is now in frank expansion and consolidation. Recent developments in computer science and in electronics have permitted the obtaining of ever more intelligent machines. The growing use of AI in all areas of human life will have (and is already having) an enormous impact on the ways we live in society. But as AI expands and gives rise to the sort of technical, legal, ethical issues above discussed, a number of questions will necessarily emerge, to which we are not yet prepared to give a full response.

For example:

(1) Will intelligent machines evolve from *things* into *beings*?
(2) Will intelligent machines cease being considered subject matter of rights and become right owners?
(3) Will intelligent machines be recognized as legal entities? As copyright owners? As patent owners?
(4) Will there be any limits as to how much, and how far, and how fast AI will evolve?

As always, humans will respond to these challenges by trial and error. Just let us hope that errors will not be too many or irreparable.

Additional Readings

This book is just an introduction to the theory and practice of Intellectual Property, and thus it is not intended to exhaust the many subjects it covers. Readers, therefore, are strongly recommended to seek deeper and more detailed information in specialized books and reviews. Additionally, various contributors of the chapters of this book have suggested complementary readings that can be found on the websites of WIPO (www.wipo.int) and UPOV (ww.upov.int). A list of those suggestions follows:

IP in General

Summaries of Conventions, Treaties and Agreements Administered by WIPO, 2013, WIPO Publication No. 442E/13, www.wipo.int/edocs/pubdocs/en/intproperty/442/wipo_pub_442.pdf.

The Effects of IP on Economic and Technological Development

Aghion, P. & Howitt, P. (1990). A Model of Growth Through Creative Destruction.

Benavente, M.J. (2006). The Role of Research and Innovation in Promoting Productivity in Chile. *Economics of Innovation and New Technology*, 15(4-5), pp. 301-315 doi: 10.1080/10438590500512794.

Benavente, J.M. & Lauterbach, R. (2008). Technological Innovation and Employment: Complements or Substitutes?. *The European Journal of Development Research*, 20, pp. 318-329 doi: 10.1080/09578810802060744.

Bresnahan, T.F. & Trajtenberg, M. (1995). General Purpose Technologies "Engines of Growth?" *National Bureau of Economic Research Working Paper Series*, No. 4148.

Bronzini, R. & Piselli, P. (2016). The Impact of R&D Subsidies on Firm Innovation. *Research Policy*, 45(2), pp. 442-457 doi: 10.1016/j.respol.2015.10.008.

Chudnovsky, D., López, A. & Pupato, G. (2006). Innovation and Productivity in Developing Countries: A Study of Argentine Manufacturing Firms' Behavior (1992-2001). *Research Policy*, 35(2), pp. 266-288 doi: 10.1016/j.respol.2005.10.002.

Cirera, X., Lage, F., & Sabetti, L. (2016). ICT Use, Innovation and Productivity: Evidence from Sub-Saharan Africa (Policy Research Working Paper No. 7868). Retrieved from World Bank website: http://documents.worldbank.org/curated/

en/997211476897844312/ICT-useinnovation-and-productivity-evidence-from-Sub-Saharan-Africa.

Cohen, W.M. & Levinthal, D.A. (1990). Absorptive Capacity: A New Perspective on Learning and Innovation. *Administrative Science Quarterly*, pp. 128-152 doi: 10.2307/2393553.

Comin, D. & Mestieri, M. (2018). If Technology Has Arrived Everywhere, Why Has Income Diverged?. *American Economic Journal: Macroeconomics*, 10(3), pp. 137-178 doi: 10.1257/mac.20150175.

Crépon, B., Duguet, E. & Mairessec, J. (1998). Research, Innovation and Productivity: An Econometric Analysis at the Firm Level. *Economics of Innovation and New Technology*, 7(2), pp. 115-158 doi: 10.1080/10438599800000031.

Crespi, G., Tacsir, E., & Vargas, F. (2016). Innovation Dynamics and Productivity: Evidence for Latin America. *Firm Innovation and Productivity in Latin America and the Caribbean: The Engine of Economic Development,* pp. 37-71 doi: 10.1057/978-1-349-58151-1_2.

Crespi, G., & Zuniga, P. (2012). Innovation and Productivity: Evidence from Six Latin American Countries. *World Development,* 40(2), pp. 273-290 doi: 10.1016/j.worlddev.2011.07.010.

Criscuolo, C., Haskel, J.E. & Slaughter, M.J. (2010). Global Engagement and the Innovation Activities of Firms. *International Journal of Industrial Organization*, 28(2), pp. 191-202 doi: 10.1016/j.ijindorg.2009.07.012.

De Long, J.B. (1988). Productivity Growth, Convergence, and Welfare: Comment. *The American Economic Review*, 78(5), pp. 1138-1154.

Edquist, C. (2013). Systems of Innovation: Technologies, Institutions and Organizations. Routledge.

Fagerberg, J., Mowery, D.C. & Nelson, R.R. (2006). The Oxford Handbook of Innovation. Oxford: Oxford University Press.

Freeman, C. (1994). Innovation and Growth. In M. Dodgson & R. Rothwell (eds.), *The Handbook of Industrial Innovation*. Cheltenham, UK: Elgar, 78-93.

Freeman, C. (1987). Technology Policy and Economic Performance: Lessons from Japan. London: Pinter.

Jones, C.I. & Romer, P.M. (2010). The New Kaldor Facts: Ideas, Institutions, Population, and Human Capital. *American Economic Journal: Macroeconomics*, 2(1), pp. 224-245 doi: 10.1257/mac.2.1.224.

Grazzi, M. & Jung, J. (2016). Information and Communication Technologies, Innovation, and Productivity: Evidence from Firms in Latin America and the Caribbean. *Firm Innovation and Productivity in Latin America and the Caribbean: The Engine of Economic Development,* pp. 103-135, doi: 10.1057/978-1-349-58151-1_4.

Griffith, R., Huergo, E., Mairesse, J. & Peters, B. (2006). Innovation and Productivity Across Four European Countries. *Oxford Review of Economic Policy*, 22(4), pp. 483-498 doi: 10.1093/oxrep/grj028.

Grossman, G.M. & Helpman, E. (1994). Endogenous Innovation in the Theory of Growth. *Journal of Economic Perspectives*, 8(1), pp. 23-44 doi: 10.1257/jep.8.1.23.

Grossman, G.M. & Helpman, E. (1991). Trade, Knowledge Spillovers, and Growth. *European Economic Review*, 35(2-3), pp. 517-526 doi: 10.1016/0014-2921(91)90153-a.

Guinet, J., Hutschenreiter, G. & Keenan, M. (2009). Innovation Strategies for Growth: Insights from OECD Countries.

Hall, B.H., Mairesse, J. & Mohnen, P. (2010). Measuring the Returns to R&D. In *Handbook of the Economics of Innovation* (Vol. 2). North-Holland: 1033-1082.

Jefferson, G.H., Huamao, B., Xiaojing, G., & Xiaoyun, Y. (2006). R&D Performance in Chinese Industry. Economics of Innovation and New Technology, 15(4-5), pp. 345-366 doi: 10.1080/10438590500512851.

Han, G., K. Kalijaran & N. Singh. (2002). Productivity and Economic Growth in East Asia: Innovation, Efficiency and Accumulation. *Japan and the World Economy*, 14(4) doi: 10.1016/S0922-1425(02)00028-2.

Khan, M. & Luintel, K.B. (2006). Sources of Knowledge and Productivity: How Robust Is the Relationship?, *OECD Science, Technology and Industry Working Papers* 2006/06.

Lundvall, B.A. (1992). National Systems of Innovation: Towards a Theory of Innovation and Interactive Learning. London: Pinter.

Mairesse, J. & Mohnen, P. (2010). Using Innovation Surveys for Econometric Analysis. In *Handbook of the Economics of Innovation* (Vol. 2). North-Holland: 1129-1155.

Raffo, J., Lhuillery, S., & Miotti, L. (2008). Northern and Southern Innovativity: A Comparison Across European and Latin American Countries. *European Journal of Development Research*, 20(2), pp. 219-239 doi: 10.1080/09578810802060777.

Reynolds, G.H. (1990), *Legislative Comment: The Patents in Space Act*, 3 Harv. J. Law & Tec 13, Spring.

Romer, P.M. (1986). Increasing Returns and Long-Run Growth. *Journal of Political Economy*, 94(5), pp. 1002-1037 doi: 10.1086/261420.

Romer, P.M. (2010). What Parts of Globalization Matter for Catch-Up Growth?. *American Economic Review*, 100(2), pp. 94-98 doi: 10.1257/aer.100.2.94.

Schumpeter, J.A. (2013). Capitalism, Socialism and Democracy. Routledge.

Vahrenwald, A. (1993), *Industrial Property on the Space Station Freedom*, 15(9) E.I.P.R.

World Intellectual Property Report (2011). The Changing Face of Innovation Geneva: *WIPO*. Available at www.wipo.int/edocs/pubdocs/en/intproperty/944/wipo_pub_944_2011.pdf.

Zhou, K. Z., Gao, G. Y., & Zhao, H. (2017). State Ownership and Firm Innovation in China: An Integrated View of Institutional and Efficiency Logics. *Administrative Science Quarterly*, 62(2), pp. 375-404 doi: 10.1177/0001839216674457.

Copyright and Related Rights

Guide to the Copyright and Related Rights Treaties Administered by WIPO and Glossary of Copyright and Related Rights Terms, prepared by Mihály Ficsor, 2004, WIPO

Publication No. 891(E), www.wipo.int/edocs/pubdocs/en/copyright/891/wipo_pub_891.pdf.

Understanding Copyright and Related Rights, 2005, WIPO Publication No. 909(E), http://www.wipo.int/edocs/pubdocs/en/wipo_pub_909_2016.pdf.

Creative Expressions: An Introduction to Copyright and Related Rights for Small and Medium-sized Enterprises, 2023, Intellectual Property for Business Series Number 4, http://www.wipo.int/edocs/pubdocs/en/wipo-pub-918-23-en-creative-expression.pdf.

The Digital Agenda: Implementation of the WIPO Copyright Treaty (WCT) and the WIPO Performances and Phonograms Treaty (WPPT) PCIPD/3/9 2002, www.wipo.int/edocs/mdocs/mdocs/en/pcipd_3/pcipd_3_9.pdf.

IP and Development

The Strategic Use of Intellectual Property for Prosperity and Development: Compendium of the Proceedings of the High-Level Forum on Intellectual Property for the Least Developed Countries, July 23 and 24, 2009, Geneva, Switzerland, 2013, WIPO Publication No. 362e, tind.wipo.int/record/28727?ln = en&v = pdf.

World Intellectual Property Report 2011: The Changing Face of Innovation, 2011, WIPO Publication No. 944E, www.wipo.int/edocs/pubdocs/en/intproperty/944/wipo_pub_944_2011.pdf.

World Intellectual Property Report 2013: Brands—Reputation and Image in the Global Marketplace, 2013, WIPO Publication No. 944E/2013, www.wipo.int/edocs/pubdocs/en/intproperty/944/wipo_pub_944_2013.pdf.

Trademarks

WIPO/STrad/INF/6, *Technical and Procedural Aspects Relating to the Registration of Certification and Collective Marks*, 2010.

Guide to the International Registration of Marks under the Madrid Agreement and the Madrid Protocol, 2014, WIPO Publication No. 455(E), www.wipo.int/publications/en/details.jsp?id = 333&plang = EN.

The Madrid Agreement Concerning the International Registration of Marks and the Protocol Relating to that Agreement: Objectives, Main Features, Advantages, 2012, WIPO Publication No. 418(E), www.wipo.int/edocs/mdocs/mdocs/en/wipo_rs_ip_be_15/wipo_rs_ip_be_15.pdf.

Enforcement

WIPO/ACE/6/7, *The Economic Effects of Counterfeiting and Piracy: A Literature Review*, prepared by C. Fink, K. Maskus, Y. Qian, 2010, www.wipo.int/meetings/en/doc_details.jsp?doc_id = 143332.

WIPO/ACE/7/5, *A Review of Statistical Information on Counterfeiting and Piracy*, prepared by C. Clift, 2011, www.wipo.int/meetings/en/doc_details.jsp?doc_id = 186997.

The Enforcement of Intellectual Property Rights: A Case Book, 4th edition, prepared by L.T.C. Harms, 2020, www.wipo.int/publications/en/details.jsp?id = 4363&plang = EN.

WIPO/ACE/6/8, *A Study Relating to Existing Methods of Disposal and Destruction of Counterfeit Goods and Pirated Goods Within the Asia-Pacific Region*, prepared by D. Blakemore, 2010, www.wipo.int/edocs/mdocs/enforcement/en/wipo_ace_6/wipo_ace_6_8.doc.

J. Soentgen, *Disposing of Counterfeit Goods: Unseen Challenges*, WIPO Magazine, 6/2012, www.wipo.int/wipo_magazine/en/2012/06/article_0007.html.

Genetic Resources, Traditional Knowledge and Traditional Cultural Expressions

Intellectual Property Needs and Expectations of Traditional Knowledge Holders: WIPO Report on Fact-finding Missions (1998-1999), 2001, WIPO Publication No. 768(E), www.wipo.int/edocs/pubdocs/en/tk/768/wipo_pub_768.pdf.

Background Brief—No. 2, *The WIPO Intergovernmental Committee on Intellectual Property and Genetic Resources, Traditional Knowledge and Folklore*, 2016, www.wipo.int/publications/en/details.jsp?id = 3861&plang = EN.

Background Brief—No. 4, *Intellectual Property and Arts Festivals*, 2016, www.wipo.int/publications/en/details.jsp?id = 3869&plang = EN.

Background Brief—No. 7, *Customary Law and Traditional Knowledge*, 2016, www.wipo.int/publications/en/details.jsp?id = 3876&plang = EN.

Background Brief—No. 8, *Alternative Dispute Resolution for Disputes Related to Intellectual Property and Traditional Knowledge, Traditional Cultural Expressions and Genetic Resources*, 2016, www.wipo.int/publications/en/details.jsp?id = 3877&plang = EN.

Background Brief—No. 9, *Documentation of Traditional Knowledge and Traditional Cultural Expressions*, 2016, www.wipo.int/publications/en/details.jsp?id = 3878&plang = EN.

WIPO/GRTKF/IC/17/INF/8, *Note on the Meanings of the Term "Public Domain" in the Intellectual Property System with Special Reference to the Protection of Traditional Knowledge and Traditional Cultural Expressions/Expressions of Folklore*, 2010, www.wipo.int/edocs/mdocs/tk/en/wipo_grtkf_ic_17/wipo_grtkf_ic_17_inf_8.doc.

WIPO-UNEP Study on the Role of Intellectual Property Rights in the Sharing of Benefits Arising from the Use of Biological Resources and Associated Traditional Knowledge, prepared by A.K. Gupta, WIPO Publ. No. 769E, www.wipo.int/edocs/pubdocs/en/tk/769/wipo_pub_769.pdf.

Draft Intellectual Property Guidelines for Access to Genetic Resources and Equitable Sharing of the Benefits arising from their Utilization, 2013, www.wipo.int/export/sites/www/tk/en/docs/resources/redrafted_guidelines.pdf.

Technical Study on Disclosure Requirements in Patent Systems Related to Genetic Resources and Traditional Knowledge, 2004, WIPO Pub. No. 786E, www.wipo.int/publications/en/details.jsp?id = 282&plang = EN.

Key Questions on Patent Disclosure Requirements for Genetic Resources and Traditional Knowledge (WIPO Pub. No. 1047).

Minding Culture: Case Studies on Intellectual Property and Traditional Cultural Expressions, prepared by Ms. T. Janke, 2004, www.wipo.int/publications/en/details.jsp?id = 286&plang = EN.

Intellectual Property and Folk, Arts, and Cultural Festivals: Practical Guide, 2018, www.wipo.int/edocs/pubdocs/en/wipo_pub_1043_2018.pdf.

Documenting Traditional Knowledge: A Toolkit (WIPO Pub. No. 1049).

Protect and Promote Your Culture: A Practical Guide to Intellectual Property for Indigenous Peoples and Local Communities (WIPO Pub. No. 1048).

Traditional Knowledge and Intellectual Property—Background Brief—No. 1.[214]

Developing a National Strategy on Intellectual Property, Traditional Knowledge and Traditional Cultural Expressions—Background Brief—No. 3.

Intellectual Property and Traditional Handicrafts—Background Brief—No. 5.

Intellectual Property and Traditional Medical Knowledge—Background Brief—No. 6.

Customary Law and Traditional Knowledge—Background Brief—No. 7.

Intellectual Property and Genetic Resources—Background Brief—No. 10.

Guide to IP Issues in Access and Benefit-Sharing Agreements (WIPO Pub. No. 1052).

Intellectual Property and the Safeguarding of Traditional Cultures: Legal Issues and Practical Options for Museums, Libraries and Archives (WIPO Pub. No. 1023).

Alternative Dispute Resolution

WIPO Mediation, Arbitration, Expedited Arbitration and Expert Determination Rules, 2021, WIPO Publ. No. 446, https://www.wipo.int/amc/en/rules.

Guide to WIPO Mediation, 2018, WIPO Publ. No. 449, https://www.wipo.int/edocs/pubdocs/en/wipo_pub_449_2018.pdf.

Guide to WIPO Arbitration, 2020, WIPO Publ. No. 919, https://www.wipo.int/edocs/pubdocs/en/wipo_pub_919_2020.pdf.

WIPO Alternative Dispute Resolution Options: A Guide for IP and Courts, 2022, https://www.wipo.int/publications/en/details.jsp?id = 4613&plang = EN.

Guidance on WIPO FRAND Alternative Dispute Resolution (ADR), 2021, https://www.wipo.int/export/sites/www/amc/en/docs/2022/wipo_adr_options_for_frand_disputes_management_resolution.pdf, https://www.wipo.int/export/sites/www/amc/en/docs/2022/wipo_adr_options_for_frand_disputes_management_resolution.pdf.

WIPO ADR Options for Life Sciences Dispute Management and Resolution, 2022, https://www.wipo.int/edocs/pubdocs/en/wipo-pub-rn2022-14-en-wipo-adr-options-for-life-sciences-dispute-management-and-resolution.pdf, https://www.wipo.int/edocs/pubdocs/en/wipo-pub-rn2022-14-en-wipo-adr-options-for-life-sciences-dispute-management-and-resolution.pdf.

214. WIPO Background Briefs on Traditional Knowledge are available at www.wipo.int/publications/en/series/index.jsp?id = 144.

Alternative Dispute Resolution Mechanisms for Business-to-Business Digital Copyright and Content-Related Disputes: A report on the results of the WIPO-MCST Survey, 2021, WIPO Publ. No. 969, https://www.wipo.int/edocs/pubdocs/en/wipo-pub-969-en-alternative-dispute-resolution-mechanisms-for-business-to-business-digital-copyright-and-content-related-disputes.pdf, https://www.wipo.int/edocs/pubdocs/en/wipo-pub-969-en-alternative-dispute-resolution-mechanisms-for-business-to-business-digital-copyright-and-content-related-disputes.pdf.

WIPO Overview of WIPO Panel Views on Selected UDRP Questions, Third Edition ("WIPO Jurisprudential Overview 3.0"), 2017, https://www.wipo.int/amc/en/domains/search/overview3.0, https://www.wipo.int/amc/en/domains/search/overview3.0.

Guide to WIPO's Services for Country Code Top-Level Domain Registries, 2021, WIPO Publ. No. 1069, https://www.wipo.int/edocs/pubdocs/en/wipo-pub-1069-22-en-guide-to-wipo-s-services-for-country-code-top-level-domain-registries.pdf, https://www.wipo.int/edocs/pubdocs/en/wipo-pub-1069-22-en-guide-to-wipo-s-services-for-country-code-top-level-domain-registries.pdf.

WIPO caseload summary, https://www.wipo.int/amc/en/center/caseload.html.

Recommended WIPO contract clauses and submission agreements, https://www.wipo.int/amc/en/clauses/index.html.

Information on WIPO ADR for specific sectors, https://www.wipo.int/amc/en/center/specific-sectors.

WIPO domain name dispute resolution statistics, https://www.wipo.int/amc/en/domains.

Information on WIPO domain name dispute resolution services for ccTLDs, https://www.wipo.int/amc/en/domains/cctld.

Patent Cooperation Treaty

PCT/GEN/7 Rev. 29, of January 1, 2009, *The Patent Cooperation Treaty (PCT) and Its Importance to Developing Countries.*

PCT FAQs: Protection your Inventions Abroad: Frequently Asked Questions About the Patent Cooperation Treaty (PCT), www.wipo.int/pct/en/faqs/faqs.html.

Patent Cooperation Treaty Yearly Review 2016, The International Patent System, WIPO Publication No. 901E, www.wipo.int/edocs/pubdocs/en/wipo_pub_901_2016.pdf.

Patents

Certain Aspects of National/Regional Patent Laws, Revised Annex II of document SCP/12/3 Rev.2: Report on the International Patent System, www.wipo.int/scp/en/annex_ii.html.

SCP/13/3, *Exclusions from Patentable Subject Matter and Exceptions and Limitations to the Rights*, 2009, www.wipo.int/edocs/mdocs/scp/en/scp_13/scp_13_3.pdf.

SCP/14/INF/2, *External Experts' Study Regarding Exclusions, Exceptions and Limitations for the Standing Committee on the Law of Patents (SCP)*, 2010, www.wipo.int/edocs/mdocs/scp/en/scp_14/scp_14_inf_2.pdf.

SCP/18/41, *Opposition* Systems and Other Administrative Revocation and Invalidation Mechanisms.

IP and New Technologies

R. Abbott (ed.), Research Handbook on Intellectual Property and Artificial Intelligence, Edward Elgar Publishing.

Paper: P. Treacy & M. Hunt, *Internet of Things (IoT): Key Legal Issues*, available at https://www.bristows.com/app/uploads/2022/10/Internet-of-Things-IoT%E2%80%94key-legal-issues-Lexis%C2%AEPSL-practical-guida.._.pdf.

D. Gervais, "Exploring the Interfaces Between Big Data and Intellectual Property Law," available at https:// papers.ssrn.com/sol3/papers.cfm?abstract_id=3360344.

P.H. Lim & P. Li, "Artificial Intelligence and Inventorship: Patently Much Ado in the Computer Program," available at https://academic.oup.com/jiplp/article/17/4/376/6562635.

V. Manzo, "The Internet of Things and Intellectual Property Rights: The Protection of Data," available at https://papers.ssrn.com/sol3/papers.cfm?abstract_id=3387417.

UPOV

UPOV/INF/13/1, *Guidance on How to Become a Member of UPOV*, 2009, www.upov.int/edocs/infdocs/en/upov_inf_13_1.pdf.

UPOV Explanatory Notes—general address: www.upov.int/explanatory_notes/en/.

UPOV/EXN/ENF, *Explanatory Notes on the Enforcement of Breeders' Rights under the UPOV Convention.*

UPOV/EXN/GEN, *Explanatory Notes on Genera and Species to be Protected under the 1991 Act of the UPOV Convention.*

UPOV/EXN/PRI, *Explanatory Notes on the Right of Priority under the UPOV Convention.*

UPOV/EXN/NOV, *Explanatory Notes on Novelty under the UPOV Convention.*

UPOV/EXN/CAL, *Explanatory Notes on Conditions and Limitations Concerning the Breeder's Authorization in Respect of Propagating Material under the UPOV Convention.*

UPOV/EXN/HRV, *Explanatory Notes on Acts in Respect of Harvested Material under the 1991 Act of the UPOV Convention.*

UPOV/EXN/EXC, *Explanatory Notes on Exceptions to the Breeder's Right under the 1991 Act of the UPOV Convention.*

UPOV/EXN/PRP, *Explanatory Notes on Provisional Protection under the UPOV Convention.*

UPOV/EXN/EDV, *Explanatory Notes on Essentially Derived Varieties under the 1991 Act of the UPOV Convention.*

TG/1/3, *General Introduction to the Examination of Distinctness, Uniformity and Stability and the Development of Harmonized Descriptions of New Varieties of Plants*, 2002, www.upov.int/export/sites/upov/resource/en/tg_1_3.pdf.

TGP/9, *Examining Distinctness*, 2008, www.upov.int/edocs/mdocs/upov/en/tc_41/tgp_9_1_draft_3.pdf.
TGP/10, *Examining Uniformity*, 2008, www.upov.int/edocs/tgpdocs/en/tgp_10.pdf.
TGP/11, *Examining Stability*, 2011, www.upov.int/edocs/tgpdocs/en/tgp_11.pdf.
UPOV/INF/12/4, *Explanatory Notes on Variety Denominations under the UPOV Convention*, 2012, www.upov.int/edocs/infdocs/en/upov_inf_12_4.pdf.

Index

D

E

F

T

U

V

W

www.ingramcontent.com/pod-product-compliance
Lightning Source LLC
Chambersburg PA
CBHW071952181025
34204CB00003B/138
9789403536361